The Politics of Protest

This collection provides a deep engagement with the political implication of Black Lives Matter. This book covers a broad range of topics using a variety of methods and epistemological approaches.

In the twenty-first century, the killings of Black Americans have sparked a movement to end the brutality against Black bodies. In 2013, #BlackLivesMatter would become a movement-building project led by Alicia Garza, Patrisse Cullors, and Opal Tometi. This movement began after the acquittal of George Zimmerman, who murdered 17-year-old Trayvon Martin. The movement has continued to fight for racial justice and has experienced a resurgence following the 2020 slayings of Ahmaud Arbery, George Floyd, Breonna Taylor, Sean Reed, Tony McDade, and David McAtee among others. The continued protests raise questions about how we can end this vicious cycle and lead Blacks to a state of normalcy in the United States. In other words, how can we make any advances made by Black Lives Matter stick?

The chapters in this book were originally published in the journal *Politics, Groups, and Identities*.

Nadia E. Brown is University Faculty Scholar and Associate Professor of Political Science and African American Studies at Purdue University, USA. Brown is a scholar of American politics whose work focuses on identity politics, legislative studies, and Black women's studies, using the theory of intersectionality to study topics across multiple disciplines.

Ray Block Jr. is Associate Professor of Political Science and African American Studies at Pennsylvania State University, USA. His research interests include racial, ethnic, and gender differences in civic involvement, the formation and mutability of social identity, campaigns and elections, and other topics.

Christopher T. Stout is Associate Professor of Political Science at Oregon State University, USA. His research interests include racial and ethnic politics, gender and politics, political behavior, representation, and Congress.

The Politics of Protest
Readings on the Black Lives Matter Movement

Edited by
Nadia E. Brown, Ray Block Jr., and Christopher T. Stout

First published 2021
by Routledge
2 Park Square, Milton Park, Abingdon, Oxon OX14 4RN

and by Routledge
52 Vanderbilt Avenue, New York, NY 10017

Routledge is an imprint of the Taylor & Francis Group, an informa business

© 2021 Taylor & Francis

All rights reserved. No part of this book may be reprinted or reproduced or utilised in any form or by any electronic, mechanical, or other means, now known or hereafter invented, including photocopying and recording, or in any information storage or retrieval system, without permission in writing from the publishers.

Trademark notice: Product or corporate names may be trademarks or registered trademarks, and are used only for identification and explanation without intent to infringe.

British Library Cataloguing in Publication Data
A catalogue record for this book is available from the British Library

ISBN 13: 978-0-367-63566-4

Typeset in Minion
by Newgen Publishing UK

Publisher's Note
The publisher accepts responsibility for any inconsistencies that may have arisen during the conversion of this book from journal articles to book chapters, namely the inclusion of journal terminology.

Disclaimer
Every effort has been made to contact copyright holders for their permission to reprint material in this book. The publishers would be grateful to hear from any copyright holder who is not here acknowledged and will undertake to rectify any errors or omissions in future editions of this book.

Contents

Citation Information viii
Notes on Contributors xi

Historical Development of the Black Lives Movement

1 American Political Development in the Era of Black Lives Matter 1
   Debra Thompson and Chloe Thurston

2 The neo-Redemption Era? APD in the age of #Black lives matter 5
   Kimberley S. Johnson

3 The Strange Fruit of American Political Development 13
   Megan Ming Francis

4 American political development and black lives matter in the age of incarceration 23
   Kirstine Taylor

5 (Re)Defining the black body in the era of Black Lives Matter: the politics of blackness, old and new 32
   Shayla C. Nunnally

6 Racial gaslighting 47
   Angelique M. Davis and Rose Ernst

Media, Politicians, Politics, and Population

7 Framing police and protesters: assessing volume and framing of news coverage post-Ferguson, and corresponding impacts on legislative activity 61
   Maneesh Arora, Davin L. Phoenix and Archie Delshad

8 Reframing racism: political cartoons in the era of Black Lives Matter 75
   Anish Vanaik, Dwaine Jengelley and Rolfe Peterson

9   Racialized differences in perceptions of and emotional responses to police killings of unarmed African Americans   89
    Ernest B. McGowen and Kristin N. Wylie

10 Scholarship on #BlackLivesMatter and its implications on local electoral politics   100
    Jamil S. Scott and Nadia E. Brown

11 Tweeting racial representation: how the congressional Black Caucus used Twitter in the 113th congress   107
    Alvin B. Tillery

12 The public's dilemma: race and political evaluations of police killings   127
    Ethan V. Porter, Thomas Wood and Cathy Cohen

13 Black Americans and the "crime narrative": comments on the use of news frames and their impacts on public opinion formation   155
    Jenn M. Jackson

14 Harbingers of unrest in Baltimore: racial and spatial cleavages in satisfaction with quality of life before the 2015 Uprising   166
    Tyson D. King-Meadows

15 Targeting young men of color for search and arrest during traffic stops: evidence from North Carolina, 2002–2013   188
    Frank R. Baumgartner, Derek A. Epp, Kelsey Shoub and Bayard Love

16 #BlackLivesDon'tMatter: race-of-victim effects in US executions, 1976–2013   213
    Frank R. Baumgartner, Amanda J. Grigg and Alisa Mastro

17 Intersectional stereotyping in policing: an analysis of traffic stop outcomes   226
    Leah Christiani

Who Participates and Why

18 Why participate? An intersectional analysis of LGBTQ people of color activism in Canada   249
    Alexie Labelle

19 Race-ing solidarity: Asian Americans and support for Black Lives Matter   268
    Julie Lee Merseth

20	Intersectional solidarity *F. Tormos*	288
21	Intersectionality at the grassroots *Michael T. Heaney*	302
	Index	323

Citation Information

The chapters in this book were originally published in various issues of *Politics, Groups, and Identities*. When citing this material, please use the original citations for each article, as follows:

Chapter 1
American Political Development in the Era of Black Lives Matter
Debra Thompson and Chloe Thurston
Politics, Groups, and Identities, volume 6, issue 1 (2018), pp. 116–119

Chapter 2
The neo-Redemption Era? APD in the age of #Black lives matter
Kimberley S. Johnson
Politics, Groups, and Identities, volume 6, issue 1 (2018), pp. 120–127

Chapter 3
The Strange Fruit of American Political Development
Megan Ming Francis
Politics, Groups, and Identities, volume 6, issue 1 (2018), pp. 128–137

Chapter 4
American political development and black lives matter in the age of incarceration
Kirstine Taylor
Politics, Groups, and Identities, volume 6, issue 1 (2018), pp. 153–161

Chapter 5
(Re)Defining the black body in the era of Black Lives Matter: the politics of blackness, old and new
Shayla C. Nunnally
Politics, Groups, and Identities, volume 6, issue 1 (2018), pp. 138–152

Chapter 6
Racial gaslighting
Angelique M. Davis and Rose Ernst
Politics, Groups, and Identities, volume 7, issue 4 (2019), pp. 761–774

Chapter 7
Framing police and protesters: assessing volume and framing of news coverage post-Ferguson, and corresponding impacts on legislative activity
Maneesh Arora, Davin L. Phoenix and Archie Delshad
Politics, Groups, and Identities, volume 7, issue 1 (2019), pp. 151–164

Chapter 8
Reframing racism: political cartoons in the era of Black Lives Matter
Anish Vanaik, Dwaine Jengelley and Rolfe Peterson
Politics, Groups, and Identities, volume 6, issue 4 (2018), pp. 838–851

Chapter 9
Racialized differences in perceptions of and emotional responses to police killings of unarmed African Americans
Ernest B. McGowen and Kristin N. Wylie
Politics, Groups, and Identities, volume 8, issue 2 (2020), pp. 396–406

Chapter 10
Scholarship on #BlackLivesMatter and its implications on local electoral politics
Jamil S. Scott and Nadia E. Brown
Politics, Groups, and Identities, volume 4, issue 4 (2016), pp. 702–708

Chapter 11
Tweeting racial representation: how the congressional Black Caucus used Twitter in the 113th congress
Alvin B. Tillery
Politics, Groups, and Identities, DOI: 10.1080/21565503.2019.1629308

Chapter 12
The public's dilemma: race and political evaluations of police killings
Ethan V. Porter, Thomas Wood and Cathy Cohen
Politics, Groups, and Identities, DOI: 10.1080/21565503.2018.1528162

Chapter 13
Black Americans and the "crime narrative": comments on the use of news frames and their impacts on public opinion formation
Jenn M. Jackson
Politics, Groups, and Identities, volume 7, issue 1 (2019), pp. 231–241

Chapter 14
Harbingers of unrest in Baltimore: racial and spatial cleavages in satisfaction with quality of life before the 2015 Uprising
Tyson D. King-Meadows
Politics, Groups, and Identities, DOI: 10.1080/21565503.2019.1674669

Chapter 15
    Targeting young men of color for search and arrest during traffic stops: evidence from North Carolina, 2002–2013
    Frank R. Baumgartner, Derek A. Epp, Kelsey Shoub and Bayard Love
    Politics, Groups, and Identities, volume 5, issue 1 (2017), pp. 107–131

Chapter 16
    #BlackLivesDon'tMatter: race-of-victim effects in US executions, 1976–2013
    Frank R. Baumgartner, Amanda J. Grigg and Alisa Mastro
    Politics, Groups, and Identities, volume 3, issue 2 (2015), pp. 209–221

Chapter 17
    Intersectional stereotyping in policing: an analysis of traffic stop outcomes
    Leah Christiani
    Politics, Groups, and Identities, DOI: 10.1080/21565503.2020.1748064

Chapter 18
    Why participate? An intersectional analysis of LGBTQ people of color activism in Canada
    Alexie Labelle
    Politics, Groups, and Identities, DOI: 10.1080/21565503.2019.1674671

Chapter 19
    Race-ing solidarity: Asian Americans and support for Black Lives Matter
    Julie Lee Merseth
    Politics, Groups, and Identities, volume 6, issue 3 (2018), pp. 337–356

Chapter 20
    Intersectional solidarity
    F. Tormos
    Politics, Groups, and Identities, volume 5, issue 4 (2017), pp. 707–720

Chapter 21
    Intersectionality at the grassroots
    Michael T. Heaney
    Politics, Groups, and Identities, DOI: 10.1080/21565503.2019.1629318

For any permission-related enquiries please visit:
www.tandfonline.com/page/help/permissions

Notes on Contributors

Maneesh Arora, Department of Political Science, Wellesley College, MA, USA.

Frank R. Baumgartner, Department of Political Science, University of North Carolina at Chapel Hill, NC, USA.

Nadia E. Brown, Department of Political Science and the Program of African American Studies, Purdue University, IN, USA.

Leah Christiani, Department of Political Science, University of North Carolina at Chapel Hill, NC, USA.

Cathy Cohen, Department of Political Science, University of Chicago, IL, USA.

Angelique M. Davis, Department of Political Science and the Program of Global African Studies, Seattle University, WA, USA.

Archie Delshad, Department of Political Science, Fullerton College, CA, USA.

Derek A. Epp, Department of Government, University of Texas, TX, USA.

Rose Ernst, Academic Editor and Writing Consultant, Seattle, WA, USA.

Amanda J. Grigg, American Political Science Association, Centennial Center, Washington, DC, USA.

Michael T. Heaney, School of Social and Political Sciences, University of Glasgow, Scotland, UK, and Institute for Research on Women and Gender, University of Michigan, MI, USA.

Jenn M. Jackson, Department of Political Science, Syracuse University, NY, USA.

Dwaine Jengelley, Honors College, Purdue University, IN, USA.

Kimberley S. Johnson, Department of Social and Cultural Analysis, New York University, NY, USA.

Tyson D. King-Meadows, Department of Political Science, University of Maryland–Baltimore County, MD, USA.

Alexie Labelle, Department of Political Science, Université de Montréal, Canada.

Julie Lee Merseth, Department of Political Science, Northwestern University, IL, USA.

Bayard Love, International Civil Rights Center and Museum, Greensboro, NC, USA.

Alisa Mastro, U.S. Department of Justice Antitrust Division, Georgetown University Law Center, DC, USA.

Ernest B. McGowen, Department of Political Science, University of Richmond, VA, USA.

Megan Ming Francis, Department of Political Science, University of Washington, WA, USA.

Shayla C. Nunnally, Department of Political Science and Institute of African American Studies, University of Connecticut, CT, USA.

Rolfe Peterson, Department of Political Science, Susquehanna University, PA, USA.

Davin L. Phoenix, Department of Political Science, University of California, CA, USA.

Ethan V. Porter, School of Media and Public Affairs, George Washington University, DC, USA.

Jamil S. Scott, Department of Government, Georgetown University, DC, USA.

Kelsey Shoub, Department of Political Science, University of South Carolina, SC, USA.

Kirstine Taylor, Department of Political Science, Ohio University, OH, USA.

Debra Thompson, Department of Political Science, University of Oregon, OR, USA.

Chloe Thurston, Department of Political Science, Northwestern University, IL, USA.

Alvin B. Tillery, Department of Political Science, Northwestern University, IL, USA.

F. Tormos, School of Public Policy, University of Maryland–Baltimore County, MD, USA, and Union of Concerned Scientists, The Center for Science and Democracy, Baltimore, MD, USA.

Anish Vanaik, Jindal Global Law School, OP Jindal Global University, Sonipat, India.

Thomas Wood, Department of Political Science, Ohio State University, OH, USA.

Kristin N. Wylie, Department of Political Science, James Madison University, VA, USA.

American Political Development in the Era of Black Lives Matter

Debra Thompson and Chloe Thurston

> **ABSTRACT**
> This Dialogues discussion explores the ways that the historical-institutional approaches of American Political Development can be useful for analyzing the ideological origins and contemporary politics of Black Lives Matter. By focusing on the evolution and impact of ideas and institutions, and the shifting relationship between the state, polity, and policy, American Political Development scholars have been crucial voices in political science working to demonstrate the intractable influence of race on the creation, maintenance, and evolution of political orders. American Political Development is, therefore, a useful lens through which to explore the era of Black Lives Matter, which is characterized by grassroots challenges to the proliferation of the American carceral state, the prison-industrial complex, the militarization of the police, and the ways that public goods are unequally distributed along racial lines. The papers presented in this Dialogues collection explore the impact of Black Lives Matter, particularly in terms of the historical processes and patterns of race politics that can contribute to our understandings of the intellectual history, contemporary politics, and future manifestations of Black Lives Matter.

The eruption of protests since 2014 condemning the police killings of African Americans throughout the United States has raised serious and pressing questions about the nature of American democracy. Amalgamated under the rallying cry, discourse, hashtag, and guiding principles of Black Lives Matter (BLM), the social movement is considered to be the "new civil rights movement" of the twenty-first century. According to BLM co-founder Alicia Garza

> Black Lives Matter is an ideological and political intervention in a world where Black lives are systematically and intentionally targeted for demise. It is an affirmation of Black folks' contributions to this society, our humanity, and our resilience in the face of deadly oppression. (Garza 2014)

Alongside the coalition of organizations that form and sustain the Movement for Black Lives, BLM challenges the proliferation of the American carceral state, the prison-industrial complex, the militarization of the police, and the ways that public goods are unequally distributed along racial lines (Taylor 2016). Above all, BLM lays bare the precarious legitimacy of American political institutions, especially those that have played a role in exacerbating racial political, economic, and social inequality.

This Dialogues discussion originated from a roundtable we organized for the 2017 annual meeting of the American Political Science Association, the original purpose of which was to explore the ways that historical-institutional approaches of American Political Development (APD) can be useful for analyzing the ideological origins and contemporary politics of BLM. By focusing on the evolution and impact of American ideas and institutions, and the shifting relationships among the state, polity, and policy, APD scholars have been crucial voices in political science working to demonstrate the intractable influence of race on the creation, maintenance, and evolution of political orders (Smith 1993; King and Smith 2005, 2011). In an early collection of work on race and APD, Lowndes, Novkov, and Warren begin with the claim that race is present at every critical moment in the United States, shaping political institutions, political discourse, public policy, and its denizen's political identities (2008, 1). And as a subfield and research agenda that takes institutions and historical development seriously, APD offers several potential insights into understanding BLM's place in political time and within the political landscape, drawing scholars' attention to issues such as the juxtaposition of an apparently "weak" or "hidden" state (Skowronek 1982; Balogh 2009) with the experience of an activist – and visible – state for those who bore the brunt of its coercive powers (Lerman and Weaver 2012; Thompson 2016; Ericson 2017; Frymer 2017); and the role of marginalized groups in modern state development (Nackenoff and Novkov 2014; Francis 2014). The strength of APD research on race and the state, Kimberley Johnson (2016) notes, is its attentiveness to understanding both the *why* and the *when* of political phenomena.

The era of BLM is marked by the increased importance of the "when" of politics, as the specters of America's racial past continue to haunt the circumstances of the present. In recent years, there have been explosive debates over whether the Confederate flag and monuments to Confederate soldiers respect southern heritage or promote white supremacy; a presidential political campaign that claimed America had lost its status as the world's most exceptional democracy and promised to return America to greatness; an election largely characterized by aggrieved whiteness, in which white people believe they are oppressed as a racial group and profess longing for a past when white supremacy was explicitly normalized and institutionalized; an intellectual and vernacular comparison between the second-class citizenship of Jim Crow segregation and the system of mass incarceration that confines and then disenfranchises substantial segments of the African American population (i.e. "the *new* Jim Crow") (Alexander 2010); comparisons drawn between the compositions, strategies, successes, and failures of the Civil Rights and Black Power movements of the 1960s and the varied manifestations of the Movement for Black Lives. Even that ubiquitously popular protest sign – "I can't believe I *still* have to protest this shit!" – speaks to the taut connection between the past and the present.

Much like the APD literature that emphasizes continuity over change, many of the seemingly nascent patterns of politics that led to the emergence of BLM have long histories. For example, Khalil Muhammad (2010) chronicles the genealogy of black criminality in nineteenth and twentieth century America while Naomi Murakawa's (2014) book, *The First Civil Right*, traces the expansion of the federal carceral state to the civil rights liberalism of the post-war era. Chris Lebron's (2017) recent exposition of the ideational foundations of BLM links it to early and important purveyors of black political thought, including Frederick Douglass, Ida B. Wells, Anna Julia Cooper, and James Baldwin, while Juliet Hooker (2016) contends that white expectations for "democratic sacrifice" that crystallized during the civil rights movement have now been stymied by the radical politics of BLM. So, too, the modes of governance that characterize what Soss and Weaver (2017) call the "second face of the state" – those activities that exercise social control through mechanisms of surveillance, coercion, containment, repression, regulation, discipline, and violence – did not come into being overnight, though some suggest that they intensified with the neoliberal turn (Soss, Fording, and Schram 2011; Spence 2015; Camp 2016). Though the strategies, leadership, composition, and politics of BLM differ from its predecessor social movements, at its core BLM is a "revival" of an appeal to Black humanity with a long history in the black freedom struggle (Harris 2015; Ransby 2015).

The papers presented in this Dialogues collection explore the impact of BLM, particularly in terms of the ways the movement raises and engages questions about the substance, breath, ethos, and limits of American democracy and its political institutions. The collection explores questions about the various historical processes and patterns of race politics that contribute to our understandings of the intellectual history, contemporary politics, and future manifestations of BLM. Together, the authors consider important theoretical and empirical questions such as: What linkages between race and American state development enabled the rise of BLM? What can APD reveal about the ideological and institutional inheritance of BLM, particularly in terms of the usefulness of theoretical tools such as intercurrence, path dependency, and policy drift? In what ways has BLM changed or challenged national and transnational racial orders? Can contemporary structures and strictures of American democracy be reformulated to create a future in which African Americans have access to substantive and meaningful forms of economic, political, and social equality? Broadly speaking, this Dialogues discussion seeks to augment APD's established strength of emphasizing the ways that race has shaped institutions, political discourse, and public policy throughout the political development of the United States, including the moment in which we currently inhabit.

Disclosure statement

No potential conflict of interest was reported by the authors.

ORCID

Debra Thompson http://orcid.org/0000-0001-6191-4461

References

Alexander, Michelle. 2010. *The New Jim Crow: Mass Incarceration in the Age of Colorblindness*. New York: New Press.
Balogh, Brian. 2009. *A Government Out of Sight: The Mystery of National Authority in the Nineteenth Century*. New York: Cambridge University Press.

Camp, Jordan T. 2016. *Incarcerating the Crisis: Freedom Struggles and the Rise of the Neoliberal State*. Oakland: University of California Press.

Ericson, David. 2017. "The United States Military, State Development, and Slavery in the Early Republic." *Studies in American Political Development* 31 (1): 130–148.

Francis, Megan Ming. 2014. *Civil Rights and the Making of the Modern American State*. New York: Cambridge University Press.

Frymer, Paul. 2017. *Building an American Empire: The Era of Territorial and Political Expansion*. Princeton, NJ: Princeton University Press.

Garza, Alicia. 2014. "A Herstory of the #BlackLivesMatter Movement." *The Feminist Wire*. Accessed October 7, 2014. http://www.thefeministwire.com/2014/10/blacklivesmatter-2/

Harris, Fredrick C. 2015. "The Next Civil Rights Movement?" *Dissent* 62 (3) (Summer 2015). https://www.dissentmagazine.org/article/black-lives-matter-new-civil-rights-movement-fredrick-harris

Hooker, Juliet. 2016. "Black Lives Matter and the Paradoxes of U.S. Black Politics: From Democratic Sacrifice to Democratic Repair." *Political Theory* 44 (4): 448–469.

Johnson, Kimberley S. 2016. "The Color Line and the State: Rae and American Political Development." In *The Oxford Handbook of American Political Development*, edited by Richard M. Valelly, Suzanne Mettler, and Robert Lieberman, 593–624. Oxford: Oxford University Press.

King, Desmond, and Rogers Smith. 2005. "Racial Orders in American Political Development." *American Political Science Review* 99 (1): 75–92.

King, Desmond, and Rogers Smith. 2011. *Still a House Divided: Race and Politics in Obama's America*. Princeton, NJ: Princeton University Press.

Lebron, Christopher J. 2017. *The Making of Black Lives Matter: A Brief History of an Idea*. New York: Oxford University Press.

Lerman, Amy E., and Vesla M. Weaver. 2012. *Arresting Citizenship: The Democratic Consequences of American Crime Control*. Chicago: University of Chicago Press.

Lowndes, Joesph, Julie Novkov, and Dorian Warren. 2008. *Race and American Political Development*. New York: Routledge.

Muhammad, Khalil Gibran. 2010. *The Condemnation of Blackness: Race, Crime, and the Making of Modern Urban America*. Cambridge: Harvard University Press.

Murakawa, Naomi. 2014. *The First Civil Right: How Liberals Built Prison America*. New York: Oxford University Press.

Nackenoff, Carol, and Julie Novkov, eds. 2014. *Statebuilding from the Margins: Between Reconstruction and the New Deal*. Philadelphia: University of Pennsylvania Press.

Ransby, Barbara. 2015. "The Class Politics of Black Lives Matter." *Dissent* 62 (4) (Fall). https://www.dissentmagazine.org/article/class-politics-black-lives-matter

Skowronek, Stephen. 1982. *Building a New American State: The Expansion of National Administrative Capacities, 1877–1920*. New York: Cambridge University Press.

Smith, Rogers. 1993. "Beyond Tocqueville, Myrdal, and Hartz: The Multiple Traditions in America." *American Political Science Review* 87 (3): 549–566.

Soss, Joe, Richard C. Fording, and Sanford F. Schram. 2011. *Disciplining the Poor: Neoliberal Paternalism and the Persistent Power of Race*. Chicago: University of Chicago Press.

Soss, Joe, and Vesla Weaver. 2017. "Police are Our Government: Politics, Political Science, and the Policing of Race-Class Subjugated Communities." *Annual Review of Political Science* 20: 565–591.

Spence, Lester. 2015. *Knocking the Hustle: Against the Neoliberal Turn in Black Politics*. Brooklyn: punctum books.

Taylor, Keeanga-Yamahtta. 2016. *From #BlackLivesMatter to Black Liberation*. Chicago: Haymarket Books.

Thompson, Debra. 2016. *The Schematic State: Race, Transnationalism, and the Politics of the Census*. New York: Cambridge University Press.

The neo-Redemption Era? APD in the age of #Black lives matter

Kimberley S. Johnson

ABSTRACT
The Black Lives Movement reflects the latest stage in the United States' racial orders. The Civil Rights State, much like the Reconstruction Period, faces significant political, institutional and ideational challenges from those who would seek to impose new kinds of inequalities along long-standing lines of racial, ethnic and gender identities. Theories of APD can be useful in tracing both how these new challenges can be identified, and how new forms of resistance can be recognized and supported. By looking at the first Redemption Era and the role it played in laying the foundation for the Jim Crow order, we can identify where and how movements like BLM can challenge efforts to create and sustain a possible neo-Redemption era.

The 2012 murder of teenager Trayvon Martin as he was walking home from a convenience store – like the murder of Emmitt Till 57 years earlier – galvanized a protest movement: Black Lives Matter (BLM). Although protests against police killings of African Americans, as well as the heightened debate over police tactics like Stop-and-Frisk policies, which targeted Black and Latinx youth, had begun to gather steam since high-profile deaths like Amadou Diallo's, it was the quasi-state sanctioned murder of Martin by a private citizen under Florida's "Stand Your Ground" law which brought into clear focus the new dangers faced by people of color. Early into Obama's administration and following in the footsteps set by his campaign's premise of racial reconciliation and progress, Obama organized a famous "beer summit" between Professor Henry Louis Gates (an African American professor at Harvard University) and James Crowley, the white police officer who detained Gates for allegedly breaking into his (Gates') home (Cooper and Goodnough 2009). With Martin's death, Obama was moved to state that Martin "could have been his son" (Thompson and Wilson 2012). With this statement (and the subsequent backlash from white conservatives), Obama inadvertently revealed that the racial progress and reconciliation of his candidacy and presidency was a fragile premise; and that his election had not overcome, but rather was revealed to be highly vulnerable to the deep political and social shifts that were restructuring American politics and society. In particular, the Obama administration was caught in the slow but now highly visible unwinding of the Civil Rights State, and the concomitant rise of white ethnonationalism that rejected the key constituent groups that made up the Obama electoral coalition (Parker and Barreto 2013).

The birth of BLM movement and the spread of mass protests against police brutality – and by extension protests against white supremacy – both during and after the administration of the U.S.'s first Black president present a puzzle for an American politics of exceptionalism predicated on the notion of racial progress and reconciliation. Theories of American Political Development (APD) can help situate the emergence of BLM movement within a broader political as well as institutional context. The emergence of the BLM movement points to not only the durability of racial political orderings; but also, the mutability of these structures. Thus, even as Obama was elected on the promise of a new era of racial progress and redemption, it also coincided with a heightened sense of lethality between the state and many of its citizens and residents of color, and more consequently moves to reshape political and institutional arrangements that had previously emerged out the civil rights movement. Indeed, Obama's election and the emergence of BLM, and in particular the latter's contestation of power and legitimacy of American policing, has engendered its own counter-reaction and mobilization – first with the emergence of the Tea Party and now the open political displays of so-called Alt-Right groups. This development – the calls for greater racial equality and justice – and movements to counter these calls have created a distinct political space that I argue bears some resemblance to earlier political eras but is also a distinctive space in its own right. I call this political space the neo-Redemption Era.

The first Redemption era (ca 1877–1900), overlapped with and was ultimately central to the unwinding of Reconstruction. The era was also the formative moment for the political, legal, institutional, and ideational structures that would undergird the southern – and also national – Jim Crow Order that would govern American politics and society from 1900 to 1965. Today's neo-Redemption era, like its predecessor, consists of not only the rolling back or dismantling of political and institutional commitments to greater racial equality and citizenship; it also entails the creation and/or strengthening of ideational, political, and institutional commitments and structures that reaffirm and/or reconstruct racial inequality. By deploying the insights of theories of APD, I explore both the historical continuities as well as present day contingencies of this neo-Redemption era and the place of the BLM movement within this era.

Placing BLM in political time and order

Before I make the claim about the contributions of theories of APD towards understanding the emergence of role of BLM, some common definitions are offered. First, when using the term "race," I draw from scholarly work which emphasize that racial identities were socially and politically constructed in the United States (Lopez 1996; Omi and Winant 1994). Thus by "race" I mean a group identity that has been shaped by a combination of social, political, and economic factors in the past; and, that is also a specific set of intertwined political legal, social, and economic identities at a particular moment in time (Omi and Winant 1994, 64). Second, "political order" is as a "constellation of rules, institutions, practices, and ideas that hang together over time, a bundle of patterns … exhibiting coherence and predictability while other things change around them" (Orren and Skowronek 2004, 14–15). Third, a "racial order" is defined as a political orders in which "political actors … adopted (and often adapted) racial concepts, commitments, and aims in order to bind together their coalitions and structure governing institutions that express and serve their architects" (King and Smith 2005). APD can thus be thought of as a process of "intercurrence," in which the U.S. can be understood as a "polity constructed through multiple, asymmetric orderings of authority" (Orren and Skowronek 2004, 182). Consequently, "racial orderings" will be used as a shorthand for the political, economic, and social arrangements structuring the interactions between and among different groups based on perceived or constructed differences (see King and Smith 2005; Lowndes, Novkov, and Warren 2008).

The relationship between race and American political orders is complex and multicausal: "race and racial orders" have at times been a causal factor in shaping institutional and political arrangements, coalitions, and orderings. In turn, "race and racial orders" has been shaped by institutional and political arrangements, organizations, and orderings. This discussion thus draws in some ways from Rogers Smith's (1993) multiple traditions arguments which suggests that APD is better understood as encompassing "multiple political traditions [and orders] that embody 'liberalism, republicanism, and ascriptive forms of Americanism.'" This multiple traditions perspective acknowledges that, "the warp of American politics is interwoven with the woof of race" (Lowndes, Novkov, and Warren 2008).

To think about "warp and woof" of American politics leads to another critical contribution of APD which is the notion of timing and periodization (Pierson 2004). How we think about politics and (political orders) as well as race and racial orders obviously changes over time, but it is also understood to have a particular meaning at a particular moment in time. This latter contribution is where APD has powerfully intersected with African American history. Scholars working within APD have contributed to our understanding of what some historians call the "long civil rights movement" by focusing on the political, institutional, and ideational arrangements and commitments that made up the Jim Crow order (Francis 2014; Frymer 1999; Hall 2005; Lowndes 2008; Valelly 2004).

Although there is sometimes a certain retrospective inevitability to the emergence of the Jim Crow order, the first Redemption Era shows that the path to Jim Crow was heavily contested. Reconstruction did not suddenly stop as opposed to slowly become undone. Over a two-decade long period, supporters and opponents of Redemption struggled over the political, economic, and ideational structures that would come to undergird the Jim Crow order. Beginning with the "beginning of the end of Reconstruction" in 1877 and culminating in the slew of new state constitutions ratified starting in 1900, the white South had effectively and "legally" purged African Americans from the political system. African Americans saw that institutional and political commitments of the Reconstruction order did not save them – indeed the Reconstruction order proved remarkably fragile as the decline in support and then the collapse of ameliorative institutions like the Freedman's Bureau (Colby 1985; Lieberman 1994). Political allies like the Northern Republicans retreated from their support for protecting the gains of Reconstruction and for beating back the counter-developments of the supporters of Redemption (Frymer 1999; Valelly 2004). Still other institutions like the Supreme Court gave support to the development of new racially punitive policies engendered in *Plessy* and new "color-blind" readings of the 14th Amendment, which gave cover to the development of second class status to African Americans – whether they were located in the South or outside of it (Brandwein 2011).

The first Redemption Era entailed not only rolling back the Reconstruction order but also entailed constituting a new order which was layered on top of the old. Alongside of quasi-publically sanctioned terrorism of lynching, a new criminal justice system using mechanisms like the convict leasing sytem, which worked to ensure the surveillance and control of black bodies in order to secure political subservience and economic exploitation (Alexander 2012; Blackmon 2009; Kato 2015). Black prisoners would supply the labor capital that would build the South's private industrial sector as well as its public infrastructure (Blackmon 2009). Finally, through the "propaganda of history," White southerners were able to justify the first Redemption Era as simply a correction, and the new Jim Crow order as inevitable and just (DuBois [1935] 1992).

The Jim Crow order would not come undone until new challenges could be formulated to confront the political, institutional, and ideational commitments that comprised it. While organizations like the NAACP seem staid and conventional to modern eyes, they (like their erstwhile descendant the BLM) were highly experimental and fluid as they groped to fashion and then mount a challenge to the particular conditions that they faced under the Jim Crow order (Francis 2014)

From the first to the second redemption

Similarly, while there is also a certain inevitability to the emergence of the modern civil rights movement; the movement, like the Civil Rights state that emerged afterwards was not at all assured, nor was its durability. As a number of APD scholars have shown the emergence (and later success) of the modern civil rights movements was one of historical contingency (Francis 2014; Johnson 2010; Parker 2009). Partisan re-orderings had to take place; institutional capacity had to be created; and political and ideational commitment to ending ascriptive inequality had to be developed and secured to political action and leadership. The establishment of a Civil Rights State (ca 1965–present), defined as a "state committed to equality," whereby state activities focus on "remedying historical injustices and securing new standards of democratic rights" (King and Lieberman 2011; Walton Jr. 1988); was also historically contingent.

For most Americans of color, the Voting Rights Act of 1965 was the most strikingly successful element of the Civil Rights state in establishing equality of political citizenship through electoral reform, oversight, and enforcement. The rise of the black electorate led to dramatic, though still significantly contested, changes at the local, state, and federal level (Grofman and Davidson 1994). This wave of democratization coupled with the programmatic efforts of the Great Society reshaped the state's engagement with those previously excluded, while creating new connections between citizens and the state (Campbell 2003). One of the most meaningful of these connections is that new electoral power could work to undo the arbitrary and aggressive policing that communities of color had been subjected to for decades (Dulaney 1996). Despite these success, the Civil Rights state has been under challenge since its formation (Lowndes 2008). However, since the turn of the twenty-first century, there have been more explicit challenges to the Civil Rights state, and attempts to supplant it with a new political ordering.

Barack Obama and a new racial ordering?

Barack Obama was elected to the presidency in 2008 with a wave of enthusiasm as the first African American president. His election – at least from the center left – portended the rise of post-racial United States as well as the emergence of a newly resurgent liberalism that would restore the failing New Deal welfare state while making the necessary adjustments to the American state needed for the twenty-first century. Others were not so sanguine about Obama's election and its impact on American politics and more broadly the impact of his election on American democracy. Conservatives argued that Obama's election merely reflected white guilt and opened the door to variously "Saul Alinsky" type radicalism. Meanwhile what is now known as the "alt-Right" experienced a resurgence as Obama's election provided visible proof that their vision of America as a "white nation" was in serious peril.

One of the most visible manifestations of this was the rejection of Obama as a legitimate president via the rise and spread of "birtherism" and the Tea Party (Parker and Barreto 2013). "Birtherism" not only rested on claims that Obama was not born in Hawaii but in Kenya; but was also rested a deep and unshakeable belief that Obama was a practicing Muslim. Thus in the post-9/11 world, Obama was seen by those on the Right as religiously and temperamentally unable to, and undesirous of, truly representing Christian America. Although political polarization was already at high levels before his election, Obama's ascension into office triggered a remarkable increase in political and racial polarization, most notably around the enactment of the Affordable Care Act, so-called Obamacare, in 2010 which some on the right positioned as a form of "racial reparation," rather than the Republican inspired reform from which it drew its policy and intellectual lineage (Parker and Barreto 2013; Tesler 2012).

Accompanying the heightened political polarization was a concerted challenge on the part of Republicans and conservative groups to limit to voter access to the ballot box – the key component that helped to establish and then secure the Civil Rights state (Roth 2016). The *Bush v. Gore* 2000 election and the aftermath of September 11th attacks yoked together "ballot integrity" and homeland security in order to justify new and growing restrictions on voter registration. The Commission on Federal Election Reform (2005) also gave a bi-partisan imprimatur to a belief that measures improving "ballot security" and "voter fraud" were important to protect American democracy. Led by Georgia, by 2007, 12 states had enacted voter ID laws. Both before 2008 and especially after, a number of states enacted legislation designed to affect voter registration and turnout through increased voter identification requirements and shifting voting times and availability. Obama's election seemed to quicken the pace with over 30 states enacting new ID laws or adding more stringent provisions to existing voter ID laws (Roth 2016).

While supporters of the first Redemption era rolled back Reconstruction in plain sight, the unfolding of the second Redemption era was hidden under the guise of a broader protection of democracy. As a result, two apparently contradictory events could take place. In 2006, George W. Bush could sign a 25-year extension to the Voting Rights Act, which had been passed in the Senate on a 98–0 vote. And not 10 years later, by 2013, the Supreme Court in *Shelby v Holder* overturned two key provisions of the act – Section 4(b) and Section 5, significantly rolling back some provisions of the Voting Rights Act. The Court justified its ruling the conclusion that "race" no longer mattered. Many on the Left including many Black activists saw this as a fundamental assault on American democracy itself. Trump's assertion that Clinton "won" the popular vote with illegal votes persists because of the growth of a governing philosophy and practice that valorized the votes of some, and delegitimized if not eliminated the votes of others (Minnite 2010; Roth 2016).

Despite the emergence of the Tea Party in Obama's first month in office and the implacable opposition of Congressional Republicans, Obama was re-elected in 2012 and left office with remarkably high approval ratings for a second-term presidency. Economic recovery, the success of Left-ish political issues such as gay marriage, immigration reform, "living wage" campaigns and the Affordable Care Act, and Obama's relatively high approval levels was not enough to help Hillary Clinton win the electoral college (even though she won the popular vote). Trump and a "conservative populism" won the election. One reigning media interpretation of Trump's win was that though Clinton won the popular vote, white voter turnout powered Trump's victory in several legacy industrial states. Key to this narrative was that the claim in these formerly heavily industrialized stated, "economic anxiety" shifted white voters away from more conventional (though not less conservative) Republican candidates to Trump. We now know that this so-called economic anxiety was intertwined and in some case was overwhelmed by "racial anxiety" (or in short – white racism) as two significant elements in motivating white voters. Added to these two factors was the deep-seated and long-standing misogyny that faced the Clinton candidacy.

A counterpoint to these battles over voting rights is the deepening of economic inequality between the wealthiest Americans and the mass public. For Black and Latinx communities, this economic inequality is categorically worse than for other groups due in part to the 2008 recession as well as fundamental economic changes including the continued loss of manufacturing jobs, cutbacks in local and state public sector employment, and the sub-prime mortgage crisis (Oliver and Shapiro 2006). Economic inequality has been accompanied by a number of other inequalities including a related wealth gap, a persistent gap in student achievement, disparities in policing and enforcement of policies like "stop-and-frisk," and dramatically higher rates of mass incarceration among communities of color. All pose quiet threats to the undermining, if not rolling back of the Civil Rights State.

The rise in visibility of black deaths at the hands of the police (and its agents) dramatically visualized the marginalization – if not threats to citizenship (and humanity) – that the neo-Redemption era poses to Blacks and other communities of color. Mass incarceration and aggressive policing techniques like stop-and-frisk; a growing Homeland Security infrastructure; a partisan and racially tinged deadlock on immigration reform and a rapid rise in deportations (particularly under Obama's term in office); all signaled not just (some sectors of) the state's indifference to black (and brown) lives, but active hostility. For many communities of color, the role of the police was not to "protect and serve," but rather to humiliate, detain, or incapacitate those seen as belonging to those communities. Rather than being seen as citizens (or citizens-in-waiting), the now hyper-visibility of police violence revealed to black and brown citizens a state that no longer was committed to racial equality, but rather a state committed to inscribing new kinds of racial inequalities. The media reflected this new moment: Black and brown victims were "no angels" as Michael Brown, another victim of police killing was called by the New York Times; while non-Christians who killed were deemed "terrorists." White males like Dylan Roof, who killed multiple black parishioners in a South Carolina church while they were praying, were accorded the status of mentally ill or a "lone wolf.'" The latter group – if not dead through the agency of their own hands – would have the opportunity experience due process and to go through the criminal justice system. Meanwhile in the former category, many of the black and brown people would experience not due process but the swift and often-lethal (in-)justice at the hands of the police officer(s) in a first and often final encounter.

Further, like the first Redemption, the second Redemption era takes place within a context where new structurings of racial inequality reflects new political and economic realities. Both eras, for example, coincide with the emergence of a "Gilded Age," where massive economic, social, and technological upheavals result in massive inequalities and the clustering of economic and political power in a small percentage (the one percent) of the population (Piketty 2014). Today's new political and economic realities come from a variety of sources ranging from the dismantling of social welfare state and public services like housing support or public education in in favor of privatized or market friendly service provision. Other changes include the possibility of mass structural unemployment of all workers of color due to combined forces of globalization and technological innovation. Still more changes more directly linked to the BLM movement include new kinds of surveillance and control from social media monitoring to algorithmic policing which leads to more precise state and private control of black and brown bodies. The BLM movement while directed at curbing the lethality of the police – also reflects long-standing activism and political struggle that Black Americans have had to employ in order to secure and protect not simply their citizenship, but also their humanity.

Conclusion

Through the lens of APD, we can powerfully see movements like Black Live Matter as not simply spontaneous eruptions of mass protest to present day crises, but also a manifestation of the struggles within – and possibly across – multiple and layered political orders. The first Redemption Era overlapped with not only the Reconstruction order that preceded it, but also the Jim Crow order that came to supplant it. The second Redemption era seems to be overlapping with and perhaps supplanting the Civil Rights State that emerged in 1965. However, whether the neo-Redemption era identified will be followed by a new Jim Crow-like order is certainly not inevitable. Rather, what is happening today may like the earlier first Redemption Era, shape what happens next. BLM is an important moment in determining the shape of America's next racial ordering.

Disclosure statement

No potential conflict of interest was reported by the author.

References

Alexander, M. 2012. *The New Jim Crow: Mass Incarceration in the Age of Colorblindness*. New York: New Press.
Blackmon, D. A. 2009. *Slavery by Another Name: The Re-enslavement of Black Americans from the Civil War to World War II*. 1st Anchor Books ed. New York: Anchor Books.
Brandwein, P. 2011. *Rethinking the Judicial Settlement of Reconstruction*. Cambridge: Cambridge University Press.
Campbell, A. L. 2003. *How Policies Make Citizens: Senior Political Activism and the American Welfare State*. Princeton, NJ: Princeton University Press.
Colby, I. C. 1985. "The Freedmen's Bureau: From Social Welfare to Segregation." *Phylon (1960)* 46 (3): 219–230.
Cooper, H., and A. Goodnough. 2009. "Over Beers, No Apologies, but Plans to Have Lunch." The New York Times, July 30.

DuBois, W. E. B. (1935) 1992. *Black Reconstruction in America, 1860–1880*. New York: Atheneum.
Dulaney, W. M. 1996. *Black Police in America*. Bloomington: Indiana University Press.
Francis, M. M. 2014. *Civil Rights and the Making of the Modern American State*. Cambridge: Cambridge University Press.
Frymer, P. 1999. *Uneasy Alliances: Race and Party Competition in America*. Princeton, NJ: Princeton University Press.
Grofman, B., and C. Davidson. 1994. *Quiet Revolution in the South: The Impact of the Voting Rights Act, 1965–1990*. Princeton, NJ: Princeton University Press.
Hall, J. D. 2005. "The Long Civil Rights Movement and the Political Uses of the Past." *Journal of American History* 91 (4): 1233–1263.
Johnson, K. S. 2010. *Reforming Jim Crow: Southern Politics and State in the Age Before Before Brown*. New York: Oxford University Press.
Kato, D. 2015. *Liberalizing Lynching: Building a New Racialized State*. New York: Oxford University Press.
King, D., and R. C. Lieberman. 2011. "The Civil Rights State: How the American State Develops Itself." Presented at the 2011 Annual Meeting of the American Political Science Association.
King, D., and R. Smith. 2005. "Racial Orders in American Political Development." *American Political Science Review* 99: 75–92.
Lieberman, R. C. 1994. "The Freedmen's Bureau and the Politics of Institutional Structure." *Social Science History* 18 (3): 405–437.
Lopez, I. H. 1996. *White by Law: The Legal Construction of Race*. New York: New York University Press.
Lowndes, J. E. 2008. *From the New Deal to the New Right: Race and the Southern Origins of Modern Conservatism*. New Haven: Yale University Press.
Lowndes, J. E., J. Novkov, and D. Warren. 2008. *Race and American Political Development*. New York: Routledge.
Minnite, L. C. 2010. *The Myth of Voter Fraud*. Ithaca, NY: Cornell University Press.
Oliver, M. and T. Shapiro, eds. 2006. *Black Wealth/White Wealth: A New Perspective on Racial Inequality*. 2nd ed. New York: Routledge.
Omi, M., and H. Winant, eds. 1994. *Racial Formation in the United States: From the 1960s to the 1990s*. New York: Routledge.
Orren, K., and S. Skowronek. 2004. *The Search for American Political Development*. Cambridge: Cambridge University Press.
Parker, C. S. 2009. *Fighting for Democracy: Black Veterans and the Struggle Against White Supremacy in the Postwar South*. Princeton, NJ: Princeton University Press.
Parker, C. S., and M. A. Barreto. 2013. *Change They Can't Believe In: The Tea Party and Reactionary Politics in America*. Princeton: Princeton University Press.
Pierson, P. 2004. *Politics in Time: History, Institutions, and Social Analysis*. Princeton: Princeton University Press.
Piketty, T. 2014. *Capital in the Twenty-first Century*. Cambridge: Belknap Press: An Imprint of Harvard University Press.
Roth, Z. 2016. *The Great Suppression: Voting Rights, Corporate Cash, and the Conservative Assault on Democracy*. New York: Crown.
Smith, R. 1993. "Beyond Tocqueville, Myrdal, and Hartz: The Multiple Traditions in America." *American Political Science Review* 87 (3): 549–566.
Tesler, M. 2012. "The Spillover of Racialization into Health Care: How President Obama Polarized Public Opinion by Racial Attitudes and Race." *American Journal of Political Science* 56: 690–704.
Thompson, K., and S. Wilson. 2012. "Obama on Trayvon Martin: 'If I had a son, he'd look like Trayvon.'" *The Washington Post*, March 23.
Valelly, R. 2004. *The Two Reconstructions: The Struggle for Black Enfranchisement*. Chicago: University of Chicago Press.
Walton Jr., H. 1988. *When the Marching Stopped: The Politics of Civil Rights Regulatory Agencies*. Albany: State University of New York Press.

The Strange Fruit of American Political Development

Megan Ming Francis

ABSTRACT
What is the relationship between black social movements, state violence, and political development in the United States? Today, this question is especially important given the staggering number of unarmed black women and men who have been killed by the police. In this article, I explore the degree to which American Political Development (APD) scholarship has underestimated the role of social movements to shift political and constitutional development. I then argue that studying APD through the lens of Black Lives Matter highlights the need for a sustained engagement with state violence and social movements in analyses of political and constitutional development.

> Southern trees bear strange fruit,
> Blood on the leaves and blood at the root,
> Black bodies swinging in the southern breeze,
> Strange fruit hanging from the poplar trees. (Billie Holiday 1954)

During the summer of 2017, the self-proclaimed "law and order" president delivered policing advice. Speaking to an assembly of law enforcement officials, Donald Trump advised: "When you see these thugs thrown into the back of a paddy wagon, you just see them thrown in – rough – I said, 'Please don't be too nice.'" Some of the officers laughed and others whistled and loudly applauded Trump's encouragement of police brutality. Black Lives Matter (BLM) activists and civil rights attorneys were quick to denounce the remarks on social media, both for violating the constitutional guarantee of due process and for condoning unlawful police force. Facing a public backlash, the administration attempted to walk the comments back, calling them "a joke." But for those who bear witness to police brutality in their communities, Trump's reckless speech reinforced the complicity of the federal government in protecting routinized forms of police violence.

What is the relationship between black social movements, state violence, and political development in the United States? Today, this question is especially important given the staggering number of unarmed black women and men who have been killed by the police. From small suburban cities like Ferguson, Missouri, to big metropolitan cities like New York, police officers have escaped punishment and in some cases, been able to keep their jobs. In response, citizens have taken to the streets in mass protest, many carrying signs that read "Black Lives Matter" as a counter to the seemingly disposability of black lives at the hands of law enforcement. But as Alicia Garza, Patrisse Cullors, and Opal Tometi, the founders of the #BlackLivesMatter movement have repeatedly underscored: the movement is not solely focused on the convictions of a few bad apple police officers – it is centered on a more expansive goal of upending the numerous manifestations of structural racism in our society:

> state violence is bigger than police terrorism. Although police terrorism plays a specific role on behalf of the state, it is not the totality of what state violence looks like or feels like in our communities. (Garza 2015)

The call to examine the way violence is embedded and continues to be exacted on black communities through the normal operation of political and legal institutions is central to the mission articulated by BLM activists (M4BL 2016).

In the short time period since the inception of the BLM movement, its impact on American politics is "undeniable" (Taylor 2016). The BLM movement has shaken the foundations of how citizens understand their relationship to government and in a few cases, shifted the actions of political elites. President Barack Obama sat down with BLM movement leaders while in office, the Department of Justice was spurred to investigate an increased number of police departments, and activists have transformed local mayoral elections in cities such as Seattle. Through an institutional focus, BLM activists have drawn attention to the way discriminatory policing practices are intertwined with persisting housing segregation, racialized welfare state policies, and political reforms that criminalize poverty.

American Political Development (APD) with its emphasis on institutional development, path dependence, and ideational change is uniquely situated to provide useful historical context to the current moment of black mobilization and racist state violence. While much of the energy of the BLM movement is centered on an analysis of the ways different institutions devalue black life; it is important to note that black citizens, long marginalized in the polity, are delivering this critique. The state is powerful but citizens are not without agency. Throughout the long arc of United States history, the fight to protect black lives from racist state violence has always been at the center of the struggle for equal rights and citizenship. And yet, these stories are largely missing in the scholarly accounts about political development and constitution building in APD. But they should not be. In APD, pattern identification is considered the "sine qua non of the enterprise" because through identifying patterns, we can better understand how the American political system operates (Orren and Skowronek 2004, 7). The pattern of black protest leading to an expansion of civil rights and the subsequent contraction of these very rights through state-sanctioned violence is durable and it is integral to the way the American political system has developed.

The mass #BlackLivesMatter protests and images of tense confrontation between police and demonstrators across the United States suggest an urgent need to peel back the well-worn layers of the triumphant liberal narrative of American development. Writing about the overwhelming tendency in APD to describe the nation in hegemonic liberal democratic terms, Smith (1993, 558–559) encourages scholars to account for the inegalitarian ideologies that shape development: "the dynamics of American development cannot simply be seen as a rising tide of liberalizing forces progressively submerging contrary beliefs and practices. The national course has been more serpentine." And Frymer

(2005, 2008) argues that development scholars more closely examine how institutions provide rules and procedures that incentivize people to behave in a racist manner. Indeed, BLM understands American political and constitutional development as a series of white supremacist political and legal projects. Drawing on a long history of black radical struggle, the BLM movement suggests this country was less a liberal democratic project than a settler colonial project (Carmichael and Hamilton 1967; Wells 1969; Rana 2010, 2015; Davis 2017; Frymer 2017).

This reorientation of American history necessitates that we ask difficult questions about the ability of our storied political and legal institutions to rectify past wrongs (Rogers 2014; Hooker 2016; Minkah 2017). BLM activists have wrestled with the central question: Is it ever possible for black lives to matter inside of racist state institutions? And if not, does it make sense for black citizens to center their equality demands from the very institutions that are responsible for the harm? The year 2018 represents a unique time to explore these sorts of questions as it marks the 50th anniversary of the Fair Housing Act and over 50 years since the Civil Rights Act of 1964 and the Voting Rights Act of 1965 were passed into law. Considered together, these three legislative achievements represent a critical juncture whereby the capacity of the state expanded to protect the rights of black citizens. The juxtaposition of these legislative anniversaries with appalling levels of racial inequality today suggests severe limits of previous institutional approaches to addressing racial injustice.

BLM poses a challenge and an opportunity to APD. The critiques brought by the BLM movement should push scholars of APD to rethink how we conduct research. Much of APD emphasizes the actions of political elites and governing institutions. Indeed, many field-defining tomes in APD center on top-down change (Skowronek 1982; Evans, Rueschemeyer, and Skocpol 1985; Bensel 1990; Liberman 1998; Carpenter 2001; Hacker 2002; Katznelson 2013). But institutions do not act in a vacuum; meaningful political development is also a product of bottom-up protest and the contestation that happens between those on the sidelines and those in power. Studying APD in the BLM era necessitates a deeper engagement with the histories of racially marginalized groups and a focus on what Nackenoff and Novkov (2014) have termed "statebuilding from the margins." In this article, I explore the degree to which APD has underestimated the role of social movements to shift political and constitutional development. I then argue that studying APD through the lens of BLM means that scholars need to center black activism and racial violence in analyses of political and constitutional development.

In 1939, Billie Holiday, a celebrated African-American jazz singer, recorded "Strange Fruit" a protest song about the horrific violence of the lynching of African-Americans.[1] Holiday endeavored to bring attention to lynchings and frequently sang the haunting song during live performances to draw attention to the precarity of black life. The singing of Strange Fruit in front of well-heeled white audiences should be read as a form of calculated resistance by Holiday meant to highlight the inescapability of spectacular racial violence that existed throughout the country. I invoke "Strange Fruit" in this article as a way to think about the violence of our silence in APD when we ignore the impact of state-sanctioned racial violence on political and constitutional development. When scholarship discounts the importance of racial violence during different moments of statebuilding, it becomes complicit in the production of a sanitized and ultimately dangerous version of history making. But as Triouillot (1995) reminds us, history is not powerless – it is created by the unconscious use of power by scholars who decide which stories to tell, what sources are credible, and what archives to cull from. By doing so, scholars decide whose lives are legible in the historical record and what histories are silenced. Trouillot implores those of us who use history as a methodology, to be attendant to the power dynamics that are ever present in our craft. What follows is an attempt to take this charge seriously.

The state of APD & BLM

APD has expanded our understanding of an important set of issues in American politics such as bureaucratization, party development, and social policy formation. However, there is an important understudied area that necessitates greater attention: APD scholars have not sufficiently examined how civil rights organizations have contested the boundaries of the American state. This absence is especially striking considering pioneering work by King (1995) has revealed the significance of the federal government as an active participant in the process of fostering and maintaining a "segregationist order" which lasted until the Civil Rights Act of 1964. And innovative scholarship by Johnson (2010) explores the role of white and black southern reformers in remaking Jim Crow institutions. Instead of civil rights organizations, however, most scholars of APD suggest that institutions and bureaucratic actors are critical for understanding the roots and dynamics of political and historical shifts and events (Orren and Skowronek 2004). Even work convinced that challenges to racial hierarchies are a persistent part of America's racial order have not focused much on how civil rights activists and organizations not only contributed to critical periods of American statebuilding but were necessary for overcoming institutional stasis (King and Smith 2005).

APD scholars link the origins of statutes guaranteeing equal citizenship and representation to macro-institutional factors like the emergence of the Cold War in 1946 instead of what social movement scholars identify as the so-called watershed events such as Bloody Sunday in Selma, the bus boycotts in Montgomery, or Freedom Summer in Mississippi. It is not that scholars have so much ignored civil rights organizations – numerous APD scholars have investigated the role of community-level civil rights mobilization to impact the development of the American state in the post-World War II era – but that these works ultimately place the determinative causal actors for changes in civil rights to be state elites motivated by exogenous issues such as foreign policy and party (Kryder 2000; Skrentny 2002; Tillery 2011). In particular, Dudziak (2000) argues that in the immediate post-World War II era, racial discrimination in the United States received increasing negative attention from other countries, which were quick to point out the contradictions between American political ideology and American practice. In other words, the need to fend off international criticism, not community-level civil rights mobilization, gave the federal government an incentive to promote social change at home. This research tradition has helped to produce richer narratives about the modernization and the development of US institutions, however, it has stumbled in conceptualizing civil rights groups as a part of the narrative, but ultimately not integral to policy changes and transformations in the American state.

The problem with these elite-driven accounts of political change is that they privilege institutions over citizen agency. African-American protest and gains in civil rights were not always a direct result of state action. In many instances, black protest drove institutional development. In other instances, white supremacist ideology and discourses about civil rights influenced the path of development (Smith 1997; Novkov 2008; Brandwein 2011a, 2011b). Just as it is important to consider the way institutions shape the landscape of American race relations, it is just as necessary to take seriously the role that black civil society via black freedom organizations can play in shifting institutions and ideas (Valelly 2004; Frymer 2008; Johnson 2010; Gillion 2013). Serious questions that have been overlooked include: What role did civil rights groups play in augmenting the capacity of the American state in the period before the peak of civil rights legislation in the 1960s? How did ideas about black liberation politics shape attempts to reconstitute the state? How does the emergence of African-American protest shape the direction of the national policy-making agenda?

Social movements and state development

Political and constitutional development was shaped by the long history of black protest. Recent work that I have conducted demonstrates the importance of incorporating social movements into analyses of APD (Francis 2014). The contemporary BLM movement is not making an entirely new set of claims about the persistence of racial violence. In general, the American public knows little about the long tradition of BLM protests. The most important figure in understanding the history of the BLM movement is newspaper editor and journalist Ida B. Wells who is responsible for exposing lynching as a tool of white supremacy (Giddings 2008). In 1892, three of Wells' friends who owned a grocery store were lynched in a railroad yard in Memphis. The lynchings of her three friends marked a transformative moment in Wells' life. The lynchings created numerous unanswered questions for Wells since they were contrary to the accepted belief that lynchings were punishment for rape. Her three friends were not even charged with the crime of rape but they were still lynched. If lynchings were not always the response to rape, then what other reasons existed for lynching African-Americans? Wells' inquiry led her to the conclusion that concerns about economic competition between the white grocer and her friends grocery store were the real reason behind the brutal lynching. After the lynching, Wells (1970, 51–52) conveys the economic underpinnings of the lynching:

> The mob took possession of the Peoples Grocery Company, helping themselves to food and drink, and destroyed what they could not eat or steal. The creditors had the place closed and a few days later what remained of the stock was sold at an auction. Thus, with the aid of the city and county authorities and the daily papers, that white grocer had indeed put an end to this rival Negro grocer as well as to his business.

For Wells, lynching was intricately linked to the protection of white economic power. It was an unofficial tool of the state to thwart black economic advancement. Understanding lynching as a tool of state economic repression, Wells encouraged black residents of Memphis to leave – taking with them their labor and capital. The linking of anti-black violence to the system of capitalism is a central issue that black radical activists would take up and place at the center of their visions of liberation in the 1960s and 1970s (Carmichael and Hamilton 1967).

Wells' inquiry into the lynching of her friends led to a more expansive investigation of lynchings across the South where she interviewed eyewitnesses and members of the community to gather information. On June 25, 1892, it became the first published exposé of lynching in America (Wells 1969). Wells reported on facts she gathered, giving names, dates, and places of many lynchings for the accused crime of rape. The *New York Age*, an African-American weekly newspaper with a substantial white following, placed the article on its front page. Wells' facts made clear lynching was not a response to rape or to a greater level of criminality among African-Americans. Lynching, Wells determined, was used as a strategy to keep African-Americans "in their place."

Building upon Wells' anti-lynching activism, in 1916, the National Association for the Advancement of Colored People (NAACP 1909–1923) led the largest movement in history against lynching and racist mob violence (Francis 2014). Focused on protecting black lives, the NAACP under the leadership of James Weldon Johnson and W.E.B. Du Bois, organized mass demonstrations in the streets and launched an extensive public outreach campaign in order to reach the "heart and conscience of the American people." This should be no surprise. Lynching and mob violence were at the top of the NAACP's issue agenda since racial violence was believed to be the greatest obstacle that African-Americans in the North and South faced to gaining equality in America. In the original NAACP platform in 1909 it was stated, "We regard with grave concern the attempt manifest South and North to deny black men the right to work and to enforce this demand with violence and bloodshed."[2] Seven years later, racial violence remained high on the list of NAACP's concerns. When concern was raised at a meeting that the NAACP's agenda was too narrowly focused on the issue of racial violence, Roy Nash, an African-American who was part of the NAACP's leadership, attempted to explain the organization's focus: "All he [the American Negro] wanted was a chance to live without a rope around his neck ... "[3] It was a sobering but necessary reminder that if the protection of black lives were not secured, all other civil rights were meaningless. As the NAACP saw it, before the organization could appropriately address other problematic areas of civil rights such as voting, labor, and housing, it was necessary to focus on ending lynching and mob violence so that African-Americans could live to enjoy the benefits of their struggle.

It was not enough for the NAACP to raise the public's awareness about mob violence and lynchings; the organization knew a lot of power lay in politic and law and felt it necessary to supplement publicity with advocacy work in the formal branches of government. The NAACP's influence was displayed most prominently in the legal effort behind the landmark Supreme Court criminal procedure decision, *Moore v. Dempsey* 261 U.S. 86 (1923), which marked the first time the federal government interfered in state criminal court proceedings. The question before the Supreme Court was whether the presence of a mob in a courtroom violated the Due Process Clause of the 14th Amendment. In a decision written by Justice Oliver Wendell Holmes, the Supreme Court ruled in favor of the African-American defendants and declared that a fair trial means freedom from mob domination. Through this ruling, the Supreme Court made history by breaking from an established tradition of federalism and shifted (ever so slightly) the federal government's position on racial violence. With this case, the Supreme Court finally moved the federal government from a rut of frustrating symbolic rhetoric to substantive legal guarantees.

Once the NAACP secured this decision from the Supreme Court, new precedent was established and the Supreme Court entered a new era of jurisprudence no longer bound by strict deference to state courts. After *Moore v. Dempsey*, the Supreme Court made clear it was no longer willing to take a hands-off policy to the blatant racism that existed in southern courtrooms. Subsequently, the Supreme Court displayed its willingness to intervene on the behalf of helpless African-American defendants in a number of precedent setting cases in the 1930s and 1940s such as *Powell v. Alabama* 287 U.S. 45 (1932); establishing that defendants in capital cases have a right to state appointed counsel, *Hollins v. Oklahoma* 295 U.S. 394 (1935); the first of many decisions declaring exclusion of African-American jurors unconstitutional, *Brown v. Mississippi* 297 U.S. (1936); ruling that confessions exacted through torture violated the Due Process Clause; and *Chambers v. Florida* 309 U.S. 227 (1940), establishing that confessions obtained under duress were illegal. Beginning with these cases in the first half of the twentieth century, the power of federal courts vis-à-vis state courts in the area of criminal law began to expand. It is important to connect this shift in constitutional development with the organizing effort of the NAACP. Without the NAACP's campaign against state violence in the public sphere and litigation in *Moore v. Dempsey*, it is unlikely the revolution in criminal procedure would have occurred when it did. What the NAACP did in a small amount of time was to push the Supreme Court in a direction it was not initially willing to go and by doing so, forever change the path of civil rights and the Supreme Court's criminal procedure jurisprudence.

Racial violence in American politics

Studying APD in the BLM era means that we need to not only center social movements – we also must incorporate the long history of racial violence in analyses. Existing APD research has helped to produce richer narratives about the modernization and development of the American state; however, it has stumbled in conceptualizing racial violence as not integral to shifts in citizenship and transformations in political and legal institutions.[4] A considerable amount of APD scholarship has relegated the persisting racial violence of the American state into the backdrop instead of treating it as a constitutive feature of statebuilding. The absence is particularly striking because much of APD scholarship centers on four periods, all of which contain staggering levels of racial violence: the founding, Civil War/Reconstruction, the Gilded Age and Progressive periods, and the emergence of the New Deal. In part, shaped by the canonical works that undergird this subfield, these are presumed to be the major periods in which the governing institutions of the United States were constructed and transformed. A focus on racial violence in the New Deal, for example, reveals the extent to which President Franklin Roosevelt bargained away the safety of black lives in order to make a pact with southern Democrats and the Jim Crow South to secure their votes. Roosevelt acutely understood the importance of racial violence to his New Deal coalition as evidenced by his refusal to support the anti-lynching bill in Congress (Zangrando 1980; Liberman 1998; Katznelson 2013). Continued state violence against black citizens in the South was a central part of what made the New Deal possible.

Racial violence does not suddenly occur and strike at certain moments – it is a foundational component of American politics. Despite noteworthy civil rights victories, black bodies have never been safe from private and state terror in the United States. For the most part, the incredible violence of slavery, the pogrom of lynchings after Reconstruction, and the extra-legal killings during the Jim Crow era are treated as aberrational features of American political and constitutional development. These were periods the United States had to get through – demons the country had to overcome – they were not institutional and certainly not enduring.

However, one need only see how racial violence figures into the Trump administration to understand its continued significance. A violent presidential administration does not suddenly appear in 2017. The work in APD suggests that institutional development is path dependent and that to understand the operation of political institutions, our work must reach back further in time. To make sense of the searing state violence already legible in the Trump administration, an engagement with the past history of racial violence is necessary. How did the militarization of local police departments happen? In what ways did the development and implementation of welfare state policies harm black communities? How were previous presidents complicit in state violence? Examining the intersection of institutional development and racial violence highlights the historical contingency of the Trump administration. For example, the rise of a formidable and destructive national security apparatus, under Presidents George W. Bush and Barack Obama, helps to explain relentless military interventions abroad and the violent undermining of the legal rights of Arab and Muslims at home in the current political moment.

We have not been here before but we have been *here* before. The increased state violence that black communities are facing in contemporary politics is not entirely unique – it was reproduced in the 1960s and 1970s when liberal and conservative politicians created new laws and policies to rollback the progress made in the heyday of the civil rights movement (Weaver 2007; Murakawa 2014; Gottschalk 2015; Hinton 2016). The pattern of politicians intentionally using law enforcement and criminal punishment to weaken black citizenship and deny representation becomes clear when we link the post-Reconstruction era with the post-segregation era of American politics. Focusing attention on the endurance of racial violence helps explain both the complicated pursuit of equal citizenship and how racism thrives inside of political and legal institutions.

To understand how to move forward, we must properly reckon with the past. APD is in a unique position to study the BLM movement as it offers an opportunity to bring together a race analysis within a historical-institutionalism framework. It also presents the opportunity to rethink the ability of marginalized citizens to transform political and legal institutions. Spurred by the lost promises of the civil rights era, black citizens are rethinking strategies of reform that have previously centered on formal electoral politics (Cohen 2010; Dawson 2013; Wright-Rigueur 2015; Taylor 2016; Minkah 2017; Thompson 2017). What the highly publicized police killings sharpened about the vulnerability of black citizenship, the election of Donald Trump crystalized: electoral politics will not save black people and new strategies are needed. In response, black activists have put their lives on the line to demand a radical transformation in the structure of government. It is too early to evaluate the full impact of the movement but it is safe to say that the BLM movement has already had a profound impact on American political and constitutional development.

Notes

1. Strange Fruit was originally written by Abel Meeropol and published as the poem 'Bitter Fruit' in 1937.
2. Platform of the National Negro Committee (1909).
3. As quoted in Kellogg (1973, 134).
4. For a significant exception, see Johnson's (2010) book on Jim Crow reformers. Johnson positions racial violence during and after World War I as central to her analysis of a southern reform movement that included black intellectuals and white moderates.

Disclosure statement

No potential conflict of interest was reported by the author.

References

Bensel, Richard. 1990. *Yankee Leviathan: The Origins of Central State Authority in America, 1859–1877*. New York: Cambridge University Press.
Brandwein, Pamela. 2011a. *Rethinking the Judicial Settlement of Reconstruction*. New York: Cambridge University Press.
Brandwein, Pamela. 2011b. "Law and American Political Development." *Annual Review of Law and Social Science* 7: 187–216.
Carmichael, Stokely and Charles Hamilton. 1967. *Black Power: The Politics of Liberation in America*. New York: Knopf.
Carpenter, Daniel. 2001. *The Forgoing of Bureaucratic Autonomy: Reputations, Networks, and Policy Innovation in Executive Agencies, 1862-1928*. Princeton, NJ: Princeton University Press.
Cohen, Cathy. 2010. *Democracy Remixed*. New York: Oxford University Press.
Davis, Angela. 2017. *Freedom is a Constant Struggle: Ferguson, Palestine, and the Foundations of a Movement*. Chicago: Haymarket Books.
Dawson, Michael. 2013. *Blacks In and Out of the Left*. Cambridge, MA: Harvard University Press.
Dudziak, Mary. 2000. *Cold War Civil Rights: Race and the Image of American Democracy*, Princeton, NJ: Princeton University Press.
Evans, Peter, Dietrich Rueschemeyer, and Theda Skocpol. 1985. *Bringing the State Back In*. New York: Cambridge University Press.
Francis, Megan. 2014. *Civil Rights and the Making of the Modern American State*. New York: Cambridge University Press.
Frymer, Paul. 2005. "Racism Revised: Courts, Labor Law, and the Institutional Construction of Racial Animus." *American Political Science Review* 99 (3): 373–387.
Frymer, Paul. 2008. *Black and Blue: African Americans, the Labor Movement, and the Decline of the Democratic Party*. Princeton, NJ: Princeton University Press.
Frymer, Paul. 2017. *Building an American Empire: The Era of Territorial and Political Expansion*. Princeton, NJ: Princeton University Press.
Garza, Alicia. 2015. "Interview with Mychael Denzel Smith." *The Nation*. March 24, 1015.
Giddings, Paula. 2008. *Ida: A Sword Among Lions*. New York: HarperCollins.
Gillion, Daniel. 2013. *The Political Power of Protest: Minority Activism and Shifts in Public Policy*. New York: Cambridge University Press.
Gottschalk, Marie. 2015. *Caught: The Prison State and the Lockdown of American Politics*. Princeton, NJ: Princeton University Press.
Hacker, Jacob. 2002. *The Divided Welfare State: The Battle Over Public and Private Social Benefits in the United States*. New York: Cambridge University Press.
Hinton, Elizabeth. 2016. *From the War on Poverty to the War on Crime: The Making of Mass Incarceration in America*. Cambridge, MA: Harvard University Press.
Holiday, Billie. 1954. *Strange Fruit. Jazz at the Philharmonic*. https://genius.com/Billie-holiday-strangefruit-lyrics.
Hooker, Juliet. 2016. "Black Lives Matter and the Paradoxes of U.S. Black Politics: From Democratic Sacrifice to Democratic Repair." *Political Theory* 44 (4): 448–469.
Johnson, Kimberley. 2010. *Reforming Jim Crow: Southern Politics and State in the Age Before Brown*. New York: Oxford University Press.
Katznelson, Ira. 2013. *Fear Itself: The New Deal and the Origins of Our Time*. New York: Liveright Publishing Corporation.
Kellogg, Charles Flint. 1973. *NAACP: A History of the National Association for the Advancement of Colored People*. Baltimore: Johns Hopkins University Press.
King, Desmond. 1995. *Separate and Unequal: Black Americans and the US Federal Government*. Oxford: Oxford University Press.

King, Desmond and Rogers Smith. 2005. "Racial Orders in American Political Development." *American Political Science Review* 88: 75–92.

Kryder, Daniel. 2000. *Divided Arsenal: Race and the American State During World War II*. New York: Cambridge University Press.

Liberman, Robert. 1998. *Shifting the Color Line: Race and the American Welfare State*. Cambridge, MA: Harvard University Press.

M4BL (Movement for Black Lives). 2016. "Platform." Accessed December 2, 2017. http://policy.m4bl.org/platform.

Minkah, Makalani. 2017. "Black Lives Matter and the Limits of Formal Black Politics." *South Atlantic Quarterly* 116 (3): 529–552.

Murakawa, Naomi. 2014. *The First Civil Right: How Liberals Built Prison America*. New York: Oxford University Press.

Nackenoff, Carol and Julie Novkov (eds). 2014. *Statebuilding from the Margins: Between Reconstruction and the New Deal*. Philadelphia: University of Pennsylvania Press.

National Association for the Advancement of Colored People Records. 1909–1923. Library of Congress, Manuscript Division, Washington, DC.

Novkov, Julie. 2008. *Racial Union: Law, Intimacy, and the White State in Alabama, 1865-1954*. Ann Arbor: University of Michigan Press.

Orren, Karen and Stephen Skowronek. 2004. *The Search for American Political Development*, 7. Cambridge: Cambridge University Press.

Platform of the National Negro Committee. 1909. NAACP Records, Manuscript Division, Library of Congress.

Rana, Aziz. 2010. *The Two Faces of American Freedom*. Cambridge, MA: Harvard University Press.

Rana, Aziz. 2015. "Colonialism and Constitutional Memory." *UC Irvine Law Review* 5 (2): 263–288.

Rogers, Melvin. 2014. "Introduction: Disposable Lives." *Theory & Event* 17 (3).

Skowronek, Stephen. 1982. *Building a New American State: The Expansion of National Administrative Capacities, 1877–1920*. New York: Cambridge University Press.

Skrentny, John. 2002. *The Minority Rights Revolution*. Cambridge, MA: Belknap Press of Harvard University Press.

Smith, Rogers. 1993. "Beyond Tocqueville, Myrdal, and Hartz: The Multiple Traditions in America." *The American Political Science Review* 87 (3), 549–566.

Smith, Rogers. 1997. *Civic Ideals: Conflicting Visions of Citizenship in U.S. History*. New Haven, CT: Yale University Press.

Taylor, Keeanga-Yamahtta. 2016. *From #BlackLivesMatter to Black Liberation*. Chicago: Haymarket Books.

Thompson, Debra. 2017. "An Exoneration of Black Rage." *South Atlantic Quarterly* 116 (3): 457–481.

Tillery, Alvin. 2011. *Between Homeland and Motherland: Africa, U.S. Foreign Policy and Black Leadership in America*. Ithaca, NY: Cornell University Press.

Triouillot, Michel-Rolph. 1995. *Silencing the Past: Power and the Production of History*. Boston, MA: Beacon Press.

Valelly, Richard. 2004. *The Two Reconstructions: The Struggle for Black Enfranchisement*. Chicago: University of Chicago Press.

Weaver, Vesla. 2007. "Frontlash: Race and the Development of Punitive Crime Policy." *Studies in American Political Development* 21 (2): 230–265.

Wells, Ida B. 1969. *On Lynchings: Southern Horrors, a Red Record, Mob Rule in New Orleans* (reprints of original pamphlets), Arno.

Wells, Ida B. 1970. *Crusade for Justice: The Autobiography of Ida B. Wells*. Chicago: The University of Chicago Press.

Wright-Rigueur, Leah. 2015. *The Loneliness of the Black Republican: Pragmatic Politics and the Pursuit of Power*. Princeton, NJ: Princeton University Press.

Zangrando, Robert. 1980. *The NAACP Crusade Against Lynching, 1909-1950*. Philadelphia: Temple University Press.

American political development and black lives matter in the age of incarceration

Kirstine Taylor

> **ABSTRACt**
> What is the use and purpose of American political development (APD) in the era of Black Lives Matter? This article clarifies the APD's role in analyzing the institutions to which the Movement for Black Lives primarily responds – racialized surveillance, policing, and incarceration. In particular, I spotlight what the discipline can offer, given the challenges of the current Trump era. The rise of Donald Trump to the presidency and the concurrent popularization of white populist nationalism in mainstream American politics present unique challenges. I argue that today, as scholars strive to understand how we arrived, or arrived again, in an era of overt white supremacist rhetoric, American political development's focus on historical institutional change offers necessary grounding. In an era of Charlottesville and chants of "Build the wall!", our collective focus is easily drawn to the spectacular and away from the long-standing and institutional, but black and brown lives also depend on our collective attention to the quieter routines of institutionalized racial violence that developed in post-civil rights era – even, and perhaps especially, in the absence of overt racial demagoguery.

What is the use and purpose of American political development (APD) in the era of Black Lives Matter? At first glance it might appear that the discipline, preoccupied as it is with apprehending the historical development of U.S. political institutions and the durability of shifts in the governing power of the American state, is perhaps less than agile at analyzing such a new, evolving, and diffuse social movement (Orren and Skowronek 2004). Indeed, as Christopher Lebron notes, unlike the Black Power Movement whose political vision is contained in Kwame Ture and Charles Hamilton's indispensable 1967 text, *Black Power*, the Movement for Black Lives has no singular text to provide it with philosophical anchorage (Lebron 2017). And in place of centralized leadership that has been a hallmark of black civil rights organizations since the birth of the National Association for the Advancement of Colored People (NAACP), the Movement instead mobilizes in real time based on a simple, urgent claim: that black lives are human lives and should not be subjected to cursory, vengeful or routine termination. These characteristics present challenges to scholars seeking to assess the Movement's precise impact on state development and state power.

At the same time, however, the precarity of African American lives in the U.S. is not a new phenomenon, nor is mobilization for the protection of those lives. When Alicia Garza, Patrisse Cullors, and Opal Tometi created the Movement for Black Lives, they responded not only to a singular event of violence perpetrated and justice denied – the 2013 acquittal of neighborhood watchman George Zimmerman for the death of Trayvon Martin – but to deeply rooted and deeply historical patterns of racialized state violence in the U.S. As Neil Roberts puts it, Martin's death "marks a moment in American political life where past and future are mutually determining" (2012).

In this sense, Garza, Cullors, Tometi and the countless advocates of #BlackLivesMatter tread in the tradition of Ida B. Wells, W. E. B. Du Bois, Audre Lorde, James Baldwin, and others who have mobilized against the vilification of blackness and for the protection of black people since the end of Reconstruction (Francis 2014; Taylor 2016; Lebron 2017).

Since Martin's death, the work of the Movement has only spread as the list of names of black and brown men, women, and children subjected to police violence grows longer. A year after Zimmerman's acquittal protests erupted in Ferguson, Missouri in response to officer Darren Wilson's fatal shooting of Michael Brown. This event crystalized state violence in black communities as a national problem and crystalized #BlackLivesMatter as, in the words of Keeanga-Yamahtta Taylor, "a movement, not a moment" (Taylor 2016). In 2016, the Movement articulated a radical platform of liberation centered on the "increasingly visible violence against Black people."[1] The platform includes the familiar problem of violent policing, but also targets what Juliet Hooker terms "the key pillars of contemporary white supremacy": mass incarceration, heightened state surveillance of black-centered organizations, the militarization of law enforcement, capital punishment, and economic injustice (Hooker 2017). While #BlackLivesMatter is best known for its attention to policing, the Movement is dedicated to fighting a complex set of interlocking institutions that render black life in the U.S. precarious. In this light, given the longstanding and ongoing nature of the problems to which the Movement responds, the question of APD's utility in the age of Black Lives Matter actually betrays a prior question that scholars of APD may yet grapple with: What is the use of APD in an age in which African Americans and other people of color are disproportionately subjected to the racialized state powers of surveillance, policing, and incarceration?

In this article, I seek to clarify APD's role in analyzing the institutions to which the Movement for Black Lives primarily responds – surveillance, policing, and incarceration. In particular, I speak to what the discipline can offer given the challenges of the current Trump era. The rise of Donald Trump to the presidency and the concurrent popularization of white populist nationalism in mainstream American politics presents unique challenges. From his 1989 insistence that the Central Park Five be executed to his suggestion that the white supremacist rally in Charlottesville, Virginia in August 2017 was attended by "very fine people," President Trump has owed his political rise in part to a form of open racial demagoguery not seen in a presidential election since Barry Goldwater's 1964 bid. What was once aberrational in the post-civil rights era is now nearly common. Today, as scholars strive to understand how we arrived, or arrived again, in an era of overt white supremacist rhetoric, APD's focus on historical institutional change offers necessary grounding. In the case of Black Lives Matter, the discipline fills out the picture of how the

U.S. carceral state, encompassing surveillance, law enforcement, and incarceration, became a primary governing institution in the U.S. – and what relation this bears to spectacular displays of white nationalism that are increasingly common today.

Rethinking racism in the age of incarceration

At the height of the 2016 presidential election, Donald Trump's then chief strategic advisor Steven Bannon commented on Black Lives Matter protests in the wake of police violence. "In the meantime, here's a thought," wrote Bannon, "What if the people getting shot by the cops did things to deserve it? There are, after all, in this world, some people who are naturally aggressive and violent" (2016). Here as elsewhere, Bannon sounds for all the world like midcentury southern segregationists who denounced the Civil Rights Movement and the implementation of *Brown v. Board of Education* by offering up well-worn images of black criminality.

Popularized in the early twentieth century, the idea of innate black criminality has buttressed a host of urban, state, and national policies regarding African Americans (Muhammad 2010). But in the 1950s and 1960s, the idea hit new heights of popularity as the nation adjusted to the Supreme Court's 1954 decision that separate did not mean equal. In September 1956, for instance, two years after Washington, D.C. desegregated its public schools, the monthly publication of the Mississippi White Citizens' Council ran a political cartoon depicting violence in the capitol city's integrated schools. In it, a schoolhouse, labeled "the nation's integrated showcase," explodes from the inside out, its roof flying off and its doors bursting open to expel white students who run with arms outstretched to the safety of nearby Virginia (The Citizens Council 1956). At the time, Virginia was the home of the massive resistance movement, so called because it sought to resist any desegregation effort in keeping with the Supreme Court's decision. The message of the cartoon is clear: white students can only be kept safe by keeping their schools free from black students. On this logic, integration and black civil rights are law-and-order issues.

The Citizens' Council was not alone in this rhetoric. Other southern publications likewise bolstered the supposed link between blackness and violence. Massive resistance literature out of Alabama darkly reported in 1961 that "Negro juvenile delinquency" in Philadelphia escalated due to black and white students attending integrated schools (George 1961). The author, the segregationist crusader W. George, linked this outcome to the "hereditary" propensity of black youth towards crime. Segregationist politicians eagerly dispensed the same rhetoric. In the months before the 1960 Civil Rights Act moved through Congress, for instance, South Carolina Senator Strom Thurmond submitted a report into the *Congressional Record* that argued there was an "incontrovertible link" between integration and crime, and accused New York senator Jacob Javits and other civil rights supporters of attempting to "'export' New York City's combination of integration, crime, and racial strife to the South" (quoted in Crespino 2012). But by the time Barry Goldwater secured the Republican nomination for the presidency in 1964, theories of innate black criminality were largely considered out of step with American values, and Goldwater's bigoted campaign lost definitively to Lyndon B. Johnson's coalition of liberals and moderates. In place of overtly racist rhetoric that sutured criminality biologically to race, colorblindness came to define the racial rhetoric of the post-civil rights era.

If the idea that African Americans are "naturally" predisposed to "aggression and violence," in Bannon's terminology, reeks of old-fashioned biological racism, scholarship in race and APD demonstrates that the expansion of state institutions that disproportionately target, police, and incarcerate African Americans and other people of color elides easy categorization. In fact, the decades of overt white supremacy's relative absence in national political campaigns are the very decades of the U.S. carceral system's most rapid expansion. Between Goldwater's campaign and Donald Trump's, the U.S. carceral population grew from two hundred thousand to over two million people. Currently, an astonishing 6.7 million adults are incarcerated in prisons or jails or are on probation or parole, and several hundred thousand more are detained in immigration detention centers and juvenile correctional facilities (Kaeble and Glaze 2016). That the U.S. carceral system has a distinctly racial character is undeniable, so much so that Michelle Alexander has termed it "the New Jim Crow" (2010). At yearend 2015, African Americans and Latinos together made up 57% of the U.S. prison population and fully half of the U.S. jail population, far outpacing their share of the general population (Carson and Anderson 2016; Minton and Zeng 2016).

What role did arguments of the Citizens Council and Strom Thurmond play in the creation of the carceral state? Some APD scholarship argues that midcentury southern segregationists played an outsized role. According to these scholars, the rise of law-and-order politics and the subsequent ballooning of the U.S. carceral system is the result of southern racial conservatives working to maintain the violent prerogatives of Jim Crow, white working class discomfiture with the scope of liberal civil rights policy, or the result of Nixonian southern strategists capitalizing on rising white anxieties of "street crime" after the riots of the 1960s (Carter 1995; Beckett 1999; Flamm 2005; Weaver 2007; Alexander 2010).

But while it is possible to draw a line from midcentury southern segregationists' rhetoric of black "criminality" to the tough-on-crime politics that popularized the War on Drugs, mandatory minimums, "three strikes" laws, and crime control legislation, recent scholarship also cautions that overt racism played only a partial role in the creation of the carceral state. Naomi Murakawa and historian Elizabeth Hinton, for instance, each document the role that liberal policymakers have played in the creation of our now expansive prison system (Murakawa 2014; Hinton 2016). Ruth Wilson Gilmore, Daniel HoSang, and Jordan Camp have separately illustrated the popularization of crime policy in the supposedly liberal bastion of California (Gilmore 2007; HoSang 2010; Camp 2016). Marie Gottschalk highlights, among other things, the surprising role victim's rights groups played in passing tough-on-crime legislation and the severely limited dent prison reform movements have made in recent efforts to reduce the prison population (2006, 2014). Judah Schept documents the steadfast commitment to prison building in the progressive university town of Bloomington, Indiana (2015). And Michael Javen Fornter and James Forman, Jr. both identify black elected officials as central figures in the twentieth century's drive to incarcerate black people (Fortner 2015; Forman 2017).

In my own research, which focuses on the development of state-level carceral policy in the post-World War II American South, I am finding that even in the nation's most racially conservative region the origins of crime policy are multiple, encompassing Old South segregationist and New South moderate legislative agendas. For instance, North Carolina, long considered the South's most progressive state, was a pioneer of carceral expansion at midcentury. Between 1951 and 1969, North Carolina substantially revised and expanded its criminal code, increased and professionalized its investigative and law enforcement agencies, increased its capacity to incarcerate juvenile offenders, and doubled its prison population, which would balloon alongside the nations in subsequent decades. African Americans felt these developments most acutely. By 2012, 56% of North Carolina's 38,385 inmates were African Americans, far outpacing their representation in their overall population in the state (Lancaster and Sullivan 2012).

These expansions took place as North Carolina politicians attempted to rein in *both* white supremacist violence and black civil rights activism, what politicians referred to as "extremism on both sides." On the one hand, the new crime legislation and increased law enforcement powers targeted the activities of the United Klans of America, a white terrorist organization who boasted a particularly large membership in North Carolina in the 1960s. Consider, for instance, Governor Terry Sanford's language in a speech denouncing the growth of the Klan in the summer of 1964:

> Because there is a growing concern across the state, I think it is necessary to remind the people involved that the Ku Klux Klan is not going to take over North Carolina. Taking the law into their hands, running people away, burning crosses, making threats, wearing hoods, are all illegal practices and are not going to be permitted... Let the KKK get this clear. I am not going to tolerate their illegal actions, and the people of North Carolina are not going to put up with it. I repeat, the KKK is not going to take over North Carolina. (Sanford 1964a)

In an effort to curtail well-worn tactics of white extralegal violence gaining speed and force in the state, the North Carolina General Assembly passed explicitly anti-Klan legislation. In the late 1950s and early 1960s, the General Assembly created special punishments for arson of public buildings, made it unlawful to use a false bomb or call in false bomb threats, outlawed the use of threats over the phone, created mandatory minimum punishments for the possession of explosives, and made it unlawful to burn schoolhouses.

Even as they outlawed the high crimes of dedicated white supremacists, North Carolina politicians also passed new legislation designed to criminalize the everyday, nonviolent political behavior of black civil rights activists. When the Greensboro Four first sat down at Woolworth's lunch counter on February 1, 1960, launching the sit-in movement that would soon spread like wildfire across the South, the governor responded not with the terminology of innate black criminality, but of public safety. He explained to a gathering of black civil rights leaders in 1963:

> These mass demonstrations also had reached the point where I, as head of the executive branch of government, responsible for law enforcement, peace and order, was required to establish a firm policy for North Carolina. My responsibility for public safety required that I take action before danger erupted into violence. I do not intend to let mass demonstrations destroy us. I hope you will not declare war on those who urge courses of reason at this time. (Sanford 1964b)

New legislation designed to criminalize civil rights protest heightened the state's power to police, apprehend, and jail black citizens. By the close of the 1960s, North Carolina had passed new criminal trespass laws, made "demonstrations or assemblies of persons kneeling or lying down in public buildings" a misdemeanor crime, and outlawed several tactics and activities relating to the Civil Rights Movement. The targeted policing of African

Americans, the purview of law enforcement since the invention of slave patrols, now took on a colorblind cast. Increasingly in the midcentury South, the racialized policing of civil rights activists, and black use of public space more generally, operated absent the old segregationist logic that African Americans are naturally violent. Instead, a surprisingly race-neutral language of "public peace" and "law and order" came to define the growing carceral regime of the New South.

In sum, the literature demonstrates that the institutional roots of U.S. carceral expansion are multiple and complex, and cannot be reduced to the presence of overt white supremacist logics. To be sure, conservative politicians have been the traditional proponents of tough-on-crime laws. Richard Nixon pioneered "law and order" as a winning political rhetoric in his Southern Strategy in 1968. Ronald Reagan famously insisted that he had an "eighteenth-century attitude on law and order." And in 2016, Donald Trump accepted the nomination to the U.S. presidency with a direct message: "I am the law-and-order candidate." But despite the ostensible link between law-and-order Republican leaders, racial conservatism, and crime policy, the institutional history of the carceral system's development in the last half of the twentieth century is far more complicated. Indeed, the two farthest-reaching crime bills in American history were the Safe Streets and Crime Control Act of 1968 and the 1994 Violent Crime and Law Enforcement Act, both signed into law under Democratic administrations. In the South, law enforcement expanded and new crime legislation passed, both falling heaviest on African Americans, at the very historical moment that Klan activity was outlawed and white supremacy derided as outdated and hateful.

Conclusions

The scholarship revealing the complex racial roots of U.S. carceral state does not stand alone in its attention to race and political development. Scholars of race and APD have for decades labored to reveal the racial underpinnings of the American state. This scholarship spans virtually every aspect of the nation's political development, and includes uneven processes of regional democratization (Lowndes 2009; Johnson 2010; Mickey 2015), segregation and city development (Sugrue 2005; Lassiter 2006; HoSang 2010; Johnson 2014; Schickler 2016), labor (Frymer 2011), law and civil rights (Brandwein 1999; Novkov 2008; Dawson 2013; Francis 2014; Thurston 2015), the formation of police (Sullivan 2008; Singh 2014), the presidency (Milkis 2008), and the way we count citizens (Thompson 2016). Despite the fact that, as Julie Novkov, Joseph Lowndes, and Dorrian T. Warren have noted, "race is present at every critical moment in political development in the United States," it is only in the last few decades the precise relationship between race and the nation's political development has been a subject of serious scholarship (Lowndes, Novkov, Warren 2008). In transgressing disciplinary norms and ideological blind spots that typically understand race, racism, and anti-racist movements as side stories rather than main features of political development, the literature on race and APD has revealed that race is a central feature in the creation, management, and governance of American political institutions.

The form of state power that the Movement for Black Lives identifies as "the war on black people" – the cocktail of racialized surveillance, policing, and incarceration that plagues black communities and other communities of color – can and has operated in the absence of racial demagoguery. To be sure, this does not lessen or alleviate the necessity of eradicating white nationalism, and particularly white nationalist violence, from our current politics, but it does suggest that vanquishing these does not "fix" the problem of racialized state violence. Indeed, if we are to learn any lessons from the history of mass incarceration's emergence and development from the APD literature, it should be that racialized state power does not require the terminology of white supremacists. In an era of Charlottesville and chants of "Build the wall!" our collective focus is easily drawn to the spectacular and away from the longstanding and institutional, but black and brown lives also depend on our attention to the quieter routines of institutionalized racial violence that have developed in post-civil rights era – even, and perhaps especially, in the absence of overt demagoguery. This is the task of APD in the age of Black Lives Matter: to provide a longer, larger, and more complicated story of the institutions and patterns of governance that render black lives uniquely precarious in American life.

Note

1. https://policy.m4bl.org/platform/

Disclosure statement

No potential conflict of interest was reported by the author.

ORCID

Kirstine Taylor http://orcid.org/0000-0001-6559-6413

References

Alexander, Michelle. 2010. *The New Jim Crow*. New York: The New Press.
Bannon, Steven. 2016. "Sympathy for the Devils: The Plot Against Roger Ailes – and America." *Breitbart.com*. July 10. http://www.breitbart.com/big-journalism/2016/07/10/sympathy-devils-plot-roger-ailes-america/.
Beckett, Katherine. 1999. *Making Crime Pay: Law and Order in Contemporary American Politics*. New York: Oxford University Press.
Brandwein, Pamela. 1999. *Reconstructing Reconstruction: The Supreme Court and the Production of Historical Truth*. Durham, NC: Duke University Press.
Camp, Jordan. 2016. *Incarcerating the Crisis: Freedom Struggles and the Rise of the Neoliberal State*. Berkeley, CA: University of California Press.
Carson, E. Ann, and Elizabeth Anderson. 2016. "Prisoners in 2015." *Bureau of Justice Statistics*.
Carter, Dan T. 1995. *The Politics of Rage: George Wallace, the Origins of the New Conservatism, and the Transformation of American Politics*. New York: Simon & Schuster.
Citizens Council. 1956, September. "The Nation's Integrated Showcase." *The Citizens Council* 1 (12).
Crespino, Joseph. 2012. *Strom Thurmond's America*. New York: Hill and Wang Publishers.
Dawson, Michael. 2013. *Blacks in and Out of the Left*. Harvard, CT: Harvard University Press.
Flamm, Michael W. 2005. *Law and Order: Street Crime, Civil Unrest, and the Crisis of Liberalism in the 1960s*. New York: Columbia University Press.
Forman, James. 2017. *Locking Up Our Own: Crime and Punishment in Black America*. New York: Farrar, Straus and Giroux.
Fortner, Michael Javen. 2015. *Black Silent Majority: The Rockefeller Drug Laws and the Politics of Punishment*. Cambridge, MA: Harvard University Press.

Francis, Megan Ming. 2014. *Civil Rights and the Making of the Modern American State.* New York: Cambridge University Press.
Frymer, Paul. 2011. *Black and Blue: African Americans, the Labor Movement, and the Decline of the Democratic Party.* Princeton, NJ: Princeton University Press.
George, W. 1961. "Race Heredity and Civilization: Human Progress and the Race Problem." *Rights for Whites* pamphlet. (North Carolina State Archives, Terry Sanford Papers, General Correspondence 1961, Box 111, Folder "Segregation, General").
Gilmore, Ruth Wilson. 2007. *Golden Gulag: Prisons, Surplus, Crisis, and Opposition in Globalizing California.* Berkeley, CA: University of California Press.
Gottschalk, Marie. 2006. *The Prison and the Gallows: The Politics of Mass Incarceration in America.* New York: Cambridge University Press.
Gottschalk, Marie. 2014. *Caught: The Prison State and the Lockdown of American Politics.* Princeton, NJ: Princeton University Press.
Hinton, Elizabeth. 2016. *From the War on Poverty to the War on Crime: The Making of Mass Incarceration in America.* Cambridge, MA: Harvard University Press.
Hooker, Juliet. 2017. "Black Protest/White Grievance: On the Problem of White Political Imaginations Not Shaped by Loss." *South Atlantic Quarterly* 116 (3): 483–504.
HoSang, Daniel. 2010. *Racial Propositions: Ballot Initiatives and the Making of Postwar California.* Berkeley, CA: University of California Press.
Johnson, Kimberley. 2010. *Reforming Jim Crow: Southern Politics and State in the Pre-Brown South.* New York: Oxford University Press.
Johnson, Kimberley. 2014. "Black Suburbanization: American Dream or the New Banlieue?" *The Cities Papers, Social Science Research Council.* July 2014.
Kaeble, Danielle, and Lauren Glaze. 2016. "Correctional Populations in the United States, 2015." *Bureau of Justice Statistics.*
Lancaster, Jennie, and Nicole E. Sullivan. 2012. *2011-2012 Annual Statistical Report.* North Carolina Department of Public Safety.
Lassiter, Matthew. 2006. *The Silent Majority: Suburban Politics in the Sunbelt South.* Princeton, NJ: Princeton University Press.
Lebron, Christopher. 2017. *The Making of Black Lives Matter: A Brief History of an Idea.* New York: Oxford University Press.
Lowndes, Joseph. 2009. *From the New Deal to the New Right.* New Haven, CT: Yale University Press.
Lowndes, Joseph, Julie Novkov, and Dorrian T. Warren. 2008. *Race and American Political Development.* New York: Routledge.
Mickey, Robert. 2015. *Paths Out of Dixie: The Democratization of Authoritarian Enclaves in America's Deep South, 1944-1972.* Princeton, NJ: Princeton University Press.
Milkis, Sydney. 2008. "The Modern Presidency, Social Movements, and the Administrative State: Lyndon Johnson and the Civil Rights Movement." In *Race and American Political Development*, edited by Joseph Lowndes, Julie Novkov, and Dorian T. Warren, 256–287. New York: Routledge.
Minton, Todd, and Zhen Zeng. 2016. *Jail Inmates in 2015. Bureau of Justice Statistics.*
Muhammad, Khalil Gibran. 2010. *The Condemnation of Blackness: Race, Crime, and the Making of Modern Urban America.* Cambridge, MA: Harvard University Press.
Murakawa, Naomi. 2014. *The First Civil Right: How Liberals Built Prison America.* New York: Oxford University Press.
Novkov, Julie. 2008. *Racial Union: Law, Intimacy, and the White State in Alabama, 1865-1954.* Ann Arbor, MI: University of Michigan Press.
Orren, Karen, and Stephen Skowronek. 2004. *The Search for American Political Development.* New York: Cambridge University Press.
Roberts, Neil. 2012. "Trayvon Martin: Introduction." *Theory and Event* 15 (3). muse.jhu.edu/article/484423.

Sanford, Terry. 1964a. "Denouncing Actions of the Ku Klux Klan as Illegal." In *Messages, Address, and Public Papers of Terry Sanford, Governor of North Carolina 1961-1965.*, edited by Memory F Mitchell, 1966. Raleigh, NC: State Department of Archives and History.

Sanford, Terry. 1964b. "First Institute for Parole Board Members." In *Messages, Address, and Public Papers of Terry Sanford, Governor of North Carolina 1961-1965*, edited by Memory F. Mitchell, 1966. Raleigh, NC: State Department of Archives and History.

Schept, Judah. 2015. *Progressive Punishment: Job Loss, Jail Growth, and the Neoliberal Logic of Carceral Expansion.* New York: New York University Press.

Schickler, Eric. 2016. *Racial Realignment: The Transformation of American Liberalism, 1932-1965.* Princeton, NJ: Princeton University Press.

Singh, Nikhil Pal. 2014. "The Whiteness of Police." *American Quarterly* 66 (4): 1091–1099.

Sugrue, Thomas. 2005. *The Origins of the Urban Crisis: Race and Inequality in Postwar Detroit.* Princeton, NJ: Princeton University Press.

Sullivan, Kathleen. 2008. "Charleston, the Vesey Conspiracy, and the Development of Police Power." In *Race and American Political Development*, 59–79. New York: Routledge. Lowndes, Novkov, and Warren.

Taylor, Keeanga-Yamahtta. 2016. *From #BlackLivesMatter to Black Liberation.* New York: Haymarket Books.

Thompson, Debra. 2016. *The Schematic State:*.

Thurston, Chloe. 2015. "Policy Feedback in the Public-Private Welfare State: Citizens Advocacy Groups and the Expansion of Access to Government Homeownership Programs." *Studies in American Political Development* 29 (2): 250–267.

Weaver, Vesla. 2007. "Frontlash: Race and the Development of Punitive Crime Policy." *Studies in American Political Development* 21 (Fall): 230–265.

(Re)Defining the black body in the era of Black Lives Matter: the politics of blackness, old and new

Shayla C. Nunnally

ABSTRACT
As a social construction, race has been defined differently for various racial groups. The construction of the "black body," over time, has been fraught with societal, scientific, biological, and educational conceptualizations about the members, who comprise this group. These racial ideas have challenged the humanity, rights, and sociolegal incorporation of "black" persons into American society. In order to grapple with contemporary understandings of the "black body," we should assess the historical discourses, public policies, and vast contexts, over time, for which the "black body" has struggled to assert its equality and liberation. Through the analysis of unconventional political contexts, such as African-American education, and particularly, historically black institutions, such as historically black colleges and universities (HBCU's) and Jim Crow black public high schools, (African)American political development can understand how race influenced the political decisions affecting the democratic experiences, agency, and responses of black Americans to their groups' racial construction and treatment. Such studies can move black sociopolitical experiences beyond historical lore and situate them within the contemporary context of Black Lives Matter's arguments, politics, and public policy interests.

Race and (African) American political development

Race is a social construction, an idea with no biological foundation (Omi and Winant 1994; Gossett 1997). As a concept, race organizes bodies into a social hierarchy, whereupon bodies are attributed different values and social statuses. In the United States, people's bodies are defined socio-legally and differently over time, distinguished as "white" and "non-white" persons (Mills 1997; Haney-Lopéz 2006). Yet, the most restrictive racial categorization has been based upon defining, by law and societal definition, those persons of African descent, who have also become known as "black" (Davis 1991).

The American racial hierarchy places whites' sociopolitical status atop nonwhites', and contemporary data continue to illustrate the extent to which whites have a higher socioeconomic status compared to most other racial and ethnic groups, barring the advancements of some Asian American ethnic groups (McClain and Carew 2017). In an era of the Black Lives Matter movement, it is important for scholars of American political development to contextualize the historical and contemporary meanings of race, in order to account for its effects on society today, and in particular, its effects on the socially-constructed "black body." In the words of political theorist, Chris Lebron, "The black body has always been at the center of racial inequality in America – how could it not, given our irrational preoccupation with skin color (Lebron 2017: 102)?"

However, through understanding the construction of the "black body" over time, we as political scientists can understand better the political contexts and policy environments in which the "black body" continues to be scripted disparately compared to the "white body," in particular. Engaging "the black body" in this way, also, assists us in understanding the contemporary political messages of black political actors, especially those who identify with the tenets of the Black Lives Matter movement.

As researchers of American political development, understanding the construction of the "black body" helps us to understand race, itself, as a larger institution with social, political, and economic processes for which people interact, according to racially-ascribed social norms, social networks, expectations, and political preferences, based upon their racial group status. In the conceptualization of King and Smith (2008), we also can render more visible the adaptation of political actors' interests based upon their situatedness in the American racial hierarchy via what they refer to as "racial institutional orders," which adapt and change over time to serve racialized political interests. Thus, it is important to comprehend the construction of the "black body," over time, in order to understand the significance of (African) American political development in times past and in an era of the Black Lives Matter movement.

How this particular "black body" has been treated lends critical analysis to the personification of bodies, once deemed "property" by the state and not recognized with personhood. Black Americans' human and civil rights had to be *accrued*, recognized, and protected by the state – a state that also historically proved complicit in their oppression. Without the knowledge of this historical treatment of the "black body," we lose sight of the various possibilities for political violation, activism, and agency to incorporate the "black body" as a full, human, rights-bearing body, in the American politic. American political development studies can provide us the contexts, over time, of state and societal discourses, laws, and the identification of specific strategic political actors, whether as perpetrators of (in)justices or as agentic actors. Hence, African-American political development assists us with tracing the processes of blacks' struggle to move beyond the constructed, corporeal "black body" towards black humanity, and what Lebron (2017) would perhaps note distinctly as "black personhood."

In my discussion of the "black body," I, first, describe the historical origins of its construction as a corporeal body, socio-legally proscribed as enslaved, devoid of liberty, "property," and without constitutional rights, until Reconstruction-era laws recognized and applied to it citizenship, voting rights, and legal protection, nonetheless, with social inequality. Next, I describe the state's legal divestment of equal protection of the laws, as applied to the "the black body," through the use of scientific racism to "prove" biological, racial differences and promote negative, black racial stereotypes that became public knowledge about black Americans and facilitated the fabricated "Negro problem." Then, I discuss how this racial "knowledge" was used to promote inequality and additional divestment of resources in different aspects of black life, most notably, in the area of education, where "separate but equal" educational facilities, in practice, were operated as under-resourced black public schools. Yet, these schools also became inadvertent sites of resistance, as black Americans sought and acquired higher education levels.

As I point to the significance of (African) American political development in understanding the agentic constitution of unconventionally-studied black institutions, such as black public high schools, I highlight the need for examining the historical context, sociopolitical engagement, and activist responses of black Americans to Jim Crow-era oppression. Through this lens (among others), I argue that we can further contextualize the historical framing, contemporary nuances, and complexities of the "black body" in the new-age, Black Lives Matter movement. It is through this movement that we see clear articulation that *all* "black bodies" can make legitimate claims for equality and justice and rightly be a part of black political agendas, whereas historically, such inclusion may have been more marginal.

Defining the "Black Body" in historical perspective: a societal denigration

Scholars of American race and politics acknowledge the extent to which, over time, white supremacy defines the relationship between white and nonwhite persons and further defines the practices that restrict nonwhite persons' behavior, and they also acknowledge how this affects incorporating the analysis of race and American political development (Lowndes, Novkov, and Warren 2008). Emerging from New World, western hemispheric contact among indigenous peoples of the Americas, Europe, and Africa, the bodies of people from each of these continents were defined by the economy of slavery, such that Europeans drove and immensely profited from trade markets built upon cheap (and mostly, unpaid) labor and production of indigenous and African peoples, beginning in the fifteenth century.

By the mid-seventeenth century, the first laws distinguishing Africans from Europeans appeared in the North American colonies, and by the century's end, slavery in colonial America became racialized and codified as synonymous with the "black body" and further characterized by lifelong stricture, based on the enslaved status of the African mother, and not patrilineage (Painter 2006; Franklin and Moss 2007). Not only could a black person, then, be born into slavery, but also, one could die in slavery, with limited options for freedom. The institution of chattel slavery further commodified and economized the "black body" as "property" and the "white (male) body" as free, citizenship-worthy (via the Naturalization Act of 1789), and importantly, protected, by the rights embodied in the U.S. Constitution (Mills 1997). Although at one point recognized as three-fifths a person for representation purposes in the U.S. Constitution, nonetheless, enslaved Africans did not have the right to vote, themselves, until codification over almost eight decades after the ratification of the Constitution.

In a slavery-based, economic system that prized human procreation to breed and maximize the reproduction of certain body parts believed to be assets for labor, the "black body" became institutionalized as a public entity, subjected to public scrutiny, violated of personal-space and privacy, and marketed for sale on public auction blocks (Hartman 1997; Johnson 1999). This public objectification further devalued the humanity and personhood of enslaved Africans, who, also as commodities sold in chattel slavery, were recognized by the U.S. courts as property to be bequeathed, even upon their slave owner's death. While freed African people existed in smatterings throughout the North and the South, the U.S. Supreme Court, nonetheless, established a different status for enslaved Africans, who lacked governance over their own "personhood," because they were deemed "property" with no rights for which the Court acknowledged or found worthy to protect; furthermore, national citizenship was barred from all descendants of enslaved Africans (*Dred Scott* v. *Sanford* 1857). Otherwise, defining this "black body" as "rights-bearing" and capable of sovereignty also challenged conventional ideological arguments that slave–owners touted as reasons to protect slavery: Slavery was declared a "societal good" because it offered structure and resources that, otherwise, enslaved Africans would be unable to provide for themselves (Faust 1981). Simply put, slavery's paternalism was seen as a public good, and while Northern abolitionists opposed slavery, many Northern blacks were discriminated against and not acknowledged as social equals to whites, in that region (Litwack 1970).

The American Civil War helped bring slavery to an end, and yet, despite passage of the Civil War Amendments, which formally prohibited slavery, provided birthright citizenship to natural-born persons, equal protection of the law, due process, and voting rights (for black men), the assumption of full-citizenship for African-Americans would not occur until the mid-twentieth century, during a Second Reconstruction era. In a society also grappling with the ideological dominance of white supremacy theories and a dominating "science of race," by the latter-nineteenth century, oppression of the "black body" occurred further by racial knowledge publicized through research, media hysteria, and (pseudo-)scientific racism that was also taught via the public education curricula (Gossett 1997; Mills 1997; Dorr 2000).

Social Darwinists openly debated what to do with the ill-fated "Negro," who also posed a societal burden (along with other racial and ethnic groups considered to be of "lower stocks") and an inconvenient pariah for whites, who, themselves, were deemed naturally "fit" to evolve and contribute to societal progress. Hence, in their view, whites were forced to solve the "Negro question," for a less "evolved" race – "the Negro." This query – what to do with the "Negro" – prevailed in the latter-nineteenth and early-twentieth centuries, because blacks, at the time, were deemed a societal threat because they were no longer bound by institutionalized slavery, which supposedly provided the paternalizing structure to tame blacks' purported inferior intelligence, depraved mentality, and disobedient deportment (Faust 1981; Taylor 2016). Without some formal, institutionalized system of containment, blacks were feared to run amok.

Indeed, this was a "condemnation of blackness," met with the perceived need to control "black behavior" through public policies that also criminalized behaviors associated with "the black body" (Muhammad 2011). These policies varied in their attempts to curb criminality, miscegenation, and reproduction (within and across races with whites), and segregation in every aspect of life. The "negro" was unaccommodated, treated second-rate, and openly violated, despite his incorporation into the American polity, via Reconstruction-era public policies. Moreover, outright disfranchisement and disavowal of protection for the "black body" during Jim Crow, further oppressed these sociopolitical advancements, post-slavery.

The psychological effects of Jim Crow, in particular, cast black bodies in ways similar to the American institution of slavery but also differently, based upon pointed second-class citizenship status. Rather, physical, psychological, and policy-driven violences obliterated the "black body" from public discourses of equality and led to divestment of Reconstruction-era (and later, twentieth century) political investments (Mills 1997; Taylor 2016). The "black body" was relegated to a racialized private sphere for which equality could only be spoken in the confines of racially-segregated spaces (the black public sphere), wherein black institutions (like the church and educational facilities) and organizational spaces in Southern states, were heavily concentrated by black Americans, prior to the Great Migration of many to Northern cities in the early-twentieth century (Dawson 2001). This black "home sphere" provided resources, wherein otherwise, the state failed to do so, based upon its own discretion (Lewis 1990).

Black Americans countered this state- and societally-sanctioned condemnation of the "black body" through their own articulation of the "New Negro" identity and politics via arts, letters, black media, and activism in the early-twentieth century, and they objected to the negative constructions of "blackness" and recast the "black body" as humane and self-articulating (Lebron 2017), as opposed to an inanimate "body" on which to project negative aspersions. Nevertheless, simultaneously, violences were onslaught against the "black body" and normalized in the form of racial etiquette, segregation, exclusion, legal re-enslavement via a convict-lease system, and extra-legal lynchings (Litwack 1998; Pinar 2001; Blackmon 2008; Lebron 2017). The racial project of a black parallel society – Jim Crow – lasted almost one-hundred years, after the conclusion of the Civil War in 1865. Second Reconstruction public policies such as the Civil Rights Act of 1964, the Voting Rights Act of 1965, and the Fair Housing Act of 1968 improved the corporeal status of how the "black body" was treated by prohibiting formal barriers to public accommodations, voting, and housing. However, these policies still did not address the economic degradation and police brutality that coupled anti-black and systemic racism, which also existed in de facto forms in the North and other predominantly black urban centers across the country (Taylor 2016), and despite policy enactments meant to address racial inequality, civil unrest erupted across the country, beginning with the riots in Watts, Los Angeles in 1965 and lasting through the latter 1960s, with unrest in other places such as Newark, Detroit, Chicago, and New Haven, but also many more. The Kerner Commission, established by President Lyndon B. Johnson, attempted to determine why these riots occurred: Put simply, it was because extreme racial inequality persisted.

By the mid- to latter- twentieth century, once civil rights policies had been implemented, white politicians used black pathological arguments to court white, anti-black animus and political outrage in opposition to rapid changes wrought by the civil rights movement and civil unrest, and they implicitly blamed black Americans for their own circumstances and civil disorder, ignoring the role the state and societal practices played in creating them (Mendelberg 2001; Taylor 2016). Yet, black political elites, over time, increasingly took similar, more moderate political tones, as they also denounced the presumed behavioral practices of the black poor, as being sociopolitically degenerative and anathema to black advancement (Taylor 2016), perhaps even changing the previously more liberal, social welfare support of the black masses by the early, twenty-first century (Tate 2010). This led to increased public policy divestment and a call for "law and order," leaving many urban black communities' problems' address unfulfilled, and practically abandoned.

The environmental effects were devastating, manifesting even today in concentrated poverty, under-performing, elementary and secondary public educational institutions, public health issues, and mass incarceration, further complicated by over-policing and racially disparate, and unfounded "War on Drugs" policies (Alexander 2012; Taylor 2016). Despite 1960s public policies meant to fight the "War on Poverty" and usher in urban redevelopment, the contexts where blacks were more heavily concentrated were not socially mobile for black urban poor people (Taylor 2016). This was not enough. With a changing economy, wherein industrial jobs no longer flourished and shifted to a service industry, black Americans, prepared for the former economy, faced fewer job opportunities in the new one (Rothstein 2017). To an eye unsympathetic to systemic racism, devoting public policies to address blacks' impoverished conditions may appear worthless and unavailing, but this thought, itself, is grounded in institutionalized thought about the Negro and the "black body."

Black futility = public divestment: publicizing the "black body" as "waste"

As white society and many white political actors of the Jim Crow era saw it, investing in "the Negro" was a doomed enterprise, because, too, "the Negro" was doomed for corruption and extinction, as Social Darwinists predicted in the latter-nineteenth century (Gossett 1997; Dorr 2000). To embolden societal knowledge and support of eugenics-based policies, sociopolitical actors encouraged biological instruction on the topic and its ideological premises in the classrooms of public high schools and colleges and universities (Dorr 2000). Disciplines such as biology and anthropology institutionalized the notion of black inferiority in their theories and research (Gossett 1997; Baker 1998). Thus, racial knowledge about the inferiority of "the black body" also evolved in the classroom – textbooks and curriculum: It was purported as *fact*.

Prevailing latter-nineteenth and early-twentieth-century discourses cast black people as "deficient" and "futile" and lacking potentiality of full investment. Pseudo-scientific and public racial knowledge supported these claims, and the "black body," formerly recognized as a valuable labor commodity, became free and assuming of personage, but also biologically and societally repugnant in ways that required regulation, legally and extra-legally, over time (Roberts 1997; Pinar 2001; Hancock 2004; Simien 2011; Threadcraft 2016; Lebron 2017). It is through these violences that the "black body" was cast as a site of "public waste," which was ultimately expendable for the better and public good of white society, through even state-sponsored eugenics projects (1930s–1970s) meant to curb reproduction among a people deemed "unfit" for reproduction and social evolution (as Social Darwinists conceived it). Their bodies were deemed ripe for medical experimentation as enslaved persons under duress (without informed consent) and at the behest of medical schools and the state (Washington 2006).

Moreover, with respect to land, black people often were segregated in resource-poor neighborhoods, poor quality land, and even exposed to environmental hazards – all indicators of environmental racism (Bullard and Wright 2012). Additional government-involved productions of casting the "black body" to racially-marginalized spaces, and sometimes environmental "wastelands" (Bullard and Wright 2012) involved legalized, geographic segregation through the housing market in the early- and mid-twentieth century, such that resources could be concentrated-out black neighborhoods (Katznelson

2005; Coates 2014) and school districts could establish demographic and economic imbalances in black and poor children's education (Highsmith and Erickson 2015). Through the government evincing what Moffett-Bateau (2014) refers to as "bureaucratic violence," today, black public housing residents experience constant, overbearing surveillance, over-regulation of their behavior, and over-exposure to violence to the point that they also feel less protected, less safe, and less empowered to advance change. Bureaucratic violence against black people also occurs when the government responds slowly, if at all, to their concerns, rendering their voices politically ineffective and serving as an affront on their political efficacy.

Casting the "black body" in public as *essentially* and *biologically* different from the "white body" also undergirded the segregationist arguments for separating blacks from whites in *every* aspect of society, including limiting and decreasing public spending on blacks' education in public schools and educators (in comparison to such spending on whites), during Jim Crow. Philanthropists and scholars (white and black) debated the capacity of black intellectualism, as they indulged larger societal questions of the "Negro problem," and questioned black inclusion based on, yet again, where the "black body" fit into Southern political economy, especially. If the "black body" were to "fit" into society, it would have to retain its place as subservient to the "white body." Thus, the "Negro problem" also became an educational question – "How (and to what extent) to educate the Negro?" As "separate and (un)equal" became part of the answer to this question for many whites, black leaders' visions varied, yet towards an eye of "black progress."

Political and educational leaders in white Northern and Southern contexts disagreed over how blacks should be educated for societal participation. They even debated black educational curricula to the effect of sustaining racially-status quo social and economic structures, wherein "black bodies" would fit into the Southern economy, mostly as agrarians and menial laborers (hence, an industrial education) and not as free-thinking labor agents and entrepreneurs (hence, a classical education). Black political leaders (a la Booker T. Washington, W.E.B. Du Bois, and later, Carter G. Woodson) of the day engaged in similar debates; however, their thinking veered towards black group advancement, and at times, curricular enhancements to defy societal beliefs about black inferiority (a la Woodson). Thinking "freely" defied Jim Crow's racial etiquette, especially in Deep South states, which were still heavily dependent upon an agricultural economy and subjugated, black labor (Anderson 1988; Fairclough 2007). The general societal mode, no matter the investment, was that the "Negro" was inferior, meanwhile "whites" were the supreme race. Various systems, including labor, medicine, housing, land concentration, and public education, thus, propagated white supremacy.

To this extent, the institutions that helped facilitate the everyday oppression of black Americans become potential research sites for race and (African) American political development, because these spaces also became politicized points of equal entry and treatment of black Americans. (Later, I emphasize this point with respect to studying African-American political development in the context of black education [and black public high schools, in particular], during Jim Crow.) However, it also becomes important for us to understand the costly effects of "forgetting" the construction of the "black body" in our political development analyses.

Forgetting the construction of the "black body": racism and institutionalized oblivion

As an ideology supported by interrelated beliefs, attitudes, societal structures, public policies, and lingering historic racial stereotypes, which stem from historic, hackneyed, and pseudo-scientific racialized knowledge, white supremacy, thus, sustains a psychology for which people comport or resist. The actions propagating white supremacy constitute racism. Through concealment of all the violences historically committed against black people, white supremacy is reified (Lebron 2017). Extracting these ideas and actions from their historical origins and relevance constitutes institutionalized oblivion and intellectual violences upon the subject, itself. It gives us un-contextualized rhetoric and attentive audiences, who arguably recognize the familiarity of white supremacy's tenets, yet reduce its components to mere liberal-conservative ideological framing, when they once were couched in racially, liberal-conservative framing for which even political actors were publicly recognized (Carmines and Stimson 1989) and for which white political actors devised code-words to evoke white fears, without using racial epithets about blacks openly, because black, civil rights activism during the 1960s influenced American society to deem them no longer socially acceptable (Mendelberg 2001; Taylor 2016). These actions culminate in a public "forgetting" of historic facts about race, ones that even inform similar patterns of systemic racism today, and thus, contribute to a society with a nebulous concept of racism, but no practicing "racists" (Bonilla-Silva 2001 and 2006).

Because of the prevailing, memetic, and ideological nature of white supremacy, we must understand how different actors (white and nonwhite) interacted, complied, perpetuated, or resisted its tenets. This is important for incorporating race in the study of new institutionalism and examining political actors' reactions to white supremacy, Jim Crow as its own institution, and other actors, whose commitment to these tenets and institutions can change over time. Again, this is similar to what King and Smith (2008) describe as "racial institutional orders." However, the way in which American political development comes to understand these interrelated processes of black–white interaction, or what Johnson (2008) refers to as "interracialisms," should be mindful of situating the black (historical) political subject more visibly in these intellectual enterprises and interrogations. (Harris-Lacewell [2003] makes a similar claim, as far as the study of racial attitudes in the U.S.)

The "black body," however, is not just an inanimate concept or political subject to be analyzed: it is an intellectually, emotive and agentic "subject" for which the people, who occupy these bodies have sought liberation for centuries in the New World, through their opposition to their perennial objectification as "things" on which to project power, anger, control, inequality, and inferiority. Simply put, rather, the "black body," beyond corporeality, is personified, and black political activism and struggles to attain equality, over time, remind us of this. Hence, we see blacks' agentic production of black civil society, black-identified and associated arts and letters, and black institutions, which assist in presenting "blacks" as "humankind" (at all times, in their own perspective) and, importantly, "citizens," especially post-Civil War proscription (Lebron 2017).

These cultural and systemic productions also occurred at different points in time from the latter-nineteenth century through the twentieth century, as black orators such as the abolitionist, Frederick Douglass, black educators such as Anna Julia Cooper, black scribes such as Ida B. Wells, Langston Hughes, Zora Neale Hurston, Audre Lorde, and James Baldwin, (re)defined conscriptions of black people through anti-slavery, anti-lynching, anti-intellectual suppression, and anti-dehumanization expressions, to the effect that "Black Lives Matter" is an *idea* that Lebron (2017) asserts predates the current movement of the same appellation. But, arguably, this enterprise of struggle and contestation to re-inscribe the value of the "black body" as equal to that of the "white body" continues in the era of Black Lives Matter, today. However, historically, this project of challenging the "deficient" characterization of blackness focused on also making invisible the secondary statuses of blacks, who were felt to be detrimental to the *positive* portrayal of blackness, and these politics also occurred intraracially. Historically, all intraracial, black group members were not recognized, valued, and equally supported in the struggle for justice and egalitarianism. Thus, it becomes important for American political development to understand in-group contestation and the scope of black political agendas and activism in various realms, within black institutions and larger black movements.

(All) Black bodies matter: studying black institutions and intraracial politics over time

Skocpol and Liazos (2006) remind us of the vast organizational networks that blacks established, during the Jim Crow era, but what about the black institutions, which also served as politically mobilizing agents to effect change in American society? Political science scholars have researched the continuing significance of the black church in political mobilization (Calhoun-Brown 1996; Harris 1999; McDaniel 2008; Tucker-Worgs 2012), but political science has a more limited view in our understanding of other black institutions, such as educational institutions (historically black colleges and universities and historically black public high schools), in the promotion of humanity, citizenship, and socioeconomic mobility among black Americans. Education was a politically contested space, wherein "black bodies" were deemed intellectually limited and incapable and deemed disruptions for whites' education. However, in their fight for humanity, black Americans struggled to acquire and obtain equal access to high-quality education, even as a political enterprise in which they developed their own, black educational institutions, in the face of Reconstruction but also the challenges of Jim Crow.

Black education historians have researched and amassed a literature on historically black colleges and universities and historically Jim Crow black schools (Randolph 2014). These institutions, of which black actors were administrators, teachers, staff, and students, who participated in an educational environment scripted by the provisos of Jim Crow. Yet, their stories of resistance or compliance varied depending upon the ideologies, beliefs, and actions of each of these actors, especially as the civil rights movement transpired. Black actors employed their tenacity, political entrepreneurship in starting their own educational institutions, and political activism to counter Jim Crow constraints. Such narratives and complexities of black Americans moving in and out black- versus white- spaces and adapting "acceptable" norms for black behavior during Jim Crow have received limited historical treatment, as far as black education politics in political science. African-American political development studies can assist with such analyses.

For example, in political science, Orr (1999) helps us to understand how black and white community networks functioned in twentieth century, Baltimore City (MD) public schools' politics, and Orr's analysis centers on the power of "black social capital" and "interracial social capital" in brokering urban education policies. Henig et al. (2001) explore the multifarious politics of race and school reform. More recently, Meier and Rutherford (2017) have provided a contemporary investigation of African-American education and its partisan politics, alerting us to the educational outcomes of black Americans, when the bureaucracies around them comprise majority Democratic or Republican political actors. However, in addition, it is pertinent to examine, over time, the racially discriminatory treatment of the "black body," as far as prohibited literacy during slavery, the Freedmen's Bureau and philanthropic support of black education during Reconstruction, its partisan discourses, public-private partnerships supporting black education during Jim Crow, and importantly, the debates over the quality, type, and level of education that should be afforded to blacks at the public's expense. Such an analysis lends itself to our understanding how black educational institutions represent sites of political resistance, as well.

It is, here, that unconventional black institutions, such as Jim Crow black public high schools, are sites for future political inquiry. Despite their comparatively dearth resources vis-à-vis white public high schools, black public high schools during this era served as politically-socializing agents that assisted black Americans (of various socioeconomic backgrounds) in challenging inferiority claims that dominated civil and political discourses about the "black body" during Jim Crow. Yet, the political resistance potential of black public high schools depended upon several factors: (1) whether secondary education was available in rural or urban areas (2) whether students were taught industrial- versus classical- curricula (3) the influence of external, northern and southern philanthropic whites and white political actors' control over the sociopolitical resources and curricula (4) the individual outlook of black administrators, staff, teachers, and students on the need for promoting challenges to Jim Crow (5) the locus of white sociopolitical actors' resistance to black civil rights and (6) the historic, black social capital in the locale, whether represented as civil rights organizations, historically black colleges and/or universities, black churches, or black-owned businesses (Fairclough 2007).

Harkening the 60th anniversary of the Little Rock Nine integrating Central High School in 1957, we also know the various cases of violences onslaught against blacks, in whites' opposition to school desegregation, post-*Brown* (1954). Understanding these "Jim Crow orders," as Johnson (2008) reminds us, will help us to comprehend the historical, racial stereotypes, political knowledge, political discourses, and political actions that were part and parcel black education. Jim Crow black public high schools, as I argue, are *political institutions* that deserve further analysis in political science, because, at times, we also lose sight of the educational experiences that blacks had prior to desegregation, again, spaces that, themselves, represent a struggle for access to education, whatsoever, despite their disparate resources. Put differently, as public institutions, depending upon the moment of Jim Crow and the "black body's" status, black public high schools represent the struggle for blacks in their respective locales to acquire a higher-level of education. In more Deep South rural areas, whites believed that secondary educations were anathema to black labor productivity (Fairclough 2007). In other areas, there was a question of whether blacks had the intellectual capacity for higher education levels.

Some black high schools also had mantras and curricula that focused on "black excellence" in ways that disrupted and challenged negative, racial stereotypes about blacks' intellectualism, while preparing them for the potential of social mobility, in the face of limited, racialized labor options, once again, more stringently enforced in the Deep South versus the Upper South (Anderson 1988; Fairclough 2007). As for "black excellence," it carried the Jim Crow psychology of knowing that as a black person, one had to be twice as good as whites to win, knowing that if one lost, one still may have been the best and had to settle with being recognized as "second-rate," and knowing that the extent of celebrating black excellence may have had to be balanced delicately with the nuances of racial etiquette in the presence of whites and exuberance in the privacy of black spaces. Differences in resources and white leaders' control of urban versus rural school schedules, curricula, and access to secondary education, also introduced inequalities within black education accessibility, especially in the latter-nineteenth and early-twentieth centuries, before secondary education became more standardized throughout the South in the early-twentieth century (Fairclough 2007).

Black education historians, furthermore, question the extent to which contemporary segregated black public schools may find exemplars for overcoming under-resources, similar to the strategies employed by Jim Crow public schools (Kelly 2009). The point is, black public high schools (and historically black educational institutions, in general) resiled *in spite of* Jim Crow, as they attempted to educate blacks with state-restricted resources.

Within black public high schools, black administrators, teachers, staff, and students surmounted limited resources to produce a respectable, well-prepared, and morally grounded black citizenry (Anderson 1988; Fairclough 2007) – all major tenets of black racial uplift (Gaines 1996). Thus, despite the accessibility of public education to black students, within these institutions, black racial uplift defined who had a clearer role in the larger group's uplift.

During the nineteenth- and early-twentieth centuries, racial uplift ideology was seminal in promoting the most talented blacks as the group for which noblesse oblige led them to represent "the best of the race," with model citizenship and comportment, to serve their communities with an eye towards "uplifting" black community members, who were downtrodden and perceived to be not yet accomplished in the vision of what constituted black group advancement (Du Bois 1903; Gaines 1996). Bourgeois in its orientation and elitist in its adaptation for who best fits the model of blackness to present to the white world, "racial uplift" castigates black group members whose behaviors violate the norms perceived to facilitate black group progress. Whether poor, ill-behaved, or indebted to society due to incarceration, such black group members were perceived to contribute to the negatively stereotypical images that whites abhorred about blacks and employed to oppress them. Thus, at times, black racial uplift ideology was interwoven in these schools' political socialization to produce racial group-focused leaders. On the face, however, black public education was purported to be a "good" for all blacks.

Black racial uplift, also a heavily, black middle-class and religious framing, rendered the "politics of respectability" that was supposed to garner blacks respect, and ultimately, grounds for better treatment and full-citizenship in whites' view (Higginbotham 1993). However, these same "respectability politics" also are known to have secondarily marginalized (a la Cohen 1999) black women, black gay people, and black poor people in particular ways that further suppressed their intraracial political interests from being at the forefront of what was deemed a black political agenda. Racial uplift ideology, and others which have been identified as African-American-focused ideologies (see Dawson 2001 and Harris-Lacewell 2004), point us to black historical subjectivity in American politics, which also further humanizes and complicates the understanding of blacks' political activism during the Jim Crow era, because intraracial differences in ideological perspectives and relationships to Jim Crow oppression made racial uplift inaccessible to some black group members.

Hence, over time, different black intellectuals and activists countered dual oppressions of racism and sexism (e.g., Anna Julia Cooper) and homophobia (e.g., Audre Lorde), as they complicated the scope of black struggle within the United States (Lebron 2017). Moreover, by challenging intraracial pathological claims about the black poor, and instead, attributing them to systemic explanations, we can shift policy agendas to consider black subgroups' interests, which otherwise, have been overshadowed by black elites, who have been often wedded to black middle class concerns (Cohen 1999; Taylor 2016). For example, with respect to education, the "talented tenth" of black Americans received special attention for their success and example to lead other blacks, the masses of whom were believed to be less polished and destined to limited success, similar to what Du Bois (1903) suggested by his "talented-tenth" theory.

Thus, as Lebron (2017) argues, the "idea of Black Lives Matter" predates the popular moniker of the movement. Because there are different black thinkers and activists, who challenged "the norm of blackness" to make it accessible to all blacks. While different black activists introduced their contributions to expand the definition of blackness and those protected by an agenda of racial justice, the contemporary Black Lives Matter movement emphasizes acknowledging all aggrieved blacks at the outset, no matter their sociodemographic backgrounds.

This is why, in an era of Black Lives Matter, contemporarily, this movement challenges the intraracially restrictive access to protection of black leadership that once characterized the often middle-class (male and hetero-normative) protections of *certain* black people. Rather, as Black Lives Matter would now have it, *all* blacks should have access to resources and become valuable in the pursuit of justice and equity. Today, Black Lives Matter presents a concerted point of departure from historic black racial uplift ideology and the politics of respectability. It creates a memetic mantra of full-citizenship and human rights protection for *all* Blacks via social media and textual and visual political activism, no matter their status or background as women, gay, differing ability, gender identification, or undocumented people (Black Lives Matter 2017). If there is a perceived legitimate disparagement or violation, then these persons should be "lifted up," in this case, in the sense of community support seeking justice for the violated black group member. These persons would not be further marginalized, such that their claims for justice render no attention or allies.

With respect to education, more specifically, in a Black Lives Matter lens, an excellent, high-quality education, thus, should be available to *all* black people, irrespective of their black leadership potential or talent. By analyzing historically (and contemporarily) black institutions, such as black colleges and universities and black public high schools, we may also find rich data, in spaces where black leaders such as Mary McLeod Bethune, Anna Julia Cooper, W. E. B. Du Bois, and Booker T. Washington foresaw the future of black socioeconomic advancement through education. Through (African) American political development, we also can learn more about how race affected the "black body" (in its various iterations) and the dynamism and ideological contestation that defined its presence (and erasures) in educational spaces over time, thus, changing the situatedness and actions of both black and white political actors.

Through the lens of *all* black bodies matter, black communities can find extended arguments to protect present-day black institutions, which continue to facilitate the advancement of black people in a continuing "anti-black" society: Over time, the "black body" has, and continues to resist societal, (extra)legal, and governmental violences against it, in pursuit of its humanity and personhood. Today, the Black Lives Matter movement recenters our thoughts about the conceptualization of all "black bodies," their treatment, and protection even in education and *all* other aspects of society. Hence, the many spaces for which black bodies exist also become politicized spaces, which should be subject to political inquiry in political science and our examinations of (African) American political development.

Disclosure statement

No potential conflict of interest was reported by the author.

Funding

This work was supported by University of Connecticut Humanities Institute [Humility and Conviction in Public Life/Public Discourse Project].

References

Alexander, Michelle. 2012. *The New Jim Crow: Mass Incarceration in the Age of Colorblindness*. New York: The New Press.
Anderson, James. 1988. *The Education of Blacks in the South, 1860-1935*. Chapel Hill: University of North Carolina Press.
Baker, Lee D. 1998. *From Savage to Negro: Anthropology and the Construction of Race, 1896-1954*. Berkeley: University of California Press.
Black Lives Matter. 2017. About. October 20. https://blacklivesmatter.com/about/.
Blackmon, Douglas A. 2008. *Slavery by Another Name: The Re-Enslavement of Black Americans from the Civil War to World War*. New York: Anchor Books.
Bonilla-Silva, Eduardo. 2001. *White Supremacy and Racism in the Post-civil Rights Era*. Boulder, CO: Lynne Rienner.
Bonilla-Silva, Eduardo. 2006. *Racism Without Racists: Color-blind Racism and the Persistence of Racial Inequality in the United States*. Lanham, MD: Rowman and Littlefield Publishers, Inc.
Bullard, Robert D., and Beverly Wright. 2012. *The Wrong Complexion for Protection: How the Government Response to Disaster Endangers African American Communities*. New York: New York University Press.
Calhoun-Brown, Allison. 1996. "African American Churches and Political Mobilization: The Psychological Impact of Organizational Resources." *Journal of Politics* 58 (4): 935–953.
Carmines, Edward G., and James A. Stimson. 1989. *Issue Evolution: Race and the Transformation of American Politics*. Princeton: Princeton University Press.
Coates, Ta-Nehisi. 2014. "The Case for Reparations." *The Atlantic* (June). Accessed October 19, 2017. https://www.theatlantic.com/magazine/archive/2014/06/the-case-for-reparations/361631/.

Cohen, Cathy. 1999. *Boundaries of Blackness: AIDS and the Breakdown of Black Politics*. Chicago, IL: University of Chicago Press.
Davis, F. James. 1991. *Who Is Black? One Nation's Definition*. University Park: Pennsylvania State University Press.
Dawson, Michael C. 2001. *Black Visions in the Mirror: The Roots of Contemporary African American Political Ideologies*. Chicago, IL: University of Chicago.
Dorr, Gregory Michael. 2000. "Segregation's Science: The American Eugenics Movement and Virginia, 1900-1980" PhD diss., University of Virginia.
Du Bois, W. E. B. 1903. The Talented Tenth. In *The Negro Problem: A Series of Articles by Representative Negroes of To-day*, Accessed October 20, 2017. http://glc.yale.edu/talented-tenth-excerpts.
Fairclough, Adam. 2007. *A Class of Their Own: Black Teachers in the Segregated South*. Cambridge: Harvard College.
Faust, Drew Gilpin. 1981. *The Ideology of Slavery: Proslavery Thought in the Antebellum South, 1830-1860*. Baton Rouge: Louisiana State University.
Franklin, John Hope, and Alfred A. Moss, Jr. 2007. *From Slavery to Freedom: A History of African Americans*. 8th ed.New York: Knopf.
Gaines, Kevin. 1996. *Uplifting the Race: Black Leadership, Politics, and Culture in the Twentieth Century*. Chapel Hill: University of North Carolina Press.
Gossett, Thomas F. 1997. *Race: The History of an Idea in America*. New York: Oxford University Press.
Hancock, Ange-Marie. 2004. *The Politics of Disgust: The Public Identity of the Welfare Queen*. New York: New York University Press.
Haney-Lopéz, Ian. 2006. *White by Law: The Legal Construction of Race*. Rev. and Updated ed. New York: New York University Press.
Harris, Fredrick C. 1999. *Something Within: Religion in African American Political Activism*. New York: Oxford University Press.
Harris-Lacewell, Melissa V. 2003. "The Heart of the Politics of Race: Centering Black People in the Study of White Racial Attitudes." *Journal of Black Studies* 34 (2): 222–249.
Harris-Lacewell, Melissa V. 2004. *Barbershops, Bibles, and BET: Everyday Talk and Black Political Thought*. Princeton, NJ: Princeton University Press.
Hartman, Saidiya V. 1997. *Scenes of Subjection: Terror, Slavery, and Self-Making in Nineteenth-Century America*. New York: Oxford University Press.
Henig, Jeffrey R., Richard Hula, Marion Orr, and Desiree S. Pedescleaux. 2001. *The Color of School Reform: Race, Politics, and the Challenge of Urban Education*. Princeton, NJ: Princeton University Press.
Higginbotham, Evelyn Brooks. 1993. *Righteous Discontent: The Women's Movement in the Black Baptist Church, 1880-1920*. Cambridge: Harvard University Press.
Highsmith, Andrew R., and Ansley Erickson. 2015. "Segregation as Splitting, Segregation as Joining: Schools, Housing, and the Many Modes of Jim Crow." *American Journal of Education* 121 (4): 563–595.
Johnson, Walter. 1999. *Soul by Soul: Life Inside the Antebellum Slave Market*. Cambridge, MA: Harvard University Press.
Johnson, Kimberley S. 2008. "Jim Crow Reform and the Democratization of the American South." In *Race and American Political Development*, edited by Joseph Lowndes, Julie Novkov, and Dorian Warren, 155–179. New York: Routledge.
Katznelson, Ira. 2005. *When Affirmative Action Was White: An Untold Story of Racial Inequality in Twentieth-Century America*. New York: Norton.
Kelly, Hilton. 2009. "What Jim Crow's Teachers Could Do: Educational Capital and Teachers' Work in Under-resourced Schools." *Urban Review* 42: 329–350.
King, Desmond S., and Rogers M. Smith. 2008. "Racial Orders in American Political Development." In *Race and American Political Development*, edited by Joseph Lowndes, Julie Novkov, and Dorian Warren, 80–105. New York: Routledge.

Lebron, Chris. 2017. *The Making of Black Lives Matter: The History of an Idea*. Oxford: Oxford University Press.

Lewis, Earl. 1990. *In Their Own Interests: Race, Class, and Power in Twentieth-Century Norfolk, Virginia*. Berkeley: University of California Press.

Litwack, Leon F. 1970. *North of Slavery: The Negro in Free States, 1790-1860*. Chicago, IL: University of Chicago.

Litwack, Leon. F. 1998. *Trouble in Mind: Black Southerners in the Age of Jim Crow*. New York: Knopf.

Lowndes, Joseph, Julie Novkov, and Dorian Warren. 2008. "Race and American Political Development." In *Race and American Political Development*, edited by Joseph Lowndes, Julie Novkov, and Dorian Warren, 1–30. New York: Routledge.

McClain, Paula D., and Jessica D. Johnson Carew. 2017. *"Can We All Get Along?" Racial and Ethnic Minorities in American Politics*. Boulder, CO: Westview Press.

McDaniel, Eric. 2008. *Politics in the Pews: The Political Mobilization of Black Churches*. Ann Arbor: University of Michigan Press.

Meier, Kenneth J., and Amanda Rutherford. 2017. *The Politics of African-American Education: Representation, Partisanship, and Educational Equity*. New York: Cambridge University Press.

Mendelberg, Tali. 2001. *The Race Card: Campaign Strategy, Implicit Messages, and the Norm of Equality*. Princeton, NJ: Princeton University Press.

Mills, Charles W. 1997. *The Racial Contract*. Ithaca, NY: Cornell University Press.

Moffett-Bateau, Alexandra. 2014. "The Development of Political Identity in Public Housing Developments". PhD diss., University of Chicago.

Muhammad, Khalil Gibrand. 2011. *The Condemnation of Blackness: Race, Crime, and the Making of Modern Urban America*. Cambridge, MA: Harvard University Press.

Omi, Michael, and Howard Winant. 1994. *Racial Formation in the United States: From the 1960s to the 1980s*. New York: Routledge.

Orr, Marion. 1999. *Black Social Capital: The Politics of School Reform in Baltimore, 1986-1998*. Lawrence: University Press of Kansas.

Painter, Nell. 2006. *Creating Black Americans: African-American History and Its Meanings, 1619 to the Present*. Oxford: Oxford University Press.

Pinar, William P. 2001. *The Gender of Racial Politics and Violence in America: Lynching, Prison Rape, and the Crisis of Masculinity*. New York: Peter Lang.

Randolph, Adah Ward. 2014. "Presidential Address: African-American Education History – A Manifestation of Faith." *History of Education Quarterly* 54 (1): 1–18.

Roberts, Dorothy E. 1997. *Killing the Black Body: Race, Reproduction, and the Meaning of Liberty*. New York: Pantheon Books.

Rothstein, Richard. 2017. *The Color of Law: A Forgotten History of How Our Government Segregated America*. New York: Liveright Publishing Corporation.

Scott v. Sandford. 60 U.S. 19 How. 393 393 (1857).

Simien, Evelyn M. 2011. "Introduction." In *Gender and Lynching: The Politics of Memory*, edited by Evelyn M. Simien, 1–13. New York: Palgrave MacMillan.

Skocpol, Theda, and Ariane Liazos. 2006. *What a Mighty Power We Can Be: African American Fraternal Groups and the Struggle for Racial Equality*. Princeton, NJ: Princeton University Press.

Tate, Katherine. 2010. *What's Going On: Political Incorporation and the Transformation of Black Public Opinion*. Washington, DC: Georgetown University Press.

Taylor, Keeanga-Yamahtta. 2016. *From #BlackLives Matter to Black Liberation*. Chicago, IL: Haymarket Books.

Threadcraft, Shatema. 2016. *Intimate Justice: The Black Female Body and the Body Politic*. New York: Oxford University Press.

Tucker-Worgs, Tamelyn. 2012. *The Black Mega-church: Theology, Gender, and the Politics of Public Engagement*. Waco, TX: Baylor University Press.

Washington, Harriet A. 2006. *Medical Apartheid: The Dark History of Medical Experimentation on Black Americans from Colonial Times to Present*. New York: Harlem Moon.

Racial gaslighting

Angelique M. Davis and Rose Ernst

ABSTRACT
How does white supremacy – the systemic covert and overt version – remain inextricably woven into the ideological fabric of the United States? We argue that racial gaslighting – *the political, social, economic and cultural process that perpetuates and normalizes a white supremacist reality through pathologizing those who resist* – offers a framework to understand its maintenance in the United States. Racial gaslighting is a process that relies on racial spectacles [Davis, Angelique M., and Rose Ernst. 2011. "Racial Spectacles: Promoting a Colorblind Agenda Through Direct Democracy." *Studies in Law, Politics and Society* 55: 133–171]: *narratives that obfuscate the existence of a white supremacist state power structure*. We trace the production of racial spectacles in *Korematsu v. United States* (1944) and *Commonwealth of Kentucky v. Braden* (1955) to highlight how micro-level individual acts are part of a macro-level process of racial gaslighting and the often-catastrophic consequences for individuals who resist white supremacy. A comparison of these cases also reveals different "functions" of gaslighting People of Color versus white people in terms of portrayal, exposure, pathologization, audience, and outcome. Although they occurred in the twentieth century, we argue that racial gaslighting is an *enduring* process that responds to individual and collective resistance. We contend that naming and clarifying racial gaslighting processes assist in building collective language and strategies to challenge this systemic violence and its manifestations.

Racial gaslighting (v)
The political, social, economic and cultural process that perpetuates and normalizes a white supremacist reality through pathologizing those who resist.
Racial spectacle (n)
Narratives that obfuscate the existence of a white supremacist state power structure.

Introduction

In the 1944 mystery-thriller film, *Gaslight*, actor Charles Boyer manipulates his home environment in an attempt to control his wife, played by Ingrid Bergman. Unbeknownst to Bergman, Boyer is a murderer and a thief who has married her in order to return to the scene of his original crime, Bergman's house. His goal is to search the attic for the treasure of his original victim. As he must keep this a secret, he leaves his wife at home, alone, while he ostensibly socializes with friends in the evenings. In reality, he creeps up to the attic, makes ominous noises – dragging trunks and furniture across the floor – and turns on the lights in the attic, thus creating a flickering effect of the gaslights in the floors below. Night after night, Bergman becomes increasingly disturbed by these unexplained occurrences. She confesses this to her husband. He dismisses her experiences as flights of fancy; when she persists in telling him about them, he begins to question her sanity. She, in turn, begins to doubt her own perceptions. Boyer isolates her from friends and family on the pretext that she is unwell. Bergman's familial and social circle gradually disappears; Boyer is able to control her through this manipulation game for his own personal gain.

Conceptual framework

The film, *Gaslight,* made the term popular, particularly among psychologists who used it to refer to a type of abusive relationship. Following the film, *The Oxford English Dictionary* defines "gaslighting" as "[t]he action or process of manipulating a person by psychological means into questioning his or her own sanity" (2016). In popular discourse, the gaslighting metaphor appears in entertainment, self-help, and more recently, social justice, and political arenas (Waltman 2016). In the field of psychology, it "describe[s] the effort of one person to undermine another person's confidence and stability by causing the victim to doubt [their] own senses and beliefs" (Kline 2006), 1148). In the area of family therapy, gaslighting describes a situation in which one partner attempts to control the other. A classic example is a philandering partner who tells their significant other that their perceptions of inappropriate or deceitful behavior are untrue. These scenarios often emerge in "male–female" relationships, though either partner may be the instigator. A typical pattern in the literature is a man's use of gendered stereotypes – such as the jealous or insecure woman – to not only deflect attention away from his activities but to also control her thoughts by causing her to doubt her perceptions (Gass and Nichols 1988).

Education scholars have used gaslighting to explain sociohistorical factors that led to the "disenfranchisement, marginalization, and overall invisibility of African American teachers writ large in the profession" (Roberts and Carter Andrews 2013, 70). They posit that the "normalized master narrative" about "the limited presence of Black teachers in teaching" has been used throughout U.S. history as an "abuse tactic" to delude the US public into believing the Black community is solely at fault for the failure of the teaching profession to recruit and retain Black teachers. This normalized master narrative fails to address structural barriers and how the presence of Black teachers benefits all students (Roberts and Carter Andrews 2013, 70).

This manipulation of perception is powerful because our reality – how we perceive the world and our place in it – is socially constructed. In the context of race politics, scholars agree that race is not biological; instead, the construct race and how it affects our perceptions are sociopolitical (Davis 2012). Interpretations of emotion can also be sociopolitical. Burrow (2005) posits that the dismissal of feminist anger is a

> key tool for leveraging women into their rightful place in society through subverting dominant ideologies .... Dismissing such anger does not then seem to be a matter of innocent oversight. Rather, dismissal silences one's political voice and, at the same time, compromises a valuable source of self-worth and self-trust. (27)

Burrow discusses how this form of judgment is used to oppress others:

> Emotional abusers often divert issues from legitimate targets by instead placing the focus on the way in which one expresses oneself. The implication is that the person raising the issue is herself inadequate to express that concern or she is to blame for how she has raised the issue. Diversion is a way of controlling the communication between the persons involved. This sort of abuse is common to women's lives. Restricting freedom of expression is a similar sort of abusive tactic used to oppress groups of persons. (31)

An example of this type of diversion is the colloquial use of the phrase "tone policing." Dominant groups use tone policing to chastise the communication style of marginalized people who challenge their oppression. It focuses on the emotion behind a message rather than the message itself. Through focusing on the manner in which the message is delivered, no matter the legitimacy of the content, tone policing prioritizes the comfort of the privileged (Hugs 2015) and minimizes marginalized peoples' experiences, "by placing sanctions on how they will or will not be heard" (Zevallos 2017). For example, tone policing emerged in media coverage of the 2017 Women's March. Mainstream media chastised Women of Color who challenged white women to think about racial divides. Women of Color's attempts to center race in dialogues about the march were criticized as "contentious." A *New York Times* article published before the march focused on the claims made by white women who felt "unwelcome," thereby prioritizing the comfort of white women (Stockman 2017). In what follows, we provide a sociopolitical contextualization of interpersonal relationships not only in individual level interactions, but also in the maintenance of white supremacy.[1]

The process of racial gaslighting

Omi and Winant's *Racial Formation in the United States* ([1986] 2014) became a classic text in race and ethnic politics, in part, because these two sociologists provided an innovative framework for understanding why and how racial categorization changes. Racial formation, first and foremost, is a *process*: "the sociohistorical process by which racial identities are created, lived out, transformed, and destroyed" (109). Unlike a system – such as capitalism, an ideology – such as colorblind racism, an institution – such as a prison, or even a political era – such as the first Reconstruction, a process does not have particular content in and of itself; rather, it is a web of relationships, perceptions, and social control mechanisms.

In the vein of Omi and Winant's focus on process, racial gaslighting offers a way to understand how white supremacy is sustained over time. We define racial gaslighting as *the political, social, economic and cultural process that perpetuates and normalizes a white supremacist reality through pathologizing those who resist*. Just as racial formation rests on the creation of racial projects, racial gaslighting, as a process, relies on the production of particular narratives. These narratives are called racial spectacles (Davis and Ernst 2011).[2] Racial spectacles are *narratives that obfuscate the existence of a white supremacist state power structure*. They are visual and textual displays that tell a particular story about the dynamics of race. For example, former President Bill Clinton gave a speech in 2012 (and again in 2016) in which he lamented the increasing number of deaths among white working-class people,

They could have said these people are dying of a broken heart .... Because they're the people that were raised to believe the American Dream would be theirs if they worked hard and their children will have a chance to do better – and their dreams were dashed disproportionally to the population as the whole. (Scheiner 2012)

This racial spectacle obfuscates how the white supremacist state power structure actively – since Bacon's Rebellion in 1676 and onward – has kept poor white people poor. If Clinton had said, "white people are dying of a broken heart because the pathology of whiteness is killing them," then this narrative would *reveal* the existence of white supremacy and call into question the role of the state as well.

Racial spectacles may be ongoing cultural narratives that generate media stories and private conversations and, in other cases, are momentary blips in the sea of media stories designed to elicit racial responses. They may become part of a larger, ongoing narrative, or they may fade from view, only to be resurrected 50 years later. Take, for example, the narratives surrounding anti-affirmative action initiative campaigns that began in the 1990s. They used the presumption of white innocence to frame the beneficiaries of affirmative action as undeserving. The synergy created between the public media campaigns and their solicitation of private "everyday opinion" formed a particularly virulent form of racial spectacle that informed voters and thereby created a direct link between the promulgation of these narratives and the creation of law (Davis and Ernst 2011).

Not all narratives about race are racial spectacles. One example of a narrative that is not a racial spectacle is the Black Lives Matter movement, emerging in response to the historical and ongoing dehumanization of Black lives in the United States. While this movement's narrative is not a racial spectacle, the colorblind-narrative in response – All Lives Matter – is. The Black Lives Matter narrative illuminates the dehumanization of Black lives and is in no way suggesting other lives do not matter – instead, it shifts the focus away from whiteness by the assertion that Black lives matter, too. The Black Lives Matter movement exposes the white supremacist state power structure and how it dehumanizes Black life in the United States. The All Lives Matter colorblind-narrative is a racial spectacle, however, because it disguises the prioritizing of white lives. The All Lives Matter movement achieves three core tasks: first, it co-opts Black social justice intellectual work; second, it pushes Black communities further to the margins of society by insisting that *all* lives in the United States are valued equally and treated as such. Consequently, it erases the centuries of brutalization and dehumanization of Black bodies. Finally, it obfuscates the role of the white supremacist state power structure by eliding over the specific targeting of Black lives by state institutions and actors, such as prisons and police.

The process of racial gaslighting invites intersectional and multiplicative understandings of domination and resistance precisely because the process is a binary of normalization versus pathologization that can take place with or without individual agency. For those who are aware of racial gaslighting, it can be almost impossible to combat their pathologization by the dominant narrative, due to the ubiquitous nature of white supremacy. Nevertheless, activists have challenged the white supremacist power structure, counted the cost, and still sacrificially engaged in acts of resistance. Some have resisted with less political motivation, but simply because they believed they were standing up for what was just. And others, like Bergman, were manipulated into believing their actions or mental state was problematic. Just as the process of white supremacy does not require those who are complicit to understand the racist nature of their actions, awareness is also not determinative of whether the process of racial gaslighting is taking place.

In the following sections, we provide examples of racial gaslighting, noting the role of racial spectacles in this process. We examine two historical court cases from Japanese American internment/incarceration and the Civil Rights Movement that highlight how micro-level individual actions are part of a larger, macro process of racial gaslighting. In both cases, *Korematsu v. United States* (1944) and *Commonwealth of Kentucky v. Braden* (1955), plaintiffs resisted white supremacist violence. As we delineate in more detail in each case discussion section, the process of racial gaslighting is markedly different for People of Color and white people who resist white supremacy in five ways: portrayal, exposure (or risk), pathologization, audience, and outcome.

Korematsu v. United States (1944): criminalizing resistance

> The two conflicting orders, one which commanded him to stay and the other which commanded him to go, were nothing but a cleverly devised trap to accomplish the real purpose of the military authority, which was to lock him up in a concentration camp. (Justice Owen Roberts, Dissent, Korematsu v. United States, 1944, 232)

Background and context

Although anti-Asian sentiment in the United States preceded the bombing of Pearl Harbor and World War II, these events resulted in the use of racial gaslighting to obfuscate state-sanctioned racism against those of Japanese ancestry. In 1942, President Roosevelt signed Executive Order 9066, which set into motion state forced removal of over 110,000 persons of Japanese ancestry from their West Coast homes. Segregated schools, anti-miscegenation laws, alien land laws, and anti-Japanese wartime propaganda pre-dated WWII, but the bombing of Pearl Harbor accelerated the level of concrete state action against them. The fact that two-thirds were US citizens by birth highlights the racism and xenophobia at play. The state did not file individual charges against them, nor was proof provided they had engaged in acts of espionage or sabotage. Failure to comply was a federal crime (Bannai 2005).

Japanese Americans who challenged these laws did so at great personal cost.[3] One of these individuals, Fred Korematsu – a US citizen of Japanese ancestry – refused to report to a detention center in San Leandro, California. He was jailed for violation of a detention order and classified as an "enemy alien." Mr Korematsu challenged the constitutionality of the order under the Fifth and Fourteenth Amendments. On December 18, 1944, the majority of the US Supreme Court upheld Executive Order 9066 and General DeWitt's orders. They acknowledged that racial discrimination should receive close scrutiny:[4] "all legal restrictions which curtail the civil rights of a single racial group are immediately suspect" (Korematsu 1944, 216). Yet, even with this acknowledgement, the majority denied the laws were a form of racial discrimination; instead, they provided a public necessity justification:

> To cast this case into outlines of racial prejudice, without reference to the real military dangers which were presented, merely confuses the issue. Korematsu was not excluded from the Military Area because of hostility to him or his race. He was excluded because we are at war with the Japanese Empire. (Korematsu 1944, 223–224)

Racial spectacle

The US government used racial spectacles at the macro-level to publicly justify its use of concrete state action against of those of Japanese ancestry during World War II. At the macro level, the federal government perpetuated and normalized its actions through the use of euphemistic language. The Supreme Court's decision and its objection to the characterization of the camps as concentration camps reflects this obfuscation: "Regardless of the true nature of the assembly and relocation centers – and we deem it unjustifiable to call them concentration camps, with all the ugly connotations that term implies – we are dealing specifically with nothing but an exclusion order" (Korematsu 1944, 223). The labels of assembly and relocation centers do not adequately explain their existence and serve to obscure reality:

> Over time, researchers and scholars, studying historical artifacts, documents, and accounts of the period, have increasingly pointed out the euphemistic nature of the language employed by the US government during WWII in relation to the concentration camps in which Japanese American citizens were incarcerated. (National JACL 2013, 8)

To authentically explain what happened to Japanese Americans requires accurate vocabulary: exclusion, or forced removal, not evacuation; incarceration, not relocation; US citizens of Japanese ancestry, not non-aliens; detention orders, not civilian exclusion orders; and American concentration camp, incarceration camp, or illegal detention center, not relocation center or internment camp (Ishizuka 2006).

Racial gaslighting

The government's use of macro-level racial spectacles to obscure the existence of a white supremacist state power structure provided a narrative that set the stage for the racial gaslighting of Japanese Americans at a micro level. In this way, the political, social, economic, and cultural process of racial gaslighting utilized racial spectacles to perpetuate and normalize a white supremacist state by pathologizing those who resisted. The government's call to engage in acts of patriotism such as military service and loyalty questionnaires compelled compliance through manipulating the requirements for Japanese Americans to be seen as loyal to the United States: "the central loyalty question was phrased in such a way that an affirmative answer implied that internees were previously loyal to the Japanese Emperor" (Fong 2013, 242). White politicians as well as leaders within Japanese American communities called for voluntary compliance with the military orders and the attendant loss of personal liberty as well as land, businesses, homes, and the majority of personal possessions. Many also joined the military to defend the United States against Japan and became highly decorated war heroes. Those who refused to comply with detention orders, such as Mr Korematsu, became convicted criminals who were ostracized by many in the Japanese American community (Bannai 2005).[5]

The use of racial spectacles and racial gaslighting by the government to hide white supremacist state action under the guise national security continues after Japanese American incarceration, albeit in different sociopolitical contexts. For decades after incarceration, the convergence of the trauma and spectacle of incarceration resulted in silence by many Japanese Americans (Roxworthy 2008). The racial gaslighting of Japanese Americans did, however, eventually subside due to ongoing advocacy efforts of the Japanese

American community. Almost 40 years after Mr Korematsu's conviction, a *writ of coram nobis* was filed to reverse his conviction based upon newly discovered evidence that was not available at the time of his trial. It revealed that the government knowingly withheld evidence that undermined its assertions of disloyalty by those of Japanese ancestry. The US Solicitor General's office did not challenge the petition. The incongruent result was the widely applauded reversal of Mr Korematsu's individual conviction in 1983 by a federal district court – a micro-level legal action – while at the macro level the 1944 Supreme Court decision remained in effect.

In *Korematsu*, the racial gaslighting of People of Color is not only symbolic – sending a message to Japanese Americans in particular – but also linked to *concrete state action*. If, for example, the Supreme Court decided to affirm Korematsu's argument, a concrete change to state action would have followed: incarceration/internment would halt. If not halted, other state action would need to occur to maintain the camps.[6] In the case of *Commonwealth of Kentucky v. Braden* (1955), however, the outcome of the case did not stifle or enable a particular state action.

Commonwealth of Kentucky v. Braden (1955): racial sedition

The process of racial gaslighting white people fundamentally differs from that of People of Color for two reasons. First, white people may be pathologized like People of Color, but the narrative is distinctive: they are viewed as traitors to their race. Second, the purpose of gaslighting individual white people is largely symbolic or pedagogical. We do not mean these individuals do not suffer harm at the hands of the state or white society – as in the case of Anne and Carl Braden, discussed in this section. Instead, they are used symbolically as an example, or warning, *to other white people*.

Background and context

On June 27, 1954, someone firebombed Andrew and Charlotte Wade's house near Louisville, Kentucky. Fortunately, the Wades were not at home when the explosion occurred; the perpetrators placed the dynamite underneath the bedroom of their child, Rosemary. This attack followed weeks of white neighbors' violent intimidation of the Wades (Braden 2001, 184, 186; Minter 2013, 362). The culprit, never brought to trial, was most likely an ex-policeman (Braden 2001, 187). We offer a brief overview of events linked to this racial terrorism, and then discuss the case through the lens of racial gaslighting.

After facing institutional practices of redlining and outright intimidation, Andrew Wade approached a white activist couple, Carl and Anne Braden, about purchasing a home in an all-white suburb on his behalf in 1954 (1989). The Bradens agreed with alacrity. After the Wades moved into their new home, white people in the neighborhood reacted violently with threats and intimidation. The Wade Defense Committee formed as a result. After the bombing attack, prosecutors charged the Bradens with orchestrating the explosion themselves. Found guilty of "teaching or advocating sedition or Criminal Syndicalism," the state of Kentucky sentenced Carl Braden to 15 years of hard labor at the State Penitentiary at LaGrange and fined him $5000 (*Kentucky v. Braden*). His $40,000 bond was the highest ever in the history of Kentucky as of 1955 (Fosl 2006). The lead prosecutor's case rested on demonstrating the Bradens were communists:

> There is no question of white and colored in this case. There has been no colored man indicted. I don't know why [defense attorney] ... wanted to harp on white supremacy and all that sort of thing .... The only question is whether or not Carl Braden advocated sedition, criminal syndicalism, or had material to circulate and display for that purpose of join assemblages of persons for that purpose. (*Braden* transcript 1955, 161)

During this period, Anne Braden described how the shape-shifting term *communist* was linked to fights against racism in the South: "To the white supremacist in the South, it means somebody fighting segregation" (Fosl 2006, 165). In the closing argument to the case, one of the prosecutors accused Braden of actually *creating racial tension* as a part of a communist plot:

> [W]e should let this be a milestone in the historic fight of America today to stop this evil pitting race against race, white against black, Catholic against Protestants, Jew against the Gentile, rich against the poor .... We must ruthlessly cut out this cancer of communism, and here is the one place to start. (*Braden* transcript 1955, 2467–2468)

Unsurprisingly, the prosecutor's argument is contradictory: white supremacy is not at issue, but then it is because communists apparently instigate the "pitting" of "white against black." Though the Bradens never considered the legal ramifications of purchasing the Wades' home, nor anticipated what followed (Fosl 2006), prosecutors and other Kentucky officials decided to use the Braden case for their own purposes:

> In my opinion, this is a test case for the white supremacists .... So far as I know, this is the first major case where an attempt has been made to place the blame for [anti-Negro] violence on the people fighting segregation. (Anne Braden, quoted in Fosl 2006, 165)

Racial spectacles

The racial intimidation culminating in the bombing of the Wades' home represented the first of many racial spectacles[7] in this case. While state entities were complicit in setting the conditions for the bombing, the characterization of this act of racial terror as an isolated *private* action served to hide the existence of a white supremacist state power structure. The prosecutor laid forth two lines of inquiry in the grand jury hearing: "[e]ither it had been set by neighbors who resented the entry of blacks into a white neighborhood or it had been an 'inside job,' part of a communist plot to stir up racial friction in an otherwise contented community" (Fosl 2006, 156). Though the prosecutor chose not to actively pursue the first theory – though it is most likely what occurred – it still comports with a narrative of private action. The same is true for the second line of inquiry. Even if Kentucky tried the ostensible white perpetrator, the "backstage" white narrative (Feagin and Picca 2007) would have been one of justification or provocation. This is in contrast to the official "frontstage" state narrative of the bomber "going too far" – which would still leave the apartheid system undisturbed.

Racial gaslighting

Individual white people may attempt to divest from or subvert their own power because they recognize what they have to gain by dismantling white supremacy (Jackson 2011). White society and the state will ignore or label them as obsessive, dangerous, or "crazy" people. Their whiteness may protect or cushion them from the violence visited upon

Table 1. Racial gaslighting.

	People of Color	White people who resist
Portrayal	The usual racist stereotypes	Race traitors and/or delusional
Exposure	Always collective and sometimes individual	Individual or small group
Pathologization	Always collective and sometimes individual	Individual or small group
Audience	People of Color and white people	White people
Outcome	Symbolic message	Symbolic message
	Individual and collective co-optation, containment, or punishment	Individual co-optation, containment, or punishment
	State action against groups of People of Color	

People of Color, and sometimes it will not (Table 1). The difference, regardless of whether or not they are individually punished, is that they are singled out as subversive individuals, not as *white* subversive individuals. Ironically, though they are seen as dangerous individuals, their punishment is a *collective message* to white people as a whole. These messages feed into the macro-level process of racial gaslighting.

One of the most important points about the *Braden* case is that the possibility of a non-prosecution or acquittal would have not had any direct concrete effect on state action. This is the opposite of possible outcomes against People of Color. The decision in *Braden* might have provoked some additional policymaking attempts and spurred further cracks in the façade of the Southern "police state" (Anne Braden, quoted in Fosl 2006, 208), but it would not have halted enforcement of segregation. This is precisely because the charges were masked as ostensibly non-racial: sedition. Again, though the process appears targeted at individual action at a micro level, the messaging to all white people fuels macro-level narratives about white supremacy.

The final important contrast is that in the case of white people resisting, the effects of gaslighting only directly harm those individual white (and People of Color as in the case of the Wades) people involved. In the case of directly gaslighting People of Color, the opposite is true. The Wades' experience with racial gaslighting illuminates this point. *Their house was bombed* – and they would have been killed if at home – and they suffered a lifetime of consequences from the case. As Anne Braden herself noted, however, it became the *Braden* case, rather than the *Wade* case. The Wades' sacrifice is invisible, but if they were somehow to contest that fact, they would be subject to ridicule and violence. Moreover, Kentucky charged the Bradens precisely because the official state version of the story was that Black people were satisfied with racial apartheid. This is the crux of racial gaslighting: to dismantle the racial spectacle that Black people were satisfied with racial apartheid, the Wades would have had to claim they bombed their own home to orchestrate a sedition campaign.

Bridging past and present

The process of racial gaslighting, as described in *Korematsu* and *Braden*, is markedly different for People of Color and white people in five ways: portrayal, exposure (or risk), pathologization, audience, and outcome. Fred Korematsu, a person of Japanese ancestry, was portrayed by state and society in a racist light. In contrast, Anne and Carl Braden, a white couple, were labeled as communists and race traitors. Second, the exposure of Fred Korematsu was both individual (to him) and to the collective of Japanese

Americans, though that collective exposure remains regardless of individual action. The Bradens' exposure was individual – white people as a whole had nothing to immediately gain or lose with the decision in the case. Third, the pathologization of Fred Korematsu, like his portrayal, was part of a process of projecting racist stereotypes on the entire group. Kentucky pathologized the Bradens as individual subversives, and also as subversives who made an active decision to become communists. Fourth, the audience for the racial spectacle of the *Korematsu* case was both People of Color and white people. In the case of the Bradens, white people were the primary audience, warned against the dangers of resisting white supremacy. Fifth, in terms of the outcome of racial gaslighting, *Korematsu* resulted in symbolic messages and concrete, racialized state-sanctioned action, in contrast to *Braden*, which resulted in individualized punishment and symbolic warnings to other white people.

The reader may be tempted to agree with our analysis of *Korematsu* and *Braden*, yet wonder how these examples are connected to the current state of white supremacy in the United States. Returning to *Korematsu*, we can see how the process of racial gaslighting continues, girded by the power of *stare decisis* and fueled by the narrative of national security. In 1988, the Civil Liberties Act provided an official apology and reparations to those individuals who were incarcerated. Mr Korematsu's resistance was recognized and he was widely considered a hero (Bannai 2005). In 1998, President Clinton awarded Fred Korematsu the Presidential Medal of Freedom.

Although the *Korematsu* decision has been undermined over time, the case has not been overturned and still has precedential value. It was used as precedent to support the Bush Administration's post-9/11 "War on Terror" (Green 2011) and the racialization of Muslims in the United States (Chon and Arzt 2005). In 2011, the Office of the Solicitor General issued a confession of error admitting it withheld reports on Japanese Americans' loyalty in the incarceration cases (Office of the Solicitor General 2011). Yet, in 2013, the Supreme Court denied certiorari to the *Hedges v. Obama* case, which challenged legislation permitting the US government to indefinitely detain people suspected of substantially supporting terrorist organizations. Review of this Second Circuit decision would have provided them the opportunity to formally overrule *Korematsu*. Add to this the plethora of state action focused on groups of People of Color, such as incarceration of immigrant families in camps in Texas and Pennsylvania (Hennessy-Fiske 2015), calls by politicians to incarcerate Syrian refugees (Varner 2015), as well as the executive order to temporarily ban travel from seven majority-Muslim countries in January 2017. These state actions underscore how the process of racial gaslighting ripples through time.

Racial gaslighting moves the ball forward in race politics scholarship in the tradition of both critical race and racial formation theories. Racial formation remains a touchstone for both theoretical and empirical scholarship (Pagliai 2009; HoSang, LaBennett, and Pulido 2012; Lawrence 2012; Feagin and Elias 2013; Golash-Boza 2013; Omi and Winant 2013; Wingfield 2013; Winant 2015), grappling with the persistence of racism in the United States. A rather heated series of exchanges in *Ethnic and Racial Studies* (2013) underlines the continuing relevance of racial formation theory. Feagin and Elias critique racial formation theory as unable to conceptualize "the deep foundation, layered complexities, and institutionalized operations of systemic racism in the USA" (2013, 931). Omi and Winant respond that Feagin and Elias' account of systemic racism as a totalizing force and as an alternative framework to racial formation theory has unintended consequences:

they dismiss the political agency of people of colour and of anti-racist whites. In Feagin/Elias's view, "systemic racism" is like the Borg in the Star Trek series: a hive-mind phenomenon that assimilates all it touches. As the Borg announce in their collective audio message to intended targets, "Resistance is futile". (2013, 962)

Our racial gaslighting framework addresses both concerns through a complementary analysis that addresses the primary critiques and rejoinders of racial formation theory. First, racial gaslighting emphasizes a structural and systemic analysis of white supremacy. Like racial formation theory, however, we view racial gaslighting as an iterative *process*. Second, while we agree with Feagin and Elias' emphasis on white supremacy, we also agree with Omi and Winant that resistance is not futile, but that certain types of resistance can be easily co-opted or have unintended consequences.[8]

Conclusion

Racial spectacles lurk everywhere, from our daily interpersonal interactions to the grotesque political theatre of the presidency. These visual and textual narratives align in a process of racial gaslighting that not only targets micro-level players in the particular story, but taps into broader historical white supremacist myths. *Korematsu* and *Braden* represent the often-catastrophic consequences of racial gaslighting for individuals who resist white supremacist violence and their subsequent effects on collectivities. While the individuals in these cases were pathologized and punished, the cases reflect the different "functions" of gaslighting People of Color versus white people in terms of portrayal, exposure, pathologization, audience, and outcome. Again, the process of racial gaslighting targets *those who resist*. By design, the survival, existence, resilience, and/or success of People of Color is an act of resistance on both macro and micro levels that results in racial gaslighting.

We contend that naming and clarifying this process of racial gaslighting enables us to build a common language in the struggle against white supremacy. Recognizing the process and developing narratives to resist the confines of gaslighting – or at the very least name it as what it is – automatically diminishes some of its power. At the close of the film *Gaslight*, Bergman regains her agency once she understands the manipulations of her husband and can clearly identify his attempts to discredit her. In the case of Fred Korematsu and the Bradens, they exercised their individual agency to challenge white supremacy in their own ways, but were pathologized for noncompliance. And, in addition to the societal structures designed to punish their noncompliance, their pathologization was facilitated by the lack of language to name and expose this duplicitous tool of white supremacy. We do not suggest that naming and clarifying are enough; rather, we posit that recognizing our collective historical and contemporary patterns is a powerful step towards building movements equipped to stop fueling white supremacy's racial gaslight.

Notes

1. We use Ellinger and Martinas' definition of white supremacy:

   White supremacy is an historically based, institutionally perpetuated system of exploitation and oppression of continents, nations and peoples of color by white peoples and nations of the European continent; for the purpose of establishing, maintaining and defending a system of wealth, power and privilege. (1994)

2. Our definition of racial spectacles builds on our previous work on the subject. The addition of the overarching process of racial gaslighting illustrates the specific role of racial spectacles in this context.
3. Others also resisted the incarceration through the court system, such as Yosh Kuromiya and Gene Akutsu (Bannai 2005).
4. While this is the first case to introduce the concept of strict scrutiny by the Supreme Court to equal protection analysis, it was not developed until later cases due to the majority's refusal to acknowledge the racism inherent in these orders.
5. Fred Korematsu's biography, *Enduring Conviction*, discusses his decision to resist:

   > Fred said he knew remaining in Oakland had been wrong and that he had intended to turn himself in. One might wonder now, over half a century later, why Fred didn't tell Mansfield that he had done nothing wrong – that he, as an American citizen, had a constitutional right to remain free. Maybe he was scared or intimidated or both. Maybe he wanted to protect his [girlfriend] Ida. Most importantly, however, he, as an American citizen, did not have to invoke his constitutional rights to be able to exercise them. While Fred may not have asserted his rights in words, he had asserted his right to liberty by choosing to stay. … while not quoting the Constitution, he was seeking the freedom it promised. (Bannai 2015, 42)

6. Concrete state action can also include state omission or delayed action. For example, during the 1921 Tulsa Race Riot, local public safety officials' complicity and failure to intervene allowed white mobs to injure and murder hundreds of African Americans and destroy more than 1000 Black-owned homes and businesses (Oklahoma 2001).
7. The other racial spectacles include multiple trials, arrests, hearings, press coverage, and the like.
8. Though racial gaslighting illustrates how white supremacy survives, we are aware of possible critiques of a single axis analysis along racial lines. Rather than view this framework as following a single axis analysis, however, racial gaslighting invites intersectional and multiplicative understandings of domination and resistance precisely because the process is a binary of normalization versus pathologization.

Disclosure statement

No potential conflict of interest was reported by the authors.

ORCID

Angelique M. Davis https://orcid.org/0000-0003-0270-4055
Rose Ernst http://orcid.org/0000-0003-1803-9424

References

Bannai, Lorraine K. 2005. "Taking the Stand: The Lessons of the Three Men Who Took the Japanese American Internment to Court." *Seattle Journal for Social Justice* 4 (1): 1–57.
Bannai, Lorraine K. 2015. *Enduring Conviction: Fred Korematsu and His Quest for Justice*. Seattle: University of Washington Press.
Braden, Anne. 2001. "In the Midst of the Storm." In *The Price of Dissent: Testimonies to Political Repression in America*, edited by Bud Schultz and Ruth Schultz, 184–199. Berkeley: University of California Press.
Braden v. Commonwealth. 1955. 291 S.W.2d 843
Burrow, Sylvia. 2005. "The Political Structure of Emotion: From Dismissal to Dialogue." *Hypatia* 20 (4): 27–43.

Chon, Margaret, and Donna E. Arzt. 2005. "Walking While Muslim." *Law and Contemporary Problems* 68: 215–254.

Commonwealth of Kentucky v. Braden. 1955. Court Transcript. Madison: Wisconsin Historical Society

Cukor, George. 1944. *Gaslight*. Burbank, CA: Turner Entertainment: Warner Bros.

Davis, Angelique M. 2012. "Political Blackness: A Sociopolitical Construction." In *Loving in a "Post-Racial" World: New Legal Approaches to Interracial Marriages and Relationships*, edited by Kevin Noble Maillard and Rose Cuison Villazor, 169–180. New York: Cambridge University Press.

Davis, Angelique M., and Rose Ernst. 2011. "Racial Spectacles: Promoting a Colorblind Agenda Through Direct Democracy." *Studies in Law, Politics and Society* 55: 133–171.

Ellinger, Mickey, and Sharon Martinas. 1994. "The Culture of White Supremacy." *Challenging White Supremacy Workshop*. http://whgbetc.com/mind/culture-white-sup.html.

Feagin, Joe, and Sean Elias. 2013. "Rethinking Racial Formation Theory: A Systemic Racism Critique." *Ethnic and Racial Studies* 36 (6): 931–960.

Feagin, Joe, and Leslie H. Picca. 2007. *Two-faced Racism: Whites in the Backstage and Front Stage*. New York: Routledge.

Fong, Edmund. 2013. "Beyond the Racial Exceptionalism of the Japanese Internment." *Politics, Groups, and Identities* 1 (2): 239–244.

Fosl, Catherine. 2006. *Subversive Southerner: Anne Braden and the Struggle for Racial Justice in the Cold War South*. Lexington: University Press of Kentucky.

"Gaslighting, n.2." 2016. OED Online. Oxford University Press, March. http://www.oed.com/view/Entry/255555?rskey=qdZFWb&result=2&isAdvanced=false.

Gass, Gertrude Z., and William C. Nichols. 1988. "Gaslighting: A Marital Syndrome." *Contemporary Family Therapy* 10 (1): 3–16.

Golash-Boza, Tanya. 2013. "Does Racial Formation Theory Lack the Conceptual Tools to Understand Racism?" *Ethnic and Racial Studies* 36 (6): 994–999.

Green, Craig. 2011. "Ending the Korematsu Era: An Early View from the War on Terror Cases." *Northwestern University Law Review* 105 (3).

Hedges v. Obama. 2013. 724 F.3d 170, 173-74, *cert. denied*, 2014. 572 U.S. 5.

Hennessy-Fiske, Molly. 2015. "Immigrant Family Detention Centers Are Prison-Like, Critics Say, Despite Order to Improve." *Los Angeles Times*. http://www.latimes.com/nation/nationnow/la-na-immigration-family-detention-20151020-story.html.

HoSang, Daniel Martinez, Oneka LaBennett, and Laura Pulido. 2012. *Racial Formation in the Twenty-First Century*. Berkeley: University of California Press.

Hugs, Robot. 2015. "No, We Won't Calm Down – Tone Policing Is Just Another Way to Protect Privilege." *Everyday Feminism*. http://everydayfeminism.com/2015/12/tone-policing-and-privilege/.

Ishizuka, Karen L. 2006. *Lost and Found: Reclaiming the Japanese American Incarceration*. Urbana: University of Illinois Press.

Jackson, Taharee Apirom. 2011. "Which Interests Are Served by the Principle of Interest Convergence? Whiteness, Collective Trauma, and the Case for Anti-racism." *Race Ethnicity and Education* 14 (4): 435–459.

Kline, Neal A. 2006. "Revisiting Once Upon a Time." *American Journal of Psychiatry* 163 (7): 1147–1148.

Korematsu v. United States. 1944. 323 U.S. 214.

Lawrence, Charles. 2012. "Listening for Stories in All the Right Places: Narrative and Racial Formation Theory." *Law & Society Review* 46 (2): 247–258.

Minter, Patricia Hagler. 2013. "Race, Property, and Negotiated Space in the American South: A Reconsideration of *Buchanan v. Warley*." In *Signposts: New Directions in Southern Legal History*, edited by Sally E. Hadden and Patricia Hagler Minter, 345–368. Athens: University of Georgia Press.

National JACL (Japanese Americans Citizens League). 2013. *Power of Words Handbook: A Guide to Language about Japanese Americans in World War II*. National Japanese American Citizens

League Power of Words II Committee. https://jacl.org/wordpress/wp-content/uploads/2015/08/Power-of-Words-Rev.-Term.-Handbook.pdf.

Office of the Solicitor General, U.S. Department of Justice. 2011. "Confession of Error: The Solicitor General's Mistakes During the Japanese-American Internment Cases." https://www.justice.gov/opa/blog/confession-error-solicitor-generals-mistakes-during-japanese-american-internment-cases.

Oklahoma Commission to Study the Tulsa Race Riot of 1921. 2001. *A Report by the Oklahoma Commission to Study the Tulsa Race Riot of 1921.* http://www.okhistory.org/research/forms/freport.pdf.

Omi, Michael, and Howard Winant. (1986) 2014. *Racial Formation in the United States.* 3rd ed. New York: Routledge.

Omi, Michael, and Howard Winant. 2013. "Resistance Is Futile?: A Response to Feagin and Elias." *Ethnic and Racial Studies* 36 (6): 961–973.

Pagliai, Valentina. 2009. "Conversational Agreement and Racial Formation Processes." *Language in Society* 38 (5): 549–579.

Roberts, Tuesda, and Dorinda J. Carter Andrews. 2013. "A Critical Race Analysis of the Gaslighting of African American Teachers: Considerations for Recruitment and Retention." In *Contesting the Myth of a Post Racial Era: The Continued Significance of Race in U.S. Education*, edited by Dorinda J. Carter Andrews and Franklin Tuitt, 69–94. New York: Peter Lang.

Roxworthy, Emily. 2008. *The Spectacle of Japanese American Trauma: Racial Performativity and World War II.* Honolulu: University of Hawaii Press.

Scheiner, Eric. 2012. "Bill Clinton: White Americans Without H.S. Diplomas Are 'Dying of a Broken Heart.'" CNSnews.com. http://cnsnews.com/news/article/bill-clinton-white-americans-without-hs-diplomas-are-dying-broken-heart.

Stockman, Farah. 2017. "Women's March on Washington Opens Contentious Dialogues About Race." nytimes.com. https://mobile.nytimes.com/2017/01/09/us/womens-march-on-washington-opens-contentious-dialogues-about-race.html?smid=fb-nytimes&smtyp=cur&referer=http%3A%2F%2Fm.facebook.com%2F.

Varner, Natasha. 2015. "Anti-refugee Rhetoric and Justifications for WWII-Era Mass Incarceration: Is History Repeating Itself?" Densho Blog. http://www.densho.org/5-alarming-similarties-between-anti-syrian-refugee-rhetoric-and-justifications-for-world-war-ii-era-mass-incarceration/.

Wade, Andrew. 1989. "Interview with Andrew Wade, November 8, 1989 [Catherine Fosl]." https://kentuckyoralhistory.org/catalog/xt7mcv4bpp1t.

Waltman, Katy. 2016. "From Theater to Therapy, the Eerie History of Gaslighting." Slate.com. http://www.slate.com/blogs/lexicon_valley/2016/04/18/the_history_of_gaslighting_from_films_to_psychoanalysis_to_politics.html.

Winant, Howard. 2015. "Race, Ethnicity and Social Science." *Ethnic and Racial Studies* 38 (13): 2176–2185.

Wingfield, Adia Harvey. 2013. "Comment on Feagin and Elias." *Ethnic and Racial Studies* 36 (6): 989–993.

Zevallos, Zuleyka. 2017. "Intersectionality and the Women's March." *The Other Sociologist.* https://othersociologist.com/2017/01/25/intersectionality-womens-march/#more-5512.

Framing police and protesters: assessing volume and framing of news coverage post-Ferguson, and corresponding impacts on legislative activity

Maneesh Arora, Davin L. Phoenix and Archie Delshad

ABSTRACT
The 2014 killing of Michael Brown in Ferguson, MO intensified debates on policing in Black and minority communities and served as a major catalyst for protest movements such as Black Lives Matter (BLM). We assess the degree to which the volume and tone of news media coverage of policing and protests changed in the post-Ferguson environment. We also examine the impact of this volume and framing of news coverage on the legislative activity on policing across all 50 state legislatures. Observational analyses from two original data sets yield two key observations. First, the initial increase and subsequent decline in news media attention devoted to policing post-Ferguson are associated with corresponding rises and wanes in the amount of policing legislation proposed and passed across state legislatures. Second, the relative proportions of news stories framing either the police or protesters demanding police reform as legitimate correspond with the amounts of state bills working to either enhance police autonomy or increase police accountability, respectively. We discuss what these trends imply about the capacity of mainstream news media to influence policy responsiveness to the demands of protesters.

Introduction

During August 2014, striking images of unrest and clashes between police and protesters were transmitted from Ferguson, Missouri onto front pages, television screens, and social media feeds across the nation. These images transformed "Black Lives Matter," (BLM) originally a movement organized by three Black women in the aftermath of the George Zimmerman acquittal in the Trayvon Martin trial, to a national rally cry – and lightning rod for controversy. In the three years since protests erupted in response to the killing of unarmed Black teen Michael Brown by police officer Darren Wilson, the issue of police treatment of racial minorities (particularly, although not limited to African Americans) has been propelled to the national stage of political discourse.

Ferguson was far from the first time police violence against vulnerable communities surfaced in the national agenda. Police brutality received prominent attention after the 1919 passage of the Volstead Act, culminating in the Wickersham Commission's claim that "the use of physical brutality, or other forms of cruelty, to obtain involuntary confessions or admissions – is widespread" amongst police officers. In the 1940s, police targeted Mexican-Americans with physical violence in the Zoot Suit Riots. During the height of the Civil Rights Movement, Black Civil Rights leaders were targeted by J. Edgar Hoover's FBI through COINTELPRO, which included wiretapping conversations, intimidation, infiltrating organizations, and even assassinations of leaders within the Black Panther Party. In the early 1990s, police brutality against Blacks returned to salience after the acquittal of the officers in the Rodney King beating trial. The events in Ferguson, MO in 2014 were another instance in the long-running contested political discourse over policing and violence.

Technological advances and the rise of social media may have provided activists and advocates in Ferguson with a new platform to press for legal and political action to increase accountability mechanisms for police officers. But also prominent during this era are efforts to frame the movement for Black lives as either divisive or threatening to the well-being of police officers. The rise of counter-frames such as "All Lives Matter" and "Blue Lives Matter" exemplify challenges faced by advocates for racial minorities, as they face uphill struggles both to get their issues considered on the mainstream political agenda and then to "own" the framing of those issues once they are finally considered.

We endeavor to ask which frames traditional mainstream media outlets employed in reporting on the movement for police accountability in the post-Ferguson era. Do news reports on BLM and related advocacy movements paint such efforts as legitimate and justified, or menacing and ineffectual? Correspondingly, do reports on police units and officers paint these actors as above reproach, or worthy of critical scrutiny?

We expect that the dominant frames employed in news depictions of the major players in the debate over policing have clear implications for the volume and content of policy actions taken on the issue. Since the Ferguson unrest catapulted this issue once again to the forefront of the political agenda, lawmakers across the nation have sought to stake out their positions. To which competing sub-constituencies these lawmakers seek to provide responsiveness should be a function, in part, of their perceptions of the relative legitimacy of the groups' respective claims.

We argue these perceptions are meaningfully shaped by the lenses offered by media reporting on police and protesters. If the motives or methods of advocates for police accountability are constantly called into question in news media accounts, legislators face less incentive to respond to their demands. Alternately, if news reporting casts police units as prone to racial bias or abuse of power, then legislators may feel pressure to signal their efforts to enact tighter control over the police in their jurisdiction.

Using two original datasets, we provide preliminary tests of the claim that the volume and framing of media coverage around policing and policing-related protests have an effect on the legislative output on policing. We trace the correlation between the amount *and* framing of coverage of policing controversies by prominent newspaper outlets pre- and post-Ferguson and the amount and type of policing-related bills proposed and passed by all 50 state legislatures during the same period. From such trends can be drawn key inferences about the political significance of the news media's agenda setting and agenda building functions in a racially polarizing issue area.

Our trends suggest that both amount and framing of media coverage on policing have an association with the volume of state legislative activity on policing. News frames depicting protesters favorably are met with state bills that increase accountability mechanisms on police. Conversely, news stories depicting positive portrayals of police are met with state bills enhancing autonomy of police. Finally, once news attention to policing subsides, so too does the amount of state legislative activity on policing. We present here the opening stage of a project aimed at making nuanced inferences about the role of news media as a political actor, either brightening or dimming the prospects for marginalized communities seeking to assert their issues onto the national agenda.

Media as agenda setter and agenda builder

The Civil Rights-era removal of formal barriers to electoral participation heralded forceful calls for African Americans to shift their collective political strategy from protest to electoral politics (Browning, Marshall, and Tabb 1984; Tate 1994). But despite the absence of legal barriers, informal obstacles remain to Black Americans receiving adequate political responsiveness to their demands.

Such obstacles include lessened efforts by partisan elites to mobilize Black Americans, dampening Black participation (Rosenstone and Hansen 1993). Additionally, Blacks are underrepresented among the economic elite class, to which policymakers are most responsive (Gilens and Page 2014). Furthermore, as evidenced by experimental work by Butler and Broockman (2011), constituents perceived to be Black receive less consideration from state legislators than those perceived to be White.

In light of these barriers to responsiveness through conventional political channels, African Americans and other racial minorities often issue calls for greater police accountability through means of protest and demonstration. Scholarship has emerged demonstrating those protest tactics indeed translate to policy responsiveness from legislative actors. Gillion (2012) finds a positive association between protest activity by minorities within a district and roll call votes registered by members of Congress representing those districts. Gause (2016) finds that members of Congress are more likely to cast votes in support of low-resource groups engaged in protest actions. Gause operationalizes protest via news coverage from *The New York Times*. Hence, prior work indicates protesting does engender legislative responsiveness while suggesting that media reporting on protests is a mechanism through which protesters effectively transmit their preferences to responsive legislators.

Assessing scholarship on the functions and political influence of news media provides insight into how the intense media scrutiny that descended upon Ferguson could either help or harm the cause of advocates demanding police reform. As Lippmann (1922) observed, politicians view the media as a spotlight that illuminates specific issues that are salient to the public at given times. Consistent with Mayhew's (1974) account of legislators as rational actors, we expect state lawmakers to assign more of their resources and attention to the issues they deem to be salient. In a political climate Strömbäck (2008) asserts is "mediated," the news media are the primary vehicle signaling to policymakers which issues should demand more or less of their attention. Thus, a greater preponderance of news stories devoted to policing controversies in the wake of Ferguson should signal to state legislators the increased significance of the issue, resulting in greater time and resources being devoted to addressing it.

Increased media coverage of policing can also shape the prioritization given to the issue by rank and file people, who, in turn, communicate their preferences to their state officials. Brummett (1994) notes that individuals rely on media coverage of issues to help them guide and sort their political interests. Dunaway, Branton, and Abrajano (2010) find that increased media coverage of a locally relevant issue causes people to rank the issue as more important than people in areas receiving less media coverage of the issue.

In addition to the ability to set the agenda for elites and the public, the news media can also shape the public's perceptions of the varying sides of the issue, thus painting the competing sets of actors advancing their interests as legitimate or unworthy. Smith et al. (2001) assess this agenda building power of the media in their review of the predominant frames employed by news outlets covering protests in Washington D.C. They contend that news coverage de-emphasizes the underlying social issues being addressed by the protesters, applying instead an episodic lens focused solely on the protest events themselves.

This trend is consistent with Bennett's (1983) claim that news coverage generally trends toward more sensational stories focused on the individual players, as opposed to the broader issues represented by the stories. Media frames that filter depictions of protesters through sensationalized and individualistic lenses can have the dual effects of decreasing the audience's empathy with protesters – who they perceive to be social deviants – and reinforcing public support for the status quo the protesters seek to challenge (see Hertog and McLeod 1995; McLeod and Detenber 1999). Overall then, trends in how news media portray protests can prove diametrically opposed to the ideologies and goals of the protesters.

This prevalent framing device has clear implications for the patterns we may find in the news coverage of policing and protests post-Ferguson. Stories devoted mainly to dissecting the short life of Michael Brown, interrogating the record and racial attitudes of Darren Wilson, or sensationalizing the visceral images of clashes between protesters and police officers fail to offer substantive thought on the fundamental issues underlying the Ferguson unrest, such as racial profiling, political and economic disenfranchisement of Black people, and lack of sufficient mechanisms to hold police legally accountable for abuses of power against racial minorities. The focus on the individual players over the broader legal, political, and social forces comprising the bigger picture works to the detriment of the police accountability activists who represent Lee's (2002) concept of a counter-public seeking to insert their demands for action onto the mainstream sphere of political discourse. This notion finds corroboration in Davenport's (2010) analysis of police repression of the Black Panther Party. Davenport finds that variation in media framing of dissidents has an outsized effect on the public's perception of the counter-public seeking redress through insurgent activity.

News framing decisions not only affect whether the issues being advocated by Ferguson activists are elevated, obscured, or perceived to be ideologically deviant, but also whether the protesters and the issue are "racialized" – that is, conflated with age-old stereotypes that associate Blackness with violence and criminality. Numerous empirical works show that regular viewers of local news both over-report the amount of violent crime in the U.S. and overestimate the proportion of crimes committed by African Americans (Gilliam et al. 1996; Gilliam and Iyengar 2000; Dixon 2017). These studies are part of a larger body of work examining how prevalent news frames have reinforced the public's perceptions that compared to Whites, African Americans have a less legitimate claim to policy goods (e.g., Gilens 1999). If the prevalent frames applied to news depictions of Ferguson portray the protesters as riotous or menacing, not only is the cause of police accountability activists diminished, but the coverage can prime racial stereotypes among the broader public, strengthening their opposition to the policy interventions sought by the activists (see Mendelberg 2001; Valentino, Hutchings, and White 2002; Hurwitz and Peffley 2005).

It is apparent, then, that both the volume and the type of news coverage can influence whether advocates of greater police accountability are met with more or less policy responsiveness from state lawmakers in the post-Ferguson era. Accordingly, we find it worthwhile to explore how trends in news media coverage of policing and protests post-Ferguson comport with the legislative activity on policing across state legislatures. In this first phase of that exploration we ask, is there an apparent correlation between the bills proposed and passed by state legislatures and the volume and framing of policing coverage from major news outlets? In the sections that follow, we describe the original data sets created for this project, and describe the observational trends from this first phase, and discuss the implications for our understanding of the role of mainstream news media in facilitating or hindering the cause of racial justice advocates in the post-Ferguson era.

Data

Our first original data set is the State Legislative Action on Policing (SLAP) database, a comprehensive archive of every policing-related bill proposed and passed by all 50 state legislatures between 2013 and 2016. Using the LexisNexis State Capital database, a team of research assistants searched for and coded all state-level bills related to policing during this time period. The team coded multiple variables associated with the bill, including whether the bill passed, date of introduction in the chamber, characteristics of the bill sponsors, and substantive bill type.

The substantive coding of the legislation includes categorizing whether the bills increase accountability mechanisms for police, or loosen the reins on them, thereby increasing police autonomy. We view the dichotomy between *police accountability* and *police autonomy* bills as reflecting the competing constituencies to which state policymakers may seek to signal responsiveness – either those declaring that BLM, or those insisting that Blue lives matter.[1]

Police accountability bills purport to tighten regulations of police conduct, increase oversight of police activity, or create or strengthen accountability protocols for officers accused of abusive, illegal, or unethical behavior. An example is the "End Racial Profiling Act of 2015" (MO H.B. 395), introduced by Representative Joshua Peters in the Missouri legislature soon after the outbreak of unrest in Ferguson. *Police autonomy* legislation is aimed at expanding the authority of police, loosening restrictions on their conduct, or increasing their legal protection. One such example is H.B. 953, introduced by Representative Lance Harris and passed in the Louisiana legislature in 2016. Dubbed the "Blue Lives Matter bill" (Izadi 2016), this was the first of its kind to give law enforcement officers protection under hate-crime law.

Only a small subset of policing-related legislation was specifically related to perceived overreaches of police authority. Beyond identifying the bills with a clear impact on the accountability or autonomy of police units (as opposed to policing-related bills addressing unrelated issues, such as pensions), our team further identified whether the purported effects of the bills would be more substantive or symbolic. Accordingly, we created six total categories for policing legislation: strong police accountability, strong police autonomy, symbolic police accountability, symbolic police autonomy, unrelated police accountability, and unrelated police autonomy.

For this initial exploration, we aggregated the different categories of accountability and autonomy bills into two respective variables. We expect that pro-police media framing should influence the adoption of police autonomy bills, regardless of the strength of the bill. Conversely, pro-protester-framed news coverage should associate with proposal and passage of police accountability bills. While we do not grapple here with the potential tangible effects of the state legislation on the state of policing in minority communities, we can still assess the political influence of news coverage on the overall state of legislative activity on this issue.

Our second data set is the *Media Perspectives on Policing* (MPOP) database. The MPOP is a comprehensive archive of every news article from the 25 largest newspapers in circulation that addresses policing and police-related protests, between the years 2013 and 2016. As the MPOP is still under construction, we present here the results from an abridged version focusing on the policing coverage from four flagship newspapers with national or significantly regional readerships – *The New York Times*, *Washington Post*, *Wall Street Journal* and *Los Angeles Times*. While these papers do not provide us with the nuanced variations in coverage that come from a greater geographic spread of news outlets, they provide news accounts generally viewed as authoritative to rank and file news consumers and policy-makers alike.

Our team conducted content analysis on all articles addressing policing from each of these newspapers, coding for an extensive set of variables, including frames applied to police and protesters, calls for changing policing procedures (body cameras, training/evaluation, complaint processes, public release of documents, diversity, etc.), and article type (i.e., reporting or editorial). The category of *pro-protester* was assigned to two types of articles: those framing the actions or demands of police accountability advocates as just and legitimate *and* those framing the actions of police as problematic. Conversely, the category of *pro-police* was assigned to articles depicting protesters as acting illegitimately or their demands as unreasonable *and* articles that paint police as acting justifiably or above reproach. We compared the over-time volume of news stories employing these respective frames.

Both the SLAP and MPOP datasets contain a small subset of cases that are coded as containing elements of both competing elements. We assigned two assistants the same sets of data to code to determine intercoder reliability. This process determined coding errors were minimal, with differing codes being assigned less than five percent of the time.

Below we present the results of observational analyses of the across-time trends in newspaper coverage of policing and the volume and type of legislative activity from state legislatures on policing. The overlapping trends between news coverage and state-level policymaking suggest a clear role played by news media in providing legislators with signals about the salience of policing, as well as the proper legislative response to the issue.

Results

Table 1 displays the number of policing-related articles per year from the four newspapers between 1 January 2013 and 31 December 2016. It also displays the number of articles categorized as pro-protester and pro-police. Not surprisingly, the number of articles addressing policing skyrocketed in 2014. Out of the total media articles, 32% (271) were categorized as pro-police, while 42% (356) were labeled pro-protester.[2] There is a noticeable increase in pro-protester articles in the aftermath of the Ferguson protests in August, 2014. These numbers suggest that the intensified media spotlight provided the protesters in Ferguson with an elevated platform to make their claims against police brutality. Furthermore, there was a preponderance of news coverage that did not adhere to predominant racialized frames, which would either paint police as unimpeachable or depict those protesting their actions as disorderly.

Table 2 displays the number and type of policing-related bills across all fifty state legislatures over the same time period. The number of bills introduced in state legislatures increases from 97 in 2014 to 406 in 2015. This time lag is important, as it indicates that the substantial increase in legislative activity on policing is indeed preceded by an increase in media attention devoted to policing issues. In another pattern following the media coverage trends, a greater proportion of bills being introduced are categorized as increasing police accountability (449 bills, or 59% of all bills) opposed to increasing police autonomy (210 bills, or 27%).[3]

Finally, turning to bills that were actually passed, we find 74 accountability bills, versus 47 autonomy bills. Again, we see suggestive evidence that state lawmakers across the nation are heeding the media signals about the salience of the issue. And the direction of their legislative responses appears to be relatively consistent with the pro-protester framing employed by the majority of news stories.

Figure 1 below displays the month-to-month trends in policing-related news coverage and legislative activity. The sharp rise in news reports on policing from the four major newspapers, illustrated by the solid lines marked with dots, reflect the catalyzing role of two key flashpoints on race and the legal system. Prior to July 2013, when George Zimmerman was acquitted for the slaying of Trayvon Martin, the four major papers had produced

Table 1. Descriptive summary of media articles.

	2013	2014	2015	2016	Total
Media articles	23	327	360	124	834
Police frame	3	104	117	47	271
Protester frame	8	94	202	52	356

Table 2. Descriptive summary of policing bills.

	2013	2014	2015	2016	Total
Bills introduced	56	97	406	196	755
Bills passed	7	24	83	45	159
Autonomy bills introduced	16	25	103	66	210
Accountability bills introduced	33	57	256	103	449
Autonomy bills passed	2	4	28	13	47
Accountability bills passed	4	11	43	16	74

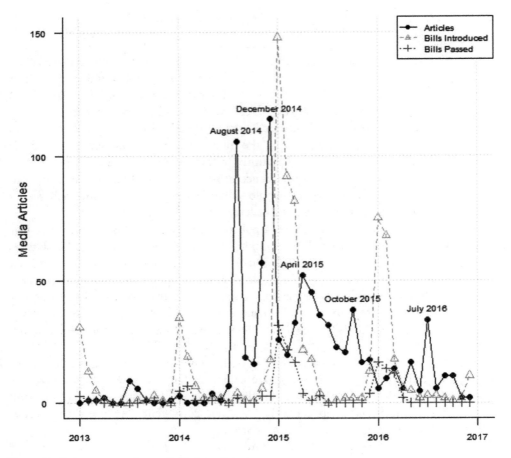

Figure 1. State response to media (total articles).

only seven articles about policing. Newspaper coverage of policing tripled in the second half of 2013. The Michael Brown slaying and its aftermath in August 2014 bring about a seismic increase in policing news coverage. Prior to August, the papers devoted 46 articles to policing. From August through December, 281 articles were written.

We can trace the other peaks in media coverage to specific high-profile instances of police killings of African Americans: Tamir Rice in November, 2014, Freddie Gray in April, 2015, and Alton Sterling and Philando Castile, both in July, 2016. With the exception of the Rice case, which occurred just three months after the Brown slaying, these incidents do not incite the same volume of coverage as Ferguson. We attribute the diminishing attention paid to these post-Ferguson incidents to two factors. First, the protest activities incited by these officer-involved killings did not match the levels of intensity or contentiousness of the Ferguson insurgency. Second, the somewhat steady decrease in policing-related coverage with each subsequent incident reflects the fatigue that his characteristic of news media's coverage of repeated events.

Turning attention from the solid to the dashed and dotted lines, we see that peaks in policing-related legislative activity appear to lag behind peaks in policing news coverage in response to inciting events. The highest spike in legislation passed and proposed comes in January 2015, about five and two months after the highest spikes in media coverage of policing in light of the Ferguson and Rice incidents, respectively.

We cannot draw causal inferences from these time trends. But we observe clear patterns at work. The slaying of Michael Brown and subsequent protests engendered a substantial increase in policing coverage from the four major newspapers. This attention was reignited about three months later by the officer slaying of 12-year-old Tamir Rice. Months after this major spike in newspaper coverage, there was a surge in policing-related bills proposed and passed throughout the nation's state legislatures. Post-Ferguson, there is a less clear pattern of smaller spikes in newspaper coverage being complemented months later by surges in legislative activity on policing. While Ferguson appears to be a flashpoint generating intensive media coverage and legislative responsiveness, subsequent racial policing controversies appear unable to achieve similar results.

The trends in Figure 1 suggest that the volume of policing-related news coverage in the aftermath of Ferguson may have signaled to state lawmakers that policing was deserving of legislative action. Figure 2 displays the month-to-month changes in the numbers of *pro-protester* and *pro-police* framed articles, as well as the changes in the numbers of *police*

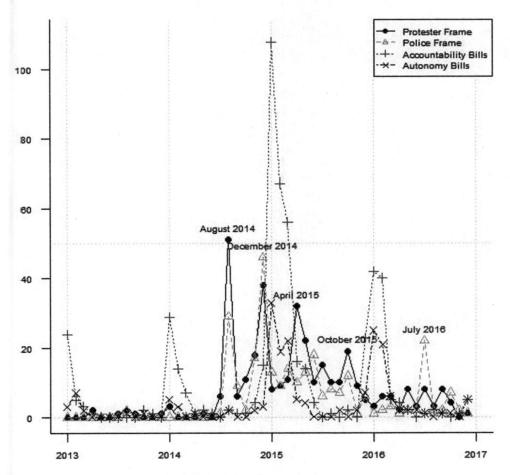

Figure 2. State response to media (bills introduced).

accountability and *police autonomy* bills introduced in state legislatures. The overlapping patterns on display here suggest an association between the framing of police and protesters and the type of policing-related legislative output emanating from statehouses.

As shown by the trend lines marked by circles and triangles, which display the number of pro-protester and pro-police framed articles, respectively, pro-police articles from the four major newspapers exceeded pro-protester articles in only 7 of the 48 months under study. Prior to Ferguson, the numbers of pro-police and pro-protester-framed articles are virtually equivalent. But with few exceptions, after the inciting events in Ferguson, articles sympathetic to protesters or skeptical of police become a more prominent feature of news coverage of policing. This trend suggests that activists advocating for greater police accountability in the Ferguson era were not just successful at inserting their agenda in the national conversation, they were largely able to drive the conversation on policing.

As shown by the respective lines marked by crosses and *x*'s displaying the numbers of accountability and autonomy bills introduced, the number of autonomy bills introduced exceeded the number of accountability bills in only five months. Overall, the national

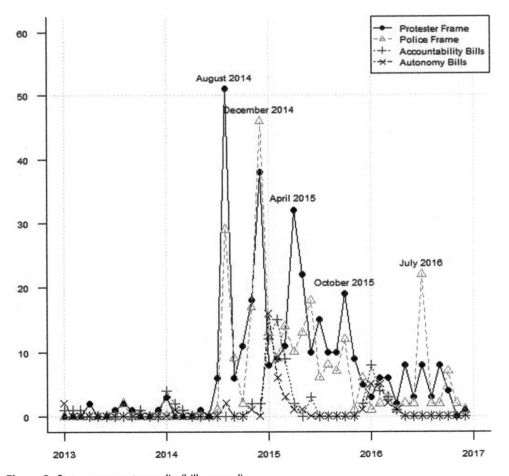

Figure 3. State response to media (bills passed).

trends in output from state legislatures are consistent with the trends in newspaper coverage. Both the news coverage and bills introduced on policing appear to be sympathetic to the demands of police accountability advocates in the immediate aftermath of Ferguson. The substantive impact of this apparent sympathy remains to be seen. This point is corroborated by Figure 3, which displays the month-to-month changes in *pro-protester* and *pro-police* articles, changes in the numbers of *police accountability* and *police autonomy* bills actually passed by state legislatures. While many more police accountability bills were proposed than autonomy bills, the proportions of both sets of bills actually passed are much closer.

Altogether, these observational trends indicate that Ferguson represented a flashpoint that shifted the volume and tone of news coverage of policing. Furthermore, that coverage likely provided an important signal to lawmakers across the nation of whether and how they should act on the issue. Notably, subsequent high-profile policing controversies that did not produce insurgent activity on par with Ferguson did not generate the same amount of media coverage. Not incidentally, the amount of policing-related legislative output also failed to reach the same heights as in the immediate post-Ferguson era.

Discussion and conclusion

Even in the absence of certainty about the causal arrow, we believe the trends we observe in media coverage are contributing to an overall political environment in which the policing of minorities is more or less salient. And policymakers are sensitive to perceptions of that issue salience. State legislation offers but one type of institutional response to the policing issue. Responses from local municipalities or the federal government may more effectively shape the overarching climate in which police units operate.

Nonetheless, the state legislature is a unit of analysis offering rich variation in key factors determining the capacity of competing sub-constituencies to get their interests advanced. Our set of 50 state legislative bodies differs along lines of partisan control, concentration of racial minorities, professionalization of the legislature, and strength, scope and size of policing units (and police unions). These types of factors meaningfully shape the decisions individual lawmakers make about the groups to which they will – and will not – provide policy responsiveness. We, therefore, consider state legislatures a valuable source of insight into how policymakers respond to racially contentious issues such as policing.

The agenda-setting power of the news media appears evident from these observations. The relative intensity or idleness of policing-related news coverage correlates with the ebbs and flows of attentiveness state lawmakers devote to the issue. Additionally, we can note that Ferguson marked a significant flashpoint in promoting and shaping the ensuing narrative around policing in minority communities. Not only does the increase in news articles about policing skyrocket in August 2014, but the tone of the coverage appears to shift, with frames sympathetic to protesters becoming more prominent.

One could be skeptical that a high volume of news coverage framed as pro-protester rather than pro-police would actually translate to greater legislative activity aimed at increasing police accountability. For instance, polls have revealed White Americans – to whom the aforementioned research indicates state lawmakers will be most responsive – remain steadfast in their support for and trust in police officers (Fingerhut 2017).

Additionally, as Marenin (1985) contends, "police forces are the capstone in the construction of the modern state." This symbiotic relationship between police and political actors could be expected to preclude many lawmakers from taking legislative positions that appear to oppose police units, who are viewed as allies.

Yet despite these attitudinal and ideological dispositions, which should privilege the political position of police within state assembly halls, we find state lawmakers prioritizing policies that would rein in rather than expand police power. We propose that this policy focus is likely influenced by the predominant frames evident in news coverage.

Our observations appear to highlight the potential political power of policing protests. The activists in Ferguson endeavored upon a sustained and intensive insurgent response to the Michael Brown killing that produced interactions and visuals so captivating that news media outlets were compelled to take note. Building on aforementioned work, we find conditions in which protest activity does appear to translate to policy responsiveness. Furthermore, we identify a specific mechanism through which such activity translates to policy change – through extensive and agreeable media coverage that signals to lawmakers the urgent and legitimate demands of groups whose views are often compromised within conventional electoral channels.

Yet, these observations also raise questions about the conditions under which police protests can effectively change the national political agenda. What were the distinguishing characteristics that made the protests in Ferguson a major turning point in the national conversation, yet not the demonstrations in response to the aforementioned slayings of Freddie Gray or Philando Castile? Why did the death of Sandra Bland in custody of officials in a Texas jailhouse in July 2015 not engender an increase in newspaper coverage of policing? Does the relative lack of media scrutiny in this instance reflect the lessened salience of women of color who are victims of alleged police wrongdoing? Or did the circumstances surrounding Bland's death not conform to established scripts about racial policing controversies? Raising such questions emphasizes the long road faced by protesters to achieve sufficient media attentiveness (and subsequently policy responsiveness) to their aims, even in sociopolitical climates with a heightened awareness of the issues for which they agitate.

As we build on this initial exploration, we will examine how the state legislative responses to media framing of policing are affected by factors such as the racial composition of the electorate and legislative body, and the geographic proximity to Ferguson. By accounting for more of these distinguishing features of state legislatures, we aim to pinpoint more precisely which characteristics make state lawmakers more or less susceptible to prevalent media frames in policing coverage.

In addition to broadening the scope of newspapers to better account for how political culture, racial diversity and urbanicity shape news coverage of policing post-Ferguson, we will examine the influences of policing coverage from other news outlets, including television broadcasts and social media. Finally, future projects will disaggregate the accountability and autonomy bills to determine how the policing legislation passed will tangibly alter relationships between police and minority communities.

In summary, analyses from our two original datasets indicate the insurgent activity in Ferguson that firmly etched "BLM" onto the national consciousness had a meaningful effect on the ensuing media narratives about policing. Along with these media, narratives was an increase legislative activity on policing issues, seemingly responsive both to the volume and tone of the news coverage on policing. The protests in the immediate aftermath of Ferguson appeared to be effective at shaping the conversation on policing in prominent newsrooms, and subsequently within the halls of state legislatures.

Notes

1. Not included in either of these categories are policing bills that address aspects of policing unrelated to substantive issues of police authority, scope, and power. For example, bills centered on increasing police training and recognition of persons with disabilities. Although this policy may improve policing, it is unrelated to the central issues of police misconduct raised by Ferguson.
2. The remaining 207 articles were categorized as having no distinguishable pro- or anti-frame in their depictions of police or protesters.
3. The remaining 97 bills are categorized as unrelated to both accountability and autonomy.

Acknowledgments

The authors would like to thank our team of undergraduates who worked tirelessly to collect the data for the two original data sets used in this study.

Disclosure statement

No potential conflict of interest was reported by the authors.

References

Bennett, W. L. 1983. *News: The Politics of Illusion*. Chicago: University of Chicago Press.
Browning, R. P., D. R. Marshall, and D. H. Tabb. 1984. *Protest Is Not enough: The Struggle of Blacks and Hispanics for Equality in Urban Politics*. Berkeley: University of California Press.
Brummett, B. 1994. *Rhetoric in Popular Culture*. Thousand Oaks, CA: Sage.
Butler, D. M., and D. E. Broockman. 2011. "Do Politicians Racially Discriminate Against Constituents? A Field Experiment on State Legislators." *American Journal of Political Science* 55 (3): 463–477.
Davenport, C. 2010. *Media Bias, Perspective, and State Repression: The Black Panther Party*. Cambridge: Cambridge University Press.
Dixon, T. L. 2017. "Good Guys Are Still Always in White? Positive Change and Continued Misrepresentation of Race and Crime on Local Television News." *Communication Research* 44 (6): 775–792.
Dunaway, J., R. P. Branton, and M. A. Abrajano. 2010. "Agenda Setting, Public Opinion, and the Issue of Immigration Reform." *Social Science Quarterly* 91 (2): 359–378.
Fingerhut, H. 2017. *Deep Racial, Partisan Divisions in Americans' Views of Police Officers*. PEW Research Center. http://www.pewresearch.org/fact-tank/2017/09/15/deep-racial-partisan-divisions-in-americans-views-of-police-officers/.
Gause, L. 2016. The Advantage of Disadvantage: Legislative Responsiveness to Collective Action by the Politically Marginalized (Dissertation). Retrieved from Deep Blue Dissertations and Theses Database. https://deepblue.lib.umich.edu/handle/2027.42/133207.
Gilens, M. 1999. *Why Americans Hate Welfare: Race, Media, and the Politics of Anti-poverty Policy*. Chicago: University of Chicago Press.
Gilens, M., and B. I. Page. 2014. "Testing Theories of American Politics: Elites, Interest Groups, and Average Citizens." *Perspectives on Politics* 12 (3): 564–581.

Gilliam Jr, F. D., and S. Iyengar. 2000. "Prime Suspects: The Influence of Local Television News on the Viewing Public." *American Journal of Political Science* 44: 560–573.

Gilliam Jr, F. D., S. Iyengar, A. Simon, and O. Wright. 1996. "Crime in Black and White: The Violent, Scary World of Local News." *Harvard International Journal of Press/Politics* 1 (3): 6–23.

Gillion, D. Q. 2012. "Protest and Congressional Behavior: Assessing Racial and Ethnic Minority Protests in the District." *The Journal of Politics* 74 (4): 950–962.

Hertog, J. K., and D. M. McLeod. 1995. "Anarchists Wreak Havoc in Downtown Minneapolis: A Multi-level Study of Media Coverage of Radical Protest." *Journalism & Mass Communication Monographs* 1 (151): 1.

Hurwitz, J., and M. Peffley. 2005. "Playing the Race Card in the Post–Willie Horton Era: The Impact of Racialized Code Words on Support for Punitive Crime Policy." *Public Opinion Quarterly* 69 (1): 99–112.

Izadi, E. 2016. This State Is About to Become the First Where Targeting Police Is a Hate Crime. *The Washington Post.* https://www.washingtonpost.com/news/post-nation/wp/2016/05/21/this-state-is-about-to-become-the-first-where-targeting-police-is-a-hate-crime/.

Lee, T. 2002. *Mobilizing Public Opinion: Black Insurgency and Racial Attitudes in the Civil Rights Era*. Chicago: University of Chicago Press.

Lippmann, W. 1922. *Public Opinion*. New York: Harcourt, Brace, and Company.

Marenin, O. 1985. "Policing Nigeria: Control and Autonomy in the Exercise of Coercion." *African Studies Review* 28 (1): 73–93.

Mayhew, D. R. 1974. *Congress: The Electoral Connection*. New Haven: Yale University Press.

McLeod, D. M., and B. H. Detenber. 1999. "Framing Effects of Television News Coverage of Social Protest." *Journal of Communication* 49 (3): 3–23.

Mendelberg, T. 2001. *The Race Card: Campaign Strategy, Implicit Messages, and the Norm of Equality*. Princeton: Princeton University Press.

Rosenstone, S. J. H., and J. M. Hansen. 1993. *Mobilization, Participation, and Democracy in America*. Basingstoke: Macmillan Publishing Company.

Smith, J., J. D. McCarthy, C. McPhail, and B. Augustyn. 2001. "From Protest to Agenda Building: Description Bias in Media Coverage of Protest Events in Washington, DC." *Social Forces* 79 (4): 1397–1423.

Strömbäck, J. 2008. "Four Phases of Mediatization: An Analysis of the Mediatization of Politics." *The International Journal of Press/Politics* 13 (3): 228–246.

Tate, K. 1994. *From Protest to Politics: The New Black Voters in American Elections*. Cambridge: Harvard University Press.

Valentino, N. A., V. L. Hutchings, and I. K. White. 2002. "Cues That Matter: How Political Ads Prime Racial Attitudes During Campaigns." *American Political Science Review* 96 (1): 75–90.

Reframing racism: political cartoons in the era of Black Lives Matter

Anish Vanaik, Dwaine Jengelley and Rolfe Peterson

ABSTRACT
The Black Lives Matter movement gained national prominence after highly publicized protests turned the spotlight on police violence in the US. We explore how this complex, multi-vocal movement is framed in the media using an original dataset of over 500 editorial cartoons by award-winning syndicated cartoonists. We find that every cartoonist in our sample increased their frequency of cartooning about racism in the BLM period with the greatest increases from those who had previously drawn the least about racism. Cartoons of this period also focused on police brutality to a hitherto unprecedented extent. When they did so, they emphasized the systemic nature of police brutality. Cartoons about movements having an impact on racism significantly increased. Movements were usually portrayed in a sympathetic light. Despite these gains for the advocacy of BLM activists, the engagement with the movement was superficial, indicated most clearly in the exclusion of women from cartoonists' framing of the movement. Nevertheless, the cartoons drawn in the wake of BLM demonstrate a clear break, in imagery and meaning, from the presence of post-racial tropes typical of editorial cartoons in the preceding period.

Black Lives Matter: a multi-vocal arena

The Black Lives Matter (BLM) movement, which developed after the killing of Michael Brown in August 2014, has had resounding significance. As with similar mobilizations – mass-based, part-spontaneous part-organized, and rooted in a long history – the nature of participation, demands, and outcomes of the movement are complex. Scholars have focused on the movement's root causes (Rickford 2015), connected it to the historical struggle for equality (Taylor 2016), and assessed its impact on the country's political development (Francis 2018; Johnson 2018; Taylor 2018). It is clear, however, that the scope and legacy of the BLM movement are ongoing. We investigate the framing of BLM in public discussion, asking: has BLM transformed the imagery of racism in mainstream editorial cartoons?

Black Lives Matter was a hashtag created in 2013 by Alicia Garza, Patrisse Cullors and Opal Tometi in the wake of Trayvon Martin's killing (Garza 2014). It was after August 2014, however, that both media attention and mobilizations grew decisively larger (Freelon, Mcilwain, and Clark 2016). Since fall 2014, the country witnessed a series of flashpoints as well as continuing protests and mobilizations in major cities, universities, and the world of sports and entertainment.

The framing of BLM in public discussion has been varied. One key issue has been whether BLM ought to be defined in narrow or expansive terms. At its narrowest are calls for institutional police reform with enhanced training and technology (e.g. body cameras). A more extensive program of action has been demanded on the basis that the causes of police violence against black people are structural. Here demands range from reparations to Palestine solidarity (Movement for Black Lives 2017). The balance of these narrow and expansive framings is one critical determinant of the legacy of BLM.

BLM has also had critics, especially among police and right-wing commentators. Two lines of criticism of the movement were particularly prominent (Anderson and Hitlin 2016). First, the accusation that BLM protests lowered the bar on attacks against police personnel – the so-called "Ferguson Effect." The other staple criticism was encapsulated in the slogan "All Lives Matter." Proponents of this claimed that BLM was divisive and promoted sectional interests. Milder criticism of the movement questioned whether all BLM uprisings met standards of "respectable" protest. Within the movement, a loose conglomeration of groups and individuals, differences of opinion about specific demands as well as broader strategy remain salient. BLM, in short, is a multi-vocal and contested terrain.

In this dialogue, we explore the framing of this contested terrain in political cartoons of the period. Beginning with a description of how the movement influenced cartoonists and cartoons about racism, we then examine the shifts in imagery during the period of BLM mobilizations.

BLM in the media

Emerging qualitative and quantitative research into the public discussion of BLM use social media (especially Twitter) as source material (Bonilla and Rosa 2015). One trend is to study participation in online discussions of BLM. "Black Twitter," scholars have found, was a leader in the online discussion of BLM over 2014–2015 (Freelon, Mcilwain, and Clark 2016; Olteanu, Weber, and Gatica-Perez 2016). Places with histories of police violence against black communities were also more likely to participate in BLM online activism (De Choudhury et al. 2016). Closer to the kinds of questions that we raise are studies that analyze content. Ince, Rojas and Davis (2017, 1825) find that hashtags that express solidarity and approval of the movement are more common among Twitter users than the adoption of the "movement's specific grievances." Langford and Speight (2015) argue that BLM hashtags have made the black body present and newsworthy, thereby undercutting political colorblindness. Scholars have also pointed to the highly contested nature of the online discussion (Langford and Speight 2015; Carney 2016).

Despite the strengths of these studies, important limitations remain. First, Twitter content loses the richness of extended engagement and expertise that reportage and opinion pieces supply. Elmasry and el-Nawawy (2017) as well as Clayton (2018), illustrate these advantages through their study of articles in the *New York Times* and *St. Louis Post-Dispatch*. Their conclusions support the major findings of the social media analyses: most critically, that the framing of the movement was largely positive. Elmasry and el-Nawawy (2017) point out, that newspapers are more likely to quote protesters than police and government officials. They also find that even when looting is mentioned in articles a net positive framing persists (albeit with a higher proportion of negative framing). Clayton (2018) found that the *New York Times* was more likely to present the issues raised by the movement in the form of "Human Rights statements" than its coverage of the Civil Rights Movement of the 1960s had done at a comparable stage. Studies based on mainstream news outlets, thus, allow researchers to pose critical questions that cannot be explored through social media.

Another gap in the existing literature is that most studies have not effectively integrated visual content into their analysis (Freelon, Mcilwain, and Clark 2016). Entman and Rojecki (2000, xv) underline the importance of these media by pointing out that "the subject of race is peculiarly visual." Research about cultures of racism in the period before BLM have extensively and effectively employed cartoons (Rossing 2011; Wingfield and Feagin 2012; Howard 2014). Probing the patterns of cartooning that emerged in the period of BLM, then, would join a larger conversation about racism in the US.

Why political cartoons?

The literature on political cartoons spans a variety of disciplines – rhetoric, political science, art history, sociology and anthropology (Gamson and Stuart 1992; Greenberg 2002; Baumgartner 2008; Conners 2010). Within political science, analysis of editorial cartoons remains an under-studied sub-field within the area of satire and political communication (Worcester 2007). This research suggests that satire is an effective purveyor of information as well as an argument (Caufield 2008).

Editorial cartoons are a good medium to study public discussion of political issues. For one, cartoonists actively discuss the subject and form of their cartoons with editors – they are insiders to the opinion-making segment of the media (Gamson and Stuart 1992). Second, editorial cartoonists operate with both complexity and an economy of expression (Abraham 2009). They do this largely through employing effective and multi-layered visual metaphors, a great advantage to the social scientist seeking clear and non-simplistic forms of articulation. Third, cartoons span the domains of reasoned argument and imagination. Thus, they can speak directly to aspects of implicit bias that are otherwise difficult to assess – e.g. how are victims or police officers imagined? No surprise, then, that they are often used to discuss racial stereotypes (Howard 2014). Finally, cartoons are a staple of print media and circulate quite widely on social media as well.

Racism in political cartoons

Recent research on the Obama presidency explores what depictions of the Obamas in cartoons reveal about the nature of contemporary racism. Discussing caricatures of Obama as a monkey, Wingfield and Feagin (2012) suggest that the election of a black president was met with the resurgence of "hard racial frames" that openly referenced ideas of the racial inferiority of black people. Absent any "counterframing" in mainstream outlets, they argue, public terrain is occupied by "soft racial frames." The latter diminish the role of structural racism in US life, arguing in "colorblind" terms while eschewing overtly racist terminology. Examples of this kind of speech, Wingfield and Feagin argue, include many of President Obama's own statements.

PSS Howard's (2014) analysis of similar cartoons takes seriously the fact that they are often accompanied by denial of any racist intent. He draws on David Goldberg's work to explain this pattern – producing explicitly racist imagery while denying racist intention – as typical of a period of heightened neo-liberal individualism and post-racialism. Rossing (2011) examines reactions to the July 2008 *New Yorker* cover cartoon that parodied racist fears about the Obamas – depicting the Obamas as a Radical Muslim, and Black nationalist militant. He argues that the spectrum of reactions, "revealed ideologies and habits that erect obstacles to racial justice" (Rossing 2011, 433).

Taken together, these studies point to a culture of images in which racist stereotypes have been widely propagated since 2008. In both, the content of cartoons and in the responses to them, the literature suggests that there is a preponderance of a post-racial denial of structural racism. The caricatural culture of the current moment, these studies suggest, consists of images that either reinforce or ignore structural racism.

Methodological departures

Our use of political cartoons departs from the existing literature in significant ways. First, most studies of cartoons in politics focus on personalities (Conners 2010; Zurbriggen and Sherman 2010). Each of the recent studies of racism in cartoons discussed above is based on a similar focus: they probe the ways in which deep-seated forms of racism in US political culture are projected onto depictions of the Obamas. The focus on personalities, however, offers little traction to study whether cartoonists have depicted racism in non-individualized contexts. Our study offers a fuller set of objects of analysis by bringing in the anonymous, representative, and metaphorical figures deployed by cartoonists. Our effort is to capture structural depictions of racism as they are directly portrayed rather than generate inferences based on depictions of particular personalities.

Second, most studies that analyze political movements, phenomena or processes through cartoons gather data around various flashpoints (Gamson and Stuart 1992).[1] In contrast, we study the entire period of BLM and offer a comparison with the period before. Our approach, therefore, allows us to better capture the deeper effects of a movement against racism on the depiction of a structure of racism than more narrowly targeted studies.

Data and methods

To examine the influence of BLM on political cartooning we use an original dataset of over 500 editorial cartoons about racism drawn by 23 active award-winning cartoonists from August 2012 to January 2016. Our data set includes cartoons from two years before the agreed start of the BLM movement – August 10, 2014 – until January 2016. We distinguish between cartoons drawn before August 9, 2014, as pre-BLM and those created after that date as BLM. The former allows us to have a baseline to track the changes in the latter period. For both periods we reviewed every cartoon drawn by the cartoonists in our sample. We then selected for coding every cartoon whose subject was racism. Our database is the population of cartoons about racism for the reference period from our cartoonist sample. We have also maintained a count of the total number of cartoons drawn by each cartoonist during this period.

We identify cartoonists for this study using purposive selection. To be included, a cartoonist must be a recipient in the 10 years preceding 2015 of either the Pulitzer or Herblock, the two apex prizes awarded for editorial cartooning. Winners of these prizes are respected cartoonists whose work attains a level of proficiency and acclaim. The Pulitzer and Herblock serve as a proxy for reach, as award-winning cartoonists are usually widely syndicated. We felt it important to include cartoonists with reach because syndicated cartoonists are reputable, aim for a wide audience, and have the ability to influence cartooning at smaller newspapers. Based on these aspects of peer recognition and reach we often refer to the cartoonists in our sample as "mainstream."

We sourced most of the cartoons from gocomics.com, politicalcartoons.com, and from the Association of American Editorial Cartoonists (AAEC) http://editorialcartoonists.com/aaecweb/, all online repositories of editorial cartoons. In some cases, we relied on newspaper websites and cartoonists' personal websites. We excluded award-winning cartoonists whose work during the period of study is not available online.

There are drawbacks to only including award-winning cartoonists. First, most award-winners are men and only two women cartoonists appear in our sample. This number reflects the state of the industry. Our sampling strategy also tends to exclude younger and early career cartoonists, who are unlikely to win these awards. Finally, most award-winning mainstream cartoonists in our data describe themselves as politically left of center. And while most cartoonists are left-leaning (Lamb 2004), there are many active center-right editorial cartoonists.

A more significant exclusion derives from the absence of active award-winning African American cartoonists. This is problematic given that previous research (Kinder and Sanders 1996) suggests, race-specific differences exist when it comes to valuing and framing racism. We include Darrin Bell, a syndicated African American cartoonist as a point of comparison outside our sample of mainstream cartoonists. We have not included any cartoonist from the Black Press, another possible area where the pattern of framing BLM might differ.

Frames and coding procedures

When editorial cartoonists draw cartoons about political issues, they usually prescribe meaning and evaluate the issue. By providing meaning or emphasizing a particular position through visual imagery, a cartoonist is engaging in the exercise of framing (Gamson and Stuart 1992; Entman 1993; Nelson, Clawson, and Oxley 1997). Frames "promote a particular problem, definition, causal interpretation, moral evaluation and/or treatment recommendation for the item described" (Entman 1993, 52). Cartoonists are, in this respect, more akin to editorial commentators than to reporters.

Based on a preliminary analysis of the broader debate around BLM, we identified five key framing areas in these cartoons about racism: Police, Media, General Racism, Movements, and Solutions. Table 1 lists the five key frames and sub-frames associated with each

Table 1. Frames and sub-frames used to code the sample of cartoons on race.

Police	Media bias	General	Movement	Solutions
Systemic	Systemic racism	Multi-dimensional cause	Part of the political landscape	Racial harmony
Individualizing-bad victim	Sensationalism	Mass incarceration	Systematically misrepresented	Improving symbolisms
Individualizing-one bad cop	Misplaced priorities	Voter suppression	Protestors raised consciousness	Mainstream politics
	Ideologically driven	Economic	Tribute to pioneers	Approval of administrative action
	Expand democracy: mainstream media	Party politics	Women play a leading role in BLM	Police reforms
	Expand democracy: social media	Post-racial society	Movement a positive development	Radical
		Shared blame	Defining legitimate protest	
		Black responsibility	Endangering law enforcement	
		Other specific causes	BLM is a negative development	

frame. The first three frames cover diagnoses of the problems that spurred protests, the fourth takes up the depiction of the movement itself, and the fifth concerns solutions being offered. Within each frame, sub-frames encompass a full range of political positions – from those hostile to claims of systemic racism, to others that favor a structural view of racism and demand a radical response. Some sub-frames are based on current literature, while others were created or refined for this study.

Cartoons that bring up the issue of racism through images that reference police activity were classified as employing a "Police" frame. Instances of police brutality were the immediate cause of BLM protests. There is also a long history in the U.S. suggesting that police forces are structurally predisposed to racism and that policing methods perpetuate racism (Vitale 2017). Within the Police frame, the sub-frames are drawn directly from Regina Lawrence's (2000) work on the coverage of police brutality incidents in the 1990s. Lawrence argues that there is strong sponsorship of individualizing frames by authorities seeking to defend their conduct – promoting the idea that the instance of brutality was because of a bad or unfortunate victim, or, more rarely, because of the one bad policeman. In contrast, activists and academics opposing police violence sponsor frames that argue for the systemic character of police racism and demand larger transformations in policing.

"Media" frames linked racist or anti-racist activity with the representations of race in media – television, social media or print media. The sub-frames here range from those condemning the media as a purveyor of stereotypes to ones that celebrate the media – including social media – as ameliorating racism.

The "General Racism" frame has an omnibus character. It contains a variety of non-media and non-police related representations of the causes of racism in public life. Common to all the cartoons in this frame is the identification of phenomena considered to be a cause of racism in the U.S. Some General Racism sub-frames capture diagnoses of racism that are broad-ranging. Examples of these include suggesting that racism is multi-causal, that there is shared blame between Black and White folks for racism, or that Black people bear responsibility for their own predicament. Other sub-frames identify more specific linkages between racism and social institutions: e.g, mass incarceration, voter suppression, and party politics.

Cartoons that addressed the issue of racism through concentrating on mass mobilizations that oppose racism were classified as employing the "Movements" frame. This frame includes the range of collective action frames: "injustice, agency and identity" outlined by Gamson (1992, 7). In the pre-BLM period, the depiction of a variety of movements against racism would result in a cartoon being classified as using a movement frame: from the Civil Rights movement to mobilizations about Trayvon Martin. Sub-frames in the Movements frame can be divided into those that framed the movement in a sympathetic light – as being misrepresented, opposing mischaracterizations promoted by opponents (e.g. that they disturb public peace), or emphasizing movements' ability to transform the public debate. Other sub-frames include those that are hostile to the movements framing them, for instance, as an illegitimate pressure group.

Finally, discussions during this period also suggested solutions to the problem of racism. The "Solutions" frame captured cartoons that explicitly advocated for ways of redressing racism. Typically, cartoons included here would offer a diagnosis of the problem and a solution at the same time. The range of sub-frames for the Solutions frame went from diffuse calls for racial harmony to the precise advocacy of police or administrative reforms (e.g. the induction of body cameras or inclusion of black personnel in administration or police). Another range of sub-frames within the solution frame went from advocating radical, often movement-based, transformations of race relations, to solutions that were framed in terms of mainstream politics.

These frames capture the entire range of discussion of racism that appeared in editorial cartoons in the pre-BLM and BLM periods. Coders were instructed to select only one sub-frame within a frame. However, in rare circumstances, one sub-frame each from multiple frames could be selected. Consequently, the number of frames in our data exceeds the number of cartoons.

Findings

Figure 1 displays the increase in productivity on racism from Pre-BLM to BLM. Cartoonists are grouped in two categories based on their productivity on the issue: *less frequent referencers* of racism and *more frequent referencers* of racism. Cartoonists whose output on racism is below average in the pre-BLM era are categorized as *less frequent referencers*, and cartoonists whose percentage of cartoons in the pre-BLM era are above the average are categorized as *more frequent referencers*. This delineation allows us to show how cartoonists responded to BLM based on the rate they previously addressed race. The figure also shows the average change in our overall data.

The findings are stark. In the pre-BLM period, only 3% of the cartoonists' body of work is about racism. After the BLM protests began, cartoonists produced significantly more cartoons about racism (10%). In the BLM period, cartoons about racism are also a broad-based phenomenon – every cartoonist in our sample produces more racism cartoons – testifying to the agenda-setting influence of BLM. In the pre-BLM era, in contrast, a relatively small number of cartoonists (5 of the 23) drew the majority of cartoons about racism.

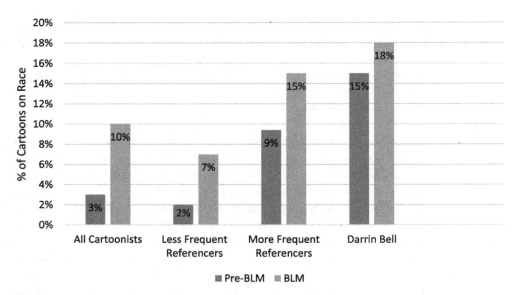

Figure 1. Increase in Productivity on Racism from Pre-BLM to BLM.
Notes: Bars are the percentage of overall cartoons about race by cartoonist. "More Frequent Referencers" are cartoonists that in the Pre-BLM era drew more race cartoons on average than the sample. "Less Frequent Referencers" drew race cartoons at a lower rate than the average in the sample in the Pre-BLM era. Darrin Bell is a black cartoonist that is not part of our sample. BLM era cartoons are cartoons produced after August 9, 2014.

Even though every cartoonist produces more cartoons on racism, an interesting result emerges when we look at just the *less frequent referencers*. These cartoonists increased the frequency of racism-related cartoons from 2% pre-BLM to 7% in the BLM era. In comparison to this 350% increase, the *more frequent referencers* of racism group increased their output on racism only 66% (from 9% to 15%). This is evidence that BLM was not "preaching to the converted." BLM amplified the issue of racism in all cartooning but had a greater impact on those who were less likely to broach the subject before the movement. Overall, however, the topic of racism was amplified: more cartoonists were speaking out about the issue and they spoke about it more often than before. Even with this increased productivity, none of the award-winning cartoonists outperformed Darrin Bell, an African American cartoonist we used as a reference point. Bell moved from 15% to 18% of racism cartoons after BLM.

The frames

What is the substance of this amplified conversation about racism? Table 2 presents the frequency of frames in pre-BLM and BLM cartoons. The most striking finding about frames in the BLM era is the increase in the frequency of the Police Frame, jumping from 6% to 33% of all racism cartoons in the BLM period. The imagery here portrays the police as quick to use excessive force in their encounters with black citizens, increasingly militarized, and overwhelmingly white, and lacking diversity. These are structural criticisms of the police system rather than individualizing ones singling out the police officer responsible for a given killing.

Table 2. Frequency of frames in cartoons in the pre-BLM vs. BLM era.

	Pre-BLM		BLM	
	Frame count	% of Total cartoons*	Frame count	% of Total Cartoons*
Police	7	6	110	33
General racism	96	76	170	51
Movement	2	2	35	11
Media bias	17	13	22	7
Solutions	12	9	20	6
Total frame count	134		357	
Total cartoon count*	127*		331*	

Notes: The total number of cartoons in our Mainstream Cartoonist dataset is 458. Frames are not mutually exclusive because cartoons can have multiple frames. Percentages are calculated using the total cartoon count.

Mike Luckovich's, August 15, 2014, cartoon "Mayberry 2014," illustrates the multiple dimensions of this systemic critique. Luckovich draws the popular police officers Andy and Barney (from the Andy Griffith show's fictional town of Mayberry) surreally dressed in riot gear and carrying assault rifles on a normal day in front of a barbershop. A black man walks past them, however, he has raised his hands in the air to demonstrate that he's unarmed. Luckovich is simultaneously reflecting on the BLM movement (with their slogan "Hands Up, Don't Shoot"), police militarization, and America's idyllic perception of local police versus the current reality.[2]

In both periods, cartoonists largely present police brutality as a systemic problem. The key distinction between the periods is the increasing number of police brutality cartoons that appear in the era of BLM. The rise in cartoons about the police is statistically significant. Lawrence (2000) demonstrates that in cases of police brutality, individualizing frames (bad victim or bad cop) are strongly sponsored by officials, while anti-police brutality movements sponsor systemic frames. The nature of the discussion of the police in these cartoons implies that editorial cartoonists weren't adopting frames typical of administration officials and that the BLM movement may have focused the conversation about police as a structural problem.

Two other shifts in Table 2 are also noteworthy. The number of cartoons that adopt a Movements frame jumps from 2% to 11%. On the one hand, it appears that cartoonists are beginning to picture a role for movements in eradicating racism. On the other hand, 11% represents a relatively small proportion of the output of racism cartoons in the BLM period. Cartoons were more likely to depict the issues raised by BLM than the movement itself. The third shift is the decline of the proportion of cartoons in the General Racism frame. As we shall see a lot is going on beneath the surface of this large frame.

The general frame

More than half of the BLM cartoons in our sample fall into the General Racism frame. As noted above, this represents a significant decline from the proportion of racism cartoons that adopt a General Racism frame pre-BLM. Speaking of racism in general terms was being replaced by the sharper critique of police and attention paid to movements. This, by itself, is an interesting finding. However, it is worth digging deeper. In contrast to the other frames, the "General Racism" frame has a large, umbrella character and therefore numerous sub-frames. Table 3 indicates the frequency of sub-frames of cartoons that were coded as falling into the General Racism frame.

Table 3. Percentage of General Racism sub-frames in cartoons in pre-BLM and BLM era.

Subframes	Pre-BLM % of Frame	BLM % of Frame
Multi-dimensional causes	36	46
Party politics	27	28
Voter suppression	19	6
Shared blame	1	5
Black responsibility	1	4
Economic	0	2
Post-racial	1	0
Individual racist	3	0
Mass incarceration	3	2
Other	8	7

Notes: Total number of cartoons with a General Racism frame are 265 (95 in the pre-BLM and 170 in the BLM era). Table 3 depicts the use of General Racism sub-frames in the pre- and BLM era. BLM era cartoons are cartoons produced after August 9, 2014. Percentages may not sum to 100% due to rounding.

While there is no appreciable change in many sub-frames, the voter suppression sub-frame declines significantly. This is interesting given that about half the BLM cartoons in our sample were produced in 2015, during the cycle of primaries for the 2016 election. The electoral arena (especially depictions of events on the campaign trail) was both topical and the subject of many cartoons that weren't about racism. It is surprising, therefore, that, during BLM, the sub-frames that linked racism to the voter suppression fell from 19% of General Racism cartoons in the Pre-BLM period to about 6%. The emergence of BLM protests appears to reduce the inclination of cartoonists to link racism to the electoral arena.

The other major change in the proportion of sub-frames within the General Frame concerns the increase in number of cartoons that identify the causes of racism as being multi-dimensional. This went from being just over a third of General Racism cartoons in the pre-BLM to just under half of General Racism cartoons in the BLM period. Similar to the increase in cartoons using police frames and those using movement frames, the rise in the identification of racism as multi-causal can be seen as the mainstreaming of the social critique offered by BLM movement.

Women and BLM

The BLM movement would not have gained national prominence were it not for black women who, through social media and grassroots organizing, brought national attention to the problem of police brutality. Scholars have suggested that the decentralized leadership structure and attention paid to the issues of black women, queer black people, black transgendered, and other marginalized groups are one of the distinctive features of BLM (Clayton 2018). Given this central role played by women, we might expect them to occupy a prominent place in the imagery of the BLM movement. Quite the opposite is the case. Our codebook has a sub-frame to register cartoons that depict that women had taken a lead in the movement. No cartoons in our sample employed this sub-frame. This is an instructive silence. Leaving the leadership role of women out of their cartoons indicates the relative superficiality in mainstream cartoonists' engagement with the BLM movement.

Women do, however, appear in the cartoons in a few other ways. Table 4, provides percentage on the presence of men and women in the cartoons during the BLM movement.

Table 4. Percentage of men and women in cartoons in the BLM Era.

Cartoon element	Men (%)	Women (%)	Both (%)	# Cartoons
Police	84	1	15	109
Victims	85	5	11	66
Everyman	93	5	3	42
Protesters	43	13	43	26
Generic politician	94	0	6	17
Public figures	93	7	NA	95

Notes: Total number of BLM cartoons is 331. More than one element can be in a cartoon.

Cartoonists frequently depict people in conflict with police, victims, protesters, public figures, politicians, and generic "everyman" archetypes. In each case, we code whether women are included in these roles.

The comparison reveals that women are rarely presented in the political cartoons. Of the 109 cartoons that include depictions of the police, 84% are men with only 1% women. Fifteen percent of the time both male and female police officers are drawn. This result is, perhaps, expected since the majority of high-profile incidents with the police and people of color involve male police officers. The cartooning of victims, however, is similar to that of police. Women victims were present only 5% of the time – higher than in the police category, but hardly a significant proportion. Most depictions of female victims are also in the context of a single incident in McKinney, Texas.

Most remarkable about this is that many of the victims drawn in the cartoons are not those whose deaths became the spur for the movement. Rather, these are figures imagined by the cartoonist. There is, one would imagine, no bar on imagining each of these as women.[3] The erasure of women's experiences of police brutality when victims are imagined as male has been mentioned by other scholars (Chatelain and Asoka 2015; Scott and Brown 2016). Within the movement, the #SayHerName campaign emerged to address this silence. No reflection of these concerns can be found in the cartoons in our sample.

As protestors women fare better. Thirteen percent of the cartoons that depict protests have only women protesters, 43% show men only, but 43% show both men and women. It is likely that a cartoon depicting a protest includes women protesters. Here, drawing women does serve to underline the community-wide support for BLM actions. Ironically enough, however, this is happening in an arena where women have been not just participants, but leaders. As such, these depictions are a diminishment of the actual role of women.

Discussion

The changes in the frames prevalent in cartoons depicting racism indicate a measure of success for BLM. A relative silence about racism has been broken. Most cartoonists throughout the period of BLM draw cartoons about racism. Consequently, the overall output of cartoons about racism increased significantly through this period. The second ground for optimism is that some frames promoted by the movement seem to have seen a significant increase. Notably, the Police Frame (33%) – the central issue raised by BLM protesters – was widely adopted by mainstream cartoonists. There was also a more-modest but, nevertheless a significant increase in the identification of racism as a multi-dimensional problem. Third, frames that run contrary to the spirit of BLM have little weight among the cartoonists we studied. Individualizing police frames are nearly absent. Only 5% of General Frame cartoons apportioned shared blame to black and white communities or shifted responsibility onto Black people for their own marginalization. One percent of cartoons attribute racism to individual racists, and a meager 0.33% suggest that America is now a post-racial society.

Cartoons, thus, present the sources of racism as complex and broad-based. Potentially, this lends force to the BLM movement's call for action on multiple fronts. Compared to the period preceding, the problem of racism in the US in the BLM era is presented in images that are more prepared to point to structural causes, less confident about solutions and coming to grips with the presence of a social movement.

Perhaps most significant of all, this pattern of framing represents a decided break from our findings of the pre-BLM era and the scholarly consensus about political cartoons in the earlier portions of Obama's presidency. As we noted, every study suggested that cartoons about the Obamas prevented the highlighting of structural racism or the need for collective action against it. The pattern of frames indicated here suggests something quite different is happening.

While there was an increase in the number of cartoons about movements, they still constitute only 11% of the overall number. One could also take note, for instance, of some of the frames to which BLM has given prominent attention that have a marginal presence in the cartoons in our sample. As shown in Table 3, mass incarceration and exclusion from economic activity were only seen in 3% of cartoons combined. These issues are central to a discussion of contemporary Black oppression. The absence of mass incarceration or economics sub-frames indicates that the engagement with the movement has been superficial. Further evidence of this is in the fact that the leadership role of women in the BLM demonstrations and protests has not been registered. While the mainstream cartoonists in our sample have been quick to view racism as a problem with structural causes, they have been less nimble-fingered in their attention to the BLM movement as pointing a way forward.

Conclusion

In this dialogue, we expanded the conversation about the framing of the BLM movement in the media. Our analysis suggests that the imagery of the cartoons in the BLM era is an important departure from the post-racial imagery characteristic of the period preceding. Silence about racism has been broken, and the cartoons align with many of the aims of BLM. Systemic police brutality and the increase of sympathy for movements are real gains of the mass mobilization.

Nevertheless, significant frames promoted by the BLM movement found little traction and, though drawn more often than before, the movement itself is rarely the subject of racism-related cartoons. The lack of success in catapulting the movement to center stage is manifested in the depiction of women. In contrast to the prominent role women have played in the movement, they are mostly absent in political cartoons. This conspicuous absence is partly a systematic feature of media representations generally and cartoons specifically. But the lack of women also has consequences for our understanding of the tremendous toll police violence takes in communities of color and the reality of activism in the BLM.

Notes

1. Analysis of news stories about BLM and social media content employ this approach of sampling from moments of heightened significance for the movement (Elmasry and el-Nawawy 2017; Freelon, Mcilwain, and Clark 2016).
2. The polysemic nature of this cartoon also shows the potential of cartoons as an object of study and the challenge of developing a method that captures the positions taken in the debates about BLM while protecting the complexity and depth of the cartoons.
3. By imagining the victim (or police officer) cartoons allow us to evaluate the degree to which the figure of the victim is assumed to be male.

Disclosure statement

No potential conflict of interest was reported by the authors.

ORCID

Dwaine Jengelley http://orcid.org/0000-0002-9459-3622

References

Abraham, Linus. 2009. "Effectiveness of Cartoons as a Uniquely Visual Medium for Orienting Social Issues." *Journalism and Communication Monographs* 11 (2): 117–165.
Anderson, Monica, and Paul Hitlin. 2016. "Social Media Conversations About Race." 1–34. Pew Research Center.
Baumgartner, Jody C. 2008. "Polls and Elections: Editorial Cartoons 2.0: The Effects of Digital Political Satire on Presidential Candidate Evaluations." *Presidential Studies Quarterly* 38 (4): 735–758.
Bonilla, Yarimar, and Jonathan Rosa. 2015. "#Ferguson: Digital Protest, Hashtag Ethnography, and the Racial Politics of Social Media in the United States." *American Ethnologist* 42 (1): 4–17.
Carney, Nikita. 2016. "All Lives Matter, but so Does Race: Black Lives Matter and the Evolving Role of Social Media." *Humanity & Society* 40 (2): 180–199.
Caufield, R. P. 2008. "The Influence of "Infoenterpropagainment": Exploring the Power of Political Satire as a Distinct Form of Political Humor." In *Laughing Matters: Humor and American Politics in the Media Age*, edited by J. C. Baumgartner, and Jonathan S. Morris, 3–20. New York: Routledge.
Chatelain, Marcia, and Kaavya Asoka. 2015. "Women and Black Lives Matter." *Dissent* 62 (3): 54–61.
Clayton, Dewey M. 2018. "Black Lives Matter and the Civil Rights Movement: A Comparative Analysis of Two Social Movements in the United States." *Journal of Black Studies* 49 (5): 448–480. https://www.ncbi.nlm.nih.gov/pubmed/28840078.
Conners, Joan L. 2010. "Barack Versus Hillary: Race, Gender, and Political Cartoon Imagery of the 2008 Presidential Primaries." *American Behavioral Scientist* 54 (3): 298–312.
De Choudhury, Munmun, Shagun Jhaver, Benjamin Sugar, and Ingmar Weber. 2016. "Social Media Participation in an Activist Movement for Racial Equality." *International Conference on Web and Social Media* May: 92–101. https://www.ncbi.nlm.nih.gov/pubmed/28840078. Association for the Advancement of Artificial Intelligence.
Elmasry, Mohamad Hamas, and Mohammed el-Nawawy. 2017. "Do Black Lives Matter?" *Journalism Practice* 11 (7): 857–875.
Entman, Robert M. 1993. "Framing: Toward Clarification of a Fractured Paradigm." *Journal of Communication* 43 (4): 51–58.
Entman, Robert M., and Andrew Rojecki. 2000. *The Black Image in the White Mind: Media and Race in America*. Chicago, IL: University of Chicago Press.

Francis, Megan Ming. 2018. "The Strange Fruit of American Political Development." *Politics, Groups, and Identities* 6 (1): 128–137.

Freelon, Deen, Charlton Mcilwain, and Meredith Clark. 2016. *Beyond the Hashtags: #Ferguson, #Blacklivesmatter, and the Online Struggle for Offline Justice*. Washington, DC: Center for Media and Social Impact: American University.

Gamson, William. A. 1992. *Talking Politics*. Cambridge: Cambridge University Press.

Gamson, William A., and David Stuart. 1992. "Media Discourse as a Symbolic Contest: The Bomb in Political Cartoons." *Sociological Forum* 7 (1): 55–86.

Garza, Alicia. 2014. "A Herstory of the #BlackLivesMatter Movement." *The Feminist Wire* 7.

Greenberg, J. 2002. "Framing and Temporality in Political Cartoons: A Critical Analysis of Visual News Discourse*." *Canadian Review of Sociology* 39 (2): 181–198.

Howard, Philip SS. 2014. "Drawing Dissent: Postracialist Pedagogy, Racist Literacy, and Racial Plagiarism in Anti-Obama Political Cartoons." *Review of Education, Pedagogy, and Cultural Studies* 36 (5): 386–402.

Ince, Jelani, Fabio Rojas, and Clayton A. Davis. 2017. "The Social Media Response to Black Lives Matter: How Twitter Users Interact with Black Lives Matter Through Hashtag Use." *Ethnic and Racial Studies* 40 (11): 1814–1830.

Johnson, Kimberley S. 2018. "The Neo-Redemption Era? APD in the Age of #Black Lives Matter." *Politics, Groups, and Identities* 6 (1): 120–127.

Kinder, Donald R., and Lynn M. Sanders. 1996. *Divided by Color: Racial Politics and Democratic Ideals, American Politics and Political Economy*. Chicago, IL: University of Chicago Press.

Lamb, Chris. 2004. *Drawn to Extremes: The Use and Abuse of Editorial Cartoons*. New York: Columbia University Press.

Langford, Catherine L, and Monteé Speight. 2015. "#BlackLivesMatter: Epistemic Positioning, Challenges, and Possibilities." *Journal of Contemporary Rhetoric* 5 (3/4): 78–89.

Lawrence, Regina G. 2000. *The Politics of Force: Media and the Construction of Police Brutality*. Berkeley: University of California Press.

The Movement for Black Lives. 2017. "Platform of the Movement for Black Lives." Accessed June 15, 2017. https://policy.m4bl.org/platform/.

Nelson, Thomas E., Rosalee A. Clawson, and Zoe M. Oxley. 1997. "Media Framing of a Civil Liberties Conflict and Its Effect on Tolerance." *American Political Science Review* 91 (3): 567–583.

Olteanu, Alexandra, Ingmar Weber, and Daniel Gatica-Perez. 2016. "Characterizing the Demographics behind the #BlackLivesMatter Movement." Symposia on Observational Studies of Social Media and other Human Generated Content. Stanford University. http://arxiv.org/abs/1512.05671.

Rickford, Russell. 2015. "Black Lives Matter." *New Labor Forum* 25 (1): 34–42.

Rossing, Jonathan P. 2011. "Comic Provocations in Racial Culture: Barack Obama and the 'Politics of Fear'." *Communication Studies* 62 (4): 422–438.

Scott, Jamil S, and Nadia E Brown. 2016. "Scholarship on #BlackLivesMatter and its Implications on Local Electoral Politics." *Politics, Groups, and Identities* 4 (4): 702–708.

Taylor, Keeanga-Yamahtta. 2016. *From #BlackLivesMatter to Black Liberation*. Chicago, IL: Haymarket Books.

Taylor, Kirstine. 2018. "American Political Development and Black Lives Matter in the Age of Incarceration." *Politics, Groups, and Identities* 6 (1): 153–161.

Vitale, Alex. 2017. *The End of Policing*. London: Verso Books.

Wingfield, Adia Harvey, and Joe Feagin. 2012. "The Racial Dialectic: President Barack Obama and the White Racial Frame." *Qualitative Sociology* 35 (2): 143–162.

Worcester, Kent. 2007. "Introduction." *PS: Political Science & Politics* 40 (2): 223–227.

Zurbriggen, Eileen L, and Aurora M Sherman. 2010. "Race and Gender in the 2008 US Presidential Election: A Content Analysis of Editorial Cartoons." *Analyses of Social Issues and Public Policy* 10 (1): 223–247.

Racialized differences in perceptions of and emotional responses to police killings of unarmed African Americans

Ernest B. McGowen and Kristin N. Wylie

ABSTRACT
Widespread attention to, and mobilization against, police killings of unarmed African Americans shatter any lingering myths of a post-racial America. We argue that the entrenched racial divide in the lived experiences and perceptions of whites and African Americans is mediated by emotions. Continuing research about the perceptions of and emotions attached to political events by people of different races, we draw on an embedded experiment. We contend that stories about police killings will elicit distinct emotions from whites and African Americans. The experiment varies the race of a victim of a police-involved shooting as well as whether the victim was suspected of criminality. We find that the majority of respondents express disappointment without regard to condition and that African Americans are more likely than whites to express anger as an emotional response. We see in-group/out-group psychological tendencies, with whites who read about a white victim (regardless of criminality) more likely to recommend criminal charges for the officer versus those who received a black victim. The findings highlight how identity moderates the connection between emotions and politics while also contributing to our understanding of race relations today.

In the wake of the 2013 acquittal of George Zimmerman for the 2012 murder of Trayvon Martin, an unarmed 17-year-old, many Americans were compelled to collectively assert the value of Black lives. That watershed event was followed in 2014–2015 by several high-profile police killings of unarmed African Americans including Michael Brown, laying bare institutional and societal devaluing of Black lives and serving as a catalyst for the Black Lives Matter (BLM) movement and broader Movement for Black Lives. The widespread attention to and BLM mobilization against police killings of unarmed African Americans seem to shatter any lingering myths of a post-racial America. We examine disparities in the emotional response to such events and the connection between these emotional responses and assessments of blame and proposed punishment.

Such disparities appear to have increased in recent years. In the midst of economic recovery, political dysfunction, and a host of challenges related to foreign policy, a striking 15% of African American respondents in a late 2014 Gallup poll indicated race relations as the most important problem facing the US. That was up from just 3% in early 2014 and stands at five times the rate of mentions by white respondents (3%), opening up the widest gap in Black-white mentions of race relations as the country's top problem in over a decade (Brown 2015). Although more recent data suggest increasing awareness of racial inequality among white respondents (Pew 2016),[1] the racial divide in the lived experiences and perceptions of white and nonwhite Americans remains entrenched.

In this article, we use the familiar police script to analyze how those divergent perceptions and media frames based on race and criminality mediate individual behavior affect respondent opinions toward police. Continuing our previous research (Philpot et al. 2010; White et al. 2007), we contend that police killings will elicit distinct emotional responses from whites versus Blacks contingent upon the race of the victim. The findings highlight how identity moderates the connection between emotions and politics while also contributing to our understanding of race relations today.

Theoretical expectations

While there are many reasons for a differential response to events such as the Trayvon Martin and Michael Brown killings, particularly ideas about how people sort themselves into in-groups and out-groups (Tajfel 1981) and the high levels of group consciousness (Miller et al. 1981) or linked fate (Dawson 1994) among African Americans, we believe that media framing elicits group-based responses through racialized frames of criminality. Often, media present stereotypical depictions of African Americans as criminals. African Americans and Latinos are more likely to be shown as lawbreakers, while whites are most often depicted as law defenders (Dixon and Linz 2000; Dixon 2015). Entman and Rojecki (2001) also find that whites are most often shown as victims and Blacks as perpetrators. The Black criminals also are more likely to be unnamed, have their mugshots shown, and be shown in prison jumpsuits. Gilliam and Iyengar (2000) explain these components are so prevalent that they have become a crime "script" recognizable to viewers of all races.

Jackson (2019) gives a comprehensive account of how media frames such as the typical crime script produce different opinions and behaviors for African Americans and whites. Yet regardless of the frame, non-Black respondents are less likely than African Americans to blame police for police-involved shootings (Boudreau, MacKenzie, and Simmons 2019). Different groups often seek out information to confirm their preconceived notions of blame (Jefferson, Neuner, and Pasek, n.d.). Gilliam et al. (1996) find that the public believes African Americans bear most of the responsibility for societal criminality, to the point that when a description of a crime is devoid of any mention of race, respondents still believe the perpetrator is Black, and that these feelings negatively influence other attitudes about African Americans (Gilliam and Iyengar 2000). African Americans, however, tend to reject these scripts, which, along with the narratives proffered by the police, are processed amidst historical and recent experiences engendering distrust of police. More generally, racialized issues can activate group-based responses (Valentino, Hutchings, and White 2002).

Tuch and Weitzer (1997) speak to racialized differences in perceptions of and reactions to police, focusing on the shooting of Eulia Love in 1979 and the recorded beating of Rodney King in 1991. Experimental studies echo those findings: Mbuba (2010) finds that blame toward police actions varies based on the race of the respondent, with whites less likely to assess blame toward officers in similar incidents, and Yadon and Crabtree (n.d.) find that whites express stronger reactions to a white victim or even a dog than an African American victim. Such differences in opinion have policy implications. Burge and Johnson (2018), for example, find that the race of the victim affects support for increased prison sentences.

There has been less consideration, however, of the mediating role of emotions (but see Phoenix 2018). We believe examining the affect produced by familiar police incidents highlights an intervening variable between identity (e.g. race) and behavior (e.g. placing blame, advocating for punishment). More generally, this article contributes to the growing literature previewed in this special issue on the influence of emotions in Black politics.

Design and hypotheses

To test how emotion and racial identity affect opinion about police actions we employ an embedded survey experiment. We gave students at the University of Richmond and James Madison University a fictional news article about a male youth being shot in a confrontation with a police officer. The conditions varied the race and criminality of the victim, with the control condition specifying neither. Our randomization by condition had a high of 48 respondents and a low of 43. We then asked respondents about their emotional response to the incident, which party was to blame, and whether the officer should face charges as well as standard demographics. The experiment was conducted between March 18, 2016, and April 5, 2016.[2]

Respondents were given the following prompt: "We are going to ask you a few questions about the following news story where a male youth named Keith Simmons is encountered by a police officer and was subsequently shot." The treatments vary the race of the victim between Black and white. We also vary the encounter between the victim being "suspected of having completed a drug deal" in which the officer "noticed an exchange between two individuals and proceeded to inquire of one of them" or "was asked by police why he was in an area known for drug dealing" as the officer had "noticed two men talking and proceeded to inquire of one of them." In the familiar narrative, the police chief reports "the officer feared for his life." Community officials express concern and officials indicate that the victim was unarmed. The article informs that the officer had been on the police force for six years and has submitted to an interview. There is no mention of disciplinary action in the story, nor is there mention of the officer's race.

Following the story, respondents answered a battery of questions about the incident. We asked about their primary emotional reaction to the incident. The answer choices were (in order): anger, disappointment, indifference, satisfaction, or none of these (see White et al. 2007; Gallup/USA Today September 2005, and Pew September 2005, December 2017 for similar emotion questions). Next, we asked who was to blame (the police officer, Keith Simmons, or both), and what should happen to the officer (nothing, suspension, termination, or criminal charges). Hypotheses:

> **H1**: The modal emotion chosen will be disappointment, followed by anger for all respondents regardless of condition or race.

H1a: The prevalence of these emotions will differ by race as African Americans will be more likely than whites to express anger, regardless of condition.

As stated, we believe these stories fall into a familiar pattern where the tragedy of a death would trigger some negative emotion. However, as previous research has shown, African Americans and whites react differently. We expect African Americans to have the more reactive response.

H2: Across all conditions we expect African Americans to be more likely to blame the police officer for the shooting (as opposed to the victim, "both," or "none of these").

H3: Across all conditions African Americans will be more likely to recommend criminal charges.

Hypotheses 2 and 3 fit into the influence of repeated incidents and familiarity with the media narrative around these events. This particular treatment is presented without any thematic prompt about previous incidents. However, we believe the sheer consistency of this narrative lends itself to a punitive or acquitting projection based on the identity of the respondent in even the most generic descriptions of police killings.

H4: We expect white respondents will be less likely to blame the officer or recommend criminal charges when the victim is Black (regardless of criminality).

Hypothesis 4 is rooted in the in-group/out-group psychology when race is prompted. Suspected culpability is an undercurrent in the reactions to police action against African Americans, at times divorced from the facts of the incident. We believe white respondents will be more punitive against actions against their in-group versus the stereotyped out-group.

Experimental results

We use independent sample t-tests of means to analyze differences between racial groups and experimental conditions. One emotion was most prevalent – disappointment. Most respondents chose this emotion irrespective of the suspect's race or purported level of culpability. Given the tacit acceptance of police-related shootings by many whites indicated in public opinion polls (Woodly 2016), it is interesting that most (56%) respondents chose disappointment (Table 1). The white-crime condition had the highest rate of indifference at 29.2% – nearly double the rate for the next highest conditions, white-no crime (15.2%) and the control (14.9%). The Black-no crime condition had the highest proportion of respondents choosing "none of these" at 20.9%. Respondents choosing "none of these [emotions]" to police shootings occurred at an average 19.7% with a Black victim and just 6.5% with a white victim. Anger was actually the third most commonly expressed emotion (15.0%) behind the aforementioned disappointment and indifference (15.9%).

Emotional response, blame, and punishment

Stratification by race shows the same disparities from previous research. Across conditions, 37.5% of African Americans expressed anger at the incident compared to just 14.4% of white respondents, a statistically significant gap of 23.1 percentage points (Table 2). African Americans were also 14.3 percentage points less likely to express disappointment. Looking deeper into this finding, we examine who the respondents blamed for

Table 1. Emotional response to police killings, by condition.

	White no crime	Black no crime	White crime	Black crime	Control	Total
Anger	19.6%	7%	8.3%	25.6%	14.9%	15.0%
	(0.401)	(0.257)	(0.279)	(0.441)	(0.359)	(0.357)
Disappointment	52.2%	65.1%	60.4%	44.2%	57.5%	56.0%
	(0.505)	(0.482)	(0.494)	(0.502)	(0.499)	(0.497)
Indifference	15.2%	7%	29.2%	11.6%	14.9%	15.9%
	(0.363)	(0.257)	(0.459)	(0.324)	(0.359)	(0.366)
Satisfied	0%	0%	0%	0%	0%	0%
	(0.000)	(0.000)	(0.000)	(0.000)	(0.000)	(0.000)
None of these	10.9%	20.9%	2.1%	18.6%	12.8%	12.8%
	(0.314)	(0.411)	(0.144)	(0.393)	(0.337)	(0.334)
N	46	43	48	43	47	227

Note: Mean response displayed as percent; standard deviations appear in parentheses.
Source: Embedded experiment at University of Richmond and James Madison University, April 2016.

the incident. Overall, 46.7% of respondents blamed only the officer[3] and 29.5% recommended criminal charges (Table 2).[4] However, any ambiguity about this finding disappears when accounting for race. A full 68.7% of African Americans faulted the officer compared to only 44.9% of whites, a difference of 23.8 percentage points with a p-value of .069. The difference was even starker as to the suggested punishment. When asked whether the officer should face criminal charges, the African American rate of agreement was 62.5% compared to only 26.9% for white respondents, a statistically significant difference of 35.6 percentage points. Again, this is without regard to the race of victim or perceived criminality.

In an interesting twist of the randomization, half of our African American respondents received the control condition. For whites, there is little change between their responses from the control and the treatments: in the control condition, disappointment is almost unchanged and indifference is slightly higher, as would be expected. In addition, fewer white respondents fault the officer. For African Americans, half of the sample (8 of 16) received the control condition. This is proportionally higher than the Black representation

Table 2. Emotional response to police killings (across conditions), by racial identity.

	African American	White	Total	Difference	
Emotional response					
Anger	37.5%	14.4%	15.0%	23.1%	*
	(0.500)	(0.351)	(0.357)		
Disappointment	43.8%	58.1%	56.0%	−14.3%	
	(0.512)	(0.494)	(0.497)		
Indifference	12.5%	16.2%	15.9%	−3.7%	
	(0.341)	(0.369)	(0.366)		
Satisfied	0.0%	0.0%	0.0%	0.0%	
	(0.000)	(0.000)	(0.000)		
None of these	6.3%	10.8%	12.8%	−4.5%	
	(0.250)	(0.311)	(0.334)		
Accountability					
Officer at fault	68.7%	44.9%	46.7%	23.8%	+
	(0.478)	(0.498)	(0.500)		
Criminal charges	62.5%	26.9%	29.5%	35.6%	*
	(0.500)	(0.445)	(0.457)		
N	16	167	227		

*$p < .05$; +$p < .10$ (two-tailed difference in proportion tests).
Note: Mean response displayed as percent; standard deviations appear in parentheses.
Source: Embedded experiment at University of Richmond and James Madison University, April 2016.

at our respective universities. The control is devoid of any explicit racial or criminality cues. One can view respondents' reactions as similar to hearing a news story about a police interaction with little information and no constructed racialized narrative. Examining the responses to the control by race, we see that Blacks' affect is still one of anger (Table 3). African Americans in the control condition were nearly three times more likely to express anger (37.5%) than whites (12.9%), a difference that approximates statistical significance (p-value = .112). The racial gap between faulting the officer was also larger when compared to all other conditions (control difference = 30.3; all other conditions difference = 26.8%). African Americans in the control condition were also more likely to recommend criminal charges for the officer (75.0%) than were whites (25.8%), a statistically significant difference of 49.2 percentage points compared to just 22.3% cross all other conditions. Despite the low number of Black respondents, the substantively and statistically significant differences are suggestive and warrant further examination.

Race of victim and criminality

As stated earlier, the vast majority of our respondents identify as white. This makes a closer examination of their responses by condition appropriate. When one of these incidents happens, the response from the African American community, its elites, and its institutions is almost monolithically one of outrage. What follows is a demand for change and the hope that the white mainstream sees the persistence of these inequalities and will work to address them. As they understand this to be rooted in systemic racism, the exact circumstances of the encounter are not paramount and do not mediate the response. The data show this is different from the white mainstream. In most instances, white respondents will err on the side of defending the police, who society tasks with the maintenance of the status quo, privileging whites at the expense of minorities. Therefore, examining when and where whites change their responses to a situation will help us understand better why whites react how they do and what type of events may lead to societal, and eventually, policy changes.

There is no significant difference between the emotions of white respondents based on the race of the victim (Table 4). However, predicted differences emerge when assessing blame and recommending punishment. As alluded to earlier, whites who read about a Black victim (without respect to criminality) are more likely to choose no emotion ("none of these") as a response compared to whites in the white-victim condition (Black victim = 18.0%; white victim = 5.3%). As hypothesized, white respondents were statistically less likely to fault the police officer for the shooting. While the majority of white respondents who read about a white victim blamed the officer (56.0%), white respondents who read a story about an African American young man were almost 20 percentage points less likely to fault the officer (37.7%). There were also no differences between whites in the crime versus no crime conditions. Multivariate analysis based on the race of victim or criminality did not reach the conventional levels of statistical significance. However, the relationships were in the hypothesized directions. Particularly, white respondents who read about a Black victim were less likely to say the officer was to blame (p-value = .111) or recommend criminal charges as punishment (p-value = .141). Again, the evidence is clear that for whites confronted with an African American victim they are less likely to blame the officer or recommend criminal charges. We saw this same

Table 3. Emotional response to police killings control condition, by racial identity.

	African American	White	Difference
Emotional response			
Anger	37.5%	12.9%	24.6%
	(0.517)	(0.340)	
Disappointment	50%	54.8%	−4.8%
	(0.534)	(0.505)	
Indifference	0%	22.5%	−22.5%
	(0.000)	(0.425)	
Satisfied	0%	0%	0.0%
	(0.000)	(0.000)	
None of these	12.5%	9.6%	2.9%
	(0.353)	(0.300)	
Accountability			
Officer at fault	62.5%	32.2%	30.3%
	(0.517)	(0.475)	
Criminal charges	75.0%	25.8%	49.2%
	(0.462)	(0.444)	
N	8	31	

*$p < .05$ (two-tailed difference in proportion tests).
Note: Mean response displayed as percent; standard deviations appear in parentheses.
Source: Embedded experiment at University of Richmond and James Madison University, April 2016.

Table 4. White emotional response to police killings, by race of victim.

	Black Victim	White Victim	Difference	
Emotional response				
Anger	16.3%	13.3%	3.0%	
	(0.373)	(0.342)		
Disappointment	55.7%	61.3%	−5.6%	
	(0.500)	(0.490)		
Indifference	9.8%	18.6%	−8.8%	
	(0.300)	(0.392)		
Satisfied	0%	0%	0.0%	
	(0.000)	(0.000)		
None of these	18.0%	5.3%	12.7%	*
	(0.387)	(0.266)		
Accountability				
Officer at fault	37.7%	56.0%	−18.3%	*
	(0.488)	(0.499)		
Criminal charges	21.3%	32.0%	−10.7%	
	(0.412)	(0.469)		
N	61	75		

Note: Mean response displayed as percent; standard deviations appear in parentheses.
Source: Embedded experiment at University of Richmond and James Madison University, April 2016.
*$p < .05$ (two-tailed difference in proportion tests).

phenomenon in public opinion surveys (Woodly 2016) and in the real-life actions of the majority white grand juries like in the Michael Brown case.[5]

Conclusion

In Megan Ming Francis' poignant examination of the BLM movement and American Political Development scholarship, she reminds us that "racial violence … is a foundational component of American politics" (2018, 134). Yet as demonstrated in this article, racial disparities in responses to racial violence persist, at once illustrating broader patterns of group-based responses to racialized political events and the salience of emotions in Black politics. The differential emotional responses to police killings have important implications for race relations generally, and the societal demands on police specifically. When individuals perceive these incidents as normal occurrences, done by sanctioned authority figures, to protect "the people," then they assume the system is doing its job and criminals are being punished. However, if these events signal a larger (even if unconscious) bias toward African Americans, then the justice system – particularly the use-of-force guidelines for police officers – exacerbates these issues. In such an environment excised attention, protest, and anger are warranted responses. Decades of surveys have proven that racially disparate views of society exist and it does not appear this divide is dissipating; rather, with each subsequent event that takes on a racialized frame, the gap appears to be widening. The documentation and explanation of the causes and consequences of such racial disparities is a critical step in the truth and reconciliation process, and implore a long-overdue societal reckoning with how the state's coercive power "shape(s), reinforce(s), and then naturalize(s) patterns of racial inequality" (Thurston 2018, 162).

Future studies should further examine connections between individual attention, perceptions, and emotional responses to racialized political events, which will enhance our comprehension of such divides and the role media play in sustaining racial tensions. The costs of such disparities carry profound political implications.[6] When group-based responses condition empathy to such an extent that the pain of "others" is naturalized, and cross-racial interactions remain shaped by media narratives reifying stereotypes rather than open intergroup dialogue and personal relationships, the possibilities for cultivating inclusion and dismantling the legacies of racial hierarchy are diminished.

Notes

1. Pew asked respondents in 2009, 2011, 2014, 2015, and 2016 to choose which of two statements came closer to their view, either "our country has made the changes needed to give blacks equal rights with whites" or "our country needs to continue making changes to give blacks equal rights with whites." The 2015 iteration marked the first time in that series that a majority (59%) agreed with the latter statement, up from 43% in 2009 (Pew 2016).
2. Full survey, treatments, and demographics are available by request.
3. This compares to 46.3% who blamed both and just 7% who blamed the victim.
4. This compares to 33% who recommended suspension, 26.4% who recommended termination and 10.1% who recommended no punishment.
5. See appendix for full regression tables.
6. Several studies have, for example, spoken to the *weathering* process or physiological costs of structural inequities and related emotional distress and coping, and its political consequences (Geronimus et al. 2006; Rodriguez et al. 2015).

Disclosure statement

No potential conflict of interest was reported by the author(s).

References

Boudreau, Cheryl, Scott A. MacKenzie, and Daniel J. Simmons. 2019. "Police Violence and Public Perceptions: An Experimental Study of How Information and Endorsements Affect Support for Law Enforcement." *Journal of Politics*. doi:10.1086/703540.

Brown, Alyssa. 2015. "Views of Race Relations as Top Problem Still Differ by Race." *Gallup,* June 11. https://news.gallup.com/poll/183572/race-divides-views-race-relations-top-problem.aspx.

Burge, Camille D., and Gbemende Johnson. 2018. "Race, Crime, and Emotions." *Research and Politics* 5 (3): 1–9.

Dawson, Michael. 1994. *Behind the Mule: Race and Class in African-American Politics.* Princeton, NJ: Princeton University Press.

Dixon, Travis L. 2015. "Good Guys are Still Always in White? Positive Change and Continued Misrepresentation of Race and Crime on Local News." *Communication Research* 44 (6): 775–792.

Dixon, Travis L., and Daniel Linz. 2000. "Overrepresentation and Underrepresentation of African Americans and Latinos as Lawbreakers on Television News." *Journal of Communication* 50: 131–154.

Entman, Robert, and Andrew Rojecki. 2001. *The Black Image in the White Mind: Media and Race in America.* Chicago, IL: University of Chicago Press.

Geronimus, Arline, Margaret Hicken, Danya Keene, and John Bound. 2006. "'Weathering' and Age Patterns of Allostatic Load Scores among Blacks and Whites in the United States." *American Journal of Public Health* 96 (5): 826–833.

Gilliam, Franklin, and Shanto Iyengar. 2000. "Prime Suspects: The Influence of Local Television News on the Viewing Public." *American Journal of Political Science* 44 (3): 560–573.

Gilliam, Franklin, Shanto Iyengar, Adam Simon, and Oliver Wright. 1996. "Crime in Black and White: The Violent, Scary World of Local News." *Harvard International Journal of Press/Politics* 1: 6–23.

Jackson, Jenn M. 2019. "Black Americans and the 'Crime Narrative:' Comments on the use of News Frames and Their Impacts on Public Opinion Formation." *Politics, Groups, and Identities* 7 (1): 231–224.

Jefferson, Hakeem J., Fabian G. Neuner, and Josh Pasek. n.d. "Seeing Blue in Black and White: Race and Perceptions of Officer-Involved Shootings."

Mbuba, Jospeter M. 2010. "Attitudes Toward the Police: The Significance of Race and Other Factors Among College Students." *Journal of Ethnicity in Criminal Justice* 8: 201–215.

Miller, Arthur, Patricia Gurin, Gerald Gurin, and Oksana Malanchuk. 1981. "Group Consciousness and Political Participation." *American Journal of Political Science* 25 (3): 494–511.

Ming Francis, Megan. 2018. "The Strange Fruit of American Political Development." *Politics, Groups, and Identities* 6 (1): 128–137.

Pew Research Center. 2016. "On Views of Race and Inequality, Blacks and Whites Are Worlds Apart." June 27. https://www.pewsocialtrends.org/wp-content/uploads/sites/3/2016/06/ST_2016.06.27_Race-Inequality-Final.pdf.

Philpot, Tasha S., Ismail K. White, Kristin Wylie, and Ernest B. McGowen. 2010. "Feeling Different: Racial Group-Based Emotional Response to Political Events." In *African-American Political Psychology,* edited by Tasha S. Philpot and Ismail K. White, 55–70. New York: Palgrave Macmillan.

Phoenix, Davin. 2018. "Black Hope Floats: Racial Emotion Regulation and the Uniquely Motivating Effects of Hope on Black Political Participation." (Manuscript submitted for publication).

Rodriguez, Javier, Arline Geronimus, John Bound, and Danny Dorling. 2015. "Black Lives Matter: Differential Mortality and the Racial Composition of the U.S. Electorate, 1970–2004." *Social Science & Medicine* 136-137: 193–199.

Tajfel, Henry. 1981. *Social Identity and Intergroup Relations.* Cambridge: Cambridge University Press.

Thurston, Chloe. 2018. "Black Lives Matter, American Political Development, and the Politics of Visibility." *Politics, Groups, and Identities* 6 (1): 162–170.

Tuch, Steven A., and Ronald Weitzer. 1997. "The Polls – Trends: Racial Differences in Attitudes Toward the Police." *Public Opinion Quarterly* 61 (4): 642–663.

Valentino, Nicholas, Vince Hutchings, and Ismail White. 2002. "Cues That Matter: How Political Ads Prime Racial Attitudes During Campaigns." *American Political Science Review* 96 (1): 75–90.

White, Ismail, Tasha Philpot, Kristin Wylie, and Ernest McGowen. 2007. "Feeling the Pain of My People: Hurricane Katrina, Racial Inequality, and the Psyche of Black America." *Journal of Black Studies* 37 (4): 523–538.

Woodly, Deva. 2016. "Black Lives Matter: The Politics of Race and Movement in the 21st Century." *Public Seminar*, January 18. http://www.publicseminar.org.

Yadon, Nicole, and Kiela Crabtree. n.d. "Breeding Contempt: White's Reactions to Police Violence Against Men and Dogs." Working paper.

Appendix

	Officer to Blame	Criminal Charges
Black Victim	-0.693 (0.435)	-0.700 (0.475)
Party Identification	-2.856 * (0.790)	-1.604 * (0.801)
Age	0.908 * (0.472)	0.409 (0.476)
Female	-0.195 (0.426)	0.911 (0.460)
Income	0.515 (0.996)	0.164 (1.085)
-2LL	131.787	121.439
N	112	112

Note: Standard errors are in parentheses
* $p < 0.05$, + $p < 0.10$ (two-tailed test)

Scholarship on #BlackLivesMatter and its implications on local electoral politics

Jamil S. Scott and Nadia E. Brown

August 9 2016 marked the second anniversary of Mike Brown's murder at the hands of Darren Wilson in Ferguson, Missouri. This anniversary affords scholars the opportunity to reflect on the nature of Black life in the closing Age of Obama. At present, our society is faced with the juxtaposition of repeated assaults on Black and Brown bodies at a time when a self-identified Black man holds the highest elected position in the United States. Consequently, our nation has witnessed the rise of the Black Lives Matter Movement and the resurgence of protest politics. #BlackLivesMatter is a hashtag used by a network of activists, scholars, and practitioners that seek to create a world where "Blacks lives are no longer systematically and intentionally targeted for demise" (blacklivesmatter.com/about). The Black Lives Matter movement works to affirm Blacks' humanity while simultaneously calling attention to the continued brutality that Blacks endure at the hands of the state, institutions, and oppressive structures. Seeking to "(re)build the Black liberation movement," Black Lives Matter is a national organization with several chapters that are working toward ending anti-Black racism (blacklivesmatter.com/about). Founded by Patrisse Culors, Opal Tometi, and Alicia Garza after George Zimmerman was acquitted for the murder of 17-year-old Trayvon Martin, #BlackLivesMatter became a political intervention – more than a mere social media hashtag – that called national attention to the dehumanization of Black lives. The Black Lives Matter Movement is a social justice movement that embraces the lives of all Blacks – including queer, transgender, undocumented, women, and those within the criminal justice system.

The works of Glaude (2016), Hill (2016), and Taylor (2016) provide scholars with insightful analysis, engaging theoretical frameworks, and comprehensive connections to the historical and modern-day realities of Black Americans as they skillfully reflect on why and how the Black Lives Matter Movement emerged after the July 2013 acquittal of George Zimmerman. These scholars simultaneously question how much Black lives are valued in the United States under a system of White supremacy. Glaude, Hill, and Taylor conclude that Black lives indeed matter by forcefully illustrating the continued salience of structural racism, classism, sexism, and transphobia.

In the following essay, we address four prominent themes that emerge across *Democracy in Black: How Race Still Enslaves the American Soul* (Glaude); *Nobody: Casualties of America's War on the Vulnerable, From Ferguson to Flint and Beyond* (Hill); and *From #BlackLivesMatter to Black Liberation* (Taylor). Using our recent work that is centered on the 2016 Baltimore Mayoral Democratic Primary, we explore the implications for electoral politics as #BlackLivesMatter activist DeRay Mckesson sought to transition the movement from protest to politics. We conclude by discussing the role of the Black Lives Matter Movement in electoral politics as well as our thoughts on direction for future research.

Disposable citizens

Glaude, Hill, and Taylor point to the death of Mike Brown as the visible birth of a resistance movement, yet note that Brown was neither the first nor the last victim of state sanctioned violence. As of 2015, 381 Blacks have been killed by on-duty police officers (Lowery 2016). This is a staggering number given that African Americans are only 13% of the US population yet account for 24% of victims that are fatally shot and killed by the police. Analysis by reporters at the *Washington Post* concluded that Blacks are 2.5 more likely than Whites to be shot and killed by police. These statistics are not new. Indeed, those familiar with American history are able to place these killings firmly in the national memory and trajectory which recognizes that Black deaths at the hands of police – as well as a number of instances of police brutality – are frequently all too common (Zack 2015). Taylor adroitly connects this adversarial relationship between the police and the Black community to policing practices that have roots in the nineteenth century. Laws such as the Black codes and practices such as convict leasing worked in tandem to associate Blacks with criminality and inferiority. These associations have followed Blacks across time and space to create what Glaude calls "racial habits" – actions that inadvertently place greater value on White lives than Black ones. This phenomenon is not lost on Hill who demonstrates that Black men, women and Latinos make up an ever-growing proportion of the prison population. Furthermore, the prospects for these groups upon release are grim. It is in this context that Hill dedicates his work to and highlights the lives of the "nobodies," those individuals, like Mike Brown, who are victims of state violence in all of its forms. The prevalence of over policing, punishment, and incarceration is a daily reminder to Black "nobodies" that equality and justice are luxuries singularly afforded to White citizens. Taylor, Glaude, and Hill cleverly weave together instances in American history in which Blacks have been subject to unequal treatment. Although many popularly center #BlackLivesMatter movement around the life and deaths of Trayvon Martin and Mike Brown, the authors' analysis show that their stories are not unique.

Obama and black lives matter

At a time when some Blacks are making historic gains politically, economically, and socially, the reality is that the majority of Blacks in the United States are facing economic hardship, homophobia, and racial discrimination. What is clear from the authors' analysis is that the Black Lives Matter Movement is both a national wake-up call and a call to action. While Americans have twice elected Barack Obama, the nation's first Black president, racial relations have failed to progress. Indeed, the nation is witnessing a regression in race relations. A recent poll found that 57% of Americans say race relations are getting worse (Graham 2015). Glaude, Taylor, and Hill provide stinging indictments of President Obama's inaction and hesitancy to address race relations and structural racism. While President Obama has asserted that he is not the President of Black America, but America as a whole, these authors seem to argue that his self-identification as a Black man *should* carry some allegiance or responsibility to his racial group. Glaude further insists that Black politicians have become complicit in the oppression of their own Black constituencies. Take for example, Obama's commencement speech at Howard University in May 2016, in which he suggested that graduates must do more than be aware of systematic injustices. The president encouraged graduates to bring about structural change, however, this type of change that could only be accomplished by being willing to listen and compromise – even with those who do not agree with you. He added that progress is not perfect by providing examples from the Civil Rights Movement. President Obama commended Brittany Packnett, a member of Black Lives Matter and a legislative assistant to Rep. Wm. Lacy Clay (D-MO), for participating in the White House Task Force on policing, though also underscoring that her fellow activists questioned her participation. In this way, President Obama implicitly suggested that attacking racial habits might lend itself to a moral high ground, but not necessarily a way forward in achieving progress.

Through interactions with the leaders of the Black Lives Matter Movement and analysis of the events in Ferguson, MO, Glaude and Taylor depict the divisions between the current protest leaders and the older guard of Black politicians and leaders. Hill, in particular, highlights how the Black Lives Matter Movement has engaged young people not only in mass protest, but also through social media and public dialogue. As such, the new vanguard of Black leaders is asserting that the "Nobody" is a "Somebody". Glaude, Hill, and Taylor smartly draw parallels to the protests and civic engagement of Black youth during the Civil Rights Era, nevertheless, the three authors demonstrate the ways in which the Black Lives Matter Movement is distinct. The Black Lives Matter Movement has called a new guard of Black Leaders who demand that *all* Black lives matter. Sub-marginalized group members – such as women, transgender, and queer Blacks – are both seen and heard within Black Lives Matter in ways that pointedly differ from past activism that challenged racism as a singularly defined issue. While novel in mainstream Black American social justice organizing, the focus on *all* Black lives within this movement is by design. Two of the three female founders of Black Lives Matter identify as queer and seek to center the voices and experiences of women and queer Blacks (Garza 2015).

Value gap/color blindness

The Black Lives Matter Movement is a catalyst and plays an important role in exposing what Glaude terms the "value gap." Intimately related to his concept of "racial habits," the value gap refers to the actual beliefs that sustain White superiority and drive American racial habits. Both Glaude and Taylor demonstrate that the historic gains of the Civil Rights Movement were systematically taken away with the enactment of "color-blind" policies. These policies led to the rise of a culture-based argument that justified Black poverty as a social ill which is endemic to a group that was unfit and too lazy to reap the benefits of the American dream. Glaude, Hill, and Taylor point to the logical fallacy of color blindness as wholly rooted in White supremacist, neoliberal and capitalist arguments of moral responsibility for one's own condition. These policies have created the current need to assert Black Lives Matter. Furthermore, because these policies have severely marginalized poor Black communities, this population have been reduced to using "weapons of the weak" to assert their humanity and challenge the repressive system that governs their lives (Scott 1985). To counteract these racial habits, "nobodies" are using new technologies such as social media and video sharing applications as a way to present their narratives to the world as evidence of their continued marginalization. The overt racist and oppressive structures that intimately govern the lives of America's discarded and forgotten citizens are openly being challenged by the victims of Reagan-era neoliberal politics. Asserting that Black Lives Matter is a direct challenge to color-blind doctrines that have eroded the gains of the Civil Rights Movement. Black Lives Matter activists are attempting to reclaim their humanity by documenting how state policies and its authorized actors are systematically targeting Black lives for destruction. Blacks remained disadvantaged in American political life. In summary, the election of Barack Obama did little to change the material realities of many Black Americans.

Importance of saying their name

Perhaps Marc Lamont Hill presents the most humanizing depictions of victims of state violence of the three books reviewed in this essay. While the #BlackLivesMatter movement challenges us to recall the names of those who have fallen victim to police brutality – especially that of the female victims who are often forgotten through the hashtag #SayHerName – Hill calls us to know their stories and wrestle with the political, social, and economic circumstances that led to the demise of these victims. Indeed, the founders of #BlackLivesMatter are three women who insist upon an intersectional approach to understanding and dismantling state sponsored violence against Black communities. Hill's analysis shows readers why some of the most notable victims of state sponsored violence have become casualties to America's policies and political structures that led to their deaths. In a complementary fashion, Glaude and Taylor illustrate through their analyses the particular political, historical, and psychological factors that have converged to allow this assault on Black bodies. All authors challenge the assumptions that these individuals have been complicit in their own demise.

Moving from protest to electoral politics

Black Lives Matter directly challenges the political, economic, and social realities that prioritizes White lives. This value gap skews how Americans think and talk about race relations, making it difficult to recognize the differing circumstances that lead to disproportionate deaths of Blacks at the hands of the police. Furthermore, these realities are shaped by policies, cultural beliefs, and systemic structures that undercut Blacks humanity and ability to live fulfilling lives free of oppression and marginalization. Glaude, Hill, and Taylor convincingly combine historical analysis, personal accounts, as well as political and social analysis to demonstrate the myriad ways that Blacks are continually denied justice, freedom, and equality. However, these texts fall short in making explicit connections to local electoral politics and the #BlackLivesMatter.

Scholars of Black politics may aptly reference Bayard Rustin's (1965) *From Protest to Politics: The Future of Civil Rights Movement* as a historical signpost for the future of the Black Lives Matter movement. Rustin asks if protests can successfully transform into a political movement. Citing similar factors that continue to beleaguer Black communities today, Rustin's writing points to the possibilities of a protest movement turning into a social and then political movement that challenges the socioeconomic order that calls for equality and opportunity for all Black Americans. At time of his writing, the electoral benefits of Voting Rights Act (VRA) had yet to be fully realized and Rustin is understandably reduced to writing about the Negro vote as a way to build coalitions with allies who support the Negro agenda. The VRA helped to usher the elections of Black lawmakers to local and national governing bodies that may have been difficult for Rustin to predict at the time of his essay. Indeed, many of the protest leaders – such as John Lewis, Julian Bond, Walter Fauntroy, and Andrew Young – would go on to win elections and physically embody the move from protest to politics.

The Black Lives Matter movement has yet to have its John Lewis, no protest leader has successfully won election to Congress, a state legislature, or statewide executive office. However, the move from protest to politics is a strategy that is being pursued by some #BlackLivesMatter activists. Our research focuses on the 2016 Baltimore Democratic Mayoral Primay. This race provided a unique opportunity to gauge how voters coalesced around particular Black candidates after a race-based incident, that is, the murder of Freddie Gray, which led to several #BlackLivesMatter demonstrations. While our research is centered on Black women candidates, the Baltimore Democratic Mayoral Primary provided a unique lens to examine if and how the social media activism of #BlackLivesMatter would translate into electoral politics. Here, we focus on the candidacy of DeRay Mckesson, a prominent Black Lives Matter activist, who unsuccessfully sought the Democratic nomination of mayor of Baltimore.

Mckesson, born and raised in Baltimore, was an educator and founded a youth organization in his native city, came in sixth in the April primary by garnering only 2% of the vote. Mckesson received national attention as #BlackLivesMatter activist. His allies praised his efforts and financially supported Mckesson's campaign. However, citizens of the Charm City viewed Mckesson's last minute bid for mayor akin to carpet bagging as he had not recently lived in the city nor had been involved in city or state politics in a sustained manner. Indeed, city residents viewed Mckesson's motives with suspicion and labeled the Baltimore native as an outsider. One of the most retweeted articles about the Black Lives Matter activist was published by Mother Jones, the progressive magazine, entitled "The Political Miseducation of DeRay Mckesson." Another popular article that enjoyed many retweets was entitled "Black Lives Matter gave him fame, but Baltimore isn't biting: DeRay Mckesson the Black Lives Activist" which was published in several AP news outlets.

Our current study, an analysis of twitter data to evaluate if and how Black mayoral candidates' race and gendered identities influence voters perceptions of one's ability to effectively handle a race-based crisis, has found that voters rarely included race- and gender-based stereotypes in their evaluation of candidates' leadership styles and qualifications for the position. Furthermore, though DeRay Mckesson has been outspoken about his identity as a gay Black man, his sexuality was rarely a topic of conversation amongst tweeters. Instead, we find that tweeters are more concerned with the leadership qualities of each of the candidates and preferred a candidate who would overhaul the current system that proliferates racial- and economic-based injustices. Unfortunately for DeRay Mckesson, tweeters (as well as voters) felt that he did not possess the necessary political skills and leadership traits to enable him to successfully turn the city around.

A postmortem of Mckesson's campaign may be fruitful for other Black Lives Matter activists who want to hold elected office. Voters prefer candidates with proven political experience, a set of skills that can be honed through protesting and organizing, but needs to be fine tuned through holding smaller offices prior to running for high profile offices. Our study also found that tweeters valued candidates who can easily translate revolutionary ideas – such as Black lives matter – into tangible policy prescriptions such as economic justice that manifests itself into advocating for a livable wage, affordable childcare, and rent subsidies for high-quality housing. Lastly, tweeters evaluated candidates based on perceived authenticity and one's ability to relate to everyday citizens. Others retweeted an article posted on nytimes.com titled "DeRay Mckesson Won't Be Elected Mayor of Baltimore, But Why is He Running?" The majority of tweets that mentioned Mckesson asked why the Black Lives Matters activist thought that he would be the solution to fix Baltimore. The tweeters showed an outright disdain for his entry into Baltimore politics in which he had little political currency or contemporary connections. DeRay McKesson was challenged by these last two points and, consequently, failed to win over the majority of Baltimore Democratic voters.

It is important to note, however, that the ideals expressed by the tweeters (and voters) are not uncommon in any political race, yet they are unique given the context of the Baltimore Democratic primary mayoral race. The death of Freddie Gray cast a long shadow on how Black mayoral candidates discussed race relations in the city that was distinctly colored by police brutality. In a city that was accustomed to Black leadership, and leadership by Black women mayors, Baltimore residents challenged those that sought to lead the city to directly address policing, crime, economic justice, and educational opportunities that would impact poor Black communities. These issues, among others, are cornerstones of the Black Lives Matter mission statement. As such, #BlackLivesMatter activists who want to move from protest to politics should have an advantage in talking with Black communities about these issues, especially young Black voters who are more likely to be reached from a social media platform. Conversely, their challenge may be getting Whites to interrogate this value gap as noted by Glaude, rather than primarily speaking to Blacks (even in a minority–majority city) who tacitly recognize oppressive structures as denying them the full rights and privileges of American citizenship.

DeRay Mckesson's campaign, though unsuccessful, represents an attempt on the part of the Black Lives Matter Movement to usher in a new era of Black Power in the ways defined by Ture and Hamilton (1992). Through the notion of Black Power, Ture and Hamilton call Blacks to define their own goals, develop their own organizations, and reject an unjust value structure and political system. The authors underscore that Black Power is more than a Black face in office. In the Afterword, Hamilton notes that Black Power and Black visibility have often been confused in the popular discourse. Instead, real Black Power stems from Blacks infiltrating the system to make it better for Black masses. It is yet to be seen what electoral gains leaders of the Black Lives Matter Movement can make. Others may learn from Mckesson's mistakes coupled with Bayard Rustin's adages to use electoral politics to challenge the prevailing racial order. These ideals are what make the #BlackLivesMatter Movement a political, social, and economic necessity.

Disclosure statement

No potential conflict of interest was reported by the authors.

References

Garza, A. 2015. *HISTORY: A Herstory of the #BlackLivesMatter Movement.* Accessed 12 August 2016. http://www.thefeministwire.com/2014/10/blacklivesmatter-2/.

Glaude Jr, E. S. 2016. *Democracy in Black: How Race Still Governs the American Soul.* New York, NY: Crown Publishing Group.

Graham, D. A. 2015. "Are Americans More Pessimistic About Race – or More Realistic?" July 25. Accessed 12 August 2016. http://www.theatlantic.com/politics/archive/2015/07/are-americans-more-pessimistic-about-raceor-more-realistic/399569/.

Hill, M. L. 2016. *Nobody: Casualties of America's War on the Vulnerable, From Ferguson to Flint and Beyond.* New York, NY: Simon and Schuster.

Lowery, W. 2016. "Aren't More White People Than Black People Killed by Police? Yes, But No." July 11. Accessed 12 August 2016. https://www.washingtonpost.com/news/post-nation/wp/2016/07/11/arent-more-white-people-than-black-people-killed-by-police-yes-but-no/?utm_term=.69cef1f52a03.

Rustin, B. 1965. "From Protest to Politics: The Future of the Civil Rights Movement." *Commentary* 39 (2): 25–31.

Scott, J. C. 1985. *Weapons of the Weak: Everyday Forms of Peasant Resistance.* New Haven: Yale University Press.

Taylor, K. Y. 2016. *From #BlackLivesMatter to Black Liberation.* Chicago, IL: Haymarket Books.

Ture, K., and C. V. Hamilton. 1992. *Black Power: The Politics of Liberation in America: With New Afterwords by the Authors.* New York, NY: Vintage Books.

Zack, N. 2015. *White Privilege and Black Rights: The Injustice of U.S. Police and Racial Profiling and Homicide.* Lanham, MD: Rowman & Littlefield.

Tweeting racial representation: how the congressional Black Caucus used Twitter in the 113th congress

Alvin B. Tillery

ABSTRACT
The social media and microblogging site Twitter has emerged as both a vehicle for political expression and a powerful tool for political organizing within the African American community. This paper examines the extent to which members of the Congressional Black Caucus (CBC) utilize Twitter to communicate with their constituents about racial issues. An analysis of CBC members' tweets during the 113th Congress (2013–2014) shows that the organization's members do talk about race and occasionally use racially distinct hashtags. Moreover, statistical analyses show that the best predictors of a CBC members' engagement with racial issues on Twitter are being a woman legislator, the size of their margin of victory in the 2012 elections, and the percentage of whites living within the boundaries of their district.

Introduction

The rise of social media in the last two decades has transformed human social interactions in a number of ways (Couldry 2012; Lovejoy and Saxton 2012; O'Keeffe and Clarke-Pearson 2011; Van Dijck 2013). In the political arena, social media platforms like FaceBook and Twitter have become important resources for organizing protest activities (Della Porta and Mosca 2005; Eltantawy and Wiest 2011 Langman 2005). These tools have also emerged as important means for politicians in advanced democracies to directly communicate with the public during their campaigns for office and as they carry out their representative duties once elected (Conway, Kenski, and Wang 2013; Druckman, Kifer, and Parkin 2007; Graham, Jackson, and Broersma 2014; Grant, Moon, and Grant 2010; Towner and Dulio 2012).

This paper examines how members of the Congressional Black Caucus used Twitter to communicate their ideas about racial issues during the 113th Congress (2013–2014). Twitter is a popular social networking and microblogging website. The service allows registered users to send text messages of 140 characters or less or share photos and videos. The process of posting messages or visual media to the service is called "tweeting" in the parlance of the social network. Twitter also allows registered users to follow the accounts of other users in the network for the purpose of reading their public "tweets" and or engaging in direct communications.

During the first quarter of 2017, the site reported that it averaged 328 million users per month. Given Twitter's reach, it is not surprising that members of Congress have embraced the website as a means of direct communication with their constituents (Golbeck, Grimes, and Rogers 2010; Peterson 2012; Shogan 2010). The scholarly consensus on the Twitter usage by members of Congress is that they primarily turn to the service to engage in forms of communication aimed at bolstering their prospects for reelection (Druckman, Kifer, and Parkin 2010; Golbeck, Grimes, and Rogers 2010; Peterson 2012). In other words, the social network is utilized for both the "position-taking" statements that Mayhew (1974) describes as essential for all members of Congress hoping to win reelection and for engaging in the empathetic rhetoric that Fenno (1978) claims is a key component of developing what he calls a "home style." For Fenno, developing and maintaining a "home style" – which encompasses self-presentation, delivery of resources, and explanations of one's work in Washington, DC – that fits with one's district was the primary task of a member of Congress.

Scholars have long-noted how important it is for African American members of Congress to engage in position-taking on racial issues and deploy empathetic speech about race relations in order to develop and maintain robust "home style" connections with their constituents (Fenno 2003; Sinclair-Chapman 2002; Singh 1998; Smith 1981; Tate 2001; Tate 2003; Tillery 2006). The main questions asked in this paper are: Do African American members of Congress use Twitter to take positions on racial issues? Do they use racially distinct hashtags to communicate with the African American community? Finally, is Twitter usage to engage racial issues uniform across the membership of the Congressional Black Caucus or do some African American legislators use it more than others for these purposes?

Why study the tweets of CBC members? There are three answers to this question. First, Twitter is heavily utilized within the African American community (Smith 2014). Indeed, African Americans are 25% of the population of the American Twittersphere despite the fact that they are only 13.5% of the population of the United States (Brock 2012). Moreover, several recent studies have shown that African Americans access the service on a daily basis at a much higher rate than their white counterparts (Fox, Zickuhr, and Smith 2009; Horrigan 2009; Smith 2010; Smith and Brenner 2012). In short, Twitter is the space where the digital divide between African Americans and whites evaporates. It is important to understand the extent to which African American members of Congress are aware of this reality and seek to capitalize on it to expand their opportunities to communicate with their constituents. Ardoin (2013) has argued, based on his analysis of the volume of tweets generated by Congressional Black Caucus members between 2006 and February 20, 2012, that there is a significant "digital divide" between African American and white legislators in terms of both their utilization of Twitter and their impact on the social media site. Dancey's and Masand's (2017) study of the ways that African American and white members of Congress responded to the deaths of Michael Brown and Eric Garner on Twitter in the summer of 2014 found that African American members were actually more communicative than their white counterparts during these events. This study has the potential to adjudicate between these competing findings by tracking how CBC members utilize Twitter over the entire run of the 113th Congress.

The second reason to study the behavior of Congressional Black Caucus members on Twitter is the fact that – as both Ardoin (2013) and Dancey and Masand (2017) agree – it is a space where African Americans are deeply engaged in a truly national conversation about both the meaning of race and race relations (Carney 2016; Nakamura 2008). Several studies have demonstrated that African American discourse on Twitter tends to replicate the unique idioms and verbal patterns – known in both common parlance and academic studies as "signifyin" (Gates 1983; Mitchell-Kernan and Caponi 1999) – that have long circulated in the community's oral traditions (Brock 2012; Florini 2014; Manjoo 2010). Some of these same studies also assert that, just as with their face-to-face speech acts, signifyin' on Black Twitter is often a form of resistance to racism and racial exclusions (Brock 2012; Florini 2014). Recent studies have also elaborated how the use of hashtags that make reference to racial issues – so called "Blacktags" – can quickly transform Black Twitter into a counterpublic sphere where African Americans can join debates about the important issues affecting their racial group in real time (Carney 2016; Sharma 2013). As stated above, Dancey's and Masand's (2017) study of the period between August 9th and August 25th of 2014 has provided compelling evidence that CBC members do seek to participate in these national conversations about race. The aim of this study is to determine how much CBC members seek to drive these conversations on Black.

Finally, studying the tweets of Congressional Black Caucus members also provides us with an opportunity to further develop predictive models of racial representation in the US Congress. The Congressional Black Caucus was founded in 1971. Studies of the organization in this period have shown that the thirteen African Americans serving in the House of Representatives a that time had a set of experiences in the Civil Rights Movement that gave them very similar ideas about how to achieve racial progress (Barnett 1975; Barnett 1982; Henry 1977; Singh 1998). In this context, it was not very difficult for individual CBC members to achieve what Representative William Clay, one of the founders of the organization, called in his memoir a "solidarity of purpose and program" to advance the racial group interests of African Americans (Clay 1993, 117).

A number of studies have revealed how both the growth and diversification of the CBC's ranks in terms of age, experience, and representational context over the past four decades have generated cross-pressures that make it more challenging for the larger group to hang together on racial issues of national import (Canon 1999; Singh 1998; Tate 2003; Tate 2014; Tillery 2011, 125–149; Whitby 2007). The statistical analyses presented in this paper will allow us to ascertain whether these same trends hold in the Twittersphere as well or if other patterns of cleavage emerge.

To answer these questions, I present a systematic analysis of the tweets of the 41 members of the Congressional Black Caucus who served in the House of Representatives during the 113th Congress. The 113th Congress provides an excellent window to explore the ways that CBC members use Twitter for several reasons. First, at the time that its members were sworn in, the 113th Congress was the most diverse in the history of the republic (Hicks 2013). Moreover, for the first time in U.S. history, women and minorities comprised the majority of the Democratic Party's caucus in the House of Representatives. Second, the 113th Congress was the first seated after Barack Obama won reelection to a second term as president of the United States of America. Finally, the rise of the #BlackLivesMatter movement at the start of the 113th Congress placed a national spotlight on how the issues of hate crimes, police brutality, and state violence affected the African American community (Garza 2014; Rickford 2016; Taylor 2016).

If CBC members use Twitter in the same strategic ways that they now pursue legislative activities, we can expect these dynamics to generate incentives for individual African American legislators to talk about race on Twitter.

The article proceeds as follows. The next section places this study within the theoretical context of the extant literature on African American representation and articulates the hypotheses that will be evaluated through quantitative analyses. The paper then shifts to a description of the data and methods. From there, the paper presents both the summary statistics about CBC members' Twitter usage and statistical models of the factors that predict the behavior of African American members of Congress in the Twittersphere. The concluding section describes the relevance of the main findings for ongoing debates about the nature of African American representation and the internal dynamics of the Congressional Black Caucus.

Theoretical context and hypotheses

The Congressional Black Caucus was formed in 1971 (Barnett 1975; Bositis 1994; Singh 1998). The organization was predicated upon the 260% increase in the ranks of African American legislators serving in the House of Representatives between the passage of the Voting Rights Act (VRA) in 1965 and the 1970 elections. From its inception, the formation of the CBC garnered considerable attention from scholars seeking to understand the relationship between African American legislators and their constituents. Indeed, the formation of the Congressional Black Caucus ushered in the rise of the modern tradition of legislative studies within the fields of African American politics and racial and ethnic politics (REP). There have been three waves of scholarship on how membership in the Congressional Black Caucus shapes both the legislative behavior of African American members of Congress and the representation that they provide to their constituents. Although most of this literature has elided the formal study of the rhetoric of African American legislators in favor of foci on bill sponsorship and roll-call votes, the four hypotheses tested in this paper are derived from key insights developed in these three waves of scholarship.

The first wave of academic studies of the Congressional Black Caucus were largely qualitative case-studies that focused on the group's decision to organize along racial lines and how this form of organization shaped African American legislators' legislative behavior (Barker and McCorry 1976; Barnett 1975; Henry 1977).[1] These studies were the first to chronicle the fact that the founders of the CBC saw their organization's role as an explicitly racial one – providing representation to both a national African American constituency and their home districts (Barnett 1975; Henry 1977). These same studies also highlighted the concerns that some African American legislators raised in this early period – what Barnett (1975, 1977) calls the "collective stage" of the CBC's development – about their ability to balance between their desires to provide "symbolic leadership" to all African Americans and to deliver "tangible benefits" to their districts (Henry 1977, 150–152).

Barnett's (1975, 1977) landmark studies of the internal dynamics of the Congressional Black Caucus during the 93rd and 94th Congresses traced the growing realization among the charter group of CBC members that striking the right balance would require them to pare down their extra-institutional activities aimed at providing symbolic representation and focus more on passing legislation. Thus, Barnett reports that at the start of the 94th Congress, the CBC entered an "ethnic stage" of development in which African American legislators began to behave as if there was a "parallel between the political assimilation of blacks and the political assimilation of white ethnic groups" (Barnett 1975, 40). In other words, CBC members began to adopt the attitude that their legislative profiles in service of their individual constituencies were their top priorities and that some degree of political assimilation within the House of Representatives would be necessary to achieve these profiles. At the start of the 94th Congress, the CBC adopted a series of reforms aimed at smoothing their assimilation into the Democratic Party Caucus and boosting their effectiveness as legislators within the House chamber (Barnett 1975, 41–44; Barnett 1977, 23–25).

Barnett saw the CBC's efforts to focus more on legislation in the 94th Congress as a success. Despite this fact, she remained somewhat circumspect about the future prospects of the CBC for two reasons. First, she believed that racial politics in the United States would always create conditions that would make it necessary for African American legislators to "oscillate" between the "collective" and "ethnic" representational styles (1977, 48–50). Second, Barnett feared that the cross-pressures African American legislators faced to "represent blacks collectively as a holistic unit" and deal with their "individual political circumstances" might stifle their ability to pass legislation (1977, 50).

A second wave of largely quantitative scholarship on African American legislators has taken up the question of their status within the Democratic Party's caucus in the House of Representatives. The consensus within the literature is that Barnett's fears about the Congressional Black Caucus achieving only a tenuous institutionalization in the House of Representatives were not realized. On the contrary, African American legislators are now fully integrated into the Democratic Party's Caucus in the House of Representatives. Indeed, CBC members routinely serve as the chairs of powerful standing committees and in senior leadership posts within the Democratic Party's hierarchy (Bositis 1994, 18–21; Haynie 2005; Minta 2011, 62–64; Singh 1998, 175–178; Tate 2014, 22–25; Tillery Jr 1999). Moreover, a raft of recent quantitative studies examining the roll-call votes of CBC members have found that more often than not they take their cues from the Democratic leadership on most pieces of legislation (Canon 1999; Sinclair-Chapman 2002; Tate 2003; Tate 2014). In short, African American legislators have achieved a level of integration into the Democratic Party in the House of Representatives that could not have been foreseen in the 1970s.

The fact that the median members of the CBC and the Democratic Party's Caucus in the House of Representatives now tend to converge on roll-call votes does not mean, as Swain (1995) has argued, that African American and white legislators provide identical representation to African American constituents. On the contrary, the second wave literature has identified several ways in which African American legislators provide distinctive representation and unique benefits to their African American constituents and the entire nation. Tate's (2003) analyses of the 103rd and 104th Congresses, for example, found that "Black Democrats' voting behavior as measured by Poole and Rosenthal [was] significantly more consistent with the liberal Democratic party agenda than that of White and other minority Democratic legislators" (p. 85). In other words, despite voting with their party on the overwhelming majority of roll-call votes, African American legislators have demonstrated a persistent willingness to break ranks in order to promote and defend liberal policies on the floor of the House of Representatives. Moreover, several studies have shown that African American legislators are far more likely than their white counterparts to introduce and champion bills advancing the interests of African Americans in both committees and on the House floor (Canon 1999; Gamble 2007; Grose 2011; Minta 2009; Minta and Sinclair-Chapman 2013; Anderson, Box-Steffensmeier, and Sinclair-Chapman 2003; Tate 2003; Whitby 2000).

The fact that African American legislators as a group demonstrate a higher level of commitment to representing the interests of African Americans does not mean that there is unanimity within the CBC on every policy matter. On the contrary, Brown, Minta, and Sinclair-Chapman (2016) have illustrated through an analysis of C-SPAN oral histories that the founding generation of CBC members strived to develop distinct legislative styles on both racial and nonracial issues. It is also clear that not every CBC member demonstrates an equal commitment to carrying the burden of representing African American interests in Congress. Indeed, there is broad consensus within recent studies of the Congressional Black Caucus that the expansion and institutionalization of the group has led to greater fragmentation on policy matters (Bositis 1994; Singh 1998; Tate 2003; Tate 2014; Tillery 2011).

The extant literature suggests that this fragmentation became particularly acute after the 1992 national elections. The results of this first election after the 1990 reapportionment of Congress boosted the number of African Americans serving in the House of Representatives from 24 to 38. The fourteen-seat pickup was the largest gain in African American membership in a single electoral cycle in the history of the House of Representatives (Bositis 1994; Singh 1998). Several studies have pointed to the incredible heterogeneity in terms of the ages, career trajectories, and political experiences of the CBC members that arrived after 1992 (Bositis 1994; Singh 1998; Tate 2003). Moreover, the literature argues that the fact that most of the new African American members elected to the 103rd Congress were from southern districts with higher proportions of both white and rural residents would moderate their tendencies to speak out on racial issues (Canon 1999; Champagne and Rieselbach 1995; Singh 1998; Tate 2003).

Although Tate (2003) was initially a proponent of the view that the growing southern bloc within the CBC after the 1992 elections was a source of moderation and fragmentation, her recent work has initiated a third wave of literature on African American legislative behavior that casts doubt on this thesis. Indeed, Tate's (2014) landmark study of the roll-call activity of African American legislators between 1977 and 2010 shows that:

> The [CBC's] move from more radically Left positions to more moderate ones and the move to vote more frequently with the House majority when their party is in power has occurred independently of the change in membership brought about by the election of new black moderates from the South. (4)

Tate argues that when you view the legislative activity of CBC members over the longer term, it becomes clear that "incorporation in the system has made Black legislative leaders less radical and more pragmatic" and "less likely to challenge party and Democratic presidential leadership through ideological debate" (2014, 4–5). As Tate (2014) notes, African American women legislators are an important caveat in her results (134). "Gender," she writes, "may also be an ideological force among Black lawmakers" (2014, 134). Tate's statistical analyses of the impact of gender on Pool-Rosenthal scores for African American legislators serving in the House of Representatives between 1993 and 2009 confirmed that African American women are more liberal than their male counterparts in the CBC (2014, 136).

Tate's (2014) findings nest within a larger turn within the literature on African American politics over the last two decades that attempts to account for the role of gender. Simien (2006) found that African American public opinion is often stratified based on how much survey respondents believe that a policy will affect the lives of African American women as a distinct subset of the community. Smooth (2006) has also shown that African American women are more active than African American men on all measures of political behavior. Moreover, several studies of African American women serving in state legislatures show that they are more progressive than African American men serving in these bodies (Orey et al. 2007; Orey and Larimer 2008). It is also true that African American women tend to take an "intersectional approach" to their legislative activities in the Congress (Bratton and Haynie 1999; Brown and Banks 2014 ; Hawkesworth 2003).[2] Indeed, Brown (2014) argues that the work that African American women do as legislators is informed by "representational identities" that "are simultaneously subordinated by the larger society because of their race and gender" (5).

As stated above, the rich literature on racial representation in the US House of Representatives that has emerged since the founding of the CBC in 1971 has largely elided the rhetoric of African American legislators. This is not surprising given the traditional barriers associated with constructing comprehensive datasets of the speech acts of members of Congress from government documents and media sources. While technological developments like computer-assisted content analysis now make it possible to evaluate large volumes of text in a short time, the digitization of public records and local media sources remains spotty at best. Although tweets – with their 140 character limits – are not a perfect representation of all of the complex speech acts that members of Congress likely engage in during a session, the wide accessibility and public-facing nature of tweets make them an excellent proxy for the rhetorical profiles of legislators. In other words, since members of Congress know that their tweets are public, it is likely that they approach the Twittersphere with the same strategic lens that they apply to their speech acts on the floor of the House and other dimensions of their legislative behavior. Moreover, the findings of one recent study lend credence to this argument by demonstrating that the tweets generated by members of Congress are an excellent source of data for estimating their Bayesian ideal points (Barberá 2015).

The three waves of literature on African American legislative behavior have left us with the key insights that district composition, electoral cohorts, and gender all shape the ways that CBC members approach their work in the House of Representatives. Building on these insights,

I test the following four hypotheses about African American legislators' usage of Twitter during the 113th Congress:

H1: CBC members from more rural districts are likely to talk less about race on

Twitter than their colleagues from districts with urban geography.

H2: CBC members from districts with higher concentrations of white voters are likely to talk less about race on Twitter.

H3: CBC members elected after 1992 (the 102nd Congress) are likely to talk less about race on Twitter than their colleagues elected before this time.

H4: Women members of the CBC are likely to talk about race on Twitter more than their male counterparts.

I will test these hypotheses as part of statistical models that utilize control variables to approximate other member-level and district-level characteristics. Confirmation of these hypotheses will suggest that there is verisimilitude between the ways African American members of Congress approach their legislative activities and Twitter usage. It will also provide evidence that the institutionalization of the CBC shapes the way that African American members communicate with their constituents. The following section explicates the data sources and methods that I utilize to test these hypotheses (see the appendix).

Data and methods

The systematic study of media representations or content analysis has long been a tool employed by social scientists in multiple fields (Lasswell 1965; Holsti 1969; Krippendorff 2004; Franzosi 2008). Scholars of racial and ethnic politics have become particularly adept at using the method in recent years (e.g., Caliendo and McIlwain 2006; Entman 1997; Grose 2006; Tillery 2011). This study used content analysis to determine how members of the Congressional Black Caucus used Twitter during the 113th Congress.

Two independent coders read the entire universe of 71,905 tweets that appeared on the public feeds of the 41 members of the CBC during the 113th Congress (which was in session between January 3, 2013 and January 5, 2015). The most comprehensive study of Congressional Twitter usage to date found that members of Congress tend to use the service more to share information about government services and their daily activities with their constituents than to discuss political or policy problems (Golbeck, Grimes, and Rogers 2010). This study reinforces this finding, as 70% of the universe of tweets conforms to this pattern of behavior. Moreover, the vast majority of these informational tweets were initially generated by other users – i.e., federal government agencies, state and municipal agencies, and news organizations – and subsequently shared (or "retweeted") by CBC members.

Since the main goal of this study is to glean whether CBC members use their Twitter feeds to communicate directly about racial issues, only the 21,692 original tweets authored by the member and or their personnel are included in the dataset. The coders culled the tweets about race from this larger sample and categorized them by issue area, the racial group (or groups) referenced in the tweet, and whether its content was symbolic or substantive. The coders also indicated whether or not the tweet used a hashtag to make it more visible on Twitter; and recorded the content of these hashtags when they were utilized.

The intercoder reliability for the 41 content analyses that serve as the foundation for this paper is .81%. In the 19% of cases where the coders disagreed with one another, a third coder was engaged to break these ties. Once the tweet dataset was completed, I conducted regression analyses in order to test the four hypotheses described above. As is often the case with count data, the distribution of the observations is non-normal. To account for this problem, I utilize the Poisson regression technique, which is a common method for correcting for overdispersed data (Frome 1983; Gardner, Mulvey, and Shaw 1995; Lawless 1987), to develop the statistical models presented below.

Findings

Some very interesting results emerged from the analysis of the subset of 21,692 original tweets made by CBC members during the 113th Congress. The first important finding is that Congressional Black Caucus members do indeed talk about racial issues on Twitter. The entire universe of race tweets was 2,403 or 11% of the total number of original content tweets. This means that the average CBC member tweeted about race only 59 times during the 113th Congress. As Figure 1, which displays the universe of CBC members' tweets by content category, tweets about economic issues (29%), symbolic politics (18%), and constituency service (16%) are larger percentages of the total than are tweets about racial issues.

This does not mean that communicating about racial issues is unimportant to CBC members. On the contrary, as Figure 1 also shows, they tweet about race more than they tweet about partisan politics (10%), legislative activities on the floor of the House of Representatives (7%) and their own campaigns for reelection (2%). Moreover, given Dancey's and Masand's (2017) finding that white members of Congress almost never tweet about race – even in the middle of crises like the Ferguson uprising – there is little doubt that African American legislators are driving the discourse about race relations on Twitter that emanates from the US Congress.

The content analyses conducted for this study also found evidence that CBC members engage in the practice of using racially distinct hashtags or "Blacktags" for some of their tweets. Indeed, thirty-one CBC members – 76% of the caucus – used at least one Blacktag

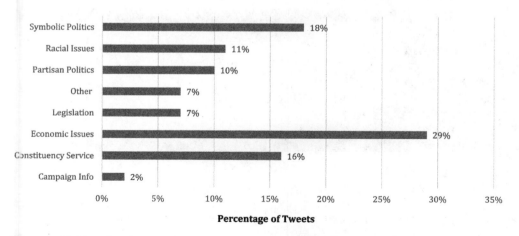

Figure 1. CBC Members' Tweets by Content Category (113th Congress).
Source: Twitter.

during the 113th Congress. As Figure 2 shows, the most frequently used Blacktag was #TrayvonMartin, which CBC members tweeted a total of 55 times during the 113th Congress. This is not surprising given the fact that Trayvon Martin's tragic death at the hands of George Zimmerman ignited a national conversation within the African American community about racial profiling and racial bias in the justice system (Hodges 2015; Schmittel and Sanderson 2015).

The second most frequently used Blacktag was #BlackMenEnroll. CBC members marked their tweets using this racially distinct hashtag 55 times during the 113th Congress. The #BlackMenEnroll marker was created by CBC members to encourage African American men to sign up for coverage under the Affordable Care Act.

What is missing from the Blacktags of CBC members during the 113th Congress is also interesting. The hashtag #BlackLivesMatter was created by Alicia Garza, Patrisse Cullors, and Opal Tometti in 2013 in direct response to the Trayvon Martin murder case (Garza 2014). Since that time, it has become one of the most widely utilized Blacktags on Twitter (Freelon and McIlwain 2016). Despite the fact that many CBC members took part in BLM rallies and other activities throughout the country, the hashtag had not gained any traction with CBC members by the close of the 113th Congress. Indeed, only one member, Representative Frederica Wilson (D-FL), marked a tweet #BlackLivesMatter during the term of the 113th Congress.

It is not surprising that Representative Wilson was the first CBC member to use #BlackLivesMatter in one of her tweets. She is the most active tweeter on racial issues in the Congressional Black Caucus. Again, the average CBC member tweeted 59 times about racial issues during the 113th Congress. Representative Danny Davis's (D-IL) eight tweets represented the minimum number in the sample. Representative Wilson's 420 tweets about race was seven times the average number.

So, what separates frequent tweeters about racial issues like Representative Wilson from average and low commitment tweeters in the Congressional Black Caucus? To answer this question, I used negative binomial regressions to develop a model of the behavior of CBC

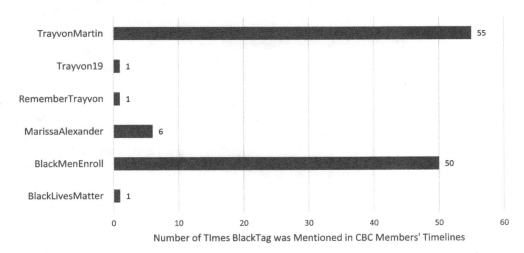

Figure 2. Distribution of Blacktags in CBC Members' Tweets (113th Congress).
Source: Twitter.

members in the Twittersphere. The dependent variable is the number of tweets about race generated by members of the Congressional Black Caucus. I utilize negative binomial regression because the dependent variable is a count variable and there is overdispersion in the data (Cameron and Trivedi 1986; Gardner, Mulvey, and Shaw 1995). The model includes variables that aimed at testing the four hypotheses related to cohort effects, district composition effects, and gender. It also includes several control variables. The results from the negative binomial regression model are displayed in Table 1.

As Table 1 illustrates, gender is the strongest predictor of how frequently a member of the Congressional Black Caucus will tweet about racial issues. The coefficient on the gender dummy variable is .695 and it is statistically significant at the .01% level. In order to get a sense of the substantive significance of this finding it is necessary to convert the negative binomial regression coefficient – which is the log form – to an incident rate. The incident rate tells us that women members of the CBC are likely to tweet about race 2.5 times more than their male counterparts. In other words, while the average CBC members tweeted 59 times during the 113th Congress, the average woman in the group did so 62 times. Moreover, these results hold even when Representative Frederica Wilson, who, as we have seen, is the most prolific tweeter in the CBC, is removed from the analysis.[3] These results provide strong support for confirmation of H4 (women members of the CBC will tweet more about race).

Table 1. Negative binomial regression model of CBC members' race tweets.

Variable	Negative binomial regression coefficients	Incident rates
Age	−.006	−.993
	(.010)	(.010)
CBC Founder	1.14*	3.14*
	(.622)	(1.95)
Gender	.937***	2.55***
	(.285)	(.730)
Leadership	.989	1.10
	(.356)	(.393)
MOV2012	.016***	1.01***
	(.005)	(.005)
Post-1992 Cohort	.566	1.76
	(.377)	(.665)
%Foreign Born	.001	1.00
	(.010)	(.010)
%Homeowners	.008	1.00
	(.015)	(.038)
%Poverty	.004	1.00
	(.038)	(.038)
%Rural	−.018*	−.982*
	(.011)	(.010)
%Unemployed	.067	1.06
	(.056)	(.060)
%White	032***	032***
	(.009)	(.009)
Median age	.129**	1.30**
	(.055)	(.063)
Southern district	.719**	2.05**
	(464)	(464)
Constant	−4.82**	−.007**
	(2.29)	(.018)
R^2	.07	.07

Sources: Twitter; US Census Bureau.
Note: Standard errors are reported in parentheses.
*$p \leq .10$; **$p \leq .05$; ***$p \leq .01$.

The results of the negative binomial model also confirmed H1. As Table 1 shows, CBC members with more rural districts tweeted less about race. The coefficient was significant at the .10% level. The incident rate on the model shows that for every one unit change in the percentage of rural residents within the district, a 1% decrease in race tweets will occur. Surprisingly, the dummy variable for "Southern District," which was a control variable in the model, is also a statistically significant positive predictor of the likelihood that a CBC member will tweet about race. The incident rate of the variable shows that CBC members representing districts in the South will tweet about race 2 times more in the 113th Congress than their colleagues representing districts located in other parts of the United States. This finding suggests that the burgeoning conservatism that legislative studies scholars have observed among CBC members since 1992 is perhaps more a function of the influx of member representing more rural districts than southern ones. It also lends support to Tate's (2014) argument that ideological moderation was more a function of integration into the Congress than a spike in the number of new CBC members from the South.

The negative binomial model also illuminated the importance of three other district-level variables. First, contrary to the expectations conveyed through H2, having higher than average concentrations of white voters within their district actually increases the likelihood that CBC members will tweet about race. For every unit increase in the white population above the mean level of 36%, a CBC member was 1% more likely to tweet about race in the 113th Congress. This result, which was significant at the .01% level, suggests that African Americans serving more racially diverse districts feel compelled to engage more on racial issues. Beyond undermining support for H2, this finding suggests that perhaps Orey (2006) is correct to argue that it is time to rethink the conventional wisdom that African American politicians need to "deracialize" their rhetoric as their districts grow increasingly white.[4]

The control variable for median age is also a statistically significant predictor of the likelihood that CBC members will tweet about race. The median age of the districts represented by CBC members is 34 years. For every one-year increase above this average, there is a 1% increase in the incident rate for race tweets. That CBC members representing older districts tweet more about race makes sense in light of the facts that older voters have constituted a growing and more reliable share of the electorate in the United States in every election since 1996 (Binstock 2000; Putnam 2001; Schulz and Binstock 2008). Moreover, Nunnally (2012) has demonstrated that older African Americans have had more experiences with racism and report a greater degree of "racial protectiveness" than younger African Americans (111-113). In light of these dynamics, it makes perfect sense that CBC members would expand their commentary on racial issues on Twitter as the median age of their districts increase.

Finally, CBC members that had larger margins of victory in the 2012 elections were more likely to tweet about racial issues. For every 1% increase in the margin of victory above the CBC's overall average of 56% that a CBC member experienced in 2012, there was a 1% increase in the incident rate of race tweets. As we have seen, the first wave studies on the Congressional Black Caucus argued that the organization's charter members consistently struggled with cross-pressures due to their desires to provide symbolic representation to the entire African American community and deliver tangible benefits to their entire community. This finding shows that as CBC members' confidence about their safety within their districts increases so does the incidence of race tweets.

The tests for cohort effects in the negative binomial model yielded some very interesting results. First, contrary to the predictions of H3, CBC members elected after 1992 were not less likely to tweet about race. Moreover, the sign on the coefficient for the post-1992 cohort is positive. Serving on the Democratic Party's leadership team during the 113th Congress also was not a statistically significant predictor of tweets about race. The only cohort effect that was statistically significant predictor variable is whether the member was a founder of the Congressional Black Caucus. Both Representative John Conyers (D-MI) and Representative Charles Rangel (D-NY) generated more race tweets than the average CBC member. Indeed, they had an incident rate that is 3.1 times higher than other CBC members. This finding suggests that despite the overall integration and moderation of the African American legislators, the founding members of the CBC remembered the organization's roots and remained committed to talking explicitly about racial issues.

Conclusion

This study examined the behavior of CBC members on the micro-blogging site Twitter during the 113th Congress. Given the overall popularity of Twitter and its sustained growth and reach within the African American community, I wanted to know if individual CBC members used their accounts to talk about racial issues. I also wanted to know what variables made CBC members more or less likely to tweet about racial issues.

Previous studies had found that members of Congress tend to use Twitter to make statements designed to bolster their prospects for reelection by sharing information about the services they are providing to their districts (Druckman, Kifer, and Parkin 2010; Golbeck, Grimes, and Rogers 2010; Peterson 2012). This study confirms that the behavior of CBC members on Twitter follows a similar pattern. As we have seen, 35% of the tweets originating from the accounts of CBC members fall into content categories that enhance their ability to claim credit on an issue or otherwise reinforce their home styles. Moreover, an additional 18% of the CBC members' tweets during the 113th Congress are crafted to reinforce their standing as symbolic representatives of their districts. The analysis also showed that CBC members' tweets about racial issues comprised 11% of their total activity on the site during the 113th Congress. This figure made it the fourth most frequent content category after economic issues (29%), symbolic politics (18%), and constituency service (16%).

As stated above, there is considerable discussion in the extant literature on the role that Twitter plays as a component of the black counterpublic sphere (Carney 2016; Nakamura 2008). A good deal of this discussion revolves around the ways that African Americans replicate their distinct cultural idioms on the site through "signifyin" behaviors and the use of racially distinct hashtags (or "Blacktags"). This study found that CBC members do not tend to "signify" on Twitter. Moreover, while they do use "Blacktags," they do so quite sparingly. For example, in the same year that #BlackLivesMatter burst into the national consciousness on Twitter, only one CBC member, Representative Frederica Wilson (D-FL), who was the most active Twitter user in the CBC during the 113th Congress, marked a tweet with the #BlackLivesMatter designation.

The empirical results from the negative binomial regression analysis show that gender is the best predictor of how frequently a CBC member will speak about race on Twitter. The women in the Congressional Black Caucus spoke out on racial issues with greater regularly than their male colleagues throughout the 113th Congress. Moreover, this finding maintains its robustness even when you remove Representative Frederica Wilson (D-FL), who tweets about race at six times the rate of the average CBC member, from the analysis. The finding that the women of the CBC are the most outspoken about racial issues on Twitter is consistent with several recent studies about the importance that African American women attach to providing racial representation within legislative bodies as part of their intersectional politics (Brown 2014; Brown and Gershon 2016; Minta and Brown 2014; Smooth 2008, 2011).

The two other most important predictors of CBC members' tweets about race during the 113th Congress were their margins of victory during the 2012 election and the percentage of whites living within the boundaries of their districts. Since the literature on legislative studies has long held that politically safe members of deliberative bodies are freer to assume political risks (Fiorina 1973; Mayhew 1974; Sullivan and Uslaner 1978), the finding that winning by a larger margin in the previous election freed up CBC members to talk more about race on Twitter is not at all surprising. By contrast, the finding that higher concentrations of whites within their districts encouraged CBC members to talk more about race on Twitter does cut against the conventional wisdom within legislative studies about the need for African American politicians to "deracialize." The fact that CBC members whose districts had higher concentrations of white voters during the 113th Congress tweeted more about racial issues than their counterparts suggests that it is time to rethink this axiom. Perhaps CBC members who represent districts with high concentrations of white voters even see it as in their interests to talk more about race on Twitter in order to keep their African American constituents mobilized against electoral threats.

The findings that the cohort of CBC members elected after 1992 does not speak less about racial issues on Twitter and that CBC members representing southern districts tweet more about race both challenge the conventional wisdom about the nature of ideological change within the organization. As we have seen, roll-call voting studies done in the 1990s and early 2000s found that the expansion of the CBC after the 1992 election shifted the nature of the group because more conservative southern members joined the organization (Bositis 1994; Canon 1999; Tate 2003). Tate's (2014) landmark study of the roll-call voting behavior of African American legislators between 1977 and 2010 has raised questions about the validity of these assumptions because the cohort that entered Congress in 1992 does not look substantially different within the broader context of the data. In other words, the longer time horizon of Tate's study shows that many of the assumptions formed by studying the one or two Congresses that clustered around the election of 1992 were snapshots that applied only to those particular moments in the history of the CBC. While this study bolsters Tate's claims, it is important to note that as a study of CBC members' rhetoric in one Congress it faces the same limitations as the studies of roll-call voting referenced above.

It is also important to recognize that this study is a snapshot that was taken in a moment just after the CBC had experienced a higher than average number of retirements. In order to build truly durable theories about the public-facing racial rhetoric of CBC members in the post-Civil Rights Era, it will require scholars to examine the group's behavior over multiple Congress. As stated above, even with advances in computer-assisted content analysis, building such a multi-Congress database will require a considerable investment of time and intellectual resources. This study should serve as a baseline for these efforts.

Notes

1. Gripping first hand accounts of this period in the history of the CBC are provided by Clay (1993) and Dellums (2000).
2. For excellent overviews of the intersectionality concept as a paradigm in political science research, see Hancock (2007) and Smooth (2006).
3. When Representative Frederica Wilson (D-FL) is removed from the sample, gender remains a statistically significant predictor variable at the .01% level. The negative binomial regression coefficient is .801 (standard error = .264) and the incident rate is 2.22 (standard error = .589).
4. For studies that developed this conventional wisdom on deracialization, see McCormick and Jones (1993), Perry (1991), and Wright (1996).

Acknowledgements

I would like to thank Laura Day, Ana Estrada, and Alice Welna for their assistance with this research.

Disclosure statement

No potential conflict of interest was reported by the author.

References

Anderson, William D., Janet M. Box-Steffensmeier, and Valeria Sinclair-Chapman. 2003. "The Keys to Legislative Success in the US House of Representatives." *Legislative Studies Quarterly* 28 (3): 357–386.
Ardoin, Phillip J. 2013. "Why Don't You Tweet? The Congressional Black Caucus' Social Media Gap." *Race, Gender & Class* 20 (1/2): 130–140.
Barberá, Pablo. 2015. "Birds of the Same Feather Tweet Together: Bayesian Ideal Point Estimation Using Twitter Data." *Political Analysis* 23 (1): 76–91.
Barker, Lucius J., and Jesse J. McCorry. 1976. *Black Americans and the Political System*. Cambridge, MA: Winthrop Publishers.
Barnett, Marguerite Ross. 1975. "The Congressional Black Caucus." *The Proceedings of the Academy of Political Science* 32 (1): 35–50.
Barnett, Marguerite Ross. 1977. "The CBC and the Institutionalization of Black Politics." *Journal of Afro-American Issues* 5: 201–227.
Barnett, Marguerite Ross. 1982. "The Congressional Black Caucus: Illusions and Realities of Power." In *The New Black Politics*, edited by Michael B. Preston, Lenneal J. Henderson, and Paul L. Puryear, 28–39. New York: Longman.
Binstock, Robert H. 2000. "Older People and Voting Participation: Past and Future." *The Gerontologist* 40 (1): 18–31.
Bositis, David. 1994. *The Congressional Black Caucus in the 103rd Congress*. Washington, DC: Joint Center for Political and Economic Studies.
Bratton, Kathleen A., and Kerry L. Haynie. 1999. "Agenda Setting and Legislative Success in State Legislatures: The Effects of Gender and Race." *The Journal of Politics* 61 (3): 658–679.

Brock, Andre. 2012. "From the Blackhand Side: Twitter as a Cultural Conversation." *Journal of Broadcasting and Electronic Media* 56 (4): 529–549.

Brown, Nadia. 2014. *Sisters in the Statehouse: Black Women and Legislative Decision Making*. New York: Oxford University Press.

Brown, Nadia, and Kira Hudson Banks. 2014. "Black Women's Agenda Setting in the Maryland State Legislature." *Journal of African American Studies* 18 (2): 164–180.

Brown, Nadia, and Sarah Gershon. 2016. "Intersectional Presentations: An Exploratory Study of Minority Congresswomen's Websites' Biographies." *Du Bois Review: Social Science Research on Race* 13 (1): 85–108.

Brown, Nadia E., Michael D. Minta, and Valeria Sinclair-Chapman. 2016. "Personal Narratives and Representation Strategies: Using C-SPAN Oral Histories to Examine key Concepts in Minority Representation." In *Exploring the C-SPAN Archives: Advancing the Research Agenda*, 139–164. West Lafayette, IN: Purdue University Press.

Caliendo, Stephen M., and Charlton D. McIlwain. 2006. "Minority Candidates, Media Framing, and Racial Cues in the 2004 Election." *Harvard International Journal of Press/Politics* 11 (4): 45–69.

Cameron, A. Colin, and Pravin K. Trivedi. 1986. "Econometric Models Based on Count Data. Comparisons and Applications of Some Estimators and Tests." *Journal of Applied Econometrics* 1 (1): 29–53.

Canon, David T. 1999. *Race, Redistricting, and Representation*. Chicago: University of Chicago Press.

Carney, Nikita. 2016. "All Lives Matter, but so Does Race: Black Lives Matter and the Evolving Role of Social Media." *Humanity and Society* 40 (2): 180–199.

Champagne, Richard A., and Leroy N. Rieselbach. 1995. "The Evolving Congressional Black Caucus: The Reagan-Bush Years. Blacks and the American Political System." In *Blacks and the American Political System*, edited by Huey L. Perry, and Wayne Parent, 130–161. Gainesville: University of Florida Press.

Clay, William L. 1993. *Just Permanent Interests*. New York: Amistad.

Conway, Bethany Anne, Kate Kenski, and Di Wang. 2013. "Twitter Use by Presidential Candidates During the 2012 Campaign." *American Behavioral Scientist* 57 (11): 1596–1610.

Couldry, Nick. 2012. *Media, Society, World: Social Theory and Digital Media Practice*. Cambridge, UK: Polity.

Dancey, Logan, and Jasmine Masand. 2017. "Race and Representation on Twitter: Members of Congress' Responses to the Deaths of Michael Brown and Eric Garner." *Politics, Groups, and Identities* 1–20.

Della Porta, Donatella, and Lorenzo Mosca. 2005. "Global-net for Global Movements? A Network of Networks for a Movement of Movements." *Journal of Public Policy* 25 (1): 165–190.

Dellums, Ronald V. 2000. *Lying Down with the Lions: A Public Life From the Streets of Oakland to the Halls of Power*. Boston, MA: Beacon Press.

Druckman, James, Martin J. Kifer, and Michael Parkin. 2007. "The Technological Development of Congressional Candidate Web Sites: How and Why Candidates Use Web Innovations." *Social Science Computer Review* 25 (4): 425–442.

Druckman, James, Martin J. Kifer, and Michael Parkin. 2010. "Timeless Strategy Meets New Medium: Going Negative On Congressional Campaign Web Sites, 2002-2006." *Political Communication* 27: 88–103.

Eltantawy, Nahed, and Julie B. Wiest. 2011. "The Arab Spring| Social Media in the Egyptian Revolution: Reconsidering Resource Mobilization Theory." *International Journal of Communication* 5: 1207–1224.

Entman, Robert M. 1997. "Manufacturing Discord: Media in the Affirmative Action Debate." *Harvard International Journal of Press/Politics* 2 (4): 32–51.

Fenno, Richard F. 1978. *Home Style: House Members in Their Districts*. New York: Harper Collins.

Fenno, Richard F. 2003. *Going Home: Black Representatives and Their Constituents*. Chicago: University of Chicago Press.

Fiorina, Morris P. 1973. "Electoral Margins, Constituency Influence, and Policy Moderation." *American Politics Quarterly* 1 (4): 479–498.

Florini, Sarah. 2014. "Tweets, Tweeps, and Signifyin' Communication and Cultural Performance on "Black Twitter"." *Television & New Media* 15 (3): 223–237.

Fox, Susannah, Kathryn Zickuhr, and Aaron Smith. 2009. Twitter and Status Updating. *Pew Internet and American Life Project*. http://pewinternet.org/Reports/2009/17-Twitter-and-Status-Updating.aspx.

Franzosi, Roberto. 2008. "Content Analysis: Objective Systematic, and Quantitative Description of Content." *Content Analysis* 1 (1): 21–49.

Freelon, Deen, and Charlton McIlwain. 2016. Beyond the Hashtags: #Ferguson, #Blacklivesmatter, and the Online Struggle for Offline Justice.

Frome, Edward L. 1983. "The Analysis of Rates Using Poisson Regression Models." *Biometrics* 39 (3): 665–674.

Gamble, Katrina L. 2007. "Black Political Representation: An Examination of Legislative Activity Within U.S. House Committees." *Legislative Studies Quarterly* 32: 421–447.

Gardner, William, Edward P. Mulvey, and Esther C. Shaw. 1995. "Regression Analyses of Counts and Rates: Poisson, Overdispersed Poisson, and Negative Binomial Models." *Psychological Bulletin* 118 (3): 392–404.

Garza, Alicia. 2014. "A Herstory of the #Blacklivesmatter Movement." *The Feminist Wire* 7.

Gates, Jr., Henry Louis. 1983. "The "Blackness of Blackness": A Critique of the Sign and the Signifying Monkey." *Critical Inquiry* 9 (4): 685–723.

Golbeck, Jennifer, Justin M. Grimes, and Anthony Rogers. 2010. "Twitter Use by the US Congress." *Journal of the American Society for Information Science and Technology* 61 (8): 1612–1621.

Graham, Todd, Dan Jackson, and Marcel Broersma. 2014. "New Platform, Old Habits? Candidates' Use of Twitter During the 2010 British and Dutch General Election Campaigns." *New Media & Society* 18 (5): 765–783.

Grant, William J., Brenda Moon, and Janie Busby Grant. 2010. "Australian Politicians Use of The Social Network Tool Twitter." *Australian Journal of Political Science* 45 (4): 579–604.

Grose, Christian R. 2006. "Bridging the Divide: Interethnic Cooperation; Minority Media Outlets; and the Coverage of Latino, African-American, and Asian-American Members of Congress." *Harvard International Journal of Press/Politics* 11 (4): 115–130.

Grose, Christian R. 2011. *Congress in Black and White: Race and Representation in Washington and at Home*. New York: Cambridge University Press.

Hancock, Ange-Marie. 2007. "When Multiplication Doesn't Equal Quick Addition: Examining Intersectionality as a Research Paradigm." *Perspectives on Politics* 5 (1): 63–79.

Hawkesworth, Mary. 2003. "Congressional Enactments of Race–Gender: Toward a Theory of Raced–Gendered Institutions." *American Political Science Review* 97 (4): 529–550.

Haynie, Kerry L. 2005. "African Americans and the New Politics of Inclusion: A Representational Dilemma?" In *Congress Reconsidered, 8th Edition*, edited by Lawrence C. Dodd, and Bruce I. Oppenheimer, 395–401. Washington, DC: CQ Press.

Henry, Charles. 1977. "Legitimizing Race in Congressional Politics." *American Politics Quarterly* 5: 149–176.

Hicks, Josh. 2013. Interesting Demographic Facts about the 113th Congress. *The Washington Post*.

Hodges, Adam. 2015. "Ideologies of Language and Race in US Media Discourse About Trayvon Martin Shooting." *Language and Society* 44: 401–423.

Holsti, Ole R. 1969. *Content Analysis for the Social Sciences and Humanities*. Reading, MA: Addison-Wesley.

Horrigan, John. 2009. Wireless Internet Use. *Pew Internet and American Life Project*. http://pewinternet.org/Reports/2009/12-Wireless-Internet-Use.aspx.

Krippendorff, Klaus. 2004. "Reliability in Content Analysis." *Human Communication Research* 30 (3): 411–433.

Langman, Lauren. 2005. "From Virtual Public Spheres to Global Justice: A Critical Theory of Networked Social Movements." *Sociological Theory* 23 (1): 42–74.

Lasswell, Harold. 1965. "Why Be Quantitative?" In *Language of Politics: Studies in Quantitative Semantics*, edited by Nathan Leites. Cambridge, MA: MIT Press.

Lawless, Jerald F. 1987. "Negative Binomial and Mixed Poisson Regression." *Canadian Journal of Statistics* 15 (3): 209–225.

Lovejoy, Kristen, and Gregory D. Saxton. 2012. "Information, Community, and Action: How Nonprofit Organizations Use Social Media." *Journal of Computer-Mediated Communication* 17: 337–353.

Manjoo, Farhod. 2010. How Black People Use Twitter: The Latest Research on Race and Microblogging. *Slate.com*.

Mayhew, David. 1974. *Congress: The Electoral Connection*. New Haven: Yale University Press.

McCormick, Joseph, and Charles E. Jones. 1993. "The Conceptualization of Deracialization: Thinking Through the Dilemma." In *Dilemmas of Black Politics*, edited by Georgia Persons, 66–84. New York: Harper Collins.

Minta, Michael D. 2009. "Legislative Oversight and the Substantive Representation of Black and Latino Interests in Congress." *Legislative Studies Quarterly* 34 (2): 193–218.

Minta, Michael D. 2011. *Oversight: Representing Black and Latino Interests in Congress*. Princeton: Princeton University Press.

Minta, Michael D., and Nadia E. Brown. 2014. "Intersecting Interests: Gender, Race, and Congressional Attention to Women's Issues." *Du Bois Review: Social Science Research on Race* 11 (2): 253–272.

Minta, Michael D., and Valeria Sinclair-Chapman. 2013. "Diversity in Political Institutions and Congressional Responsiveness to Minority Interests." *Political Research Quarterly* 66 (1): 127–140.

Mitchell-Kernan, Claudia, and Gena Dagel Caponi. 1999. "Signifying, Loud-Talking and Marking." In *Signifyin (g), Sanctifin', & Slam Dunking: A Reader in African-American Expressive Culture*, 309–330. Amherst: University of Massachusetts Press.

Nakamura, Lisa. 2008. *Digitizing Race: Visual Culture and the Internet*. Minneapolis: University of Minnesota Press.

Nunnally, Shayla C. 2012. *Trust in Black America: Race, Discrimination, and Politics*. New York, NY: NYU Press.

O'Keeffe, Gwenn Schurgin, and Kathleen Clarke-Pearson. 2011. "The Impact of Social Media on Children, Adolescents, and Families." *Pediatrics* 127 (4): 800–804.

Orey, Byron D'Andra. 2006. "Deracialization or Racialization: The Making of a Black Mayor in Jackson, Mississippi." *Politics & Policy* 34 (4): 814–836.

Orey, Byron D'Andra, and Christopher W. Larimer. 2008. "The Role of Race, Gender, Party, and Structure in State Policymaking." *Journal of Race & Policy* 4 (1): 22–33.

Orey, Byron D'Andra, Wendy Smooth, Kimberly S. Adams, and Kisha Harris-Clark. 2007. "Race and Gender Matter: Refining Models of Legislative Policy Making in State Legislatures." *Journal of Women, Politics & Policy* 28 (3-4): 97–119.

Perry, Huey. 1991. "Deracialization as an Analytical Construct in American Urban Politics." *Urban Affairs Quarterly* 27 (2): 181–191.

Peterson, Rolfe Daus. 2012. "To Tweet or Not to Tweet: Exploring the Determinants of Early Adoption of Twitter by House Members in the 111th Congress." *The Social Science Journal* 49: 430–438.

Putnam, Robert D. 2001. *Bowling Alone: The Collapse and Revival of American Community*. New York: Simon and Schuster.

Rickford, Russell. 2016. "Black Lives Matter: Toward a Modern Practice of Mass Struggle." *New Labor Forum* 25 (1): 34–42.

Schmittel, Annelie, and Jimmy Sanderson. 2015. "Talking About Trayvon in 140 Characters: Exploring NFL Players' Tweets About the George Zimmerman Verdict." *Journal of Sport and Social Issues* 39 (4): 332–345.

Schulz, James H., and Robert H. Binstock. 2008. *Aging Nation: The Economics and Politics of Growing Older in America*. Baltimore: Johns Hopkins University Press.

Sharma, Sanjay. 2013. "Black Twitter? Racial Hashtags, Networks and Contagion." *New Formations: A Journal of Culture/Theory/Politics* 78 (1): 46–64.

Shogan, Colleen. 2010. "Blackberries, Tweets, and YouTube: Technology and the Future of Communicating with Congress." *PS: Political Science and Politics* 43 (2): 231–233.

Simien, Evelyn M. 2006. *Black Feminist Voices in Politics*. Albany, NY: SUNY Press.

Sinclair-Chapman, Valeria. 2002. *Symbols and Substance: How Black Constituents are Collectively Represented in the United States Congress through Roll-Call Voting and Bill Sponsorship*. Ph.D. Dissertation. The Ohio State University.

Singh, Robert. 1998. *The Congressional Black Caucus: Racial Politics in the U.S. Congress*. Thousand Oaks, CA: Sage Publications.

Smith, Robert C. 1981. "The Black Congressional Delegation." *Western Political Quarterly* 34: 203–221.

Smith, Aaron. 2010. Mobile access 2010. *Pew Internet and American Life Project*. http://pewinternet.org/Reports/2010/Mobile-Access-2010.aspx.

Smith, Aaron. 2014. "African Americans and Technology Use: A Demographic Portrait." *Pew Research Center*. http://www.pewinternet.org/2014/01/06/african-americans-and-technology-use/.

Smith, Aaron, and Joanna Brenner. 2012. Twitter Use in 2012. *Pew Internet and American Life Project*. http://pewinternet.org/Reports/2012/Twitter-Use-2012.aspx.

Smooth, Wendy. 2006. "Intersectionality in Electoral Politics: A Mess Worth Making." *Politics & Gender* 2 (3): 400–414.

Smooth, Wendy. 2008. "Gender, Race, and the Exercise of Power and Influence." In *Legislative Women: Getting Elected, Getting Ahead*, edited by Beth Reingold, 175–196. Boulder, CO: Lynne Rienner Publishing.

Smooth, Wendy. 2011. "Standing for Women? Which Women? The Substantive Representation of Women's Interests and the Research Imperative of Intersectionality." *Politics & Gender* 7 (3): 436–441.

Sullivan, John, and Eric M. Uslaner. 1978. "Congressional Behavior and Electoral Marginality." *American Journal of Political Science* 22 (3): 536–553.

Swain, Carol Miller. 1995. *Black Faces, Black Interests: The Representation of African Americans in Congress*. Cambridge, MA: Harvard University Press.

Tate, Katherine. 2001. "The Political Representation of Blacks in Congress: Does Race Matter?" *Legislative Studies Quarterly* 26 (4): 623–638.

Tate, Katherine. 2003. *Black Faces in the Mirror: African Americans and Their Representatives in the US Congress*. Princeton, NJ: Princeton University Press.

Tate, Katherine. 2014. *Concordance: Black Lawmaking in the U.S. Congress From Carter to Obama*. Ann Arbor: University of Michigan Press.

Taylor, Keeanga-Yamahtta. 2016. *From# BlackLivesMatter to Black Liberation*. Chicago, IL: Haymarket Books.

Tillery, Jr., Alvin B. 2006. "Foreign Policy Activism and Power in the House of Representatives: Black Members of Congress and South Africa, 1968-1986." *Studies in American Political Development* 20 (1): 88–103.

Tillery, Jr., Alvin B. 2011. *Between Homeland and Motherland: Africa, US Foreign Policy and Black Leadership in America*. Ithaca, NY: Cornell University Press.

Tillery Jr, Alvin B. 1999. ""Black Americans and the Creation of America's Africa Policies: The De-Racialization of Pan-African Politics." In *The African Diaspora: African Origins and New World Identities*, edited by Isidore Okpewho, Carole Boyce-Davies, and Ali A. Mazrui, 504–524. Bloomington, IN: Indiana University Press.

Towner, Terri L., and David A. Dulio. 2012. "New Media and Political Marketing in the United States: 2012 and Beyond." *Journal of Political Marketing* 11 (1-2): 95–119.

Van Dijck, Jose. 2013. *The Culture of Connectivity: A Critical History of Social Media*. Oxford, UK: Oxford University Press.

Whitby, Kenny J. 2000. *The Color of Representation: Congressional Behavior and Black Interests*. Ann Arbor, MI: University of Michigan Press.

Whitby, Kenny J. 2007. "Dimensions of Representation and the Congressional Black Caucus." In *African American Perspectives on Political Science*, edited by Wilbur C. Rich, 195–211. Philadelphia, PA: Temple University Press.

Wright, Sharon. 1996. "The Deracialization Strategy and African American Candidates in Memphis Mayoral Elections." In *Race, Politics and Governance in the United States*, edited by Huey Perry, 151–164. Gainesville: University of Florida Press.

Appendix

Description of independent variables and coding

The coding schemes for the independent variables utilized in the Poisson regression analyses are listed below. The variables are listed in alphabetical order.

(1) Age: This is a ratio variable; the range is from 38 to 85.
(2) CBC Founder: This is a dummy variable; coded 0 for members who were not part of the founding cohort and 1 for members who were founders.
(3) Gender: This is a dummy variable; coded 0 for male and 1 for female.
(4) Leadership: This is a dummy variable; coded 0 for members who do not serve in the Democratic Party's leadership and 1 for members who serve as leaders.
(5) Margin of Victory 2012: This is a ratio variable; the range is from 30 to 88.
(6) Post-1992 Cohort: This is a dummy variable; coded 0 for members elected before 1992 and 1 for members elected after this time.
(7) %Foreign Born: This is a ratio variable; the range is from 3 to 52.
(8) %Homeowners: This is a ratio variable; the range is from 10 to 66.
(9) %Poverty: This is a ratio variable; the range is from 0 to 28.
(10) %Unemployed: This is a ratio variable; the range is from 8 to 18.
(11) %White: This is ratio variable; the range is from 10 to 66.
(12) Median Age: This is a ratio variable; the range is from 31 to 40.
(13) Southern District: This is a dummy variable; coded 0 for members who represent districts outside of the South and 1 for members who represent southern districts.

The public's dilemma: race and political evaluations of police killings

Ethan V. Porter, Thomas Wood and Cathy Cohen

ABSTRACT
This paper explores perceptions of the killings of African-Americans by police officers. We show how characteristics of the victim, officer and surrounding environment, as well as political cues, shape such perceptions. In the first study, we employ a conjoint survey experiment, wherein subjects are exposed to descriptions of hypothetical police killings. Focusing on subjects who score high on the Symbolic Racism Scale (SRS), we identify what leads such subjects to view shootings as more justified. We replicate and extend these effects in a second study in which subjects read fictitious newspaper articles. We find that exposing high SRS subjects to primes related to Black Lives Matter can decrease their belief in shootings' justifiability.

1. Introduction

Shortly after noon on August 9, 2014, in Ferguson Missouri, Darren Wilson, a white police officer, shot and killed Michael Brown, an African-American teenager. Almost as soon as the news was reported, a debate began in the media and among the public about the role race had played in the shooting, and whether details of the incident somehow made it justified. This debate was hardly unfamiliar. Only the previous summer, George Zimmerman, a "neighborhood watch" patrol man in Florida, had been acquitted of murdering Trayvon Martin, an unarmed African-American teenager. While the list of African-Americans brutalized or otherwise murdered by police stretches back longer from slavery through Jim Crow to more recent victims including Amadou Diallo and Rodney King, the debate over the issue has become newly intense. The summer of Brown's killing inaugurated a morbid parade of death. Eric Garner, an African-American man selling individual cigarettes was choked to death by police officers; Tamir Rice, a 12-year-old African-American boy, was killed when officers said they mistook a toy gun for a real gun, an incident also caught on videotape; Freddie Gray, 25, died in police custody after being arrested for possession of a switchblade; Sandra Bland, 28, died in police custody in Waller Country, Texas. Widely disseminated video footage of the first two incidents helped propel them to the national spotlight. Members of the public and Black communities in particular have protested, elected officials have issued policy proposals, and a social movement, called "Black Lives Matter" (BLM) by the public but organized under the label "Movement for Black Lives," has attracted domestic and worldwide attention.

Yet even as police killings of African-Americans have unsettled American politics, we know little about the causal determinants behind mass public perceptions of such incidents. To be sure, we have observational data on perceptions of race and the police, with attitudes often splintering sharply along racial lines. Fifty percent of whites believe African-Americans are treated fairly by the police; 84% of African-Americans say otherwise (Pew 2016). There were also sharp divisions along racial lines in response to the Garner and Brown cases (Pew 2014). Yet the available survey evidence provides little insight into the precise reasons why some police shootings are regarded as justified – and others are not, especially by white Americans. What available evidence there is, is often from the the perspective of police officers, in studies that examine what, and why, they are more likely to shoot at African-Americans, comes largely from the perspective of the police officer – not the average citizen (Correll et al. 2002; Greenwald, Oakes, and Hoffman 2003).

Such work has tended to focus on the role that stereotypes play in police decisions and how they structure everyday interactions (Allport 1954; Steele 2010). Stereotypes linking blacks to crime are especially well-documented. Research indicates that mere exposure to the faces of black people can lead one to think about crime; conversely, thinking about crime can itself lead one to think of black Americans (Eberhardt et al. 2004). Priming exercises can also result in increased public support for harsh punitive policies among white respondents (Hetey and Eberhardt 2014). In experiments that place subjects in the role of a police officer via video game, white players were quicker to shoot African-American targets, with the degree of racial bias related to the extent to which players relied on stereotypes (Correll et al. 2002). Work in similar simulated environments corroborates this bias (Greenwald, Oakes, and Hoffman 2003).

In the latter two studies, researchers presented subjects with environments meant to mimic those in which police officers make decisions. In this paper, we broaden the scope of the simulated environment. We ask: Given the limited information at their disposal, how do citizens make judgments about police killings? Do their judgments rely on stereotypes alone? How does racism affect their judgments? What specific attributes best explain their beliefs about whether specific killings seem justified? To help answer these questions, we mount two studies. In Study 1, we employ a conjoint survey experiment, wherein subjects are presented with descriptions of hypothetical situations in which police shoot and kill individuals. While we understand the sensitivity of this work, we are interested in what happens in terms of evaluations of the justification of such shootings when we vary the characteristics assigned to the victim, perpetrator and context.

Conjoint experiments have recently come to the fore of survey research in political science (Hainmueller, Hopkins, and Yamamoto 2014). The virtue of conjoint survey experiments is straightforward: Many experiments present respondents with treatments that consist of multiple constituent parts. Disentangling what, specifically, about the treatment provoked the observed effects is a difficult task. In contrast, a conjoint experiment allows researchers to isolate the causal effects of specific attributes. By randomizing the information vended about each attribute, and compelling subjects to evaluate paired scenarios, data emerges about what precisely motivates outcomes.

In Study 1, we presented subjects with paired profiles of hypothetical police shootings. We randomized information about each shooting, including the victim's age, the location where it occurred, and the background of the police officer. Subjects were then asked to evaluate the perceived justifiability of each killing. Such a request, to determine whether a shooting was justifiable based on a very limited information, may seem artificial, but the public routinely makes decisions about whether police shootings are justifiable with less information. Following the procedure outlined by Hainmueller, Hopkins, and Yamamoto (2014), we isolate the effects of each level on beliefs about justifiability. Moreover, as we collected information about subjects' racial attitudes and their attitudes toward the police weeks before administering this experiment, we can understand how such attitudes intersect with beliefs about justifiability.

Across all subjects, we found that a victim's described criminal background, his or her age, his or her reported recent drug use, and the weapon possibly in his or her possession all played powerful roles in beliefs about justifiability. Thus, how the media reports on these issues when describing a shooting has an effect on perceived justification. The picture becomes more complicated when we separate subjects based on their scores on the Symbolic Racism Scale (SRS). SRS is premised on the idea that, as the most hostile forms and violent forms of anti-black racism have become socially taboo, racist attitudes have persisted by other means. In place of what is often called "old fashioned racism" whites have expressed their anti-black attitudes by focusing on Blacks' supposed deficiencies in upholding "traditional" American values such as individualism and hard work (Kinder and Sanders 1996; Henry and Sears 2002; Kinder and Sears 1981. There are, of course, other ways to explore the impact of race and racism on political attitudes. Some researchers focus on group conflict and threat (Bobo, Kugel, and Smith 1997; Bobo and Hutchings 1996; Quillian 1995); while others explore the manifestation of color-blind racism (Bonilla-Silva and Forman 2000). Still others have found the reemergence in some domains of old-fashioned racism (Tesler 2012). We are using SRS because of its dominance in the field, making our findings easily accessible and replicable to other researchers. We find that those who score high on the SRS scale react more sharply to the location of a shooting.

In Study 2, we tested whether our observations about justifiability can be replicated with a different treatment deployed outside of a conjoint setting, and what, if any, effects social and political primes have on beliefs about justifiability. Eight weeks after Study 1, we recontacted the same subject pool and randomly vended them a news article about a hypothetical police shooting. Based on the conjoint results, each article described one of the two hypothetical victims. One victim was described as displaying all the characteristics that our conjoint results indicated would lead a respondent to perceive her death as being unjustified; the other victim was described as displaying all the characteristics that our results indicated would lead to the death being perceived as more justified. In some of the articles, we embedded primes related to and Donald J. Trump. In the BLM prime, a movement supporter describes the victim as a beloved family and community contributor; in the Trump prime, the then-presidential candidate urged people not to blame the police.

Study 2 both corroborates and enriches our findings from Study 1. The death of the victim who was described with seemingly unjustifiable characteristics was regarded as unjustified, while the death of the victim described with seemingly justifiable characteristics was regarded as justified. Additionally, the political primes had differential effects based on respondents' SRS levels. High SRS subjects exposed to a BLM prime viewed a police shooting of a hypothetical undeserving victim as *less* justified than all other subjects. A similar pattern is observed when we isolate responses by ideology and partisanship. We speculate that this pattern is owed to a seminal finding of the research into new kinds of racism, wherein individuals whose racial attitudes are most conservative are in fact more supportive of black Americans when blacks are described as meeting traditional American values – because those with conservative racial attitudes are surprised that black Americans can confirm to their supposed standards (Sniderman et al. 1991). It seems the facts confront them with the humanity of black Americans.

Our results speak to how individuals, and especially how high SRS individuals, make use of stereotypes. In Study 1, high SRS individuals were uniquely responsive to the location of the shooting, suggesting that they are more willing to extrapolate from environmental evidence than their low SRS counterparts. It seems that high SRS individuals are looking for a reason to believe the shooting by a police officer is justified. And while all subjects were responsive to the individual characteristics offered in ourscenarios – the age of the victim, his use of drugs, his criminalhistory – high SRS subjects were alone in the effect that the"evidence" offered by the shooting location increased their belief in the justifiable nature of the shooting. Indeed, the difference between locations in our study had no effect on low SRS subjects. High SRS subjects make inferences about police shootings not only based on characteristics of the shooting victim himself, but characteristics of the victim's environment. In Study 2, we show that the same high SRS subjects regard the shooting of hypothetical unjustified victims as less justified when they are described as meeting traditional American values.

2. Theoretical motivation

In U.S. courts of law, jurors are given detailed instructions on how to assess a defendant's guilt. In the court of public opinion, no such instructions exist. Instead, individuals make use of the limited information available to them, as well as their own biases, to answer the question at hand. Their judgments often reflect their acceptance of racist stereotypes – which by definition are formed on the basis of incomplete information (Allport 1954) about particular groups. To resort to stereotypes is to make a judgment quickly and imperfectly (Tajfel 1969), failing to account for the ways in which individual members of a group do not conform to all external characteristics and narratives of that group. Stereotypes surrounding African-Americans abound. As Allport (1954) recognized, stereotypes can begin with a grain of truth but quickly take on a life of their own. Consider the stereotype which holds African-Americans in possession of superior athletic ability. It may be the case that African-Americans make up a disproportionate share of players in the National Basketball Association. Individuals take this limited information and seek to confirm the stereotype. In Stone et al. (1999), survey participants were randomly told that some basketball players on a radio broadcast were black, and others were white. Players randomly described as black were subsequently rated as more athletic than players randomly described as white.

This form of confirmation bias is hardly limited to athletics. A robust literature shows that, given the racist stereotype that blacks are more violent, blacks will be considered more violent in ostensibly ambiguous situations. Duncan (1976) randomly assigned subjects to watch an interaction in which people physically shove each other. When the shove was performed by a black person, it was perceived as more violent than when it was performed by a white person. Eberhardt et al. (2004) shows that criminal defendants rated as more "stereotypically black" than others were more likely to be sentenced to death. In Hetey and Eberhardt (2014), respondents were asked to sign a petition calling for stricter punitive laws. Those who had been shown pictures that made it seem that blacks comprised an even larger share of the prison population than they do became more likely to sign. Once activated, racist stereotypes of blacks as more violent led to calls for more punitive policies.

These consequences extend to interactions between individuals and law enforcement. Several studies have used simulations to evaluate how police officers react to race in potentially violent settings. In Correll et al. (2002), subjects played a video game in which they had to decide whether to shoot a target. Players shot targets with guns more quickly if the target was black. When players were instructed to fire as fast as possible, players shot unarmed black targets more often than unarmed white targets. Greenwald, Oakes, and Hoffman (2003) use a similar video game to show that subjects have greater trouble distinguishing violent objects from non-violent objects when in the hands of a black target.

While stereotypes may be an inescapable component of the human categorization process (Tajfel 1981), reliance on stereotypes leads to prejudice and racism (Devine 1989). From the perspective of a member of the stereotyped group, stereotypes are particularly pernicious. Steele (2010) describes "stereotype threat," wherein members of a stereotyped group anticipate that they will be stereotyped and respond accordingly. This threat looms over their lives and compels them to change their behavior. Steele quotes journalist Brent Staples on his experience of walking as a black man in Chicago:

> I became an expert in the language of fear. Couples locked arms or reached for each other's hand when they saw me I whistled popular tunes from the Beatles and Vivaldi's *Four Seasons*. The tension drained from people's bodies when they heard me. A few even smiled as they past me in the dark.

For Staples, "whistling Vivaldi" was a low-cost way to signal to passer-bys that he was harmless. He was black, but contrary to stereotypes, he was not violent; the disjunction between expectation and reality disarmed Staples' neighbors.

Our task in this paper is more morbid. We are trying to identify the details of police shootings that are likely to make people think of the shootings as more justifiable. We are spurred on by the fact that in many of the high-profile shootings, seemingly small details about the victim have played central roles in the subsequent public debate. For example, in the aftermath of the Michael Brown killing, commentator noted the marijuana that toxicology reports indicated Brown had consumed. Also noted was the shoplifting Brown had engaged in prior to his encounter. Both of these factors were used to justify the shooting and killing of Michael Brown in media reports. We outline additional examples of much-discussed details used to justify shootings in the design section.

3. Empirical expectations

While some whites likely react to police shootings with barely disguised racial animus toward blacks, this form of out-and-out or old-fashioned racism is likely not as prevalent as "modern" (McConahay 1986) or "symbolic" (Kinder and Sears 1981) racism. For those who score high on the SRS, blacks are regarded negatively for being perceived as failing to work as hard as other minority groups have done (Henry and Sears 2002). Yet harboring high levels of symbolic racism does not necessarily mean that one always expresses racially hostile attitudes. In their investigation of new forms of racism, Sniderman et al. (1991) found that conservatives are *more likely* than liberals to believe that the government should offer to aid to laid-off black workers. However, their research suggests that this generosity is contingent upon the laid-off black worker being described as a "dependable worker." By exhibiting a strong work ethic, the black worker is demonstrating her fealty to the American value of hard work; the authors assert that conservatives support the worker in part because she confounded their expectations. The so-called racial novelty can push people, particularly whites or those who score high on SRS, toward supporting blacks more so than they would otherwise (Porter and Wood 2016).

We believe the anti-black attitudes measured by SRS are not just individual assessments but are similarly shaped by perceptions of group threat. As Ash (1993, 308) writes, "there is reason to identify symbolic racism with group-based, emotion-linked appraisals." Thus our measures of SRS help us to understand how race and racism assessed through an individual and collective lens, influences whether an individual will believe the killing of another individual by the police is justified.

With all this in mind, so as to be precise about our expectations, we offer the following hypotheses:

Hypothesis 1: The extent to which one relies on stereotypes when forming perceptions of police killings will fluctuate dependent on one's level of symbolic racism.

Hypothesis 2: Among those who exhibit high levels of symbolic racism, victims of police killings who appear to come closer to meeting what has been represented as "traditional" American values will be regarded as more sympathetic, and thus their shootings will be viewed as less justified, among those who exhibit high levels of symbolic racism.

We use Study 1 to evaluate Hypothesis 1. Hypothesis 2 is evaluated in Study 2.

4. Study 1: experimental design

We administered Study 1 over two waves in July 2016. The study was conducted over Mechanical Turk, a popular, low-cost means of subject acquisition (Berinsky, Huber, and Lenz 2012). As described in the supporting information, we cross-validated the Mechanical Turk sample against face-to-face government survey data; our sample compares favorably. To run a two-wave panel on Mechanical Turk, we followed Christenson and Glick (2013). In wave one, we asked standard demographic questions, as well as the SRS scale of Henry and Sears (2002). Following a two-week washout period, we recontacted subjects and administered the conjoint experiment. In creating a lag between waves 1 and 2, we were simply adhering to the standard of Hainmueller, Hopkins, and Yamamoto (2015) study of immigration attitudes.

4.1. Wave 1

We recruited 1700 subjects for Wave 1 in July 2016, paying each subject $.50, a standard level of incentive pay on the Mechanical Turk platform. Wave 1 consisted of a standard demographic battery, including questions about subjects' age, race, party identification, household income and gender, and the SRS. Table 1 provides the demographic composition for all three waves (Study 1 comprised waves one and two, while Study 2 comprised wave 3). Study 2 is disaggregated by the condition. The top row (in italics) reports the number of respondents. Subsequent rows report the distribution of demographic characteristics by wave. We have evaluated white and people of color subjects simultaneously. However, while our sample includes whites, African-Americans, Latino and other people of color, there are not enough respondents outside of whites to rigorously analyze each racial and ethnic group separately.

4.2. Wave 2

At the beginning of the second wave, subjects were then told that they would be evaluating descriptions of videos, with each video showing the police killing a person. We explained to subjects that they would not actually be able to see the videos but wanted them to make the best decision they could about the justifiable nature of the killing with the limited information we presented to them. The full text read:

> In this study, we are going to describe several videos. Each video shows a policeman killing a person. We know that you are used to actually watching videos, but we want you to make the best decision you can with the limited information we give you.

By describing the profiles as related to videos of police killing individuals, we aimed to increase the verisimilitude of the study, given that many of the more high-profile police killings involved videos of the incident.[1]

In a conjoint experiment, a respondent is compelled to evaluate a series of paired profiles. Each profile consists of attributes, under which exist a set of levels. The forcedresponse – with subjects choosing between the two profiles – is repeated multiple times. In our case, each profile contained attributes about a hypothetical police killing. We selected attributes that might be driving attitudes about police killings. Each profile contained attributes about the gender of the person killed, the age of the person killed, if the person killed had a criminal record, if the person killed was in possession of a weapon and if so what type, the policeman's disciplinary record, the location of the shooting, if the person killed had taken an illegal substance, the race of the person killed and the race of the police officer.[2]

The attributes remain the same across each profile. What randomly varies is the "level" of each attribute, within each profile. For example, a level of the "age" attribute was 21; a level of the "criminal record of person killed attribute " was "no criminal record." Table 4 displays all attributes and levels. Upon telling subjects that they would see description of videos of police killings, we described each level. Subjects then were confronted with five sets of two profiles. Upon seeing each set of two profiles, subjects were asked how justified they believed the killing described in the first profile was, and how justified they believed the killing described in the second profile was. To assess justifiability, subjects answered a seven-point scale, ranging from "entirely justified" to "entirely unjustified."[3] To construct the conjoint experiment, we relied on software by Hainmueller, Hopkins, and Yamamoto (2014). Figure 1 displays an example of what a paired profile would look like to respondents. Table 2 displays all attributes and levels.

Table 1. Experimental balance, by wave and prime (for third wave.) first row indicates count of respondents. subsequent entries are column percentages.

		Study 1		Hypothetical Justified Victim			Study 2 Wave 3 Hypothetical Unjustified Victim			Balance
		Wave 1	Wave 2	None	BLM	Trump	None	BLM	Trump	
n		1723	1352	146	153	155	130	143	143	
Age	18–34	60	57	53	50	48	51	46	42	$\chi^2 = 6.2(10)$
	35–54	32	34	37	36	39	40	42	42	$p = .78$
	55+	8	9	10	14	13	10	12	16	
Education	HSD or Less	12	11	12	16	9	12	9	15	$\chi^2 = 13.4(10)$
	Some College	38	37	31	31	29	36	34	43	$p = .19$
	BA+	50	52	57	54	62	52	57	43	
Employment	Full-Time Employee	63	64	68	59	61	67	63	69	$\chi^2 = 9.8(20)$
	Self Employed	19	19	15	18	20	20	19	14	$p = .97$
	Unemployed	8	8	8	10	9	6	6	8	
	Not Working	10	9	9	13	10	8	11	9	
Gender	Female	45	45	47	46	46	48	46	49	$\chi^2 = .45(5)$
	Male	55	55	53	54	54	52	54	51	$p = .99$
Income	0–35k	43	43	42	53	40	39	32	45	$\chi^2 = 17.9(10)$
	35–75k	40	39	39	30	44	37	50	41	$p = .06$
	75k+	18	18	19	17	16	25	18	14	
Ideology	Conservative	24	24	19	24	25	33	26	27	$\chi^2 = 12.9(15)$
	Moderate	19	19	23	16	17	18	21	14	$p = .61$
	Liberal	56	57	59	60	58	48	53	59	
Partisanship	Republican	24	24	20	21	26	27	23	27	$\chi^2 = 6.47(15)$
	Independent	25	24	28	23	21	26	26	23	$p = .97$
	Democrat	52	53	52	56	53	47	51	50	
Race	White	78	78	85	77	80	81	82	80	$\chi^2 = 6.38(15)$
	Black	6	6	5	8	6	6	5	7	$p = .97$
	Hispanic	6	5	5	8	7	5	6	3	
	Other	10	10	6	7	8	8	7	9	
Region	North Central	20	21	20	21	20	14	27	17	$\chi^2 = 19.13(25)$
	Northeast	14	13	11	14	15	13	17	16	$p = .79$
	South	31	30	29	32	24	30	31	34	
	West	35	35	38	32	40	42	24	33	

	Shooting 1	Shooting 2
Age of Person Killed	27	27
Race of Person Killed	White	Black
Policeman's Disciplinary Record	Some complaints	Some Complaints
Race of Policeman	White	White
Substances Taken by Person Killed	Alcohol	Alcohol
Weapon in Possession of Person Killed	Gun	Knife
Location of Shooting	Middle class neighborhood	Middle class neighborhood
Gender of Person Killed	Transgender	Transgender
Criminal Record of Person Killing	No Criminal Record	Short Criminal Record

Which shooting is more justified?   (Shooting 1)   (Shooting 2)

Figure 1. Indicative conjoint options facing each respondent.

The attributes and levels were not chosen accidentally. Each attribute could, on its own, warrant an investigation. For example, the relationship between stereotypes and gender has a robust literature (e.g. Cadinu et al. 2005; Carr and Steele 2010). So too does the relationship between stereotypes and race (e.g. Nelson, Sanbonmatsu, and McClerking 2007; Steele 2010). By using a conjoint, we are able to precisely distill the exact effect that each attribute has on attitudes. Our choice of attributes was owed to two factors. First, as our ambition was to unpack the determinants of attitudes toward police killings,

Table 2. Conjoint survey design.

Attribute	Levels
Age of Person Killed	12, 15, 18, 21, 24, 27, 30
Gender of Person Killed	Male, Female, Transgender
Criminal Record of Person Killed	No Criminal Record, Short Criminal Record, Extensive Criminal Record
Weapon in Possession of Person Killed	No weapon, gun, knife
Policeman's Disciplinary Record	Spotless record, Some complaints, many complaints
Location of Shooting	Middle-class neighborhood, known gang area
Substances Taken By Person Killed	No substances taken, Marijuana, alcohol, PCP
Race of Person Killed	White, Latino, Black
Race of Policeman	White, Latino, Black

we believed that our attributes should include details that featured prominently in media discussions of such killings. The role of media coverage in shaping racial attitudes is well-documented (e.g. Iyengar 1991; Entman and Rojecki 2000). Each level we tested had featured prominently in discussions about at least one of the more prominent shootings. Tamir Rice's youth was highlighted by multiple media accounts (Blow 2015). The public dwelled on Michael Brown's supposed criminal activity before the shooting (Roller 2014). The race of the police officers was featured prominently in coverage of the Freddie Gray case, as photographs of the officers led news accounts, highlighting that police officers from different races were involved in this incident (Stolberg and Oppel 2015). The shooting of Laquan MacDonald was followed by stories about the drugs in his system, and the knife he allegedly wielded – but did not actually wield – at officers (Gorner 2015).

We also tested attributes that might signal whether the victim was or was not conforming to race-related stereotypes about crime. This was tested most directly by including the attribute about the victim's supposed criminal history, and it was tested more by including the reference to the location. Previous work has found that perceptions of the police are often tied up with the location of the respondent, with residents of middle-class neighborhoods perceiving the police differently than residents of lower-class neighborhoods (Weitzer 1999). With that in mind, describing a shooting as occurring in a middle-class neighborhood might spur respondents to regard that shooting as more justified. The victim's age, often mentioned in media reporting of police killings, might also relate to perceptions of innocence, given the relationship between age, crime and jury outcomes (e.g. Farrington 1986; Anwar, Bayer, and Hjalmarsson 2014). In sum, the attributes we tested both increased our ability to shed empirical light on real-life incidents as people might have heard about them through media and helped us speak to a variety of attributes that scholarship suggests could have played a role in affecting attitudes.

In this study, a conjoint design also offered several methodological advantages. Consider what kind of standard survey experiment could have been designed to answer these questions. Before administering the survey, we would have had to make predictions informed by the literature about the specific characteristics (or "levels") that drive the public's attitudes about police killings. Perhaps people believe shootings of young children are especially unjustified; perhaps they think reported marijuana use by the victim makes a shooting more justifiable. We could have constructed fictitious news articles or vignettes around those predictions and judged responses accordingly. But just as our treatments would have been byproducts of informed guesswork, so too would our understanding of their effects in relationship to other possible characteristics. To understand one level's effect in relationship to others, we would have had to conduct multiple follow-up studies. A level of precision that would have taken multiple rounds with standard survey experiments is achieved with the conjoint design in one fell swoop.

4.3. Study 1 results

Exactly 1352 subjects completed Waves 1 and 2. We are estimating the *Average Marginal Component Effect* (AMCE) of each attribute, which is best thought of as the difference in probability that one attribute, compared to another, will lead to a shooting being perceived as justified. As each level is randomly assigned within each profile, each displayed level is orthogonal to one another, allowing us to make inferences about the effects of any level on our outcome variable. Hainmueller, Hopkins, and Yamamoto (2015) helpfully compare the inferences drawn from a conjoint survey to the inferences researchers make when reviewing results from survey questions vended in random order. To make our estimates, we run regressions in which a benchmark level is regressed against all other levels within the attribute. For additional details on the procedure, consult Hainmueller, Hopkins, and Yamamoto (2014).

Figure 2 displays the effects of each attribute on the probability that respondents will regard a shooting as justified. To understand how to interpret the figure, turn to the results for the "age" attribute at the top of the plot. The result for a hypothetical 12-year-old victim,.16, indicates that just being shown a profile of a shooting in which the victim was aged 12 years reduces the likelihood that the shooting will be regarded as justified by 16%, in comparison to the baseline level (in this case, 21). Similarly, the result for the "gun" level, within the "victim" attribute, shows that being shown a profile in which the victim is described as having a gun increases the likelihood that the shooting will be regarded as justified by 34%. In this case, that number is in comparison to the baseline level of having no gun.

Across the sample, we see respondents making inferences about the shooting's justifiability based on individual traits of the victim. Shootings with young victims are less likely to be regarded as justified; shootings in which victims are said to have guns or knives are likely to lead respondents to think of the shooting as more justified. Criminal records matter too – shootings in which the victim is reported to have an extensive criminal record are 16% more likely to be regarded as justified than shootings in which the victim has no criminal record. Equally as interesting as what we do observe is what we do not observe. The race of the police officer did not matter in our analysis. The number of complaints a police officer had received mattered somewhat, but hardly so in comparison to the criminal record of the victim. Respondents seem conditioned to believe the police irrespective of conditions. This is an especially important finding because it raises the question of what individuals need to know about a police officer involved in a shooting to move the burden of proof of innocence from the victim to the officer. The finding also suggests that without controlling for trust in the police, it appears that most individuals are willing to give the police the benefit of doubt when it comes to police officers killing civilians.

In contrast, when we vary the purported gender of the victim, we observe significant effects, suggesting that shootings with male victims are regarded as more justifiable

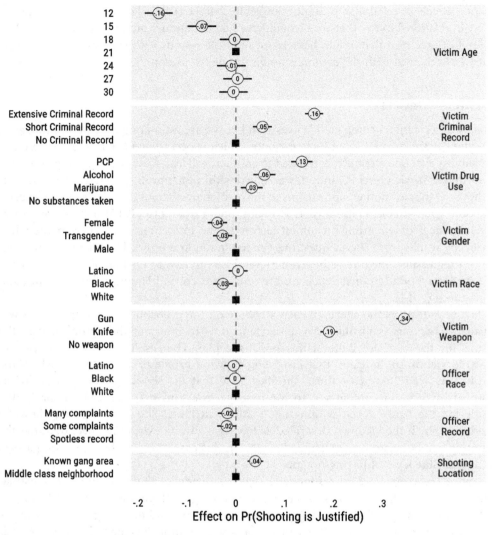

Figure 2. Overall conjoint experiment results. Points to the right of the dashed horizontal indicate shootings with this characteristic were more likely to be deemed justified, relative to the baseline levels indicated by the square. Within each attribute, the square indicates the reference level.

than shootings with female/transgender victims, but only slightly. Finally, we saw effects on race of the victim, but in the opposite direction anticipated; shootings with black victims were seen as slightly *less* justifiable than shootings with white or Latino victims. The negative effect is small and could be explained by some combination of social desirability bias, wherein subjects know the socially "correct" answer, and an awareness caused by actual shootings which led subjects to think that shootings with black victims are less justified. It is possible that the constant stream of news about police shooting, and possibly protests over police shootings, had conditioned subjects to be especially skeptical of such shootings of black victims.

4.4. Symbolic racism

While the first analysis tells us how varying characteristics impacts the general trend in justifiability, we are also interested in how individuals who hold greater anti-black attitudes respond to the varying characteristics. We disaggregated SRS scores into quartiles, regarding subjects in the bottom quartile as scoring low on the SRS scale and those in the top quartile as high on the SRS scale. Figure 3 displays the effects for each level on the probability that respondents will regard a shooting as justified. For each attribute, the benchmark level in the regression is noted by a square. Hollow circles denote effects for those who score low on SRS, while solid circles denote effects for those who score high.

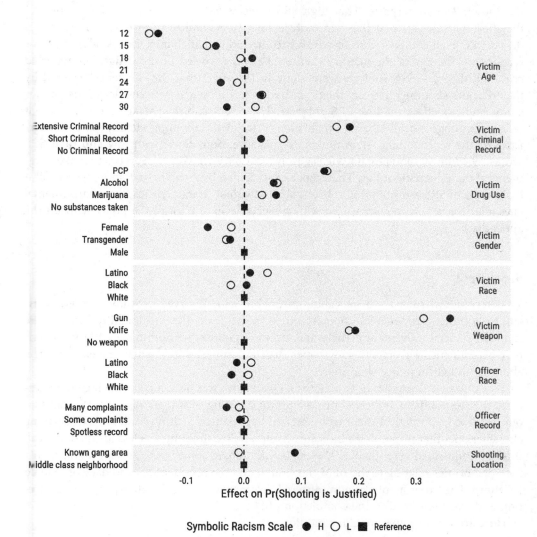

Figure 3. Subgroup conjoint experiment – effect of conjoint attributes for respondents of high symbolic racism (indicated by the solid points) and low symbolic racism (hollow points). Within each attribute, the square indicates the reference level, shared between the model types.

The circles largely follow one another, with most differences between high and low SRS respondents registering as statistically significant but substantively small. The reader should pay special attention to the marked difference on the question of shooting location. High SRS respondents become 10% more likely to view a shooting as justified merely on the basis of its location, with high SRS respondents more likely to think of a shooting as justified if it occurred in a "known gang zone." We also observe effects on the race of the victim and the race of the police officer. On the race of the victim, high SRS respondents were more likely to view a shooting as justified if the victim were Black or Latino/a. On the race of the officer, we observe effects, but in the opposite direction; high SRS subjects regarded shootings by Black or Latino/a officers as less justifiable.

These results suggest that high SRS subjects make use of stereotypes differently than their low SRS counterparts. That high SRS subjects were responsive to the location of the shooting suggests that they are more willing to generalize from environmental evidence. While all subjects were responsive to the individual characteristics offered in our scenarios – the age of the victim, whether she was reported to use drugs, her reported criminal history – SRS subjects were alone in the effect that the "evidence" offered by the location shooting had on them. Indeed, the difference between locations in our study had no effect on low SRS subjects. High SRS subjects make inferences about police shootings not only based on characteristics of the shooting victim, but characteristics of the surrounding environment. To be sure, both those with low and high SRS scores relied on stereotypes; no one is absolved from relying on stereotypes to make judgments about police shootings. That said, as anticipated by *Hypothesis 1*, those who exhibit high levels of SRS are willing to rely on non-individual characteristics like environmental cues. (To see how responses varied with subjects' level of trust in the police, consult the appendix.)

5. Study 2

To determine whether the beliefs about justifiability we observed in Study 1 would translate to another experimental context and to evaluate whether justifiability beliefs were shaped by social movement activity and electoral politics, we administered Study 2. For this experiment, we created newspaper articles, modeled on actual media coverage, about hypothetical police shootings.

We constructed profiles of two victims. One victim was described as having characteristics that respondents indicated made a police shooting seemingly justified. We call that our Justified Hypothetical Victim. Our second hypothetical victim was described as having characteristics that respondents indicated made a police shooting was less justified. We call this our Unjustified Hypothetical Victim. In addition, in some of the articles we randomly included primes relating to the BLM movement and the presidential candidacy of Donald J. Trump. The experiment was administered three weeks before the 2016 presidential election and two months after the completion of Study 1.

Here are the six experimental conditions:

(1) *Unjustified Hypothetical Victim/No Prime:* The article relayed a story about the police shooting of a 12-year-old girl with no prior convictions, who did not appear to be on

any substances, that occurred in a middle-class neighborhood, by a police officer who had previously received civilian complaints.
(2) *Unjustified Hypothetical Victim/Black Lives Matter Prime:* The article relayed a story about a police shooting of the same victim as described above. The article also contained a hypothetical statement of mourning from the local Black Lives Matter chapter.
(3) *Unjustified Hypothetical Victim/Trump Prime:* The article again relayed a story of the same victim. This time, the article contained a hypothetical quote from Donald J. Trump about the shooting, in which he urged his listeners not to blame police.
(4) *Justified Hypothetical Victim/No Prime:* The article relayed a story about the police shooting of a 30-year-old man with an extensive criminal record, who witnesses said appeared high on PCP, with a gun in a known gang area, by a police officer with no known record of complaints.
(5) *Justified Hypothetical Victim/Black Lives Matter Prime:* The article relayed a story about the police shooting of the same victim described above. The article also contained a hypothetical statement of mourning from the local BLM chapter.
(6) *Justified Hypothetical Victim/Trump Prime*: The article relayed a story about the police shooting of the same victim, while also containing a hypothetical quote from Donald J. Trump, in which he urged his listeners not to blame police.

The test of the resultant articles is provided in Figure 4 on page 22.

Given the well-known relationship between media coverage and racial attitudes (e.g. Iyengar 1991; Entman and Rojecki 2000), we based our treatments on articles that appeared in U.S. media. We modeled our treatments on an article about the Michael Brown shooting (O'Neil 2014) and an article about the Alton Sterling shooting (Stole 2016); the latter article featured a family member describing Sterling in ways similar to the description we used in the BLM prime. We edited the articles somewhat; the variation in the final paragraph of each treatment is owed to concerns about differential length. The longer version of the paragraph was used in those conditions without additional primes. The study was administered on the same subjects who participated in Study 1, recontacting them eight weeks later.

After reading their article, subjects evaluated the justifiability of the victim's death, using the Study 1 scale. They were then asked how important they believed the issue of "police shootings of black people" is. We presented subjects with feeling thermometers of Donald Trump and the BLM movement. As a manipulation check, we asked subjects how old the victim they saw was, and as an attention check, we asked what time the press conference would occur. The latter was an especially aggressive attention check, given that the information was conveyed at the end of the article.

5.1. Study 2 results

Exactly 826 subjects from our original sample were recruited and successfully completed Study 2. Subjects were significantly more likely to view a killing as justified if the victim was described with the high deserving attributes identified from the conjoint data. On our 1–7 scale, higher values indicate greater belief in justifiability. Subjects in the *Justified Hypothetical Victim/No Prime* condition reported a mean response of 4.54, or

Police Shoot and Kill [*30-Year-Old Man/12-Year-Old Girl*]

Details are slowly emerging regarding the police-involved shooting death of [*30-year-old Aaron Jones/12-year-old Melissa Jones*] around noon yesterday. The shooting occurred on Garrison Avenue at the Wilson Apartment Complex, [*a known gang area/a middle class neighborhood*].

According to a police department source, a police officer had an encounter on the street with Jones before the shooting. Jones, [*an African-American male with an extensive criminal record / an African American girl with no criminal record*], [*was in possession of a gun/ was not in possession of any weapons*]. While compete toxicology tests will take about six weeks to complete, [*witnesses say nothing appeared unusual about Jones in her interaction with the police officer/multiple witnesses says that Jones appeared to be high on PCP, or "angel dust," during his interaction with police officers*].

[BLM PRIME: *The local Black Lives Matter Chapter released the following statement: [Aaron/Jessica] had dreams, goals, and a family who loved them and counted on them. Instead of contributing to their community, [Aaron's/Jessica's] life was cut short by a racist police department that sees Black people as a threat. They did not deserve to die like this."*]

[TRUMP PRIME: Campaigning nearby, GOP Presidential Nominee Donald Trump denounced those who are protesting the shooting. "We count on the police to protect us. Why do we instinctively blame the police? It's sick. The only long-term solution is to expect these people to take some responsibility for their own behavior," he said.]

The police officer in question has [*complaints on his/a spotless*] record. When asked about the officer's record, a police spokesman declined to comment. The city's Bureau of Crimes against Persons will conduct an independent investigation.

It is not yet known what precisely led the officer to kill Jones. More details will be shared at [*a police press conference tomorrow./a police press conference tomorrow at City Hall, currently scheduled for 1 PM. City Hall was last renovated in 2007. The press conference should last for 30 minutes to an hour. The weather forecast for tomorrow calls for gray clouds with a chance of sun in the afternoon.*]

Figure 4. Text scheme for study 2 treatments. Italicized text indicates article characteristics which have were randomized for either a high (the first entry) or low justifiability (the second entry). The second dimension of random assignment – whether respondents saw a BLM or Trump prime – are captured in the paragraphs inside brackets. Across both randomization types, each respondent saw *either* a description of a low or high justifiability shooting, and a Trump or a BLM prime.

in between "Neither Justified and Justified " and "Somewhat Justified." Meanwhile, subjects in the *Unjustified Hypothetical Victim/No Prime* reported a mean response of 2.13, close to the "Unjustified" choice. This 2.4 difference is significant by conventional standards ($p<.000$). The Justified Hypothetical Victim's shooting was regarded as more justified when paired with either the Trump or BLM prime. The same was true of the Unjustified Hypothetical Victim's shooting – regardless of the prime associated with it,

Table 3. Overall study 2 estimates of treatment effects on perceived justifiability of shooting. Column 1 includes all respondents. Columns 2 only includes respondents who passed manipulation check. Intercept omitted for simplicity.

	All respondents	Passed manipulation check
Unjustified Victim No Prime	2.41***	2.64***
	(.15)	(.16)
Justified Victim BLM Prime	2.46**	2.59***
	(.15)	(.16)
Unjustified Victim BLM Prime	−.13	.05
	(.16)	(.18)
Justified Victim Trump Prime	2.39***	2.57***
	(.15)	(.17)
Unjustified Victim Trump Prime	.04	.09
	(.15)	(.17)
n	826.	602.
r^2	.48	.53
Adjusted r^2	.38	.52

people were comparatively skeptical that the shooting was justified. The statement of mourning voiced by BLM did not change subjects' attitudes in one direction or another, nor did Trump's defense of the police.

An OLS model of the results further affirms this finding. In column 1 in Table 3, we estimate an OLS model of the perceived justifiability of the shooting, with the *Justified Hypothetical Victim/No Prime* condition omitted. The coefficients for the Justified Hypothetical Victim are large and significant, regardless of the prime. (The coefficients for this victim across conditions are not statistically distinct from one another.) The coefficients for the Unjustified Hypothetical Victim, meanwhile, are small and insignificant across conditions. In column 2 in Table 3, we restrict the model to those who passed the hardest manipulation check, for which correct answers could be obtained by reading to the end of the treatment. Our results remain robust to this restriction.

Next, we consider how subjects' pre-treatment characteristics interacted with their susceptibility to the BLM and Trump primes. In Figure 5, we show how the primes mattered for the Hypothetical Justified and Unjustifiable and victims by SRS, by confidence in police, by partisanship, by ideology and by level of education. The plots each reflect separate OLS models with the unjustified/no prime condition as the excluded condition. First, consider SRS related to responses to Hypothetical Justified and Unjustified victims. Of special interest are the responses of high SRS subjects to the Hypothetical Unjustifiable Victim. Such subjects are motivated by the Trump prime to view this victim's shootings as more justifiable – but the BLM prime pushes them significantly in the other direction. The BLM prime makes high SRS subjects view the shooting of a hypothetical unjustifiable victim as significantly *less* justified than a Trump prime. For the Hypothetical Justified Victim, high SRS subjects who are exposed to the BLM prime effectively come to view the shooting as more justified than the version with the Trump prime (though the difference for the Hypothetical Justified Victim is not significant). For no other condition, and for no other level of SRS, did seeing the BLM prime deflate subjects' belief in the justifiability of the shooting. It only did so for high SRS subjects.[4]

What first might appear to be an especially surprising result makes more sense when we consider the content of the BLM prime. Subjects in the BLM prime were exposed to one

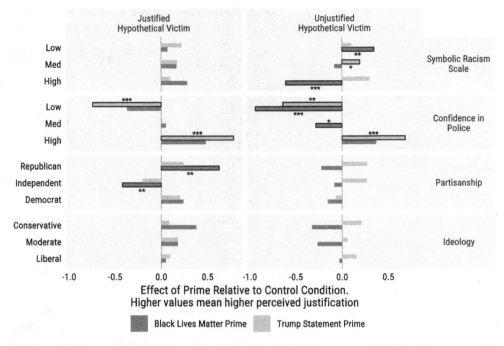

Figure 5. Treatment effects as a function of Trump (light bars) or and BLM (dark bark) frames. Each bar shows the mean difference compared to demographically similar respondents (indexed on the y-axis) exposed to no frame. Differences are measured on a seven point scale. Significant differences to control ($p<.05$) are indicated by a black border. Redundantly, significant differences are also labeled with asterisks (* $p<.05$, ** $p<.01$, *** $p<.001$). Column facets show the effect of changing the shooting's circumstance either to encourage respondents to justify the shooting – "justified hypothetical victim" – or to believe the shooting was not justified – "unjustified hypothetical victim." Row facets interact different respondent characteristics with the treatments. The regression models which provide these estimates are described in Table 4 in the appendix.

specific example of BLM rhetoric. In his prime, (based on how Sterling's father described him (Stole 2016), BLM mentioned the victim's family and made clear that the victim had been loved. Had the victim not been shot, he or she would be "contributing to their community." For high SRS subjects, this rhetoric may have been unusually effective in turning the victim into a person deserving of sympathy. Recall Sniderman et al. (1991) finding that conservatives are *more likely* than liberals to be sympathetic toward a laid-off black worker, contingent on upon the worker being described as a "dependable worker." A similar dynamic may be at play in high SRS subjects' responses to the BLM prime when attached to the Unjustified Hypothetical Victim. The victim described – a beloved family member, a community contributor – arguably conforms to "traditional" American values of hard work and nuclear family dynamics. High SRS subjects may find this combination novel and re-evaluate the victim as one who has met traditional values. They thus object more to her death than they would otherwise. There are limits to this finding; a similar response to the BLM prime was not observed when the prime was used in relationship to the Justified Hypothetical Victim. We should not interpret this finding as evidence of high SRS subjects' broad sympathy for BLM. A different example of BLM rhetoric may have produced much different results. Further research on the relationship between attitudes toward BLM and SRS is needed.

6. Discussion

We live in a time when increased attention is being paid to the shooting of civilians, in particular black Americans, by the police. Individuals are provided limited information and are being asked to draw conclusions on these shootings. We believe that researchers must explore what factors shape how individuals view these shootings. What causes people to view such shootings as justifiable? And can such evaluations be affected by politicians and social movements? To evaluate the causal determinants of mass attitudes about police shootings, we employed a two-wave conjoint survey experiment in which we varied attributes of hypothetical police killings. Across the sample, we observed subjects drawing inferences about the justifiability of such shootings based on their knowledge of the individuals involved in the shooting. Shootings in which the victim had an extensive criminal record, had a gun, or was reported to be using psychedelic drugs were especially likely to be viewed as justified. Conversely, shootings with young victims were more likely to be viewed as unjustified.

In addition, we find individuals who exhibit high SRS levels heavily weighing environmental evidence. This suggests that SRS levels condition what kind of stereotypes individuals use when evaluating police shootings. Those who demonstrate high SRS need only environmental evidence to judge the shooting as more justifiable, while those who exhibit low SRS dwell more on individual-level information. Our results indicate that SRS also relates to the kinds of evidence subjects use when evaluating racially charged and racist events. This lends credence to our first hypothesis, which anticipated that SRS levels would affect subjects' beliefs about justifiability.

We corroborate these initial findings about justifiability by administering another experiment. For Study 2, we showed subjects fictitious newspaper articles about police shootings, in which we varied shooting descriptions by hypothetical justifiability and included BLM or Trump primes. We find that the results from Study 1 hold. Across conditions, the shooting of the Justified Hypothetical Victim was regarded as much more justified.

Our results over both studies speak to how individuals, especially high SRS individuals, make use of stereotypes, in particular racist stereotypes. In Study 1, high SRS individuals were uniquely responsive to the location of the shooting, suggesting that they are more willing to extrapolate from environmental evidence than their low SRS counterparts. It may be that high SRS individuals are looking for a reason to believe the shooting by a police officer is justified. While all subjects were responsive to the individual characteristics offered in our scenarios, high SRS subjects were alone in the effect that the "evidence" offered by the location shooting had on their assessment of justifiability. Indeed, the difference between locations in our study had no effect on low SRS subjects. High SRS subjects make inferences about police shootings not only based on characteristics of the shooting victim himself, but characteristics of the victim's environment.

In Study 2, we show that the same high SRS subjects are less likely to view the shooting of a hypothetical unjustified victims as justified when they are described as meeting traditional American values. Study 2 demonstrates that what we observed from the conjoint holds in a more traditional survey experiment environment. In addition, in a variation of prior research into new racism, we find that those with high SRS view the shooting of a Unjustified Hypothetical Victim as *less justified* than those who have lower SRS scores when a BLM prime is included. The same is true when we compare conservatives to liberals and Republicans to other partisans. When BLM describes victims as meeting "traditional" American values, they may be able to allow conservatives and Republicans to see the humanity of black Americans. This lends support to our second hypothesis, which posited that there might be a relationship between how high SRS subjects perceived shootings and the extent to which victims were reported to conform to what are thought to be traditional American values.

Our studies are not without their limitations. First, our findings may have been contingent on the precise time of each study's administration. Study 1 was fielded in mid-July 2016, shortly after the high-profile shootings of Alton Sterling and Philando Castile. The tragic fact is that police killings have long been prominent in mass media and salient in the public mind. It is possible that, were police killings not as common as they are, respondents' attitudes would have been less well-developed than we observed. If, for example, no police killings had been widely reported around the time of the study, more inchoate attitudes might have resulted in less cogent responses. Yet, sadly, that is not the world we live in. Study 2 was fielded in early October 2016, when the presidential campaign was nearing its end. If we had run the study after the election of President Trump, it stands to reason that the treatments related to him might have yielded different effects.

We were also limited by our decision to frame the treatments in Study 1 as stemming from videos, without actually showing subjects the videos. As discussed above inNote 1, we did so in order to balance experimental realism with experimenter control. Similarly, in Study 2, we were limited by existing news articles and descriptions of victims, limiting our ability to separate the effects of a BLM prime from a traditional values prime. Our evidence only suggests that people are willing to set aside some concerns they may have about BLM, as they are moved by traditional value primes. Finally, while our use of a conjoint design permits us to test a large number of potential determinants, we did not test all possible factors. There may be more at work beyond how the victim, the police and the location of the shooting are described. Future research should pursue these lines of inquiry.

6.1. Appendix study 1: results and trust in police

In Study 1, because we believed that subjects' trust in police might shape their responses, we asked them a question from Gallup's battery of questions about trust in institutions. Subjects were asked: "As an institution, how much confidence do you have in the police in the United States?" and allowed answers on a five-point scale. Next, we adopt the same procedure to that we used when evaluating the relationship between Study 1 results and symbolic racism. We anticipated that those with higher levels of trust in the police will be less likely to see most killings as unjustifiable. Figure 6 displays the effects for each level on the probability that respondents will regard a shooting as justified, separating the bottom quartile of trust in police respondents from the top. Again, squares denote the benchmark level for each regression, solid points represent effects for those who score high and hollow points represent effects for those who score low. Once

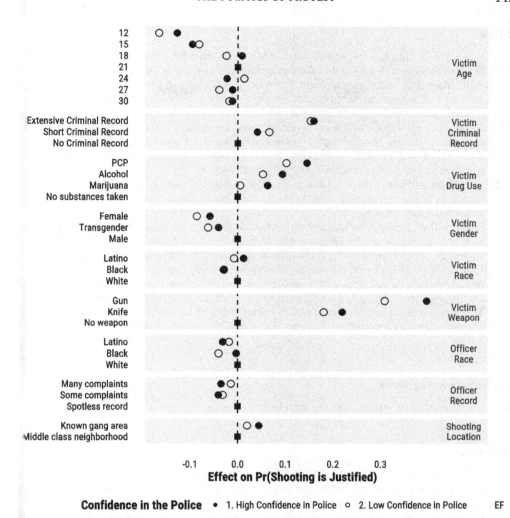

Figure 6. Subgroup conjoint experiment—effect of conjoint attributes for respondents with high confidence in the police (indicated by the solid points) and low confidence in the police (hollow points). Within each attribute, the square indicates the reference level, shared between the model types.

again, the effects for low scores tend to lag behind the effects for high scores. Subjects who reported high trust in the police have a lower evidentiary threshold for believing a shooting was justified. The difference in the effects on marijuana is especially pronounced. Respondents with low trust in the police effectively disregarded marijuana consumption. In contrast, high trust respondents were nearly 10% more likely to regard a shooting as justified if the victim had consumed marijuana. In addition, though the difference is smaller than that observed in the symbolic racism section, those who are very trusting of police take away more from the location of the shooting than those with low trust in police. Also worth noting are the effects on victim; those who trust police are more likely to view shootings as justified if the victim is Latino. One possible explanation for this is that, while subjects believe that race matters, social desirability effectively constrains their responses to a black victim. Speculatively, they may transfer their remaining racial anxiety to Latino victims.

Notes

1. Although we did not have actual videos, the aim in claiming otherwise was to increase the chance that respondents would take the hypotheticals seriously and engage with them as if they reflected an underlying incident. Otherwise, we feared that participants would generally disregard all differences we presented to them. There is always a trade-off between experimental realism and experimenter control. We tried to balance those two objectives, using descriptions of videos to enhance realism but not actually showing videos to maintain control. It remains possible that responses may have been confounded by people thinking about real-world incidents in response to our experimental treatments but that would also have been a risk had we shown fictionalized videos.
2. The reader will notice that we have made a decision not to identify those killed by the police as victims in the survey, as describing them as victims might have affected results. This was a difficult decision to make.
3. This is a novel survey item we constructed for this study. It is strongly related, in the expected direction, to scores on symbolic racism, ideology, and confidence in the police. Different responses on this perceived justifiability scale related to significant differences on these related scales. These mean differences by scale are depicted in the appendix, in Figure 1.
4. A reviewer speculated SRS and confidence in the police were actually tapping the same underlying dimension, and that their effect on perceived justifiability might be interactive. The two variables are in fact only weakly correlated (.28) and their interaction does not significantly predict perceived justifiability. A regression estimate is included in the appendix, in Table 5.

Disclosure statement

No potential conflict of interest was reported by the authors.

References

Allport, Gordon. 1954. *The Nature of Prejudice*. New York: Basic Books.
Anwar, Shamena, Patrick Bayer, and Randi. Hjalmarsson. 2014. "The Role of Age in Jury Selection and Trial Outcomes." *Journal of Law, Economics and Organization* 57 (4): 1001–1030.
Berinsky, Adam J., Gregory A. Huber, and Gabriel S. Lenz. 2012. "Evaluating Online Labor Markets for Experimental Research: Amazon.com's Mechanical Turk." *Political Analysis* 20 (3): 351–368. doi:10.1093/pan/mpr057.
Blow, Charles. 2015. "Tamir Rice and the Value of Life." *The New York Times*, January 11.
Bobo, Lawrence, and Vincent L. Hutchings. 1996. "Perceptions of Racial Group Composition." *American Sociological Review* 61: 951–972.
Bobo, Lawrence, James R. Kugel, and Ryan A. Smith. 1997. "Laissez-faire Racism: The Crystallization of a Kinder, Gentler, Antiblack Ideology." In *Racial Attitudes in the 1990s: Continuity and Change*, edited by Steven A. Tuch and Jack K. Martin. New York, NY: Russell Sage Foundation.
Bonilla-Silva, Eduardo, and Tyrone A. Forman. 2000. "I Am Not A Racist, But…." *Discourse and Society* 11 (1): 50–85.
Cadinu, Mara, Anne Maass, Alessandra Rosabianca, and Jeff Kiesner. 2005. "Why Do Women Underperform Under Stereotype Threat?: Evidence for the Role of Negative Thinking." *Psychological Science* 16 (7): 572–578.
Carr, Priyanka B., and Claude Steele. 2010. "Stereotype Threat Affects Financial Decision Making." *Psychological Science* 21 (10): 1411–1416.
Christenson, Dino P., and David M. Glick. 2013. "Crowdsourcing Panel Studies and Real-Time Experiments in MTurk." *The Political Methodologist* 20 (2): 27–32.

Correll, Joshua, Bernadette Park, Charles M. Judd, and Bernd Wittenbrink. 2002. "The Police Officer's Dilemma: Using Ethnicity to Disambiguate Potentially Threatening Individuals." *Journal of Personality and Social Psychology* 83 (6): 1314–1329.

Devine, Patricia G.. 1989. "Stereotypes and Prejudice: Their Automatic and Controlled Components." *Journal of Personality and Social Psychology* 56 (1): 5–18.

Duncan, Birt L.. 1976. "Differential Social Perception and Attribution of Intergroup Violence: Testing the Lower Limits of Stereotyping of Blacks." *Journal of Personality and Social Psychology* 34 (4): 590–598.

Eberhardt, Jennifer L., Valerie Purdie, Phillip Goff, and Paul Davies. 2004. "Seeing Black: Race, Crime, and Visual Processing." *Journal of Personality and Social Psychology* 87 (6): 876–893.

Entman, Robert, and Andrew. Rojecki. 2000. *The Black Image in the White Mind*. Chicago, IL: University of Chicago Press.

Farrington, David P.. 1986. "Age and Crime." *Crime and Justice* 7: 189–250.

Gorner, Jeremy. 2015. "PCP Found in Body of Teen Shot 16 Times by Chicago Cop". April 15.

Greenwald, Anthony G., Mark A. Oakes, and Hunter G. Hoffman. 2003. "Targets of Discrimination: Effects of Race on Responses to Weapons Holders." *Journal of Experimental Social Psychology* 39: 399–405.

Hainmueller, Jens, Daniel Hopkins, and Teppei. Yamamoto. 2014. "Causal Inference in Conjoint Analysis: Understanding Multi-Dimensional Choices via Stated Preference Experiments." *Political Analysis* 22 (1): 1–30.

Hainmueller, Jens, Daniel Hopkins, and Teppei Yamamoto. 2015. "The Hidden American Immigration Consensus: A Conjoint Analysis of Attitudes toward Immigrants." *American Journal of Political Science*59 (3): 529–548.

Henry, P. J., and David O. Sears. 2002. "The Symbolic Racism 2000 Scale." *Political Psychology* 3 (2): 253–283.

Hetey, Rebecca, and Jennifer L. Eberhardt. 2014. "Racial Disparities in Incarceration Increase Acceptance of Punitive Policies." *Psychological Science* 25 (10): 1949–1954.

Iyengar, Shanto.. 1991. *Is Anyone Responsible? How Television Frames Political Issues*. Chicago, IL: University of Chicago Press.

Kinder, Donald R., and Lynn Sanders. 1996. *Divided by Color: Racial Politics and Democratic Ideals*. Chicago, IL: University of Chicago Press.

Kinder, D. R., and D. O. Sears. 1981. "Prejudice and politics: Symbolic racism versus racial threats to the good life." *Journal of Personality and Social Psychology* 40 (3): 414–431.

McConahay, John B.. 1986. "Modern Racism, Ambivalence, and the Modern Racism Scale." In *Prejudice, Discrimination, and Racism*, edited by John F. Dovidio, and Samuel L. Gaertner. San Diego, CA: Academic Press..

Nelson, Thomas, Kira Sanbonmatsu, and Harwood K McClerking. 2007. "Playing a Different Race Card: Examining the Limits of Elite Influence on Perceptions of Racism." *Journal of Politics* 69 (2): 416–429.

O Neil, Bridjes. 2014. "STL County Police Chief Claims Struggle With Gun Lead to Fatal Shooting of Michael Brown." *St. Louis Dispatch*, August 10. http://www.stlamerican.com/news/local_news/article_86cdc228-20c9-11e4-984c-001a4bcf887a.html

Pew. 2014. "Sharp Racial Divisions in Reactions to Brown, Garner Decisions." *Pew Research Center*, Dec 8. http://www.people-press.org/2014/12/08/sharp-racial-divisions-in-reactions-to-brown-garner-decisions/.

Pew. 2016. "On Views of Race and Inequality, Blacks and Whites Are Worlds Apart." 2016. *Pew Research Center*, June 27. http://www.pewsocialtrends.org/2016/06/27/on-views-of-race-and-inequality-blacks-and-whites-are-worlds-apart/.

Porter, Ethan, and Thomas J. Wood. 2016. "Race, Interracial Families, and Political Advertising in the Obama Era: Experimental Evidence." *Political Communication* 33 (3): 481–502.

Quillian, Lincoln. 1995. "Prejudice as a Response to Perceived Group Threat." *American Sociological Review* 60 (4): 586–611.

Roller, Emma. 2014. "The Character Assassination of Michael Brown." *The Atlantic*, Aug 19. https://www.theatlantic.com/politics/archive/2014/08/the-character-assassination-of-michael-brown/455124/.

Sniderman, P. M., T. Piazza, P. E. Tetlock, and A. Kendrick. 1991. "The New Racism." *American Journal of Political Science* 35 (2): 423–447.

Steele, Claude. 2010. *Whistling Vivaldi: How Stereotypes Affect Us and What We Can Do.* New York, NY: W.W Norton and Company.

Stolberg, Sheryl, and Richard Oppel. 2015. "Suspects in Freddie Gray Case." *The New York Times*, May 9.

Stole, Bryn. 2016. "Alton Sterling's Son Says Father 'Was Good Man,' Calls For Peaceful Protests." *The Advocate*, July 13. https://www.theadvocate.com/baton_rouge/news/alton_sterling/article_d28eafa4-48f1-11e6-93d3-e333aa7efd80.html.

Stone, Jeff, Mike Sjomeling, Christian Lynch, and John Darley. 1999. "Stereotype Threat Effects on Black and White Athletic Performance." *Journal of Personality and Social Psychology* 77 (6): 1213–1227.

Tajfel, Henri. 1969. "Cognitive Aspects of Prejudice." *Journal of Social Issues* 25 (4): 79–97.

Tajfel, Henri. 1981. *Human Groups and Social Categories.* New York, NY: Cambridge University Press.

Tesler, Michael. 2012. "The Return of Old-Fashioned Racism to White Americans' Partisan Preferences in the Early Obama Era." *Journal of Politics* 75 (1): 110–123.

Weitzer, Ronald. 1999. "Citizens' Perceptions of Police Misconduct: Race and Neighborhood Context." *Justice Quarterly* 16 (4): 819–846.

Appendix

Table A1. Regression models which provide the estimates for the differences in Figure 5.

<table>
<tr><th></th><th colspan="6">Variable interacted with condition</th></tr>
<tr><th></th><th>Education</th><th>Ideology</th><th>Partisanship</th><th>Conf. Police</th><th>Symb.Racism</th><th>No Interactions</th></tr>
<tr><td>High Deserving Victim, No Prime</td><td>−.32 (.44)</td><td>−.04 (.2)</td><td>−.24 (.21)</td><td>.59 (.58)</td><td>−.16 (.15)</td><td>−.13 (.15)</td></tr>
<tr><td>High Deserving Victim, Trump Prime</td><td>.52 (.47)</td><td>.05 (.2)</td><td>−.04 (.21)</td><td>−.54 (.57)</td><td>0 (.15)</td><td>−.02 (.14)</td></tr>
<tr><td>Low Deserving Victim, BLM Prime</td><td>−3.35*** (.49)</td><td>−2.6*** (.21)</td><td>−2.75*** (.22)</td><td>−2.8*** (.61)</td><td>−2.67*** (.15)</td><td>−2.69*** (.15)</td></tr>
<tr><td>Low Deserving Victim, No Prime</td><td>−2.48*** (.43)</td><td>−2.57*** (.21)</td><td>−2.58*** (.22)</td><td>−1.55*** (.57)</td><td>−2.58*** (.15)</td><td>−2.56*** (.15)</td></tr>
<tr><td>Low Deserving Victim, Trump Prime</td><td>−2.92*** (.41)</td><td>−2.41*** (.2)</td><td>−2.66*** (.22)</td><td>−2.53*** (.58)</td><td>−2.39*** (.15)</td><td>−2.39*** (.15)</td></tr>
<tr><td>Some College</td><td>−.07 (.35)</td><td></td><td></td><td></td><td></td><td>−.14 (.14)</td></tr>
<tr><td>BA +</td><td>−.2 (.32)</td><td></td><td></td><td></td><td></td><td>−.16 (.14)</td></tr>
<tr><td>High Deserving Victim, No Prime x Some College</td><td>.2 (.53)</td><td></td><td></td><td></td><td></td><td></td></tr>
<tr><td>High Deserving Victim, Trump Prime x Some College</td><td>−.64 (.56)</td><td></td><td></td><td></td><td></td><td></td></tr>
<tr><td>Low Deserving Victim, BLM Prime x Some College</td><td>.8 (.57)</td><td></td><td></td><td></td><td></td><td></td></tr>
<tr><td>Low Deserving VictimNo Prime x Some College</td><td>.09 (.51)</td><td></td><td></td><td></td><td></td><td></td></tr>
<tr><td>Low Deserving Victim, Trump Prime x Some College</td><td>.42 (.49)</td><td></td><td></td><td></td><td></td><td></td></tr>
<tr><td>High Deserving Victim, No Prime x BA +</td><td>.21 (.49)</td><td></td><td></td><td></td><td></td><td></td></tr>
<tr><td>High Deserving Victim, Trump Prime x BA +</td><td>−.55 (.52)</td><td></td><td></td><td></td><td></td><td></td></tr>
<tr><td>Low Deserving Victim, BLM Prime x BA +</td><td>.78 (.54)</td><td></td><td></td><td></td><td></td><td></td></tr>
<tr><td>Low Deserving Victim, No Prime x BA +</td><td>−.01 (.48)</td><td></td><td></td><td></td><td></td><td></td></tr>
<tr><td>Low Deserving Victim, Trump Prime x BA +</td><td>.82 (.47)</td><td></td><td></td><td></td><td></td><td></td></tr>
<tr><td>Moderate</td><td></td><td>.31 (.31)</td><td></td><td></td><td></td><td>.31* (.13)</td></tr>
<tr><td>Conservative</td><td></td><td>1*** (.27)</td><td></td><td></td><td></td><td>.44* (.2)</td></tr>
<tr><td>High Deserving Victim, No Prime x Moderate</td><td></td><td>−.11 (.41)</td><td></td><td></td><td></td><td></td></tr>
<tr><td>High Deserving Victim, Trump Prime x Moderate</td><td></td><td>−.04 (.43)</td><td></td><td></td><td></td><td></td></tr>
<tr><td>Low Deserving Victim, BLM Prime x Moderate</td><td></td><td>.34 (.43)</td><td></td><td></td><td></td><td></td></tr>
<tr><td>Low Deserving Victim, No Prime x Moderate</td><td></td><td>.57 (.43)</td><td></td><td></td><td></td><td></td></tr>
<tr><td>Low Deserving Victim, Trump Prime x Moderate</td><td></td><td>.47 (.45)</td><td></td><td></td><td></td><td></td></tr>
<tr><td>High Deserving Victim, No Prime x Conservative</td><td></td><td>−.3 (.4)</td><td></td><td></td><td></td><td></td></tr>
<tr><td>High Deserving Victim, Trump Prime x Conservative</td><td></td><td>−.33 (.38)</td><td></td><td></td><td></td><td></td></tr>
<tr><td>Low Deserving Victim, BLM Prime x Conservative</td><td></td><td>−.6 (.39)</td><td></td><td></td><td></td><td></td></tr>
<tr><td>Low Deserving Victim, No Prime x Conservative</td><td></td><td>−.3 (.36)</td><td></td><td></td><td></td><td></td></tr>
<tr><td>Low Deserving Victim, Trump Prime x Conservative</td><td></td><td>−.24 (.37)</td><td></td><td></td><td></td><td></td></tr>
<tr><td>Independent</td><td></td><td></td><td>−.17 (.27)</td><td></td><td></td><td>−.15 (.13)</td></tr>
<tr><td>Republican</td><td></td><td></td><td>.92** (.29)</td><td></td><td></td><td>−.2 (.2)</td></tr>
<tr><td>High Deserving Victim, No Prime x Independent</td><td></td><td></td><td>.66 (.38)</td><td></td><td></td><td></td></tr>
<tr><td>High Deserving Victim, Trump Prime x Independent</td><td></td><td></td><td>.27 (.39)</td><td></td><td></td><td></td></tr>
</table>

(Continued)

Table A1. Continued.

	\multicolumn{6}{c	}{Variable interacted with condition}	
	Education	Ideology	Partisanship	Conf. Police	Symb.Racism	No Interactions
Low Deserving Victim, BLM Prime x Independent			.72 (.39)			
Low Deserving VictimNo Prime x Independent			.63 (.38)			
Low Desert, Trump Prime x Independent			.99* (.39)			
High Deserving Victim, No Prime x Republican			−.4 (.41)			
High Deserving Victim, Trump Prime x Republican			−.36 (.39)			
Low Desert, BLM Prime x Republican			−.45 (.41)			
Low Desert, No Prime x Republican			−.38 (.39)			
Low Desert, Trump Prime x Republican			−.04 (.39)			
Confidence in Police				.34** (.13)		.14** (.05)
High Deserving Victim, No Prime x Confidence in Police				−.22 (.18)		
High Deserving Victim, Trump Prime x Confidence in Police				.17 (.17)		
Low Desert, BLM Prime x Confidence in Police				.05 (.18)		
Low Desert, No Prime x Confidence in Police				−.28 (.17)		
Low Desert, Trump Prime x Confidence in Police				.06 (.17)		
Symbolic Racism					.63*** (.11)	.45*** (.05)
High Deserving Victim, No Prime x Symbolic Racism					−.06 (.16)	
High Deserving Victim, Trump Prime x Symbolic Racism					−.09 (.15)	
Low Desert, BLM Prime x Symbolic Racism					−.35* (.16)	
Low Desert, No Prime x Symbolic Racism					−.08 (.15)	
Low Desert, Trump Prime x Symbolic Racism					−.02 (.14)	
r.squared	.49	.52	.52	.52	.58	.58
adj.r.squared	.48	.51	.51	.51	.58	.58
statistic	4.49	45.59	44.61	7.21	9.31	78.47
BIC	2497.45	2453.73	2461.97	2423.8	2323.18	2318.99

Table A2. Regression estimates for study two testing for the possibility that confidence in police and the symbolic racism scale have an interactive effect on perceived justifiability of a shooting. for simplicity, the intercept is omitted.

High justifiability victim, no prime	−.12 (.15)
High justifiability victim, Trump prime	.01 (.14)
Low justifiability victim, BLM prime	−2.67*** (.15)
Low justifiability victim, no prime	−2.55*** (.14)
Low justifiability victim, Trump prime	−2.37*** (.14)
Symbolic racism scale	2.16*** (.36)
Confidence in police	.99*** (.36)
SRS × Conf. in police	−.71 (.61)
Observations	725
R^2	.59
Adjusted R^2	.58

Note: *$p<0.1$; **$p<0.05$; ***$p<0.01$

Table A3. Racial differences in study 2.

	Perceived justifiability of shooting
Condition: High justifiability, no prime	.15 (.36)
Condition: High justifiability, Trump prime	−.48 (.31)
Condition: Low justifiability, BLM prime	−2.76*** (.34)
Condition: Low justifiability, no prime	−2.38*** (.31)
Condition: Low justifiability, Trump prime	−2.19*** (.32)
Symbolic Racism Scale (SRS)	.20 (.24)
Race: White	.29 (.24)
Condition: High justifiability, no prime * SRS	.26 (.44)
Condition: High justifiability, Trump prime * SRS	.41 (.30)
Condition: Low justifiability, BLM prime * SRS	−.14 (.38)
Condition: Low justifiability, no prime * SRS	.13 (.37)
Condition: Low justifiability, Trump prime * SRS	.53 (.32)
Condition: High justifiability, no prime * White	−.40 (.39)
Condition: High justifiability, Trump prime * White	.59 (.41)
Condition: Low justifiability, BLM prime * White	.08 (.38)
Condition: Low justifiability, no prime * White	−.26 (.35)
Condition: Low justifiability, Trump prime * White	−.25 (.36)
SRS * White	.54** (.27)
Condition: High justifiability, no prime * White * SRS	−.41 (.47)
Condition: High justifiability, Trump prime * White * SRS	−.65 (.55)
Condition: Low justifiability, BLM prime * White * SRS	−.31 (.42)
Condition: Low justifiability, no prime * White * SRS	−.29 (.40)
Condition: Low justifiability, Trump prime * SRS	−.70 (.48)
Observations	724
R^2	.59
Adjusted R^2	.58
Residual std. error	1.13 (df = 700)
F-statistic	44.49*** (df = 23; 700)

Note: *$p < 0.1$; **$p < 0.05$; ***$p < 0.01$.

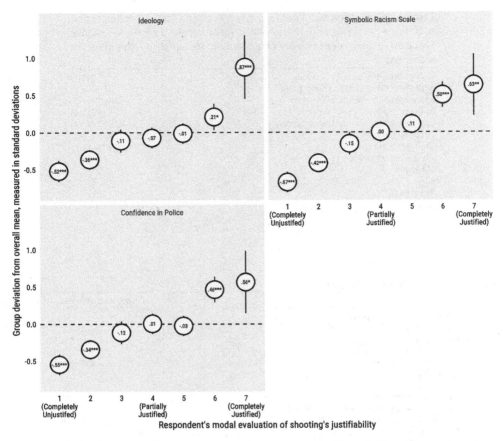

Figure A1. Relationship between our dependent variable (perceived justifiability of some police shooting) and three related attitudinal scales. The *x*-axis categorizes respondents by their *modal* evaluation of each described shooting. The *y*-axis shows that group of respondents' deviation from some related scale – specifically, ideology, symbolic racism, and confidence in the police. Each related variable is rescaled to be mean centered and measured by standard deviations.

Black Americans and the "crime narrative": comments on the use of news frames and their impacts on public opinion formation

Jenn M. Jackson

ABSTRACT
News framing choices remain critical components in the formation of political attitudes and public opinion. Early findings, which indicated that episodic framing of national issues like poverty and unemployment informed public opinion about minority group members, asserted that these framing choices often resulted in the attribution of societal ills to individuals rather than society at-large. Moving this analytical framework into the twenty-first century, I engage with literature on racial messaging to show that shifting social norms surrounding implicit versus explicit racism have transformed the ways that news frames function in mass media. As such, this essay examines the canonical theory of news frames as falling along a *thematic-episodic* continuum. Fundamentally, I argue that implicit and explicit racial messaging in news media coverage of crime could change the way viewers form opinions of Black Americans and criminality. Thus, it is critical to revisit longstanding theories of news frames to accommodate the present political moment.

Introduction

Television news stories remain critical vehicles for the transmission of political messages. In his seminal work *Is Anyone Responsible?* Shanto Iyengar examined the effects of television news frames on public opinion formation in the late-twentieth century – a period that he called the "age of the television" (1991). Since his work was published, television news consumption has decreased from roughly 52 million viewers in 1980 to 26 million viewers in 2014 (Pew Research Center 2014).[1] Increasing media choice – in the form of cable and Internet news – has diversified the news environment while preserving the general messages, angles, and types of stories that are covered. According to the Pew Research Center, the consumption gap between traditional television news and digital sources is narrowing, dropping from a 19-percentage point difference in August 2016 to only a 7-percentage point difference in August 2017, with television news narrowly remaining the leading source of viewership (Bialik and Matsa 2017). In response to this new demand, most mass media companies and local newspapers have created "cross-media sources" which give traditional news outlets a path into the 24-hour news cycle (Iyengar 2011, 60). Thus, traditional news sources are adapting to the changing media landscape rather than becoming obsolete. As consumers' choices have changed, news messaging and framing choices have remained relatively constant.

While investigating the influence of television news on public opinion formation between 1981 and 1986,[2] Iyengar found that framing of newsworthy topics as episodic – focusing on "specific events or particular cases" – versus thematic – placing "political issues and events in some general context" – greatly affects how viewers attribute responsibility for social issues (Iyengar 1991, 2). Media framing choices have a critical impact on the ways that stories about racial minorities shape public opinion on issues of immigration, race, and healthcare in the U.S., among other issues (Brader, Valentino, and Suhay 2008; Spence 2010; Abrajano and Hajnal 2015). These contemporary changes are of primary salience as highly publicized instances of police brutality against Black Americans have become mostly virtual phenomena (Freelon, McIlwain, and Clark 2018). As such, this essay seeks not only to chronologically update Iyengar's work but also to place it in a context of increasingly dynamic racial attitudes and public opinion formation.

In this essay, I review the extant literature on news frames, racial messaging, and crime narratives. I argue that the canonical *thematic-episodic* framing theory is insufficient in fully capturing the contemporary impacts of news frames on political attitudes concerning racial minorities, specifically Black Americans. Fundamentally, what remains unanswered by this framework is the tension between the episodic frame and the pervasiveness of implicit and explicit racial messaging in news production.[3] Building upon existing framing literature (e.g., Gross 2008; Spence 2010; Aarøe 2011), I provide a typology of implicit-explicit media framing which provides greater depth and contextualization for assessing the impacts of framing choices in influencing political attitudes toward marginalized groups. As a starting point, I locate this work within a broader review of existing literature concerning the effects of framing on public opinion of violent crime and Black Americans. My objective is to provide a framework for future scholarly work on the role of frames in today's racially and technologically diverse environment.

A brief discussion of news frames and political context

The term "frame" is still in its nascence in the social sciences. Only since the 1980s and 90s have scholars used the term to describe the ways that issues are selected, articulated, relayed, and packaged for mass consumption (Gamson and Modigliani 1987; Gamson and Modigliani 1989; Iyengar 1991; Gamson 1992; Druckman 2001; Gross 2008). This literature theorizes that it is not just the content of news messages that matters but also the way these messages are transmitted to consumers. Thus, there is no doubt that Shanto Iyengar's work on racial attitudes and responsibility attribution remains a key contribution to the public opinion and political communication literature. He noted, "television's unswerving focus on specific episodes, individual perpetrators, victims, or other actors at the expense of more general, thematic information inhibits the attribution of political responsibility to societal factors and to the actions of politicians such as the president" (Iyengar 1991, 5). Further, Iyengar describes the episodic frame as taking

[t]he form of a case study or event-oriented report and depicts public issues in terms of concrete instances (for example, the plight of a homeless person or a teenage drug user, the bombing of an airliner, or an attempted murder). The thematic frame, by contrast, places public issues in some more general or abstract context and takes the form of a "takeout," or "backgrounder," report directed at general outcomes or conditions. (Iyengar 1991, 14)

For example, stories of Black poverty were framed to shift the responsibility for these economic issues to individuals and away from societal structures like policy and political leaders (Iyengar 1991, 61; Iyengar and Kinder 2010). These findings echo a vast body of literature which suggests that racialized messages often negatively shape public opinion about Black Americans (Schuman et al. 1985; Kinder and Sanders 1996; Sears, Sidanius, and Bobo 2000). However, this framework paints an incomplete picture, especially considering the implications of these framing choices in the current socio-political landscape.

A question which emerges from the literature is, simply: *What is the role of news frames in today's multifaceted media environment?* To this end, recent scholarship on the role of news frames in shaping political beliefs and attitudes has made valuable theoretical interventions concerning the increasingly competitive media environment. In particular, Dennis Chong and James N. Druckman provide a compelling analysis of framing effects[4] which finds that, in a competitive framing environment where multiple frames exist, the structure and persuasiveness of news frames predict whether or not they will be effective in shaping ideas about the issues and topics framed (2007). Rather than the perceived strength of the frame, Chong and Druckman instead focus on the effects. This theoretical intervention is critical in understanding the relationship between emotion and framing choices given changes in the forms of news coverage and technological access that enable news consumers to receive and share stories in real-time. Specifically, in recent years, police and citizen involved shootings of Black Americans like Rekia Boyd, Eric Garner, Aiyana Stanley-Jones, Trayvon Martin, and Tamir Rice, present highly publicized instances where the "crime narrative," news frames, and individual viewers' assessments of responsibility collide. Questions regarding the legitimacy of police force trigger racially coded primers already existing in the minds of news consumers. Moreover, these violent cases – which often involve police authorities, are the types of news stories for which framing choices may affect how viewers form opinions of individual responsibility, racial resentment, and social policy concerning Black Americans. This has been increasingly apparent with the growing media interest in the Black Lives Matter Movement, which gained national attention after Michael Brown was killed by then-Officer Darren Wilson on August 9 2014 (Taylor 2014). These news stories and framing choices occur within an increasingly racially tense environment where media consumers often rely on mobile and digital sources to interpret events (Freelon, McIlwain, and Clark 2018). Simultaneously, this political moment is marked by growing political distance between racial groups and evidence of the pervasive influence of race on voting and political participation (Tesler 2016). Given this political context, existing theories on the role of news frames in shaping public opinion, specifically concerning Black Americans, require another look.

Placing the episodic frame in dialogue with racial messaging theory

A great deal of literature has examined the shifts in the types of racial messaging and social norms surrounding race since the 1990s (Bonilla-Silva and Forman 2000; Mendelberg

2001; Valentino, Hutchings, and White 2002; Prior 2007; Banks 2014; Woodly 2015; Tesler 2016). These works situate changes in the formation of political beliefs within a dynamic societal setting with many competing factors, namely race. Of particular interest is Tali Mendelberg's findings which suggest that overtly racist sentiments, norms, and messages expressed in the public sphere were supplanted by racially coded language in accordance with new social norms of equality between white and Black Americans (2001). However, this turn away from explicitly racist sentiments in public did not signify the eradication of racist beliefs writ large. Rather, the changing expectations of public decorum necessitated ancillary changes in the ways that racial messages were conveyed. Mendelberg claims that shifts in public social customs around race have created two distinct norms: (1) the norm of racial inequality and (2) the norm of equality (2001). The former, existing through the late nineteenth and early twentieth centuries, was characterized by "explicitly racial appeals" (Mendelberg 2001, 63). The latter emerged when,

> [f]irst, public commitment to basic racial equality reached immense proportions starting in the late 1960s. Second, notwithstanding this commitment, racial resentment continues to thrive among a significant portion of the white public. Third, in response to the first two factors, implicit appeals to racial stereotypes, fears, and resentments have been, since 1968, an important tool for mobilizing support from white voters. (Mendelberg 2001, 111)

These social norms were not limited to private citizens, but also include news outlets who subscribe to socially acceptable forms of racial messaging (Mendelberg 2001). What is vital to take from Mendelberg's contribution, which is also absent from Iyengar's, is that the implicit racial frame operates on racial predispositions differently than the explicit racial frame.

Mendelberg refers to the post-civil rights moment as the "norm of equality" – a period underscored by a social norm of rebuking explicit racial appeals. However, the episodic frame cannot properly account for explicit or implicit racial priming. This is mainly because of its binary relationship as the antithesis to the more objective news coverage of the thematic frame. Further, the episodic frame alone does not account for measuring how implicit messages shape public opinions primarily because implicit messages are coded to invoke responses only from individuals who are primed to receive and act upon them (Albertson 2015). Likewise, Deva R. Woodly found that political messages and social actions were more likely to gain acceptance and traction if they utilized framing language to which target groups were already primed (2015). Thus, the *implicit-explicit* categorization, or the "IE model," suggests that existing racial cues temper public dialogue and corral interracial interactions so as to avoid the consequences of seeming expressly racist (Mendelberg 2001). While thematic-episodic news framing and implicit-explicit racial messaging are not typically in direct conversation with one another, a key objective of this essay is to re-situate these paradigms given the contemporary social world.

Updates to the IE model suggest that the "norm of equality" and its dampening effect on the expression of overtly racial opinions has changed in recent years. For example, Gregory A. Huber and John S. Lapinski found that the use of implicit racial messaging was effective for more educated social groups. They say, "Among less-educated individuals, either implicit or explicit appeals appear somewhat effective in activating racial predispositions in opinion formation on non-race-related policy … Moreover, more-educated individuals do react more negatively to explicit appeals than implicit ones" (2006, 438). These findings are imperative since digital media consumers are increasingly older, non-white, and less educated (Bialik and Matsa 2017). Thus, while political candidates may not be incentivized to use implicit messages over explicit messages to appeal to mass publics, there is still much to be learned regarding how framing choices by news organizations inevitably shape public opinion, especially where race is concerned.

To this end, Valentino, Neuner, and Vandenbroek find that the increasing racial tensions of this political moment have reduced the impact of explicit racial appeals. They note, "Many whites now view themselves as an embattled and even disadvantaged group, and this has led to both strong in-group identity and a greater tolerance for expressions of hostility toward out-groups" (2017, 768). The increased tolerance for explicitly racial messages, as outlined by Valentino, Neuner, and Vandenbroek, suggests that news outlets may be incentivized to produce more episodic news coverage using overtly racialized messages to align with consumer media tastes. James N. Druckman and Michael Parkin refer to this process as media "slant," a framing choice which can work to subconsciously influence voters' preferences (2005). This suggests that the IE model, while it may be less effective in understanding racial resentment and political attitudes in the aggregate, can be particularly helpful in assessing the increasing distance between deracialized, objective news frames (thematic), covertly racialized, subjective news frames (implicit episodic), and overtly racialized, subjective news frames (explicit episodic). Thus, I suggest a move beyond the thematic-episodic continuum, towards an analysis of news framing that captures implicit and explicit racial cues as well.[5]

A typology of the episodic frame

While each possible combination of the thematic-episodic and IE Model is shown in the cross-tabular relationship chart illustrated in Figure 1, this project is primarily concerned with the attitudinal effects associated with the episodic frame. This theoretical emphasis

	Implicit	Explicit
Thematic	Structural explanations Coded through non-overt racial language	Structural explanations Coded through overtly racial language
Episodic	Individual explanations Coded through non-overt racial language	Individual explanations Coded through overtly racial language

Figure 1. Typology of implicit-explicit media framing.

stems from key findings that the episodic frame more consistently and effectively triggers intense emotional reactions (Gross 2008; Aarøe 2011), and personal responsibility attribution (Iyengar 1991; Spence 2010). The episodic frame is also most likely to be used immediately following a highly publicized social event when viewers are first gathering information about the newsworthy phenomenon (Dimitrova 2006).

Thus, the fundamental structure of the thematic frame (e.g., focusing on structural and societal explanations for political phenomena) does not lend itself to the bifurcation of IE Model. Thematic framing focuses on structural explanations of phenomena even when those stories center the experiences of racial minorities. Moreover, a potential thematic-explicit frame would employ overtly racial messaging, which focuses on individuals and communities, making it identical to the episodic frame. For example, thematically framed news stories may mention the racial demographics of actors involved but do not contextualize their racial characteristics as correlative with the social interactions at the heart of the news story (Jackson, n.d.). Thus, the mere mention of race in a thematically framed news story does not preclude a story from remaining objective and non-episodic.

Crime narratives and public opinion formation

While there are a great many ways to measure racial predispositions and their resulting impacts on political attitudes, the intersections of race and criminality present an especially salient site for this investigation. When compared to non-blacks, scholars have found that Black Americans have been mischaracterized as particularly violent in both mass media and public opinion (Stark 1993; Gilens 1996; Peffley, Hurwitz, and Sniderman 1997; Entman and Rojecki 2000; Dixon and Maddox 2005). As such, this essay engages directly with the "myth of black violence" and its influence on news coverage of black assailants and victims of violent crime (Davis 1981; Stark 1993; Hill Collins 2000; Hutchings 2015; Shelby 2016). In Iyengar's research, the black crime narrative reliably triggered individualistic attributions of responsibility whereas the white crime narrative triggered societal attribution (1991). He says that even "modest amounts of exposure" to news about crime "proved sufficient to induce significant shifts in viewers' attributions" (1991, 45). These contradictions in attribution of responsibility are a result of the pre-dispositional effects of racial social norms. Importantly, they have a disproportionately negative association of criminal behaviors with the category of "blackness" (Mendelberg 2001; Shelby 2005). Thus, the effects of implicit and explicit episodic framing contribute to an ongoing narrative of black violence at the individual level and shape public opinion towards Black Americans in general.

This point is buttressed by public opinion literature linking news coverage to attitudes toward Black Americans and social policy. On the issues of poverty and welfare, Martin Gilens found that news media (both television and print) portrayed poor Americans as more black than real figures suggested (1999). These choices, he found, also shaped Americans' views about welfare policy because, when race is introduced, Americans are more likely to make negative associations with black welfare recipients than their white counterparts (1996). In this way, racial animus operates as a latent variable triggering personal opposition to social policy. News frames are central to this process. Some scholars have argued that these influences happen without prior knowledge or personal intervention by those who consume racial-primed messages. For example, Mark Peffley, Jon Hurwitz and Paul Sniderman speculate that these negative associations, which they also refer to as "stereotypes," might actually be the result of unconscious bias. They say, "under most circumstances, such individuals are likely to avoid prejudice and even actively reject stigmatizing responses" (1997, 54). Essentially, they find that political actors who are predisposed to negative racial attitudes can be interrupted if exposed to discordant messaging, thus nullifying the predisposition effects. Conversely, Bethany Albertson suggests that, while predispositions are important, racially coded messages work on their receivers (e.g., viewers) precisely because they target those individuals who are primed to respond positively to the message (2015).[6] Understood in this way, the same message might seem explicit to some individuals and implicit to others.

Historical narratives of Black criminality as news media cues

Underlying this analysis is the primacy of perceptions of black criminality in shaping public opinion. In 1965, Daniel Moynihan suggested that black families were inherently dysfunctional and out of alignment with acceptable familial social norms. He termed this process the "culture of poverty." Nearly a half century later, William Julius Wilson (2012) suggested that poorer blacks deviate from centrally accepted racial and gender norms in American society, creating a "ghetto underclass." However, these efforts to identify Black Americans as inherently deviant do not comport with U.S. crimes statistics. Murder, homicide, rape, robbery, and aggravated assault are each considered violent crimes.[7] According to the FBI, the homicide rates between whites and blacks were not materially different when race was known, at 44% for the former and 54% for the latter in 2013 (Stark 1993; Federal Bureau of Investigation 2014a). Despite these statistics, a narrative of inherent black criminality continues to be reproduced in mass media, thereby influencing attribution of violence to individual black actors rather than societal conditions (Stark 1993; Entman and Rojecki 2000; Oliver 2003; Shelby 2005). These scholars echo Iyengar's findings that "[m]ore than 60 percent of all causal attributions were directed at individuals when the news reported on black violent crime" (1991, 43). Therefore, a key component of this research is unearthing the ways that crime messaging involving Black Americans works to reproduce and reinforce personal attribution assessments and negative racial attitudes.

Many scholars have made connections between news coverage of crime and public opinion on race in America. Gilliam and Iyengar found that "exposure to local news coverage of crime conditions attitudes toward crime and race ... the racial element of the crime script (as opposed to the violence element) has the most demonstrable impact" (2000, 571) in increasing support for punitive crime policies. Consequently, it is not the news coverage of crime alone but the qualifying component of racial affiliation that influences public opinion. Similarly, Entman and Rojecki have argued that news

> presents a face of black disruption, of criminal victimizing and victimization that compares unfavorably with whites. Such depictions may increase Whites' fear of entering Black neighborhoods, as it reduces their sympathy for Blacks – who are in fact far more afflicted by violence and crime than most Whites. (2000, 209)

These sentiments of racial animus toward Black Americans, which are pre-existing conditions to news media exposure, make the work of studying race, news media, and crime all the more critical.

Discussion: an agenda for future research

Scholars who are committed to studying the intersections of news media, race, and crime will find this essay heartening. It provides a new perspective of news frames that accounts for the complex socio-political processes that order daily life. Simultaneously, it posits the present research on racial messaging as existing in conversation with the canonical *thematic-episodic* news framework. Yet, while this essay provides theoretical depth in field of political communication, there remains a great deal of future scholarship that can and should build upon this analysis.

There are many research questions which emerge from this combined approach. First, if news media coverage of the crime narrative frames Black Americans as inherently violent, how does this framing influence public opinion towards Black Americans in general? Second, if news outlets' framing of Black Americans involved in violent crime affects whites' propensity to understand the complexities of violent crime in the U.S., how do white Americans who consume this media view government intervention programs focused on social welfare issues, gun control, and drug mediation? And, third, to what degree can the effects of news media framing be parsed out from the feedback effects of other racial messaging? These questions are imperative in developing future research on the role of news frames in public opinion about Black Americans and crime.

Figure 2 outlines several possible research agendas stemming from this theoretical intervention. The theoretical focus outlined seeks to examine how implicit or explicit episodic frames may have varying impacts on support for race-related issues. By analyzing frequency-based groupings of episodic stories, we can better understand how to clearly delineate stories using implicit and explicit racial messaging from one another. A final mode of research might take up the experimental approach. Using this method, researchers could test message receptivity based on the types of outlets delivering the stories.

Although there remain a great many questions regarding the role of news media frames in the shaping of public opinions on racial matters, it is clear that racial predispositions, news media, and societal realities like criminality remain prescient concerns for social scientists of all disciplines. By adapting the canonical thematic-episodic framing theory

Theorization	Does the use of implicit or explicit episodic frames in race-related news stories affect support for social protest (e.g. Black Lives Matter), police interventions, or political candidates?
Quantification	Of the episodically framed stories presented by news outlets, what proportion rely on implicit or explicit racial messaging?
Experimentation	How is receptivity to episodic-implicit, episodic-explicit, and thematic-implicit framing moderated by the reputation of the news outlet broadcasting the story?

Figure 2. Potential future research questions.

to accommodate today's media landscape, this work provides a new pathway for researchers interested in the intersections of race, political communications, and public opinion.

Notes

1. However, the decrease in television news consumption does not mean that viewers no longer consume news or are less influenced by political messages the news provides (Prior 2007).
2. This was the content analysis portion of Shanto Iyengar's work. The field experiments were performed between June 1985 and September 1987.
3. See Shanto Iyengar (1991, Appendix A, 145). Coding of the news content is described in percentages but there is no investigation of how the varying percentages change the outcomes of the episodic news frame on viewer opinions and attitudes.
4. See James N. Druckman's discussion of the role of "frames of communication" in influencing "frames in thought," the former being a discursive process of selection and focus and the latter being a process of cognition. The intersection of these processes is what Druckman refers to as "framing effects" (2001, 227–228).
5. My primary intervention is on the episodic frame because Iyengar notes that the episodic frame is the most prevalent news frame leveraged by news sources. To add, it carries the greatest consequences for "blaming the victim" (1991, 46).
6. See also Tali Mendelberg's experiment (*The Race Card*, Chapter 8). She specifically calls out "highly resentful people" who face issues when relying on their racial predispositions to make political decisions. The context of implicit and explicit messages then carries great meaning when recipients of the messages have varying levels of resentment.
7. These terms were utilized by the Federal Bureau of Investigation. Retrieved from http://www.fbi.gov/about-us/cjis/ucr/crime-in-the-u.s/2013/crime-in-the-u.s.-2013/violent-crime/violent-crime-topic-page/violentcrimemain_final on March 8 2015.

Acknowledgements

I would like to thank Cathy J. Cohen, Michael C. Dawson, John Brehm, Linda Zerilli, Justin Grimmer, Alysia Mann Carey, Marcus Board, and the editors and anonymous reviewers of *Politics, Groups, and Identities* for their vital insights and feedback on various iterations of this article. I would also like to thank the Center for the Study of Race, Politics, and Culture, the Center for the Study of Gender and Sexuality, and the Department of Political Science at the University of Chicago for their continued support of this research.

Disclosure statement

No potential conflict of interest was reported by the author.

ORCID

Jenn M. Jackson http://orcid.org/0000-0002-0049-515X

References

Aarøe, Lene. 2011. "Investigating Frame Strength: The Case of Episodic and Thematic Frames." *Political Communication* 28 (2): 207–226.
Abrajano, Marisa, and Zoltan L. Hajnal. 2015. *White Backlash: Immigration, Race, and American Politics*. Princeton, NJ: Princeton University Press.

Albertson, Bethany. 2015. "Dog-Whistle Politics: Multivocal Communication and Religious Appeals." *Political Behavior* 37: 3–26.

Banks, Antoine. 2014. *Anger and Racial Politics: The Emotional Foundation of Racial Attitudes in America*. New York: Cambridge University Press.

Bialik, Kristin, and Katerina Eva Matsa. 2017. "Key Trends in Social and Digital News Media." Pew Research Center, October 4. http://www.pewresearch.org/fact-tank/2017/10/04/key-trends-in-social-and-digital-news-media/.

Bonilla-Silva, Eduardo, and Tyrone A. Forman. 2000. "I am Not a Racist But." *Discourse Society* 11 (1): 50–85.

Brader, Ted, Nicholas A. Valentino, and Elizabeth Suhay. 2008. "What Triggers Public Opposition to Immigration? Anxiety, Group Cues, and Immigration Threat." *American Journal of Political Science* 52 (4): 959–978.

Chong, Dennis, and James N. Druckman. 2007. "A Theory of Framing and Opinion Formation in Competitive Elite Environments." *Journal of Communication* 57 (1): 99–118.

Davis, Angela Y. 1981. *Women, Race, & Class*. New York: Random House.

Dimitrova, Daniela V. 2006. "Episodic Frames Dominate Early Coverage of Iraq War in the NYTimes. com." *Newspaper Research Journal* 27 (4): 79–83.

Dixon, Travis L., and Keith B Maddox. 2005. "Skin Tone, Crime News, and Social Reality Judgments: Priming the Stereotype of the Dark and Dangerous Black Criminal." *Journal of Applied Social Psychology* 35 (8): 1555–1570.

Druckman, James N. 2001. "The Implications of Framing Effects for Citizen Competence." *Political Behavior* 23 (3): 225–256.

Druckman, James N., and Michael Parkin. 2005. "The Impact of Media Bias: How Editorial Slant Affects Voters." *Journal of Politics* 67 (4): 1030–1049.

Entman, Robert M., and Andrew Rojecki. 2000. *The Black Image in the White Mind*. Chicago, IL: Chicago University Press.

Federal Bureau of Investigation. 2014a. "Expanded Homicide Data Table 3: Murder Offenders, 2013." Uniform Crime Report, Crime in the United States, 2013. Accessed March 8, 2015. https://www.fbi.gov/about-us/cjis/ucr/crime-in-the-u.s/2013/crime-in-the-u.s.-2013/offenses-known-to-law-enforcement/expanded-homicide/expanded_homicide_data_table_3_murder_offenders_by_age_sex_and_race_2013.xls.xls.

Freelon, Deen, Charlton McIlwain, and Meredith Clark. 2018. "Quantifying the Power and Consequences of Social Media Protest." *New Media & Society* 20 (3): 990–1011.

Gamson, William A. 1992. *Talking Politics*. New York: Cambridge University.

Gamson, William A., and Andre Modigliani. 1987. "The Changing Culture of Affirmative Action." In *Research in Political Sociology*, edited by Richard D. Braungart, Vol. 3, 137–177. Greenwich, CT: JAI.

Gamson, William A., and Andre Modigliani. 1989. "Media Discourse and Public Opinion on Nuclear Power: A Constructionist Approach." *American Journal of Sociology* 95 (1): 1–37.

Gilens, Martin. 1996, Winter. "Race and Poverty in America: Public Misperceptions and the American News Media." *The Public Opinion Quarterly* 60 (4): 515–541.

Gilens, Martin. 1999. *Why Americans Hate Welfare: Race, Media, and the Politics of Antipoverty Policy*. Chicago, IL: Chicago University Press.

Gilliam, D. Franklin, Jr., and Shanto Iyengar. 2000. "Prime Suspects: The Influence of Local Television News on the Viewing Public." *American Journal of Political Science* 44 (3): 560–573.

Gross, Kimberly. 2008. "Framing Persuasive Appeals: Episodic and Thematic Framing, Emotional Response, and Policy Opinion." *Political Psychology* 29 (2): 169–192.

Hill Collins, Patricia. 2000. *Black Feminist Thought: Knowledge, Consciousness, and the Politics of Empowerment*. New York: Routledge.

Huber, Gregory A., and John S. Lapinski. 2006. "The 'Race Card' Revisited: Assessing Racial Priming in Policy Contests." *American Journal of Political Science* 50 (2): 421–440.

Hutchings, Vincent. 2015. "Race, Punishment, and Public Opinion." *Perspectives on Politics* 13 (3): 757–761.

Iyengar, Shanto. 1991. *Is Anyone Responsible?* Chicago, IL: University of Chicago Press.

Iyengar, Shanto. 2011. *Media Politics: A Citizen's Guide*. 2nd ed. London: W.W. Norton.
Iyengar, Shanto, and Donald R. Kinder. 2010. *News that Matters: Television & American Opinion*. Chicago, IL: University of Chicago Press.
Jackson, Jenn M. n.d. "Race, News Frames, and Implicit-Explicit Racial Messaging."
Kinder, Donald R., and Lynn M. Sanders. 1996. *Divided by Color: Racial Politics and Democratic Ideals*. Chicago, IL: University of Chicago Press.
Mendelberg, Tali. 2001. *The Race Card: Campaign Strategy, Implicit Messages, and the Norm of Equality*. New Jersey: Princeton University Press.
Moynihan, Daniel P. 1965. "The Negro Family: The Case for National Action." *African American Male Research*.
Oliver, Mary Beth. 2003. "African American Men as 'Criminal and Dangerous': Implications of Media Portrayals of Crime on the 'Criminalization' of African American Men." *Journal of African American Studies* 7 (2): 3-18.
Peffley, Mark, Jon Hurwitz, and Paul Sniderman. 1997. "Racial Stereotypes and Whites' Political Views of Blacks in the Context of Welfare and Crime." *American Journal of Political Science* 41: 30-60.
Pew Research Center (Nielsen Media Research). 2014. "Network TV: Evening News Overall Viewership Since 1980." November, 2014. Accessed November 6, 2015. http://www.journalism.org/media-indicators/network-tv-evening-news-overall-viewership-since-1980/.
Prior, Marcus. 2007. *Post-Broadcast Democracy*. Cambridge: Cambridge University Press.
Schuman, Howard, Charlotte Steeh, Lawrence Bobo, and Maria Krysan. 1985. *Racial Attitudes in America: Trends and Interpretations*. Rev. ed. Cambridge: Harvard University Press.
Sears, David O., Jim Sidanius, and Lawrence Bobo. 2000. *Racialized Politics*. Chicago, IL: Chicago University Press.
Shelby, Tommie. 2005. *We Who Are Dark: The Philosophical Foundations of Black Solidarity*. Cambridge, MA: Belknap Press of Harvard University.
Shelby, Tommie. 2016. *Dark Ghettos: Injustice, Dissent, and Reform*. Cambridge, MA: Belknap Press of Harvard University.
Spence, Lester K. 2010. "Episodic Frames, HIV/AIDS, and African American Public Opinion." *Political Research Quarterly* 63 (2): 257-268.
Stark, Evan. 1993, July. "The Myth of Black Violence." *Social Work* 38 (4): 485-490.
Taylor, Keeanga-Yamahtta. 2014. *From #BlackLivesMatter to Black Liberation*. Chicago, IL: Haymarket Books.
Tesler, Michael. 2016. *Post-Racial or Most-Racial: Race and Politics in the Obama Era*. Chicago, IL: University of Chicago Press.
Valentino, Nicholas A., Vincent L. Hutchings, and Ismail K. White. 2002. "Cues that Matter: How Political Ads Prime Racial Attitudes During Campaigns." *The American Political Science Review* 96 (1): 75-90.
Valentino, Nicholas A., Fabian G. Neuner, and L. Matthew Vandenbroek. 2017. "The Changing Norms of Racial Political Rhetoric and the End of Racial Priming." *The Journal of Politics* 80 (3): 757-771.
Wilson, William Julius. 2012. *The Truly Disadvantaged: The Inner-City, the Underclass and Public Policy*. Chicago, IL: University of Chicago Press.
Woodly, Deva R. 2015. *The Politics of Common Sense: How Social Movements Use Public Discourse to Change Politics and Win Acceptance*. Oxford: Oxford University Press.

Harbingers of unrest in Baltimore: racial and spatial cleavages in satisfaction with quality of life before the 2015 Uprising

Tyson D. King-Meadows

ABSTRACT
The 2015 Baltimore Riots, which occurred following clashes between residents and police during anti-police brutality protests, were the most widespread acts of civil unrest to grip the city since 1968. The civil unrest raised questions about whether policymakers had misdiagnosed the intensity of resident dissatisfaction with neighborhood conditions or the ease at which the death of a black resident in police custody would ignite outrage. I use data from the 2014 Baltimore Citizen Survey, a city-commissioned satisfaction survey, to examine resident perceptions of police a year before the unrest and to examine which individual and contextual factors shaped dissatisfaction with quality of life in the city. Results from one-way ANOVA, factor analysis, and multivariate regressions show that race and economic distress were significant predictors of dissatisfaction. Furthermore, blacks, Millennials, and residents of certain planning districts were highly dissatisfied with police and with the availability of resources. High levels of dissatisfaction were reported by areas which would become flashpoints of the 2015 unrest. I discuss the implications of racial, spatial, and social cleavages in satisfaction for city governance, including how citizen surveys, as policy feedback devises, can attune policymakers to the attitudinal, demographic, and experiential profiles typically correlated with civil unrest.

Introduction

Commonly referred to as the 2015 Baltimore Riots or the 2015 Baltimore Uprising, the events occurring in Baltimore City, Maryland on April 27 and spanning into the early morning on April 28 2015, reignited discussions about the ways in which race and socio-economic status shape resident encounters with law enforcement officials. While it is clear that the injury to and death of Freddie Gray while in police custody played a pivotal role in animating outrage about police brutality in the City, narratives that anchored the unrest to a single factor discounted how resident dissatisfaction with one area of city services might have influenced attitudes about other areas. Likewise, such narratives also implied that the protestors were anomalies: they were attitudinal outliers in general (i.e., most dissatisfied) or they were issue-specific attitudinal outliers (i.e., most dissatisfied about police). Furthermore, narratives which focused on the race of protestors discounted other factors which might have correlated with dissatisfaction. Because incidents of civil unrest shape national conversations about economic disadvantage and government legitimacy (Snow, Vliegenthart, and Corrigall-Brown 2007; Gillion 2013), it is important to consider which storylines frame narratives about what happened in Baltimore and why. An examination of resident opinion about city services prior to the unrest is vital to understanding how, and in what specific ways, the arrest, injury, and death of Gray may have exemplified unaddressed grievances. Knowing what happened to Gray is thus as vital a storyline to understanding the 2015 Baltimore Uprising as is knowing how race, class, and location may have shaped perceptions about quality of life prior to the unrest.[1]

That "Freddie Gray" became shorthand for denoting the cause of the Baltimore unrest is understandable. On April 18, 2015, a ruckus but non-violent protest occurred outside the Baltimore City Police Department's (BPD) Western Police District station. Residents gathered to protest Freddie Gray's arrest and injury. Gray, a 25-year-old black male resident of Sandtown-Winchester, was arrested on April 12 and soon needed emergency spinal surgery for injuries sustained in custody. The protest occurred blocks away from where Gray was arrested. On April 19, Gray died. Protests continued over the next few days – outside the Western station, throughout the Western district, outside City Hall, and outside Baltimore City police headquarters. Developments ostensibly characterized as attempts to address the protestors' concerns did not stymie resident outrage: a US Department of Justice investigation into the death of Gray; Mayor Stephanie Rawlings-Blake's meetings with black civic organizations and clergy members; a meeting between protestors and Police Commissioner Anthony Batts; press conferences by city officials; urges for calm by officials and community leaders; announcements that the officers involved were suspended; and increased media attention to the protests. A daytime funeral for Gray on April 27 was heavily attended. By mid-afternoon on April 27, media sources began broadcasting a violent encounter at Mondawmin Mall between young people (many reportedly from Frederick Douglass High School) and police dressed in tactical gear. Debris was thrown at police; however, the police did not engage with direct force. Other encounters between police and residents, vandalism, looting, violence, non-violent marches, and ruckus demonstrations punctuated that day. By 20:00, the Mayor announced a State of Emergency, an upcoming curfew, and a request for the National Guard. By early April 28, the widespread unrest in 2015 had arguably eclipsed what happened in the city 47 years earlier following the assassination of Martin Luther King, Jr. in April 1968. Damage estimates hovered around $20 million and the City reported more than 250 arrests and numerous injuries to officers (Wenger 2015).

Observers offered competing explanations about *why* the 2015 Baltimore Uprising happened. Explanations targeted micro-level factors (e.g., outrage; alienation), mezzo-level factors (e.g., neighborhood conditions; gangs), and macro-level factors (e.g., racism; bureaucratic ineptitude; Ferguson spillover). I refer to a common thread connecting these explanations as "Baltimore Exceptionalism," whereby unparalleled social stratification or unmet racialized expectations causes the unrest. Observers privileging stratification framed Baltimore as an inequality outlier, asserting that the city outpaced other similarly sized cities in poverty, segregation, health disparities, and economic divesture (Graham

2015; Linskey 2015; Vey and Berube 2015). These observers contended that poverty and inequality, not race, primarily shaped quality of life. The Uprising was the city's destiny; the unrest was predictable, if not necessary, given the ubiquity of deprivation. Observers privileging expectations, on the other hand, framed Baltimore as a racial leadership outlier, asserting that black economic and political clout outpaced that of similar cities. Age and affluence mattered most. The Uprising was an anomaly; deprivation in Baltimore was typical of other cities, but the alienation of young blacks was unique (Berube 2015; Mozingo and Phelps 2015; Vey 2015). Journalist Michael Fletcher, in an April 28th *Washington Post* op-ed, effectively channeled the Baltimore Exceptionalism framework. Fletcher wrote, "Baltimore is not Ferguson and its primary problems are not racial. The mayor, city council president, police chief, top prosecutor, and many other city leaders are black, as is half of Baltimore's 3,000-person police force." He continued, "The city has many prominent black churches and a line of black civic leadership extending back to Frederick Douglass." Fletcher added, "Yet, the gaping disparities separating the haves and the have nots in Baltimore are as large as they are anywhere. And, as the boys on the street will tell you, black cops can be hell on them, too" (Fletcher 2015).

Remarks by black elected officials also trafficked in the Baltimore Exceptionalism framework. President Barack Obama linked the protest to concerns about inequalities, noted "the multiple days of peaceful protests that were focused on entirely legitimate concerns of these communities in Baltimore," and referenced "impoverished communities that have been stripped away of opportunity, where children are born into abject poverty" (US White House 2015). However, Obama, like Mayor Rawlings-Blake before him, referred to some individuals as "criminals and thugs." That both black elected officials characterized some protestors as "criminals and thugs" especially shocked those observers who saw parallels between the April 2015 Uprising and the race-related unrest of 1967 in cities across America and the unrest of April 1968 in Baltimore following news that Dr. Martin Luther King, Jr. had been assassinated. Whether incidents of civil unrest across various cities and time periods share similar causes is highly debatable. And it is outside the scope of this article to address whether and how similar concerns energized the unrest in Baltimore in April 1968 and in April 2015 (Hooker 2016). However, some participants, local observers, news outlets, and social media broadcasts *did* frame the 2015 Uprising as being animated by concerns found to have energized the racial unrest of the 1960s: black outrage over poverty, systemic injustices, state-sanctioned anti-black violence, economic immobility, and government unresponsiveness. Drawing such parallels was not without controversy, especially since an individual's beliefs about the underlying cause for the 2015 Uprising were partially shaped by their news attentiveness and their racial and political identities (Haider-Markel et al. 2018). Indeed, it is precisely because "conflicting narratives" about civil unrest and anti-black violence do persist that I aim to subject the Baltimore Exceptionalism framework to empirical scrutiny.

Narratives about Baltimore Exceptionalism often made unsubstantiated claims about the link between protest, resident opinion, and neighborhood conditions. For instance, these narratives sidestepped any confounding effects of race, age, class, and location on propensity to protest (Traister 2015). If socioeconomic status determined propensity to protest, location would not necessarily predict dissatisfaction nor epicenters of protest (Weffer 2017). Also, Baltimore Exceptionalism narratives predominantly drew upon impressionistic accounts, aggregate data, and reports from advocacy groups. While this evidence was not superficial, it was not dispositive either. If a confluence of factors shaped dissatisfaction, the 2015 unrest would be neither exceptional nor preventable.

Indeed, no scholarly consensus exists on the link between resident dissatisfaction, sociodemographic status, and unconventional political behavior (Johnson and Farrell 1993; Gillion 2012). Racial cleavages in satisfaction with quality of life (e.g., available resources, city services, or economic prospects) could reflect differences in knowledge about or engagement with agencies. Cleavages could also correlate with social stratification across groups and within locales. However, even if cleavages did correlate with individual- and neighborhood-level circumstances, the link between dissatisfaction and protest is tenuous at best (Fine 2007; Weffer 2017). Some highly dissatisfied neighborhoods will become sites of protest, others will not. Perceptional cleavages do not predestine any action (Fine 2007; Zuberi et al. 2016). Nonetheless, dissatisfaction has analytic value in the study of protest behavior. Persistent, intense, and (geographically) localized dissatisfaction about quality of life is substantively different than discontent. Outrage could flourish amongst highly dissatisfied residents concentrated in high poverty neighborhoods in ways separate and apart from how perceptions might typically correlate with individual and neighborhood factors.

That class rather than race can shape resident outrage about quality of life is a theme prominent in the work of Adolph Reed, Jr. (2016) and Cedric Johnson (2016) on the rhetoric and strategies of activists aligned with Black Lives Matter and the movement's protests against police killings of black Americans. After examining data on police shootings from the *Washington Post*, Reed (2016) argued that racism could not explain the high rate of white deaths at the hands of police. He further contended that attention to the "racial" disparity in police killings "demand[s] that we disattend from other possible causal disparities," like the location of poor blacks in the economy. In championing economic exploitation over race as the cause for police anti-black violence, Reed (2016) asserted that police violence "emerges from an imperative to contain and suppress the pockets of economically marginal and self-employed working-class populations produced by revanchist capitalism." For Reed (2016), the consequence of ignoring class is undeniable: individuals who organize principally around race and place, rather than around economic exploitation, uncritically embrace "the premise of neoliberal social justice that the problem of inequality ... is whether or not is its distributed in a racially equitable way." Endorsing a similar view, Johnson (2016) argued that Black Lives Matter as the "dominant framing, which presupposes that blacks are the primary, and for some, exclusive targets of mistreatment and violence by police has had the effect of mystifying social reality" that "police violence is widely felt across racial and ethnic groups." Johnson (2016) further asserted that "police violence and the carceral state are experienced more broadly across the working class, and more intensively among the most submerged segments of the black population," and contended that "[p]olicing emerged as a mechanism for defending capitalist property relations" not "exclusively as a means of securing white domination." Johnson (2016) thus concluded: "Despite their rhetorical power, antiracist arguments are too imprecise to describe the origins and dynamics of the current policing crisis." Overall, both Johnson and Reed contend that economic exploitation is the best explanation of police killings and is the only viable organizing principle by which (poor) blacks and their allies can sustain and advance movement politics.

Yet, while Johnson (2016) and Reed (2016) are most aligned with the class-first version of Baltimore Exceptionalism, their work also calls into question whether deprivation in Baltimore City could be exceptional in any way given the ubiquitous "ravages of neoliberalism" and the pro-capitalist origins of policing. Moreover, accusations that the carceral state in Baltimore feeds primarily but not exclusively on economic vulnerability is somewhat corroborated by evidence that poor and working-class residents of all races often reported negative interactions with city police (Dizard 2015).[2] Nonetheless, the question of whether class status mattered more than racial identity in shaping Baltimore City residents' perceptions about quality of life, especially evaluations of the police, prior to the 2015 Uprising is an empirical question as much as it is a philosophical one.

To test theories related to resident satisfaction in Baltimore prior to the April 2015 unrest, I examine the 2014 Baltimore City Survey, a scientific "citizen satisfaction survey" of adult residents. Specifically, I assess the degree to which race, socioeconomic status, and location structured perceptions about city services and neighborhood conditions. Did black residents express higher levels of dissatisfaction with services and conditions than other racial groups? Did residents in economically distressed locales express higher levels of dissatisfaction? Were the most dissatisfied locations in 2014 also sites of the 2015 Uprising? While the 2014 survey did not contain items related to protest, I ascertain what clues, if any, about the 2015 unrest could be gleamed from examining perceptions a year before the disturbance.

Why citizen surveys matter

Citizen surveys are vital to evaluating service delivery and resident satisfaction with bureaucratic performance (Stipak 1979; Stipak 1980; Poister and Thomas 2007; James and Moseley 2014). By centering the experiences and perceptions of residents, "citizen surveys" provide information that cannot be gathered from aggregate data (Hero and Durand 1985; Van Ryzin and Immerwahr 2007; Van Ryzin, Immerwahr, and Altman 2008). Policymakers and scholars thus turn to citizen surveys to learn from the "wisdom of crowds" (Poister and Thomas 2007), to test the correlation between satisfaction and objective measures used to assess neighborhood quality, and to ascertain if bureaucratic performance affects perceptions about services (James and Moseley 2014).

Yet, crowd wisdom (Poister and Thomas 2007) can be misleading: opinion can be uninformed and myopic, can exclude emergent services, and can be influenced by motivated reasoning. Discourses around what constitutes a problem and how to solve said problem are not immune from the macro-level about the "distinctiveness of cities" (Barbehön et al. 2016), about the externalities of neoliberalism (Spence 2015), and about the racial makeup and affluence of taxpayers and tax recipients (Henricks and Seamster 2017; Walsh 2017). Thus, the mechanisms driving resident views about social and political phenomena also drive resident evaluation of city services and leadership. Those mechanisms include racialized trust (Van Ryzin 2007; Bradbury and Kellough 2008; Nunnally 2012), resident strategies to gather information about city services (James and Moseley 2014), and social differences in engagement (Hajnal and Trounstine 2014). Relatedly, the mechanisms driving government response to resident demands are the same which impact any principal-agent relationship. Residents who perceive that officials have been unresponsive to their demands are less likely to engage in conventional politics. Attentive publics are more likely to influence officials. Given the relationship between socioeconomic status and civic engagement, resident dissatisfaction with neighborhood conditions might reflect alienation as much as it reflects objective circumstances (Hajnal and Trounstine 2013). Hence, if elections are weak policy feedback devices (cf. Riker 1982), so are citizen satisfaction surveys. Policymakers may be unable to defend changes in services as being responsive to well-informed popular demands.

Policymakers must also account for race, as a heuristic and emotive prism (Dawson 1994; Tesler 2012), when using satisfaction surveys as diagnostic tools. While the literature on race has primarily dealt with elections and policy preference, its application to unpacking satisfaction is straightforward. Race can undermine the wisdom of crowds by distorting perceptions of neighborhoods (Krysan and Bader 2007; Haveke, Bader, and Krysan 2016) and evaluations of potential neighbors (Schwartz, McClure, and Taghavi 2016). Race can also prefigure dissatisfaction. In a study of Chicago residents, Swaroop and Krysan (2011) demonstrate the extent of this prefiguration and its impact on neighborhood satisfaction by referring to the "racial proxy perspective." The "racial proxy perspective" is when individuals of a certain race prefer to live in same-race predominant neighborhoods because they want to avoid "the social problems" they believe are more likely to occur in mixed-race neighborhoods or in neighborhoods in which another race predominates. Swaroop and Krysan (2011) find that whites report less satisfaction in more diverse neighborhoods, but that objective neighborhood conditions are weakly correlated with dissatisfaction. Moreover, because race is correlated with "cumulative advantage" (DiPrete and Eirich 2006), neighborhood conditions result from non-random processes which affect where and how individuals and groups live, work, and play (Vemuri et al. 2011; Hur and Nasar 2014; Holtan, Dieterlen, and Sullivan 2015; Troy, Nunery, and Grove 2016). In Baltimore City, this racial proxy perspective cannot be disentangled from the vestiges of racial segregation that have shaped which neighborhoods are more likely to attract white and affluent home seekers and which neighborhoods are more likely to garner political and economic investment (Pietila 2010; Beilenson and McGuire 2012). The "racial proxy perspective" is thus problematic on multiple levels.

Here the theory of "relative deprivation" can demystify as well as obscure the link between dissatisfaction and civil unrest. According to Ted Gurr (2011), communities with prolonged frustrations or grievances about suffered injustices, a belief that there is a discrepancy between what they deserve and what they receive, will engage in political protest and violence once angered. Gurr (2011) explains that the potency of relative deprivation, however, depends in part upon how individuals interpret their socioeconomic and political circumstances and whether the capacity to repel or support protest and violence rests with government forces or with communities, respectively. Even so, as Gurr (2011) acknowledges, anger does not preordain protest and violence because leaders, narratives, and the motives of government matter (Gurr 2011; Grasso and Giugni 2016). Not all aggrieved community members will act and not all leaders have the acumen to effectively mobilize members. The implication of this is that prolonged dissatisfaction might not be a harbinger of future violence; dissatisfaction can also lead to alienation and self-loathing.

Relatedly, racialized narratives about neighborhoods can enhance dissatisfaction by privileging dispositional or situational explanations of inequality (Swaroop and Krysan 2011). One result of privileging dispositional explanations is that differences become normalized. Normalization depresses outrage about inequities, dampens the effectiveness of calls for ameliorative action, and further isolates groups. In addition, normalization can lead certain identity groups to underestimate health status, neighborhood conditions, personal and communal distress (Bediako and Moffitt 2011; Rizzo and Kintner 2013) and overstate dissatisfaction with government services (Hero and Tolbert 2004). Residents could be more dissatisfied than objective measures suggest that they should be (Bradbury and Kellough 2011; Hajnal and Trounstine 2013; Batson and Monnat 2015).

The *Baltimore Citizen Survey*

As a citizen satisfaction survey, four facets of the 2014 Baltimore Citizen Survey (BCS) make it uniquely positioned to provide insights into resident satisfaction with city services and perceptions about city life before the unrest. First, Baltimore City commissioned an external entity to conduct the annual satisfaction survey. The survey was inaugurated in 2009 and suspended in 2015. According to city documents, the BCS was intended to help policymakers understand "quality of life indicators, [resident] awareness of and satisfaction with City services, general trends in behavior and identified future needs for and current gaps in City services."[3] The BCS was also designed to "[establish] a baseline understanding of what living in Baltimore is like for the average citizen" for the purposes of improving life in Baltimore. Policymakers believed the BCS would provide "feedback [that] may be used to inform future policy or budgetary decisions in Baltimore City government, which means that the survey respondents may have a very real effect on the quality of life in Baltimore." Second, creation of the BCS underscored the limitations of prior research findings. Prior research on Baltimore utilized aggregate data, principal investigator-driven surveys, geospatial analysis, cross-sectional survey data collected at sporadic intervals, or from some combination thereof. However, that research could not address residents' perceptions of service areas. Nor could that research reveal cleavages in satisfaction across time and location. Third, the BCS contained the question depth, regularity, and coverage to conduct robust statistical analysis. Fourth, city officials and media outlets were familiar with BCS findings. Officials were provided topline results and final reports from each survey. Reports were disseminated. Policymakers could turn to BCS reports for confirmatory evidence that dissatisfaction correlated with race and place.

Data and methods

I examine the 2014 BCS to examine resident satisfaction with city services in the year before the 2015 Uprising. The 2014 BCS was fielded from September 2nd through September 30th, had a ±3.9% margin of error, averaged 26 minutes in length, was available in Spanish and English, and was weighted to reflect the city's demographic distribution on age, gender, and race. The sample was gathered using a random-digit-dial household technique, was augmented with a sample of cellphone users, and was done to assure a representative sample from each of the city's nine planning districts. The 2014 BCS yielded 680 respondents: non-Hispanics Whites (184); non-Hispanic Blacks (403); Other Racial Minorities (62); and Refused (32). The 2014 BCS is invaluable for ascertaining the predictive value of age, race, and location for satisfaction.

Dependent variables

Following the conceptual roadmap of the BCS designers, I use multiple items to measure resident perceptions about quality of life and city services. The first dependent variable is *Availability of Resources Index* comprised of answers to seven items rating "availability of good jobs," "cleanliness of the city," "cleanliness of their neighborhood," "amount of green space in their neighborhood," "amount of green space in the city," "availability of cultural activities in the city," and "availability of recreational opportunities in the city" (0 = Poor, 1 = Fair, 2 = Good, 4 = Excellent). Responses were normalized to range from 0 to 1, and then summed to create an index. Higher scores reflected a stronger belief in the availability of resources. Diagnostic tests confirmed the factorability of these seven items: two factors explained 61.26% of the variance; factor loadings were above 0.60 and generated a Kaiser–Meyer–Olkin measure of sampling adequacy at 0.754; and the Cronbach's alpha statistic was strong ($\alpha = 0.804$). Answers to items about jobs, cultural activities, and recreational activities comprised one factor, *Lifestyle Resources*. Another factor, *Physical Resources*, consisted of answers to the other four items. I generated predicted factor scores and rescaled them to have a mean of 100 and a standard deviation of 10 (see Appendix Table 1). These rescaled factor scores are the second and third dependent variables. The fourth dependent variable, *Perception of Safety Index*, was derived from answers to five items: "safety in neighborhood in daytime," "safety in neighborhood at night time," "safety downtown in daytime," "safety downtown at night time," "safety in city parks in daytime" (1 = Very Unsafe, 2 = Unsafe, 3 = Safe, 4 = Very Safe). Responses were normalized to range from 0 to 1, and then summed to create an index where 1 was the highest number ($\alpha = 0.745$).[4]

Finally, I examine resident evaluation of the BPD using two variables: *Favorability of Police* (1 = Very Unfavorable; 2 = Somewhat Unfavorable, 3 = Neither Favorable or Unfavorable, 4 = Somewhat Favorable, 5 = Very Favorable) and *Evaluation of Police Protection* (0 = Poor, 1 = Fair, 2 = Good, 4 = Excellent). These constitute the fifth and sixth dependent variable, respectively. Responses were normalized to range from 0 to 1, with the highest value representing strong favorable assessments of police protection.

Independent variables

The independent variables of interest are racial identification (*White, Black, Other Minority*); age cohort (*Age 1* = 18–34, *Age 2* = 35–44, *Age 3* = 45–44, *Age 4* = 55–64, and *Age 5* = 65 and over); *Income* (1 = less than $25k, 2 = $25–$50k, 3 = $50,001–$75k, 4 = $75,001–$100k, and 5 = Over $100k); and *Length of Residency in Baltimore* (1 = 1 year or less, 2 = 2–5 years, 3 = 6–10 years, 4 = 11–19 years, and 5 = 20 years or longer). The survey also captured other respondent demographics, e.g., education, income, gender, and marital status. The survey did not measure traditional ideology or support for government policies. Response of "don't know" and "refused" were excluded and not imputed.

To assess the effect of contextual forces on respondent perceptions, I controlled for several locational, temporal, and historic circumstances. First, I controlled for cumulative disadvantage (DiPrete and Eirich 2006) by utilizing the Distressed Communities Index created by the Economic Innovation Group, Inc.[5] The DCI aggregates items measuring economic and social conditions which ostensibly shape mobility and neighborhood dynamics in America. Seven metrics comprise the index: (1) No high school degree: Percent of the population 25 years and over without a high school degree; (2) Housing vacancy: Percent of habitable housing that is unoccupied, excluding properties that are for seasonal, recreational, or occasional use; (3) Adults not working: Share of the population 16 years and over that is not currently employed; (4) Poverty: Percent of population living under the poverty line; (5) Median income relative to state: Ratio of the geography's median income to the state's median income; (6) Change in employment: Percent change in the number of individuals employed between 2010 and 2013; and (7) Change in business establishments: Percent change in the number of business establishments between 2010 and 2013. DCI scores range from 0 to 100. Higher scores indicate more economic distress.[6] I appended the DCI's zip code-level distress scores (*Distress Scores*) to the individual-level dataset. Second, I adopted a strategy from Perkins and Sampson (2015) to control for concentrated poverty. Individuals with household incomes of less than $25,000 and living in a zip code with a poverty rate of 30% or higher were identified (*Concentrated Poverty* 1 = yes, 0 = no). Third, I controlled for exposure to crime within and beyond respondents' environs by appending average reported crime at the police district level. I used the 2011–2013 average of total reported violent and property crime (*3-YR Crime Average*) listed in the city's Comstat Data Reports. This statistic has three advantages: first, averages are preferable over single year sums; second, reported crime is a better approximation of exposure than is number of arrests; and third, while the 2014 planning districts shared the same name as the 2014 police districts, the boundaries did overlap in many places across the city.[7] Fourth, and finally, I controlled for residency in one of the nine planning districts because the socioracial and economic profiles of the Planning Districts varied considerably (see Appendix Table 2). For example, the Northern District had the lowest unemployment rate (8.42%), the highest median household income ($65,855), and the highest percentage of white residents (44.26%). By contrast, the Western District had the lowest percentage of white residents (2.25%), the second highest unemployment rate (15.18), and the fourth lowest median household income ($42,244). In other ways, the Southern District stood out from the other districts: it had the highest unemployment rate (16.60), the second highest percentage of residents below poverty (34.19), and the highest percentage of households receiving public assistance (10.59).

Analytic strategy

I employed univariate, bivariate, and multivariate analysis on the weighted 2014 BCS data. First, I compared the 2009 results to the 2014 results to assess shifts in resident perceptions. Second, I used one-way ANOVA to test whether race was a significant predictor of mean differences. Third, I estimated six models. I employed weighted OLS hierarchical regression to test the relative impact of crime and economic distress (Distress Model), individual demographics (Basic Model), concentrated poverty (Poverty Model), and of region plus distress (Full Context) on dissatisfaction (See Appendix Table 3). To account for clustering at the planning district level, I estimated the Full Context model using both robust regression and multilevel/mixed-effects modeling. Here I only present tables with the Full Context models. Fourth, I estimated subpopulation equations on white and black respondents to examine the differential influence of certain variables. Fifth, I generated predicted probabilities from the Full Models to estimate socioeconomic and location effects. Sixth, I plotted zip code- and planning district-level predicted probabilities onto city maps.[8]

Findings and discussion

Data from the 2009 and 2014 satisfaction surveys show deep cleavages in perceptions about neighborhood and city conditions. Table 1 shows that residents were largely dissatisfied with quality of life in both years. By 2014, there was a 19-point downward shift in overall satisfaction, an eleven point upward shift in perceptions that neighborhoods were unsafe during the daytime, and a 14-point downward shift in overall ratings of police. Results also show an increase in dissatisfaction with neighborhood cleanliness, a large increase in perceptions that city parks were unsafe in the daytime, and no movement in resident satisfaction with the availability of cultural and recreational activities. Taken together, the results in Table 1 suggest that residents were concerned about the availability of safe and clean public spaces in 2009 and 2014.

Perceptions about resources and police in 2014

Table 2 reveals the extent to which perceptual differences in 2014 correlated with racial identity, location, and socioeconomic status. Whites were more likely than were blacks

Table 1. Percentage indicating dissatisfaction with select neighborhood and city quality of life measures, 2009 and 2014.

Measure	2009	2014
Overall satisfaction with city services		
City services: satisfied/very satisfied	63%	44%
Perceptions of safety		
Neighborhood in daytime: unsafe/very unsafe	7	18
Neighborhood at nighttime: unsafe/very unsafe	30	39
Downtown in daytime: unsafe/very unsafe	12	23
Downtown at nighttime: unsafe/very unsafe	57	65
City parks in daytime: unsafe/very unsafe	10	21
Perceptions of police in neighborhood		
Rating: good/excellent	51	37
Favorability: somewhat unfavorable/very unfavorable	na	36
Level of police presence: unsatisfied/very unsatisfied	26	na
Responsiveness: unsatisfied/very unsatisfied	24	na
Approachability: unsatisfied/very unsatisfied	25	na
Ability to prevent crime: unsatisfied/very unsatisfied	35	na
Lifestyle resources and physical recourses		
Availability of good jobs: poor and fair	81	76
Availability of green space in city: poor and fair	57	65
Availability of green space in neighborhood: poor and fair	42	57
Availability of cultural activities: poor and fair	46	44
Availability of recreational activities: poor and fair	62	62
Cleanliness of city: poor and fair	72	79
Cleanliness of neighborhood: poor and fair	41	55

Notes: Excludes don't knows, refusals, and those with no experience. NA means "not asked" on survey.
Source: Author calculations, *BCS*, relevant years.

Table 2. Racial differences in resident perceptions about quality of life in baltimore and in resident socioeconomic circumstances, 2014.

	All	White	Black	Other Minority
Availability of Resources Index (1 = Excellent)[a]	0.40	0.50	0.35	0.41
Rescaled factor score for lifestyle resources[a]	99.83	103.66	97.30	104.74
Rescaled factor score for physical resources[a]	98.91	102.26	98.13	93.39
Perception of Safety Index (1 = Very safe)	0.62	0.62	0.63	0.59
Neighborhood in daytime (1 = Very safe)	0.76	0.79	0.75	0.72
Neighborhood at nighttime (1 = Very safe)[a]	0.57	0.52	0.60	0.48
Downtown in daytime (1 = Very safe)	0.70	0.71	0.69	0.71
Downtown at nighttime (1 = Very safe)	0.39	0.35	0.41	0.35
City parks in daytime (1 = Very safe)	0.70	0.70	0.72	0.62
Perceptions of Police				
Favorability of police (1 = Very favorable)[a]	0.49	0.59	0.46	0.42
Evaluation of police protection (1 = Excellent)[a]	0.41	0.49	0.37	0.43
Objective Neighborhood Characteristics				
Zip code distress score (0–100)[a]	76.7	64.8	81.4	81.4
Zip code Herfindahl–Hirschman Index (0–1)[a]	0.58	0.52	0.60	0.60
Planning district 3-YR (11–13) crime average[a]	4347	4469	4375	3798

Notes: Results exclude unknown/refused. An HHI of 1.0 is the highest level of racial homogeneity.
Source: BCS 2014.
[a]ANOVA results indicate that differences across groups are statistically significant at $p < .01$

and other racial minorities to express a belief that the availability of physical resources and lifestyle resources was excellent. The whites-blacks gap on *Availability of Resources Index* was statistically significant (a difference of 0.15, $p < .001$). The gap between other racial minorities and whites was also significant (a difference of 0.09, $p < .10$). Perceptual gaps are further illuminated by mean differences on the rescaled factor scores. The *Physical Resources* score for whites was four points higher than it was for blacks and eight points higher than it was for other minorities. The *Lifestyle Resources* score for whites was six points higher than it was for blacks. However, there were no statistically significant racial differences in aggregate perceptions about safety, except for the measure on neighborhood safety at night.[9] Whites and non-black racial minorities were less likely than were blacks to feel safe in their neighborhoods at night. The racial gaps in perception about the police are important to note in that regard: Whites were more likely than other groups to perceive the Baltimore City police as "very favorable" and as "excellent" in providing protection. The white-black gap on favorability was 0.13 ($p < .001$) and the whites-other racial minorities gap was wider (a 0.17 difference, $p < .001$). Furthermore, Whites were more likely than were blacks to view police as excellent (a 0.12 difference, $p < .003$). Such racial differences were not disconnected from socioeconomic status. Respondents in the 2014 BCS lived under different socioeconomic circumstances. On average, whites lived in less economically distressed zip codes, lived in more racially/ethnically heterogenous zip codes, and lived in police districts with higher reported crime than did other respondents.[10]

Table 3 reports results from OLS models assessing the impact of respondent characteristics and location on perceptions about lifestyle and physical resources. The first model ("random") controls for locational effects, but does not control for correlated opinions within planning districts. The two subsequent models control for clustering and multilevel effects, respectively. Results for *Lifestyle Resources* reveal that black respondents had a low mean lifestyle resources score relative to other racial minorities (the reference category). Living longer in Baltimore, being a Baby Boomer, and living in the Western, Southern,

Table 3. Estimating impact of race, region, age, and zip code distress on perceptions about availability of lifestyle resources and physical resources in 2014.

	Lifestyle Resources			Physical Resources		
	Random	Cluster	MLM	Random	Cluster	MLM
White	−2.87	−2.87	−2.56	7.67**	7.67**	7.61**
	(2.51)	(2.24)	(2.17)	(2.48)	(1.82)	(1.68)
Black	−7.10**	−7.10**	−7.24**	4.79*	4.79	4.96
	(2.41)	(1.72)	(1.67)	(2.41)	(3.42)	(3.08)
18–34	−1.05	−1.05	−1.29	−2.33	−2.33	−2.34
	(1.72)	(2.25)	(2.27)	(1.71)	(1.92)	(1.93)
35–44	−2.56	−2.56	−2.62	−3.35+	−3.35+	−3.37*
	(1.72)	(1.63)	(1.59)	(1.94)	(1.69)	(1.63)
45–54	−2.29	−2.29	−2.57+	−1.04	−1.04	−0.99
	(1.41)	(1.38)	(1.43)	(1.56)	(1.47)	(1.53)
55–64	−2.61+	−2.61+	−2.79*	0.70	0.70	0.61
	(1.38)	(1.18)	(1.23)	(1.76)	(2.35)	(2.19)
Eastern District	−4.04+	−4.04**		−4.94+	−4.94**	
	(2.12)	(0.78)		(2.76)	(0.65)	
Northeast District	−5.84*	−5.84**		0.60	0.60	
	(2.37)	(1.48)		(3.53)	(0.96)	
Northern District	−3.02	−3.02+		−1.86	−1.86	
	(2.51)	(1.39)		(3.06)	(1.05)	
Northwest District	−3.96	−3.96*		−0.08	−0.08	
	(2.98)	(1.33)		(3.82)	(1.27)	
Southeast District	−0.38	−0.38		−3.04	−3.04+	
	(2.62)	(1.03)		(2.97)	(1.44)	
Southern District	−5.56*	−5.56**		−5.18+	−5.18**	
	(2.34)	(1.58)		(2.88)	(1.02)	
Southwest District	−5.46*	−5.46*		0.49	0.49	
	(2.28)	(1.65)		(3.16)	(0.89)	
Western District	−6.12**	−6.12**		−7.12*	−7.12**	
	(2.35)	(1.27)		(2.99)	(0.82)	
Zip distress Score	0.00	0.00	0.00	−0.09*	−0.09*	−0.10**
	(0.03)	(0.03)	(0.02)	(0.04)	(0.03)	(0.03)
Constant	113.34**	113.34**	110.44**	101.06**	101.06**	99.78**
	(5.78)	(4.70)	(5.60)	(6.92)	(6.14)	(6.05)
Districts: sd(cons)			1.70+			2.35**
			(0.52)			(0.47)
Districts: sd(Residual)			8.60**			9.28**
			(0.31)			(0.21)
Control for clustering	No	Yes	Yes	No	Yes	Yes
Control for hierarchy	No	No	Yes	No	No	Yes
Observations	491	490	490	491	490	490
R-squared	0.233	0.233		0.212	0.212	

Note: Select parameters reported. See Table A6 for all parameters. Dependent Variables are rescaled predicted factor scores (M = 100, SD = 10). Excluded categories are Other Minority, Age: 65 and older, and Central District. Standard errors are linearized in model without control for clustering at district; standard errors are robust cluster for model with control for clustering at district; standard errors are robust for mixed-effects multilevel model.
+$p < .10$, *$p < .05$, **$p < .01$.

and Eastern planning district lowered the mean lifestyle resources score. Results for *Physical Resources*, on the other hand, show that white respondents had a significantly higher physical resources score compared to other respondents. Zip code distress was a significant predictor of perceptions about physical resources, but not about lifestyle resources. Results from the multilevel models also show that district residency shaped perceptions.[11] Diagnostic tests for these models, however, showed them to be no more useful than robust cluster models.[12] In total, the models show that being black and living in specific locations significantly reduced belief in the availability of lifestyle and physical resources.

Table 4. Determinants of racial differences in perceptions about available resources.

	All Random	All Cluster	Whites Random	Whites Cluster	Blacks Random	Blacks Cluster
White	0.032 (0.060)	0.032 (0.052)	–	–	–	–
Black	−0.075 (0.060)	−0.075 (0.058)	–	–	–	–
Education	0.003 (0.013)	0.003 (0.011)	0.031* (0.013)	0.031** (0.007)	0.002 (0.016)	0.002 (0.016)
18–34	−0.070+ (0.038)	−0.070 (0.043)	−0.042 (0.049)	−0.042 (0.054)	−0.098* (0.049)	−0.098* (0.041)
35–44	−0.101** (0.037)	−0.101** (0.030)	−0.085+ (0.050)	−0.085** (0.025)	−0.074 (0.047)	−0.074+ (0.036)
45–54	−0.075* (0.034)	−0.075* (0.030)	−0.014 (0.038)	−0.014 (0.044)	−0.080* (0.036)	−0.080* (0.030)
55–64	−0.060 (0.036)	−0.060* (0.025)	−0.042 (0.034)	−0.042 (0.044)	−0.018 (0.039)	−0.018 (0.030)
Residency length	−0.014 (0.016)	−0.014 (0.020)	−0.040* (0.017)	−0.040+ (0.019)	−0.020 (0.027)	−0.020 (0.034)
Eastern District	−0.126* (0.051)	−0.126** (0.016)	−0.043 (0.065)	−0.043+ (0.021)	−0.184** (0.068)	−0.184** (0.026)
Northeast District	−0.077 (0.067)	−0.077** (0.022)	0.032 (0.081)	0.032 (0.064)	−0.074 (0.083)	−0.074** (0.019)
Northern District	−0.058 (0.054)	−0.058* (0.022)	0.069 (0.069)	0.069 (0.072)	−0.111 (0.076)	−0.111** (0.026)
Northwest District	−0.048 (0.078)	−0.048 (0.028)	0.008 (0.086)	0.008 (0.093)	−0.053 (0.102)	−0.053+ (0.026)
Southeast District	−0.061 (0.053)	−0.061* (0.024)	0.028 (0.069)	0.028 (0.051)	−0.124 (0.099)	−0.124** (0.020)
Southern District	−0.140* (0.056)	−0.140** (0.031)	−0.061 (0.078)	−0.061 (0.067)	−0.150* (0.075)	−0.150** (0.037)
Southwest District	−0.073 (0.056)	−0.073* (0.030)	−0.005 (0.078)	−0.005 (0.065)	−0.019 (0.079)	−0.019 (0.031)
Western District	−0.163** (0.061)	−0.163** (0.021)	−0.154 (0.116)	−0.154** (0.046)	−0.157* (0.072)	−0.157** (0.024)
Zip distress score	−0.001+ (0.001)	−0.001+ (0.001)	−0.001+ (0.001)	−0.001 (0.001)	−0.003* (0.001)	−0.003+ (0.001)
Constant	0.704** (0.157)	0.704** (0.152)	0.657** (0.126)	0.657** (0.094)	0.848** (0.208)	0.848** (0.198)
Control for clustering	No	Yes	No	Yes	No	Yes
Observations	575	574	253	253	297	297
R-squared	0.205	0.205	0.244	0.244	0.190	0.190

Note: Select parameters reported here. See Table A7 for all parameters. DV is 0 (Poor) to 1 (Excellent). Excluded categories for first two models are Other Minority; Age: 65 and older; and Central District. Standard errors are linearized in model without control for district; standard errors are robust cluster for model with control for district.
+$p < .10$, *$p < .05$, **$p < .01$.

Table 4 depicts results from a multivariate OLS regression analysis of perceptions about overall available resources. Race was an insignificant predictor. Age cohort and location, however, were significant predictors. Respondents 35–44 years of age and 45–54 years of age were less likely than other age groups to view available resources as excellent. Residents living in the Western, Eastern, and Southern planning districts were less likely than residents in the Central district to view resources as excellent. Separate estimations for white and black respondents revealed that economic distress was strongly and significantly associated with perceptions about resources. Moving across the range of the distress score resulted in a 0.247 decrease in the probability for black respondents.

District residency and length of residency in Baltimore did not have uniform impacts: residency length mattered for whites, but not for blacks. Blacks and whites living in the same district did not share the same perspective, save for residents in the Western and Eastern districts. There are five possible explanations for why length of residency did not matter for blacks. First, white residents with long tenure in Baltimore experienced life in the city in drastically different ways than did their equally resourced black counterparts. Second, black residents could have been disproportionately situated in informational networks that promote dissatisfaction with quality of life in Baltimore or that highlight racial disparities as an explanation for poor quality of life. Third, on balance, black residents could have had a greater number of negative encounters with Baltimore institutions and actors than did white residents. Fourth, white residents may have become more despondent about quality of life with each passing year while their black counterparts remained despondent. Fifth, white residents with long tenure in Baltimore may have fondly remembered quality of life under mayoral administrations prior to that of Mayor Stephanie C. Rawlings-Blake whereas their black counterparts did not have such fond memories.

Finally, being a Millennial mattered for blacks, but not for whites; young blacks were more likely to be dissatisfied than were their white counterparts. Figure 1 depicts the marginal effect of residing in each planning district on the probability of having perceived resources as excellent. Residents in the Central District were estimated to have a mean probability of 0.48 and residents in the Western District were estimated to have a mean probability of 0.32.

Determinants of perceptions about police in 2014

Table 5 reports results from the Full Context models estimating the determinants of perceptions about the police in 2014. Whites were statistically more likely than were other respondents to view the police as very favorable (column 3). Zip code distress, education, gender, income, residency length and homeowner status were not significant predictors. These findings run counter to narratives that class, not race, predominately shaped

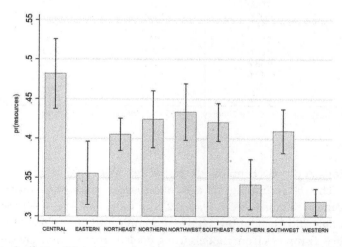

Figure 1. Marginal effects of living in a planning district on perceptions that available resources are excellent in 2014.
Note: Estimates from Table 4, cluster model, all respondents. Variables held at sample mean.

Table 5. Effects of race, planning district, and age on shaping perceptions about police.

	Very Favorable		Protection is excellent	
	Random	Cluster	Random	Cluster
White	0.192*	0.192*	0.103	0.103
	(0.080)	(0.083)	(0.079)	(0.096)
Black	0.040	0.040	−0.058	−0.058
	(0.079)	(0.069)	(0.075)	(0.109)
Female	0.047	0.047	−0.018	−0.018
	(0.042)	(0.034)	(0.041)	(0.041)
Married	−0.076	−0.076	−0.068	−0.068
	(0.048)	(0.060)	(0.052)	(0.091)
Education	0.004	0.004	0.010	0.010
	(0.020)	(0.019)	(0.018)	(0.016)
Income	0.004	0.004	0.023	0.023
	(0.021)	(0.031)	(0.021)	(0.029)
Homeowner	0.055	0.055	0.004	0.004
	(0.051)	(0.030)	(0.048)	(0.052)
18–34	−0.221*	−0.221*	−0.161*	−0.161*
	(0.056)	(0.074)	(0.054)	(0.063)
35–44	−0.156*	−0.156+	−0.162*	−0.162*
	(0.054)	(0.069)	(0.050)	(0.054)
45–54	−0.102*	−0.102	−0.149*	−0.149*
	(0.050)	(0.057)	(0.044)	(0.048)
55–64	−0.077	−0.077	−0.043	−0.043
	(0.049)	(0.046)	(0.046)	(0.033)
Residency length	0.007	0.007	0.027	0.027
	(0.021)	(0.028)	(0.025)	(0.026)
Eastern District	−0.046	−0.046+	−0.000	−0.000
	(0.066)	(0.022)	(0.065)	(0.026)
Northeast District	0.041	0.041	0.095	0.095*
	(0.095)	(0.035)	(0.084)	(0.018)
Northern District	−0.044	−0.044+	0.039	0.039
	(0.081)	(0.020)	(0.079)	(0.037)
Northwest District	−0.036	−0.036	0.060	0.060+
	(0.096)	(0.049)	(0.095)	(0.026)
Southeast District	−0.008	−0.008	−0.006	−0.006
	(0.069)	(0.025)	(0.072)	(0.021)
Southern District	−0.141*	−0.141*	−0.056	−0.056*
	(0.071)	(0.038)	(0.077)	(0.022)
Southwest District	−0.118	−0.118*	0.002	0.002
	(0.093)	(0.031)	(0.093)	(0.024)
Western District	−0.027	−0.027	−0.017	−0.017
	(0.080)	(0.034)	(0.079)	(0.026)
Zip distress score	−0.001	−0.001	0.001	0.001
	(0.001)	(0.001)	(0.001)	(0.001)
Constant	0.585*	0.585*	0.260	0.260
	(0.194)	(0.128)	(0.210)	(0.215)
Observations	571	570	566	565
R-squared	0.145	0.145	0.114	0.114

Note: Excluded baseline categories are Other Minority; Age: 65 and older; and Central District.
+$p < .10$, *$p < .05$.

residents' opinions and that economic distressed residents held stronger negative evaluations of police. The robust findings for age cohort largely support narratives highlighting age as a significant predictor (*18–34*: $B = -0.221$, $p < .05$, *35–44*: $B = -0.156$, $p < .05$). On average, Millennials and Generation Xers were significantly more likely to hold negative views of the police. Estimates from models using pooled cross-sections, nested regressions, and subpopulations confirmed the impact of race and place (See Appendix Table 4 and Table 5a/5b). Blacks residing in the Southwest District or in the Southern District were more likely than other blacks to hold negative views. Whites at higher levels of education were more likely to hold positive views. Age cohort effects were most pronounced for blacks.

To illustrate the impact of individual circumstances and location on perceptions about city police, I mapped planning district-level specific mean predicted probabilities from the cluster models in Table 5 (see Appendix Figure 1 for zip code maps). Figure 2 depicts predicted probabilities by planning district. Residents in the Northern District were predicted to report the highest probability for favorability (0.574) and for excellence (0.492). The Southern District had the lowest mean predicted probability for favorability (0.371) and for excellence (0.334). The second lowest mean probabilities for excellence and for favorability were predicted for the Western District (0.376) and the Southwest District (0.397), respectively. The mapped results are doubly illustrative: the most recognizable sites of the initial 2015 protest events – the Sandtown-Winchester neighborhood and the Mondawmin Mall – are in the Western District, which is near the Southwest District.

All things considered, the above analysis of the 2014 BCS supports two summary conclusions about the ways in which individual and neighborhood circumstances shaped resident perceptions about quality of life a year prior to the 2015 Uprising. Both conclusions emphasize the role of race and political economy in shaping resident dissatisfaction. These conclusions are consistent with prior research showing that race and social location affect how residents view city services and how residents interact with and think about the police (Brunson 2007; Hinton 2016). First, there were substantial differences in the lived experiences across racial groups. Blacks and other racial minorities were more likely than were whites to live in economically distressed and in racially homogenous zip codes. Whites

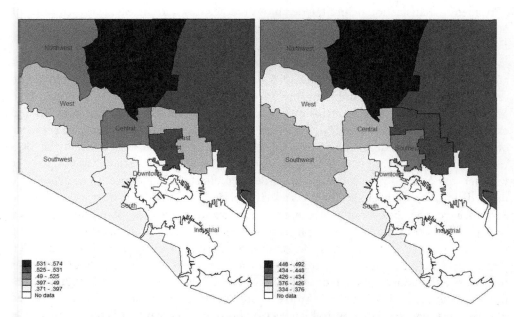

Figure 2. Map of predicted probabilities of perceptions about police by planning district. (a) Viewing police as very favorable. (b) Viewing police protection as excellent.

Note: Estimates from Table 5, cluster model. Variables held at their planning district-level mean. Darker colors indicate higher probability.

were also more likely than their counterparts to live in planning districts with high reported crime figures. Second, there were stark racial differences in perceptions about city and neighborhood life and about police in the year prior to the unrest. Whites were more likely than their counterparts to have favorable impressions of city and neighborhood amenities and were more likely to have favorable impressions of the police. Young people and residents living in certain planning districts also expressed unfavorable impressions. Such circumstances undoubtedly both fueled and reflected racial differences in patterns of engagement with government services and actors. Consequently, it is highly likely that residents were predisposed to view the death of Freddie Gray and the subsequent protests through racial, experiential, and ideological lens. While it is unsurprising that such perceptual and experiential cleavages existed prior to 2015, this reality complicates narratives about Baltimore Exceptionalism. The findings presented here thus should give individuals pause about reductionist treatments of the 2015 unrest which summarily privilege race over class, or vice versa.

Conclusion

The 2015 Baltimore Uprising intensified interest in the cumulative effects of segregation, economic displacement, and political alienation on young adults. Many narratives about the unrest depicted Baltimore as an exceptional case study for understanding the racial and economic correlates of urban unrest and the limitations of black political empowerment. Narratives also opined about how much Baltimore officials knew about the sociocultural and environmental circumstances shaping residents' quality of life. The 2015 Baltimore Uprising, in short, raised the question of whether policymakers had misdiagnosed both the intensity of resident dissatisfaction before the death of Freddie Gray and the ease at which resident outrage could ignite protest.[13] The germination of protests inside the Western District raised the question of whether resident dissatisfaction was widespread.

To excavate the association between individual- and neighborhood-level circumstances and resident perceptions prior to the 2015 Baltimore Uprising, I conducted multivariate regressions on a dataset combining the 2014 BCS, city data, and Census Bureau data. My findings support three conclusions about the potential attitudinal, contextual, and experiential factors shaping the 2015 unrest. First, the unrest could be considered evidence of a failed policy feedback loop. It is unclear whether policymakers deemed the BCS reports to be unpersuasive, whether officials enacted policy changes after any report, or whether any enacted policy changes were deemed effective. Nonetheless, residents were more dissatisfied with quality of life and city services in 2014 than they were in 2009. Second, race, age, and location mattered in direct and indirect ways. Whites expressed high levels of positive views about physical and lifestyle resources, even after accounting for socioeconomic characteristics, neighborhood distress, and residential location. Yet, young black respondents were often, but not always, more pessimistic about resources than were older counterparts. Household income and education were not significant predictors about available resources. Third, exposure to crime and residency length mattered in different ways. Blacks living in high reported crime areas expressed lower satisfaction with police than did similarly situated white respondents. But age moderated perceptions about police. Also, white long-term residents expressed higher dissatisfaction than did white recent arrivals. Residency length was not a significant predictor for blacks.

In conclusion, racial and spatial cleavages in resident perceptions about quality of life in Baltimore City in 2014 provide insight into both the 2015 unrest and the value of citizen surveys. On the one hand, whether labeled a rebellion, an uprising, or a riot, one could characterize the events of April 27–28 2015 as prototypical of what can happen when policymakers discount the perceptions of urban residents. On the other hand, the April 2015 events also confirm the value of satisfaction surveys as diagnostic tools. The cleavages were evident before April 2015 and were not predominantly shaped by neighborhood circumstances or by individual socioeconomic status. The bottom line is that narratives about the 2015 Baltimore Uprising which privilege race, class, or location are insufficient when viewed separately and are incomplete when viewed sequentially. Although no one could predict the 2015 unrest, that it happened should not have been such a surprise to city leaders or to close observers of Baltimore. Residents had signaled their deep and pronounced dissatisfaction with a range of quality of life issues prior to and in 2014, thereby complicating the storyline of class-based black outrage about the death of Freddie Gray as *the* catalyst.

Urban policymakers looking to gleam lessons from the 2015 Baltimore Uprising or from the *BCS* would be well served by viewing persistent and localized dissatisfaction as harbingers of unrest. While it is true that every resident will not engage in protest behavior, city officials who ignore deep cleavages in perceptions about quality of life jeopardize much more than public confidence in local governance and in electoral accountability.

Notes

1. I do not use the word "riot" in deference to the nomenclature preferred by most city residents who are unaffiliated with the police or city government. City reports refer to what happened as the "Baltimore City's April 2015 Civil Unrest." The Fraternal Order of Police refer to what happened as "the 2015 Baltimore Riots."
2. See also Jackson (2016).
3. Schaefer Center for Public Policy, University of Baltimore, *Baltimore City Citizens Survey Final Report* (October 2009), 3.
4. PCA not supported: KMO was 0.617 and only 50% of variance explained by one factor.
5. The Distressed Communities Index, "including the licensed dataset, constitute confidential and propriety information of EIG" and "cannot be disseminated or disclosed to a third party." EIG provided the author the dataset under limited nontransferable use as defined by a university-approved data use agreement.
6. Per the EIG documentation, "[t]he DCI is based on data from the American Community Survey (5-year estimates 2010–2014) and the 2010 and 2013 Zip Code and County Business Pattern data." Distress scores are calculated based on a geography's rank on each of the seven equally weighted variables. The ranks are then averaged and normalized to be equivalent to percentiles, resulting in the distress score – the higher the score, the greater the economic distress.
7. BCS data identified only the respondents' planning district, not respondent's police district. Planning districts and police districts were organized for different purposes (Mike Galdi, GIS Analyst, Baltimore City Department of Planning, personal communication with author, September 20 2017). See Appendix Table 2 for descriptive statistics on districts. See Appendix Figure 2 for side-by-side comparison. Crime reports at the zip code level were also less reliable.
8. See Appendix Table 8 for descriptive statistics.
9. *Perception of Safety Index* means were 0.62 for all, 0.62 for whites, 0.63 for blacks, and 0.59 for other minorities.

10. Zip code level Herfindahl–Hirschman Index (HHI) scores computed using four racial categories: non-Hispanic whites, non-Hispanic blacks, Hispanics, and non-Hispanic other racial minorities ($M = 0.55$, $SD = 0.15$, range 0.37–0.93). A 1.0 HHI indicates a locale where everyone has the same race; a 0.0 HHI indicates a racially/ethnically diverse locale. ANOVA results for race and HHI index were significant: $F(2, 643) = 19.92$, $p < .001$, $\eta^2 = 0.06$. Zip code distress and zip code HHI were strongly positively correlated ($r = 0.229$; $p < .000$).
11. The MLM intercept standard deviation of 1.7 for *Lifestyle Resources* suggested that respondents could have regional specific intercepts up to 3.4 higher or lower than average about 95% of the time. Likewise, the deviation of 2.35 for *Physical Resources* meant that respondents could have regional specific intercepts up to 4.7 higher or lower than average.
12. Interclass correlations were 0.04 (*Lifestyle Resources*) and 0.06 (*Physical Resources*). These low ICC estimates suggested that (1) the IVs were not significantly different across the planning districts, (2) any variance in the DVs was due to respondent differences within the districts rather than between them, and (3) multilevel modeling was unnecessary.
13. US Department of Justice, Civil Rights Division, *Investigation of the Baltimore City Police Department*, August 10 2016.

Acknowledgements

I thank representatives from Baltimore City's Bureau of the Budget and Management Research for providing the anonymized survey data and associated reports. I thank Mike Galdi and Christian O'Neill in the Baltimore City Department of Planning for providing shapefiles and other data. I thank Rhoanne Esteban, University of California Santa Barbara, for assistance with geocoding locations related to the unrest. I thank Candis Watts-Smith, Christopher Stout, Loren Henderson, Derek Musgrove, Kimberly Moffitt, the anonymous reviewers, and the editors for helpful comments and suggestions. Any remaining errors are my own. Earlier versions of this manuscript were presented at the 2017 annual meetings of the National Conference of Black Political Scientists and of the Midwest Political Science Association.

Disclosure statement

No potential conflict of interest was reported by the author.

References

Barbehön, Marolon, Sybille Münch, Petra Gehring, Andreas Grossmann, Michael Haus, and Hubert Heinelt. 2016. "Urban Problem Discourses: Understanding the Distinctiveness of Cities." *Journal of Urban Affairs* 38 (2): 236–251.

Batson, Christie D., and Shannon M. Monnat. 2015. "Distress in the Desert: Neighborhood Disorder, Resident Satisfaction, and Quality of Life During the Las Vegas Foreclosure Crisis." *Urban Affairs Review* 51 (2): 205–238.

Bediako, Shawn M., and Kimberly R Moffitt. 2011. "Race and Social Attitudes About Sickle Cell Disease." *Ethnicity and Health* 16: 423–429.

Beilenson, Peter L., and Patrick A. McGuire. 2012. *Tapping into the Wire: The Real Urban Crisis*. Baltimore, MD: Johns Hopkins University Press.

Berube, Alan. 2015. "Beyond Baltimore: Thoughts on Place, Race, and Opportunity." *The Brookings Institution*, September 29.

Bradbury, Mark, and J. Edward Kellough. 2008. "Representative Bureaucracy: Exploring the Potential for Active Representation." *Journal of Public Administration Research and Theory* 18: 697–714.

Bradbury, Mark, and J. Edward Kellough. 2011. "Representative Bureaucracy: Assessing the Evidence on Active Representation." *The American Review of Public Administration* 41 (2): 157–167.

Brunson, Rod K. 2007. "'Police Don't Like Black People': African American Young Men's Accumulated Police Experiences." *Criminology & Public Policy* 6 (1): 71–101.

Dawson, Michael C. 1994. *Behind the Mule: Race and Class in American Politics*. Princeton, NJ: Princeton University Press.

DiPrete, Thomas A, and Gregory M Eirich. 2006. "Cumulative Advantage as a Mechanism for Inequality: A Review of Theoretical and Empirical Developments." *Annual Review of Sociology* 32 (1): 271–297.

Dizard, Wilson. 2015. "Baltimore's Poor White Residents also Feel Sting of Police Harassment." *America.Aljazeera.Com*, May 1. http://america.aljazeera.com/articles/2015/5/1/class-not-race-the-engine-of-police-harassment-in-baltimore.html.

Fine, Sidney. 2007. *Violence in the Model City: The Cavanagh Administration, Race Relations, and the Detroit Riot of 1967*. East Lansing: Michigan State University Press.

Fletcher, Michael. 2015. "What You Really Need to Know About BALTIMORE, from a Reporter Who's Lived There for Over 30 Years." *Washington Post*, April 28.

Gillion, Daniel Q. 2012. "Protest and Congressional Behavior: Assessing Racial and Ethnic Minority Protests in the District." *Journal of Politics* 74 (4): 950–962.

Gillion, Daniel Q. 2013. *The Political Power of Protest: Minority Activism and Shifts in Public Policy*. New York: Cambridge University Press.

Graham, David A. 2015. "The Baltimore Riot Didn't Have to Happen." *The Atlantic*, April 30.

Grasso, Maria T., and Marco Giugni. 2016. "Protest Participation and Economic Crisis: The Conditioning Role of Political Opportunities." *European Journal of Political Research* 55: 663–680.

Gurr, Ted Robert. 2011. *Why Men Rebel*. New York: Routledge.

Haider-Markel, Donald P., Mark R. Joslyn, Ranya Ahmed, and Sammy Badran. 2018. "Looters or Political Protesters? Attributions for Civil Unrest in American Cities." *Social Science Research* 75 (September): 168–178.

Hajnal, Zoltan L., and Jessica L. Trounstine. 2013. "Identifying and Understanding Perceived Inequities in Local Politics." *Political Research Quarterly* 67 (1): 56–70.

Hajnal, Zoltan L., and Jessica L. Trounstine. 2014. "What Underlies Urban Politics? Race, Class, Ideology, Partisanship, and the Urban Vote." *Urban Affairs Review* 50 (1): 63–99.

Haveke, Esther, Michael Bader, and Maria Krysan. 2016. "Realizing Racial and Ethnic Neighborhood Preferences? Exploring the Mismatches Between What People Want, Where They Search, and Where They Live." *Population Research and Policy Review* 35: 101–126.

Henricks, Kasey, and Louise Seamster. 2017. "Mechanisms of the Racial Tax State." *Critical Sociology* 43 (2): 169–179.

Hero, Rodney E., and Roger Durand. 1985. "Explaining Citizen Evaluations of Urban Services: A Comparison of Some Alternative Models." *Urban Affairs Quarterly* 20 (3): 344–354.

Hero, Rodney E., and Caroline J. Tolbert. 2004. "Minority Voice and Citizen Attitudes About Government Responsiveness in the American States: Do Social and Institutional Context Matter?" *British Journal of Political Science* 34 (1): 109–121.

Hinton, Elizabeth. 2016. *From the War on Poverty to the War on Crime: The Making of Mass Incarceration in America*. Cambridge: Harvard University Press.

Holtan, Meghan T., Susan L. Dieterlen, and William C. Sullivan. 2015. "Social Life Under Cover: Tree Canopy and Social Capital in Baltimore, Maryland." *Environment and Behavior* 47 (5): 502–525.

Hooker, Juliet. 2016. "Black Lives Matter and the Paradoxes of U.S. Black Politics: From Democratic Sacrifice to Democratic Repair." *Political Theory* 44 (4): 448–469.

Hur, Misun, and Jack L. Nasar. 2014. "Physical Upkeep, Perceived Upkeep, Fear of Crime and Neighborhood Satisfaction." *Journal of Environmental Psychology* 38: 186–194.

Jackson, Lawrence. 2016. "The City That Bleeds: Freddie Gray and the Makings of An American Uprising." *Harper's Magazine*, July.

James, Oliver, and Alice Moseley. 2014. "Does Performance Information About Public Services Affect Citizens' Perceptions, Satisfaction, and Voice Behaviour: Field Experiments with Absolute and Relative Performance Information." *Public Administration* 92 (2): 493–511.

Johnson, Cedric. 2016. "Ending the Violence." *Jacobin*, July 2016. https://www.jacobinmag.com/2016/07/dallas-police-shootings-castile-sterling-class-workers/.

Johnson Jr, James H., and Walter C. Farrell Jr. 1993. "The Fire This Time: The Genesis of the Los Angeles Rebellion of 1992." *North Carolina Law Review* 71(5): 1403–1420.

Krysan, Maria, and Michael Bader. 2007. "Perceiving the Metropolis: Seeing the City Through a Prism of Race." *Social Forces* 86 (2): 699–733.

Linskey, Annie. 2015. "There Are No 'Two Baltimores'." *Boston Globe*, May 10.

Mozingo, Joe, and Timothy M. Phelps. 2015. "Black Power in Baltimore: When African American Leaders Confront Racial Unrest." *Los Angeles Times*, April 29.

Nunnally, Shayla C. 2012. *Trust in Black America: Race, Discrimination, and Politics.* New York: New York University Press.

Perkins, Kristin L., and Robert J. Sampson. 2015. "Compounded Deprivation in the Transition to Adulthood: The Intersection of Racial and Economic Inequality Among Chicagoans, 1995–2013." *RSF: The Russell Sage Foundation Journal of the Social Sciences* 1 (1): 35–54.

Pietila, Antero. 2010. *Not in My Neighborhood: How Bigotry Shaped a Great American City.* Chicago, IL: Ivan R. Dee.

Poister, Theodore H., and John Clayton Thomas. 2007. "The Wisdom of Crowds: Learning From Administrators' Predictions of Citizen Perceptions." *Public Administration Review* 67 (2): 279–289.

Reed, Adolph. 2016. "How Racial Disparity Does Not Help Make Sense of Patterns of Police Violence." *Non-Site.Org*, September 16. https://nonsite.org/editorial/how-racial-disparity-does-not-help-make-sense-of-patterns-of-police-violence.

Riker, William H. 1982. *Liberalism Against Populism: A Confrontation Between the Theory of Democracy and the Theory of Social Choice.* Illinois: Waveland Press.

Rizzo, Victoria M., and Evelyn Kintner. 2013. "Understanding the Impact of Racial Self-Identification on Perceptions of Health-Related Quality of Life: A Multi-Group Analysis." *Quality of Life Research* 22: 2105–2112.

Schwartz, Alex, Kirk McClure, and Lydia B. Taghavi. 2016. "Vouchers and Neighborhood Distress: The Unrealized Potential for Families with Housing Choice Vouchers to Reside in Neighborhoods with Low Levels of Distress." *Cityscape: A Journal of Policy Development and Research* 18 (3): 207–227.

Snow, David A., Rens Vliegenthart, and Catherine Corrigall-Brown. 2007. "Framing the French Riots: A Comparative Study of Frame Variation." *Social Forces* 86 (2): 385–415.

Spence, Lester K. 2015. *Knocking the Hustle: Against the Neoliberal Turn in Black Politics.* New York: Punctum Books.

Stipak, Brian. 1979. "Citizen Satisfaction with Urban Services: Potential Misuse as a Performance Indicator." *Public Administration Review* 39 (1): 46–52.

Stipak, Brian. 1980. "Local Governments' Use of Citizens Surveys." *Public Administration Review* 40 (5): 521–525.

Swaroop, Sapna, and Maria Krysan. 2011. "The Determinants of Neighborhood Satisfaction: Racial Proxy Revisited." *Demography* 48: 1203–1229.

Tesler, Michael. 2012. "The Spillover of Racialization into Health Care: How President Obama Polarized Public Opinion by Racial Attitudes and Race." *American Journal of Political Science* 56 (3): 690–704.

Traister, Rebecca. 2015. "The Violence in Baltimore Didn't Start with the Riots." *The New Republic*, April 28.

Troy, Austin, Ashley Nunery, and J. Morgan Grove. 2016. "The Relationship Between Residential Yard Management and Neighborhood Crime: An Analysis From Baltimore City and County." *Landscape and Urban Planning* 147: 78–87.

US White House. 2015. "President Barack Obama's Remarks on Baltimore Riots." April 28.

Van Ryzin, Gregg G. 2007. "Pieces of a Puzzle: Linking Government Performance, Citizen Satisfaction, and Trust." *Public Performance & Management Review* 30: 521–535.

Van Ryzin, Gregg G., and Stephen Immerwahr. 2007. "Importance-Performance Analysis of Citizen Satisfaction Surveys." *Public Administration* 85 (1): 215–226.

Van Ryzin, Gregg G., Stephen Immerwahr, and Stan Altman. 2008. "Measuring Street Cleanliness: A Comparison of New York City's Scorecard and Results From a Citizen Survey." *Public Administration Review* 68 (2): 295–303.

Vemuri, Amanda W., J. Morgan Grove, Matthew A. Wilson, and William R. Burch Jr. 2011. "A Tale of Two Scales: Evaluating the Relationship Among Life Satisfaction, Social Capital, Income, and the Natural Environment at Individual and Neighborhood Levels in Metropolitan Baltimore." *Environment and Behavior* 43 (1): 3–25.

Vey, Jennifer S. 2015. "The Challenges of Baltimore (and the Nation) in Context." *The Brookings Institution*, May 7.

Vey, Jennifer S., and Alan Berube. 2015. "Yes, There Are Two Baltimores." *The Brookings Institution*, May 15.

Walsh, Camille. 2017. "White Backlash, the 'Taxpaying' Public, and Educational Citizenship." *Critical Sociology* 43 (2): 237–247.

Weffer, Simón E. 2017. "Are the Truly Disadvantaged Truly Demobilized? Neighborhood Disadvantage and Protest in Chicago, 1970–1990." *Critical Sociology* 43 (2): 267–289.

Wenger, Yvonne. 2015. "Unrest Will Cost City $20 Million, Officials Estimate." *Baltimore Sun*, May 26. Accessed April 25, 2017. http://www.baltimoresun.com/news/maryland/baltimore-city/bs-md-ci-unrest-cost-20150526-story.html.

Zuberi, Anita, Waverly Duck, Bob Gradeck, and Richard Hopkinson. 2016. "Neighborhoods, Race, and Health: Examining the Relationship Between Neighborhood Distress and Birth Outcomes in Pittsburgh." *Journal of Urban Affairs* 38: 546–563.

Targeting young men of color for search and arrest during traffic stops: evidence from North Carolina, 2002–2013

Frank R. Baumgartner, Derek A. Epp, Kelsey Shoub and Bayard Love

ABSTRACT
North Carolina mandated the first collection of demographic data on all traffic stops during a surge of attention to the phenomenon of "driving while black" in the late 1990s. Based on analysis of over 18 million traffic stops, we show dramatic disparities in the rates at which black drivers, particularly young males, are searched and arrested as compared to similarly situated whites, women, or older drivers. Further, the degree of racial disparity is growing over time. Finally, the rate at which searches lead to the discovery of contraband is consistently lower for blacks than for whites, providing strong evidence that the empirical disparities we uncover are in fact evidence of racial bias. The findings are robust to a variety of statistical specifications and consistent with findings in other jurisdictions.

The US has been in a period of intense discussion of police shootings and relations with minority communities for the past three years. Beginning with the acquittal of George Zimmerman for the killing of Trayvon Martin (July 2013), through the killings by police officers of Eric Garner in Staten Island, NY (17 July 2014), Michael Brown in Ferguson, MO (9 August 2014), and Freddie Gray in Baltimore, MD (12 April 2015), these four unarmed black men have become symbols of a national movement made apparent with the #BlackLivesMatter and the "Hands up, don't shoot" slogans that have now become commonplace. Unequal treatment of black and white citizens is of course nothing new, as can be attested to by such works as those of Alexander, whose *New Jim Crow* (2010) dramatically and forcefully traced the history of racial disparities in the criminal justice system, brought, she argues, to a new level through the mass incarceration movement in the 1980s and beyond. As Stevenson (2014) notes, the US Department of Justice (DOJ) reported almost 7 million American adults were under some form of judicial control at the end of 2013 (see also Glaze and Kaeble 2014). This marked a dramatic shift from historical trends, as state and federal prisoners were no more in 1973 than they had been in 1960 (see BJS 1982). The dramatic shift toward mass incarceration began in 1974 and accelerated during the 1980s and the 1990s when the war on drugs generated not only large increases in incarceration rates overall, but also an increased focus on the minority community.

Gary Webb's journalistic exposes of the "driving while black" phenomenon made clear in 1999 the extent to which black and brown drivers were subjected to systematic profiling as part of the war on drugs, also stressing the degree to which a previous police focus on safe driving was diverted into one focused on a needle-in-the-haystack search for drug couriers and largely reliant on very inefficient "behavioral" and racial profiles (see Webb 2007 [1999]).

The US Drug Enforcement Agency (DEA) promoted the use of profiles largely on the basis of the work of Florida state trooper Bob Vogel, later elected Sheriff of Volusia County, Florida. In a laudatory profile in the *Orlando Sentinel*, Fishman (1991) explains Vogel's laser-like focus on drug couriers, in spite of the fact that they typically were only in transit through his rural stretch of I-95 near Daytona Beach. Fishman writes:

> The pipeline wasn't causing much of a law enforcement problem for Vogel. (An early element of the courier profile, in fact, was that cars obeying the speed limit were suspect – their desire to avoid being stopped made them stand out.)

In fact, according to Webb (2007), Vogel's early work on drug interdiction was thrown out by various judges who considered his "hunch" that drugs may be in the car an unconstitutional violation of the need to have a probable cause before conducting a search. Vogel responded by studying the Florida vehicle code, finding that there were hundreds of reasons why he could legally pull a car over.

> He found them by the hundreds in the thick volumes of the Florida vehicle code: rarely enforced laws against driving with burned-out license plate lights, out-of-kilter headlights, obscured tags, and windshield cracks. State codes bulge with such niggling prohibitions, some dating from the days of the horseless carriage.
>
> "The vehicle code gives me fifteen hundred reasons to pull you over", one CHP [California Highway Patrol] officer told me. (Webb 2007)

In a major victory for this police strategy in the war on drugs, the Supreme Court decided in *Whren v. United States* (1996) that *any* traffic violation was a legitimate reason to stop a driver, even if the purported violation (e.g. changing lanes without signaling) was clearly a pretext for the officer's desire to stop and search the vehicle for other reasons, such as a general suspicion. There was no requirement that speeding laws, for example, be equitably enforced; if all the drivers are speeding, it is constitutionally permissible, said the Justices, to pick out just the minority drivers and enforce the speeding laws selectively. Of course, once a car is stopped, officers are often able to conduct a "consent" search when drivers do not object to the officer's request to search the vehicle. The *Whren* decision opened the floodgates to pretextual stops. Thus, tens of thousands of black and brown drivers have routinely been stopped and searched in an effort to reduce drug use. As Provine (2007) has pointed out, drug use is no different across race, though drug arrests differ dramatically.

Peffley and Hurwitz (2010) document the dramatic disparities in how white and black Americans experience, perceive, and relate to the police. Given the trends described above, it is no surprise that members of minority communities feel much less trustful of the police as compared to white Americans. Epp, Maynard-Moody, and Haider-Markel (2014) have provided the most comprehensive analysis of citizen interactions with the police in the particular context of traffic stop. They demonstrate that when blacks are stopped for legitimate reasons such as speeding, they show no difference in attitudes about the lawfulness and appropriateness of the traffic stop nor in the behavior of the officer, as compared to whites. However, they note that drivers have a sense of when the stops are pretextual and that being subjected to these pretextual stops is humiliating, threatening, and unjustified. It dramatically reduces the driver's sense of belonging in the community and belief that they are equal citizens awarded the same level of respect and protection by the police as whites. Thus, the racialized character of traffic stops, as in other elements of the criminal justice system, may have dramatic consequences not just for traffic safety, crime, drugs, and incarceration, but for the nature of American democracy itself. It goes to the heart of the question of whether all Americans feel that they are part of a single nation rather than living in separate communities divided by color and subject to differing rights and burdens.

Recent studies by Burch (2013), Lerman and Weaver (2014), and Moore (2015) have further documented the adverse effects of such disparate police practices (see also the studies included in Rice and White (2010)). Burch shows the collective impact on entire neighborhoods stemming from high levels of police interaction and incarceration. While feelings of trust toward the police are highly related to neighborhood crime rates (which *increase* trust in the police, who are seen as helping solve the problem), the nature of those interactions matters as well. As Epp and colleagues argued, where individuals feel they cannot count on being treated fairly by the police, social connections, efficacy, voting, and participation in politics all decline, as does a full sense of citizenship. Lerman and Weaver document a wide variety of social ills stemming from adverse interactions with police, including reduced willingness to use relevant government programs, fear of reprisals that keeps individuals from asking for services to which they are entitled, and further involvement with the criminal justice system. In fact, they find that a mere interaction with a police officer (not resulting in arrest) is associated with a reduction in the probability of voting of almost 10% (223). Moore (2015, 5–7) documents relatively similar levels of interactions with the police, in particular in traffic stops, but significant differences in the reasons for the traffic stops and their outcomes, with black drivers much more likely to see adverse outcomes such as search and arrest. Interactions with the criminal justice system can have dramatic and adverse outcomes to individuals and to entire communities, as these scholars show.

For many, the first and most straightforward interaction with a criminal justice official comes in the context of a routine traffic stop. In this article we explore the degree to which motorists in North Carolina experience different outcomes when stopped by the police and add to our collective understandings about the degree of racial difference apparent in this most common form of police–citizen interaction. For most whites, a speeding ticket is unpleasant, certainly unwelcome, perhaps understandable, and most likely attributed to a perhaps inadvertent lead foot. For many members of minority communities, traffic stops and their aftermaths represent something distinctly more alienating.

The US DOJ report on Ferguson

In March of 2015, the US Department of Justice released the results of its investigation of the Ferguson Police Department (FPD) (US DOJ 2015). The investigation took two lines of inquiry. The first was a qualitative assessment of department practices, based on interviews with Ferguson residents, police officers, and city officials; reviews of court documents, arrest records, and municipal budgets; and ride-alongs with on-duty officers. The second component was a quantitative analysis of patterns of police enforcement that compared the rate at which blacks were cited, arrested, and searched relative to whites.

Results from these inquiries were complementary and showed flagrant and systematic civil rights violations by the FPD. Among the most egregious violations was that city officials put great pressure on the police department to raise revenues by issuing traffic citations, and that these efforts were directed disproportionately toward the minority community. In effect, the city was subverting its traffic laws to balance municipal budgets, and doing so through the pockets of its black residents. Investigators also found that black motorists were more than twice as likely to be searched as whites following a traffic stop, but were 26% less likely to be found in the possession of contraband. The report concludes that

> the lower rate at which officers find contraband when searching African Americans indicates either that officers' suspicion of criminal wrongdoing is less likely to be accurate when interacting with African Americans or that officers are more likely to search African Americans without any suspicion of criminal wrongdoing. Either explanation suggest bias, whether explicit or implicit. (US DOJ 2015, 65)

The Department of Justice's logic in juxtaposing search rates with contraband hit rates as an indicator of racial discrimination finds support in the criminal justice literature. If studies discover that minority drivers are more likely to be searched, but less likely to be found with contraband, this disparity is taken as evidence of racial bias in police practice (Lamberth 1996; Harris 1999; Meehan and Ponder 2006; Persico and Todd 2008; Bates 2010). Conversely, when evidence shows that contraband hit rates are equal or higher among minorities, then the differences in search rates are considered to be part of good policing, not bias (Knowles, Persico, and Todd 2001). Others have used more complicated multivariate models that control for estimated rates of participation in crime across racial groups (Gelman, Fagan, and Kiss 2007). (Of course, higher contraband hit rates for relatively minor substances, such as user-amounts of marijuana, may not be an appropriate police focus, but this is a discussion beyond the scope of this analysis. We do not distinguish among the various types or amounts of contraband found here, which is a limitation we share with many previous analyses.)

Theory and expectations

We replicate the empirical component of the Ferguson investigation for North Carolina. North Carolina maintains the longest and most detailed record of traffic stops in the nation, allowing a wholescale replication of the quantitative segment of the report. We also push forward and measure the effects of other demographic factors that data limitations prevented the Department of Justice from considering in the Ferguson case. In particular, we consider how police enforcement varies not only by race, but also by age and gender. We determine that for North Carolina, racially disparate policing is predominantly a male-oriented phenomenon; female motorist experience only marginally different outcomes across racial lines.

We focus on particular empirical questions and draw out theoretical expectations from the literature on race and criminal justice as well as findings discussed above concerning the diversion of traffic control into part of the war on drugs. Our expectations are simply that the war on drugs has led to a sharp, but unjustified, focus on young men of color. Further, given that attention has only recently focused on the politically sensitive nature of these activities, and that no previous studies have given reason to expect any changes over time in the degree of racial disparities we might observe, we hypothesize no changes over time in these levels of disparity. Further, if the process is related to unjustified targeting, then any changes over time, if observed, should be uncorrelated with changes in contraband hit rates. Finally, we expect nothing in North Carolina to be exceptional. The Ferguson report showed an extreme case, perhaps, but incidents of racial profiling by the nation's police departments do not lend themselves to the conclusion that there is a single "hot spot" – rather there seems to be a broad and widespread institutional system at play. With that in mind, we lay out these hypotheses for testing:

> H1: Young men of color will be subjected to harsher outcomes following a traffic stop compared to any other demographic group.
> H2: These patterns are institutional rather than the results of individual "bad apple" police officers.
> H3: A focus on young men of color goes beyond what can be explained by higher rates of contraband found in those groups.
> H4: Trends over time will show no significant change in the degree of focus on young men of color over the study period of 2002–2013.
> H5: Any trends over time in the degree of disparity will not be justified by corresponding changes in contraband hit rates.
> H6: To the extent that it can be tested, the results from North Carolina analysis will be consistent with simple tests in other jurisdictions.

Data and preliminary analysis

North Carolina was the first state in the nation to mandate the collection of police-stop data, after public attention surged to this issue in the late 1990s. At least 15 states considered legislation during 1999 mandating the collection of police-stop information, and North Carolina was the first in the nation to pass such a law (GAO 2000, 15). Since 1 January 2002, the NC DOJ has collected information on every traffic stop from law-enforcement agencies throughout the state.[1] Our Supplemental Materials include a copy of the "SBI-122 Form", the two-page paper form which the officers fill out after any traffic stop. Data are relayed to the state DOJ and made available to the public in an online searchable database: http://trafficstops.ncdoj.gov/. Though the underlying legislation required the state to collect the data, police departments to report it, and the Attorney General to analyze it and issue reports on a biennial basis (see Mance 2012, fn. 3), the state has never issued any official analysis of the trends and patterns associated with the data collected. Because of the highly detailed nature of the NC database, we can add to the literature not only by exploring trends in stops, searches, and arrests as others have done (e.g. Moore 2015, using national data), but also with a multivariate analysis with controls not possible in other databases. We also note significant differences from one agency to the next (and from officer to officer), so we control for these in our statistical analyses as has not previously been possible in other studies.

North Carolina now makes an enormous amount of data available to the public: over 18 million traffic stops are documented in the NC DOJ database across the entire state, from 2000 to present. Before conducting any analysis, we drop observations from years where the data are incomplete. These include 2000 and 2001 when only the State Highway Patrol was reporting data, and 2014, which was the year of the last data update we received from the NC DOJ. We also drop observations relating to passengers and checkpoint stops. NC law requires these records to be collected only in the case when a search occurs, not for every stop. Therefore, we do not know how many drivers were stopped at a checkpoint, or how many passengers were in vehicles that were stopped. Table 1 presents an overview of the data.

The top part of Table 1 shows first how we move from 18.2 million observations to 15.99 million by eliminating years with incomplete data, checkpoint stops, and passengers. Then, based on the remaining cases, the bottom half of the table reports the number of times various outcomes have occurred following a traffic stop, with the right column showing the associated rates. Most traffic stops in NC result in a citation; this takes place in 66% of all cases. Searches occur in approximately 3% of the cases; arrests in 2.1%; and contraband in 0.8% of all stops, just 129,000 stops out of 16 million. The overall contraband hit rate (simply the number of contraband finds divided by the number of searches) is 25%. So a quarter of the searches conducted by NC officers are successful in the sense that they lead to contraband.[2]

Officers record the reason for each traffic stop and the State Bureau of Investigation (SBI) form allows for 10 different possibilities. For example, drivers can be stopped for speeding, safe movement violations, or not having their seat belt buckled. Table 2 shows how the 16 million stops are distributed across 9 of these stop purposes, excluding checkpoint stops. By far the most common reason NC motorists are pulled over is for speeding, followed by vehicle regulatory issues (having expired registration tags, for example). Other outcomes are less common. The table also shows the racial breakdown associated with each type of stop, making clear that the majority of motorists stopped for each type of violation are white. As whites greatly outnumber blacks in NC, this is not surprising. (The US Bureau of the Census reports that in 2013, 71.7% of North Carolinians identified as white, and 22.0% as black.) Overall 31% of stopped motorists are black and 63% are white, with the remainder belonging to other races. Reading down the two rightmost columns of the table tells us what types of stops break in a black or white direction relative to these baseline percentages. Vehicular issues skew strongly in the black direction. Blacks make up 31% of total stops, but 38% of stops relating to regulatory violations, 38% of those relating to

Table 1. Overview of the data.

Data subsets	Observations	Rates (%)
Total stops	18,194,110	–
2000	641,397	–
2001	598,733	–
2014	515,852	–
Passengers	298,459	–
Checkpoint stops	183,691	–
Stops for analysis	15,992,317	–
Citations	10,616,581	66.3
Searches	511,813	3.2
Arrests	349,136	2.1
Contraband	128,918	0.8

Table 2. Racial composition of traffic stops by purpose.

Purpose	Number	% Total	% White	% Black
Total stops	15,992,305	–	62.85	30.64
Driving impaired	158,264	0.99	66.22	22.32
Seat belt	1,492,624	9.33	66.88	26.56
Speed limit	6,665,939	41.68	66.64	26.65
Safe movement	886,090	5.54	62.93	29.82
Stop light/sign	758,136	4.74	62.63	31.18
Investigation	1,130,736	7.07	59.13	31.43
Other vehicle	851,550	5.32	57.49	33.53
Vehicle equipment	1,422,461	8.89	56.50	38.12
Vehicle regulatory	2,626,505	16.42	57.55	38.41

equipment issues, and 34% of "other vehicle" stops. The table also shows that some stops skew toward white drivers. These include speeding, seat belt violations, and driving impaired; white drivers are more likely to be stopped for one of these violations relative to their baseline rate of 63%. The data in Table 2 are for descriptive purposes only. As we do not know what percent of the driving public is black or white, or what percent of drivers engaging in various infractions are white or black, we do not interpret these results in any way at all, except to note dramatic differences in the proportions of blacks pulled over for various reasons (from 22% for driving while impaired to 38% for regulatory issues).

The Ferguson report focused on the rate at which blacks were searched, cited, and arrested relative to whites. We do the same in Table 3. For each of the nine stop purposes, the table shows the racial breakdown for experiencing these different outcomes. We also calculate a "percent difference", which describes the likelihood that a black driver experiences an outcome relative to a white driver. For example, if 10% of black motorists are searched following a stop for speeding and 5% of whites are searched, then the percent difference between them is 100%, indicating that blacks are 100% more likely to experience a search following a stop for speeding.[3] Percent differences will feature prominently in subsequent analysis as they highlight how black and white experiences with police differ. Table 3 thus starts our analysis of who experiences a relatively harsh outcome following their traffic stop. In contrast to Table 2, where we are limited because we do not know who was engaged in the behavior that led to the traffic stop, in Table 3 we know both the numerator and the denominator in the equation. Given all the people pulled over for a given reason, what was the outcome? And how does that differ by race?

Black drivers are much more likely to be searched or arrested than whites following each type of stop, with the exception of driving impaired. Blacks are 200% more likely to be searched and 190% more likely to be arrested after being pulled over for a seat belt violation; 110% are more likely to be searched or arrested following a stop for vehicle regulatory violations; and 60% are more likely to be searched or arrested after being stopped for equipment issues. In contrast, citations appear almost race-neutral. For six of the stop purposes, white motorists are slightly more likely to receive a citation and the only double-digit disparity is for driving impaired where black drivers are 11% more likely to be ticketed. Driving impaired appears to be an outlier; whites are more likely to be arrested and blacks more likely to be cited.

The only demographic distinction the Ferguson report makes is for race; but because the data for NC is more detailed and extensive than what is available for MO, we can

Table 3. Percent of drivers searched, cited, and arrested by race and purpose of stop.

	Searched			Cited			Arrested		
Purpose	Percent white	Percent black	Percent difference	Percent white	Percent black	Percent difference	Percent white	Percent black	Percent difference
Total	2.61	4.57	75	66.88	63.43	−5	1.90	2.71	43
Driving impaired	37.24	30.51	−18	24.56	27.25	11	56.26	46.82	−17
Safe movement	5.54	7.41	34	38.29	37.50	−2	3.25	3.62	11
Investigation	5.79	9.57	65	48.05	47.15	−2	4.03	6.39	59
Vehicle equipment	4.39	6.88	57	31.50	31.06	−1	1.75	2.78	59
Speed limit	0.95	1.67	76	78.35	79.16	1	0.69	1.12	62
Stop light/sign	2.31	4.55	97	57.03	56.89	0	1.42	2.33	64
Other vehicle	3.68	6.52	82	56.70	58.42	3	2.43	4.14	70
Vehicle regulatory	2.39	4.95	107	64.92	61.70	−5	1.23	2.56	108
Seat belt	1.09	3.30	203	90.00	84.21	−6	0.53	1.54	191

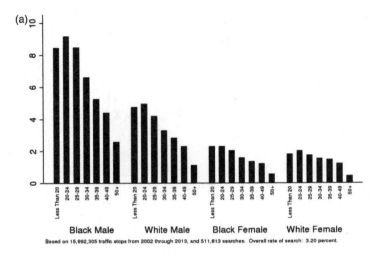
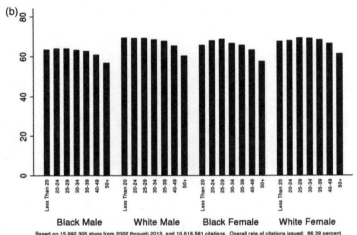
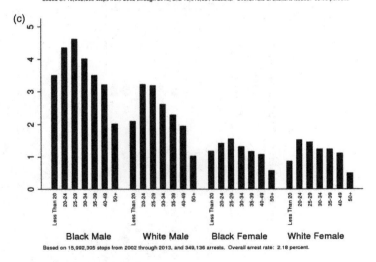

Figure 1. Rates by race, gender, and age group.

also separate motorists by age and gender, and still retain enough observations to ensure robust calculations. Figure 1 presents this analysis in a series of bar charts that show the rate at which different groups are searched, cited, or arrested following a stop. Looking first at searches, there are dramatic age disparities; older motorists are less likely to be searched and this holds true across racial and gender groups. There are also stark gender disparities. Male motorists of both races are more likely to be searched than their female counterparts. Comparing extremes, 9% of the black men between the ages of 20 and 24 years who are stopped are searched, while less than 1% of white women over the age of 50 years are searched. Young black men are 1800% more likely to be searched after a traffic stop than older white women.

Of particular interest is that the racial disparities so clearly visible between black and white males are only very modest for female drivers. In fact, black and white females are searched at a roughly equivalent rate across each age group and the same is true when looking at Panel C for arrests. This signals an important point of departure for our analysis from the Ferguson report. In NC, it appears that racially disparate policing predominately affects male drivers. Subsequent analysis will therefore focus only on males. Complementary analysis looking at female drivers is available in the appendix.

Finally, looking at Panel B it is clear that NC police approach citations differently than either searches or arrests. Table 2 indicates that ticketing was neutral with respect to race and Panel B suggests that it is also age- and gender-neutral. Black men of any age are actually marginally less likely to be ticketed than their white or female counterparts. In this respect, policing in NC and Ferguson is very different. Furthermore, the conventional wisdom that women are less likely to be ticketed after being pulled over appears to be false. Having established that pronounced disparities exist for searches and arrests (but not for citations), and having narrowed our focus to male drivers, we turn now to documenting trends over time and assessments of racial disparities.

Twelve years of NC policing

Table 2 shows that black drivers (men and women) are 75% more likely to be searched than whites, 5% less likely to be ticketed, and 43% more likely to be arrested. Figure 2 shows how these differences have varied over time, for male motorists. In 2002, black men were 70% more likely to be searched than whites and this disparity has grown steadily over the period of study. Beginning in 2007, black men were twice as likely to be searched and by 2013 this difference had grown to over 140%. Black men are also more likely to be arrested; however, this disparity has remained stable at about a 60% increased likelihood. We also see that black men are marginally less likely to receive citations and there is almost no variance; NC police are highly consistent over time in their relative treatment of whites and black men when it comes to ticketing.

Figure 3 shows the percent differences for citations, arrests, and searches across the various stop purposes. (Table 2 presents the same information for men and women combined.) Isolating men does little to change the overall pattern, except that the disparities are greater when we focus only on men. Compared to white men, black men are more likely to be searched and arrested for every type of stop, with the exception of driving while impaired. Disparities in ticketing are comparatively minor and fluctuate around zero.

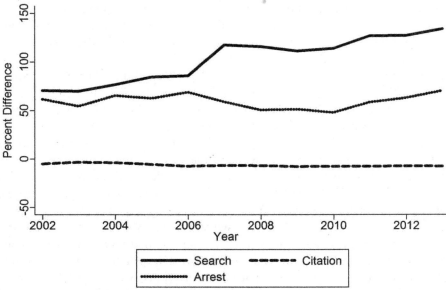

The figure shows the percentage difference in the likelihood of different outcomes for Blacks as compared to Whites.

Figure 2. Percent difference in the likelihood of search, citation, or arrest for black men.

There are two possible explanations for the disparities documented in Figures 2 and 3. One is racially differential policing and the other is racially differential possession of contraband.[4] Both explanations could account for higher search and arrest rates of black men, but they point to very different problems so we want to distinguish between them. To do so, we first take a closer look at the types of searches to which NC motorists are subjected. The SBI form lists five different search types and Table 4 shows the rate at which each type of search occurs. The three most common types of search are those based on driver consent, searches that occur incident to an arrest, and searches based on probable cause. Searches conducted when executing a warrant or as protective frisks are very rare. The top cell of the rightmost column shows the overall percent difference; black men are 97% more likely to be searched than white men. Reading down this column reveals how different types of search deviate from this baseline rate. Probable cause searches skew strongly toward blacks, indicating that officers are much more likely to be suspicious of criminal wrongdoing when interacting with black motorists. Black men are also twice as likely to be searched with consent. This indicates either that black men

Table 4. Rates of search by race for men.

Search type	Number	% Total	% White	% Black	Percent difference
Total stops	10,320623				
Total searches	427,677	4.14	3.23	6.38	97
Incident to arrest	148,326	1.44	1.23	1.90	55
Search warrant	1,127	0.01	0.01	0.01	61
Protective frisk	14,316	0.14	0.11	0.21	94
Consent	194,236	1.88	1.47	2.94	100
Probable cause	69,672	0.68	0.42	1.33	216

THE POLITICS OF PROTEST 199

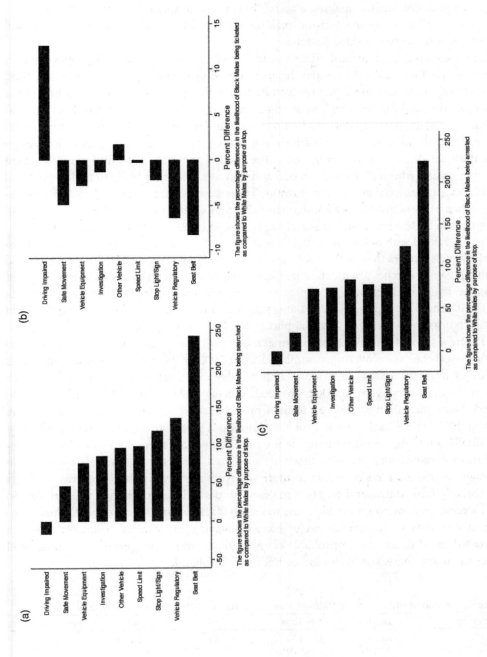

Figure 3. Percent difference in the likelihood of outcomes for blacks, by purpose of stop.

are more willing to give their consent to be searched or that officers are more likely to request consent after stopping a black driver. The other types of search take place under prescribed circumstances and in these instances may be a mandatory component of police protocol, such as making a search in conjunction with an arrest. They therefore have less to tell us about the decision-making of NC police, as officers have less discretion about when to carry out these searches.

Are the suspicions that lead officers to search black drivers at such disproportionately high rates justified? Table 5 provides the answer by showing the rates at which officers find contraband on drivers subsequent to conducting each type of search. Looking first at the row labeled "Total Contraband", we see that overall officers are 2% more likely to find contraband on black drivers after conducting a search. However, reading down the column shows that this increased likelihood is driven entirely by the searches where officers exercise the least discretion. For example, police are 9% more likely to find contraband on black motorists whom they have arrested and they are 11% more likely to find contraband on blacks after exercising a search warrant. These searches are mandated, not discretionary. When officers must make a judgment call about whether or not to search a motorist, they tend to be less successful at searching blacks; in other words, they use a lower probability threshold with blacks or have a "hunch" that is less likely to be accurate with regard to black male drivers than with others. Moreover, we know from Table 4 that consent and probable cause searches are much more likely to be employed on black motorists; so, taken together, these results paint a bleak picture of NC officer's abilities to discern when a black motorist should be searched. Indeed, it is just such a disparity that the US Department of Justice points to as evidence of racial bias in the Ferguson report.

Figure 4 shows trends in the differential use of probable cause searches and the success of these searches at recovering contraband from 2002 to 2013 between white and black males. A dramatic change is evident. Police today are much more suspicious of black motorists than they were in 2002. In 2002, officers were almost 125% more likely to search black men than white men using a probable cause search. By 2013, officers were almost 250% more likely to use probable cause as a justification for searching blacks – essentially doubling the disparity in the use of probable cause searches. Tracking the contraband hit rate associated with this type of search reveals that officers' suspicions of wrongdoing have always been less accurate when engaging with black motorists; officers consistently find contraband on black males at modestly lower rates than white males. So the increased reliance on probable cause to search blacks is not associated with more accurate assessments of the likelihood of blacks engaging in criminal behavior. And the increased racial disparities in probable cause searches over time appear to be unjustified in terms of any increased likelihood of finding contraband.

Table 5. Likelihood of finding contraband given a search for men, by race and type of search.

Search type	Number	% Total	% White	% Black	Percent difference
Total searches	427,677	4.14	3.23	6.38	97
Total contraband	108,198	25.30	25.64	26.07	2
Consent	194,236	20.91	23.30	19.13	−18
Probable cause	69,672	52.81	56.39	50.68	−10
Incident to arrest	148,326	18.92	18.68	20.39	9
Search warrant	1127	39.31	38.19	42.28	11
Protective frisk	14,316	15.95	15.79	17.76	12

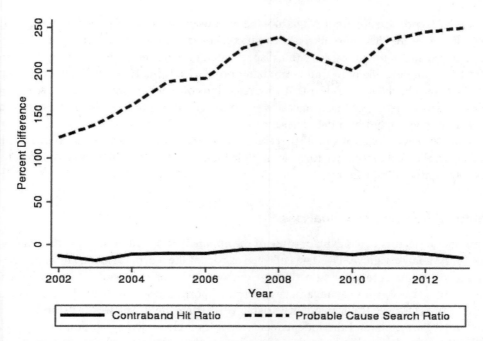

Figure 4. Percent difference in the likelihood of probable cause searches and finding contraband for black men.

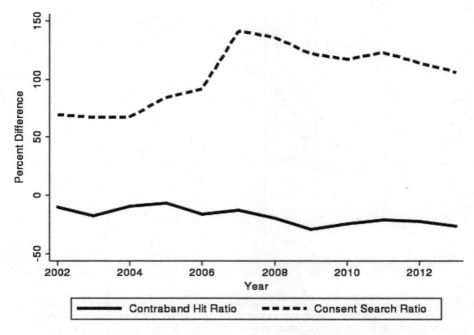

Figure 5. Percent difference in the likelihood of consent searches and finding contraband for black men.

Similar trends are apparent when looking at consent searches. Figure 5 shows that in 2002 officers were 75% more likely to conduct a consent search on a black man as compared to a white man, but by 2013 this disparity had grown even higher. During this time officers became less likely to find contraband on blacks; from 10% less likely in 2002 to 25% in 2013. The data make clear that with regard to consent and probable cause searches, an increased targeting of black males was completely unjustified by any corresponding increase in contraband hit rates. These were either flat or declining.

So far, we have looked at simple percentage differences in searches and contraband hits by race. In the next section we turn to multiple logistic regressions in order to control for possibly confounding factors.

Multivariate regression analyses

A number of factors could explain some of the apparent racial differences that we uncovered in the analyses above. The data collected as part of the North Carolina law allow us to control for the purpose of the stop, the time of day and day of week, and a number of other factors. In Table 6, we take advantage of these opportunities to present three statistical models. In each case, the dependent variable is whether the driver was (a) searched, (b) cited, or (c) arrested, and the independent variables include demographics, the purpose of the stop, the day and hour of the stop, whether the individual officer conducting the

Table 6. Predicting the occurrence of a search, citation, or arrest for men.

Variable	Search	Citation	Arrest
Demographics			
Black	1.75*(0.01)	1.08*(0.00)	1.51*(0.01)
Hispanic, not black	1.16*(0.01)	1.83*(0.01)	1.72*(0.01)
Age	0.97*(0.00)	0.99*(0.00)	0.99*(0.00)
Stop purpose			
Speed limit	–	–	–
Stop light	1.45*(0.01)	0.52**(0.00)	1.25*(0.02)
Impaired	23.65*(0.24)	0.08*(0.00)	59.21*(0.68)
Movement	2.96*(0.02)	0.21*(0.00)	2.04*(0.02)
Equipment	2.38*(0.02)	0.17*(0.00)	1.27*(0.01)
Regulatory	1.90*(0.01)	0.55*(0.00)	1.57*(0.01)
Seat belt	2.10*(0.02)	0.89*(0.00)	1.26*(0.02)
Investigation	5.38*(0.04)	0.27*(0.00)	3.98*(0.04)
Other	2.61*(0.02)	0.47*(0.00)	2.38*(0.03)
Officer type			
Black disparity[a]	1.20*(0.01)	0.98*(0.00)	1.12*(0.00)
White disparity[a]	0.84*(0.01)	0.97*(0.01)	1.32*(0.02)
Contraband			
Contraband Found	–	0.88*(0.01)	23.49*(0.19)
Time			
Hour of Day	Included	Included	Included
Day of Week	Included	Included	Included
Constant	0.09*(0.00)	2.63*(0.02)	0.03*(0.00)
N	4,752,908	4,752,908	4,752,908
Psuedo R^2	0.10	0.10	0.23

Notes: Entries are odds-ratios, with standard errors in parentheses. The number of observations is smaller than the total number of male stops because the "hour of stop" variable is missing in some cases. Race is coded in mutually exclusive categories here, with "White, non-Hispanic" being the reference category. "Other" race drivers are omitted in this table.
*$p < .05$.
[a]High disparity officers search white (black) drivers at more than twice the rate of a black (white) driver. Additionally, the office must have stopped at least 50 black drivers, 50 white drivers, and have a search rate greater than the statewide average of 3.20%.

stop was a "high disparity" officer, and, for the citation and arrest models, whether contraband was found. The models exclude a small number of motorists coded as "other" in the race category, so coefficients for the black and Hispanic variables can be interpreted as the differential likelihood of these groups experiencing a search, citation, or arrest relative to whites. Furthermore, we focus only on male drivers. Our appendix presents similar results for females, and a model in which we include a fixed-effects term for the agency conducting the stop, since different agencies have different overall rates of search, on average. (These robustness checks produce very similar results to those presented here, though the results for females show much lower levels of racial disparity.)

Table 6 provides clear evidence that the comparisons of percentages presented in earlier sections are robust to a more sophisticated set of controls. Coefficients indicate the percent difference in likelihood from a baseline of 1.00 that a search, arrest, or citation occurs. In the first model, black men are shown to have a 75% increased likelihood of search compared to white men, controlling for all other factors in the model, and based on over 4.7 million observations. The officer-disparity variables allow us to control for a "bad apple" hypothesis. While it is true that a driver stopped by an individual officer who tends to search many more blacks than whites will be more likely to be searched, inclusion of this variable in the model allows us to see if the race-of-driver variable remains significant even when that is controlled for. So the 75% increased likelihood can be interpreted as the increased chance, after controlling for all the other factors, including the "bad apple" hypothesis. Clearly, there are some officers with great disparities in their behaviors. However, the patterns we document here cannot be explained away with reference only to these individuals; these are widespread patterns of differential treatment.

The single greatest predictor of being searched, it is important to note, is being stopped for impaired driving. Overall 32.77% of male drivers stopped for impaired driving are searched, as compared to 3.2% of drivers overall, and the large coefficient for this variable accurately reflects this huge increase in likelihood. In fact, all the search purpose variables are relatively large (and of course are all significant, which we expect since there are almost five million observations); this means that the baseline category, speeding, is significantly less likely to lead to a search than any other type of traffic stop. Safe movement, equipment, and seat belt violations have high coefficients in the search model, and of course stops relating to investigations have very high rates of both search and arrest.

Looking at the citation model, as speeding tends to lead to a ticket, all the other stop purposes have low coefficients (a coefficient of 0.90 would indicate a 10% lower likelihood of that outcome, compared to the baseline, which in our model is speeding). Driving while impaired has an extremely low coefficient for citation, and a very high one for arrest, indicating that such drivers are more likely to be searched and/or arrested, not simply given a ticket. These common-sense outcomes are evidence that the models are indeed capturing the results of most traffic stops, giving confidence that the other coefficients can similarly be interpreted with confidence.

In the second (citation) and third (arrest) models, we include a variable for whether contraband was found. Again, consistent with common sense, these coefficients indicate that the presence of contraband is a strong predictor that the driver will be arrested, not ticketed. In the citation and arrest models, we can see that blacks are marginally more likely to be cited (with an 8% increased likelihood) and much more likely to be arrested (51% increased likelihood), all other factors equal. Hispanic males show a 16%

increased likelihood of search; 83% increased likelihood of citation, and 72% increased chance of arrest. In all cases, the odds of these outcomes decline with age.

In general, the results from Table 6 present a stark picture of the odds of negative outcomes for black and Hispanic male drivers in North Carolina. Controlling for why and when they were stopped, which officer pulled them over, and whether or not they had contraband in the car, young men of color are much more likely to see adverse outcomes. Of course, the analysis is limited in that we do not know the extent to which motorists were breaking the law when they were pulled over. It may be that minorities systematically break the law in more egregious ways than whites, as the Lange, Johnson, and Voas (2005) study found. In part, we account for this possibility by controlling for contraband, but this is incomplete as there are many ways to break law beyond carrying contraband. Still, these multivariate results corroborate and extend the findings from our earlier presentations of simple percentage differences in the rates of search or arrest. Minorities are much more likely to be searched and arrested than similarly situated whites, controlling for every variable that the state of North Carolina mandates to be collected when traffic stops are carried out.

Conclusion

The war on drugs comes with readily apparent costs, both fiscal and in lost human opportunity. Much has been written about the price of incarcerating minor drug users and the effects on community development of "missing black men". Burch's (2013) careful work has shown the enormous collective costs to entire communities of mass incarceration. Epp, Maynard-Moody, and Haider-Markel (2014) have clearly documented how pretextual traffic stops alienate, humiliate, and demean minority drivers, depriving them of a full sense of citizenship and promoting distrust with government. An insidious but growing consequence of the war on drugs, we believe, has been the gradual alienation of minority communities whose residents feel that the police unreasonably target them; a trend that recent events in Ferguson, New York, and Baltimore have forced the nation to confront. Having conducted an extensive statewide analysis of traffic stops using state-of-the-art data, we can conclude that blacks in North Carolina appear to have good reasons to be mistrustful of the police, and that these trends appear to be growing over time. This is particularly true for North Carolina's black men, who are searched at much higher rates than their white counterparts, but are less likely to be found with contraband in discretionary police searches. If we follow the precedent used by the US Department of Justice in the Ferguson report, then this discrepancy points strongly toward racial bias in the policing of NC motorways.

Our most surprising and worrisome finding is that evidence for racial discrimination appears to be growing stronger over time. Black motorists today are much more likely to be searched relative to whites than they were 10 years ago and these higher search rates find no justification in contraband hit rates. This is a trend that deserves immediate attention by NC and national policy-makers. In a recent study of the Texas Department of Highway Safety (their Highway Patrol), Baumgartner et al. (2015) show that black drivers in Texas were subject to search 51% more often than white drivers in 2003, but that this disparity has also grown over time, reaching 97% in 2011, and 86% in 2014, the most recent year available. If the US DOJ report on Ferguson was troubling, these two statewide reports document something perhaps even more troubling: these racial disparities are increasing over time.

Our findings confirm all of our hypotheses but one, and all of the findings are troubling, if not all unexpected. Young men of color are indeed targeted for harsher outcomes (searches and arrest); these patterns cannot be explained by our high disparity officer variable, debunking a "bad apple" hypothesis; this targeting cannot be explained by contraband hit rates; trends over time disconfirm our naïve hypothesis that there would be no trends, as disparities are sharply increasing; these disparities are uncorrelated with contraband hit rates and therefore cannot be explained by them; and the findings in North Carolina are similar to the extent that they can be replicated in Texas, with the limited data available there.

Notes

1. The law exempts only police departments in towns with fewer than 10,000 population. The State Highway Patrol has been subject to the law since 1 January 2000, but it was phased in for other agencies in 2002.
2. Other outcomes that can result from a traffic stop include verbal or written warnings and "no enforcement action". In concert with the Ferguson report, we focus on only citations, arrests, and searches because they are the most invasive and punitive of the possible outcomes.
3. The mathematics behind this calculation are straightforward: ((10/5)*100)−100.
4. For example, a study by Lange, Johnson, and Voas (2005) of drivers on the New Jersey Turnpike found that speeders were more likely to be black and that patterns of police traffic stops accurately reflected the racial make-up of speeders, rather than the racial composition of the surrounding communities.

Disclosure statement

No potential conflict of interest was reported by the authors.

References

Alexander, Michelle. 2010. *The New Jim Crow: Mass Incarceration in the Age of Colorblindness*. New York: The New Press.
Bates, Timothy. 2010. "Driving While Black in Suburban Detroit." *Du Bois Review: Social Science Research on Race* 7: 133–150.
Baumgartner, Frank R., Bryan D. Jones, Julio Zaconet, Colin Wilson, and Arvind Krishnamurthy. 2015. "Racial Disparities in Texas Department of Public Safety Traffic Stops, 2002–2014." Testimony presented to the Texas House of Representatives Committee on County Affairs, November 18. http://www.unc.edu/~fbaum/TrafficStops/Baumgartner-TexasDPS-Nov2015.pdf.
Burch, Traci. 2013. *Trading Democracy for Justice*. Chicago, IL: University of Chicago Press.
Bureau of Justice Statistics. 1982. *Prisoners, 1925–81*. Washington, DC: US DOJ. http://www.bjs.gov/content/pub/pdf/p2581.pdf.
Epp, Charles R., Steven Maynard-Moody, and Donald Haider-Markel. 2014. *Pulled Over: How Police Stops Define Race and Citizenship*. Chicago, IL: University of Chicago Press.
Fishman, Charles. 1991. "Sheriff Bob Vogel: He's The Mayor of I-95, and a Terror to Drug Smugglers." *Orlando Sentinel*, August 11. Accessed June 6, 2015. http://articles.orlandosentinel.com/1991-08-11/news/9108091173_1_bob-vogel-drug-trade-drug-traffic.
GAO (Government Accounting Office). 2000. *Racial Profiling: Limited Data on Motorist Stops*. Washington, DC: US General Accounting Office.

Gelman, Andrew, Jeffrey Fagan, and Alex Kiss. 2007. "An Analysis of the New York City Police Department's "Stop-and-Frisk" Police in the Context of Claims of Racial Bias." *Journal of the American Statistical Association* 102: 813–823.

Glaze, Lauren E., and Danielle Kaeble. 2014. *Correctional Populations in the United States, 2013*. Washington, DC: US DOJ. http://www.bjs.gov/content/pub/pdf/cpus13.pdf.

Harris, David A. 1999. *Driving While Black: Racial Profiling on Our Nation's Highways*. New York: American Civil Liberties Union.

Knowles, John, Nicola Persico, and Petra Todd. 2001. "Racial Bias in Motor Vehicle Searches: Theory and Evidence." *Journal of Political Economy* 109: 203–229.

Lamberth, John. 1996. *A Report to the ACLU*. New York: American Civil Liberates Union.

Lange, James E., Mark B. Johnson, and Robert B. Voas. 2005. "Testing the Racial Profiling Hypothesis for Seemingly Disparate Traffic Stops on the New Jersey Turnpike." *Justice Quarterly* 22: 193–223.

Lerman, Amy E., and Vesla M. Weaver. 2014. *Arresting Citizenship*. Chicago, IL: University of Chicago Press.

Mance, Ian A. 2012. *Racial Profiling in North Carolina: Racial Disparities in Traffic Stops 2000 to 2011*. Raleigh, NC: North Carolina Advocates for Justice.

Meehan, Albert J. and Michael C. Ponder. 2006. "Race and Place: The Ecology of Racial Profiling African American Motorists." *Justice Quarterly* 19: 399–430.

Moore, Nina M. 2015. *The Political Roots of Racial Tracking in American Criminal Justice*. New York: Cambridge University Press.

Peffley, Mark, and Jon Hurwitz. 2010. *Justice in America: The Separate Realities of Blacks and Whites*. New York: Cambridge University Press.

Persico, Nicola and Petra Todd. 2008. "The Hit Rates Test for Racial Bias in Motor-Vehicle Searches." *Justice Quarterly* 25 (1): 37–53.

Provine, Doris Marie. 2007. *Unequal Under Law: Race in the War on Drugs*. Chicago, IL: University of Chicago Press.

Rice, Stephen K., and Michael D. White, eds. 2010. *Race, Ethnicity and Policing: New and Essential Readings*. New York: New York University Press.

Stevenson, Bryan. 2014. *Just Mercy: A Story of Redemption*. New York, NY: Spiegel & Grau.

United States Department of Justice, Civil Rights Division. 2015. *Investigation of the Ferguson Police Department*. March 4. Washington: US DOJ.

Webb, Gary. 2007. "Driving While Black: Tracking Unspoken Law-Enforcement Racism." *Esquire*, January 29. Accessed May 21, 2015. www.esquire.com/news-politics/a1223/driving-while-black-0499. [Originally published as: DWB, Esquire 131, 4 (April 1999): 118–127].

Appendix 1. Alternative model specifications

Table 6 presented a model for the entire state. Each agency has a different baseline rate of search, however, so it may be appropriate to include fixed effects for the agency. We do so in Table A1, limiting our analysis in this case to the 25 largest police agencies in the state. Note that the N here declines from 4.75 million in Table 6 to just over 3 million, as we exclude many smaller agencies. Results in Table A1 suggest that the findings in Table 6 are highly robust.

Table A1. Predicting the occurrence of a search, citation, or arrest for men for the top 25 agencies.

Variable	Search	Citation	Arrest
Demographics			
Race	2.08*(0.01)	0.94 *(0.00)	1.61*(0.01)
Hispanic	1.23*(0.01)	1.70*(0.01)	1.78*(0.02)
Age	0.97*(0.00)	0.97*(0.00)	0.99*(0.00)
Stop purpose			
Speed limit	–	–	–
Stop light	1.62*(0.02)	0.45*(0.00)	1.23*(0.02)
Impaired	29.44*(0.42)	0.05*(0.00)	75.48*(1.18)
Movement	2.85*(0.03)	0.20*(0.00)	2.11*(0.03)
Equipment	2.52*(0.02)	0.15*(0.00)	1.28*(0.02)
Regulatory	1.98*(0.02)	0.43*(0.00)	1.49*(0.02)
Seat belt	2.55*(0.03)	0.68*(0.00)	1.35*(0.03)
Investigation	5.52*(0.05)	0.22*(0.00)	4.07*(0.05)
Other	2.96*(0.03)	0.39*(0.00)	2.59*(0.04)
Officer type			
Black disparity[a]	1.30*(0.01)	0.92*(0.00)	1.10*(0.00)
White disparity[a]	0.90*(0.02)	1.07*(0.01)	1.42*(0.03)
Contraband			
Contraband found	–	0.76*(0.01)	26.90*(0.30)
Time			
Hour of day	Included	Included	Included
Day of week	Included	Included	Included
Agency fixed effects	Included	Included	Included
N	3,052,024	3,052,024	3,052,024
Log likelihood	−627,322.11	−1,839,413.2	−366,595.01

Notes: Entries are odds-ratios, with standard errors in parentheses. Constant suppressed. The number of observations is smaller than the total number of male stops because the "hour of stop" variable is missing in some cases.
*$p < .05$.
[a]High disparity officers search white (black) drivers at more than twice the rate of a black (white) driver. Additionally, the office must have stopped at least 50 black and white drivers, and have a search rate greater than 3.20%.

Appendix 2. Analysis of female drivers

Our main text focuses on males. Here we provide parallel information for female drivers, generally showing much more muted racial disparities. Figure A1 presents basic information on the differential likelihood of various outcomes of a stop for black women as compared to white women. As can be seen, women have essentially the same likelihood of being cited; this remains constant over the time period of the study. Over time, black women are increasingly more likely to be searched after being stopped than white women; in 2002 there was no difference, but by 2013 there is a 25% increased likelihood of being searched. The difference in the likelihood of being arrested fluctuates over this time.

Moving on from the basic trends in time of differences in stop outcomes, Figure A2 presents the percent difference in the likelihood of outcomes for black women as

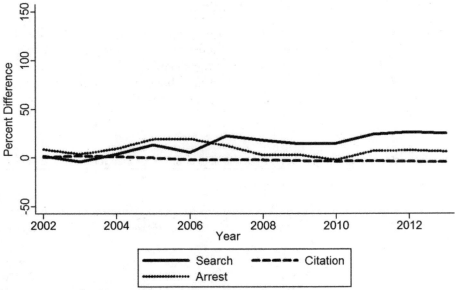

The figure shows the percentage difference in the likelihood of different outcomes for Blacks as compared to Whites.

Figure A1. Percent difference in the likelihood of traffic stop outcomes for black women.

compared to white women by purpose of stop. Unlike for men, there is more variation in the percent differences by purpose and outcome. White women are more likely to be searched after being stopped for driving while impaired, safe movement violations, and vehicle equipment. Black women have an essentially equal rate of search when stopped for an investigation. Black women are more likely to be searched following any other type of stop. All women are roughly as likely as being cited following any of type of stop; the differences are all within 5%. Finally, black women are consistently more likely to be arrested following a stop except for driving while intoxicated and safe movement stops.

These differences in the likelihood of being searched following a stop once again lead us to examine whether this difference is being driven by the differential use of specific types of searches. Table A2 begins to answer this question. While there are modest differences for consent searches, searches executed per a search warrant, and incident-to-arrest searches, the real differences are in the use of probable cause searches. In these cases, black women are much more likely to be subject to search.

Table A3 extends this line of enquiry by presenting the contraband hit rates following a search-by-search type. In every case, the police are less to find contraband on black women. This is emphasized in Figures A3 and A4 where the percent difference in the likelihood of a consent and probable cause searches are presented alongside the percent difference in the likelihood of finding contraband following a search for black women as compared to white women. While these trends are more dramatic than those for men, they are smaller and fluctuate more over time.

Table A4 presents the same model from Table 6 for women. Findings indicate much more muted racial disparities: Black women are 10% less likely to be searched, 21%

THE POLITICS OF PROTEST 209

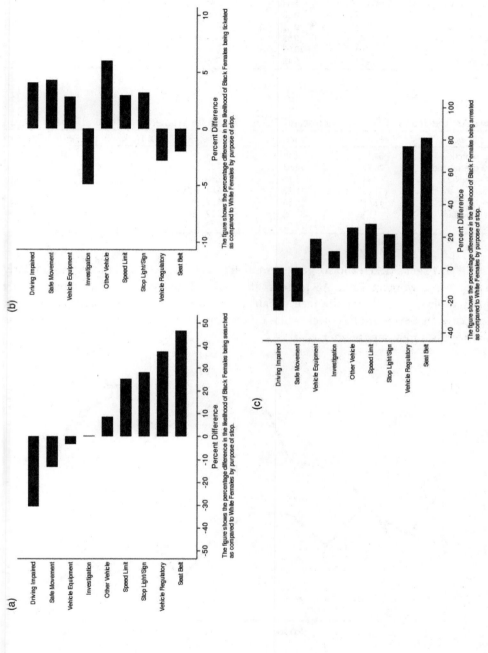

Figure A2. Percent difference in the likelihood of outcomes for black women by purpose of stop.

Table A2. Rates of search by race for women.

Search type	Number	% Total	% White	% Black	Percent difference
Total stops	5,671,694	–	62.42	33.06	–
Total searches	84,136	1.48	1.45	1.63	12
Consent	36,974	0.68	0.68	0.65	−5
Search warrant	218	0	0	0	0
Incident to arrest	31,457	0.55	0.55	0.59	7
Protective frisk	1917	0.03	0.03	0.04	33
Probable cause	13,570	0.19	0.19	0.35	84

Table A3. Likelihood of Finding Contraband Given a Search for Women, by Race and Type of Search.

Search type	Number	% Total	% White	% Black	Percent difference
Total searches	84,136	1.48	1.45	1.63	12
Total contraband	20,720	24.63	25.75	23.03	−11
Protective frisk	1917	12.26	12.49	11.99	−32
Incident to arrest	31,457	15.43	16.88	13.21	−22
Probable cause	13,570	50.36	54.22	46.29	−21
Search warrant	218	31.65	35.17	23.94	−15
Consent	36,974	23.61	25.48	20.23	−11

more likely to get a ticket, and six percent more likely to be arrested, compared to similarly situated white women. Table A5 presents the fixed-effects agency model showing only slightly different results for the race variable: 12%, 6%, and 14% increased likelihoods. In no case, however, are the black/white differences among women close to as great as those we document among men.

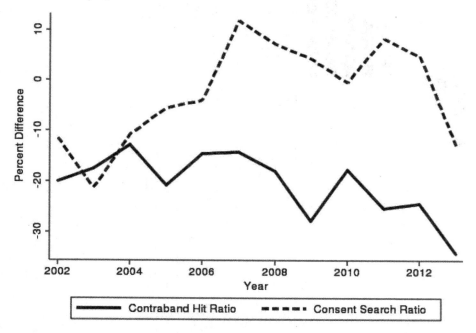

Figure A3. Percent difference in the likelihood of probable cause searches and finding contraband for black women.

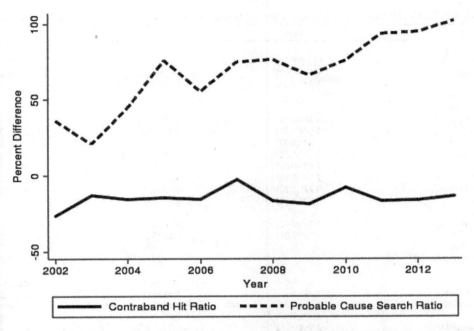

Figure A4. Percent difference in the likelihood of consent searches and finding contraband for black women.

Table A4. Predicting the occurrence of a search, citation, or arrest for women.

Variable	Search	Citation	Arrest
Demographics			
Race	0.90*(0.01)	1.21*(0.00)	1.06*(0.01)
Hispanic	0.48*(0.01)	1.80*(0.01)	0.69*(0.02)
Age	0.97*(0.00)	0.99*(0.00)	0.99*(0.00)
Stop purpose			
Speed limit	–	–	–
Stop light	1.63*(0.03)	0.45*(0.00)	1.36*(0.03)
Impaired	37.05*(0.75)	0.08*(0.00)	93.64*(2.01)
Movement	3.77*(0.06)	0.19*(0.00)	2.90*(0.06)
Equipment	3.06*(0.05)	0.13*(0.00)	1.65*(0.04)
Regulatory	2.44*(0.03)	0.50*(0.00)	1.99*(0.03)
Seat belt	2.79*(0.07)	0.89*(0.01)	1.68*(0.06)
Investigation	9.70*(0.15)	0.26*(0.00)	7.14*(0.14)
Other	3.86*(0.07)	0.43*(0.00)	3.51*(0.08)
Officer type			
Black disparity[a]	1.12*(0.01)	0.96*(0.00)	1.16*(0.02)
White disparity[a]	0.96*(0.03)	0.95*(0.01)	1.24*(0.04)
Contraband			
Contraband Found	–	1.24*(0.02)	35.93*(0.68)
Time			
Hour of Day	Included	Included	Included
Day of Week	Included	Included	Included
Constant	0.04	2.26	0.01
N	2,906,964	2,906,964	2,906,964
R^2	0.12	0.11	0.24

Notes: Entries are odds-ratios, with standard errors in parentheses. The number of observations is smaller than the total number of male stops because the "hour of stop" variable is missing in some cases.
*$p < .05$.
[a]High disparity officers search white (black) drivers at more than twice the rate of a black (white) driver. Additionally, the office must have stopped at least 50 black and white drivers, and have a search rate greater than 3.20%.

Table A5. Predicting the occurrence of a search, citation, or arrest for women for the top 25 agencies.

Variable	Search	Citation	Arrest
Demographics			
Race	1.12*(0.01)	1.06*(0.00)	1.14*(0.01)
Hispanic	0.52*(0.02)	1.60*(0.01)	0.69*(0.02)
Age	0.97*(0.00)	0.99*(0.00)	0.98*(0.00)
Stop purpose			
Speed limit	–	–	–
Stop light	1.76*(0.05)	0.39*(0.00)	1.36*(0.04)
Impaired	45.54*(1.27)	0.06*(0.00)	112.24*(3.26)
Movement	3.49*(0.08)	0.17*(0.00)	2.93*(0.09)
Equipment	2.96*(0.06)	0.11*(0.00)	1.61*(0.05)
Regulatory	2.40*(0.04)	0.38*(0.00)	1.90*(0.04)
Seat belt	2.94*(0.10)	0.74*(0.01)	1.72*(0.08)
Investigation	9.27*(0.20)	0.20*(0.00)	7.35*(0.19)
Other	3.90*(0.10)	0.36*(0.00)	3.75*(0.11)
Officer type			
Black disparity[a]	1.23*(0.02)	0.91*(0.00)	1.15*(0.02)
White disparity[a]	1.13*(0.04)	1.06*(0.01)	1.36*(0.06)
Contraband			
Contraband Found	–	1.03*(0.03)	45.13*(1.20)
Time			
Hour of Day	Included	Included	Included
Day of Week	Included	Included	Included
Agency fixed effects	Included	Included	Included
N	1,905,026	1,905,026	1,905,026
Log likelihood	−154,994.72	−1,122,016.30	−106,235.63

Notes: Entries are odds-ratios, with standard errors in parentheses. Constant suppressed.
The number of observations is smaller than the total number of male stops because the "hour of stop" variable is missing in some cases.
*$p < .05$.
[a]High disparity officers search white (black) drivers at more than twice the rate of a black (white) driver. Additionally, the office must have stopped at least 50 black and white drivers, and have a search rate greater than 3.20%.

#BlackLivesDon'tMatter: race-of-victim effects in US executions, 1976–2013

Frank R. Baumgartner, Amanda J. Grigg and Alisa Mastro

> This paper examines the role of racial bias in the implementation of capital punishment. First, our analysis of existing literature confirms higher rates of capital punishment for those who kill Whites, particularly for Blacks who kill Whites. Second, we compare homicide victim data with a newly collected data set including information on the victims of every inmate executed in the USA from 1976 through 2013, some 1369 executions. These data reveal that Black males have been the primary victims of homicides, but their killers are much less likely to be put to death. While previous scholars have emphasized the over-representation of killers of White women, we shed additional light on another aspect of the racial and gender biases of the US death penalty. Capital punishment is very rarely used where the victim is a Black male, despite the fact that this is the category most likely to be the victim of homicide.

The USA routinely experiences over 10,000 homicides in a single year but in the modern period (post-1976) has never executed as many as 100 individuals; death is not and never has been the likely consequence for murder. In spite of the low rates of usage of capital punishment, its symbolic and emotional power are immense. In this article, we focus on one particular element of that power: the great odds against being executed if one's victim is a Black male. Black men, especially among the relatively young, have a statistical risk of homicide victimization many times higher than any other racial or gender group, but their killers rarely face the death penalty. We explore the extent of these discrepancies here first by reviewing the literature and second by presenting the results of a newly collected database of all US executions from 1976 through 2013.

The single most reliable predictor of whether a defendant in the USA will be executed is the race of the victim. Blacks make up about half of the total homicide victims in the USA though they represent only about 12% of the population. Yet, among convicted murderers who have been executed, only 15% of victims have been Black. A substantial body of academic research has confirmed a persistent racial bias in death sentencing in favor of White victims. Further, research suggests that among defendants charged with killing White victims, Blacks are more likely than Whites to receive a death sentence. Just 9.5% of executions for interracial murders involve White killers with non-White victims (DPIC 2015). One statistic is particularly stark: since the reinstatement of capital punishment in 1976 through the end of 2013, 1359 inmates were executed. Among this group were 534 White inmates executed for killing a single victim. Just 9 of that group of 534 had a Black male victim.[1] Including killers with multiple victims, just 16 Whites executed had a Black male victim (these 16 cases are listed in Appendix B in Supplementary material). It has long been widely known that racial disparities affect criminal justice, of course. Academics and activists have for years argued that the judicial system places more value on the lives of Whites, resulting in disproportionately harsh treatment of Black criminals who have White victims (ACLU 2007; Baldus, Pulaski, and Woodworth 1983; NAACP 2013). Our goal in this paper is to draw attention to the scope of existing disparities in treatment, and in particular to focus on a group which is nearly invisible in this system: Black male victims.

Our work offers new evidence in efforts to document racial bias in the implementation of capital punishment, providing both a systematic review of existing literature and a new, comprehensive review of all 1359 executions in the modern era. We would certainly expect to uncover patterns in the direction of what we observe, given the robust literature documenting bias in capital punishment. However, the scope of the disparity identified is greater than even the existing body of scholarship would lead one to expect. In addition, our findings are not based on a sample or an estimate; they come from a complete list of every execution in the modern area and detailed information about each victim. The thorough nature of our evidence allows us to make substantial conclusions about the state of capital punishment in the USA; it is clearly a racial project, and a highly gendered one as well.

The influence of victim race in capital sentencing

Of course, suggesting that the race of the victim has an impact on the likelihood of a death sentence is hardly new. It is one of the most consistent findings in all empirical legal scholarship relating to capital punishment. The landmark work on the influence of victim race in death penalty sentencing was conducted by Baldus, Pulaski, and Woodworth (1983). Their work examined over 2000 murders in Georgia, controlling for over 230 variables. They found that those accused of killing White victims were four times as likely to be sentenced to death as those accused of killing Black victims (Baldus, Pulaski, and Woodworth 1983).[2] Research has continued on this topic apace, and by 1990 the federal Government Accounting Office (GAO) had issued a report reviewing the substantial body of scholarship on racial bias in capital punishment. According to the GAO, 82% of studies found that those who murdered Whites were more likely to be sentenced to death than those who murdered Blacks (GAO 1990).

In the years following the GAO report, academic research has continued to demonstrate that victim race is a strong determinant of whether defendants are sentenced to death, and done so with increasingly sophisticated methods (Baldus and Woodworth 2003; Bowers, Pierce, and McDevitt 1984; Donohue 2014; Paternoster and Brame 2003; Pierce and Radelet 2005; Radelet 1989). These more recent works have found that even after controlling for aggravating factors, defendants with White victims are as much as four times as likely to be sentenced to death than those with Black victims (Baldus and Woodworth 2001; Paternoster et al. 2004). Donohue (2014) was particularly complete in assessing the degree of heinousness of the crimes for all death-eligible homicides in Connecticut. His conclusion was that death sentences were not reserved for the "worst of the worst" – many not sentenced to death had committed more heinous or aggravated murders than those sentenced; rather, victim race and geography were major predictors. Similar disparities have been found across the death penalty states.[3]

Though victim race is the key determinant, certain combinations of victim race and defendant race can result in even greater bias. Donohue's study of over 4600 murders in Connecticut found that African-American defendants received the death penalty at three times the rate of White defendants in cases where the victims are White (Donohue 2014). The race of a defendant and victim can play a role even after the death sentence has been imposed. Among those already on death row, minority inmates convicted of killing Whites are more likely to be executed than any other perpetrators (Jacobs et al. 2007).

Several US states, even among those that are substantial users of capital punishment, have never seen a White inmate executed for killing a Black man. In his 1981 study of the death penalty in Florida, Zeisel found that not only were there no Whites on death row for killing only a Black person, but also that there had "never been such a person on Florida's death row in living memory" (Zeisel 1981). In Texas and Alabama, the execution of a White man for the murder of a Black man has occurred only once in living memory, in both cases within the last decade. The men executed in those two cases, Lee Taylor and Henry Francis Hays, were both White supremacists convicted of particularly gruesome and racially motivated murders.[4]

Meta-analysis of race-of-victim bias

As the preceding review of the literature suggests, race-of-victim bias has been a topic of great interest to scholars. To better understand the scope of race-of-victim effects in capital prosecution and sentencing, we conducted a meta-analysis of existing research. In so doing we expand on the work of Baldus and Woodworth whose 2005 article provides an excellent overview of empirical research on racial bias in the death penalty, with an emphasis on post-1990 research.

To begin, we produced a comprehensive inventory of the body of research, identifying 236 sources, of which 72 listed empirical estimates. The articles included are empirical analyses and discussions of race- and gender-based differences in death penalty prosecution and sentencing. This review is limited to works from academic journals, governmental studies, and state-commissioned reports.[5] The review is also limited to works published after 1972, which was the year the Supreme Court of the United States decided in *Furman v. Georgia* that states had to reevaluate their death penalty statutes to eliminate arbitrariness. Michael Radelet (1989) has argued that much of the research conducted before the *Furman* decision failed to consider important controls, including the effect of prior criminal records, and employed methodologies that have since become outmoded due to their simplicity. The periods under study range from 1972 to 2008 and jurisdictions include the U.S. Armed Forces, Federal Courts, and 33 current and prior death penalty states from all regions of the USA. Notably, the controls used in the studies under review varied widely.

In every study of racial bias in capital prosecution, prosecutors were more likely to charge killers of Whites with capital crimes than those who were killers of Blacks.[6] Studies of bias in death sentencing (in the penalty phase of a capital trial) covered an even greater range than those of capital prosecution.[7] The vast majority of these studies found that killers of Whites were more likely than killers of Blacks to receive a death sentence.[8] Though existing scholarship would certainly lead us to expect to find frequent documentation of racial bias, the enormous range of methods, time frames, geographic foci, and control variables used make finding consistent evidence of anything far more difficult. In light of this, the persistent presence of bias is both striking and extremely robust.

Figure 1 illustrates the collective findings of all the studies we reviewed. Part A summarizes the race-of-victim findings for published studies on the prosecutor's decision to charge a defendant capitally, and Part B does so for studies looking at sentences of death after a trial. The bars indicate the number of studies that found each level of bias. A value of 1.00 would indicate that

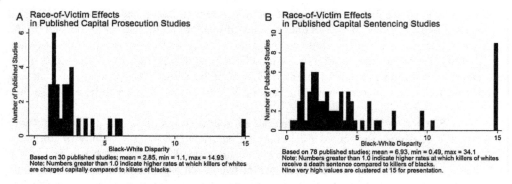

Figure 1. Race-of-victim effects found in published studies (A) capital prosecutions and (B) death sentences. Note: For a list of sources and more details on the findings, see Appendix A in Supplementary material.

Black and White victims are equally likely to see the crime proceed capitally (Part A), or lead to a sentence of death (Part B). As Figure 1 makes clear, almost all published studies find some degree of racial bias, and, for the decision to prosecute, this was unanimous.

In the studies summarized in Figure 1(A), none found a value below 1.00. That is, each of the 30 studies identified found that killers of Whites were more likely than killers of Blacks to face a capital prosecution. These studies cover a wide range of geographic areas and time periods, and include different sets of statistical controls. In Figure 1(B), we see almost the same pattern, with some slight differences. Though the vast majority of studies found that killers of Whites are sentenced to death at higher rates than killers of Blacks, there were cases in which this was not found.[9] Nine studies found a negative effect or no significant effect (ratios below 1.09), and 69 studies found significant and substantial race-of-victim effects. As the captions to the figures show, the average bias in the charging studies (Part A) was 2.85, and in the sentencing studies (Part B), 6.93. These are very high racial disparities, and as Appendix A in Supplementary material makes clear they have been found in many time periods, geographical areas, and with different statistical models controlling for legally relevant factors. Note that Part B includes nine studies where ratios could not be calculated because no Whites had been sentenced to death for killing Black victims. Overall, then, our comprehensive review of past studies shows ample evidence of racial biases in the vast majority of cases. The unique contribution of the current study is to examine all US executions since 1976. We turn to those findings in the next section.

Methodology

The USA has executed 1359 inmates from 1977 through 31 December 2013.[10] Each of these executions is the object of considerable public record, and several web sites make available information about each of them. Most prominent is that of the Death Penalty Information Center (DPIC), a Washington-based clearinghouse of information related to the modern death penalty. Another prominent and near-comprehensive source is the website of the Clark County (IN) Office of the Prosecuting Attorney. This site, in fact, links to newspaper coverage, legal documents, and other sources relating especially to the underlying crimes that lead to the death penalty in each case. Beginning with these two sources, the senior author of this article, working with a team of research assistants, compiled a database listing the race and gender of each of the victims of these executions. For cases from 2000 through 2013, the Clark County

Prosecutor's Office site contains full information; for earlier cases, extensive web and legal database searches were conducted to ascertain information about the victims, dates of crimes, dates of sentencing, and county of crime and conviction; this article makes use only of the victim information. With information about the inmate easily available, and information about the victims now compiled, our analysis is relatively straightforward; we simply want to know the number of cases with various combinations of offender–victim race and gender. These can then be compared with US Department of Justice (Bureau of Justice Statistics – BJS) statistics about homicides overall.[11] BJS statistics come from "Homicide Trends in the United States" and are available only through 2005. The time coverage of our execution database is therefore slightly longer than that of homicides, but we report the full series available. Limiting our execution database to 2005 would show similar results; executions typically follow homicides by more than 10 years in any case.

It is important to recognize some limitations to our comparisons of execution cases with all US homicides; the key point is that we do not know which homicides are capital-eligible and which are not. Here, we follow the examples of Blume, Eisenberg, and Wells (2004) and Fagan, Zimring, and Geller (2006), who looked at particular states (eight states where offender and victim race and gender data were available for Blume, and Texas in the case of Fagan) and compared death-sentence cases with homicides more generally. For example, Blume et al. calculated the number of death sentences per homicide (using the same BJS statistics that we use) and showed these rates per 1000 homicides: Black Offender–Black Victim, 8.4; White Offender–Black Victim, 19.3; White Offender–White Victim, 30.1; Black Offender–White Victim, 65.4 (calculated from Blume, Eisenberg, and Wells 2004, 197; note that for Arizona, the comparisons are Minority–Majority rather than Black–White). Our results are highly consistent and use a similar methodology to those, with these differences: Blume et al. looked at death sentences where we look at executions; they looked at just eight states where we look at all US jurisdictions; and they reviewed statistics from 1977 through 2000 and we go through 2013.

Fagan, Zimring, and Geller (2006, 1825, Figure 2) compare homicide trends with capital homicide trends and show that capital homicides represent roughly 15–25% of all homicides

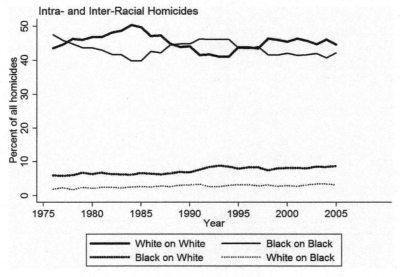

Figure 2. Percent of homicides by offender–victim race.
Source: Bureau of Justice Statistics 2008, 2011.

in death penalty states from 1976 through 2005, or 22–28% of homicides nationally. The percentage of homicides eligible for capital prosecution increases slightly over time nationally as well as in death penalty states. As our interest is in proportions and trends over time, these numbers suggest that a national analysis based on all homicides will show similar trends as one limited to death-eligible homicides (since these represent a relatively constant percentage of all homicides), and to look at national data rather than to limit our assessment to death penalty states only (since the trends are highly similar in both).

Systematic data on capital-eligible homicides are not available, but the number of capital-eligible homicides is generally related to the number of homicides more broadly, as Fagan, Zimring, and Geller (2006) demonstrate. Further, a number of carefully controlled studies reviewed above have looked at individual-level factors including victim and defendant socio-economic status, number of victims, egregiousness of crime, and aggravating and mitigating factors statutorily considered in death penalty sentencing and reached findings broadly similar to our own (Baldus and Woodworth 2003; Donohue 2014; Paternoster and Brame 2003; Pierce and Radelet 2005).[12] And, finally, a review of the White-on-Black killings that did lead to an execution in Appendix B in Supplementary material makes clear, even to a reader accustomed to the violent nature of capital homicides, that these cases are indeed particularly heinous.

Results

To begin, we examine overall homicide rates in order to determine how many executions of each racial combination we would expect in the absence of bias. Using data from the Department of Justice on all US homicides, available from 1975 through 2005, we find that the vast majority of homicides are intra-racial (between two people of the same race). As shown in Figure 2, White-on-White homicide and Black-on-Black homicide each consistently make up over 40% of all homicides. Interracial crimes, White-on-Black and Black-on-White homicides, each make up less than 10%.

In the absence of legally permissible factors that are relevant to death sentencing, we would expect that most executions would be the result of White-on-White or Black-on-Black crime, and that executions for White-on-Black and Black-on-White crime would be infrequent, and roughly equal to their proportion of all homicides (10%). However, literature on race-of-victim bias suggests that executions for Black-on-White crime will be relatively common while executions for White-on-Black crime will be rare (see our meta-analysis above). Our analysis confirms that this is the case, but extends the evidence to a larger historical period, with greater geographic coverage than has been done before, and shows that the bias is larger than had been previously estimated. Figure 3 provides a visual representation. The dark bars show the number of victims of White killers who were later executed; grey bars show the number of victims of Black killers who were later executed.

While 17 Whites have been executed for killing a Black, 230 Blacks have been executed for killing a White. In fact, twice as many Blacks have been executed for killing Whites (230) as have been executed for killing Blacks (108). This is in spite of the fact that the vast majority of all homicides committed by Blacks have a Black victim.[13]

Figure 4 compares execution rates for intra-racial (White-on-White and Black-on-Black) and interracial homicides. Figure 2 showed that the vast majority of homicides occur between individuals of the same race, and this is reflected in the right-most columns of Figure 4, which show that 94% and 85%, respectively, of Whites and Blacks have victims of the same race. The left-most columns in Figure 4 show that patterns of intra-racial homicide are not reflected in executions. As in the case of homicides, the vast majority of Whites have victims of the same race. There is no such correspondence in the case of Black defendants. While 85% of all Blacks found guilty of

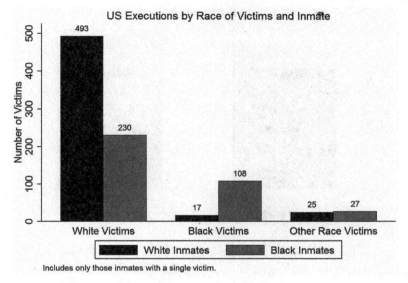

Figure 3. Race of victim for Blacks and Whites executed.

homicide have Black victims, fewer than 40% of Blacks executed for homicide have Black victims.

We see the same phenomenon in Figure 5 which compares the race of all homicide victims (on the right) with the victims of individuals later executed (on the left).

Figure 5 shows that Blacks make up 47% of all homicide victims, but just 17% of the victims of those executed. This suggests that Blacks are not only over-represented among the executed (as scholars have long argued) but are also vastly under-represented among victims of those executed. Analysis of the 2128 victims of all individuals executed between 1977 and 2013, and all 401,650

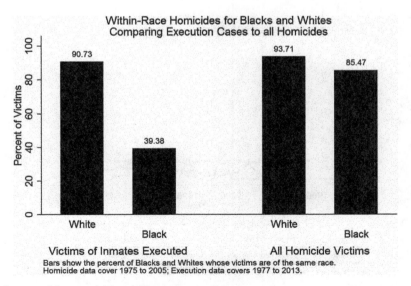

Figure 4. Inter- and intra-racial homicides and executions.

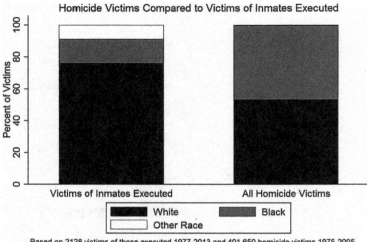

Figure 5. Race of homicide victims compared to race of victims of those executed.

homicide victims between 1975 and 2005 reveals that although Blacks make up almost half (47%) of all homicide victims, they represent just a small proportion (17%) of the victims of crime where the perpetrator is later executed by the state. Conversely, Whites are over-represented among victims of those executed as compared to homicides in general. These findings suggest that race-of-victim bias can work not only to increase the perceived seriousness of crimes against White victims, but also to decrease the perceived seriousness of crimes against Black victims.

Figure 6 shows the ratio of executions to homicides, by year, for the different combinations of inmate and victim race. It calculates the ratio of percent of all homicides in a given offender–victim race category to the percentage of execution-related homicides for that same category. If an equal percentage of homicides led to execution, the ratio would be 1.00. Numbers below

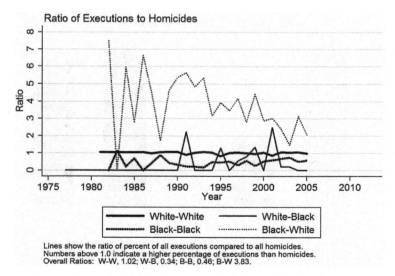

Figure 6. Ratio of executions to homicides by race of offender and victim.

1.00 indicate that such homicides are relatively unlikely to lead to an execution, and numbers above 1.00 show where the executions are statistically more likely.

The thick Black line in Figure 6 shows that White-on-White crime is consistently treated in a proportionate manner, with an overall ratio 1.02. Roughly the same percentage of these homicides leads to execution as not. This is what we would expect in the absence of any kind of bias for or against victims or perpetrators. In both of the victim/perpetrator combinations with Black victims, however, overall ratios are well below 1, meaning that killers of Black victims are substantially less likely than killers of Whites to be executed. Of course, the low odds of execution are particularly stark in the case of White-on-Black crime, for which the overall ratio is 0.34. In fact, as the thin solid line makes clear, there are many years where this ratio is 0.00: no Whites were executed killing Blacks in many of the years shown. (A quick perusal of Appendix B in Supplementary material gives a feel, in fact, of just how horrific these crimes need to be in order to lead to execution.) The dotted line at the top of the graph shows the opposite for Black-on-White crime. In this case, Black-on-White murders make up a far larger proportion of all executions than they do of all homicides. While Whites who killed Blacks are vastly under-represented in the list of those executed, Blacks with White victims are dramatically over-represented. These trends are stark, consistent over time, and overwhelming in their magnitude.

Conclusion

Strong race-of-victim effects have consistently been found in post-*Furman* studies indicating that individuals with White victims are treated more harshly than those with Black victims. Our own data consisting of all reported homicides and executions in the modern era (from 1976 onwards) confirm that there are very few cases in which Whites are executed for killing Blacks, and a disproportionately high number of cases in which Blacks are executed for killing Whites. Researchers have tended to focus on the latter cases, specifically as evidence of a troubling bias in favor of White victims. In fact, our data suggest that an exploration of both kinds of cases presents even more compelling evidence of the power of race-of-victim bias.

A long line of scholarship documents persistent racial bias in the implementation of capital punishment. In *McCleskey v. Kemp*, the United States Supreme Court ruled that even the most convincing evidence of racial bias is not enough to demonstrate a violation of constitutional rights unless it presents proof of intentional, conscious discrimination. Such evidence is nearly impossible to come by barring an outright admission. Further, as the magnitude and scope of racial bias documented in our findings suggests, a focus on intentional discrimination by individuals ignores the ways in which bias might be built into the system or operate unconsciously across multiple individuals and processes. Recent litigation regarding the retention of the death penalty in Connecticut included the compilation of extensive statistics in a massive data collection effort by Donohue (2014) covering every death-eligible homicide in recent years in that state, and confirming important racial and geographic biases in the application of the penalty. (From 1973 through 2007, Donohue's analysis showed that Connecticut had 4979 homicides, 205 death-eligible homicides, 12 death sentences, 9 death sentences sustained after appeals, and 1 execution.) The court, as in *McCleskey*, threw out the argument that such evidence was persuasive. Scheidegger (2011, 2012) argued that if crimes occur in urban areas, and urban juries have Blacks, and Blacks are unwilling to impose the death sentence, then "racial disparities would shrink to insignificance if legitimate factors, *including jurisdiction*, could properly be taken into account" (2011, 22).[14] In another article (2012, 164) he asks: "To the extent that a race-of-the-victim disparity exists, is it due to racial animus of the decision makers?" If this cannot be demonstrated, then his logic suggests that there can be no finding of disparity, and that was the finding in *McCleskey* as well as in the Connecticut litigation.

The idea that racial disparities require the demonstration of racial animus and intent is what Eduardo Bonilla-Silva (1997) refers to as the "prejudice problematic" – the expectation that we should identify a single racist villain to explain an outcome that could well be due to more structural causes. To a large extent, the courts have remained true to this "prejudice problematic," unwilling to confront implicit bias and structural differences. Further, as Scheidegger (2011) suggests, they take geographic disparities – which of course can be related to racial outcomes – as signs of appropriate "local control" properly to be left to the discretion of locally elected prosecutors, judges, and juries and in fact a sign of healthy variation rather than a challenge to the equal protection clause of the Constitution.

Despite the rejection of powerful evidence by the courts, scholarship continues to document the presence of racial bias in capital punishment. Numerous studies, such as those by Bonilla-Silva (1996, 1997) and Bonilla-Silva, Lewis, and Embrick (2004) and Eberhardt with various colleagues (Eberhardt et al. 2004, 2005/2006; Hetey and Eberhardt 2014; Rattan et al. 2012; Williams and Eberhardt 2008), convincingly show the subconscious bias that underlies many decisions in the criminal justice system from traffic stops to eyewitness ID procedures to prosecutors' decisions about capital punishment to whether an offender should be tried as a child or an adult, to the imposition of the ultimate penalty. Our work builds on these important theoretical works, providing both a systematic review of existing empirical literature and a new, comprehensive review of all 1359 executions in the modern era. In both cases the results are stunning. The trend is certainly expected given the large body of scholarship documenting bias. However, the scope of the disparity is greater than even the existing literature would lead one to expect. Further, our findings are not based on a survey or an estimate; we have assembled a complete list of every execution in the modern era, and looked up information on each of the victims. The comprehensive nature of our evidence allows some strong conclusions about the state of capital punishment in the USA now almost 40 years since its re-establishment in 1976.

The enormous scope of racial bias identified here, in both the review of existing literature and analysis of all modern-era executions, suggests that we question the standard for evidence presented in *McCleskey v. Kemp*. It is clear that significant, troubling, racial disparities exist without proof of intentional discrimination by state actors. These disparities are not, as Justice Powell suggested, "an inevitable part of our criminal justice system" (*McCleskey v. Kemp* 1987). More pressingly, these findings suggest that we reevaluate the death penalty itself. At a minimum, we must recognize its strongly racialized character.

The justices have recognized these facts. In fact, in an internal memorandum from Justice Scalia to the conference during consideration of Justice Powell's draft decision quoted above, he wrote:

> Since it is my view that unconscious operation of irrational sympathies and antipathies, including racial, upon jury decisions and (hence) prosecutorial decisions is real, acknowledged in the decisions of this court, and ineradicable, I cannot honestly say that all I need is more proof. (quoted in Gross 2012, 1921)

In other words, no evidence could change his mind: he already believes that "irrational sympathies," and even their "unconscious operation" (i.e., with no explicit intent), are powerful factors in the criminal justice system. And, furthermore, he thinks this is a fact we simply have to become accustomed to, as it cannot be avoided.

Whether or not Justice Scalia's opinion that racial factors in the criminal justice system are both real and "ineradicable" remains the operating assumption on the US Supreme Court, the degree of racial disparity demonstrated here is powerful enough to cause many others to find it unacceptable. In a time when support for capital punishment among legislators and the public has reached record lows, our study adds another reason to oppose the practice. In its modern history as in its use in previous eras, racial bias in its application is consistently high. In addition to the threat to the equal protection of the law that these numbers suggest, such overwhelming evidence of differential treatment erodes public support for the judicial system. Further, the strength of these biases makes clear that complaints of unequal treatment are real, not imagined. If the ultimate and highly symbolic punishment is meted out in such a disparate manner with regard to race, and with these patterns of racial bias so similar in the modern period to the overtly racist practices of previous generations, the statistical patterns laid bare in this study can only lead to a decline in support and efficacy of the judicial system overall.

Notes

1. Eight had Black female victims.
2. It was notably the central evidence presented in the 1987 Supreme Court decision *McCleskey v. Kemp*, which alleged widespread racial bias in the implementation of the death penalty in Georgia. In the end, the Supreme Court ruled that even strong statistical evidence of racial bias in sentencing did not render the death penalty unconstitutional.
3. Examinations of capital punishment in Texas have found the death penalty more likely in cases with White victims after controlling for a large number of potential explanatory values (Bowers, Pierce, and McDevitt 1984; Ekland-Olson 1988). Similar results were found in studies of death penalty sentencing in North Carolina and Florida (Unah 2011; Zeisel 1981). In North Carolina, the rate of death penalty sentencing for White victim cases was almost twice as high of that of non-White victim cases between 1993 and 1997. A study of California executions found that those convicted of killing White victims were 3.7 times as likely to receive a death sentence as those with Black victims (Pierce and Radelet 2005).
4. See Appendix B for a list and short description of the cases where a White has been executed for the crime of killing a Black man.
5. We make one exception to this rule, including a piece from the *Los Angeles Times*, which details the results of a study commissioned by the newspaper.
6. Thirty studies examined race-of-victim bias in prosecutor's decisions to charge defendants capitally. In addition, the literature covered 16 current and past death penalty states including states in the geographic West, South, and Northeast as well as cases prosecuted within the judicial branch of the US Armed Forces. Studies covered a period of over 30 years with periods studied ranging from 1976 to 2007.
7. Researchers collectively examined cases over a period of 35 years, from 1972 to 2008, and from 33 states as well as cases conducted within the US Armed Forces.
8. Appendix A lists each of the studies reviewed, indicates the geographic scope and time coverage of the study, and lists the findings.
9. One study, in Delaware, found a value of 0.49; a second, from South Carolina, found 0.54; 7 studies found values in the range of 0.93–1.09; 60 studies found race-of-victim disparities ranging from 1.19 to 34.1; and 9 studies found an infinite ratio, as there were no death sentences handed down for any killers of Blacks (these are clustered at a value of 15 in the graph).
10. The modern period starts with the reinstitution of the death penalty by the US Supreme Court in *Gregg v. Georgia* in 1976; the first execution occurred in 1977. The most recent before that had been in 1965.
11. The usual caveats apply to the use of homicide data reported by the BJS, as it comes from local jurisdictions and may not always be a full census. However, for homicides, the data are more fully reported than for lesser crimes. And, most importantly, we are concerned with percentages of victims and offenders of different race and genders. These percentages may vary somewhat in the real world from those reported by BJS, but as the reader will see, the differences we report are so large that we are confident they cannot be due to measurement error in the BJS reports. Further, to

the extent that crimes are not closed and therefore offender data are missing, this may be expected disproportionately to affect Black-on-Black crimes, rather than others. If this were the case, it would make our findings stronger rather than weaker.
12. As noted earlier, we expand on these works here both in our use of a new, more comprehensive national data set of modern-era executions as well as in our focus on bias against Black victims (and in favor of White defendants with Black victims).
13. Note that our analysis here focuses on those cases where there was only a single victim. Including all 1359 cases shows a similar pattern but the results are clouded because many with multiple victims included victims of different races. Blume, Eisenberg, and Wells (2004) note that race-of-offender effects often are not found because Black offenders typically have Black victims, and crimes with Black victims are unlikely to lead to a death sentence. Blacks who kill Whites, however, are greatly over-represented on death row.
14. He obviously ignores Houston, Dallas, and Fort Worth as top 10 counties nationally by executions, and Philadelphia and Los Angeles, top counties by death sentences imposed. The "death qualification", limiting jury participation only to those with abstract support of the death penalty, mitigates his concerns at the same time as it eliminates many Blacks from capital juries.

References

American Civil Liberties Union Capital Punishment Project. 2007. "The Persistent Problem of Racial Disparities in the Federal Death Penalty." June 25, 2007. Web. March 19, 2014.

Baldus, David C., Charles Pulaski, and George Woodworth. 1983. "Comparative Review of Death Sentences: An Empirical Study of the Georgia Experience." *Journal of Criminal Law and Criminology* 74: 661–753.

Baldus, David C., and George Woodworth. 2001. "Race of Victim and Race of Defendant Disparities in the Administration of Maryland's Capital Charging and Sentencing System (1979–1996). Preliminary Finding."

Baldus, David C., and George Woodworth. 2003. "Race Discrimination in the Administration of the Death Penalty: An Overview of the Empirical Evidence with Special Emphasis on the Post-1990 Research." *Criminal Law Bulletin* 39 (2): 194–226.

Blume, John, Theodore Eisenberg, and Martin T. Wells. 2004. "Explaining Death Row's Population and Racial Composition." *Journal of Empirical Legal Studies* 1 (1): 165–207.

Bonilla-Silva, Eduardo. 1996. "Rethinking Racism: Toward a Structural Interpretation." *American Sociological Review* 62 (June): 465–480.

Bonilla-Silva, Eduardo. 1997. "Rethinking Racism: Toward a Structural Interpretation." *American Sociological Review* 62 (3): 465–480.

Bonilla-Silva, Eduardo, Amanda Lewis, and David G. Embrick. 2004. "I Did Not Get That Job Because of a Black Man … : The Story Lines and Testimonies of Color-blind Racism." *Sociological Forum* 19 (4): 555–581.

Bowers, W. J., G. L. Pierce, and J. F. McDevitt. 1984. *Legal Homicide: Death as Punishment in America, 1864–1982*. Boston, MA: Northeastern University Press.

Death Penalty Information Center. 2015. "Facts About the Death Penalty." Accessed March 3, 2015. http://www.deathpenaltyinfo.org/documents/FactSheet.pdf.

Donohue III, John J. 2014. "An Empirical Evaluation of the Connecticut Death Penalty System Since 1973: Are There Unlawful Racial, Gender, and Geographic Disparities?" *Journal of Empirical Legal Studies* 11 (4): 637–696.

Eberhardt, Jennifer L., Paul G. Davies, Valerie J. Purdie-Vaughns, and Sheri Lynn Johnson. 2005/2006. "Looking Deathworthy: Perceived Stereotypicality of Black Defendants Predicts Capital-sentencing Outcomes." *Psychological Science* 17 (5): 383–386.

Eberhardt, Jennifer L., Phillip Atiba Goff, Valerie J. Purdie, and Paul G. Davies. 2004. "Seeing Black: Race, Crime, and Visual Processing." *Journal of Personality and Social Psychology* 87 (6): 876–893.

Ekland-Olson, Sheldon. 1988. "Structured Discretion, Racial Bias, and the Death Penalty: The First Decade after 'Furman' in Texas." *Social Science Quarterly* 69 (4): 853–873.

Fagan, Jeffrey, Franklin E. Zimring, and Amanda Geller. 2006. "Capital Punishment and Capital Murder: Market Share and the Deterrent Effects of the Death Penalty." Accessed August 4, 2014. http://ssrn.com/abstract=928649.

Government Accountability Office. 1990. *Death Penalty Sentencing: Research Indicates Pattern of Racial Disparities* (GAO Publication No. 90-57). Washington, DC: US Government Printing Office.

Gross, Samuel R. 2012. "David Baldus and the Legacy of McCleskey v. Kemp." *Iowa Law Review* 97 (6): 1906–1924.

Hetey, Rebecca C., and Jennifer L. Eberhardt. 2014. "Racial Disparities in Incarceration Increase Acceptance of Punitive Policies." *Psychological Science* 25 (10): 1949–1954.

Jacobs, David, Zhenchao Qian, Jason T. Carmichael, and Stephanie L. Kent. 2007. "Who Survives on Death Row? An Individual and Contextual Analysis." *American Sociological Review* 72 (4): 610–632.

McCleskey v. Kemp. 1987. 481 US 279.

NAACP Criminal Justice Project. 2013. "Death Row U.S.A." Accessed March 3, 2015. http://www.naacpldf.org/files/publications/DRUSA_Fall_2013.pdf.

Paternoster, Raymond, and Robert Brame. 2003. *An Empirical Analysis of Maryland's Death Sentencing System with Respect to the Influence of Race and Legal Jurisdiction*. College Park: University of Maryland.

Paternoster, Raymond, Robert Brame, Sarah Bacon, and Andrew Ditchfield. 2004. "Justice by Geography and Race: The Administration of the Death Penalty in Maryland, 1978–1999." *University of Maryland Law Journal of Race, Religion, Gender and Class* 4 (1): 1–97.

Pierce, Glenn L., and Michael L. Radelet. 2005. "The Impact of Legally Inappropriate Factors on Death Sentencing for California Homicides, 1990–1999." *Santa Clara Law Review* 49: 1–31.

Radelet, Michael L. 1989. "Executions of Whites for Crimes against Blacks: Exceptions to the Rule?" *The Sociological Quarterly* 30 (4): 529–544.

Rattan, A., C. S. Levine, C. S. Dweck, and J. L. Eberhardt. 2012. "Race and the Fragility of the Legal Distinction between Juveniles and Adults." *PLoS ONE* 7 (5): 1–5.

Scheidegger, Kent S. 2011. "Mend It Don't End it: A Report to the Connecticut General Assembly on Capital Punishment." Accessed August 4, 2014. http://www.cjlf.org/deathpenalty/deathpenalty.htm.

Scheidegger, Kent S. 2012. "Rebutting the Myths about Race and the Death Penalty." *Ohio State Journal of Criminal Law* 10 (1). Accessed August 4, 2014. http://www.cjlf.org/deathpenalty/deathpenalty.htm.

Unah, Isaac. 2011. "Empirical Analysis of Race and the Process of Capital Punishment in North Carolina." *Michigan State Law Review* 609: 610–658.

Williams, Melissa J., and Jennifer L. Eberhardt. 2008. "Biological Conceptions of Race and the Motivation to Cross Racial Boundaries." *Journal of Personality and Social Psychology* 94 (6): 1033–1047.

Zeisel, Hans. 1981. "Race Bias in the Administration of the Death Penalty: The Florida Experience." *Harvard Law Review* 95 (2): 456–468.

Intersectional stereotyping in policing: an analysis of traffic stop outcomes

Leah Christiani

ABSTRACT
Identity-based stereotyping often operates on perceptions about the intersection of multiple identities. Intersectional stereotyping predicts that certain combinations of attributes lend themselves more readily to perceived suspicion than others. In this paper, I test the way that suspicion-evoking stereotypes affect police-citizen interactions. Through the use of traffic stop data from Illinois spanning ten years and amounting to more than 20 million observations, I am able to produce accurate estimates for the relative degree of targeting that individual drivers face based on their racial, gender, age, and class-based perceived identities. Overall, I find both theoretical and methodological support for the necessity of intersectional analyses of identity-based profiling.

The 2013 acquittal of George Zimmerman in the shooting of Trayvon Martin sparked the development of the #BlackLivesMatter (BLM) movement, which brought focus to charges of racial profiling and brutality against people of color in the United States. One year later, public interest in racial profiling was amplified by the police shooting of Michael Brown in Ferguson, Missouri, which sent Google searches for "police brutality" up by 300%.[1] In 2014, the #SayHerName campaign was launched to direct attention specifically to the way that black women and girls have been victimized by the police. Such accusations of police brutality have captured media attention ever since and subsequent incidents of alleged targeting have been highly publicized.

Leaders of these movements argue that the police target people of color in their enforcement of the law. This charge has been backed up by empirical research, confirming that there is significant bias against racial minorities and, in particular, young African American men, in policing (Bates 2010; Baumgartner et al. 2017a, 2017b; Fagan and Davies 2000; Fagan et al. 2010; Meehan and Ponder 2002; Tomaskovic-Devey, Mason, and Zingraff 2004). One study demonstrates that in North Carolina, young, black men are about twice as likely to be searched following a traffic stop compared to similarly situated whites (Baumgartner et al. 2017b).

Despite #BlackLivesMatter and #SayHerName's explicit focus on the intersection of multiple identities, research on racial profiling largely focuses on outcomes for individuals in the most highly targeted group (i.e., young men of color). However, we know that there are persistent stereotypes associated with a host of other identity-based groups as well (Fiske et al. 2002) that likely produce relative degrees of targeting and leniency by police. As police are encouraged to investigate "suspicious" actors to proactively seek out and eradicate crime (Epp, Maynard-Moody, and Haider-Markel 2014), widely held stereotypes about race, gender, age, and class, likely inform this process. Intersectional identity-based stereotypes lead to heavy targeting of certain identity groups and to more lenient treatment of other identity groups.

In this paper, I propose that we conceive of racial profiling as explicitly grounded in an intersectional understanding of identity and stereotyping. I analyze identity-based profiling in the context of police traffic stops, with a dataset from Illinois that spans ten years, resulting in over 20 million observations. My analysis demonstrates that a driver's race, gender, age, and class all play an interactive role in whether a police officer decides to search a car following an initial traffic stop and in whether or not that driver receives a warning. Tested against an additive model, I find that an intersectional model is better equipped to explain the disparate outcomes that drivers face, both theoretically and methodologically. Analyzing multiple, intersecting identities allows for a clearer understanding of profiling and the way that group-based stereotypes operate, individually and institutionally, to produce both targeting and leniency in policing.

Intersectional stereotypes

Stereotypes are generalizations about a group of people that are both individual and collective; they are the "pictures in the head" that individuals have about others, but they are also conceptions about groups of people that are widely shared among a culture (Stangor and Shaller 1996). The most readily available and visible categories are used most frequently, like race (Devine 1989; Devine and Elliot 1995), age, and gender (Brewer and Lui 1989). Stereotyping does not operate on one identity at a time, but rather across multiple identities simultaneously (Fiske 1993). Each individual has an identity that is a result of the manner in which their multiple identities interact. Rather than an additive relationship, these factors are seen as mutually constructing an identity (Collins 1990; Crenshaw 1989, 1991; Hancock 2004; Harris-Perry 2011).

Crenshaw (1989, 1991) first coined the term intersectionality to describe the way that black women were unable to make use of *either* race-based antidiscrimination claims *or* gender-based antidiscrimination claims, though the concept itself extends back much further (see, e.g., Combahee River Collective [1983] 1983; Hancock 2016). Because discrimination against black women does not operate solely on the basis of their race or solely on the basis of their gender, their experience differs from those for whom the policies were designed to protect. It was impossible for the black women in Crenshaw's case studies to untangle whether their race or gender disadvantaged them and, as a result, they tended to be unsuccessful in their antidiscrimination claims (Crenshaw 1989).

Recent work has emphasized the importance of context in understanding how subgroups are stereotyped. McConnaughy (2018) demonstrates the way that identity-based stereotypes affect the perceived legitimacy of non-violent protestors. Black men, often stereotyped as violent and aggressive, are the least likely race-gender subgroup to be viewed as legitimate, while white women, conversely stereotyped as moral and peaceful, are considered most legitimate. The context here, a question of the level of legitimacy that a group possesses, determines how powerful and relevant certain stereotypes will become in the decision-making process (McConnaughy 2018). In this instance, black males experience the most negative outcomes; while in Crenshaw's work, it was black women who were disadvantaged at the intersection. It is not that there is always one most highly targeted group in every situation, but instead that the context shapes which intersectional stereotypes will be most influential in determining outcomes.

Stereotypes of suspicion

In the context of policing, stereotypes that evoke suspicion are most relevant, as the police are charged with seeking out and eradicating crime. Especially since the growth of proactive policing in the 1980s, officers have been encouraged to approach and question "suspicious" people in order to prevent crime – to be *proactive* rather than reactive (Epp, Maynard-Moody, and Haider-Markel 2014; Fagan and Geller 2015; Harcourt 2003). However, it is impossible to investigate every single person on the street. Instead, this has led to both relying on and codifying into practice stereotypes about suspicion (Epp, Maynard-Moody, and Haider-Markel 2014; Fagan and Geller 2015).

Epp, Maynard-Moody, and Haider-Markel (2014) describe the "institutional practices" that result in disparate policing. These practices are "common ways of doing things that, while not required by any specific official policy, are supported and legitimated by rules, training, and law, and that spread widely to become commonly accepted activity" (11). The authors argue that institutional practices that dictate what constitutes reasonable suspicion are informed by culturally held racial stereotypes about black criminality and are the source of much of the racial disparities in police-citizen interactions (Epp, Maynard-Moody, and Haider-Markel 2014). These commonly held beliefs amount to "scripts of suspicion" that informally define who is suspicious – in ways that are race and neighborhood dependent (Fagan and Geller 2015). Then, such suspicion becomes a self-fulfilling prophecy (Harris 2003). When law enforcement focus their efforts on certain populations and define crime in ways that target certain populations, they inevitably end up finding more crime there (Harcourt 2003, 2009; Harris 2003).

According to one police training manual cited in Epp, Maynard-Moody, and Haider-Markel (2014), police officers are taught to use investigatory traffic stops as a way to "'sniff out' possible criminal behavior" (36). Often, the police are looking for drug offenders. The traditional profile of a drug courier, developed and taught during the War on Drugs, is that of a young, poor, black male. While officers are now taught that racial profiling is not legal, a section of a recent police training manual reads: "Traditional profile characteristics still *do* correlate closely with a sizeable portion of drug couriers" (Epp, Maynard-Moody, and Haider-Markel 2014, 40). African Americans are often stereotyped as linked with crime, criminality, and violence (Epp, Maynard-Moody, and Haider-Markel 2014; Gilliam and Iyengar 2000; Loury 2008; Muhammad 2010; Welch 2007) and youths who "look tough" are often assumed to have committed crimes (Fagan and Geller 2015, 57). Because officers are taught to act on notions of suspicion to seek out drug offenders that are informed by culturally held stereotypes, young black men experience undue scrutiny by the police.

Women of color are also caught up in the push to seek out drug offenders. While men, especially men of color, are still most likely to be incarcerated, the rate of which women are being incarcerated is growing at a faster pace than men. This surge in growth is largely due to nonviolent drug offenses and has disproportionately impacted poor women of color. 70% of women in prison are black, Latina, Native American, or Asian, and most are working class. Black women are four times as likely to be incarcerated as white women, and twice as likely as Latinas (Lawston 2008). While black men may fill the traditional drug courier profile, black and Latina women are likely similarly profiled for committing drug offenses, and thus treated with more suspicion than their white counterparts.

In addition to seeking out drug offenders, officers are increasingly asked to prioritize immigration enforcement. In her analysis of the Nashville Police Department, Armenta (2017) finds that, "Through [the officers'] implementation of the MNPD's policing priorities, officers subject Latino residents to lengthier inspections, sanctions, and sometimes arrest" (92). The integration of immigration enforcement into the day-to-day criminal justice operations results in heightened scrutiny of Latinx drivers. Again, often minor traffic violations are used as a way in to investigate the driver more closely. This leads to harsher treatment of Latinx drivers by the police, as they are often stereotyped as immigrants, who warrant suspicion on the part of the officer (Armenta 2017).

Finally, location informs suspicion that officers develop. Poorer neighborhoods with larger black and Latinx populations are targeted, as biased ideas about increased criminality in these areas guide police practice. In their analysis of New York City's stop and frisk policy, Fagan and Geller (2015) find that "most stops were concentrated in a relatively small number of neighborhoods with high crime rates, concentrations of non-White residents, and severe socioeconomic disadvantage" (62). The pressure to make as many stops as possible leads officers to concentrate their efforts in certain contexts – especially those in which a potential arrest seems easiest. While there is no difference in drug dealing rates between black and white communities, deals tend to occur outdoors in black communities and indoors in white communities (Epp, Maynard-Moody, and Haider-Markel 2014). This, combined with the way that crime is defined and sought out (Harcourt 2009; Harris 2003), anti-black stereotypes (Epp, Maynard-Moody, and Haider-Markel 2014), and a penal system developed to criminalize blacks (Loury 2008) leads to heavy targeting of poor, non-white areas. Indeed, poverty and racial makeup of a location predict police presence more than crime rates (Fagan and Davies 2000; Fagan et al. 2010).

Stereotypes based on race, class, age, and gender shape suspicion that police may develop about particular citizens. Often, the focus is on the most highly targeted groups (young, poor, black and Latino men). However, there are a host of culturally-held stereotypes about identities beyond race, and about racial groups beyond blacks and Latinx. Stereotypes about these identities interact to generate differential levels of perceived suspicion.

Counter to blacks or Latinx, whites are often stereotyped positively and associated with wealth or hard work (Winter 2006), as whiteness was developed from a privileged position and continues to occupy and reap the benefits of that position – including better treatment by police (Alcoff 2015). Gender conditions this stereotype, as white women tend to be viewed as victims who deserve empathy rather than punishment (Dirks, Heldman, and Zack 2015). Because Asian Americans tend to have higher levels of education and income than other racial minorities (in the aggregate), they are often stereotyped as the "model minority" (Kim 2003; Chou and Feagin 2015). They are held up as the example to other minority groups, like blacks and Latinx, as justification for the individualistic notion that hard work will lead to success in America (Kim 2003; Lee and Fiske 2006; Taylor and Stern 1997; Wong et al. 1998). While this stereotype is damaging and casts Asians as permanent outsiders (Kim 2003), it does not evoke suspicion in ways that stereotypes about black and Latinx people do.

While often overlooked, Native Americans have been negatively stereotyped in ways that evoke suspicion – as they have been stereotyped as welfare dependent and economically depressed, while simultaneously undeserving of the wealth they have accumulated through casinos and the gaming industry (D'Errico 2000). In the context of policing, Native Americans are the racial group is most likely to be killed by police (Revesz 2016), These class-based stereotypes of poverty and police targeting evoke suspicion, as they are closely linked to criminality.

Race, gender, age, and class are tied together as they work jointly to produce stereotypes that evoke relative levels of perceived suspicion. Depending on the intersectional combination of identities, these stereotypes may be magnified or mitigated and influence the perception of suspicion about an individual. Perhaps the most recognized stereotype of the "criminal predator" is that of the poor, young, black or Latino male (Baumgartner et al. 2017b; Welch 2007, 276). This stereotype is so inextricably tied with suspicion that it is likely that as an individual's identity approaches this criminal trope, they come under increasing suspicion. This intersectional identity group is often the focus of empirical work on policing, since members are so highly targeted. But all of the stereotypes outlined above demonstrate that there are likely degrees of targeting and leniency produced by stereotypes beyond that of the often-recognized "criminal predator."

A reconception of identity-based profiling

There is a well-documented bias against people of color in policing, especially young men (Bates 2010; Baumgartner et al. 2017b; Epp, Maynard-Moody, and Haider-Markel 2014; Fagan and Davies 2000; Fagan et al. 2010; Meehan and Ponder 2002; Warren et al. 2006). Baumgartner et al. (2017b) demonstrate through the use of over 18 million traffic stops in North Carolina that young black and Latino men are consistently targeted for searches and arrests. They find that this disparity persists even after controlling for the "bad apple" hypothesis, the notion that disparities result from the actions of a few, racist police officers. Instead, the racial disparities that they find are prevalent throughout the entire police force (Baumgartner et al. 2017b). Such outcomes may instead rely on policing practices that codify widely shared stereotypes about young, black and Latino men as suspicious and thus lead to targeting by the police.

While there has been substantial work demonstrating the high level of police targeting that young, poor, black and Latino males face, the consequences of this targeting for other identity groups is often overlooked. Sampaio (2014) analyzes immigration enforcement through a raced and gendered lens. She finds that while men are more likely to be the target of immigration enforcement, their experience with immigration enforcement differs dramatically than that of women, who are often exposed to harassment and sexual violence when they are detained (Sampaio 2014). Sampaio's findings illustrate the importance of a broad, intersectional lens: a singular focus on the most highly targeted group (in this case, men) obscures and conceals the treatment that women receive in immigration enforcement.

Steffensmeier, Painter-Davis, and Ulmer (2017) similarly take an intersectional perspective in their analysis of criminal sentencing. They find that race, gender, and age are all critical components in understanding sentencing and that the effects of age vary by race and gender. Black and Latino men experience harsher sentences regardless of age, while age has a curvilinear effect for females – younger and older females receive the most lenient treatment. Age has a different effect on sentencing, depending on race and gender (Steffensmeier, Painter-Davis, and Ulmer 2017).

Such evidence points to the need to broaden our understanding of racial profiling in a way that incorporates intersectional identity and stereotyping beyond an analysis of the most highly targeted group. It also demonstrates the importance of quantitative analysis that is informed and motivated by theory. Here, following intersectionality theory leads to conclusions that might have otherwise been overlooked with an additive approach (Collins 1990).

The context of traffic stops

While traffic stops may be brief interactions with law enforcement and, overall, occur fairly rarely, such interactions still have substantial, political effects on the individual driver and on their community. Direct contact with law enforcement leads to political demobilization (Burch 2011; Lerman and Weaver 2014a; Weaver and Lerman 2010; though see Lawless and Fox 2001) – especially when this contact involves searches or the use of force (Lerman and Weaver 2014b). Effects of contact with law enforcement can ripple throughout a community, though there is mixed evidence about whether it mobilizes or suppresses political participation (Burch 2013, 2014; Owens and Walker 2018; Walker 2014; Walker and García-Castañon 2017).

Traffic stops are the most common way that people interact with the police. Individuals from a variety of racial, gender, age, and class groups are stopped – allowing for a test of intersectional identity-based profiling that is fairly inclusive. The stop is usually a quick and surface interaction, which provides a good context with which to test the use of stereotypes, whether those held by the individual officer or those reinforced through policing norms and training, as stereotypes act as heuristics that can be used when full information is not available (Fagan and Geller 2015; Fiske 1993).

Police officers are trained to search a driver or vehicle based on suspicion (Epp, Maynard-Moody, and Haider-Markel 2014; Fagan and Geller 2015). Officers take in the entire context in which the stop occurs, such as the time of day, the reason the driver was stopped, as well as the identity of the driver (Fagan and Geller 2015). When a car or driver is perceived as suspicious, the officer is more likely to search that vehicle or its occupants.

Substantively, race, gender, age, and class all evoke stereotypes that may result in relative levels of perceived suspicion by the officer. My measure of suspicion is the officer's decision to search the vehicle or driver following an initial traffic stop. This measure captures suspicion, as it directly measures whether the officer wants more information about the person with whom they are interacting. As a secondary outcome variable, I operationalize the officer's leniency with their decision to give the driver a warning. While less directly linked to suspicion, this outcome measures the degree to which an officer feels the driver warrants some leniency – a perception that is at least partially determined by the officer's training and culturally held stereotypes. While there may be slightly less discretion in terms of whether the officer can give a warning, compared to their decision to search a car, there is nevertheless a degree of discretion at work.

The data contain the race, gender, and age of the driver stopped. In addition, I use the age of the vehicle stopped as a proxy for class. While not a perfect measure, it is likely the case that on average, individuals who drive newer cars are perceived as having higher socioeconomic status than those who drive older cars. A better measure would include not only the age of the vehicle, but also the make and model, which combine to create a broader perception about class. Illinois does collect data on the make of the vehicle (though not model), but it is recorded as a write-in variable – resulting in more than 63,000 unique values and thus making it unusable for analysis. Another downfall to using vehicle age to approximate class is that it assumes linearity both in movement from year to year and in its translation to a linear measure for class. Overall though, it is the best approximation for perceived class that the data provides.

I follow previous research and expect black and Latino males to be most highly targeted for searches. Native Americans, while often overlooked, are the racial group that is most likely to be killed by the police (Revesz 2016), so I expect that their probability of harsh treatment to follow. Whites should come next, followed by Asians, who are the least likely to be targeted. Of course, these race-based expectations will be conditioned by other identities. Young (compared to old), male (compared to female), and drivers with old vehicles (compared to those with new vehicles) should experience higher levels of targeting, based on stereotypes that both produce and suppress suspicion. In terms of leniency, the same expectations should hold but in the reverse. Those drivers who are perceived as least suspicious should be most likely to receive a warning from the police.

In sum, the crux of my expectations lies in two realms. First, there should be a spectrum of targeting (rather than a bimodal distribution of those who are targeted versus those who are not). Instead, intersectional identities should produce varying levels of targeting as a consequence of the way that stereotyping results in a range of suspicion. Second, I expect that suspicion compounds. Drivers who possess more and more suspicious identities should also experience higher and higher degrees of targeting. As individuals' racial, gender, age, and class characteristics approach those of the "criminal profile," they are likely subject to harsher treatment by police.

Data and methods

The data[2] I analyze is comprised of every individual traffic stop from every agency in Illinois over the years 2004–2014, collected by the state Department of Transportation. This large amount of data offers some benefits. It allows for accurate estimates of traffic stop outcomes for minority racial groups that are often omitted due to their low sample size, like Asians and Native Americans. Further, it is a dataset that is high in naturalism. It involves police officers making probabilistic decisions in the field, and thus, it is a potentially useful venue for testing the way that stereotyping functions in a real-world context. The data records whether or not the officer searched the car, which makes for a relatively good indicator of the level of perceived suspicion. It also records the outcome of the stop, which allows me to operationalize leniency afforded to the driver by whether or not s/he receives a warning.

I use the presence or absence of a search as my main dependent variable and whether or not the driver receives a warning as a secondary dependent variable.[3] Of course, merely analyzing the outcome of a traffic stop does not account for other factors that could be working to produce biased outcomes, such as the true level of warranted suspicion. It may be appropriate that certain groups evoke more suspicion, as they tend to be more likely to be breaking the law. I test for this explanation with analysis of whether the search results in the discovery of contraband, presented in Online Appendix H. This analysis demonstrates that the heightened targeting of certain drivers based on identity is not justified as they are no more likely to be carrying contraband than those who are not being targeted. Still, it could be that groups' latent risk distributions of carrying contraband differ. While I do not account for this explanation in this paper, work by Simoiu, Corbett-Davies, and Goel (2017) has demonstrated that even when these risk distributions can be estimated, the discrimination detected in benchmarking and outcome tests remains. As such, there is reason to have some confidence that while not perfect, a test of differential probabilities of search does indeed estimate the direction of the bias appropriately.

Further, recent work has demonstrated that if the police discriminate when choosing who to investigate, analyses that use administrative records are statistically biased. So, if the police are racially motivated when they decide who to pull over for a traffic stop in the first place, any subsequent analyses using data on traffic stops likely underestimate the racial bias present (Knox, Lowe, and Mummolo 2019). Any racial discrimination that is revealed from this analysis then, likely underestimates the true level of bias present in policing.

Searches are rare, they only comprise about 4.1% of the data. While the search of a car or driver is not a frequent occurrence, it is nevertheless an impactful one that takes a toll both on the individual driver and more broadly on the relationship between individuals and law enforcement (Burch 2011, 2013, 2014; Lerman and Weaver 2014a, 2014b; Weaver and Lerman 2010). Warnings, on the other hand, are much more common: about 38.8% of traffic stops in this dataset result in a warning. These are not mutually exclusive, you could both be searched and receive a warning.

The main independent variables of interest are the race, gender, and age of the driver and the age of the vehicle. For my first analysis, I use a categorical variable that identifies the intersectional identity of the driver in terms of race, gender, age, and class (measured by vehicle age). I split the driver's age variable at its median (32 years old) and recode it into two groups: old drivers and young drivers. I then split the vehicle age variable at its median (8 years old)[4] and recode it into two groups: old car and new car. This leads to 40 separate identity categories. The breakdown of this intersectional identity measure is presented in Table 1. In subsequent analyses, I estimate models that preserve age and vehicle age as continuous variables, and interact these terms with race and gender for an intersectional and continuous estimate.

The dataset includes a variety of contextual factors for which I control, including the hour, day of the week, and year of the stop. If individuals driving at late hours or on the weekend are more likely to be searched, I will capture that effect in this control. I also control for the purpose of the stop (collected by Illinois as a registration, equipment, or moving violation) to capture the effect of the type of offense on the outcome the driver receives (Epp, Maynard-Moody, and Haider-Markel 2014). As a robustness check, I

Table 1. Number of stops, searches, and warnings for all intersectional identity groups.

Demographic	Stop N	Search N	Search rate	Warning N	Warning rate
Old, white, male, old vehicle	3,184,994	41,800	0.013	1,437,961	0.451
Young, white, male, old vehicle	2,867,287	151,221	0.053	1,250,202	0.436
Old, white, male, old vehicle	2,459,323	81,846	0.033	11,79,131	0.479
Young, white, male, new vehicle	2,327,746	71,298	0.031	878,879	0.378
Old, white, female, new vehicle	2,033,518	16,515	0.008	941,281	0.463
Young, white, female, new vehicle	1,617,979	25,378	0.016	677,794	0.419
Young, white, female, old vehicle	1,401,416	46,183	0.033	658,285	0.470
Old, white, female, old vehicle	1,151,330	26,841	0.023	576,987	0.501
Young, black, male, old vehicle	934,082	120,066	0.129	357,779	0.383
Young, Latino, male, old vehicle	824,808	125,213	0.152	251,400	0.305
Old, black, male, old vehicle	717,101	62,844	0.088	302,251	0.421
Old, Latino, male, old vehicle	590,056	51,608	0.088	218,871	0.371
Old, black, male, new vehicle	555,122	22,109	0.040	223,805	0.403
Young, black, male, new vehicle	511,261	44,153	0.086	177,501	0.347
Young, black, female, old vehicle	474,380	28,411	0.060	179,167	0.378
Young, Latino, male, new vehicle	422,812	36,264	0.086	130,630	0.309
Old, black, female, new vehicle	398,193	6,008	0.015	152,789	0.384
Young, black, female, new vehicle	367,628	11,507	0.031	123,875	0.337
Old, black, female, old vehicle	340,847	13,776	0.040	145,701	0.427
Old, Latino, male, new vehicle	311,804	11,905	0.038	117,645	0.377
Young, Latina, female, old vehicle	235,345	15,683	0.067	83,680	0.356
Young, Latina, female, new vehicle	191,015	6,224	0.033	64,302	0.337
Old, Asian, male, new vehicle	169,901	1,575	0.009	62,750	0.369
Old, Latina, female, old vehicle	168,849	8,270	0.049	65,353	0.387
Old, Latina, female, new vehicle	142,416	2,649	0.019	53,545	0.376
Young, Asian, male, new vehicle	136,570	2,853	0.021	47,354	0.347
Old, Asian, male, old vehicle	111,094	1,864	0.017	46,259	0.416
Old, Asian, female, new vehicle	95,589	404	0.004	35,758	0.374
Young, Asian, male, old vehicle	93,988	3,351	0.036	37,484	0.399
Young, Asian, female, new vehicle	65,843	604	0.009	24,253	0.368
Old, Asian, female, old vehicle	48,252	348	0.007	20,039	0.415
Young, Asian, female, old vehicle	34,429	574	0.017	14,451	0.420
Old, Native American, male, new vehicle	9,968	182	0.018	3,643	0.365
Young, Native American, male, new vehicle	8,308	308	0.037	2,556	0.308
Young, Native American, male, old vehicle	8,243	651	0.079	2,942	0.357
Old, Native American, male, old vehicle	8,133	339	0.042	3,236	0.398
Old, Native American, female, new vehicle	4,590	53	0.012	1,694	0.369
Young, Native American, female, new vehicle	4,113	73	0.018	1,364	0.332
Young, Native American, female, old vehicle	3,111	121	0.039	1,161	0.373
Old, Native American, female, old vehicle	3,063	87	0.028	1,255	0.410
Total stops, searches, and warnings	25,034,507	1,041,159		10,555,013	
Mean search rate and warning rate			0.041		0.388

Note: demographic groups ordered from high to low in terms of the total number of stops.

estimate models predicting searches with fixed effects for police agencies in order to control for disparate agency-level policing behavior. Online Appendix C reports and compares these models with the categorical additive and intersectional models presented in the body of the paper. The results are nearly identical. These controls and additional tests isolate the effect that identity plays in the outcome of traffic stops.

For my main dependent variable (whether or not the driver is searched), I estimate three models: an additive categorical model, an intersectional categorical model, and an intersectional continuous model. The first two models will be used to compare the utility of an intersectional approach against an additive approach. Specifying the identity of the driver as a categorical variable makes for an easier comparison of the different estimates produced from each model. Further, it allows for a subsequent analysis of the treatment of the driver based on the number of "suspicious" identities held. Then, the third model makes it possible to estimate treatment of the driver across a range of vehicle and driver ages. This is helpful because it does not require any decisions be made about which ages classify as "old" or "young" (for driver age) or "old" or "new" (for vehicle age). Instead, it estimates the level of targeting a driver receives at each age.

The additive categorical model treats identity as additive, rather than interactive, and includes separate indicators for the driver's race, gender, age, and the age of the vehicle. This constrains each variable to a single effect, regardless of the value of the other identity-based variables. For example, in this model, the effect of the driver being black is constrained to having one, single effect on the dependent variable (whether the driver is searched), regardless of whether the driver is male or female, old or young, or driving a new or old car.

The second model I estimate is the intersectional categorical model. This model uses an intersectional identity categorical variable with every combination of identity (age, race, gender, and vehicle age), which allows the effects of one identity to vary based on the particular combination of other identities. Here, the effect of race on the dependent variable can vary based on the driver's gender, age, and vehicle age. For example, the effect of being black on the probability of being searched can be different for males than it is for females. This model allows for identity to vary in an interactive way and as such, does not expect that a single identity will have a uniform effect, but rather that the effect of one identity will vary based on the presence of other identities. I will be able to compare this model with the first model to determine whether an intersectional measure of identity is methodologically necessary.

Next, I estimate an intersectional continuous model, in which vehicle age and driver age are preserved as continuous variables. These are then interacted with a categorical measure of race and gender. Preserving the variation in these continuous variables allows for a clearer understanding of the effect of vehicle age and driver age on the probability of search, and the way that these effects vary by race and gender. It also means that I do not need to make any decisions about what is considered an old or new vehicle or an old or young driver.

Because my comparison of the additive and intersectional models reveals that the intersectional model is more methodologically appropriate, I then specify the two intersectional models (one categorical and one continuous) to predict whether or not a driver receives a warning following an initial traffic stop (my secondary dependent variable). Taken together, these models demonstrate that intersectional modeling is important, both methodologically and theoretically, to properly estimating and understanding the experience that individuals have with the police, based on their group membership.

Analysis and findings

The first, additive model treats race, gender, age, and vehicle age as discrete categories and allows each to have a single effect. The second, intersectional model includes a categorical variable with every combination of identity, allowing the effects of an identity to vary based on the particular combination of identities. The results of these logistic regressions are presented in Online Appendix B. The fit statistics produced from each model indicate that the intersectional model fits the data better (i.e., it has a higher log likelihood, lower AIC, and lower BIC). However, this is at least partly due to the fact that the intersectional model estimates so many more parameters than the additive model. That is, the intersectional model estimates different effects for forty different intersectional identity groups (rather than for seven) – so by design, it will be more accurate in its estimates.

To better test the performance of these models, I split the data into training and testing sets. 80% of the data is used to estimate the additive and intersectional models: the training set. The models' fit statistics are then calculated using the remaining 20% of the data that was never used to estimate the models: the testing set. These statistics determine which model fits the data better, divorced from their role in generating the models. Then, I compare the actual values of the dependent variable (whether or not a driver was searched) to the predicted values. The better performing model gets these predictions right more often. Table 2 reports the results from all of these tests and Appendix E discusses the specifics of these tests in greater detail.

The intersectional model consistently performs better than the additive model, across all indicators. Because the intersectional model estimates so many more parameters (compare the 49 degrees of freedom in the additive model to the 81 in the intersectional model), there may have been concern that the model was simply overfitting this particular dataset. If that were the case, it would not perform better on data that was not used to generate the model. Even though the intersectional model only does slightly better than the additive model (i.e., it correctly predicts the dependent variable 0.17% more often), it performs no worse despite estimating nearly double the number of parameters. The intersectional model allows us to study the mechanism implied by intersectionality: the notion that the effect of one identity will depend on the value of other identities held by the individual driver – and even still, does no worse than the additive model despite the additional demands it places on the data.

In order to truly determine the utility of the intersectional model, I calculate and compare predicted probabilities for each identity group using both models (these are reported in Online Appendix D). All of the estimates are statistically significant from zero. Even a cursory examination of this table demonstrates that there is a spectrum of targeting. The distribution does not appear to be bimodal – with some groups targeted and others not targeted. Instead, there seem to be relative degrees of targeting that exist, based on an intersectional conceptualization of identity.

Upon further inspection, a pattern emerges in these estimates. Estimates for the probability of search for black and Latino male drivers from the intersectional model tend to exceed those in the additive model. Accordingly, estimates of the probability of search for black and Latina female drivers from the intersectional model tend to be lower than those of the additive model. Figure 1 plots the predicted probabilities of search for all black and

Table 2. Fit statistics for additive and intersectional models using the testing set of data.

	Additive model	Intersectional model	Better fit?
Degrees of freedom	49	81	
Log Likelihood	−778,415	−777,185	Intersectional
AIC	1,556,929	1,554,532	Intersectional
BIC	1,557,655	1,555,732	Intersectional
AUC	0.7572 (75.72%)	0.7589 (75.89%)	Intersectional

Note: Models with higher log likelihoods, lower AICs, and lower BICs have a better fit. The AIC and BIC penalize models for the number of parameters estimated. AUC refers to the area under the curve. This is the proportion of observations for which the predicted values gained from the regression successfully match the true value of the dependent variable. Here, a higher value means the model gets the outcome right more often.

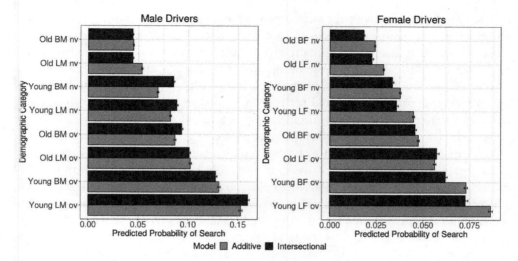

Figure 1. Comparing predicted probabilities from additive and intersectional models for black and Latinx drivers.

Latinx identity groups. The y-axis indicates the identity of the driver with respect to age, race, gender, and vehicle age (in that order). Racially, W = white, B = black, L = Latinx, A = Asian, and N = Native American; and in terms of gender, M = male and F = female. New vehicles are abbreviated with "nv" and old vehicles, with "ov." So, the observation for "Young BF ov" refers to a young, black, female driver with an old vehicle.

Figure 1 demonstrates that the additive model systematically overestimates the probability of search for black and Latina female drivers, but underestimates the probability of search for black and Latino male drivers. For young black and Latina females with old vehicles, the additive model overestimates the probability of search by 0.011 and 0.013, respectively. When the average probability of search is only 0.044, these differences are sizable. The same is true for every black and Latina female identity group – no matter the age of the driver or vehicle. For males, the probability of search for young black and Latino drivers with new vehicles are overestimated by 0.015 and 0.007, respectively. For almost every black and Latino male identity group, with the exception of two, the additive model underestimates the probability of search.

This illustrates the pitfall with treating race as an additive variable that has a single effect on all drivers, regardless of other identities that those drivers may hold. Here, the effect of race for black and Latinx drivers is higher for males than for females. As such, its value needs to be permitted to vary based on gender. This demonstrates that an intersectional conception of profiling may not only be theoretically relevant, but methodologically necessary as well, as allowing the effect of race to vary based on other identities, such as gender, is paramount to obtaining the most accurate estimates.

Targeting across class and age

Continuing with an intersectional approach, I then estimate the intersectional continuous logistic regression; results are presented in Online Appendix B. Instead of splitting age and vehicle age at their medians, they are preserved as continuous variables. The predicted probabilities of search by race and gender, over vehicle age is presented in Figure 2. Covariates were held at their modes, and driver age was held at its mean. Vehicle age is plotted here from 0 to 30 years old for ease of interpretation, though the variable itself extends beyond 30 years. As vehicle age moves from low to high, the predicted probability of search increases, for all gender and racial groups. This suggests that older vehicles may signal class-based stereotypes that result in higher levels of suspicion.

Male drivers experience significantly higher predicted probabilities of search than their female counterparts – some reaching beyond a 0.2 probability of search (for Latino males in 30-year-old vehicles). Female drivers, on the other hand, experience a high of 0.152 probability of search. But, this single-axis interpretation is not sufficient. While males, as a group, have higher probabilities of search than females, Latina and black females' probabilities of search exceed that of white and Asian males. With 30-year-old vehicles, Latina women have a 0.152 probability of search and black women have a 0.111 probability. Contrast this with that of white men (0.083) and Asian men (0.055).

For both genders, the order of racial groups in terms of the probabilities of search is the same: Latinx drivers experience the highest probability of search, followed by blacks, Native Americans, whites, and Asians. Racially, this is in line with expectations. Latinx and black drivers, who experience stereotyping that makes them prone to suspicion, experience the highest probabilities of search following a traffic stop. For males, black and Latino drivers with 30-year-old vehicles have a 0.171 and 0.216 probability of search, respectively. That means, for this particular subgroup, a search is likely to occur approximately every one in five stops. Stereotypes of criminality make these drivers prone to undue scrutiny, when all other contextual factors are taken into consideration.

While black and Latinx drivers are most prone to searches, on the other end of the spectrum, Asians' probabilities of search fall below that of white drivers. While Asians are a negatively stereotyped group, the associated stereotypes do not particularly elicit

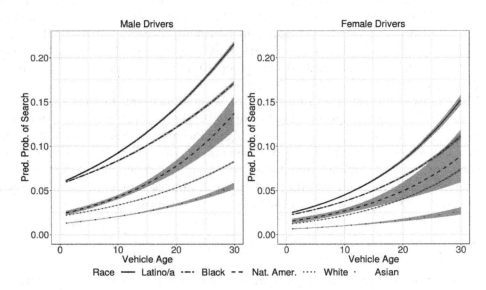

Figure 2. Predicted probabilities of experiencing a search, by racial group, over vehicle age.

suspicion. This illustrates two points. First, context matters for the way that stereotyping will produce outcomes. Asians are negatively stereotyped in the US, but their particular stereotypes do not happen to elicit suspicion, which is likely the dominant consideration in whether to search a car. Second, stereotypes do not solely operate to produce targeting, but also to produce a lack of targeting. A singular focus on the most highly targeted misses this inverse function of stereotypes.

With the newest vehicles, female drivers' predicted probabilities of search are all fairly clustered, with probabilities ranging from 0.006 to 0.025. Male drivers do cluster closer when they have newer vehicles than when they have older vehicles, but black and Latino male drivers are in their own group above the others from the beginning. While white, Native American, and Asian male drivers all begin in the 0.013–0.025 range, similar to the female drivers, the probabilities of search for black and Latino males never get this low, no matter the vehicle age. Instead, they begin above 0.06; a probability that Native American male drivers do not reach until vehicle age is 16 years old. White male drivers do not exceed this probability until their vehicle age is 23 years old. Asian males' probability never exceeds 0.06 for any range of vehicle age in this plot (it caps at 0.055 for 30-year-old vehicles). At no point are black and Latino male drivers' probability of search comparable to any other group.

For both male and female drivers, the average differences in probabilities of search between racial groups with newer vehicles are much smaller than those that emerge with older vehicles. For males, the average difference in probability of search between minority drivers and white drivers is 0.038 points when vehicle age is 1 year old. When it is 30 years old, this difference increases by about 43%, to 0.088 points. For females, there is a similar but less dramatic increase. When vehicle age is 1 year old, the average difference in probabilities of search is 0.011. This increases by about 28% percent to 0.037 at a vehicle age of 30 years old. This points to the expectation that disadvantage mounts. First, the increase in the spread of the probabilities of search is much more dramatic among men (the more suspicious gender identity) than women. Second, the difference in probabilities of search is greater for drivers with old vehicles (the more suspicious identity) than those with new vehicles. As suspicion-evoking identities grow (in this case, as vehicle age gets larger), the differences in search grow. Vehicle age matters more – in the sense that it functions to produce greater probabilities of search – for those subgroups that already experience higher levels of searches because they also possess racial or gender identities that are suspicion-evoking.

For age, an opposite but theoretically consistent pattern emerges. Figure 3 plots the predicted probabilities of search for male and female drivers, by racial group, across a range of ages. The y-axis represents the probability of search and the x-axis plots this probability over ages 15 through 70.

Of course, male drivers are searched more than female drivers. Racially, Latinx drivers are searched the most, followed by black, Native American, white, and finally by Asian drivers. Though, note that the predicted probability line for black and Latino male drivers switch places around age 50. Similar to vehicle age, the differences between racial and gender subgroups are largest when age is at its "most" suspicious – meaning, when drivers are young. At older ages, these differences start to shrink. For males, the mean difference in the probability of search between minority and white drivers when age is 70 years old is 0.022. When age is 16 years old, the average difference

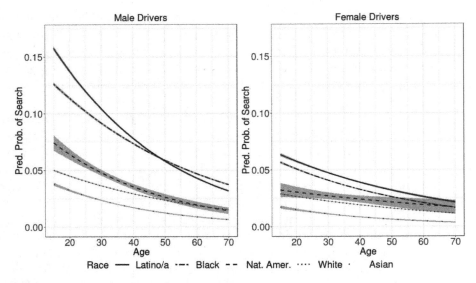

Figure 3. Predicted probabilities of experiencing a search, by racial group, over driver age.

in probabilities increases by 29%, to 0.075. For female drivers, when age is 70 years old, the mean difference in probabilities of search by racial group is 0.005, which grows by 19% to 0.027 when the driver's age is 16 years old. The differences in the probabilities of search is largest for young drivers, compared to older drivers, and for male drivers, compared to female drivers. The more and more suspicious identities that a person holds, the level of targeting grows. The effect of being younger or being in an old vehicle is largest for those drivers who already experience targeting based on their suspicion-evoking racial and gender identities.

Leniency in traffic stops

Whether a driver receives a warning following a traffic stop measures leniency afforded by the officer. The logistic regressions predicting a warning are presented in Online Appendix F. Predicted probabilities of receiving a warning are plotted over a range of vehicle ages in Figure 4.

First note that women receive more warnings than men, by about 0.02 on average, though this ranges from a difference of 0.043 for whites to 0.002 for blacks, when the vehicle is new. Racially, whites receive by far the most warnings, which is counter to my expectation that Asian drivers would be most apt to receive warnings. Asians are the second most likely group to receive a warning, which may be due to negative stereotyping of Asians, divorced from notions of suspicion, that result in harsher treatment during a traffic stop. After Asians, Native Americans and blacks are likely to receive a warning, followed by Latinx drivers, who experience the least amount of warnings, by far. A Latino male in a 30-year-old vehicle has a 0.173 probability of receiving a warning while a white male is almost double that (a 0.312 probability). For females, the difference is similarly stark: white females in a 30-year-old vehicle have a 0.335 probability of receiving a warning while Latina females only have a 0.203 probability. Disparities

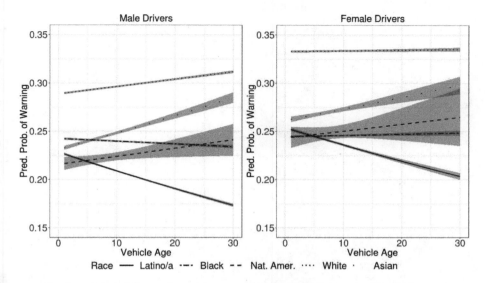

Figure 4. Predicted probabilities of receiving a warning, by racial group, over vehicle age.

between racial minority groups are smaller at newer vehicle age values, but they grow as vehicle age increases (that is, as vehicle age starts to signal a more "suspicious" identity); for men, the difference between the most likely and least likely group to receive a warning grows from 0.063 to 0.138 and for women, from 0.088 to 0.132.

For whites, Asians, and Native Americans, the probability of receiving a warning increases with vehicle age – though the trend is most pronounced among Asians. This is unexpected, as theory would dictate that older vehicles would signal lower class status and result in less leniency. The expected trend does hold for black and Latinx, though most prominently among Latinx drivers, who appear to be punished most heavily for having an older vehicle. This finding illustrates the importance of intersectional analyses. An additive model would not have allowed vehicle age to have different effects depending on race and gender.

Figure 5 plots predicted probabilities from the same model, computed over a range of driver ages. Here, women consistently receive more warnings than men, when compared within racial groups by about 0.3, on average. Again, this depends on the racial group. White females' probability of receiving a warning is about 0.040 higher than their male counterparts, while for blacks, the difference is only 0.004. Whites receive the most warnings, again followed by Asians. Similar to the plots for vehicle age, the disparities between racial groups are more prominent at younger ages (the more "suspicious" group) than at older ages. After about age 50, all racial minorities have a similar probability of receiving a warning, following a traffic stop, though whites are still much more likely to experience this leniency – by a probability of about 0.062 for male drivers and 0.088 for female.

The disparities between all groups within warnings are less pronounced than those among searches, potentially because the decision to search a car is much more closely tied to perceptions of suspicion than the decision to issue a warning. Nevertheless, there are clear, theoretically consistent disparities that emerge in whether or not the officer gives the driver a warning. Female drivers receive more leniency than their

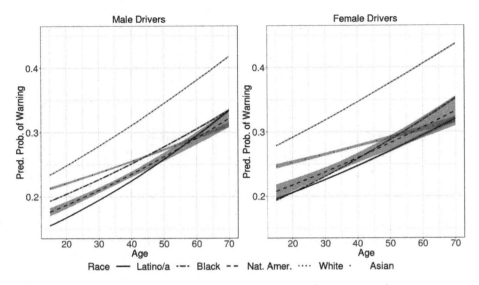

Figure 5. Predicted probabilities of receiving a warning, by racial group, over driver age.

within-race male counterparts. Whites receive the most leniency, by far. Then, Asians receive leniency followed by blacks and Native Americans. Latinx drivers consistently receive the least leniency. Leniency increases with driver age, but its effect with vehicle age depends on the racial and gender group analyzed. Most notably, whites are significantly advantaged in this arena, across gender, vehicle age, and class.

Categorical compounding of suspicion

To illustrate this targeting one final way, I return to the intersectional categorical models. Recall that these models include indicators for each of the 40 different identity categories (for which vehicle age and driver age were split at their medians into new/old vehicles and young/old drivers). I assign a suspicion-level to each of the 40 identity categories. This level ranges from 0 to 4 and represents the number of suspicion-evoking identities that the group holds. Recall the suspicious identities are male (versus female), young (versus old), and old vehicles (versus new vehicles). Racially, I consider black, Latinx, and Native American drivers to hold suspicion-evoking identities and white and Asian drivers to hold non-suspicious identities. This dichotomy, of course, is a gross generalization and there is much room for debate about these categories. The mean probability of search and warning, by the number of suspicion-evoking identities that a driver holds, is plotted in Figure 6. Broad trends in both outcomes are immediately apparent: as the number of suspicious identities that a driver holds increases, their probability of being searched increases and their probability of receiving a warning decreases.

The mean probability of receiving a warning when a driver holds no suspicion-evoking identities is 0.323. This drop to 0.289 when the driver holds one of these identities, and then to 0.258 (for two), 0.225 (for three), and 0.196 (for four). The mean probability of warning drops by about 0.03 points with each addition of another suspicion-evoking identity, though the difference slightly grows as the number of suspicious identities increases

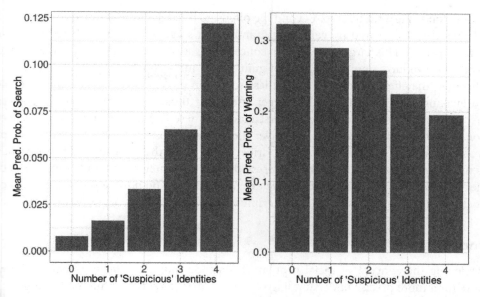

Figure 6. Predicted probabilities of traffic stop outcomes (search or warning), by the number of "suspicious" identities held by the driver.

(e.g., the difference is 0.029 when moving from zero to one suspicious identity, but 0.034 when moving from three to four). The more suspicion-evoking identities held by the driver, the less likely they are to experience lenient treatment by the officer.

Drivers with no suspicion-evoking identities experience a mean predicted probability of search of 0.008. For drivers with one suspicion-evoking identity, the mean probability is 0.016. For those with two, it is 0.033; with three, it is 0.066; and with four, 0.122. Note that the differences produced in the mean search rate gets larger and larger as the number of suspicion-evoking identities increase. Moving from 0 suspicion-evoking identities to one produces a difference of 0.008. From one to two, the difference jumps up about 49%, to 0.017. The difference in mean probability of moving from two suspicion-evoking identities to three is 0.032: a 53% increase. Finally, the largest increase in the mean probability of search is produced by moving from three suspicion-evoking identities to four. The difference jumps up to 0.057, which is a 57% increase. The differences in gaining one more suspicion-evoking identity are most prominent for those groups that already have highly suspicious identities. The jump in the probability of search for drivers with one suspicious identity to two is lower than that of the jump from three to four. Again, this points to the notion that disadvantage mounts as suspicion compounds for an individual driver.

Overall, we can conclude that certain intersectional identity groups do experience higher probabilities of search – and lower probabilities of receiving a warning – following a traffic stop than others, even once all confounding variables that the data provides are taken into account. These disparate probabilities cannot be accounted for with the reason the driver was stopped, the time of day, or any other variables for which the regression controlled. Instead, even after these confounding variables were accounted for, identity remains a significant explanatory and predictive variable for a search or a warning following a traffic stop. Beyond the often-analyzed identities of race and gender, I find that class (measured by vehicle age) and driver's age are important predictors for police targeting. This targeting is better conceived as a spectrum, in which stereotyping operates to produce a presumed level of guilt *and* of innocence for drivers.

Further, the effect of moving from a less suspicion-evoking identity to a more suspicion-evoking identity generally has larger effects for those groups that already possess other suspicion-evoking identities. Intersectionally, these identities compound the effect of one another and are larger as the driver moves more closely to the targeted profile of a young, black or Latino, poor, male driver. The effect that targeting this trope has extends beyond the individuals that possess this specific intersectional identity. Instead, other individuals are effected to a relative extent, depending on how closely their intersectional identity approaches the targeted criminal trope.

Conclusion

Broadening the concept of racial profiling to include multiple, intersectional identities allows for a more precise understanding of the way that stereotyping and police targeting operate. Stereotypes can result in both increased and depressed levels of targeting. Rather than conceiving of profiling as a dichotomy between who is targeted and who is not, we should think of targeting as a spectrum. The degree to which a certain identity group approaches the criminal trope of a young, black or Latino, poor man determines the degree to which they will be targeted.

Even though searches are relatively rare in traffic stops, the consequences that they have can ripple throughout a community. After controlling for a myriad of factors, it is clear that certain racial, gender, age, and class groups are much more heavily targeted than others. Racially, black and Latinx drivers are targeted most heavily, with Native American, white, and Asian drivers following behind. Males are targeted more than females, young drivers are targeted more than old drivers, and those with old vehicles are targeted more than those with new vehicles. An analysis of whether or not the driver receives a warning demonstrates that stereotypes do not only result in harsh treatment or targeting, but in leniency as well. Those drivers who are more likely to be searched are also less likely to receive a warning – and those who are not likely to be searched, are likely to receive warnings.

What does this mean for police-citizen relations for these communities? This analysis focused on individual drivers, but the effect of police contact extends to an individual's network (Owens and Walker 2018; Walker 2014; Walker and García-Castañon 2017) and neighborhood (Burch 2013, 2014; Lawless and Fox 2001; Lerman and Weaver 2014b). When someone experiences harsh treatment by the police, they likely talk about their experience with friends and family. When certain groups are more heavily targeted than others, such experiences start to build and animosity likely grows. Being searched less than one in 200 times that an individual is stopped (like old, Asian females with new vehicles) results in a much different lived experience than being searched 15 in 100 times (like young, Latino males with old vehicles). These experiences are tangible disparities that result in different realities for individuals in the United States.

Further, these experiences have concrete political consequences. Lerman and Weaver (2014b) find that police contact that involves searches or the use of force leads to decreased neighborhood-level outreach to local government. Burch (2011, 2014) finds consistently that contact with law enforcement demobilizes voter turnout at the individual and neighborhood level. Further, she finds that this demobilizing effect extends to other forms of political participation as well, such as signing petitions, protesting, volunteering, and participating in community groups (Burch 2013). At the same time, there is some evidence that proximal contact with an individual who has experienced contact with the criminal justice system may produce political mobilization (Walker 2014).

This study demonstrates that intersectional models of identity can help obtain more precise estimates of targeting and a deeper understanding of identity itself – at least with respect to traffic stop outcomes in Illinois. Further work should seek to expand the scope of this study, both geographically and contextually. The police operate in many contexts beyond traffic stops that may produce different outcomes. Further, there are likely important geographical differences in perceived suspicion that identities evoke, and expanding the scope of the study beyond one state would help outline these differences. Finally, this study makes headway by studying the intersection of four visible identities: race, gender, age, and class. However, there are many more unmeasured identities that likely combine to have an effect on how an individual is treated. For example, Burch (2015) finds that lighter-skinned blacks receive prison sentences that are not statistically significantly different from those received by whites, even though medium and dark-skinned blacks receive sentences that are about 4.8 percent higher than whites. Stereotypes associated with darker skin tone likely lead to increased police targeting and are another element of intersectional identity that could be explored further. Apart from race, gender identity (beyond the binary male/female) and sexual orientation have been absent from this paper, as the data do not include such information, but may contribute to the way that an individual is stereotyped, and potentially to the outcome from contact with law enforcement that they ultimately experience.

Intersectionality emphasizes the need to study the interaction of multiple identities, and this paper demonstrates that this claim is both theoretically and methodologically warranted. Intersectional models, without any constraints on the way that a single identity's effect can vary, produce better estimates than additive models. Theoretically, intersectional understandings of identity allow for a more specific understanding of the way that stereotyping operates – beyond a singular focus on the most highly targeted group. All in all, conceiving of profiling as intersectional is paramount to accurate analyses when studying identity-based disparities in the United States.

Notes

1. See Online Appendix A for more details.
2. Only eight states collect and report individual-level traffic stop data at the moment. Within those, Illinois is the only state that includes both a variable for vehicle age and for driver's age, in addition to the driver's racial and gender identity.
3. I also analyze whether or not the driver receives a ticket – the other outcome recorded in the data. The ticket analysis largely mirrors the search analysis, as it is also a harsh outcome, though there are less disparities – see Online Appendix G for a lengthier discussion.
4. Robustness checks compare this model to those estimated with different driver age cut points (21 years old and 25 years old) and different vehicle age cut points (at 3 and 5 years old) and results are nearly identical. See Online Appendix C. Further secondary analyses in the paper preserve driver age and vehicle age as continuous.

Disclosure statement

No potential conflict of interest was reported by the author(s).

References

Alcoff, Linda Martin. 2015. *The Future of Whiteness*. Malden, MA: Polity Press.
Armenta, Amada. 2017. "Racializing Crimmingration: Local Law Enforcement Agencies and the Institutional Production of Immigrant Criminality." *Sociology of Race and Ethnicity* 3 (1): 82–95.
Bates, Timothy. 2010. "Driving while Black in Suburban Detroit." *Du Bois Review: Social Science Research on Race* 7 (1): 133–150.
Baumgartner, Frank R., Leah Christiani, Derek A. Epp, Kevin Roach, and Kelsey Shoub. 2017a. "Racial Disparities in Traffic Stop Outcomes." *Duke Forum for Law & Social Change* 9: 21–56.
Baumgartner, Frank R., Derek A. Epp, Kelsey Shoub, and Bayard Love. 2017b. "Targeting Young Men of Color for Search and Arrest During Traffic Stops: Evidence from North Carolina, 2002–2013." *Politics, Groups, and Identities* 5 (1): 107–131.
Brewer, Marilynn B., and Layton N. Lui. 1989. "The Primacy of Age and Sex in the Structure of Person Categories." *Social Cognition* 7 (3): 262–274.
Burch, Traci. 2011. "Turnout and Party Registration among Criminal Offenders in the 2008 General Election." *Law & Society Review* 45 (3): 699–730.
Burch, Traci. 2013. *Trading Democracy for Justice: Criminal Convictions and the Decline of Neighborhood Political Participation*. Chicago, IL: University of Chicago Press.
Burch, Traci R. 2014. "Effects of Imprisonment and Community Supervision on Neighborhood Political Participation in North Carolina." *The ANNALS of the American Academy of Political and Social Science* 651 (1): 184–201.
Burch, Traci. 2015. "Skin Color and the Criminal Justice System: Beyond Black-White Disparities in Sentencing." *Journal of Empirical Legal Studies* 12 (3): 395–420.
Chou, Rosalind S., and Joe R. Feagin. 2015. *The Myth of the Model Minority: Asian Americans Facing Racism*. New York: Routledge.
Collins, Patricia Hill. 1990. "Black feminist thought in the matrix of domination." In *Black Feminist Thought: Knowledge, Consciousness, and the Politics of Empowerment*. Boston, MA: Unwin Hyman.
Combahee River Collective. 1983. "The Combahee River Collective Statement." In *Home Girls: A Black Feminist Anthology*, edited by Barbara Smith, 264. New Brunswick, NY: Rutgers University Press.
Crenshaw, Kimberle. 1989. "Demarginalizing the Intersection of Race and Sex: A Black Feminist Critique of Antidiscrimination Doctrine, Feminist Theory and Antiracist Politics." *University of Chicago Legal Forum* 140: 139–167.
Crenshaw, Kimberle. 1991. "Mapping the Margins: Intersectionality, Identity Politics, and Violence against Women of Color." *Stanford Law Review* 43: 1241–1299.
D'Errico, Peter P. 2000. "Introduction: Native Americans in American Politics." In *Encyclopedia of Minorities in American Politics, Volume II: Hispanic Americans and Native Americans*, edited by Jeffrey D. Schultz, Kerry L. Haynie, Anne M. McCulloch, and Andrew L. Aoki, 569–580. Phoenix, AZ: Oryx Press.
Devine, Patricia G. 1989. "Stereotypes and Prejudice: Their Automatic and Controlled Components." *Journal of Personality and Social Psychology* 56 (1): 5–18.
Devine, Patricia G., and Andrew J. Elliot. 1995. "Are Racial Stereotypes Really Fading? The Princeton Trilogy Revisited." *Personality and Social Psychology Bulletin* 21 (11): 1139–1150.
Dirks, Danielle, Caroline Heldman, and Emma Zack. 2015. "'She's White and She's Hot, So She Can't Be Guilty': Female Criminality, Penal Spectatorship, and White Protectionism." *Contemporary Justice Review* 18 (2): 160–177.
Epp, Charles R., Steven Maynard-Moody, and Donald P. Haider-Markel. 2014. *Pulled Over: How Police Stops Define Race and Citizenship*. Chicago: University of Chicago Press.

Fagan, Jeffrey, and Garth Davies. 2000. "Street Stops and Broken Windows: Terry, Race, and Disorder in New York City." *Fordham Urban Law Journal* 28: 457.

Fagan, Jeffrey, and Amanda Geller. 2015. "Following the Script: Narratives of Suspicion in *Terry* Stops in Street Policing." *The University of Chicago Law Review* 82: 51–88.

Fagan, Jeffrey, Amanda Geller, Garth Davies, and Valerie West. 2010. "Street Stops and Broken Windows Revisited." In *Race, Ethnicity, and Policing*, edited by Stephen K. Rice, and Michael D. White, 309–348. New York: New York University Press.

Fiske, Susan T. 1993. "Social Cognition and Social Perception." *Annual Review of Psychology* 44 (1): 155–194.

Fiske, Susan T., Amy JC Cuddy, Peter Glick, and Jun Xu. 2002. "A Model of (Often Mixed) Stereotype Content: Competence and Warmth Respectively Follow from Perceived Status and Competition." *Journal of Personality and Social Psychology* 82 (6): 878–902.

Gilliam Jr, Franklin D., and Shanto Iyengar. 2000. "Prime Suspects: The Influence of Local Television News on the Viewing Public." *American Journal of Political Science* 44 (3): 560–573.

Hancock, Ange-Marie. 2004. *The Politics of Disgust: The Public Identity of the Welfare Queen*. New York, NY: New York University Press.

Hancock, Ange-Marie. 2016. *Intersectionality: An Intellectual History*. Oxford, UK: Oxford University Press.

Harcourt, Bernard E. 2003. "The Shaping of Chance: Actuarial Models and Criminal Profiling at the Turn of the Twenty-First Century." *The University of Chicago Law Review* 70 (1): 105–128.

Harcourt, Bernard E. 2009. "Henry Louis Gates and Racial Profiling: What's the Problem?" Paper presented at the Malcolm Wiener Inequality and Social Policy Program, Chicago, IL, September 14, 2009.

Harris-Perry, Melissa V. 2011. *Sister Citizen: Shame, Stereotypes, and Black Women in America*. New Haven, CT: Yale University Press.

Harris, David A. 2003. *Profiles in Injustice: Why Racial Profiling Cannot Work*. New York, NY: The New Press.

Kim, Claire Jean. 2003. *Bitter Fruit: The Politics of Black-Korean Conflict in New York City*. New Haven, CT: Yale University Press.

Knox, Dean, Will Lowe, and Jonathon Mummolo. 2019. "The Bias is Built In: How Administrative Records Mask Racially Biased Policing." Available at *SSRN*: https://papers.ssrn.com/sol3/papers.cfm?abstract_id=3336338.

Lawless, Jennifer L., and Richard L. Fox. 2001. "Political Participation of the Urban Poor." *Social Problems* 48 (3): 362–385.

Lawston, Jodie Michelle. 2008. "Women, the Criminal Justice System, and Incarceration: Processes of Power, Silence, and Resistance." *NWSA Journal* 20 (2): 1–18.

Lee, Tiane L., and Susan T. Fiske. 2006. "Not an Outgroup, Not Yet an Ingroup: Immigrants in the Stereotype Content Model." *International Journal of Intercultural Relations* 30 (6): 751–768.

Lerman, Amy E., and Vesla M. Weaver. 2014a. *Arresting Citizenship: The Democratic Consequences of American Crime Control*. Chicago, IL: University of Chicago Press.

Lerman, Amy E., and Vesla Weaver. 2014b. "Staying Out of Sight? Concentrated Policing and Local Political Action." *The ANNALS of the American Academy of Political and Social Science* 651 (1): 202–219.

Loury, Glenn C. 2008. *Race, Incarceration, and American Values*. Cambridge, MA: The MIT Press.

McConnaughy, Corrine. 2018. "Black Men, White Women, and Demands from the State: How Race and Gender Jointly Shape the Public's Expectations of Protestors and Legitimate State Response." Paper presented at the Policy Research Group, UNC-Chapel Hill. Chapel Hill, NC.

Meehan, Albert J., and Michael C. Ponder. 2002. "Race and Place: The Ecology of Racial Profiling African American Motorists." *Justice Quarterly* 19 (3): 399–430.

Muhammad, Khalil Gabran. 2010. *The Condemnation of Blackness: Race, Crime, and the Making of Modern Urban America*. Cambridge, MA: Harvard University Press.

Owens, Michael Leo, and Hannah L. Walker. 2018. "The Civic Voluntarism of 'Custodial Citizens': Involuntary Criminal Justice Contact, Associational Life, and Political Participation." *Perspectives on Politics* 16 (4): 1–24.

Revesz, Rachael. 2016. "Native Americans Most Likely Ethnic Group to Be Killed by Police." *Independent.co*. Accessed October 3, 2018. https://www.independent.co.uk/news/world/americas/native-americans-police-death-murder-investigation-jacqueline-salyers-a7371861.html.

Sampaio, Anna. 2014. "Racing and Gendering Immigration Politics: Analyzing Contemporary Immigration Enforcement using Intersectional Analysis." *Politics, Groups, and Identities* 2 (2): 202–221.

Simoiu, Camelia, Sam Corbett-Davies, and Sharad Goel. 2017. "The Problem of Infra-Marginality in Outcome Tests for Discrimination." *The Annals of Applied Statistics* 11 (3): 1193–1216.

Stangor, Charles, and Mark Shaller. 1996. "Stereotypes as Individual and Collective Representations." In *Stereotypes and Stereotyping*, edited by Neil C. Macrae, Charles Stangor, and Miles Hewstone, 64–82. New York, NY: Guilford Press.

Steffensmeier, Darrell, Noah Painter-Davis, and Jeffery Ulmer. 2017. "Intersectionality of Race, Ethnicity, Gender, and Age on Criminal Punishment." *Sociological Perspectives* 60 (4): 810–833.

Taylor, Charles R., and Barbara B. Stern. 1997. "Asian-Americans: Television Advertising and the 'Model Minority' Stereotype." *Journal of Advertising* 26 (2): 47–61.

Tomaskovic-Devey, Donald, Marcinda Mason, and Matthew Zingraff. 2004. "Looking for the Driving While Black Phenomena: Conceptualizing Racial Bias Processes and their Associated Distributions." *Police Quarterly* 7 (1): 3–29.

Walker, Hannah L. 2014. "Extending the Effects of the Carceral State: Proximal Contact, Political Participation, and Race." *Political Research Quarterly* 67 (4): 809–822.

Walker, Hannah L., and Marcela García-Castañon. 2017. "For Love and Justice: The Mobilizing of Race, Gender, and Criminal Justice Contact." *Politics & Gender* 13 (4): 541–568.

Warren, Patricia, Donald Tomaskovic-Devey, William Smith, Matthew Zingraff, and Marcinda Mason. 2006. "Driving While Black: Bias Processes and Racial Disparity in Police Stops." *Criminology; An interdisciplinary Journal* 44 (3): 709–738.

Weaver, Vesla M., and Amy E. Lerman. 2010. "Political Consequences of the Carceral State." *American Political Science Review* 104 (4): 817–833.

Welch, Kelly. 2007. "Black Criminal Stereotypes and Racial Profiling." *Journal of Contemporary Criminal Justice* 23 (3): 276–288.

Winter, Nicholas J. G. 2006. "Beyond Welfare: Framing and the Racialization of White Opinion on Social Security." *American Journal of Political Science* 50 (2): 400–420.

Wong, Paul, Chienping Faith Lai, Richard Nagasawa, and Tieming Lin. 1998. "Asian Americans as a Model Minority: Self-Perceptions and Perceptions by Other Racial Groups." *Sociological Perspectives* 41 (1): 95–118.

Why participate? An intersectional analysis of LGBTQ people of color activism in Canada

Alexie Labelle

ABSTRACT
The recent Black Lives Matter disruptions of Pride marches in Toronto and Montreal have brought to light a persistent conflict over the exclusion of people of color within LGBTQ movements in Canada, the United States, and elsewhere. Yet, they also reflect a recurrent form of organizing observed in these movements, namely the creation and mobilization of LGBTQ organizations formed around specific racialized identities. Using Canada and more specifically Montreal as a case study, this paper aims to understand what drives activists of color to engage in LGBTQ movements in general, and in particular within LGBTQ organizations formed around specific racialized identities. Previous work on social movement participation has underlined structural and identity-related processes that explain participation, such as networks, social ties, and collective identity. However, I argue that with its emphasis on marginalization and politically excluded identities, intersectionality as a theoretical framework is more suitable to fully grasp why activists of color participate in the Canadian LGBTQ movement today. Drawing from in-depth interviews conducted with 15 activists in Montreal, results show that experienced marginalization at the intersection of gender, sexuality, and race, shape structural and identity-related processes in specific ways, thereby acting as a driving force of social movement participation.

Introduction

In July 2016, *Black Lives Matter* (BLM) staged a sit-in during Toronto's Pride march to demand an increased inclusion of people of color within the organizing committee, the banning of police officers in uniforms during the march, and the acknowledgement of the overarching racism within LGBTQ[1] communities in Canada (Battersby 2016). The creation of a Montreal chapter of the organization soon ensued, and on August 2017, BLM Montreal interrupted the minute of silence during the city's Pride march to honor trans women of color victims of police repression. These disruptive actions not only bring to light a persistent conflict over racialization[2] and the exclusion of people of color within LGBTQ movements in Canada, in the United States, in France, and in the United Kingdom (Boston and Duyvendak 2015; Trawalé and Poiret 2017), but also point to a recurrent form of organizing that has been observed in Canada's LGBTQ movement since the late 1980s, namely the creation and mobilization of LGBTQ organizations formed around specific racialized identities. Using Canada, and more specifically Montreal as a case study, this paper aims to understand what drives activists of color to engage in LGBTQ movements in general, and in particular within LGBTQ organizations formed around specific racialized identities.

Previous work on social movement participation has shed light on some of the structural and identity-related processes that explain why individuals engage in collective actions, in particular the role of networks, social ties (McAdam and Paulsen 1993; Passy and Giugni 2001; Diani 2004), and collective identity (Taylor and Whittier 1992; Melucci 1995). Others have furthered social movement participation theorizing by developing middle-range theories that go beyond a structure/identity binary (Dauvin and Siméant 2002; Schussman and Soule 2005; Corrigall-Brown 2012; Viterna 2013; Ward 2016). However, while middle-range and interactionist theories provide useful avenues in understanding social movement participation, I argue that they fall short of explaining people of color's engagement within the Canadian LGBTQ movement. Instead, I hold that with its emphasis on marginalization and politically excluded identities, intersectionality as a theoretical framework is more suitable to fully grasp why activists of color take part in the Canadian LGBTQ movement today.

Considering the fragmented nature of the LGBTQ movement at a pan-Canadian scale (M. Smith 2015; Tremblay 2015b), and bearing in mind that Canadian urban milieus act as converging spaces for LGBTQ activism of color (M. Grundy and Smith 2005; Smith 2005), I focus my analysis on the city of Montreal. Building on in-depth interviews conducted with 15 activists involved in a range of LGBTQ organizations formed around specific racialized identities, including *Gay and Lesbian Asians of Montreal, Arc-en-ciel d'Afrique, Helem Montréal*, and *Black Lives Matter*, results show that experienced marginalization at the intersection of gender, sexuality, and race, acts as a driving force of social movement participation.

The paper is divided as follows. First, I provide an overview of the different collective actors, events, and issues that have shaped LGBTQ activism in Montreal. Second, I review the current literature on social movement participation, introduce intersectionality, and outline my theoretical framework. Third, I specify my methodological design, and in the final section I present and discuss my results.

LGBTQ activism in Montreal

In the 1950s and the early 1960s, cabarets, burlesque shows, and other social and cruising networks acted as sites of gender and sexual resistance throughout Canada (see Namaste 2005; Gentile, Kinsman, and Rankin 2016). Yet, gay and lesbian communities at that time remained not only "isolated by both class and gender" (Auger and Krug 2013, 27), but were also racially homogeneous (Warner 2002). While previous work points to the significance of the 1969 federal Bill C-150 partially decriminalizing homosexuality in Canada in the development of a politicized sexual identity and in the emancipation of a visible Canadian LGBTQ community (Smith 1999, 2015), its heritage remains contested. For instance, Hooper (2019) speaks of a "recriminalization of homosexuality" rather than a "partial decriminalization," referring to the latter as a myth. As such, he specifies that not only did the Criminal Code maintain buggery, bestiality, and gross indecency as punishable offenses, but it also "added an exception that allowed individuals to commit these crimes under specific circumstances."[3] (Hooper 2019, 258). Additional studies have further brought to light the intensification of police repression towards LGBTQ communities in the years that followed the passing of the 1969 Bill C-150 (Gentile, Kinsman, and Rankin 2016). Nonetheless, this reform, which also maintained a higher age of consent for same-gender sexual practices, was followed by the organization of the first Canadian public gay and lesbian protest in 1971 on Parliament Hill in Ottawa (Gentile, Kinsman, and Rankin 2016).

Scholars remain reluctant to speak of a gay and lesbian movement in Quebec prior to the 1970s as few homophile activities and organizing could generate and sustain activism prior to the partial decriminalization of homosexuality in 1969 (Higgins 1999; Tremblay 2015a). Referring to Quebec's particular sociopolitical context, Tremblay (2015a) underlines the importance of the Quiet Revolution, namely a "vast movement of social, cultural, and economic modernization and national affirmation" (107) in the development of lesbian and gay activism in the 1970s. As such, Québécois nationalism "played an indirect role in the expression of lesbian and gay activism in the early 1970s by advancing a modernizing nationalism with which lesbian and gay groups could associate" (Tremblay, 2015a: 107), hence the creation of the *Front de libération homosexuel*[4] (FLH), which shared an affinity to Quebec's independence movement (see Gentile 2016).

Following the dismantling of the FLH in 1972 (Podmore 2015), gay and lesbian organizing in Montreal intensified in the second half of the decade, prompted by two major events: the Olympic Games "cleansing" in 1975–1976,[5] and the Truxx bar police raid in 1977, after which more than 200 homosexuals were arrested by the city police (Radio-Canada 2017). These events spurred massive protests and strengthened grassroots organizing, with the creation of the *Comité homosexuel anti-répression* (CHAR), later renamed the *Association pour les droits des gai(e)s du Québec* (ADGQ). Soon after, a clause prohibiting discrimination on the basis of sexual orientation was included within the Quebec Charter of Rights and Freedoms[6] in 1977 by the *Parti Québécois* (Warner 2002; Podmore 2015).

While LGBTQ activism in the 1980s was mostly marked by the HIV/AIDS pandemic, the 1990s gave rise to a number of legal battles pertaining to the federal recognition of same-sex couples. In Montreal the 1990s were once again the scene of acute repression, with the advent of the police crackdown of the Sex Garage party (Podmore 2015). This event was followed by a 150-people sit-in in the Village,[7] and a kiss-in of 400 people in front of the police station in downtown Montreal (Podmore 2015). LGBTQ activism intensified once more around the issue of police repression with the creation of *Lesbians and Gays Against Violence* and the *Table de concertation des lesbiennes et des gais du Grand Montreal*, and in the late 1990s, the first LGBTQ organization formed around a particular racialized identity was created in Montreal, namely *Gay and Lesbian Asians of Montreal* (GLAM) .[8]

Police repression diminished considerably with the advent of the new millennium, which was accompanied by major political gains. Not only did the Government of Quebec adopt Bill n°84 in 2002, instituting civil unions and thereby recognizing "joint parental rights of same-sex spouses"(Hurley 2003), but it later legally recognized same-sex marriage in 2004, followed by the Government of Canada in 2005. However, as scholars have previously exposed, such political gains tend to reflect the priorities of a movement dominated by white and cisgender activists and as such do not necessarily reflect the political grievances and demands of other marginalized groups, namely trans and people of color (Lenon 2011; Gentile, Kinsman, and Rankin 2016; DeFilippis 2018).

In this context, LGBTQ organizing around specific racialized identities diversified and became increasingly visible in Montreal in the early 2000s, with the creation of *Arc-en-ciel d'Afrique*, an LGBTQ Afro-Caribbean organization, *Helem-Montreal*, an organization for Lebanese and Arabophone sexual and gender minorities, and *Ethnoculture*, a non-profit organization that coordinated events for LGBTQ ethnic minorities, people of color, and two-spirited people (D. Smith 2010), to name a few. Meant to bring together LGBTQ individuals from particular ethnic backgrounds to provide safer spaces for LGBTQ people of color, most of these groups also aimed at fostering a greater sense of belonging within Quebec society, as well as within LGBTQ milieus. For instance, AECA participated in the annual LGBTQ Community Day hosted during Pride week and organized, until 2018, the annual Massimadi Festival that celebrates Afro-Caribbean art and filmmaking to render visible non-white LGBTQ realities.

In the last decade, race has become increasingly contentious both within Montreal's LGBTQ movement and within Quebec more generally. First, racialized activists within Montreal's LGBTQ movement have formed organizations that have openly questioned racism within and outside the movement; these groups include *Qouleur Collective*, which showcased the work of queer, trans, and two-spirited artists of color from 2012 to 2016 and which currently works at creating dialogue around issues affecting racialized communities, and *Black Lives Matter*, which aims at dismantling anti-black racism. Some of these organizations tend to embrace the QTBIPOC acronym, which stands for queer and trans, Black, Indigenous, and People of color, instead of the LGBTQ acronym. As activists interviewed for this research have underlined, this not only reflects their English-speaking character, but also points to the importance conferred to their racialized identity in their activities and actions. Second, a series of political events have rendered race more contentious in Quebec's broader public space. These include the reasonable accommodation crisis of 2006–2008,[9] the proposed Bill n°60 commonly referred to as *Charte des valeurs québécoises* introduced by the *Parti Québécois* in 2013,[10] and the recently passed *laïcité* Bill n°21 proposed by the *Coalition Avenir Québec*.[11] If these political initiatives may be seen as contemporary embodiments of Quebecois nationalism, most activists interviewed for this research nonetheless evoked how they have contributed to making race a contentious issue within society, as well as within the LGBTQ movement.

Altogether, LGBTQ activism of color organizing in Montreal is heterogeneous and should not be perceived as a monolithic entity. That said, and in spite of differences in terms of grievances, targets, and denomination, LGBTQ organizations structured around specific racialized identities have been mobilizing within the broader LGBTQ movement in Montreal since the late 1990s and early 2000s, up until today. Hence, what drives activists of color to engage and participate in Montreal's LGBTQ movement, and in particular within LGBTQ organizations formed around specific racialized identities? In the following section, I provide an overview of the recent literature on social movement participation and highlight several pitfalls of current theoretical approaches. I then build on intersectionality to fill in these gaps and develop the preliminary bases of an intersectional theoretical framework to further our understanding of LGBTQ activism of color in Montreal.

Deploying intersectionality in social movement participation theorizing

Although LGBTQ activism of color remains understudied in Canada and elsewhere, individual engagement has, on the contrary, been particularly discussed in the field of social movement studies. Following Olson's (1965) paradox on collective action participation, students of social movements have shed light on various structural and identity-related explanations to participation, such as the role of networks, social ties, ideology, collective identity, and emotions (Taylor and Whittier 1992; Melucci 1995; Passy and Giugni 2001; Polletta and Jasper 2001; Diani 2004; Chaeyoon Lim 2008). This said, another – and more recent – strand of research on social movement participation has attempted to move beyond a structure/identity and social/individual binary by looking at some of the ways in which structures and identities combine and interact in fostering social movement participation.

Such recent work has looked at patterns of protest participation by situating individual motivations within larger structural dispositions. Building on McAdam's (1986) notion of "biographical availability", defined as the "absence of personal constraints that may increase the costs and risks of movement participation, such as full-time employment, marriage, and family responsibilities" (70), Corrigall-Brown (2012) develops a trajectory model of participation wherein an individual's engagement will fluctuate through time depending on one's biographical availability, resources, and social networks, on the movement's organizational and relational context, and on the types and strength of social ties and identification with the movement. Schussman and Soule (2005) have for their part looked at the ways in which biographical availability ties in with structural availability, namely the presence of networks that facilitate recruitment, and political engagement, be it an individual's access to information or one's overall political interest. They highlight that as much as structural availability, biographical availability, and political engagement are necessary conditions to participation, being asked to protest remains the strongest indicator. While these studies provide useful avenues in combining structural and individual factors, they tend to overstate, on the one hand, the role of organizational and social ties and to understate, on the other hand, the role of identity-related processes, thus leaving aside the question of how identity factors in our understanding of what motivates individuals to mobilize. Moreover, while they do situate an individual's motivations within particular structural dispositions, they do not bring to light the ways in which individuals and structures interact.

Other studies have borrowed from interactionist approaches to explain social movement participation. For instance, Fillieule (2001) asserts that although activism constitutes a social and dynamic activity, individuals do not act independently from social structures and from the conditions in which they interact with others. Consequently, one must then look at one's biographical trajectory within a particular sociopolitical context by adopting a processual approach (Fillieule 2001). While this approach proves useful in understanding activists' trajectories, it does however understate once again the identity-related dimension of participation. Hence, drawing on Stryker's (1981) symbolic interactionism and identity theory, Viterna's (2013) study of women's engagement within El Salvador's *Farabundo Marti National Liberation Front* highlights the ways in which identity and social structures interact in fostering participation. As Ward (2016) underlines, "Viterna argues that because identities are both internally held and externally assigned, are defined through social interactions and cultural representations, and play a key role in motivating behaviors, they contribute significantly to participation in social activism" (857). To spur mobilization, identities need to become salient (Stryker 1981) in which case individuals become engaged by developing a "participation identity," defined by Gould (1995) as "the social identification with respect to which an individual responds in a given instance of social protest to specific normative and instrumental appeals" (13). For Gould (1995), the development of a participation identity is conditioned by critical and short-term events, which set the stage for the ranking of one's social identifications.

While symbolic interactionism is useful in understanding participation as it acknowledges how identities are constructed within particular contexts and interactions spurring mobilization, it remains that identities are also inscribed within specific power dynamics, wherein processes of exclusion and marginalization contribute to the shaping of identity-formation and politicization, be it individual or collective. If one is to conceptualize participation as a dynamic, on-going, and non-linear process (Ward 2016), one has to take a deeper look at the ways in which power and difference, exclusion and marginalization, discrimination and inequalities, shape personal and militant trajectories. What is more, by emphasizing the role of salient identities in explaining social movement participation, symbolic interactionism does not take a sufficient account of the ways in which identifications cross and thus lacks an intersectional perspective. Inasmuch as identities are constructed and formed through culture and interaction, they are also inscribed within specific power relations and shaped by particular instances of exclusion and marginalization. I argue that an intersectional approach can adequately overcome these theoretical pitfalls and provide useful avenues for furthering our understanding of why people of color engage within the LGBTQ movement in Montreal, particularly within LGBTQ organizations formed around specific racialized identities.

An intersectional theoretical framework to social movement participation

Coined at the end of the 1980s by Kimberlé W. Crenshaw, the term "intersectionality" refers to the idea that vectors of oppression, be it classism, racism, or sexism, intersect in such a way so as to foster discrimination. In her pioneering work on American women of color victims of violence and discrimination, she

> illustrate[d] that many of the experiences Black women face are not subsumed within the traditional boundaries of race or gender discrimination as these boundaries are currently understood, and that the intersection of racism and sexism factors into Black women's lives in ways that cannot be captured wholly by looking at the race or gender dimension of those experiences separately. (Crenshaw 1991, 1224)

While Crenshaw's work has without a doubt generated numerous studies, intersectional thinking does predate Crenshaw's work, going back to American social movements of the 1960s and 1970s, notably the *Combahee River Collective*, a group of black lesbian women activists (Yuval-Davis 2011; Hill Collins and Bilge 2016), and the works of Black feminists in the early 1980s, such as bell hooks and Angela Davis (Yuval-Davis 2011; Moreau 2015).[12]

The term has since prompted various debates pertaining mostly to its definition (Hill Collins 2000; Hancock 2007; Nash 2008; Dhamoon 2011; Mügge et al. 2018). Building on

Hill Collins and Bilge (2016), I define intersectionality as a transdisciplinary theoretical approach which sheds light on the different ways in which categories of power interlock in a given situation, interact and contribute in (re)producing inequalities; these categories of power may include gender, race, sexuality, socioeconomic status, age, ability, etc. Most importantly, it acknowledges the interconnected nature of oppressions, whereby their effects are not cumulative; one cannot add or multiply the impact that particular vectors of oppression, be it racism, sexism, cisgenderism, or homophobia, have on a particular individual, as they are not independent from one another (Hancock 2007).

Previous work on intersectionality highlights the ways in which oppressions are both *structural* and *structuring*. First, intersecting oppressions are materialized and consolidated in various institutions, be it legal, political, economic, social, or cultural, therefore taking on a *structural* character (P. Grzanka 2014), or what Crenshaw (1991) refers to as *structural intersectionality*. Second, categories of power and difference interact and institutionalize in such a way that constrains individuals' capabilities, thus situating one's positionality in society and taking on a *structuring* dimension (Crenshaw 2014).

Inasmuch as oppressions are *structural* and *structuring*, intersectionality also sheds light on the ways in which individuals navigate these structural inequalities, particularly in the field of social movements. Crenshaw's (1991) concept of *political intersectionality* is especially relevant in this sense because it "highlights the ways in which [individuals can be] situated within at least two subordinated groups that [can] pursue conflicting political agendas" (1252). Speaking specifically of Black women's situation, Crenshaw (1991) asserts that "the failure of feminism to interrogate race means that resistance strategies of feminism will often replicate and reinforce the subordination of people of color, and the failure of antiracism to interrogate patriarchy means that antiracism will frequently reproduce the subordination of women" (1252). Consequently, one can argue that individuals may respond to this *political dilemma* (Crenshaw 1991) by developing particular political identities and engaging in very specific ways. An intersectional approach can therefore be a pertinent tool in understanding social movement participation of LGBTQ activists of color. Not only does it allow for a more interactionist approach to the study of social movement participation, but it sheds light on the ways in which intersecting patterns of marginalization can drive mobilization.

Ultimately, I argue that LGBTQ activism of color is not only spurred by the continuous interaction between one's identity and the sociopolitical context in which one's personal and militant trajectories are set, but it is also driven by particular instances of marginalization and exclusion that intersect over time through multiple interactions. In the following section, I elaborate on how I intend to operationalize this framework.

Methodology

Much attention has been given to intersectional methodology in recent years (Bowleg 2008; Nash 2008; Choo and Ferree 2010), spanning mostly from McCall's (2005) pivotal work, in which she identifies three intersectional methodological approaches that consequently inform researchers' method choice: *anticategorial*, which consists of deconstructing analytical, power, and difference categories; *intercategorial*, which consists of comparing analytical categories to shed light on inequalities between social groups; and *intracategorial*, which focuses on the intersection of particular analytical categories to reveal the complexity of the lived reality of the group located at a particular intersection. This third intersectional methodological approach best characterizes this research, in which case I favor the use of qualitative methods, namely in-depth interviews. Not only does this particular method fall within intersectional feminist epistemologies in the sense that it gives voice to marginalized individuals and builds on activists' own personal narratives (Nash 2008), but it also acknowledges that activists are ultimately more aware of their own experiences, realities, and perceptions of themselves, of their environment, and of their own actions and motivations (Blee and Taylor 2002).

I conducted interviews from January to July 2018 with 15 activists who identify as LGBTQ people of color in Montreal and who have participated in a range of actions, events, and groups, from the early 2000s until now.[13] Table A1 (see Appendix) provides an overview of interviewees' profile distribution in terms of gender identity, age, and racial identity. All activists interviewed participated in at least one of the following groups: *Gay and Lesbian Asians of Montreal, Ethnoculture, Helem Montréal, AlMassir, AGIR, Arc-en-ciel d'Afrique, Qouleur, Black Lives Matter Montreal,* and *Jhalak*. These groups vary in terms of organizational structure, preferred tactics, mandate, and so forth; some do advocacy work, while others are service providers, as is the case with *Action LGBTQ avec immigrants et réfugié(e)s* (AGIR). Yet, they all engage in community-building and act as safer spaces for particular racialized communities.

Conducting intersectional research does imply several methodological concerns, one of which pertaining to my own positionality as a white sexual minority woman researcher embodying various forms of privilege. The embodiment of privilege, especially as a white academic, has contributed to limited access to the specific demographic targeted for this research, despite my own identification as a sexual minority. This limited access has manifested itself by an unwillingness to participate on the part of contacted individuals, which can be informative of the complexity of conducting empirical research on multiply marginalized individuals' activism.

Results

Evidently, one cannot expect to find a proto-typical engagement trajectory when it comes to social movement participation. However, notwithstanding each individual's personal narrative, all militant trajectories were marked by similar processes, which I have grouped into two non-mutually exclusive categories for clarity purposes: (1) *identity-related processes*, such as one's awareness, negotiation, and politicization of one's multiple vectors of identification; and (2) *structural-related processes*, such as one's social positionality, the various networks one is situated in, and the specificity of Quebec's sociopolitical context. Most importantly, and this is the core of the argument presented herein, these necessary yet non-sufficient conditions to social movement participation are inextricably interrelated through *experienced marginalization*, which consists of particular events and interactions that have contributed to one's exclusion over the course of one's lifetime. More specifically, results show that experienced marginalization at the intersection of race, sexual orientation, and (cis)gender, shapes the ways in which identity-related and structural-related processes impact one's motivation to engage in LGBTQ activism.

Identity-related processes

Despite differences in gender and age, activists interviewed for this research did share similar trajectories, both personal and militant, from which four distinct processes were identified as having shaped one's motivation to engage in social movement organizing: coming out to oneself or to others, politicizing one's sexual or gender identity, negotiating one's racialized identity, and finally, rendering visible one's multiple identifications, or what I refer to as one's "intersectional identity."

When asked to retell their debut with the LGBTQ movement, a majority of interviewees considered coming out to oneself or to others as the defining moment spurring their engagement within LGBTQ organizations. As Frédérique Duroseau, a 32-year-old activist recounts:

> I started getting involved in the LGBTQ milieu in 2008. To being with, I came out of the closet in 2005 when I was 19 years old, I didn't know any gay person around me, definitely not, so I wanted to meet some. I had heard that there were community groups, LGBT groups, so I went on the Internet and I stumbled upon Jeunesse Lambda.[14] And I went to Jeunesse Lambda.

While most interviewees share a similar account to Frédérique's, coming out narratives also involved instances of exclusion and marginalization, thus contributing to one's motivation to engage in LGBTQ groups. Florence, a 49-year-old activist who realized she was attracted to other women at 35 years old, came out to her entourage, eventually losing many friends including her best friend. Realizing how much more difficult this process can be for other people, she found it necessary to be out publicly and to render her story visible to others. She joined the GRIS-Montréal soon after. Similarly, Marlyne, who experienced multiple instances of homophobia in high school leading her to eventually change schools, coming out to her parents simultaneously marked her debut with the LGBTQ milieu:

> At the time, I had a very difficult coming out period with my parents. I must have been 25 years old. Someone suggested I go to GRIS-Montréal, that somehow by being a GRIS speaker, I would be able to work on myself and grow. In the end yes, it was a very good idea.

Engaging with social movement organizing was intrinsically linked to Marlyne's coming out process and helped her accept her own sexual identity. In recollecting their coming out stories as a way to pinpoint the beginning of their participation within Montreal's LGBTQ movement, interviewees also shared instances of marginalization that they had experienced. However, not all who experience homophobia, lesbophobia or transphobia and who come out to oneself or to others mobilize and engage in social movement organizing, which brings me to another observed identity-related process consisting of the motivation to politicize one's sexual or gender identity.

Politicizing one's sexual or gender identity involves rendering oneself visible, advocating for LGBTQ rights, sharing one's story, and connecting with other sexual and gender minorities through social movement organizing. Alan, a 46-year-old activist who has been involved in the LGBTQ community since his graduate studies, recalls his own motivation to organize within the LGBTQ movement in Montreal in the following way:

> It's important to understand your identity and feel attached to your identity because we all think of ourselves in particular ways. But I felt I needed to politicize my identity in some ways

in order to fully engage with it too, I felt like I needed to promote it, and figure out how it connected with other people's experiences so that we could share it in the movement and work together and become friends.

What stands out in Alan's narrative is the way in which politicizing his own sexual identity and publicly advocating for LGBTQ rights became a way to negotiate, consolidate, and affirm himself not only as a gay man, but as a gay man who is part of a larger LGBTQ community. This process resembles what Yuval-Davis (2011) refers to as the *politics of belonging*, which "comprise specific political projects aimed at constructing belonging to particular collectivity/ies" (10), in which case individuals can develop an emotional attachment and feel at *home*. However, when politicizing their sexual or gender identity through LGBTQ social movement organizing, all interviewees experienced some form of marginalization along racial lines, thus shaping their engagement trajectory in very particular ways.

Speaking of their militant experiences within the LGBTQ movement, and within LGBTQ spaces in general, all interviewees expressed a feeling of being relegated to the margins of the movement on the grounds of their race. Consequently, most of them shared their concerns regarding various processes of racialization that people of color are being subjected to within LGBTQ circles. For instance, the ways in which ethnocultural communities are seen as homophobic hubs within Quebec's society by mainstream white LGBTQ activists contribute to such processes. Speaking from his own experience as a 26-year-old queer trans Arab activist, Tommy recalls the following:

> We are seen as homophobic. We are seen as transphobic. And we are always seen that way. But as white *Québécois*, you're not flawless. But we are always seen as inferior, we are always seen as uneducated, as unevolved.

For Rameez, a 27-year-old South Asian Muslim gay activist, processes of racialization also manifest themselves in other realms, and not just within LGBTQ organizations:

> It's already interesting that we're ostracized for our sexual preference, but within the LGBTQ community it's amazing how much racism ... It's a little bit hard to grasp because you would think that if a community is so ostracized that they would come together, but that's not really the case. And I've learned this through speaking with a lot of members who are South Asian and are part of the community and identify as people of color and you know, they've gone through these struggles in their daily lives.

> If you take sex apps, like Grindr or Scruff, there are members in the community that haven't posted what their ethnicity is, and they'll speak to somebody and after they had mentioned their ethnicity they got blocked. I myself have seen on these apps that people are very open at posting their preferences maybe without realizing that it is racism. For example, they'll post "No Asians" or they'll post "Blacks only".

Experienced racism within the LGBTQ movement has led the activists hereby interviewed to engage differently within the movement. Building on Gould's (1995) notion of "participation identity," one could argue that these multiple forms of marginalization as experienced from within and outside the LGBTQ movement, have allowed for the development of an "intersectional participation identity," thus shifting activists' motivations to participate in social movement organizing so as to promote their intersectional identity as LGBTQ people of color.

After being involved in LGBTQ groups and having to negotiate their racialized identity, interviewees were marked by the whiteness of the LGBTQ community and the ongoing invisibilization of people of color. This has led the majority of them to render visible LGBTQ people of color's realities by engaging differently within the movement. Marc, a 38-year-old Lebanese gay man, responded to the invisibilization of Lebanese and Arab-speaking LGBTQ individuals by getting involved with *Helem Montréal*. Similarly, after noticing an acute lack of visible Black lesbian women over 40 years old, Florence joined *Arc-en-ciel d'Afrique* to work at deconstructing the image of a white masculine homosexual community:

> There is a lack of visibility of Black women of my generation, there are none who are visible. Zero. Zero visibility. Those who are visible are much younger. It's not that there are none who are gay and my age, it's just that it is hidden so that was very important for me. Because it's easier for me to live and be visible, I want to be visible for others, for those for whom it is much more difficult, even for the younger ones for whom it might be more difficult, that is why I want to be out in the public space and say yes, I'm gay.
>
> The visibility of the homosexual world is white. But Arc-en-ciel d'Afrique shows otherwise. Even before joining Arc-en-ciel d'Afrique, I thought of the homosexual world as being a white one. But now, the community is no longer white. And there is a community. It changes so many things.

The motivation to render visible one's intersectional identity was also expressed by other interviewees who either joined particular groups or launched community initiatives, as was the case for Rameez who recently founded *Jhalak*, a queer South Asian group. This process not only stems from having to negotiate one's sexual, gender, and racial identity, but also results from previous militant experience within mainstream white LGBTQ circles, wherein activists experienced instances of marginalization.

Referring to Spivak's (1988) essay *Can the Subaltern Speak?*, Yuval-Davis (2011) rightly states that "a narrative of identity is a necessary condition for any notion of agency and subjectivity to exist"(14), hence the necessity to not only engage in activism, but to also develop "a narrative of identity" to counter the predominant discourse that tends to relegate queer people of color to the margins. On a broader level, these narratives also illustrate Crenshaw's (1991) notion of *political intersectionality*, wherein LGBTQ activism of color can be thought of as a response to the LGBTQ movement's failure in (1) interrogating race as a factor of subordination within the movement itself, and instead relocating race as a factor of subordination that stands outside of the movement, and (2) portraying ethnocultural/racialized communities as inherently homophobic and transphobic.

Structural-related processes

Identity-related processes also unfold within specific contexts wherein structural-related processes contribute to shaping one's personal and militant trajectories. These include acknowledging one's privilege, building and mobilizing one's network, and finally, responding to Quebec's sociopolitical context.

While facing similar experiences with regards to their sexuality, gender, and race, most activists interviewed came from privileged socioeconomic backgrounds, and all have benefited from a post-secondary education. Yet, what particularly stood out was the interviewees' acknowledgement of their own privileged socioeconomic status as compared to other LGBTQ people of color, and their motivation to capitalize on such resources to help social movement organizations in improving their organizing skills. Speaking of privilege, Frédérique underlines the following:

> It's not by being here for a year or two that you will understand what systemic racism is and how it works. [Most of Arc-en-ciel d'Afrique's members] don't have that sort of discourse, they don't know what systemic racism is. Because people who talk about racism in Canadian and Quebec society are either from here or have studied here. They are not new comers. They are educated about that subject and read books about it. They have to know the system here. Because people who demand change regarding racism, they have to be literate, they have to have read books on that subject. Experiences aren't sufficient on their own. I mean, sometimes you live different experiences, but you need to be able to name them, to put words on them, ultimately you need that intellectual knowledge.

While Marlyne highlighted her parents' occupations and her education in private establishments as facilitating factors to her engagement, Florence underlined the way in which her organizing skills also motivated her to become *Arc-en-ciel d'Afrique*'s co-president:

> I wanted to help people carry forward their objectives, I wanted to give them tools, for me it's always been just that, to give tools. Because I'm very well organized, I have communication skills, and so for me it was to be able to provide people with tools to achieve their objectives.

Intersectional feminists, such as Gay (2018), Davis (1981), and hooks (1981), have rightly stressed that power and privilege are relational in nature, as well as multidimensional. If activists hereby interviewed considered themselves as belonging to a marginalized group and sharing multiple politically excluded identities, they also underlined their own embodiment of socioeconomic privilege. What is more, they emphasized that their motivation to participate in collective actions stemmed largely from the intersection between instances of racial, gender, and sexual marginalization, on the one hand, and their own embodiment of socioeconomic privilege, on the other hand.

Moreover, interviewees' social networks served as structures of opportunity for participation (Passy and Giugni 2001; Diani 2004). However, the acute invisibilization of LGBTQ people of color also generated a sense of isolation, spurring a certain need to break away from it and to seek a sense of belonging. Consequently, networks served a secondary function, meaning that building one's network also motivated many to participate. Alan's personal account is quite revealing in this matter:

> Just being able to be out and visible and meeting other people who kind of go through similar things with me, to be able to bring in people for events that also helped me engage with those ideas and that identity (...) I came to understand how important the social aspect of it was, and how part of it was not to feel alone, and I think that was a key aspect of the kind of work I was doing, it was to just not feel alone.

Lastly, these processes cannot be dislocated from the context in which they are set, meaning that they unfold within specific structural configurations that inform activists' motivations to mobilize. For instance, Quebec's particular status within Canada, notably in terms of its linguistic politics, as well as Quebec's provincial politics pertaining to nationalism and secularism have significantly shaped LGBTQ activism of color in Montreal. As Marlyne puts it:

Quebec's national identity makes it really hard to feel at home. Even though I grew up here, and I did all my education here, I noticed that *Québécois* are very gregarious, and it will be really hard to fully integrate their milieu. (…) In Quebec, the national identity question is so strong that it is always in a sort of protection mode. When you approach people, you need to think about the majority. And you feel it, it transpires in everything.

Therefore, provincial politics pertaining to immigration, diversity, and inclusion, significantly impact activists' experiences within the LGBTQ movement. Testament to this is Tommy's account of the effect that the 2013 *Charte des valeurs québécoises* had on LGBTQ activists of color:

There is a significant Islamophobic discourse within the LGBT community, especially when there was the proposed *Charte des valeurs québécoises*. There was a Facebook group that got created that was named "*LGBT pour la laïcité*". There's a big difference between having a secular State and compelling people to present themselves in a particular way. It gave rise to Islamophobic surges. After that, will a Muslim person feel comfortable in joining your group while you are the President of a group that is participating in "*LGBT pour la laïcité*"? When people who hold power positions in groups have that kind of discourse, I'm sorry but people will not join along.

In the end, activists' narratives highlight the interwoven nature of identity-related and structural-related processes as it relates to LGBTQ activism of color in Montreal. Personal motivations to engage in social movement organizing are driven by specific instances of marginalization as experienced from within, as well as from outside the LGBTQ movement, that unfold within a particular sociopolitical context, such as Quebec's political debate on *laïcité*.

Discussion

Ultimately, two main conclusions can be drawn from these results. First, motivations to participate do change over time, which reinforces the idea that social movement mobilization should be conceived as a dynamic and non-linear process rather than a fixed and stable phenomenon (Ward 2016). Indeed, because motivations are shaped by the dynamic interaction between identity and structural-related processes, we cannot expect motivations to be fixed in time, just as we cannot expect the interaction between these processes to be stable. Second, motivations to participate were largely shaped by the interaction between one's changing militant and personal environments, and one's different identities. However, and this is the core of the argument presented herein, one's changing militant and personal environments, and one's different identities, are interrelated through experienced marginalization at the intersection of sexuality, gender, and race.

As interviews with LGBTQ activists of color in Montreal have exposed, homophobia and transphobia triggered a need to first get involved in the LGBTQ community and find a sense of belonging. One's socioeconomic resources as well as one's network then acted as facilitating factors in activists' engagement. Racism, as experienced in Quebec's particular context of nationalist and secularist politics, accompanied by a feeling of being invisibilized within white-dominated LGBTQ organizations then contributed to shaping activists' motivations in participating in this movement. Yet, instead of contributing to their disengagement from activism, experienced marginalization within the LGBTQ movement not only shifted activists' motivations, but also impacted their overall engagement. Consequently, it spurred the need either join existing LGBTQ organizations structured along particular racialized identities or launch new initiatives, as was the case with Alan who co-founded *Qouleur Collective*. Hence, applying an intersectional analytical lens on activists' personal and militant trajectories not only enriches our understanding as to why – and to a certain extent how – people of color participate within the LGBTQ movement today, but also enlightens us on the ways in which identities and structures interact in fostering mobilization.

Conclusion

Previous work on the LGBTQ movement in Canada and elsewhere has often overlooked the contribution and the participation of people of color within the movement, even though LGBTQ organizations formed around particular racialized identities have emerged and mobilized in Montreal since the late 1990s and early 2000s. This paper sought to understand what drives activists of color to participate in Canada's LGBTQ movement in general, and within LGBTQ organizations formed around specific racialized identities in particular. While middle-range theories and interactionist approaches to social movement participation are theoretically useful, I argued that with its emphasis on politically excluded identities and marginalization, intersectionality as a theoretical framework is more suitable to fully grasp why LGBTQ people of color undertake such activism.

Using Montreal as a case study and drawing from in-depth interviews, I showed that marginalization at the intersection of race, sexuality, and gender, as experienced over the course of one's personal and militant trajectories, acts as a driving force of social movement participation. In fact, not only are identity-related processes – such as coming out to oneself or to others and needing to develop common narratives – and structural-related processes – such as building's one network or responding to one's sociopolitical context – necessary conditions to LGBTQ activism of color, they are interconnected through experienced marginalization that render salient intersecting politically excluded identities; for instance, being a queer trans Arab activist in a white male-dominated cisgender movement.

The argument developed herein furthers our understanding of activism that is situated at the intersection of marginalized and politically excluded identities, particularly race, sexuality, and gender. Nevertheless, further research should attend to the ways in which different power relations intersect within contemporary social movements and shape movements' interactions with the State. While this paper alluded to some of the power relations that are at play within Montreal's LGBTQ movement, it did not aim at explaining their effects on the movement itself, nor did it attend to explain their origins. Additional research would be needed to further unpack and understand the internal dynamics that shape LGBTQ movements in Canada, in the United State, and elsewhere.

Notes

1. I use the acronym LGBTQ to refer to people who identify as lesbian, gay, bisexual, trans, and queer.
2. The use of the term racialization serves two purposes. First, it presupposes the social construct of race. Second, it implies a categorization process undergone by a group that is in

a majority position that exerts symbolic violence on categorized groups by assigning these groups a particular essence of which are derived all social, cultural, and individual attributes (Eid 2012).
3. More precisely, "the acts had to be in private, only two people could be present, and the participants had to be at least twenty-one years old" (Hooper 2019, 258).
4. Inspired by the *Front de libération du Québec* (FLQ).
5. Police repression against gays and lesbians intensified in 1975 in anticipation of the 1976 Montreal Olympic Games (Higgins 2011), and extended from Quebec City to Toronto (Gentile 2016).
6. The Quebec Charter of Rights and Freedoms is a provincial human rights legislation that prohibits discrimination in areas that are of provincial jurisdiction. In 1985, the equality rights provision of the Canadian Charter of Rights and Freedoms came into effect and in 1996, the Canadian government adopted Bill C-33, which amended the *Canadian Human Rights Act* by adding sexual orientation as a prohibited ground for discrimination (Hurley 2005).
7. The Village refers to a part of the Montreal downtown area.
8. While there was no LGBTQ organization structured around a particular racialized identity in Montreal prior to this period, such organizations did emerge elsewhere in Canada as early as the 1980s, namely in Toronto with the founding of *Gay Asians of Toronto* and *Lesbians of Color* (Warner 2002).
9. The reasonable accommodation crisis emerged following the intensive media coverage of accommodation demands formulated by religious groups. If was followed by the Bouchard-Taylor commission in 2007, mandated to paint a portrait of reasonable accommodation practices in Quebec (Le Moing 2016).
10. Bill n°60 entitled *Charte affirmant les valeurs de laïcité et de neutralité religieuse de l'État ainsi que d'égalité entre les femmes et les hommes et encadrant les demandes d'accommodement*, was introduced by the Parti Québécois in 2013. If adopted, it would have prohibited State employees from wearing ostentatious signs and displaying any religious affiliation. The project was eventually withdrawn.
11. Bill n°21, entitled *Loi sur la laïcité de l'État* bans public sector employees from wearing religions symbols, and modifies Quebec's *Charte des droits et libertés de la personne* by clarifying that fundamental rights and freedoms must be exercised while respecting the secular nature of the State.
12. There is also a general agreement that the first expression of intersectional thinking was verbally articulated by the former slave and anti-slavery activist Sojourner Truth at the Women's Rights Convention in Ohio in 1851 (hooks 2015; Brah and Phoenix 2013).
13. Interviews with white LGBTQ activists have also been conducted as part of this research.
14. Jeunesse Lambda is a non-profit organization for French-speaking youth in Montreal, from 14 to 25 years old created in 1987.

Disclosure statement

No potential conflict of interest was reported by the author.

Funding

This work was supported and funded by the Social Sciences and Humanities Research Council.

References

Auger, Jeanette A., and Kate Krug. 2013. *Under the Rainbow: A Primer on Queer Issues in Canada*. Black Point, NS: Fernwood.

Battersby, Sarah-Joyce. 2016. "Black Lives Matter Protest Scores Victory after Putting Pride Parade on Pause." The Star. https://www.thestar.com/news/gta/2016/07/03/black-lives-matter-protest-scores-victory-after-putting-pride-parade-on-pause.html.

Blee, Kathleen M., and Verta Taylor. 2002. "Semi-Structured Interviewing in Social Movement Research." In *Methods of Social Movement Research* 16: 92–117.

Boston, Nicholas, and Jan Willem Duyvendak. 2015. "People of Color Mobilization in LGBT Movements in the Netherlands and the United States." In *The Ashgate Research Companion to Lesbian and Gay Activism*, edited by David Paternotte and Manon Tremblay, 135–148. New York: Routledge.

Bowleg, Lisa. 2008. "When Black + Lesbian + Woman ≠ Black Lesbian Woman: The Methodological Challenges of Qualitative and Quantitative Intersectionality Research." *Sex Roles* 59 (5): 312–325. doi:10.1007/s11199-008-9400-z.

Brah, Avtar, and Ann Phoenix. 2013. "Ain't I A Woman? Revisiting Intersectionality." *Journal of International Women's Studies* 5 (3): 75–86.

Choo, Hae Yeon, and Myra Marx Ferree. 2010. "Practicing Intersectionality in Sociological Research: A Critical Analysis of Inclusions, Interactions, and Institutions in the Study of Inequalities." *Sociological Theory* 28 (2): 129–149. doi:10.1111/j.1467-9558.2010.01370.x.

Corrigall-Brown, Catherine. 2012. *Patterns of Protest: Trajectories of Participation in Social Movements*. Stanford: Stanford University Press.

Crenshaw, Kimberlé W. 1991. "Mapping the Margins: Intersectionality, Identity Politics, and Violence Against Women of Color." *Stanford Law Review* 43 (6): 1241–1299. doi:10.2307/1229039.

Crenshaw, Kimberlé W. 2014. "The Structural and Political Dimension of Intersectional Oppression." In *Intersectionality: A Foundations and Frontiers Reader*, edited by Patrick R. Grzanka, 16–22. Boulder: Westview Press.

Dauvin, Pascal, and Johanna Siméant. 2002. *Le Travail Humanitaire: Les Acteurs Des ONG, Du Siège Au Terrain*. Paris: Presses de Sciences Po.

Davis, Angela Y. 1981. *Women, Race, & Class*. 1st ed. New York: Random House.

DeFilippis, Joseph Nicholas. 2018. "Introduction." In *Queer Activism After Marriage Equality*, 1–13. New York: Routledge.

Dhamoon, Rita Kaur. 2011. "Considerations on Mainstreaming Intersectionality." *Political Research Quarterly* 64 (1): 230–243. doi:10.1177/1065912910379227.

Diani, Mario. 2004. "Networks and Participation." In *The Blackwell Companion to Social Movements*, edited by David A. Snow, Sarah A. Soule, and Hanspeter Kriesi, 339–359. Oxford: Blackwell.

Eid, Paul. 2012. "Les inégalités « ethnoraciales » dans l'accès à l'emploi à Montréal : le poids de la discrimination." *Recherches Sociographiques* 53 (2): 415–450. doi:10.7202/1012407ar.

Fillieule, Olivier. 2001. "Propositions Pour Une Analyse Processuelle de l'engagement Individuel." *Revue Française de Science Politique* 51: 199–215.

Gay, Roxane. 2018. *Bad Feminist*. Impacts (Paris). Paris: Denoël.

Gentile, Patrizia. 2016. "À Bas La Répression Contre Les Homosexuels!." In *We Still Demand! Redefining Reistance in Sex and Gender Struggles*, edited by Patrizia Gentile, Gary Kinsman, and Pauline L. Rankin, 65–80. Vancouver: UBC Press.

Gentile, Patrizia, Gary Kinsman, and Pauline L. Rankin. 2016. "Introduction." In *We Still Demand! Redefining Reistance in Sex and Gender Struggles*, edited by Patrizia Gentile, Gary Kinsman, and Pauline L. Rankin, 3–25. Vancouver: UBC Press.

Gould, Roger V. 1995. *Insurgent Identities: Class, Community, and Protest in Paris From 1848 to the Commune*. Chicago, IL: University of Chicago Press.

Grundy, John, and Miriam Smith. 2005. "The Politics of Multiscalar Citizenship: The Case of Lesbian and Gay Organizing in Canada." *Citizenship Studies* 9 (4): 389–404. doi:10.1080/13621020500211388.

Grzanka, Patrick. 2014. "Systems of Oppression." In *Intersectionality: A Foundations and Frontiers Reader*, 1–4. Boulder, CO: Westview Press.

Hancock, Ange-Marie. 2007. "When Multiplication Doesn't Equal Quick Addition: Examining Intersectionality as a Research Paradigm." *Perspectives on Politics* 5 (1): 63–79.

Higgins, Ross. 1999. *De La Clandestinité à l'affirmation: Pour Une Histoire de La Communauté Gaie Montréalaise*. Montreal, QC: Comeau and Nadeau.

Higgins, Ross. 2011. "La Régulation Sociale de l'homosexualité: De La Répression Policière à La Normalisation." In *La Régulation Sociale Des Minorités Sexuelles: L'inquiétude de La Différence*, edited by Patrice Corriveau and Valérie Daoust, 67–102. Montréal, QC: Presses de l'Université du Québec

Hill Collins, Patricia. 2000. *Black Feminist Thought: Knowledge, Consciousness, and the Politics of Empowerment*. 2nd ed. New York: Routledge.

Hill Collins, Patricia, and Sirma Bilge. 2016. *Intersectionality*. Cambridge: Polity Press.

hooks, bell. 1981. *Ain't I a Woman: Black Women and Feminism*. Boston, MA: South End Press.

Hooper, Tom. 2019. "Queering '69: The Recriminalization of Homosexuality in Canada." *Canadian Historical Review* 100 (2): 257–273. doi:10.3138/chr.2018-0082-4.

Hurley, Mary C. 2003. "Sexual Orientation and Legal Rights." Law and Government Division. http://publications.gc.ca/collections/Collection-R/LoPBdP/CIR/921-e.htm#bsametxt.

Hurley, Mary C. 2005. "Sexual Orientation and Legal Rights: A Chronological Overview (PRB 04-13E)." Parliament of Canada: Parliamentary Information and Research Services. https://lop.parl.ca/content/lop/researchpublications/prb0413-e.htm.

Le Moing, Ariane. 2016. "La crise des accommodements raisonnables au Québec: quel impact sur l'identité collective?" *Mémoire(s), identité(s), marginalité(s) dans le monde occidental contemporain. Cahiers du MIMMOC* 16 (April): 1–14.

Lenon, Suzanne. 2011. "'Why Is Our Love an Issue?': Same-Sex Marriage and the Racial Politics of the Ordinary." *Social Identities* 17 (3): 351–372. doi:10.1080/13504630.2011.570975.

Lim, Chaeyoon. 2008. "Social Networks and Political Participation: How Do Networks Matter?" *Social Forces* 87 (2): 961–982. doi:10.1353/sof.0.0143.

McAdam, Doug. 1986. "Recruitment to High-Risk Activism: The Case of Freedom Summer." *American Journal of Sociology* 92 (1): 64–90.

McAdam, Doug, and Ronnelle Paulsen. 1993. "Specifying the Relationship Between Social Ties and Activism." *American Journal of Sociology* 99: 3. https://www.journals.uchicago.edu/doi/abs/10.1086/230319.

McCall, Leslie. 2005. "The Complexity of Intersectionality." *Signs: Journal of Women in Culture and Society* 30 (3): 1771–1800. doi:10.1086/426800.

Melucci, Alberto. 1995. "The Process of Collective Identity." In *Social Movements and Culture*, edited by Hank Johnston and Bert Klandermans, 41–63. Minneapolis: University of Manitoba Press.

Moreau, Julie. 2015. "Intersectional Citizenship, Violence, and Lesbian Resistance in South Africa." *New Political Science* 37 (4): 494–508. doi:10.1080/07393148.2015.1089026.

Mügge, Liza, Celeste Montoya, Akwugo Emejulu, and S. Laurel Weldon. 2018. "Intersectionality and the Politics of Knowledge Production." *European Journal of Politics and Gender* 1 (1–2): 17–36. doi:10.1332/251510818X15272520831166.

Namaste, Viviane. 2005. *C'était du spectacle!: L'histoire des artistes transsexuelles à Montréal, 1955-1985*. Montréal: McGill-Queen's Press - MQUP.

Nash, Jennifer C. 2008. "Re-Thinking Intersectionality." *Feminist Review* 89 (1): 1–15. doi:10.1057/fr.2008.4.

Olson, Mancur. 1965. *The Logic of Collective Action: Public Goods and the Theory of Groups*. Cambridge: Harvard University Press.

Passy, Florence, and Marco Giugni. 2001. "Social Networks and Individual Perceptions: Explaining Differential Participation in Social Movements." *Sociological Forum* 16 (1): 123–153. doi:10.1023/A:1007613403970.

Podmore, Julie. 2015. "From Contestation to Incorporation: LGBT Activism in Urban Politics in Montreal." In *Queer Mobilizations: Social Movement Activism and Canadian Public Policy*, edited by Manon Tremblay, 187–207. Vancouver: UBC Press.

Polletta, Francesca, and James M. Jasper. 2001. "Collective Identity and Social Movements." *Annual Review of Sociology* 27 (1): 283–305. doi:10.1146/annurev.soc.27.1.283.

Radio-Canada. 2017. "40e de la descente policière du barTruxx: un tournant pour les droits des homosexuels." Radio-Canada. https://ici.radio-canada.ca/nouvelle/1062535/40e-de-la-descente-policiere-du-bar-truxx-un-tournant-pour-les-droits-des-homosexuels.

Schussman, Alan, and Sarah A. Soule. 2005. "Process and Protest: Accounting for Individual Protest Participation." *Social Forces* 84 (2): 1083–1108. doi:10.1353/sof.2006.0034.

Smith, Miriam. 1999. *Lesbian and Gay Rights in Canada: Social Movements and Equality-Seeking, 1971-1995.* Toronto: University of Toronto Press.

Smith, Miriam. 2005. "Identités queer : diaspora et organisation ethnoculturelle et transnationale des lesbiennes et des gais à Toronto." *Lien social et Politiques* 53: 81–92. doi:10.7202/011647ar.

Smith, DeAnne. 2010. "Montreal's Ethnoculture Centres on the Experiences of Queer People of Colour." Xtra. https://www.dailyxtra.com/montreals-ethnoculture-centres-on-the-experiences-of-queer-people-of-colour-34584.

Smith, Miriam. 2015. "LGBTQ Activism: The Pan-Canadian Political Space." In *Queer Mobilizations: Social Movement Activism and Canadian Public Policy*, edited by Manon Tremblay, 45–63. Vancouver: UBC Press.

Spivak, Gayatri Chakravorty. 1988. "Can the Subaltern Speak?" In *Marxism and the Interpretation of Culture*, edited by Cary Nelson and Lawrence Grossberg, 271–313. London: Macmillan.

Stryker, Sheldon. 1981. "Symbolic Interactionism: Themes and Variations." In *Social Psychology: Sociological Perspectives*, edited by Morris Rosenberg and Ralph H. Turner, 3–29. New York: Basic.

Taylor, Verta, and Nancy Whittier. 1992. "Collective Identity in Social Movement Communities: Lesbian Feminist Mobilization." In *Frontiers in Social Movement Theory*, edited by Aldon D. Morris and Carol Mueller, 104–129. New Haven, CT: Yale University Press.

Trawalé, Damien, and Christian Poiret. 2017. "Black Gay Paris: From Invisibilization to the Difficult Alliance of Black and Gay Politics." *African and Black Diaspora: An International Journal* 10 (1): 47–58. doi:10.1080/17528631.2015.1085669.

Tremblay, Manon. 2015a. "Quebec and Sexual Diversity: From Repression to Citizenship?" In *Queer Mobilizations: Social Movement Activism and Canada Public Policy*, 106–124. Vancouver: UBC Press.

Tremblay, Manon. 2015b. *Queer Mobilizations: Social Movement Activism and Canadian Public Policy.* Vancouver: UBC Press.

Viterna, Jocelyn. 2013. *Women in War: The Micro-Processes of Mobilization in El Salvador.* New York: Oxford University Press.

Ward, Matthew. 2016. "Rethinking Social Movement Micromobilization: Multi-Stage Theory and the Role of Social Ties." *Current Sociology* 64 (6): 853–874. doi:10.1177/0011392116634818.

Warner, Tom. 2002. *Never Going Back: A History of Queer Activism in Canada.* Toronto: University of Toronto Press.

Yuval-Davis, Nira. 2011. *The Politics of Belonging: Intersectional Contestations.* London: Sage.

Appendix

Table A1. Profile of activists interviewed according to gender identity, sexual orientation, racial identity, and age.

Gender identity (n = 15)		Sexual orientation (n = 15)		Racial identity (n = 15)		Age (n = 15)	
Cisgender Men	4	Gay	4	African	1	20–29	5
Cisgender Women	4	Lesbian	5	Arab	3	30–39	6
Cisgender Non-Binary	1	Bisexual	1	Black Caribbean	2	40–49	4
Trans Men	2	Pansexual	1	Chinese	1		
Trans Woman	1	Queer	2	Haitian	2		
Trans Non-Binary	1	Heterosexual	1	Lebanese	2		
Other	2	Other	1	Latinx	1		
				South Asian	1		
				Mixed	2		

Race-ing solidarity: Asian Americans and support for Black Lives Matter

Julie Lee Merseth

> **ABSTRACT**
> What explains support for Black Lives Matter among Asian Americans? This article draws on nationally representative data from the 2016 Collaborative Multiracial Post-Election Survey to examine the contours of Asian American public opinion on Black Lives Matter and the factors that shape them. Examining intragroup and intergroup attitudes across a set of racial, ethnic/national origin, and cross-racial group measures, I show that race-based considerations are significant predictors of Asian American support for Black Lives Matter. Specifically, I find that those who support Black Lives Matter are more likely to perceive linked fate with other Asian Americans and with other non-white groups and to perceive anti-black discrimination in the United States. I argue that, while never a panacea, race-based linked fate beliefs among Asian Americans, both as Asian Americans and with other groups of color, are a viable and imperative part of building cross-racial coalitions and contemporary racial justice movements.

In the early twenty-first century, Black Lives Matter has emerged as the most visible and sustained collective mobilization for racial justice in the United States. While unequivocally centering the social, economic, and political experiences of black communities in its agendas and actions, it has also explored a commitment to working in political solidarity with other groups racialized in the U.S. as minorities, people of color, or non-whites, demonstrating the movement's potential to advance cross-racial coalitions on issues ranging from immigrant rights to environmental justice to Islamophobia.[1] Indeed, race-based movements have historically left deeper, more far-reaching imprints on American politics and society when efforts to achieve change are understood as a collective struggle across racial and ethnic lines. Yet, to date, the response that Black Lives Matter has received not only from whites but also from other communities of color has been uneven and at times reticent.

While cross-racial political work is difficult to form and sustain in general, it remains especially unclear how Asian Americans view Black Lives Matter and, in particular, why some support this movement while others do not. On the one hand, there may seem little reason to anticipate Asian American support for Black Lives Matter. As a black-led movement focused on issues that disproportionately impact or target black communities, its political agenda foregrounds experiences and articulates grievances related to anti-black racism that most Asians in the U.S. would not perceive as directly affecting their lives. As such, it is not a movement with which Asian Americans might be expected to identify or about which to form clear or strong opinions. Furthermore, a history of interracial tensions between black and Asian communities in the U.S. instructs that building cross-racial political solidarity between these two groups is fraught with challenges, particularly at intersections of race, ethnicity, and class. Many interests and issues facing African Americans and Asian Americans as they vie for greater political power and socioeconomic status continue to be perceived as unshared or even conflicting. From this perspective, Black Lives Matter may be a movement that Asian Americans have reasons decidedly to oppose. On the other hand, there is evidence that suggests Asian American communities may recognize shared stakes in Black Lives Matter. For example, Asian American support has been documented in media and organizational accounts of political activism led especially by younger generations of Asian Americans in efforts to build political solidarity with black communities. These coalition prospects are further buoyed by public opinion data confirming beliefs among Asian Americans that systemic racial inequality persists in the contemporary U.S., including and especially in the form of anti-black racism.[2]

Insofar as intragroup differences have long been a defining attribute of Asian American politics on issues of solidarity within and across groups, disagreement within Asian American communities over whether and why to support Black Lives Matter is not surprising. The definition and boundaries of the "Asian American" category itself have remained contested for half a century, as this ambitious panethnic racial grouping comprises individuals with origins across all regions of Asia.[3] However, in this particular moment of American racial and ethnic politics, when what follows the "post-racialism" of the Obama era has yet to fully take form but has already been shown to accommodate white supremacist marches and white nationalist White House advisors, Asian American responses to Black Lives Matter motivate questions with increasingly urgent implications for cross-racial coalitions and race-based movements in the twenty-first century.

This article examines the contours of Asian American public opinion on Black Lives Matter and the factors that shape them. What explains support for Black Lives Matter among Asian American communities? In particular, how do race-based considerations shape differences in this support? In what follows, I analyze new data from the 2016 Collaborative Multiracial Post-Election Survey, leveraging a large, nationally representative sample of Asian respondents across categories including ethnic/national origin, nativity, citizenship status, and language. Examining both intragroup and intergroup attitudes, I show that race-based considerations are significant predictors of support for Black Lives Matter among Asian Americans. In addition to leaning left in political ideology and partisanship, Asian Americans who support Black Lives Matter are more likely to perceive linked fate both with other Asian Americans and with other groups of color and to believe that black communities face discrimination. Ultimately, I argue that, while never a panacea, race-based linked fate beliefs among Asian Americans – as Asian Americans and with other groups of color – are a viable and imperative part of building cross-racial coalitions and contemporary racial justice movements.

#BlackLivesMatter, race, and public opinion

While the origins of Black Lives Matter can be traced back through many decades of black movement-building (Chernega 2016; Lowery 2016), they have also been located in a distinctly twenty-first century political organizing space: social media. Since 2013, through actions mobilized online with the hashtag #BlackLivesMatter and subsequently on the streets in cities across the country – Ferguson, New York City, Chicago, Baltimore, Cleveland, Minneapolis, and many others – as well as around the world, the movement has grown at a rapid pace. In so doing, it has not aimed to establish itself as an institutional entity with employees, operating budgets, and formal infrastructure – for example, Black Lives Matter can be understood as distinct in purpose and approach from organizations such as the NAACP that have played pivotal roles in black movements for racial justice (Morris 1984; Francis 2014). Rather, its decentralized organization strives to connect shifting networks of leaders and participants primarily from inside but also from outside black communities (Taylor 2016).

As a result, Black Lives Matter has arguably become the most prominent racial justice movement since the civil rights and black power movements of the mid-twentieth century. Founded and led by self-described radical black organizers, it has generated widespread interest and impact not only among marginalized communities but also in the broader public sphere, spreading its messages through both social media and news media coverage, positive and negative, of organized political actions, including direct engagement with elections. For example, much national attention was spotlighted on Black Lives Matter activists who organized protests in multiple cities during the 2016 election, strategically targeting primary campaign events for frontrunner Democratic presidential candidates, Hillary Clinton and Bernie Sanders.[4] Fueled further by endorsements and information sources as wide-ranging as conventional news outlets and social media platforms to sports stars and popular culture icons, Black Lives Matter has achieved a presence far from peripheral or obscure in the realm of mainstream American politics and society.[5] Indeed, the vast majority of the American public reports awareness of this grassroots, black youth-led movement. Recent data from the 2016 Collaborative Multiracial Post-Election Survey (discussed below in more detail) confirm that nearly 9 out of 10 U.S. citizens and residents have heard of Black Lives Matter, with only 12% indicating no knowledge at all and, moreover, minimal differences across racial groups.[6] To view this movement as fringe or fleeting would be mistaken; rather, it has undeniably entered the national landscape of American racial and ethnic politics.

Attention to Black Lives Matter among scholars also has grown as the movement's public profile and impact has deepened and sustained. Yet, while research on Black Lives Matter among scholars of political theory and American political development has established greater momentum, extremely few studies have examined the movement through a political behavior lens.[7] Some research has examined the social media dimension of Black Lives Matter by analyzing data on Twitter hashtag activity, for example, or how to incorporate social media data into the study of Black Lives Matter and other social movements (Byrd, Gilbert, and Richardson 2017; Ince, Rojas, and Davis 2017). However, there remain a host of unanswered questions concerning individual-level attitudes and behavior surrounding Black Lives Matter. Starkly missing is a greater understanding of how everyday people think about and potentially participate in this movement, built by and for communities on the ground and in the trenches.

To date, existing knowledge of public opinion on Black Lives Matter has been generated mainly from non-academic surveys fielded by polling firms or news organizations most interested in an aggregated snapshot of the American public. These polls have provided data primarily on white attitudes toward Black Lives Matter with increasing attention to black attitudes as well, for example, on surveys expressly concerned with racial issues.[8] While certainly a worthy starting point, it remains critical to press forward with moving discussions of race and public opinion in the U.S. categorically "beyond black and white" (Wu 2002). Yet the sampling constraints of the vast majority of surveys have limited or precluded analysis of Black Lives Matter attitudes among communities of color outside black communities, especially Asian Americans.[9] In contrast, this study leverages new data from a large, national sample of Asians in the U.S. to help fill this void. It is not uncommon for Asian American voices and participation to be viewed as valued but nonessential when building coalitions on issues of race and racism, particularly when those issues do not disproportionately impact or directly target Asian communities. However, as I discuss below, efforts to build racial justice movements focused on any particular group are strengthened (or weakened) by the engagement (or disengagement) of all other groups. In short, Asian American responses to Black Lives Matter, whether in support or not, have short-term consequences and far-reaching implications for the movement's outcomes.

Asian Americans, Black Lives Matter, and cross-racial coalitions

What, then, do we know about responses to Black Lives Matter among Asian communities in the U.S.? Previous knowledge of support and opposition has been derived largely from position statements issued by community organizations based in cities across the country, such as advocacy groups and online activism groups, and journalistic accounts featuring individuals interviewed by reporters, including interviews with those who support and those who oppose. For example, local and national responses by Asian American communities to the trial and subsequent conviction of NYPD police officer Peter Liang garnered widespread attention as these revealed tensions among Asian Americans on issues of racism in the criminal justice system and debates over how Asians fit into contemporary American racial politics. Liang, who is Chinese American, was charged and found guilty in the 2014 shooting of an unarmed black man, Akai Gurley. Some in Asian American communities organized rallies and protests on Liang's behalf in New York City and across the country, decrying anti-Asian discrimination in the criminal justice system and citing the numerous examples of white police officers involved in the shootings of unarmed black women and men who have not even faced indictment. Others pushed back strongly against the narrative of Liang as a racial scapegoat, instead participating even more vocally and visibly in Black Lives Matter protests with calls for unflinching attention to the disproportionate killing of black people by police officers from any racial or ethnic background.[10]

Recent examples such as the large-scale, Asian-led demonstrations surrounding the trial of Officer Liang reflect considerable disagreement and uncertainty within Asian American communities about Black Lives Matter. Such actions are consistent with prior research on Asian Americans and cross-racial coalitions, which suggests that the formation of such coalitions is certainly possible but not overwhelmingly common. Interracial coalitions that include Asian Americans have been difficult partly due to language and other cultural differences, residential patterns that shape interracial contact (e.g., social, educational, employment), and geopolitical events that impact U.S.–Asia relations (Lien 2001). Furthermore, as immigration continues to transform the demographic contours of the U.S. population, negative racial stereotypes held among minority groups about one another present an additional barrier to coalition-building on economic and especially political issues (McClain and Tauber 2001). Successful cases of Asian American multiracial alliances have formed around shared interests with Latinos, in particular, and sometimes blacks or whites, often in distinct urban settings, such as Los Angeles or New York City, and around specific issues, such as immigration-related policies or local redistricting efforts (Oliver and Grant 1995; Saito 1998; Saito 2001; Aoki and Takeda 2008).

More specifically, interracial tensions between Asian American and black communities have a complicated historical backdrop, including nationally salient conflicts that have erupted in violence and police brutality. For example, black–Korean relations in the 1990s became acutely strained, again in urban settings such as Los Angeles and New York City, fueled by political and other lived experiences rooted in racial and economic marginalization (Abelmann and Lie 1995; Kim 2000) and compelling Asian Americans from diverse backgrounds to consider how such tensions impact and implicate them. These conflicts have reinforced findings that perceived discrimination against particular racial and ethnic/national origin groups or, on the other hand, perceived closeness to other groups can strengthen or undermine the potential for cross-racial coalitions (Uhlaner 1991; Jackson, Gerber, and Cain 1994).

Influential theories of group position have also helped to explain interracial tensions, illuminating how perceived competition and threat over social and political resources influence "a sense of group position" (Blumer 1958) and examining both prejudice (especially from the dominant group) and alienation (among subordinate or minority groups) based on group-specific status in the racial order (Bobo and Hutchings 1996; Bobo 1999). An important related literature examines the role of racial hierarchy itself and, more specifically, a group's position within that hierarchy as contributing to outcomes of conflict and cooperation. In this interdisciplinary conversation spanning decades, scholars have articulated and expanded on the notion of Asian Americans as a "middleman minority" (Bonacich 1973), suggesting that they "occupy a distinctive 'third' position in the American racial hierarchy somewhere in between black and white" (Kim and Lee 2001, 633). For example, Asian Americans' positioning in the racial order has been characterized as a "racial bourgeoisie" (Matsuda 1993) or otherwise described in varied terms as a racial intermediary. Foremost, scholars have insisted on the politically distinct position of Asian Americans, arguing that "[y]ellow is emphatically neither white nor black" (Okihiro 1994, 34).

Drawing on this literature, the role of racial group positioning in Asian American responses to Black Lives Matter is particularly instructive to consider because it brings into sharper relief the ways in which Asian Americans, too, have a fundamental stake in the movement's outcomes. For insofar as Black Lives Matter aims to end white racial dominance and white supremacy as a global system of oppression,[11] differences in support for Black Lives Matter may be understood to reflect differences in support for the work of racial justice more broadly. In this view, to not support the political efforts of Black Lives Matter is effectively to endorse the status quo of American racial hierarchy.[12] Under this status quo, whites as a racialized group are positioned to control and restrict access to racial power and privilege, while those groups racialized as non-white must strategically claim and clamor for lower status positions. As Kim (2000) argues, this longstanding yet dynamic structure serves to uphold white racial power through the maintenance of relational processes that cultivate and sustain intergroup tensions among non-white groups. Critically, the status quo of racial hierarchy in the U.S. neither empowers nor protects Asian American communities; if the racial status of Asian Americans as a group is shaped over time in relation to all other groups, it must be viewed as perpetually malleable and, as such, politically precarious.[13]

Recognizing the fundamental stake that Asian Americans have in Black Lives Matter thus draws greater attention to the ostensibly competing but in fact linked logics that underlie their mixed responses. Differences in support for Black Lives Matter have foundations in how Asian Americans think about their relationship not simply to African Americans but more precisely to the racial power and status held by whites; that is, it is the result of where and how Asian Americans are relationally situated in a hierarchical racial structure. Because Asian communities in the U.S. are mutably positioned somewhere that is "neither black nor white" (Wu 1995; Ancheta 2006), beliefs in the possibility of full access to racial power and privilege – in particular, by embracing notions of Asian exceptionalism or the so-called model minority myth – may weaken and limit Black Lives Matter support. Conversely, beliefs that Asians in the U.S. are not and will never be allowed full access to racial power and privilege may motivate greater support for Black Lives Matter, reflecting a focus on transforming the structure itself rather than shifting positions within it and, toward that end, building political solidarity with other groups likewise denied this access. Attention to how racial group positioning shapes prospects for Black Lives Matter support thus serves to illuminate the underlying uncertainty within Asian American communities given their distinctly mutable group status, further underscoring the persistent challenges of building cross-racial coalitions. Moreover, it reinforces the need to examine the extent to which beliefs about race, especially group-based attitudes, influence Asian American responses to Black Lives Matter.

Asian American support for Black Lives Matter: race-based considerations

What explains support for Black Lives Matter among Asian Americans? And to what extent do race-based considerations shape differences in this support? This analysis draws on data from the 2016 Collaborative Multiracial Post-Election Survey (CMPS). The 2016 CMPS richly comprises large, nationally representative samples of respondents across four major racial group categories: Latino, Asian, black, and white (Barreto et al. 2018). The survey was fielded online in the months following the 2016 election and provided respondents the option to participate in English, Spanish, Chinese (traditional and simplified), Korean, or Vietnamese.[14] For all respondents, a vast array of demographic data was collected, making possible analysis with fine-grained attention to variation not only across categories such as gender, class, and age but also immigration-based categories such as ethnic/national origin, nativity, and citizenship status. This study employs the Asian American sample only ($n = 3,006$).

The overall distribution of Asian American attitudes toward Black Lives Matter confirms, consistent with organizational statements and journalistic reports in news and social media, that the contours of Asian American public opinion nationally on Black Lives Matter are uneven with substantial variation. While close to 40% either somewhat or strongly support (27% and 12%, respectively), a similar proportion neither support nor oppose (43%) and nearly one in five Asian Americans somewhat or strongly oppose (8% and 10%, respectively). Toward explanations of these responses, I concentrate on support for Black Lives Matter. Given the tensions that have historically defined black–Asian relations, this analysis aims to identify factors that promote the formation of cross-racial coalitions in the contemporary U.S.[15]

The central hypothesis of the study concerns the role of race-based considerations, with a focus on group-based attitudes. First, I foreground whether and how *racial group attitudes* factor in. The intuition here is that those for whom an Asian American identity is important, who report a sense of linked fate with other Asian Americans, and who perceive anti-Asian discrimination in the U.S. will be more likely to support Black Lives Matter, insofar as holding these beliefs suggests a broader racial lens through which they view American politics and society. The concept of "linked fate" refers to beliefs that connect perceived individual interests and perceived group interests – for example, as originally measured in Michael Dawson's groundbreaking study of race and class in African American politics, black respondents were asked whether and how much "what happens generally to black people in this country will have something to do with what happens in your life" (Dawson 1994). In addition, I examine a similar set of *ethnic/national origin group attitudes* to account for the possibility that these play a stronger or even singular role in determining attitudes toward Black Lives Matter, especially though not exclusively among first-generation immigrants. Furthermore, I consider the role of *cross-racial group attitudes*, in particular, linked fate beliefs with others racialized as non-white, people of color, or racial minorities. I also examine perceptions of anti-black discrimination in the U.S., another outgroup measure, given the deep roots of Black Lives Matter in African American communities and the movement's centering of systemic anti-black racism.

To be sure, previous studies have demonstrated the degree to which large numbers of Asian Americans tend not to hold group-based attitudes or to hold them conditionally, depending on political and social context (Junn and Masuoka 2008a, 2008b). In contrast to the strength and consistency of racial group identity and group consciousness among African Americans and, to a lesser degree, among Latinos, studies based on nationally representative surveys of Asian American political attitudes have found such measures to be weaker and less consistent (Lien, Conway, and Wong 2004; Masuoka 2006; Wong et al. 2011; Masuoka and Junn 2013). Furthermore, there has been relatively little attention to whether and how racial group attitudes shape extrasystemic political action such as protest and, furthermore, in the context of sustained race-based movements versus issue-specific mobilizations (but see Rim 2009). The vast majority of research that investigates links between Asian American group-based attitudes and participation has focused on outcomes related to campaigns and elections; and among studies of non-electoral participation, forms of civic engagement such as organizational activity have received the lion's share of attention (Wong 2006; Ramakrishnan and Bloemraad 2008). While the CMPS data do not allow an examination of actual participation in Black Lives Matter organized actions (respondents were not asked this question), attitudinal support for

Table 1. Race-based considerations among Asian Americans.

		Not At All Important	Not Very Important	Somewhat Important	Very Important
Identity: Race (Asian American)		6%	13%	46%	35%
Identity: Ethnic/National Origin		6%	14%	39%	41%
		None	Not Much	Some	A Lot
Linked Fate: Race (Asian American)		41%	7%	41%	11%
	Strongly Disagree	Somewhat Disagree	Neither	Somewhat Agree	Strongly Agree
Linked Fate: Ethnic/National Origin	6%	8%	40%	36%	11%
	Don't Know	None	Not Much	Some	A Lot
Linked Fate: Cross-Racial	13%	7%	27%	41%	13%
	Don't Know	Not At All	Not Much	Some	A Lot
Discrimination: Race (Asian American)	11%	6%	28%	43%	12%
Discrimination: Ethnic/National Origin	12%	7%	34%	39%	7%
Discrimination: Black	10%	5%	16%	36%	33%

Source: 2016 Collaborative Multiracial Post-Election Survey.

this movement is a productive starting place and indeed far too rare an opportunity for advancing knowledge of both Asian American extrasystemic political action and cross-racial coalitions.

Table 1 presents an overview of the full set of measures I employ to examine the role of race-based considerations in support for Black Lives Matter: the importance of racial group identity, the importance of ethnic/national group identity, racial group linked fate, ethnic/national origin group linked fate, cross-racial group linked fate, racial group discrimination, ethnic/national origin group discrimination, and anti-black discrimination. I refer broadly to this set of group-based attitudinal measures, each with a racial, ethnic/national origin, or cross-racial group reference, as "race-based considerations" insofar as all are grounded in the broader discursive and institutional landscape of race in the U.S. (see Online Appendix for exact question wordings). In addition, for the purposes of this study, I employ the terminology "Asian American" as a racial group category comprising ethnic or national origin communities such as Vietnamese, Filipino, or Chinese – that is, an aggregated panethnic category – whereas "ethnic/national origin group" is used to refer to specific ethnic or national origin communities, with the caveat and important recognition that this broad terminology glosses over complicated and nuanced distinctions between the concepts of race and ethnicity as well as politically contested definitions of the category "Asian American" itself, as noted above.

In line with previous research on Asian American group-based attitudes, this first glimpse of the data confirms a great amount of variation among Asian respondents across measures of race-based considerations. Notably, the distributions for racial group-specific and ethnic/national origin group-specific responses appear similar for both identity importance measures and linked fate measures, most evident among affirmative responses and broadly observable across the differently worded response options. The intragroup discrimination measures differ only for the strongest response categories, with 12% perceiving a lot of discrimination against Asian Americans as a group compared to 7% reporting that highest level of discrimination more specifically against their own ethnic/national group. At the same time, while Asian Americans disagree over whether their own groups face discrimination, more than two-thirds report perceiving some or a lot of anti-black discrimination in the U.S.

An initial look at the relationships between these race-based considerations and Black Lives Matter support among Asian Americans is presented in Figure 1. For ease of presentation, Black Lives Matter support is presented as a combined measure of "somewhat support" and "strongly support" responses to the question: "From what you have heard about the Black Lives Matter movement, do you strongly support, somewhat support, somewhat oppose, or strongly oppose the Black Lives Matter movement activism?"[16] Each panel in the figure shows the percentage of respondents who support Black Lives Matter for each group-based attitudinal measure across its response categories (e.g.,

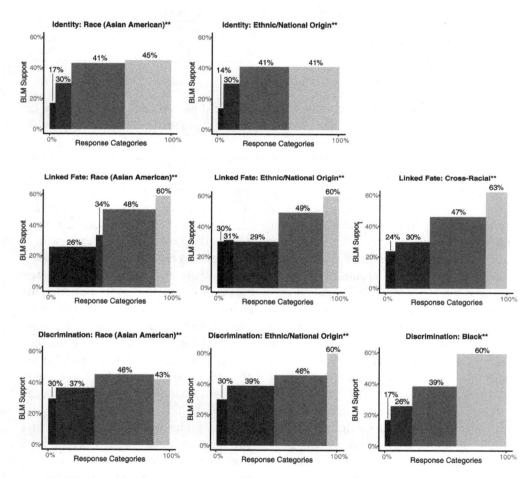

Figure 1. Race-based considerations and Black Lives Matter support among Asian Americans.
Source: 2016 Collaborative Multiracial Post-Election Survey.
Note: For each graph, bars represent response categories and bar width depicts percentage of respondents in each category. Response categories, left to right, for *identity* measures: not at all important, not very important, somewhat important, very important. Response categories, left to right, for *linked fate* measures: race – no, yes/not very much, yes/some, yes/a lot; ethnic/national origin – strongly disagree, somewhat disagree, neither disagree nor agree, somewhat agree, strongly agree; cross-racial – not at all, not much, some, a lot. Response categories, left to right, for *discrimination* measures: none at all, a little, some, a lot. Category not shown: don't know (cross-racial linked fate and discrimination measures only).
**indicates significance at the $p \leq .001$ level.

"not at all important," "not very important," "somewhat important," "very important"); the width of the bars represents the percentage of respondents in each of those categories such that wider bars convey a larger proportion of responses. For example, in the first panel, the width of the leftmost bar represents the 6% of respondents (as presented in Table 1) who answered "not at all" when asked how much being Asian or Asian American is an important part of how they see themselves; of that group, 17% reported support for Black Lives Matter. By contrast, the width of the rightmost bar represents the 35% of respondents who answered "very important" to that same question; of that group, a substantially larger 45% reported support for Black Lives Matter. Furthermore, a chi-square test of independence was performed to examine the relationship between each race-based consideration measure and Black Lives Matter support, and this relationship was significant at the $p \leq .001$ level in all cases.[17] The pattern of findings revealed is key: Asian Americans who hold stronger group-based attitudes are more likely to be those who support Black Lives Matter. Rather strikingly, for nearly every measure, Black Lives Matter support increases to some degree with each stronger response level. Ethnic/national origin group linked fate and racial group discrimination are the exceptions but unremarkably so – for the former, there is a very slight decrease in the middle of the distribution; for the latter, there is a slight decrease at the very highest end. These findings compel a closer examination of the role of race-based considerations.

Predictors of support for Black Lives Matter among Asian Americans

Certainly there are a number of explanations, some connected or even competing, that must be considered in efforts to understand differences in support for Black Lives Matter among Asian Americans. To test the relationship between race-based considerations and Black Lives Matter support controlling for other possible explanations, I add the following sets of demographic and political orientation measures to the model: first, age and immigrant generation (combined measures of respondent nativity, parent nativity, and grandparent nativity into first-generation/second-generation/third-generation and higher); and second, liberal-conservative political ideology and partisanship identification. Together, these address the common intuition that Asian American Black Lives Matter supporters, like many other Black Lives Matter supporters, are simply left-leaning youth. In addition, the model includes a measure of the perceived efficacy of protest as a participatory form. This considers the view that it is not the movement aims that Asian Americans oppose but rather its tactics – that is, pursuing change through extrasystemic political actions rather than, for example, working to improve the status of racially marginalized communities by campaigning and voting for like-minded candidates. Put another way, it is possible that Black Lives Matter supporters are simply those who believe in the efficacy of political protest. These assumptions about Asian American support for Black Lives Matter are not without sound basis, as they mirror political beliefs held by the movement's leaders and rank-and-file within black communities; rather, they have yet to be systematically examined with actual data on Asian American public opinion. As such, they represent general assumptions that are applicable across many groups and absent specific theoretical or empirical ties to the contours and histories of Asian American communities. Yet, they reflect the fact that Black Lives Matter is a movement led by young radical activists within black communities organizing marches and demonstrations, and it stands to reason that this shapes support for the movement across all racial groups, including Asian Americans. Clearly, generational differences (age-based and immigration-based) and political orientation merit examination alongside race-based considerations. In addition, the model includes controls for other salient demographic factors, including those particularly relevant to immigration-based communities: ethnic/national origin, citizenship status, income, education, and gender.

Table 2 presents the logistic regression and predicted probabilities results. The first set of findings identifies significant predictors of support for Black Lives Matter among Asian Americans, confirming the influence of three measures of race-based considerations – racial group linked fate beliefs, cross-racial linked fate beliefs, and perceived anti-black discrimination – as well as liberal-conservative ideology, partisanship, and perceived efficacy of protest. The second set of findings, in the far right column, shows the magnitude of effects for those predictors, holding all else constant at their means.

The results confirm that some common assumptions about Asian American support for Black Lives Matter are borne out empirically while others are not. Regarding the extent to which Asian American support for Black Lives Matter is driven by liberal or progressive young people, neither of the two generational measures was found to be a

Table 2. Asian American support for Black Lives Matter: logistic regression and predicted probabilities.

	Coef.	(s.e.)	First diff.
Identity: race (Asian American)	−.006	(.12)	
Identity: ethnic/national origin	.174	(.12)	
Linked fate: race (Asian American)	.254**	(.08)	.177
Linked fate: ethnic/national origin	.030	(.09)	
Linked fate: cross-racial	.189*	(.07)	.129
Discrimination: race (Asian American)	−.022	(.13)	
Discrimination: ethnic/national origin	.033	(.12)	
Discrimination: black	.552**	(.10)	.328
Age	−.073	(.06)	
Immigrant generation	.025	(.21)	
Political ideology	.368**	(.08)	.323
Party identification	.147**	(.04)	.197
Protest efficacy	.433**	(.09)	.283
Filipino	−.143	(.23)	
Indian	.488*	(.23)	.118
Japanese	.351	(.24)	
Korean	.626*	(.28)	.153
Vietnamese	−.206	(.29)	
Other	.290	(.23)	
Citizenship status	.192	(.32)	
Household income	.051	(.09)	
Education level	−.134	(.08)	
Gender	.063	(.14)	
Constant	−4.708**	(.75)	
N	2,406		
Pseudo R^2	0.211		

Source: 2016 Collaborative Multiracial Post-Election Survey.
Note: All race-based considerations measures are coded from 0 to 3, where 3 is the strongest level ("very important," "strongly agree," and "a lot"). Age is coded from 1 to 4 as follows: 18–35, 36–50, 51–70, and 71+. Immigrant generation is coded from 1 to 3, where 1 is first-generation, 2 is second-generation, and 3 is third-generation and higher. Ideology and partisanship are coded on scales of 0 to 4 (very conservative to very liberal) and 0 to 6 (strong Republican to strong Democrat), respectively. Protest efficacy is coded from 0 to 3 where 3 is "very effective." Ethnic/national origin baseline is Chinese. Household income is coded from 0 to 3 across categories from low to high as follows: less than $40,000, $40,000–80,000, and more than $8,000. Education level is coded from 0 to 4 where 0 is "less than HS grad" and 4 is "postgrad education." *indicates significance at the $p \leq .05$ level, **indicates significance at the $p \leq .01$ level.

significant predictor of Asian American support for Black Lives Matter. By contrast, both measures of political orientation were, with those who think of themselves as very liberal a substantial 32% more likely to support than those who think of themselves as very conservative; and, in parallel direction though to a lesser effect, strong Democratic identifiers 20% more likely to support than strong Republican identifiers. Second, as expected, views about how the movement organizes to achieve its goals play a large role. Beliefs in the efficacy of protest significantly predict Asian American support for Black Lives Matter, with those who view protest as an effective tactic for getting their voice heard 28% more likely to support the movement than those who view protest as not effective at all.

Turning most attentively to the role of race-based considerations, first, neither of the identity importance measures (racial group identity importance and ethnic/national origin group identity importance) was found to play a significant role in shaping Black Lives Matter support. Indeed, it is the familiarity of such null findings that perpetuates views, albeit habitually overgeneralized, that race-based considerations are weak among Asian Americans. On the other hand, among linked fate beliefs, two measures demonstrated significance in predicting Black Lives Matter support: racial group linked fate and cross-racial group linked fate. Those who hold the strongest beliefs that one's own experiences and outcomes are impacted by those of other Asian Americans are 18% more likely than those who view no such impact to support the movement; moreover, those with the strongest beliefs that one's own experiences and outcomes are impacted by those of other people of color (that is, those racialized as non-white such as blacks, Latinos, Native Americans, and Arabs and Muslims) are 13% more likely to support the movement. While the direction of these findings is not surprising, these significant effects have encouraging implications for the formation of cross-racial coalitions that politically connect Asian American communities to other communities of color. Perceptions of shared experiences and outcomes with one another and with other non-white groups make a clear and strong difference in how Asian Americans think about Black Lives Matter, suggesting that those who hold such beliefs may view the reach of the movement's impact to extend beyond black communities and potentially to Asian American communities.

Similarly, perceptions of discrimination against one's own group, whether respondents are asked to think in racial or ethnic/national origin terms, are not found to bear significantly on Asian American support for Black Lives Matter. By contrast, perceived discrimination against black communities does. While alone this point may not be surprising, together these findings speak to the weakness and inconsistency of intragroup attitudes among Asian Americans that previous research has established; in particular, that the relative absence of strong, consistent group-based attitudes – for example, compared to group-based attitudes among African Americans – need not foreclose possibilities of building cross-racial coalitions with Asian Americans on racial issues.[18] In the case of Black Lives Matter, perceived discrimination against African Americans, the group articulating the movement's core grievances, influences Asian American support, while perceived discrimination against one's own groups, racial or ethnic/national origin, does not. In fact, there is much greater agreement among Asian Americans on the question of whether black communities face discrimination.[19] Practically speaking, the discrimination findings gesture toward possibilities for greater Asian American presence in Black Lives Matter actions and race-based movements more generally; the results suggest the potential for participation in cross-racial coalitions that neither hinges on nor is hindered by strong, stable beliefs about the racial status of their own groups but instead can be fueled by a broader attentiveness to racial inequality in the U.S.

At the same time, these results highlight a larger distinction between group-based attitudes related to Asian Americans as a racial group versus group-based attitudes related specifically to one's own ethnic/national origin group. While some measures of the former were found to significantly shape Black Lives Matter support, none of the latter were. Importantly, this should be interpreted not as suggesting the irrelevance of ethnic/national group-based attitudes for Asian Americans on racial issues, but instead as pointing to the responsiveness of Asian Americans to the issue-specific contexts in which considerations based on race or ethnic/national origin can become more or less salient. Particularly in immigration-based communities, racial and ethnic/national origin identities not only coexist but can be very fluid and, moreover, activated differently depending on the context (Junn and Masuoka 2008a, 2008b). As the case of Black Lives Matter suggests, when the issues that a movement foregrounds are framed in predominantly racial terms, such as anti-black discrimination or racial inequality, it is possible that Asian Americans process their political responses more through a racial group lens than an ethnic/national origin group lens.[20]

In addition, the results do indicate the significance of ethnic/national origin for two groups, Indians and Koreans. It is important to underscore the distinction between being Indian or Korean (that is, respondents self-identifying as members of these groups) and holding particular beliefs about being Indian or Korean (for example, respondents reporting how much being Indian or Korean is an important part of how they see themselves). It is only through the former self-identification measure that Black Lives Matter support is found to be significantly shaped by ethnic/national origin. Namely, with Chinese as the baseline, both Indians and Koreans are significantly more likely to support Black Lives Matter – 12% and 15%, respectively. That Indians figure significantly into the larger Asian American story about Black Lives Matter support and in a supportive direction is not surprising. In particular, the focus of Black Lives Matter on policing and state violence resonates with the experiences of many South Asian communities in the context of policing, profiling, and state surveillance post-9/11. In contrast, it is less obvious why Black Lives Matter support among Koreans stands out significantly, especially set against the historical backdrop of black–Korean conflict. Notably, these data were collected immediately after the 2016 election, a time when nativist, xenophobic rhetoric and public support for punitive interior enforcement and hardline restrictive policies had been dramatically heightened. Because Korean communities comprise substantial numbers of first-generation immigrants as well as undocumented immigrants,[21] it is possible that Korean support for Black Lives Matter follows in part from the movement's visible and outspoken efforts to support immigrant rights, particularly for undocumented immigrants of color.

Mobilizing Asian American support for Black Lives Matter

Taken together, the findings presented above partly bear out common general narratives about support for Black Lives Matter – namely, that Asian American supporters are more likely to be those on the left end of the political spectrum and those who believe that protest makes a difference in bringing about political change. More specifically, liberal-conservative ideology and party identification are key predictors of support, with those holding liberal political views and identifying as Democrats more likely to support Black Lives Matter. Likewise, as expected, viewing protest as an efficacious form of political participation is a strong predictor of support. At the same time, race-based considerations, especially racial group-based attitudes, significantly and powerfully influence support for Black Lives Matter among Asian Americans. In particular, attitudes related to linked fate and discrimination are key predictors of support: perceptions of linked fate both as Asian Americans and with other groups of color as well as beliefs about anti-black discrimination.

These findings thus demonstrate the significance of race-based considerations in shaping Asian American responses to Black Lives Matter. While such considerations may seem straightforward in the case of a prominent racial justice movement, previous research has established that this is not to be taken for granted. For Asian Americans, the formation and mobilization of racial group-based attitudes is less apparent or consistent compared with other groups for cogent theoretical and measurement reasons (McClain et al. 2009). That race-based considerations significantly shape Asian American support for Black Lives Matter stands out particularly in the context of previous research on Asian American linked fate, with past research showing these beliefs to exist unevenly across Asian communities and without consistent strength (Lien, Conway, and Wong 2004; Masuoka 2006; Wong et al. 2011; Masuoka and Junn 2013). To be sure, this study does not lay to rest questions or concerns about the inconsistent influence of such considerations; however, contrary to stereotypes of being apolitical or politically apathetic, it presents additional evidence on a national scale that indicates Asian Americans as attuned to and potentially participatory in cross-racial coalitions.

Overall, these results advance an understanding of Black Lives Matter support among Asian Americans with less emphasis on generational cleavages, including immigrant generations, and more attention to beliefs about race and racial groups – in particular, how Asian Americans perceive themselves and the status of their communities within American racial politics. Beliefs that their social, economic, and political outcomes are linked not only with those of other Asian Americans but also with those of other people of color suggest a recognition of their mutable and precarious position in the racial hierarchy. This appears to bear significantly and substantively on the prospects for cross-racial political solidarity, for those who hold these beliefs are much more likely to support Black Lives Matter.

Thus, while never a panacea, race-based linked fate beliefs among Asian Americans, both as Asian Americans and with other groups of color, can and should be understood as a viable, imperative part of building cross-racial coalitions and contemporary racial justice movements. I do not mean to suggest that Black Lives Matter has not been or cannot be successful without Asian American support or, for that matter, Latino support or Native American support. For one thing, movements cannot afford to subscribe to such rigid prescriptions, particularly those with profoundly transformative aims. Definitions of success necessarily shift as mobilizations, large and small, emerge and evolve. A black youth-led movement with radical and intersectional foundations that has not only sustained but steadily grown for more than half a decade already constitutes an achievement against great odds. Rather, taking seriously the foundations of group positioning and racial power suggests that the potential for Black Lives Matter to shift the course of American politics and society in the direction of its vision is inherently weakened without support from other communities that have also been denied full access to this power, status, and privilege. While historically black movements have prioritized mobilizing support among whites, in theory the aims of Black Lives Matter are equally and perhaps more likely to be realized with larger, stronger coalitions of support and participation from non-white groups. Importantly, the findings of this study provide a reassuring confirmation of this possibility in practice. Among Asian Americans, perceived differences in experiences of racism across groups (e.g., anti-black racism, anti-Asian racism) alongside perceived connections between those different experiences are potentially powerful resources to cultivate and leverage in contemporary race-based movement-building.

Needless to say, it is at times painfully clear that this cultivation will require not only commitment in principle but also time, resources, and sustained work. At the outset, this article presented evidence of uneven and uncertain responses to Black Lives Matter among Asian American communities. Furthermore, activating racial and cross-racial group linked fate beliefs is a much less effective strategy when those beliefs do not reliably exist among many or even most Asian Americans. Much remains to be understood about both group-specific and intragroup-specific mechanisms of mobilizing Asian Americans on racial issues and race-based movements such as Black Lives Matter – issues and movements that inescapably impact and implicate Asian communities in the U.S., wittingly or not. The findings of this study should motivate, for example, deeper investigation of beliefs about racism itself among Asian Americans, including a closer look at beliefs about anti-Asian racism and anti-Asian discrimination, and fiercer attention to unpacking stereotypes and bias embedded in attitudes toward other marginalized groups. Without a doubt, confirming the importance of race-based considerations in Asian American support for Black Lives Matter offers valuable doses of political encouragement and political reality. The work, often uphill, of pushing forward while also pushing against promises rewards not only for Asian American communities but across communities of color.

Notes

1. Recent examples of political work in solidarity with other racialized communities include the 2016 Dakota Access Pipeline protests (#NoDAPL) on the Standing Rock Indian Reservation and mobilizations calling for "an end to all deportations, immigrant detention, and Immigration and Custom Enforcement (ICE) raids" (https://policy.m4bl.org/end-war-on-black-people/). That said, Black Lives Matter has not yet articulated a clear or definitive viewpoint on ally support – in particular, whether the movement desires or requires support from other racial and ethnic groups and, if so, which groups (e.g., whites, Latinos, Asians, Native Americans, Arabs, or Muslims). Taylor (2016) calls this an "important frontier of the movement" and rightly points out the need for Black Lives Matter to "have a real plan for building and developing solidarity among the oppressed" (186).
2. For example, according to data from the Election 2008 and Beyond Survey, 32% of Asian Americans believe that racism remains a major problem in our society and 63% believe racism exists today but is not a major problem, while just 3% believe racism once existed but no longer exists and another 3% believe racism has never been a major problem (http://www.2008andbeyond.com).

3. In an even broader formulation and, accordingly, even more politically contested, this category can further expand to include the Pacific Islands – e.g., Asian American/Pacific Islander (AAPI) and Asian Pacific Islander American (APIA).
4. See, for example, Julia Zorthian, "Black Lives Matter Activist Confronts Clinton at Fundraiser," *Time*, February, 2016; Dara Lind, "Black Lives Matter vs. Bernie Sanders, Explained," *Vox*, August 11, 2015.
5. For example, Black Lives Matter has also received and held the nation's attention on issues of racism in the criminal justice system through the intentionally politicized actions of NFL football players, led by Colin Kaepernick, and other sports figures who have "taken a knee" during the national anthem in protest of police brutality. Similarly, influential music and television/film celebrities have contributed to the momentum of the movement, with noted examples including Beyoncé's award-winning visual album, *Lemonade*, Chance the Rapper's Chicago-based community organizing and philanthropy, and actor Jesse Williams's activism through outspoken social media posts and awards speeches.
6. Among the full, nationally representative sample, the data are distributed as follows: 39% have heard a lot about Black Lives Matter, 34% some, 16% a little, and 12% nothing at all. Across racial groups, white and black respondents reported the highest levels of awareness with nearly half having heard a lot (48% and 45%, respectively) and more than three-quarters either some or a lot (79% and 81%, respectively). The two groups with large and fast-growing foreign-born populations, Asian Americans and Latinos, are the least likely to be familiar, reporting the highest percentages of having heard nothing at all (17% and 16%, respectively) and the lowest percentages of having heard a lot (27% and 39%, respectively). This is not surprising given that Asian and Latino communities include larger shares of new or recent immigrants who consume less English-language or mainstream media, lessening familiarity with Black Lives Matter and racial and ethnic politics in the U.S. generally.
7. Establishing the foundations of a richly interdisciplinary literature, recent studies have chronicled and critically engaged with the movement's visionary aims beyond short-term policy change; its intellectual lineages in black political thought, black social movements, and black resistance; its foundations in historical-institutional processes of race and state development and, in turn, its potential to shape these processes; its black feminist foundations and intersectional agenda-setting; and its expansive commitment to political solidarity with all oppressed communities worldwide (Davis 2016; Taylor 2016; Hooker 2016; Lebron 2017; Francis 2018; Johnson 2018; Thurston 2018).
8. That said, polling with modest samples of non-white respondents remains prevalent – e.g., Times/CBS News Poll (http://www.cbsnews.com/news/negative-views-of-race-relations-reach-all-time-high-cbsnyt-poll/) and NBC News/Wall Street Journal Survey (http://msnbcmedia.msn.com/i/MSNBC/Sections/A_Politics/15398%20NBCWSJ%20September%20Poll%20(2).pdf).
9. By contrast, an increasing number of surveys have featured larger samples of Latino respondents, particularly in research-oriented surveys – e.g., Pew Research Center: 2016 Racial Attitudes in America (http://www.pewsocialtrends.org/2016/06/27/on-views-of-race-and-inequality-blacks-and-whites-are-worlds-apart/) and CNN/Kaiser Family Foundation: Survey of Americans on Race (http://files.kff.org/attachment/topline-methodology-survey-of-americans-on-race).
10. See, for example, Chris Fuchs, "Thousands Rally After Conviction of Ex-Cop Peter Liang in Death of Akai Gurley," *NBC News*, February 20, 2016; Lisa Torio, "Why Are Some Asians Still Supporting the Cop Who Shot Akai Gurley?", *The Nation*, March 15, 2016; Julia Carrie Wong, "'Scapegoated?' The Police Killing that Left Asian Americans Angry – and Divided," *The Guardian*, April 18, 2016; "A Letter From Young Asian-Americans To Their Families About Black Lives Matter," *NPR Code Switch*, July 27, 2016 (also: Letter for Black Lives: An Open Project on Anti-Blackness – https://lettersforblacklives.comand#Asians4BlackLives – https://a4bl.wordpress.com); Committee Against Anti-Asian Violence (CAAAV), "Statement to Asian and Asian American Communities on the

Murder of Akai Gurley by NYPD Officer Peter Liang" – http://caaav.org/caaav-statement-to-asian-and-asian-american-communities-on-the-murder-of-akai-gurley-by-nypd-officer-peter-liang.

11. Alicia Garza (Black Lives Matter co-founder), "A Herstory of the #BlackLivesMatter Movement," *The Feminist Wire*, October 7, 2014.
12. I hold that lack of support, or "non-support," can be understood to include not only wholesale opposition but also middle ground positions expressed as uncertain or ambivalent attitudes. I discuss this further below.
13. Scholars have articulated different accounts of shifting racial paradigms that underscore the malleability and precariousness of Asian American racial status. For example, while Kim (1999) argues that Asian Americans have been racially triangulated between blacks and whites on a multidimensional "field of racial positions," Bonilla-Silva (2004) presents evidence of an emerging tri-racial stratification system that relocates Asian Americans across three tiers – namely, in which the majority of Asian subgroups are considered "honorary whites" (Japanese, Korean, Indian, Chinese, Filipino), while some become members of the lowest status group, "collective black" (Vietnamese, Hmong, Laotian), and a small handful join the "white" stratum ("a few Asian-origin people").
14. The total number of respondents across all racial group samples is 10,145, with interviews completed online between December 3, 2016, and February 15, 2017. For more details about the 2016 CMPS data collection, see http://cmpsurvey.org.
15. Importantly, I do not mean to suggest that beliefs about race cannot also predict opposition to Black Lives Matter. For example, when Asians politically align with whites or perceive no commonalities with blacks, race-based considerations may strengthen opposition. Uncertain or ambivalent attitudes ("neither support nor oppose") that might indicate a lack of strong feelings or a mixture of feelings toward Black Lives Matter merit closer examination as well. For the present purposes, results from a comparison of models that separately examine responses of support, oppose, and neither shows the latter two to be predicted by the exact same set of factors (anti-black discrimination, ideology, partisanship, protest, Indian, income), providing some reassurance that the combined category of "non-support" in this study does not mask critical differences between responses of oppose and neither.
16. As discussed above, this analysis concentrates on support for Black Lives Matter and distinguishes between support and non-support. To this end, support is examined as a dichotomous variable where "strongly support" and "somewhat support" are coded as 1.
17. For example, importance of racial group identity: $\chi^2 (3) = 74.02$, $p \leq .001$; importance of ethnic/national origin group identity: $\chi^2 (3) = 60.49$, $p \leq .001$; racial group linked fate: $\chi^2 (3) = 184.77$, $p \leq .001$; ethnic/national origin group linked fate: $\chi^2 (4) = 174.46$, $p \leq .001$.
18. To be sure, group-based attitudes among Asian Americans should be understood not just relative to other groups but as varying across contexts vis-à-vis intragroup identities, issues, and locations.
19. Without a doubt, public perceptions of anti-Asian discrimination experiences should not be conflated with actual experiences of anti-Asian discrimination, especially post-9/11, but for present purposes such perceptions are key.
20. A racial group lens and an ethnic/national origin group lens should not be understood as competing in an either/or sense; rather, they can and do operate simultaneously. Indeed, this is an empirical question for future studies to examine.
21. Jie Zong and Jeanne Batalova, "Korean Immigrants in the United States," Migration Policy Institute, February 8, 2017.

Acknowledgements

I thank Janelle Wong, Christian Collet, Deb Thompson, Al Tillery, the editors of this special issue, and anonymous reviewers for their many helpful comments, conversations, and suggestions. I also thank Alecia Richards and Jaeyoung Shin for their excellent research assistance. Earlier versions of this work were presented at the 2018 Western Political Science Association Annual Meeting and the 2018 Association for Asian American Studies Annual Conference.

Disclosure statement

No potential conflict of interest was reported by the author.

References

Abelmann, Nancy, and John Lie. 1995. *Blue Dreams: Korean Americans and the Los Angeles Riots*. Cambridge, MA: Harvard University Press.
Ancheta, Angelo N. 2006. *Race, Rights, and the Asian American Experience*. 2nd ed. New Brunswick, NJ: Rutgers University Press.
Aoki, Andrew L., and Okiyoshi Takeda. 2008. *Asian American Politics*. Cambridge, MA: Polity Press.
Barreto, Matt, Lorrie Frasure-Yokley, Edward Vargas, and Janelle Wong. 2018. "Best Practices in Collecting Online Data with Asian, Black, Latino, and White Respondents: Evidence from the 2016 Collaborative Multiracial Post-Election Survey." *Politics, Groups, and Identities* 6 (1): 171–180.
Blumer, Herbert. 1958. "Race Prejudice as a Sense of Group Position." *Pacific Sociological Review* 1: 3–7.
Bobo, Lawrence D. 1999. "Prejudice as Group Position: Microfoundations of a Sociological Approach to Racism and Race Relations." *Journal of Social Issues* 55 (3): 445–472.
Bobo, Lawrence D., and Vincent L. Hutchings. 1996. "Perceptions of Racial Group Competition: Extending Blumer's Theory of Group Position to a Multiracial Social Context." *American Sociological Review* 61: 951–972.
Bonacich, Edna. 1973. "A Theory of Middleman Minorities." *American Sociological Review* 5: 583–594.
Bonilla-Silva, Eduardo. 2004. "From Bi-Racial to Tri-Racial: Towards a New System of Racial Stratification in the USA." *Ethnic and Racial Studies* 27 (6): 931–950.
Byrd, W. Carson, Keon L. Gilbert, and Joseph B. Richardson, Jr. 2017. "The Vitality of Social Media for Establishing a Research Agenda on Black Lives and the Movement." *Ethnic and Racial Studies* 40 (11): 1872–1881.
Chernega, Jennifer. 2016. "Black Lives Matter: Racialised Policing in the United States." *Comparative American Studies* 14 (3-4): 234–245.
Davis, Angela Y. 2016. *Freedom Is a Constant Struggle: Ferguson, Palestine, and the Foundations of a Movement*. Chicago, IL: Haymarket Books.
Dawson, Michael C. 1994. *Behind the Mule: Race and Class in African-American Politics*. Princeton, NJ: Princeton University Press.
Francis, Megan Ming. 2014. *Civil Rights and the Making of the Modern American State*. New York: Cambridge University Press.
Francis, Megan Ming. 2018. "The Strange Fruit of American Political Development." *Politics, Groups, and Identities* 6 (1): 128–137.
Hooker, Juliet. 2016. "Black Lives Matter and the Paradoxes of U.S. Black Politics: From Democratic Sacrifice to Democratic Repair." *Political Theory* 44 (4): 448–469.
Ince, Jelani, Fabio Rojas, and Clayton A. Davis. 2017. "The Social Media Response to Black Lives Matter: How Twitter Users Interact with Black Lives Matter Through Hashtag Use." *Ethnic and Racial Studies* 40 (11): 1814–1830.
Jackson, Byran O., Elisabeth R. Gerber, and Bruce E. Cain. 1994. "Coalitional Prospects in a Multi-Racial Society: African-American Attitudes Toward Other Minority Groups." *Political Research Quarterly* 47 (2): 277–294.

Johnson, Kimberley S. 2018. "The Neo-Redemption Era? APD in the Age of #Black Lives Matter." *Politics, Groups, and Identities* 6 (1): 120–127.

Junn, Jane, and Natalie Masuoka. 2008a. "Asian American Identity: Shared Racial Status and Political Context." *Perspectives on Politics* 6 (4): 729–740.

Junn, Jane, and Natalie Masuoka. 2008b. "Identities in Context: Politicized Racial Group Consciousness Among Asian American and Latino Youth." *Applied Developmental Science* 12 (2): 93–101.

Kim, Claire Jean. 1999. "The Racial Triangulation of Asian Americans." *Politics and Society* 27 (1): 105–138.

Kim, Claire Jean. 2000. *Bitter Fruit: The Politics of Black-Korean Conflict in New York City*. New Haven, CT: Yale University Press.

Kim, Claire Jean, and Taeku Lee. 2001. "Interracial Politics: Asian Americans and Other Communities of Color." *PS: Political Science and Politics* 34 (3): 631–637.

Lebron, Christopher J. 2017. *The Making of Black Lives Matter: A Brief History of an Idea*. New York: Oxford University Press.

Lien, Pei-te. 2001. *The Making of Asian America Through Political Participation*. Philadelphia, PA: Temple University Press.

Lien, Pei-te, M. Margaret Conway, and Janelle Wong. 2004. *The Politics of Asian Americans: Diversity and Community*. New York: Routledge.

Lowery, Wesley. 2016. *They Can't Kill Us All: Ferguson, Baltimore, and a New Era in America's Racial Justice Movement*. New York: Little, Brown and Company.

Masuoka, Natalie. 2006. "Together They Become One: Examining the Predictors of Panethnic Group Consciousness Among Asian Americans and Latinos." *Social Science Quarterly* 87 (5): 993–1011.

Masuoka, Natalie, and Jane Junn. 2013. *The Politics of Belonging: Race, Public Opinion, and Immigration*. Chicago, IL: University of Chicago Press.

Matsuda, Mari. 1993. "We Will Not Be Used." *UCLA Asian American Pacific Islands Law Journal* 1: 79–84.

McClain, Paula D., Jessica D. Johnson Carew, Eugene Walton, and Candis S. Watts. 2009. "Group Membership, Group Identity, and Group Consciousness: Measures of Racial Identity in American Politics?" *Annual Review of Political Science* 12 (1): 471–485.

McClain, Paula D., and Steven C. Tauber. 2001. "Racial Minority Group Relations in a Multiracial Society." In *Governing American Cities: Inter-Ethnic Coalitions, Competition, and Conflict*, edited by Michael Jones-Correa, 111–136. New York: Russell Sage Foundation.

Morris, Aldon D. 1984. *The Origins of the Civil Rights Movement: Black Communities Organizing for Change*. New York: The Free Press.

Okihiro, Gary Y. 1994. *Margins and Mainstreams: Asians in American History and Culture*. Seattle, WA: University of Washington Press.

Oliver, Melvin L., and David M. Grant. 1995. "Making Space for Multiethnic Coalitions: The Prospects for Coalition in Los Angeles." In *Multiethnic Coalition Building in Los Angeles*, edited by Eui-Young Yu and Edward T. Chang, 1–34. Los Angeles, CA: Institute for Asian American and Pacific American Studies.

Ramakrishnan, S. Karthick, and Irene Bloemraad. 2008. *Civic Hopes and Political Realities: Immigrants, Community Organizations, and Political Engagement*. New York: Russell Sage Foundation.

Rim, Kathy H. 2009. "Latino and Asian American Mobilization in the 2006 Immigration Protests." *Social Science Quarterly* 90 (3): 703–721.

Saito, Leland T. 1998. *Race and Politics: Asian Americans, Latinos, and Whites in a Los Angeles Suburb*. Urbana: University of Illinois Press.

Saito, Leland T. 2001. "Asian Americans and Multiracial Political Coalitions: New York City's Chinatown and Redistricting, 1990-1991." In *Asian Americans and Politics: Perspectives, Experiences, Prospects*, edited by Gordon H. Chang, 383–408. Palo Alto, CA: Stanford University Press.

Taylor, Keeanga-Yamahtta. 2016. *From #BlackLivesMatter to Black Liberation*. Chicago, IL: Haymarket Books.

Thurston, Chloe N. 2018. "Black Lives Matter, American Political Development, and the Politics of Visibility." *Politics, Groups, and Identities* 6 (1): 162–170.

Uhlaner, Carole J. 1991. "Perceived Discrimination and Prejudice and the Coalition Prospects of Blacks, Latinos, and Asian Americans." In *Racial and Ethnic Politics in California*, edited by Byran O. Jackson and Michael B. Preston, 339–371. Berkeley, CA: Institute for Governmental Studies.

Wong, Janelle S. 2006. *Democracy's Promise: Immigrants and American Civic Institutions*. Ann Arbor: University of Michigan Press.

Wong, Janelle S., S. Karthick Ramakrishnan, Taeku Lee, and Jane Junn. 2011. *Asian American Political Participation: Emerging Constituents and Their Political Identities*. New York: Russell Sage Foundation.

Wu, Frank H. 1995. "Neither Black Nor White: Asian Americans and Affirmative Action." *Boston College Third World Law Journal* 15 (2): 225–284.

Wu, Frank H. 2002. *Yellow: Race in America Beyond Black and White*. New York: Basic Books.

Intersectional solidarity

F. Tormos

ABSTRACT
Intersectionality has gone global. The application and adoption of the concept cuts across disciplinary and territorial boundaries. How can intersectionality inform the work of social justice in the twenty-first century? This essay focuses on the practical implications of intersectionality for social movements. First, this essay reviews prominent definitions of intersectionality, identifies a series of tenets, and presents a brief history of the notion of intersectionality. Second, the essay reviews extant explanations of solidarity. This review ends with a proposal for enacting solidarity that is viable for articulating intersectionally conscious forms of solidarity – intersectional solidarity – suitable for scholars of global politics.

Introduction

Has intersectionality gone global? Intersectionality is now a global analytical framework for understanding issues of social justice and human rights (Yuval-Davis 2006; Davis 2008) and an organizing strategy within social movements (Greenwood 2008; Chun, Lipsitz, and Shin 2013; Roberts and Jesudason 2013; Collins and Bilge 2016; Hancock 2016; Laperrière and Lépinard 2016). The application and adoption of the concept transcends disciplinary, institutional, and territorial boundaries. Beginning with the writings of Maria Stewart in 1831, Savitribai Phule's intersectional advocacy in India, and Sojourner Truth's speech at the Ohio Women's Convention in 1851, the acknowledgment of the interacting, simultaneous effects of multiple axes of oppression is considered to be the most important theoretical contribution to women's and gender studies to date (McCall 2005, 1771; Davis 2008; Collins and Bilge 2016; Hancock 2016). The term's current popularity is the legacy of discursive and activist struggles by black and mestiza feminist scholars and activists that aimed to shed light over subjugated forms of knowledge production and silenced voices within advocacy efforts (Collins 1990; Combahee River Collective [1977] 1995; Crenshaw 1991; hooks 1981).

This essay focuses on the practical implications of intersectionality for transnational social movements and details the ways in which intersectionality informs global social justice work of in the twenty-first century. In this essay, I first identify a series of tenets of intersectionality and present a brief history of intersectionality. Next, I review extant explanations of solidarity in the context of intersectionality. In the final section I propose an intersectionally conscious political praxis suitable for movements engaged in transnational contentious politics.

Intersectionality

Broadly defined, intersectionality is the idea that disadvantage is conditioned by multiple interacting systems of oppression. Feminists of color developed the idea of intersectionality to disrupt the subjugation of their knowledge and to avoid the erasure of their voices (Alexander-Floyd 2012). Below, I review the major definitions and tenets of intersectionality and provide a brief historiography of intersectionality.

The term has multiple definitions and its definition is often contested (Nash 2008; Alexander-Floyd 2012; Hankivsky 2012; Collins and Chepp 2013). Patricia Hill Collins and Valerie Chepp (2013, 58) provide a working definition of intersectionality:

> [I]ntersectionality consists of an assemblage of ideas and practices that maintain that gender, race, class, sexuality, age, ethnicity, ability, and similar phenomena cannot be analytically understood in isolation from one another; instead, these constructs signal an intersecting constellation of power relationships that produce unequal material realities and distinctive social experiences for individuals and groups positioned within them.[1]

The notion of intersectionality encompasses various tenets, which reflect particular focal points of feminist debates around the understanding of oppression and identity.[2] First, intersectionality reveals and addresses policy silences and challenges experienced by marginalized groups, particularly among those whose marginalization is shaped by interacting forms of disadvantage (Crenshaw 1989; Cohen 1999; Strolovitch 2007; Hancock 2011). Second, intersectionality breaks with essentialist views of social groups by avoiding biological, static, and additive notions identity (Weldon 2006a; Hancock 2007) and proposes that the social structures that position people in multiple different groups (e.g., race, gender) interact to produce distinct lived experiences.[3] Essentialism and intersectionality are at odds because, when essentialism is practiced in efforts of devising policies and political strategies, some voices are silenced in order to privilege others (Cohen 1999). Intersectional analyses of lived experiences are open to identifying suppressed or previously unrecognized forms of marginalization by approaching relationships between different identity categories as open research questions (Hancock 2011; Hankivsky 2012). Moreover, intersectionality rejects the practice of willful blindness – the political strategy of not recognizing the privilege of one categorical group membership (e.g., a dominant race) while stressing one categorical group membership associated to oppression (e.g., a dominant gender; Hancock 2011).

Shifting nomenclatures: A brief history of intersectionality

Kimberlé Williams Crenshaw coined the term intersectionality in 1989 to stress the importance of accounting for "multiple grounds of identity when considering how the social world is constructed" (Crenshaw 1989, 1991). Yet, the notion behind the term had already been articulated in Maria Stewart's writings in the 1930s and Sojourner Truth's 1851 speech at the Women's Rights Convention in Akron, Ohio and enacted by Savitribai Phule's advocacy in India (Brah and Phoenix 2004; Collins and Bilge 2016; Hancock 2016). Sojourner Truth's speech foreshadowed campaigns by black feminists more than a century later, who referenced her challenge of black women's double bind, which in her case entailed countering notions of women as weaker than men and that enslaved black women were not real women (Brah and Phoenix 2004).

The intellectual and political project of intersectionality grew significantly with the radical feminist indictment of second-wave feminism by black feminist scholars and activists, such as the Combahee River Collective ([1977] 1995), Audre Lorde (1984), and bell hooks (1981). The project of intersectionality consisted of black, Mestiza, post-colonial, queer, and Indigenous feminists pushing social movements and scholarship to recognize previously ignored subject positions and identities (Anzaldúa 1987; Collins 1990; Cohen 1997; Valdes 1997; Bunjun 2010; Van Herk, Smith, and Andrew 2011; Hankivsky 2014). These critiques of second-wave feminism challenged the tendency to explain the experiences of women of color in an additive way (i.e., black women's oppression equals the lived experiences of black men *plus* problems of White women) (Hancock 2007; Weldon 2008).[4]

Intersectionally positioned feminist scholars also pointed to the obstacles that women of color faced in ascending to leadership roles within activist-oriented organizations and particularly within civil rights and women's movements (Harris 1990; Crenshaw 1991; Combahee River Collective [1977] 1995; Moraga 2002; Rosser-Mims 2011). Feminist and anti-racist struggles tended to privilege the experience of men of color and White women over the voices of women of color. The tendency to assume an essentialist, unitary notion of women has suppressed issues that lie at the intersection of gender and race (Harris 1990; Crenshaw 1991). Both within civil rights and women's movements, feminist women of color have pushed advocacy groups to (a) recognize variability in the experiences of women and people of color and (b) adapt political strategies and policies to reflect this variability. Their efforts to recognize within-group difference have been heralded as the most important theoretical development of second-wave feminism (Nicholson 1997).

The Combahee River Collective Statement documented a rich history of such efforts. Though the Statement decried the lack of inclusion of black lesbian feminists in the leadership of women's and civil rights movements, it did not call for separating from these movements. Instead, the Collective claimed for recognition, solidarity across differences, and inclusion within progressive movements. Overcoming oppression in the many forms that black women experienced it, they argued, was only to be achieved through coalition-building efforts with progressive organizations and movements (Combahee River Collective [1977] 1995). The Statement affirms that they

> ... do not advocate the fractionalization that white women who are separatists demand ... [W]e reject the stance of lesbian separatism because it is not a viable political analysis or strategy. It leaves [out] too much and far too many people, particularly black men, women, and children.

Combahee River Collective organizers Beverly and Barbara Smith (1981) 2002, 138–139) reiterated this stance in their contribution to Cherríe Moraga and Gloria Anzaldúa's *This Bridge Called My Back*:

> A solution to tokenism is not racial separatism ... [T]he strongest politics are coalition politics that cover a broad range of issues. There is no way that one oppressed group is going to

topple a system by itself. Forming principled coalitions around specific issues is very important.

The globalization of intersectionality

Intersectionality is not a static product of feminist debates and activism. Consequently, the term carries a contested theoretical and methodological baggage that shows both promises and limitations for understanding global phenomena. In recent times, intersectionality has been explicitly deployed to analyze global phenomena and agency (Blackwell and Naber 2002; Chan-Tiberghien 2004; Townsend-Bell 2011; Collins and Bilge 2016; Perry 2016), prompting the observation that intersectionality has gone global.[5]

A key moment for the globalization of intersectionality was the United Nations World Conference against Racism in Durban, in which intersectionality scholars and activists continued a tradition of transgressing the institutional confines of higher education and reaffirmed intersectionality's relevance as a project for social transformation (Grzanka 2014; cited in Collins and Bilge 2016). In her position paper at the Durban conference, Crenshaw (2000) affirmed that intersectionality had expanded to a human rights framework within a transnational context (Collins and Bilge 2016). Yet, intellectual histories of intersectionality recognize that intersectionality was always global (Collins and Bilge 2016; Hancock 2016).[6] Activists and intellectuals in the Global South used intersectionality without naming it as such and articulated a systemic critique of global capitalism that called for solidarity with anti-colonialist and anti-imperialist resistance to oppression (Aguilar 2012; Collins and Bilge 2016).

This discussion of intersectionality has important implications for political projects of building inclusive movements for social justice. Social movement scholars have emphasized the importance of shared identities for movements (Taylor and Whittier 1992), but intersectional scholarship problematizes these same identities. How can feminist, anti-racist, and other movements build solidarity without erasing the voices and perspectives intersectional research uncovers? The sections below review prominent explanations of solidarity and discuss how intersectionality problematizes existing accounts of how social movement identities emerge and strengthen collective action.

Solidarity

Scholars define solidarity in multiple, and at times contradictory, ways. While some explain solidarity as a result of shared identities (Taylor and Whittier 1992), others point to the presence of shared interests (Keck and Sikkink 1998; Anner 2011) or shifting opportunity structures (Williams 2010; Bieler and Lindberg 2011; Kay 2011; Bair and Palpacuer 2012) as the drivers of solidarity (Weldon 2006b). Yet, multiple studies on solidarity in women's, queer, global justice, and labor movements identify an approach to solidarity that is more congruent with an intersectional social movement organizing approach (Fantasia 1988; Caraway 1991; Cohen 1997; Cole 2008; Greenwood 2008; Marx Waterman 2001; Smith 2008; Ewig and Ferree 2013; Weldon 2006b). Below I review prominent explanations of solidarity (i.e., shared identities, shared interests, and political opportunity structures) and propose an intersectional approach to solidarity.

Shared identities

One explanation for solidarity is that shared identities are the basis of solidarity and political mobilization (Taylor and Whittier 1992). On this view, solidarity emerges in contexts in which social movement participants share identities. Yet, feminists, democratic theorists, queer theorists, social policy, and social movement scholars have criticized this explanation of solidarity. Social groups and their members' identities are not homogeneous, but rather, people identify in relation to multiple intersections of gender, class, race, sexuality, region, and nationality (Butler 1990; Epstein and Straub 1995; Rupp and Taylor 1999; Weldon 2006a). Diversity does not necessarily corrode solidarity, as social movements and policies can be structured in ways that enable groups to cope with their differences (Kymlicka and Banting 2006; Weldon 2006b). Moreover, a notion of shared identities as a basis of solidarity tends to privilege the voice and preferences of dominant groups within movements. Failing to account for social group differences has been detrimental to the sustainability and success of social movements that attempt to mobilize across group differences. Queer movements, which recognize and encourage the fluidity of sexual expression and explicitly seek to destabilize collective identities, are examples of agency and solidarity that has not developed on the basis of shared identity (Cohen 1997).

A perspective constructed in relation to social structures is a better way of understanding the process by which movement participants deliberate, constitute a group or "series," and build solidarity (Young 1994, 2000; Weldon 2011). Such structures provide a basis for social connection that cuts across group differences yet positions group members differently in relation to the intersections of their identities and lived experiences. Political mobilization is often guided by a reflective consciousness or reflexivity in practice (Frundt 2005; Rai, Forthcoming), which construct identities in the process of political mobilization and deliberation (Weldon 2006a; Collins and Bilge 2016). These constructed identities, however, are not claimed to be in existence prior to a process of political mobilization (Weldon 2006b). For the explanation of shared identities to account for the movement's success, movement participants must share identities prior to the movement's major policy achievement.

Shared interests

Scholarship on international solidarity has argued that bonds of solidarity emerge as a rational expression of shared interests (Waterman 2001; Wilde 2007). Social movement scholars add that, much like corporations, the interests of international unions can make a difference in how solidarity develops (Dreiling and Robinson 1998; Frundt 2005). Critics of this explanation point to the disparate material interests that underlie transnational political mobilization, among other modalities of coordinated social movement agency that cut across social group differences and mobilize groups from disparate material backgrounds. The transnational anti-sweatshop, environmental, LGBTQ, and human rights movements provide examples of movements that have sustained mobilization while building solidarity across multiple social group interests and identities.

Political opportunity structures

Political opportunity structure theorists do not assume shared identities or material interests, instead arguing that shifts in the structural context in which movements operate provide a basis for solidarity and political mobilization (Tarrow 1994). This prominent approach to understanding collective action, however, lacks a common definition of which structures are the most influential in shaping a movement's ability to coordinate action and promote policy change. Whereas some argue that regional trade agreements (e.g., NAFTA) contextualized the solidary actions between groups across national boundaries and social group differences (Kay 2011), others credit international trade systems emerging after World War II.

An intersectional approach to solidarity

Scholars have discussed the implications of intersectionality for different forms of collective action under distinct titles: political intersectionality (Cho, Crenshaw, and McCall 2013), intersectional conceptual approach to coalition-building (Collins and Chepp 2013), intersectional praxis (Townsend-Bell 2011), intersectional solidarity (Hancock 2011), and deep political solidarity (Hancock 2011). This notion is not novel within various social movements. In fact, the term itself is informed by a history of feminist activist experiences (Combahee River Collective [1977] 1995; Davis 2008).

This essay proposes an intersectional approach to solidarity, which consists of an ongoing process of creating ties and coalitions across social group differences by negotiating power asymmetries. An intersectionally conscious political praxis requires recognizing and representing intersectionally marginalized social groups formed by multiple interactions and linkages between different social structures and lived experiences. Moreover, an intersectional approach to solidarity may improve a movements' ability to sustain solidarity across group differences and their transformative potential (Weldon 2006b). Intersectional forms of solidarity adopt a strategy of affirmative advocacy (Strolovitch 2007), which entails redirecting the political agenda of social movement organizations, interest groups, and advocacy groups to the issues that affect intersectionally marginalized groups. Enacting affirmative advocacy requires that organizations allocate resources to issues that affect intersectionally marginalized social groups (Strolovitch 2007).[7]

Invoking intersectional approaches and understandings in the context of social movements is a useful heuristic for activists and advocates of disadvantaged groups that underscores the detrimental effects of essentialists notions of social groups and the consequent silencing of disadvantaged voices within movements and advocacy groups (Crenshaw 1991; Weldon 2006b; Strolovitch 2007; Collins and Bilge 2016). The idea of intersectional solidarity suggests that activists may act with an intersectional consciousness – a recognition of oppression as constituted by multiple and interacting social structures. Intersectionally conscious social movements may reassess their structures, internal norms, and practices in light of the recognition of social group differences (e.g., see Greenwood 2008). A collective that recognizes the intersectional contour of oppression may reassess its practices in various forms: by organizing an inclusive decision-making structure and leadership, supporting the autonomous organization of distinct social groups within the movement, and advocating for social policies that address multiple forms of oppression (Weldon 2006b; Roberts and Jesudason 2013; Laperrière and Lépinard 2016).

Intersectionality scholars have produced important insights for social movements and activists in their discussions of "political intersectionality." Cho, Crenshaw, and McCall (2013, 800) define the term as "a dual concern for resisting the systemic forces that significantly shape the differential life chances of intersectionality's subjects and for reshaping modes of resistance beyond allegedly universal, single-axis approaches." Furthermore, the authors see political intersectionality as an application of the insights of intersectionality, which offer a framework for contesting power and thereby linking theory to existent and emergent social and political struggles. Such a framework reflects a synthesis between theory and practice and open up possibilities for the development of both theoretical and practical knowledge. Cho et al. (786) recognize that throughout the history of the term, praxis "has been a key site of intersectional critique and intervention." Their definition of praxis is wide, so as to include multiple forms of agency, including: movements to demand greater economic justice for low-income women of color (e.g., Carastathis 2013; Chun, Lipsitz, and Shin 2013); legal and policy advocacy that seeks to remedy gender and racial discrimination (e.g., Carbado 2013; Verloo 2013); and state-targeted movements to abolish prisons, immigration restrictions, and military interventions that are nominally neutral with respect to race/ethnicity, gender, class, sexuality, and nationality but are in fact disproportionally harmful to communities of color, women, and non-heteronormative groups (Spade 2013).

In their analysis of the activist work of the organization Asian Immigrant Women Advocates (AIWA), Chun, Lipsitz, and Shin (2013) consider the implications of intersectionality for social movements and activism. The authors stress the importance of negotiating differences when forging coalitions within and across identity groups. Intersectionality, they argue, can be used strategically as an analytic tool "to take inventory of differences, to identify potential contradictions and conflicts, and to recognize split and conflicting identities not as obstacles to solidarity but as valuable evidence about problems unsolved and as new coalitions that need to be formed" (923). Chun et al. recognize the importance of creating collective or group identities for achieving mobilization, yet, they warn against minimizing differences within the group. Intersectionality may acknowledge both the plurality and diversity of identities that comprise any group and the common concerns that create aggregate identities (Chun, Lipsitz, and Shin 2013).

Under the title of "intersectional activism," Doetsch-Kidder (2012) examined activism that addresses more than one structure of oppression or form of discrimination (racism, classism, sexism, heterosexism, transphobia, ableism, nationalism, etc.). Doetsch-Kidder rejected the notion that engaging in solidarity across group differences is a mere strategic decision. Doetsch-Kidder (2012) echoed Sandoval (2000) to affirm that intersectional activism is a reflection of love. The notion of fighting oppression out of love for the other is not foreign to radical activism. Research on intersectional activism demonstrates how activists conceptualize their own agency as emerging out of love, spirituality, and an intersectional consciousness (Doetsch-Kidder 2012; Greenwood 2008). In a similar vein, Barvosa (2008) contends that a subject's location at the intersection of multiple disadvantaged social groups may lead them to think critically and develop ways of bridging divides within activist collectives.

Conclusion

Intersectionality has provided scholars and activists with analytical and practical tools for understanding subject positions in national and transnational contexts and identifying assemblages of lived experiences besides gender and race that conspire to oppress a group (McCall 2005; Weldon 2008; Purkayastha 2010; Collins and Chepp 2013). Collins and Chepp (2013, 72) argued that "detaching intersectionality from studies of gender might lead to other productive sites of inquiry of intersecting systems of power."

Yet, despite the politically transformative and intellectually promising trajectory and potential of intersectionality, intersectionality faces multiple challenges. These include gaps in the literature and persistent silences in social movement organizational agendas. Intersectionality also faces challenges due to limited interpretations or inadequate deployments of the term (Alexander-Floyd 2012). Below, I discuss these challenges and encourage harnessing the intellectual and political promise of intersectionality, or what Patricia Hill Collins refers to as "sharpening intersectionality's critical edge."

Recent reviews of intersectionality have identified a series of gaps in the literature and have argued that intersectionality research has given more attention to gender, race, and class than to other types of experiences emerging from intersecting frameworks of religion, spirituality, culture, geography, place, and age (Hankivsky 2012; Doetsch-Kidder 2012). Others have called for more attention to the experience of women in the global South, domestic and global divides among women, and marginalized immigrant populations within developed nations, what some have called the "inner Global South" (Crenshaw 1991; Tripp 2000; Weldon 2006b; Paxton, Kunovich, and Hughes 2007, 276). Yet, recent work has begun to fill these gaps. For instance, Wadsworth's (2011) work on religion as a basis of mobilization, identity construction, and its role in justifying and reifying racial stratification and heteronormativity is an important corrective to the lack of attention to the interaction between religion and other aspects of identity. Scholars have also addressed the gap that existed in the study of intersectionality and agency, resiliency, and resistance to domination (Kurtz 2002; Strolovitch 2007; Cole 2008; Hankvsky et al. 2010; Spade 2013; Verloo 2013; Laperrière and Lépinard 2016) and around questions of privilege, including whiteness and middle-classness (Purkayastha 2010; Hankivsky 2012).

Others have seen the concept of intersectionality as fundamentally flawed (e.g., Puar 2012; Dhamoon 2011) and have argued that "[w]e are not simply oppressed but produced through ... discourses, a production that is historically complex, contingent, and occurs through formations that do not honor analytically distinct identity categories" (Brown 1997, 86–87). Puar (2012) encourages embracing the continued mobility of subject positions that result in the continuous demands for the fine tunings of intersectionality. Yet, it is precisely this fluidity of identity and subject formation that Cohen (1997) sees as transformative and not precluding of transverse solidarity and the formation of anti-oppressive coalitions.

Such fluidity and continued motion of subject formations may lead to contradictory practical applications of intersectionality in the policymaking process. On the one hand, some have argued that it is precisely the vagueness and open-endedness of intersectionality that is responsible for its success (Davis 2008). Drawing on the insight of Murray S. Davis (1971, 1986), who argued that successful theories benefit from a degree of ambiguity and incompleteness, Davis (2008, 70) contends that intersectionality's success is due to

> its focus on a pervasive and fundamental concern in feminist theory, its provision of novelty, its appeal to the generalists as well as the specialists of the discipline, and its inherent ambiguity and open-endedness that beg for further critique and elaboration.

Davis (2008) finds that the term encourages complexity, stimulates creativity, and avoids premature closure, tantalizing feminist scholars to raise new questions and explore uncharted territory.

Conversely, some find ambiguity to be problematic, especially for how it may challenge efforts to mainstream the term and because it may affect its policy influence. Townsend-Bell (2014) reviews intersectionality's footprint in state policies and, while she recognizes the opportunities that a state's attention to intersectionality opens, she also encourages discussions in the public sphere that specify the meaning of intersectionality in each particular and historic context. In encouraging these discussions, Townsend-Bell (2014, 142) finds that "discussion over what groups constitute the most marginalized members of society and how state and nonstate actors ought to engage with and prioritize the needs of society is minimal." While many intersectionality, and feminist scholars more generally, have called for attention to the historical and contextual nuances that shape lived experiences of marginalized groups (Brown 1997; Cohen 1997; Puar 2012; Collins and Chepp 2013), perhaps it would be best to avoid a discussion over which groups constitute the most marginalized members of society, so as to avoid what Hancock (2011) and others have referred to as the Oppression Olympics. Such a discussion could be divisive for sectors that could otherwise recognize differences and reconstruct collective political claims accordingly. Smith and Smith (1981) 2002, for example, recall that black feminism has opted to avoid ranking and isolating forms of oppression in favor of targeting systems impinging on marginalized groups.

Many would like to see intersectionality as a work in progress and still hold to the promise of the concept (Hancock 2007, Weldon 2006a). However, others highlighted the promise of intersectionality research for social inquiry but argue that key questions remain unanswered. The continued practical relevance of intersectionality research will depend on the theoretical and methodological coherence employed in studies informed by intersectionality in years to come (Choo and Ferree 2010).

Notes

1. Leslie McCall (2005, 1771) provides a broader albeit contested definition of intersectionality as "the relationships among multiple dimensions and modalities of social relations and subject formations." See Alexander-Floyd (2012) for a critique of McCall's (2005) broad conceptualization of intersectionality.
2. Olena Hankivsky (2012, 1713) delineates a series of tenets for understanding intersectionality:

   [H]uman lives cannot be reduced to single characteristics; human experiences cannot be accurately understood by prioritizing any one single factor or constellation of factors; social categories such as race/ethnicity, gender, class, sexuality, and ability are socially constructed, fluid, and flexible; and social locations are inseparable and shaped by the interacting and mutually constituting social processes and structures that are influenced by both time and place.

3. Essentialist notions of social groups assume that there is a unitary, "essential" women's experience that can be isolated and described independently of race, class, sexual orientation, and other realities of experience (Harris 1990, 585). Social groups are collectives of persons differentiated from at least one other group by cultural forms, practices, or lived experiences (Young 2011, 43). On this view, people have multiple social group memberships and one

social group membership does not define personal identity (Young 2000, 99). Individuals may have affinities with more than one social group because of the intersecting social group experiences of persons, social groups do not have unified identities (Crenshaw 1991; Young 2000). Individual identity is unique and actively constituted by social relations. Individuals are agents that constitute their own identity and are conditioned by their position in structured social relations (Young 2000, 101). The positioning of individuals occurs through processes of social interaction in which individuals identify themselves in relation to others and enforce norms and expectations in relation to one another (Young 2000, 100).

4. A noteworthy effort to account for the interaction of multiple social structures in the production of oppression had also been presented by Marilyn Frye's (1983) notion of oppression as a birdcage.
5. The journal *Intersectionalities: A Global Journal of Social Work Analysis, Research, Polity, and Practice* seeks to share knowledge and facilitate collaborative discourse amongst social work theorists, activists, educators, practitioners and the communities they serve within local, regional, and global contexts.
6. Collins and Bilge (2016, 3) state "intersectionality as an analytic tool is neither confined to nations of North American and Europe nor is it a new phenomenon. People in the Global South have used intersectionality as an analytic tool, often without naming it as such." Moreover, the authors cite nineteenth century Indian feminist Savitribai Phule's anti-caste, worker, and women's rights advocacy as an example of early intersectional political activism.
7. Dara Strolovitch (2007, 11) proposes the following series of practices that movements can adopt to accomplish this redistribution of attention and resources:

> ... [C]reating decision rules that elevate issues affecting disadvantaged minorities on organizational agendas; using internal processes and practices to improve the status of intersectionally disadvantaged groups within the organization; forging stronger ties to state and local advocacy groups; promoting "descriptive representation" by making sure that staff and boards include members of intersectionally marginalized subgroups of their constituencies; resisting the silencing effects of public and constituent opinion that are biased against disadvantaged subgroups; and cultivating among advantaged subgroups of their constituencies the understanding that their interests are inextricably linked to the well-being of intersectionally disadvantaged constituents.

Acknowledgements

The author would like to thank Tiffany Willoughby-Herard, S. Laurel Weldon, and two anonymous reviewers for their insightful comments and feedback.

Disclosure statement

No potential conflict of interest was reported by the author.

References

Aguilar, Delia. 2012. "From Triple Jeopardy to Intersectionality: The Feminist Perplex." *Comparative Studies of South Asia, Africa and the Middle East* 32: 415–428.

Alexander-Floyd, Nikol G. 2012. "Disappearing Acts: Reclaiming Intersectionality in the Social Sciences in a Post-Black Feminist Era." *Feminist Formations* 24 (1): 1–25.

Anner, Mark. 2011. *Solidarity Transformed: Labor Responses to Globalization and Crisis in Latin America*. Ithaca: ILR Press, an imprint of Cornell University Press.

Anzaldúa, Gloria. 1987. *Borderlands/La Frontera: The New Mestiza*. San Francisco: Aunt Lute Books.

Bair, Jennifer, and Florence Palpacuer. 2012. "From Varieties of Capitalism to Varieties of Activism: The Antisweatshop Movement in Comparative Perspective." *Social Problems* 59 (4): 522–543.

Barvosa, Edwina. 2008. *Wealth of Selves: Multiple Identities, Mestiza Consciousness, and the Subject of Politics.* College Station, TX: Texas A&M University Press.

Bieler, Andreas, and Ingemar Lindberg. 2011. *Global Restructuring, Labour and the Challenges for Transnational Solidarity.* New York: Routledge.

Blackwell, Maylei, and Nadine Naber. 2002. "Intersectionality in an Era of Globalization: The Implications of the UN World Conference Against Racism for Transnational Feminist Practices – A Conference Report." *Meridians: Feminism, Race, Transnationalism* 2 (2): 237–248.

Brah, A., and A. Phoenix. 2004. "Ain't I a Woman? Revisiting Intersectionality." *Journal of International Women's Studies* 5 (3): 75–86.

Brown, Wendy. 1997. "The Impossibility of Women's Studies." *Differences: A Journal of Feminist Cultural Studies* 9 (3): 79–101.

Bunjun, B. 2010. "Feminist Organizations and Intersectionality: Contesting Hegemonic Feminism." *Atlantis* 34 (2): 115–126.

Butler, Judith. 1990. *Gender Trouble: Feminism and the Subversion of Identity.* New York: Routledge.

Carastathis, Anna. 2013. "Identity Categories as Potential Coalitions." *Signs* 38 (4): 941–965.

Caraway, Nancie. 1991. *Segregated Sisterhood: Racism and the Politics of American Feminism.* Knoxville: The University of Tennessee Press.

Carbado, Devon W. 2013. "Colorblind Intersectionality." *Signs: Journal of Women in Culture and Society* 38 (4): 811–845.

Chan-Tiberghien, Jennifer. 2004. "Gender-Skepticism or Gender Boom: Poststructural Feminisms, Transnational Feminisms, and the World Conference Against Racism." *International Feminist Journal of Politics* 6 (3): 454–484.

Cho, Sumi, Kimberlé Williams Crenshaw, and Leslie McCall. 2013. "Toward a Field of Intersectionality Studies: Theory, Applications, and Praxis." *Signs: Journal of Women in Culture and Society* 38 (4): 785–810.

Choo, Hae Yeon, and Myra Marx Ferree. 2010. "Practicing Intersectionality in Sociological Research: A Critical Analysis of Inclusions, Interactions and Institutions in the Study of Inequalities." *Sociological Theory* 28 (2): 129–149.

Chun, Jennifer Jihye, George Lipsitz, and Young Shin. 2013. "Intersectionality as a Social Movement Strategy: Asian Immigrant Women Advocates." *Signs* 38 (4): 917–940.

Cohen, Cathy J. 1997. "Punks, Bulldaggers, and Welfare Queens: The Radical Potential of Queer Politics?" *GLQ: A Journal of Lesbian and Gay Studies* 3: 437–465.

Cohen, Cathy J. 1999. *The Boundaries of Blackness: AIDS and the Breakdown of Black Politics.* Chicago: University of Chicago Press.

Cole, Elizabeth R. 2008. "Coalitions as a Model for Intersectionality: From Practice to Theory." *Sex Roles* 59: 443–453.

Collins, Patricia H. 1990. *Black Feminist Thought: Knowledge, Consciousness, and the Politics of Empowerment.* Boston, MA: Unwin Hyman.

Collins, Patricia H., and Sirma Bilge. 2016. *Intersectionality.* Cambridge: Polity Press.

Collins, Patricia H., and Valerie Chepp. 2013. "Intersectionality." In *Oxford Handbook of Gender and Politics*, edited by Georgina Waylen, Karen Celis, Johanna Kantola, and S. Laurel Weldon, 57–87. New York: Oxford University Press.

Combahee River Collective. [1977] 1995. "A Black Feminist Statement." In *Words of Fire: An Anthology of African American Feminist Thought*, edited by Beverly Guy-Sheftall, 232–240. New York: New Press.

Crenshaw, Kimberlé W. 1989. "Demarginalizing the Intersection of Race and Sex: A Black Feminist Critique of Antidiscrimination Doctrine, Feminist Theory and Antiracist Politics." *University of Chicago Legal Forum* 140: 138–167.

Crenshaw, Kimberlé W. 1991. "Mapping the Margins: Intersectionality, Identity Politics and Violence Against Women of Color." *Stanford Law Review* 43: 1241–1299.

Crenshaw, Kimberlé W. 2000. *Background Paper for the Expert Meeting on Gender-Related Aspects of Race Discriminations.* Zagreb: WCAR (World Conference on Racism) Documents, 21–24 November.

Davis, Murray S. 1971. "That's Interesting! Towards a Phenomenology of Sociology and a Sociology of Phenomenology." *Philosophy of the Social Sciences* 1: 309–344.

Davis, Murray S. 1986. "'That's Classic!' The Phenomenology and Rhetoric of Successful Social Theories." *Philosophy of the Social Sciences* 16: 285–301.

Davis, Kathy. 2008. "Intersectionality as Buzzword: A Sociology of Science Perspective on What Makes a Feminist Theory Successful." *Feminist Theory* 9 (1): 67–85.

Dhamoon, Rita Kaur. 2011. "Considerations on Mainstreaming Intersectionality." *Political Research Quarterly* 64 (1): 230–243.

Doetsch-Kidder, Sharon. 2012. *Social Change and Intersectional Activism: The Spirit of Social Movement.* New York: Palgrave Macmillan.

Dreiling, Michael, and Robinson Ian. 1998. "Union Responses to NAFTA in the USA and Canada: Explaining Intra- and International Variations." *Mobilization* 3 (October): 163–184.

Epstein, Julia, and Kristina Straub, eds. 1995. *Body Guards: The Cultural Politics of Gender Ambiguity.* New York: Routledge.

Ewig, Christina, and Myra Marx Ferree. 2013. "Feminist Organizing: What's Old, What's New? History, Trends, and Issues." In *Oxford Handbook of Gender and Politics*, edited by Georgina Waylan, Karen Celis, Johanna Kantola, and Laurel Weldon, 437–461. New York: Oxford University Press.

Fantasia, Rick. 1988. *Cultures of Solidarity.* Berkeley: University of California Press.

Frundt, Henry J. 2005. "Movement Theory and International Labor Solidarity." *Labor Studies Journal* 30 (2): 19–40.

Frye, Marilyn. 1983. *The Politics of Reality.* New York: The Crossing Press.

Greenwood, Ronnie M. 2008. "Intersectional Political Consciousness: Appreciation for Intragroup Differences and Solidarity in Diverse Groups." *Psychology of Women Quarterly* 32: 36–47.

Grzanka, Patrick R. 2014. *Intersectionality: A Foundations and Frontiers Reader.* Philadelphia: Westview Press.

Hancock, Ange-Marie. 2007. "When Multiplication Doesn't Equal Quick Addition: Examining Intersectionality as a Research Paradigm." *Perspectives on Politics* 5 (1): 63–79.

Hancock, Ange-Marie. 2011. *Solidarity Politics for Millennials: A Guide to Ending the Oppression Olympics.* New York: Palgrave Macmillan.

Hancock, Ange-Marie. 2016. *Intersectionality: An Intellectual History.* New York: Oxford University Press.

Hankivsky, Olena. 2012. "Women's Health, Men's Health, and Gender and Health: Implications of Intersectionality." *Social Science & Medicine* 74: 1712–1720.

Hankivsky, Olena. 2014. "Intersectionality 101." The Institute for Intersectionality Research & Policy, SFU.

Hankivsky, Olena, C. Reid, R. Cormier, C. Varcoe, N. Clark, and C. Benoit. 2010. "Exploring the Promises of Intersectionality for Advancing Women's Health Research." *International Journal for Equity in Health* 9 (5): 1–15.

Harris, Angela. 1990. "Race and Essentialism in Feminist Legal Theory." *Stanford Law Review* 42 (February): 581–616.

hooks, bell. 1981. *Ain't I a Woman: Black Women and Feminism.* Boston: South End Press.

Kay, Tamara. 2011. *NAFTA and the Politics of Labor Transnationalism.* New York: Cambridge University Press.

Keck, Margaret E., and Kathryn Sikkink. 1998. *Activists Beyond Borders: Advocacy Networks in International Politics.* Ithaca, NY: Cornell University Press.

Kurtz, Sharon. 2002. *Workplace Justice: Organizing Multi-Identity Movements.* Minnesota: University of Minnesota Press.

Kymlicka, Will, and Keith Banting. 2006. "Immigration, Multiculturalism, and the Welfare State." *Ethics and International Affairs* 20 (3): 281–304.

Laperrière, Marie, and Eléonore Lépinard. 2016. "Intersectionality as a Tool for Social Movements: Strategies of Inclusion and Representation in the Québécois Women's Movement." *Politics* 36 (4): 374–382.

Lorde, Audre. 1984. *Sister Outsider: Essays and Speeches*. California: Crossing Press.

McCall, Leslie. 2005. "The Complexity of Intersectionality." *Signs: A Journal of Women and Culture in Society* 30 (3): 1771–1800.

Moraga, Cherríe L. 2002. "From Inside the First World." In *This Bridge Called My Back*, edited by Cherríe L. Moraga, and Gloria E. Anzaldúa, xv–xliii. Berkeley: Third Woman Press Women of Color Series.

Nash, Jennifer C. 2008. "Re-thinking Intersectionality." *Feminist Review* 89: 1–15.

Nicholson, Linda. 1997. "Introduction." In *The Second Wave: A Reader in Feminist Theory*, edited by Linda Nicholson, 1–6. New York: Routledge.

Paxton, Pamela, Sheri Kunovich, and Melanie M. Hughes. 2007. "Gender in Politics." *Annual Review of Sociology* 33: 263–284.

Perry, Keisha-Khan Y. 2016. "Geographies of Power: Black Women Mobilizing Intersectionality in Brazil." *Meridians: Feminism, Race, Transnationalism* 14 (1): 94–120.

Puar, Jasbir K. 2012. "'I would rather be a cyborg than a goddess': Becoming-Intersectional in Assemblage Theory." *Philosophia* 2 (1): 49–66.

Purkayastha, Bandana. 2010. "Interrogating Intersectionality: Contemporary Globalization and Racialized Gendering in the Lives of Highly Educated South Asian Americans and Their Children." *Journal of Intercultural Studies* 31: 29–47.

Rai, Shirin. M. forthcoming. "The Good Life and the Bad: Dialectics of Solidarity." *Social Politics*.

Roberts, Dorothy, and Sujatha Jesudason. 2013. "Movement Intersectionality: The Case of Race, Gender, Disability, and Genetic Technologies." *Du Bois Review* 10 (2): 313–328.

Rosser-Mims, D. 2011. *How and Why Black Women Are Elected to Political Office*. New York: Edwin Mellen Press.

Rupp, Leila J., and Verta Taylor. 1999. "Forging Feminist Identity in an International Movement: A Collective Identity Approach to Twentieth-Century Feminism." *Signs* 24 (2): 363–386.

Sandoval, Chela. 2000. *Methodology of the Oppressed*. Minneapolis: University of Minnesota Press.

Smith, Jackie. 2008. *Social Movements for Global Democracy*. Baltimore: Johns Hopkins University Press.

Smith, Barbara, and Beverly Smith. (1981) 2002. "Across the Kitchen Table: A Sister-to-Sister Dialogue." In *This Bridge Called My Back*, edited by Cherríe L. Moraga, and Gloria E. Anzaldúa. Berkeley: Third Woman Press Women of Color Series.

Spade, Dean. 2013. "Intersectional Resistance and Law Reform." *Signs: Journal of Women in Culture and Society* 38 (4): 1031–1055.

Strolovitch, Dara. 2007. *Affirmative Advocacy: Race, Class, and Gender in Interest Group Politics*. Chicago: University of Chicago Press.

Tarrow, Sidney. 1994. *Power in Movement: Social Movements and Contentious Politics*. New York: Cambridge University Press.

Taylor, Verta, and Nancy E. Whittier. 1992. "Collective Identity in Social Movement Communities: Lesbian Feminist Mobilization." In *Frontiers in Social Movement Theory*, edited by Aldon D. Morris, and Carol McClurg Mueller, 104–129. New Haven: Yale University Press.

Townsend-Bell, Erica. 2011. "What Is Relevance? Defining Intersectional Praxis in Uruguay." *Political Research Quarterly* 64 (1): 187–199.

Townsend-Bell, Erica. 2014. "Ambivalent Intersectionality." *Politics and Gender* 10 (1): 137–142.

Tripp, Aili Mari. 2000. Rethinking "Difference": Comparative Perspectives from Africa." *Signs: A Journal of Women in Culture and Society* 25 (3): 649–675.

Valdes, Francisco. 1997. "Foreword: Poised at the Cusp: LatCrit Theory Outsider Jurisprudence and Latina/o Self-Empowerment." *Harvard Latino L. Rev.* 2 (1): 56–59.

Van Herk, Kimberley A., Dawn Smith, and Caroline Andrew. 2011. "Examining Our Privileges and Oppressions: Incorporating an Intersectionality Paradigm into Nursing." *Nursing Inquiry* 18 (1): 29–39.

Verloo, Mieke. 2013. "Intersectional and Cross-Movement Politics and Policies: Reflections on Current Practices and Debates." *Signs: A Journal of Women in Culture and Society* 38 (4): 893–915.

Wadsworth, Nancy D. 2011. "Intersectionality in California's Same-Sex Marriage Battles: A Complex Proposition." *Political Research Quarterly* 64 (1): 200–216.

Waterman, P. 2001. *Globalization, Social Movements and the New Internationalisms*. London: Continuum.

Weldon, Sirje L. 2006a. "The Structure of Intersectionality: A Comparative Politics of Gender." *Politics and Gender* 2 (2): 235–248.

Weldon, Sirje L. 2006b. "Inclusion, Solidarity and Social Movements: The Global Movement on Gender Violence." *Perspectives on Politics* 4 (1) (March): 55–74.

Weldon, Sirje L. 2008. "Intersectionality." In *Politics, Gender, and Concepts: Theory and Methodology*, edited by Gary Goertz, and Amy Mazur, 193–218. Cambridge: Cambridge University Press.

Weldon, Sirje L. 2011. *When Protest Makes Policy: How Social Movements Represent Disadvantaged Groups*. Ann Arbor: University of Michigan Press.

Wilde, Lawrence. 2007. "The Concept of Solidarity: Emerging from the Theoretical Shadows?" *The British Journal of Politics and International Relations* 9: 171–181.

Williams, Matthew S. 2010. "Strategizing Against Sweatshops: The Anti-Sweatshop Movement and the Global Economy." PhD diss., Boston College.

Young, Iris M. 1994. "Gender as Seriality: Thinking About Women as a Social Collective." *Signs: A Journal of Women in Culture and Society* 19 (3): 713–738.

Young, Iris M. 2000. *Inclusion and Democracy*. Oxford: Oxford University Press.

Young, Iris M. 2011. *Responsibility for Justice*. Oxford: Oxford University Press.

Yuval-Davis, Nira. 2006. "Intersectionality and Feminist Politics." *European Journal of Women's Studies* 13 (3): 193–209.

Intersectionality at the grassroots

Michael T. Heaney

ABSTRACT
Intersectional activism is organizing that addresses more than one structure of oppression in the struggle for social justice. The rise of the Women's March as a massive effort to mobilize women primarily on the basis of gender coincided with calls for it to pay greater attention to intersectionality. This study considers the effectiveness of the Women's March at using intersectional activism as a collective action frame. Drawing on surveys conducted at Women's March events in five cities and four other Washington, DC activist events in 2018, this study examines the extent to which activists think that the movements should place a priority on intersectional activism. The results show that participants in Women's March events were more supportive of prioritizing intersectional activism than were activists at comparable protest events that were not mobilized using intersectional collective action frames. Furthermore, the results demonstrate that ideology may be a barrier to embracing intersectional activism, with more moderate and conservative activists placing a lower priority on intersectionality than did more liberal activists. Women's March activists were more likely to prioritize intersectional activism if they were trans- or LGBTQIA+-identified, or if they had a history of backing intersectionally marginalized causes, than if they did not.

The Women's March on Washington, first held on the day after the Inauguration of President Donald Trump, has become a significant force in American politics. In its first three years of existence (2017–2019), the March spurred millions of women (and men) to protest and inspired thousands to become involved in local and electoral politics (Fisher 2019). At the same time, the March was criticized for being insufficiently inclusive of marginalized groups of women. Many grassroots activists called on the March to embrace intersectionality by centering issues that matter to these groups (Quarshie 2018). They sought for the March to become a better reflection of *intersectional activism*, which Doetsch-Kidder (2012, 3) defined as "activism that addresses more than one structure of oppression or form of discrimination (racism, classism, sexism, heterosexism, transphobia, ableism, nationalism, etc.)."

The extent to which the Women's March exemplified intersectional activism has been a matter of debate among scholars and activists. Dana Fisher and her colleagues (Fisher,

Dow, and Ray 2017; Fisher, Jasny, and Dow 2018) presented evidence that the March successfully assembled a coalition of organizations and activists with interests in a wide range of social issues, reflecting an intersectional approach to coalitions (Cole 2008). McKane and McCammon (2018) depicted the nature of the March (and its allied sister marches) more neutrally, describing it as having provided a venue for activists to gather, rather than as helping activists to define their grievances. However, Rose-Redwood and Rose-Redwood (2017) took a more critical view of the March, seeing it as defined by a "whiteness" that created barriers to solidarity building. Along the same lines, Brewer and Dundes (2018) emphasized the lack of inclusion felt by many African-American women who participated in the March. They saw the March as dominated by white women who were concerned with relatively trivial issues, such as whether they could show their nipples in public, rather than with issues of oppression, such as the shooting of unarmed black people. They were also suspicious of the loyalty of the white women present, suggesting that many of them had voted for Donald Trump, since he commanded the support of the majority of white women in the 2016 election. As Simien (2006, 24) documented, black women have historically raised similar objections when they were concerned that the women's movement "fail[ed] to address issues relevant to all women."

The goal of this article is to better understand the conflict between those who raised the Women's March as an exemplar of intersectional activism and those who depicted it as stoking divisions among women. It does so by examining the March's degree of success in using intersectionality as a *collective action frame* (Terriquez, Brenes, and Lopez 2018). David Snow and his colleagues (Snow, Vliegenthart, and Ketelaars 2019, 395) explained that collective action frames "are relatively coherent sets of action-oriented beliefs and meanings that legitimize and inspire social movement campaigns and activities." The Women's March's use of intersectional activism may have met this criterion because the March announced that it sought to be intersectional and called for women's mobilization on that basis, it presented an agenda that identified multiple forms of oppression, and it was co-chaired by women from diverse racial, ethnic, religious, and occupational backgrounds. But did the March achieve *frame alignment* in its *micromobilization processes* (Snow et al. 1986; White 1999)? That is, were participants in the Women's March motivated to participate because of the use of intersectional activism as a collective action frame, or was that frame incidental to their participation? The more that the participants prioritized intersectional activism, the greater the frame alignment in the March's micromobilization; the more that participants were divided on intersectional activism, the less successful the March was in aligning frames.

This article examines the extent of frame alignment among participants in the Women's March using an original survey of participants in the 2018 Women's March on Washington and a sample of its sister marches. Another survey of participants in comparable grassroots marches held in Washington, DC in 2018 is considered in order to evaluate the extent to which the March's embrace of intersectionality can be attributed to the March's framing, or if grassroots participants independently brought these beliefs with them to their activism. Analysis of the survey data provides support both for the view that the Women's March successfully mobilized participants who embraced intersectional activism and for the view that the issue of intersectional activism was divisive within the March. Further, the results suggest that alignment with the intersectionality frame was partly due to its deployment by the March as a collective action frame and partly due to grassroots participants bringing this frame with them to their activism. These findings illustrate how intersectionality had a complex role in helping to motivate and organize grassroots activism.

This article is organized into five parts. First, it discusses the concept of intersectionality and its extension to the related concept of intersectional activism. Second, it briefly reviews the history of the Women's March and the controversies associated with it. Third, it describes the survey, the data-collection process, and the questions addressed by the research. Fourth, it explains the data analysis. Fifth, it highlights the implications of this analysis for the Women's March and concludes by suggesting what these findings mean for future research on intersectional activism and social movements.

Intersectionality and intersectional activism

Intersectionality is an analytical tool for assessing the joint effects of power and complex social structures on people's lives (Weldon 2019). The core insight of this approach is that individuals who have multiple marginalized identities (e.g., they are both undocumented immigrants and queer) suffer from oppression from more than one direction, which creates a distinct experience of subjugation from what would be felt while having only one marginalized identity. Social critics have raised concerns along these lines for more than a century (Hancock 2016; May 2015; Tormos 2017). As May (2015) underscored, intersectionality not only involves *recognizing* these concerns, it further demands that its adherents *challenge* oppression through struggles for social justice.

The essential ideas of intersectionality theory came into sharper focus with the rise of the black-feminist movement in the 1970s and 1980s (Combahee River Collective [1977] 1995; hooks 1984). In her foundational statement on the topic, bell hooks (1984) illuminated intersectionality using the example of feminism. She explained that feminism traditionally had been dominated by the viewpoints of white, middle-class women who wrote without appreciating the life experiences of women who had been oppressed by racism and classism. hooks (1984, 15) argued that the position of being simultaneously oppressed by racism, sexism, and classism enables black women to develop a critical consciousness that reveals the consequences of multiple, interacting social structures (see also Simien 2006; White 1999). In this vein, critical race theorist Kimberlé Crenshaw (1989, 1991) coined the term "intersectionality" in her analysis of how black women suffered the consequences of racism and sexism in distinctive ways that were not recognized by existing discrimination law or programs to cope with sexual violence.

Since the 1990s, interest in intersectionality has exploded throughout legal studies, the social sciences, and society more broadly. Davis (2008) observed that this diffusion was enabled by the concept's ambiguity and incompleteness, along with the immediate recognition that it offers a compelling explanation of important social phenomena. These features give the concept a symbolic quality that enables it to be embraced by varied audiences for wide-ranging purposes. Dhamoon (2011) pointed out that this "mainstreaming" facilitated the use of intersectionality beyond sex, gender, race, and class to encompass dimensions such as territoriality, age, sexual orientation, ability, language, and culture. This type of analysis helped to develop intersectionality into a more general analytical tool for critical analysis (Collins and Bilge 2016, 4; Hancock 2007; McCall 2005).

While there is no dispute that intersectionality has been applied beyond the scope of how it was used by its progenitors, there is also no doubt that this extension has been controversial. Alexander-Floyd (2012) objected, for example, that stretching intersectionality beyond a black-feminist space serves to "disappear" the voices of women of color and, thus, re-subjugates their knowledge. According to Alexander-Floyd, this approach serves to flatten, de-historicize, de-contextualize, and tokenize intersectionality. Sumi Cho and her colleagues (Cho, Crenshaw, and McCall 2013) documented that this controversy was distributed across a variety of areas of intersectionality research.

In applying intersectionality to the context of social movements and activism, scholars have articulated a variety of similar but non-identical concepts such as "intersectional activism" (Doetsch-Kidder 2012), "movement intersectionality" (Roberts and Jesudason 2013), "intersectional mobilization" (Terriquez 2015), "affirmative advocacy" (Strolovitch 2007), and "intersectionally linked fates" (Strolovitch 2007, 186). These different terms do not necessarily correspond with variations in thinking on how intersectionality should be used in this arena. However, there were some notable differences in how scholars saw the relevance of intersectionality to social movements and activism.

Many scholars emphasized the ways that movements fail to be intersectional or the ways that intersectionality hindered the goals of social movements. Smooth and Tucker (1999) exposed how black women were relegated to behind-the-scenes roles in organizing the Million Man March in the Fall of 1995. In her analysis of the Pittston Coal strike, Beckwith (2014) reported that the intersection of class and gender served to marginalize the voices and roles of women who participated in and supported the strike. Wadsworth (2011) documented how conservative religious groups were able to use intersectionality as a way to draw the support of African Americans away from same-sex marriage rights in California. Strolovitch (2007) discovered that many advocacy organizations – even those ostensibly aimed at addressing inequalities of race, class, and gender – were often responsible for directing their efforts away from disadvantaged subgroups among their constituents.

Other scholars stressed that there are numerous ways that intersectionality can be used as a tool to improve social movements. Roberts and Jesudason (2013), Adam (2017), and Tungohan (2016) separately explained how recognizing intersectionality may aid coalition building. They each illustrated that coalitions of distinct marginalized groups may be unified around a collective identity of marginalization and experiences of oppression. They also pointed out how introducing an intersectional logic to a coalition potentially makes it harder for the coalition to put forward coherent positions and manage the balance of power among member organizations (see also Laperrière and Lépinard 2016). Laperrière and Lépinard (2016, 376) argued that intersectionality not only requires bringing together marginalized groups in coalitions, but also ensuring that "their specific needs are addressed in terms of service provision, and that they feel comfortable inside the organization." They explained that this strategy is a way to augment the power of marginalized groups within the movement. Similarly, Strolovitch (2007) advocated – consistent with the advocacy of the leaders of many social justice organizations – that addressing power asymmetries demands that social movements and other advocacy organizations affirmatively redistribute resources in the direction of disadvantaged subgroups within the movement/organization, which is what she means by "affirmative advocacy."

While many scholars emphasized the role of leaders in designing movements to address intersectionality, Terriquez (2015) also documented the importance of individual-level collective identity in addressing intersectionality. In her study of undocumented LGBTQ youth activists, she showed how individuals themselves brought consciousness of their multiple identities, as well as notions of intersectionality, with them to collective organizing. This individual-level activism thus pressured organizations to incorporate multiple identities, and their intersection, into organizational work. This study provided compelling evidence that intersectionality may flow from the bottom up, rather than only from the top down, in social movements and activism.

The Women's March and its controversies

Shortly after the election of Donald Trump as President of the United States, a clamor began for a major protest by women in the nation's capital. This clamor was instigated by Trump's misogynistic behavior and statements during the 2016 presidential campaign, as well as disgust that he defeated a more qualified woman for the office despite abundant evidence of this behavior. Organizing began by activists using Facebook. On the night after the election, Teresa Shook (a retired attorney living in Hawaii) and Bob Bland (a fashion designer living in New York) separately made posts calling for a march on Washington, DC (Tolentino 2017). The two activists quickly combined their efforts. The resulting Women's March on Washington on January 21 2017 relied on intersectionality as a collective action frame. For example, Perez (2017, 4:15–4:31), a national co-chair of the March, told the crowd that "We will be brave, intentional, and unapologetic in addressing the intersections of our identities. And, collectively, we will stand up for the most marginalized among us, because they are us." On the same weekend, hundreds of sister marches took place around the world, together consisting of millions of people, making the 2017 Women's March one of the largest (if not *the* largest) protests in history (Chenoweth and Pressman 2018). Since January 2017, the Women's March held a Women's Convention in October 2017, coordinated anniversary marches in 2018 and 2019, contributed significantly to mobilizing voters in the 2018 congressional midterm elections, and assisted in staging other grassroots marches (Fisher 2019).

While the Women's March has quickly risen as a significant political force, it has also been deeply mired in political controversy since the outset of its organizing. The proposed march initially drew criticism because its primary organizers, Shook and Bland, were both white women. Calls for including more women of color in the organizing were met by adding three women of color – Linda Sarsour, Tamika Mallory, and Carmen Perez – to the organizing committee who, along with Bland, became the national co-chairs (Tolentino 2017). The proposed march was further critiqued because its initial name, the "Million Woman March," appropriated the name of an earlier march led by African-American women in Philadelphia in 1997 (Tolentino 2017). Hence, the name was changed to the "Women's March on Washington," which still made, for some, an uncomfortable connection with the 1963 March on Washington for Jobs and Freedom, an iconic part of the civil rights movement of the 1960s. Pro-life organizations were excluded from coalescing with the March early in the organizing process in a nod to the pro-choice organizations that provided substantial funding for the March, as well as recognition by the organizers that pro-choice beliefs are central to their notion of what feminism is.

The March encountered a new round of controversy in late 2018 when leaders of the March were accused of anti-Semitism because of ties to Louis Farrakhan, the religious leader of the Nation of Islam (North 2018), who has made many negative statements about Jews. In part because of these controversies, and in part for logistical reasons, the Women's March has operated across many cities as a loose coalition – as a sisterhood – rather than as a single corporate entity.

Despite the specific incidents that have brought criticism to the Women's March and the clashing personalities of individual activists, it would be a mistake to give too much weight to these idiosyncrasies. The Women's March is the most substantial effort in several decades to organize women primarily on the basis of gender (Goss 2013). Such efforts typically prompt concerns about intersectionality, which is why women's organizations often turn to some form of hybrid organization to manage multiple-identity considerations (Goss and Heaney 2010). However, the Women's March was conceived and executed as a bold and ambitious endeavor that assembled myriad organizational and movement streams, such as supporters of Hillary Clinton's and Bernie Sanders' presidential campaigns, pro-choice organizations, the progressive Left, the remnants of Occupy Wall Street, and legal and civic advocacy organizations (Berry and Chenoweth 2018). Given the breadth of this effort, the ultimate source of divisions was more the deeply ingrained differences in understanding about how women should organize together *as women*, if at all, than the actions of people who occupied particular organizational niches or the agendas of specific organizations.

Research design

This study involved surveys at events commemorating the first anniversary of the Women's March, which were held the weekend of January 20–21, 2018. The events were a series of rallies and marches held worldwide, which were planned by independent organizations acting in solidarity with one another. For example, the event in Las Vegas was planned by Women's March "Dot Com," while the event in New York was planned by the Women's March Alliance. Collective action frames used by the organizers included intersectionality, "Power to the Polls" (i.e., voting and/or running in the upcoming midterm elections), #MeToo (i.e., stop sexual assault and harassment), and impeach President Trump. These frames were used abundantly by organizers in media interviews and speeches, on social media, and in signage at events.

While much of the attention to the Women's March has focused on its protests in Washington, DC, its sister marches also constituted regionally significant political events in many places (Beyerlein et al. 2018). A photo of an activist promoting intersectional activism at the Women's March in Lansing, Michigan is contained in Figure 1. To capture the views held by participants at these events, surveys were conducted in five cities in the United States: New York, New York; Washington, DC; Lansing, Michigan; Las Vegas, Nevada; and Los Angeles, California. These cities were selected in an attempt to represent the United States geographically as well as possible (given limited resources) and because they were advertised with sufficient advance notice to plan a survey. These rallies were among the largest Women's March events held that weekend, with hundreds of thousands attending in New York and Los Angeles, and thousands attending in Washington, Las Vegas, and Lansing (Altavena 2018; Griffiths 2018; WUSA 2018; and surveyors' observations).

Figure 1. Intersectional activism at the Women's March in Lansing, Michigan, January 21, 2018.
Note: Photo by Michael T. Heaney.

In addition to surveying at Women's March events, surveys were conducted at four comparable rallies held on other issues in Washington, DC in early 2018. None of these rallies relied on intersectionality as a collective action frame. These rallies were the March for Life (anti-abortion, January 19), the People's March on Washington (pro-impeachment, January 27), the March for Trump (March 4), and the March for Our Lives (pro-gun control, March 24). The purpose of these surveys was to assess the level of support for intersectionality among the participants, despite this issue not being a part of the collective action frame for the marches. These rallies were advertised broadly on social media and held on a weekend day, downtown in the nation's capital, around the same time as the Women's March events. Coincidentally, they yielded a desirable comparison of two liberal rallies (People's March, March for Our Lives) and two conservative rallies (March for Life, March for Trump).

The anonymous, pen-and-paper survey contained six pages of questions about topics such as political attitudes, past electoral participation, past movement participation, social identity, and socio-economic status. To assess attitudes regarding intersectional activism, the survey asked participants at the event for their opinion on how important it is for the movement to address the concerns of marginalized groups. Specifically, the question was as follows:

How important is it that the women's movement center, represent, and empower the perspectives of subgroups of women, such as women of color, LGBTQIA+ women, and low-income women? Please circle one.
- Equal to the highest priority for the movement
- A high priority, but not the highest priority

- A moderate priority
- A low priority
- Not a priority
- Don't know / No opinion

This question deliberately did not use the phrase "intersectional activism." The concern was that asking explicitly about intersectionality would test the respondents' familiarity with the term, rather than their genuine support for the concept. Instead, the question asked how much the movement should prioritize "the perspectives of subgroups of women." By prioritizing the "perspectives" of these groups, the question signaled that the movement should attend to the varied issues that they find pressing. The term "subgroups" was drawn from Strolovitch (2007) and was intended to reflect the multiple identities stressed in intersectional scholarship. For example, "black women" would constitute a subgroup of women, using this language. The terminology "center, represent, and empower" was used to reflect the fact that action should be taken by the movement's leaders (i.e., centering), that subgroups should have a seat at the table (i.e., representing), and that grassroots activists should be able to act on their own, from the bottom up (i.e., empowering).

The question did not provide an exhaustive list of marginalized groups but used the phrase "such as" to give the respondent a sense of the intended scope. For example, "black women" were not mentioned specifically, but "women of color" were mentioned. The question was written with the expectation that the reader would infer that if subgroups "such as" women of color were included, then black women were also included implicitly. By prompting the reader with "LGBTQIA+ women" and "low-income women," the hope was that the respondent would also think of other marginalized subgroups, such as disabled women and immigrant women.

By signaling a high priority when answering this question, respondents indicated that they wanted the women's movement to prioritize the concerns of those that are intersectionally marginalized. In doing so, they gave an indication of endorsing the struggle for social transformation.

The intersectional activism question was modified for the non-Women's March events to allow for differences in the context. At the March for Life, it read "How important is it that the pro-life movement center, represent, and empower the perspectives of members of disadvantaged groups, such as African Americans, women of color, LGBTQIA+ persons, and low-income persons?" The other rallies used this wording but substituted the names of the pertinent movement (e.g., "impeachment movement" for "pro-life movement").

The intersectional activism question provides relevant insight into the degree to which respondents support intersectional activism. However, a skeptical reader might prefer questions about other aspects of intersectionality. For example, some readers might have preferred to see the question mention black women specifically, since the foundational analyses of intersectionality focused on black women. Or, some readers might have preferred for the question to include language about marginalization and oppression. Given these considerations, it is important to acknowledge that a limitation of the empirical analysis is that it is based only on one question to measure intersectional activism. Future studies in this domain might benefit from asking multiple, intersectionality-related questions and then combining them into an index (see Dawson 2001 and

Simien 2006 for examples of this approach). Thus, the current study provides leverage on understanding relevant aspects of intersectional activism, but does not cover all aspects of intersectional activism.

To conduct surveys at each event, a team of surveyors began by positioning itself around the perimeter of the rally. Each surveyor was instructed to look out into the crowd and select one person, called "the anchor." The anchor was not surveyed because of the assumption that this person was selected with bias by the surveyor. The surveyors were instructed to count five persons to the right of their anchor and invite that person to participate in the survey. Invitations were then issued to every fifth person until three surveys were accepted, after which a new anchor was selected by each surveyor, and the process was repeated until the end of the rally. Surveyors kept a record of nonresponses, making their best guesses of the race and gender of persons refusing. This study followed the protocol established by Heaney and Rojas (2014, 2015), though similar protocols have been employed by other studies, such as Fisher et al. (2005). Research shows that when protest surveys are conducted with careful attention to selection issues, as was the case in this study, they can provide a good representation of the protest population (Walgrave, Wouters, and Ketelaars 2016; Walgrave and Verhulst 2011).

Data were gathered with the objective of answering three questions. First, did the use of intersectionality as a collective action frame correspond with greater support for intersectional activism? Second, were there divisions among participants that explained variations in frame alignment on intersectional activism? If so, what factors corresponded with these cleavages? Third, was support for intersectional activism driven by collective action frames presented by movement leaders or by frames that participants brought with them?

Data analysis

Overall support for intersectional activism

Surveys at the five Women's March events yielded a total of 521 valid responses to the intersectional activism question. Surveys at the Women's March events had a 72% response rate, while the response rate was 61% at the March for Life, 86% at the People's March, 73% at the March for Trump, and 78% at the March for Our Lives. The survey results were weighted to account for nonresponse on the basis of estimated race and gender.

The results of the survey, presented in Figure 2, indicated strong support for intersectional activism across each of the Women's March events. The most common response to the survey question was that intersectional activism should be "equal to the highest priority for the movement." Support at this level ranged from 67% in Los Angeles to 80% in New York. The next highest level of support was given to the second strongest possible answer, "a high priority, but not the highest priority." Support at this level ranged from 13% in Las Vegas to 30% in Washington, DC. All other options received less than 8% support in every city. These differences are not statistically significant ($\chi^2_{(16)} = 25.477$, $p \approx .07$). Overall, the survey responses suggested that while prioritizing intersectional activism was not universally endorsed among Women's March participants, it was viewed as important by most participants.

Surveys at the four comparison events yielded a total of 422 valid responses to the intersectional activism question. The results of the survey, presented in Figure 3, revealed varied support for intersectional activism across each of the non-Women's March events. The minimum level of support for intersectional activism was registered at the March for Trump, at which 12% of respondents said this should be equal to the highest priority for the movement. At the high end, 59% of participants in the People's March said that intersectional activism should be prioritized equal to the movement's highest priority. This percentage is sizable, but still less than the minimum support observed at any Women's March event. While hardly any (less than 3%) of Women's March participants said that intersectional activism was "not a priority," 22% of participants at the March for Life gave this response. The differences among these events are statistically significant ($\chi^2_{(12)} = 83.793$, $p \leq .05$). The differences between the liberal events (People's March, March for Our Lives) and the conservative events (March for Life, March for Trump) especially underscore that the participants at ideologically distant events had very different ways of thinking about intersectionality, if they thought about the issue at all.

The difference between the support for intersectional activism at the Women's March events and the comparison events was statistically significant ($\chi^2_{(4)} = 59.801$, $p \leq .05$). This test provides evidence in favor of the view that the Women's March gathered crowds that were more supportive of prioritizing intersectional activism than were crowds at other comparable marches in Washington, DC. This result also held when the two conservative marches were excluded from the data ($\chi^2_{(4)} = 22.228$, $p \leq .05$).

It is important to note that some respondents may not have supported intersectional activism as strongly as they indicated in answering this question. For example, some respondents may have simply acquiesced to the survey question (Wright 1975). Or, respondents may have underreported their support even if they were more directly

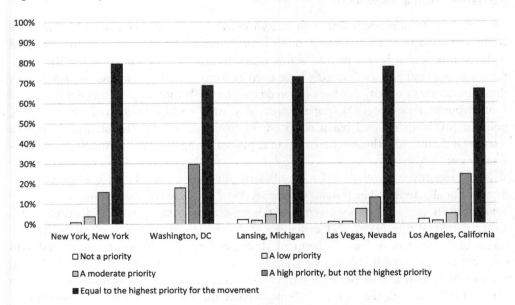

Figure 2. Support for intersectional activism at Women's March events, 2018.
Note: $N = 521$.

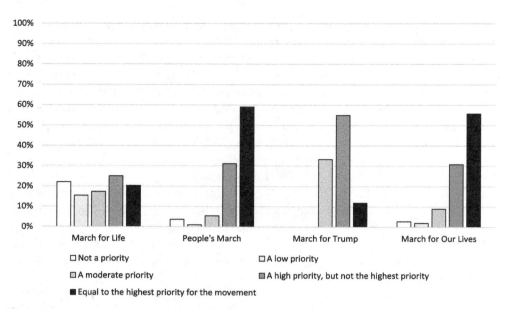

Figure 3. Support for intersectional activism at comparative events in Washington, DC, 2018.
Note: $N = 422$.

concerned with marginalization and oppression. Nonetheless, the results are consistent with the conclusion that participants in the Women's March considerably agreed with prioritizing intersectional activism, much more than was typically the case at other activist events.

Barriers to frame alignment

The previous section documents that not all participants in the Women's March, or in comparable marches in Washington, DC, participated for reasons that were aligned with the intersectional activism collective action frame. This section considers the structural and political factors that may have been barriers to that alignment, as well as how those barriers may or may not have differed between the Women's March and other grassroots protests. Four potential sources of division were social identity, political attitudes, political involvement, and participants' socio-economic status. The statistical analysis tests these factors for whether they help to explain alignment with the intersectional activism frame.

Social identity is the first and most obvious potential explanation for cleavages over intersectional activism. The pursuit of intersectional activism was potentially of deep personal importance to activists who embraced intersectionally marginalized identities (Tungohan 2016). White (1999, 77) explained that experiences of marginalization help to promote the success of frame alignment strategies linked to "racialized, gendered, and class-based micromobilization." McCormick and Franklin (2000) demonstrated that micromobilization may depend on participants' degree of racial consciousness (see also Dawson 1994). Swank and Fahs (2013) documented that these strategies were also relevant for sexual minorities. Of course, it is not necessarily the case that there are differences in support for intersectionality between members of marginalized and advantaged groups.

Instead, members of advantaged groups may choose to see themselves as allies to marginalized groups, and vice versa, thus potentially muting the effects of the difference (Droogendky et al. 2016).

Political attitudes are a second potential source of division regarding support for intersectional activism. Beliefs about activism are likely to be embedded within a broader package of ideas that individuals have been offered by political elites, which are generally presented as existing along the liberal-conservative continuum and/or through the platforms of political parties (Converse 1964; Noel 2013).

Political involvement is a third potential source of divisions. Activists' views may be developed through contact with activist and advocacy organizations (Munson 2008; Walker 1991, 129–130). As Heaney and Rojas (2015) argued, movement organizations may play a notable role in advising activists about how to think about contemporary political issues and partisan politics. As a result, it is reasonable to expect that activists who identify themselves with parties, ideologies, and/or activist organizations may align their views on intersectionality with these entities (Mason 2018). Individual activists may be inclined to take what they learn through one social movement and use it to shape their involvement in future movements (Meyer and Whittier 1994).

Fourth, socio-economic status may play a role in whether activists support intersectionality. Schlozman, Brady, and Verba (2018) document that persons with lower socio-economic status are less likely to be recruited by social movement organizations and less likely to volunteer on their own to participate in activism than are persons with higher socio-economic status (but see Schussman and Soule 2005 for contrary evidence). As a result, persons of lower socio-economic status may feel more isolated within social movements and, therefore, may be more sympathetic with appeals to intersectionality and inclusion.

The relevance of these four factors to frame alignment was examined using an Ordered Probit model of responses to the question on intersectional activism. Table 1 contained two models. Model 1 used data from the Women's March events and Model 2 used data from the four comparison events. Event dummy variables were included to account for average differences across events, with the Women's March in Washington, DC excluded as the base event in Model 1 and the March for Our Lives excluded as the base event in Model 2. The estimates were weighted to account for variations in survey nonresponse by gender and race and adjusted for stratification across events. Missing values were imputed using complete-case imputation, which is an appropriate method when there is a relatively low incidence of missing data, as was the case in this study (King et al. 2001; Little 1988; Wood et al. 2004). Descriptive statistics for these models are provided in Table 2, including survey-weighted means, standard deviations, and the percentage of observations imputed.

The results reported in Model 1 indicate the factors that were associated with support for intersectional activism in the Women's March. Trans- and LGBTQIA+-identified individuals were more likely than people with other social identities to support intersectional activism, suggesting that they may have seen a greater urgency for these issues than did cisgendered and straight individuals. However, there were no differences in support for intersectional activism between men and women, between nonwhites and whites, or on the basis of age, indicating that these groups had relatively close agreement on the prioritization of intersectional activism. Given the controversies surrounding the Women's March,

Table 1. Factors associated with support for intersectional activism.

Independent variable	Model 1 Women's March events	Model 2 Comparison events
Social identity		
Gender is female = 1	0.258	0.356*
	(0.144)	(0.131)
Gender is trans = 1	1.658*	1.002
	(0.723)	(0.554)
Race is nonwhite = 1	0.297	−0.008
	(0.158)	(0.191)
LGBTQIA+ = 1	0.563*	0.273
	(0.206)	(0.196)
Age in years	−0.008	−0.004
	(0.004)	(0.005)
Political attitudes		
Ideology (Conservative to Liberal 1–9)	0.232*	0.132*
	(0.053)	(0.049)
Party identification (Republican to Democrat 1–7)	0.492	−0.004
	(0.469)	(0.041)
Political involvement		
Member of political organization = 1	−0.186	0.070
	(0.136)	(0.138)
Past movement participation (Count of marginalized movements, 0–4)	0.182*	0.139
	(0.066)	(0.076)
Socio-economic status		
Income in thousands of dollars	0.000	0.001
	(0.001)	(0.001)
Level of education (Less than High School Grad. to Grad. Degree 1–6)	−0.046	0.043
	(0.051)	(0.051)
Event		
New York Women's March = 1	0.235	
	(0.174)	
Lansing, Michigan Women's March = 1	−0.030	
	(0.204)	
Las Vegas Women's March = 1	0.063	
	(0.188)	
Los Angeles Women's March = 1	−0.208	
	(0.180)	
March for Life = 1		−0.520
		(0.299)
People's March = 1		0.109
		(0.136)
March for Trump = 1		−0.100
		(0.339)
Cut points		
Cut Point 1	0.653	−0.923
	(1.379)	(0.453)
Cut Point 2	0.970	−0.617
	(1.142)	(0.462)
Cut Point 3	1.617	−0.067
	(1.398)	(0.464)
Cut Point 4	2.698	0.945
	(1.395)	(0.470)
Model statistics		
Sample size	521	422
F Statistic	4.04*	5.21*
F degrees of freedom	15, 502	14, 405

Notes: *$p \leq .05$. Models estimated using an Ordered Probit estimator. Standard errors in parentheses.

a significant difference between white and nonwhite respondents was expected. However, the results hint that the March may have been more unified on the basis of race at the grassroots level than among movement elites.

Table 2. Descriptive statistics – survey-weighed mean/(standard deviation)/[percent imputed].

Variable	Women's March events		Comparison events	
Dependent variable				
Support for addressing intersectionality (1–5)	4.648 (0.671)	N.A.	4.192	N.A.
Social identity				
Gender is female = 1	0.789 (0.400)	[13.13%]	0.625 (0.480)	[17.50%]
Gender is trans = 1	0.006 (0.076)	[13.13%]	0.016 (0.129)	[17.50%]
Race is nonwhite = 1	0.268 (0.453)	[12.46%]	0.193 (0.401)	[16.90%]
LGBTQIA+ =+1	0.212 (0.411)	[36.36%]	0.171 (0.386)	[38.77%]
Age in years	43.610 (17.398)	[14.48%]	41.942 (18.417)	[19.48%]
Political attitudes				
Ideology (Conservative to Liberal 1–9)	7.552 (1.325)	[15.15%]	6.702 (2.007)	[19.88%]
Party identification (Republican to Democrat 1–7)	6.226 (1.156)	[8.08%]	5.475 (1.749)	[10.74%]
Political involvement				
Member of political organization = 1	0.474 (0.500)	[10.94%]	0.334 (0.472)	[11.53%]
Past movement participation (Count of marginalized movements, 0–4)	1.561 (1.277)	[13.97%]	1.122 (1.213)	[16.90%]
Socio-economic status				
Income in thousands of dollars	99.257 (104.233)	[16.67%]	102.189 (100.640)	[22.27%]
Level of education (Less than High School Grad. to Grad. Degree 1–6)	4.506 (1.439)	[12.29%]	4.323 (1.660)	[16.90%]
Event				
New York Women's March = 1	0.213 (0.410)	[0.00%]		
Washington, DC Women's March = 1	0.300 (0.458)	[0.00%]		
Lansing, Michigan Women's March = 1	0.123 (0.327)	[0.00%]		
Las Vegas Women's March = 1	0.179 (0.386)	[0.00%]		
Los Angeles Women's March = 1	0.184 (0.389)	[0.00%]		
March for Life = 1			0.177 (0.366)	[0.00%]
People's March = 1			0.226 (0.424)	[0.00%]
March for Trump = 1			0.031 (0.176)	[0.00%]
March for Our Lives = 1			0.565 (0.494)	[0.00%]

In contrast to the Women's March, Model 2 indicates that gender was the only statistically significant social identity variable for the comparison events. Women attending the comparison events were more likely than men to say that they supported intersectional activism for the movements behind the comparison events that they attended, even though the organizers of those events did not stress intersectionality in their collective action frames. It appears that women were more inclined than men to bring intersectionality with them to their non-gender-focused activism.

The Women's March exhibited similarity with comparison events with respect to the relevance of political attitudes. In both models, the coefficient on ideology was positive and statistically significant, though the coefficient on partisan identification was not statistically significant. These results demonstrated that ideology was a factor that tended to divide activists in their views on intersectional activism. More liberal ideological views were associated with a greater desire to prioritize intersectional activism. As a result, the Women's March – which was heavily dominated by activists on the left side of the political spectrum – may expect that less liberal or more moderate women may be more likely than activists on the far Left to resist initiatives that are motivated by intersectional considerations.

Past political involvement was associated with prioritizing intersectional activism among Women's March activists but not among those activists at the comparison marches. The results of Model 1 show that activists who had participated in a greater number of movements for marginalized constituencies (specifically, Black Lives Matter, civil rights, immigrant rights, and women's rights) tended to assign a higher priority to intersectional activism than did activists who participated in fewer of these movements. This finding also lends support to the view that activists brought their interest in intersectionality with them from past activism to the Women's March.

Neither socio-economic status nor event dummy variables were significantly associated with variations in prioritization for intersectional activism.

Were framing effects top-down or bottom-up?

A final question to address using the survey data is whether activists prioritized intersectional activism because movement leaders emphasized this concept in their collective action frames? Or, did activists bring this idea with them to the activist events that they choose to participate in? An Ordered Probit analysis on the combined Women's March and comparison events data indicated that Women's March participants were significantly more likely to be aligned with the intersectional activism frame, holding constant the independent variables included in the regression, than were participants in other marches ($t = 2.94$, $p \leq .05$). Figure 4 reports the marginal effects in this equation of participation in the Women's March on the prioritization of intersectional activism. It illustrates that most of the marginal effects were on increasing the probability of observing "equal to the highest" and decreasing the probability of "high, but not highest," with other effects being relatively

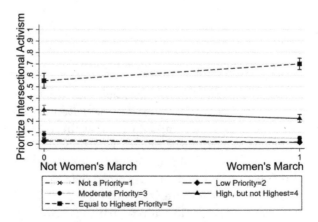

Figure 4. Marginal effects of women's March participation on prioritization of intersectional activism.

flat. A problem with this analysis, however, is that it did not account for the fact that activists participating in the Women's March may have been compositionally different from those participating in comparison events. That is, was the Women's March attended by people who prioritized intersectional activism, or did the March convince attendees to prioritize intersectional activism?

Propensity-score matching is a statistical technique that provides some leverage on the top-down, bottom-up question (Dehejia and Wahba 2002). This procedure weights the data so that Women's March participants were effectively compared with comparison-event participants as if they were statistically alike in all respects except having attended the Women's March. For example, a young, nonwhite woman who had participated in two prior movements for marginalized constituencies at the Women's March is compared with a weighted-equivalent person at a comparison event. When this method was applied, the average treatment effect indicated that a Women's March participant was likely to assign a higher priority to intersectional activism than was a weighted-equivalent participant at a comparison event ($t = 2.05$, $p \leq .05$). This result also held if the conservative events were excluded from the data ($t = 3.70$, $p \leq .05$). The implication of these findings is to support the view that attendance at the Women's March amplified the priority attached to intersectional activism. Thus, the evidence suggests that the collective action frame used by the Women's March leadership had at least some positive effect on encouraging participants to prioritize intersectional activism at the grassroots.

It would be incorrect to assume, however, that the effect of top-down framing rules out the possibility of bottom-up frame alignment. As is reported in the previous section, Women's March participants gave higher priority to intersectional activism the more that they had previously participated in movements for the interests of marginalized groups. These findings together indicate that processes of both bottom-up and top-down alignment were simultaneously at work.

Conclusion

Efforts at organizing women primarily on the basis of gender have historically prioritized the concerns of white, middle class, straight women. Thus, when the Women's March began a massive effort at organizing along these lines after the election of President Trump, activists concerned about intersectional marginalization raised red flags. They pressured the March to modify its organizing plans to accommodate the interests of marginalized constituencies. In response, the March adopted intersectionality as a collective action frame and took other concrete steps to align with an intersectional approach to activism. Subsequently, the March staged protests that – as demonstrated in this study – mobilized large groups of women (and others) that signaled their desire to see intersectionality as a high priority for the women's movement. This preference was greater at Women's March events than was the case of other comparable activist events held in Washington, DC. Thus, it is justified to conclude that the March achieved some reasonable degree of frame alignment with respect to intersectionality. While credit is owed to the March's leaders for projecting this frame, the evidence suggests that grassroots participants also learned about intersectionality from their prior activism.

It would be a misreading of this study, however, to claim that the Women's March transcended the problems of intersectional marginalization that tend to emerge when large groups of women organize together *as women*. As Blee (2012) and Lichterman (1995) emphasized in their research on grassroots organizational processes, collaborating on problems that differently affect vulnerable groups requires trust, which is often lacking between communities that do not frequently work together. Ideology was a factor that divided Women's March participants regarding intersectional activism, with more liberal activists placing a higher priority on this cause than did more moderate and conservative activists. Similarly, intersectional activism was not as important to cis-gendered and straight Marchers as it was to trans and queer Marchers. Activists with a history of involvement in movements for marginalized communities were more prone to endorse intersectional activism than were those without this background.

This research deepens what is known about the relationship between intersectionality and the politics of social movements. It highlights the importance of march organizers and grassroots participants in adopting collective action frames. It demonstrates how this process is both organizationally and ideologically driven. It raises the question of the relevance of participants' views about intersectionality, not only in movements that are focused on multiple axes of oppression, but also in movements that are not framed around these issues. With the mainstreaming of dialogues about intersectionality, this topic – along with imperatives to struggle against oppression and injustice – is likely to pervade social movement organizing at every level.

At the same time that it advances our understanding of intersectionality at the grassroots, this article leaves numerous questions unresolved for future research to address. For example, this study considered the support that respondents gave to intersectional activism but did not probe the diverse ways that activists may be oriented toward intersectionality or feminism (Greenwood 2008; Harnois 2005). How do participants understand the need to embrace the concerns of subgroups? How do participants understand the ways that issues are intersectionally constituted? These and other questions may be addressed not only by developing more complex batteries of survey questions about intersectionality but also by incorporating more qualitative analysis of movement activity into future studies.

Acknowledgements

The author is grateful for helpful comments from Sara Angevine, Rhiannon Auriemma, Lisa Disch, Dana Fisher, Anna Kirkland, Dara Strolovitch, Sid Tarrow, three anonymous reviwers, and participants in symposia of the Institute for Research on Women and Gender at the University of Michigan in 2017 and 2018 and the 2018 Women's History Month Symposium at Wayne State University. An earlier version of this paper was presented at the 114th Annual Meeting of the American Political Science Association, Boston, Massachusetts, August 30–September 2, 2018. Special thanks are owed to many surveyors, research assistants, and anonymous survey respondents who contributed to this research.

Disclosure statement

No potential conflict of interest was reported by the author.

Funding

This work was supported by Institute for Research on Women and Gender, University of Michigan; National Center for Institutional Diversity, University of Michigan; Organizational Studies Program, University of Michigan; Undergraduate Research Opportunity Program, University of Michigan; National Institute for Civil Discourse, University of Arizona.

References

Adam, Erin. 2017. "Intersectional Coalitions: The Paradoxes of Rights-based Movement Building in LGBTQ and Immigrant Communities." *Law & Society Review* 51 (1): 132–167.

Alexander-Floyd, Nikol. 2012. "Disappearing Acts: Reclaiming Intersectionality in the Social Sciences in a Post-black Feminist Era." *Feminist Formations* 24 (1): 1–25.

Altavena, Lily. 2018. "Las Vegas Women's March 2018 Draws Thousands to Sunday Event." *Azcentral*, January 21. Accessed September 3, 2018. https://www.azcentral.com/story/news/nation/2018/01/21/2018-womens-march-las-vegas-nevada-draws-thousands/1052368001/

Beckwith, Karen. 2014. "Gender, Class, and the Structure of Intersectionality: Working-class Women and the Pittston Coal Strike." *Politics, Groups, and Identities* 2 (1): 17–34.

Berry, Marie, and Erica Chenoweth. 2018. "Who Made the Women's March?" In *The Resistance*, edited by David S. Meyer and Sidney Tarrow, 75–89. New York: Oxford University Press.

Beyerlein, Kraig, Peter Ryan, Aliyah Abu-Hazeem, and Amity Pauley. 2018. "The 2017 Women's March: A National Study of Solidarity Events." *Mobilization: An International Quarterly* 23 (4): 425–449.

Blee, Kathleen. 2012. *Democracy in the Making*. New York: Oxford University Press.

Brewer, Sierra, and Lauren Dundes. 2018. "Concerned, Meet Terrified: Intersectional Feminism and the Women's March." *Women's Studies International Forum* 69: 49–55.

Chenoweth, Erica, and Jeffrey Pressman. 2018. "One Year after the Women's March on Washington, People are Still Protesting en Masse." *Washington Post*, January 21, 2017. Accessed February 9, 2019. https://www.washingtonpost.com/news/monkey-cage/wp/2018/01/21/one-year-after-the-womens-march-on-washington-people-are-still-protesting-en-masse-a-lot-weve-counted/.

Cho, Sumi, Kimberlé Crenshaw, and Leslie McCall. 2013. "Toward a Field of Intersectionality Studies: Theory, Applications, and Praxis." *Signs: Journal of Women in Culture and Society* 38 (4): 785–810.

Cole, Elizabeth. 2008. "Coalitions as a Model for Intersectionality: From Practice to Theory." *Sex Roles* 59 (5): 443–453.

Collins, Patricia, and Sirma Bilge. 2016. *Intersectionality*. Cambridge: Polity Press.

Combahee River Collective. [1977] 1995. "A Black Feminist Statement." In *Words of Fire*, edited by Beverly Guy-Sheftall. New York: New Press.

Converse, Philip. 1964. "The Nature of Belief Systems in Mass Publics." In *Ideology and Discontent*, edited by David E. Apter, 206–261. New York: Free Press.

Crenshaw, Kimberlé. 1989. "Demarginalizing the Intersection of Race and Sex." *University of Chicago Legal Forum* 140: 139–167.

Crenshaw, Kimberlé. 1991. "Mapping the Margins: Intersectionality, Identity Politics, and Violence Against Women of Color." *Stanford Law Review* 43 (6): 1241–1299.

Davis, Kathy. 2008. "Intersectionality as Buzzword: A Sociology of Science Perspective on What Makes a Feminist Theory Successful." *Feminist Theory* 9 (1): 67–85.

Dawson, Michael. 1994. *Behind the Mule*. Princeton: Princeton University Press.

Dawson, Michael. 2001. *Black Visions*. Chicago: University of Chicago Press.

Dehejia, Rajeev, and Sadek Wahba. 2002. "Propensity Score-matching Methods for Nonexperimental Causal Studies." *Review of Economics and Statistics* 84 (1): 151–161.

Dhamoon, Rita. 2011. "Considerations on Mainstreaming Intersectionality." *Political Research Quarterly* 64 (1): 230–243.

Doetsch-Kidder, Sharon. 2012. *Social Change and Intersectional Activism*. New York: Palgrave MacMilan.

Droogendky, Lisa, Stephen Wright, Micah Lubensky, and Winnifred Louis. 2016. "Acting in Solidarity: Cross-group Contact Between Disadvantaged Group Members and Advantaged Group Allies." *Journal of Social Issues* 72 (2): 315–334.

Fisher, Dana. 2019. *American Resistance*. New York: Columbia University Press.

Fisher, Dana, Dawn Dow, and Rashawn Ray. 2017. "Intersectionality Takes It to the Streets." *Science Advances* 3, September 20: 1–8.

Fisher, Dana, Lorien Jasny, and Dawn Dow. 2018. "Why are We Here? Patterns of Intersectional Motivations Across the Resistance" *Mobilization: An International Quarterly* 23 (4): 451–468.

Fisher, Dana, Kevin Stanley, David Berman, and Gina Neff. 2005. "How Do Organizations Matter? Mobilization and Support for Participants at Five Globalization Protests" *Social Problems* 52 (1): 102–121.

Goss, Kristin. 2013. *The Paradox of Gender Equality*. Ann Arbor: University of Michigan Press.

Goss, Kristin, and Michael T. Heaney. 2010. "Organizing Women *as Women*: Hybridity and Grassroots Collective Action in the 21st Century." *Perspectives on Politics* 8 (1): 27–52.

Greenwood, Ronni. 2008. "Intersectional Political Consciousness: Appreciation for Intragroup Differences and Solidarity in Diverse Groups." *Psychology of Women Quarterly* 32 (1): 36–47.

Griffiths, Brian. 2018. "Hundreds of Thousands Protest in D.C., Across Country on Women's March Anniversary." *Politico*, January 20. Accessed September 3, 2018. https://www.politico.com/story/2018/01/20/womens-march-anniversary-dc-352231.

Hancock, Ange-Marie. 2007. "When Multiplication Doesn't Equal Quick Addition." *Perspectives on Politics* 5 (1): 63–79.

Hancock, Ange-Marie. 2016. *Intersectionality*. New York: Oxford University Press.

Harnois, Catherine. 2005. "Different Paths to Different Feminisms? Bridging Multiracial Feminist Theory and Quantitative Sociological Gender Research" *Gender & Society* 19 (6): 809–828.

Heaney, Michael T., and Fabio Rojas. 2014. "Hybrid Activism: Social Movement Mobilization in a Multimovement Environment." *American Journal of Sociology* 119 (4): 1047–1103.

Heaney, Michael T., and Fabio Rojas. 2015. *Party in the Street*. New York: Cambridge University Press.

hooks, bell. 1984. *Feminist Theory*. Boston, MA: South End Press.

King, Gary, James Honaker, Anne Joseph, and Kenneth Scheve. 2001. "Analyzing Incomplete Political Science Data." *American Political Science Review* 95 (1): 49–69.

Laperrière, Marie, and Eléonore Lépinard. 2016. "Intersectionality as a Tool for Social Movements: Strategies of Inclusion and Representation in the Québécois Women's Movement." *Politics* 36 (4): 374–382.

Lichterman, Paul. 1995. "Piecing Together Multicultural Community: Cultural Differences in Community Building among Grass-roots Environmentalists." *Social Problems* 42 (4): 513–532.

Little, Roderick. 1988. "Missing Data Adjustments in Large Surveys." *Journal of Business and Economic Statistics* 6 (3): 287–296.

Mason, Lilliana. 2018. *Uncivil Agreement*. Chicago, IL: University of Chicago Press.

May, Vivian. 2015. *Pursuing Intersectionality, Unsettling Dominant Imaginaries*. New York: Routledge.

McCall, Leslie. 2005. "The Complexity of Intersectionality." *Signs: Journal of Women in Culture and Society* 30 (3): 1771–1800.

McCormick, Joseph, and Sekou Franklin. 2000. "Expressions of Racial Consciousness in the African American Community." In *Black and Multiracial Politics in America*, edited by Yvette Alex-Assensoh and Lawrence Hanks, 315–336. New York: New York University Press.

McKane, Rachel, and Holly McCammon. 2018. "Why We March: The Role of Grievances, Threats, and Movement Organizational Resources in the 2017 Women's Marches." *Mobilization: An International Quarterly* 23 (4): 401–424.

Meyer, David, and Nancy Whittier. 1994. "Social Movement Spillover." *Social Problems* 41 (2): 277–298.

Munson, Ziad. 2008. *The Making of Pro-life Activists*. Chicago: University of Chicago Press.

Noel, Hans. 2013. *Political Ideologies and Political Parties in America*. New York: Cambridge University Press.

North, Anna. 2018. "The Women's March Changed the American Left." *Vox*, December 21. Accessed February 8, 2019. https://www.vox.com/identities/2018/12/21/18145176/feminism-womens-march-2018-2019-farrakhan-intersectionality.

Perez, Carmen. 2017. "CARMEN PEREZ Speech." *YouTube*, February 2. Accessed August 23, 2018. https://www.youtube.com/watch?v=32uPDwdKGQ8.

Quarshie, Mabinty. 2018. "Is the Women's March More Inclusive this Year?" *USA Today*, January 20. Accessed February 9, 2019. https://eu.usatoday.com/story/news/2018/01/18/womens-march-more-inclusive-year/1038859001/.

Roberts, Dorothy, and Sujatha Jesudason. 2013. "Movement Intersectionality." *Du Bois Review: Social Science Research on Race* 10 (2): 313–328.

Rose-Redwood, CindyAnn, and Reuben Rose-Redwood. 2017. "'It Definitely Felt Very White': Race, Gender, and the Performative Politics of Assembly at the Women's March in Victoria, British Columbia." *Gender, Place & Culture* 24 (5): 645–654.

Schlozman, Kay, Henry Brady, and Sidney Verba. 2018. *Unequal and Unrepresented*. Princeton: Princeton University Press.

Schussman, Alan, and Sarah Soule. 2005. "Process and Protest: Accounting for Individual Protest Participation." *Social Forces* 84 (2): 1083–1108.

Simien, Evelyn. 2006. *Black Feminist Voices in Politics*. Albany: State University of New York Press.

Smooth, Wendy, and Tamelyn Tucker. 1999. "Behind but Not Forgotten." In *Still Lifting, Still Climbing*, edited by Kimberly Spring, 241–258. New York: New York University Press.

Snow, David, Burke Rochford, Steven Worden, and Robert Benford. 1986. "Frame Alignment Processes, Micromobilization, and Movement Participation." *American Sociological Review* 51 (4): 464–481.

Snow, David, Rens Vliegenthart, and Pauline Ketelaars. 2019. "The Framing Perspective on Social Movements." In *The Wiley Blackwell Companion to Social Movements*, edited by David Snow, Sarah Soule, Hanspeter Kreisi, and Holly McCammon, 2nd ed., 392–411. Hoboken, NJ: John Wiley & Sons.

Strolovitch, Dara. 2007. *Affirmative Advocacy*. Chicago, IL: University of Chicago Press.

Swank, Eric, and Breanne Fahs. 2013. "An Intersectional Analysis of Gender and Race for Sexual Minorities Who Engage in Gay and Lesbian Rights Activism." *Sex Roles* 68 (11–12): 660–674.

Terriquez, Veronica. 2015. "Intersectional Mobilization, Social Movement Spillover, and Queer Youth Leadership in the Immigrant Rights Movement." *Social Problems* 62 (3): 343–362.

Terriquez, Veronica, Tizoc Brenes, and Abdiel Lopez. 2018. "Intersectionality as a Multipurpose Collective Action Frame: The Case of the Undocumented Youth Movement." *Ethnicities* 18 (2): 260–276.

Tolentino, Jia. 2017. "The Somehow Controversial Women's March on Washington." *The New Yorker*, January 18. Accessed February 5, 2018. https://www.newyorker.com/culture/jia-tolentino/the-somehow-controversial-womens-march-on-washington.

Tormos, F. 2017. "Intersectional Solidarity." *Politics, Groups, and Identities* 5 (4): 707–720.

Tungohan, Ethel. 2016. "Intersectionality and Social Justice: Assessing Activists' Use of Intersectionality Through Grassroots Migrants' Organizations in Canada." *Politics, Groups, and Identities* 4 (3): 347–362.

Wadsworth, Nancy D. 2011. "Intersectionality in California's Same-sex Marriage Battles: A Complex Proposition." *Political Research Quarterly* 64 (1): 200–216.

Walgrave, Stefaan, and Joris Verhulst. 2011. "Selection and Response Bias in Protest Surveys." *Mobilization* 16 (2): 203–222.

Walgrave, Stefaan, Ruud Wouters, and Pauline Ketelaars. 2016. "Response Problems in the Protest Survey Design: Evidence From Fifty-one Protest Events in Seven Countries*." *Mobilization: An International Quarterly* 21 (1): 83–104.

Walker, Jack. 1991. *Mobilizing Interest Groups in America*. Ann Arbor: University of Michigan Press.

Weldon, Laurel. 2019. "Power, Exclusion and Empowerment: Feminist Innovation in Political Science." *Women's Studies International Forum* 72: 127–136.

White, Aaronette. 1999. "Talking Feminist, Talking Black." *Gender & Society* 13 (1): 77–100.

Wood, Angela, Ian White, Melvyn Hillsdon, and James Carpenter. 2004. "Comparison of Imputation and Modeling Methods in the Analysis of a Physical Activity Trial with Missing Outcomes." *International Journal of Epidemiology* 34 (1): 89–99.

Wright, James. 1975. "Does Acquiescence Bias the 'Index of Political Efficacy?'" *Public Opinion Quarterly* 39 (2): 219–226.

WUSA. 2018. "Thousands Gather for 2018 Women's March in DC." *WUSA9*, January 20, 2018. Accessed September 3, 2018. https://www.wusa9.com/article/news/local/dc/thousands-gather-for-2018-womens-march-in-dc/509711469.

Index

Note: Figures are denoted by *italic* text and tables are shown in **bold**. Notes are indicated by "n" and the note number after the page number e.g., 297n6 refers to note number 6 on page 297. American Political Development is abbreviated to APD, Black Lives Matter to BLM, and Congressional Black Caucus to CBC.

9/11 9, 56, 280, 284n19

AAEC (Association of American Editorial Cartoonists) 79
accountability, police 61, 62, 63, 64, 65, 66, 67, 70, 71
activism 11, 33, 36; anti-lynching 18; Asian American 269; black 15, 27, 39, 40, 43; BLM 76, 86, 102, 104, 276; intersectional *see* intersectional activism; LGBTQ people of color 249–263; political 40, 43, 269, 297n6
additive model 227, 234, 235–237, **236**, *237*, 241
advocacy 52–53, 62, 81, 169, 256, 271; affirmative 293, 305; BLM 75; intersectional 288, 289, 290, 294, 293, 297n6, 297n7, 307, 313
affirmative advocacy 293, 305
Affordable Care Act 9, 10, 116
African American legislators 108, 110–114, 115, 119, 120
African American politics 32, 110, 113, 118, 120, 274
African American women 112–113, 120, 303, 306
age: Asian American support for BLM 273, 277, 278, **278**; Baltimore Exceptionalism framework 168; grassroots intersectionality 304, 313, **314**, **315**; of incarceration 23–29; intersectional solidarity 289, 295; intersectional stereotyping in policing 226–245, **234**, **236**, *237*, *238*, *240*, *241*, *242*, *243*, 245n2, 245n4; LGBTQ people of color, activism in Canada 255, 256, 257, 259, 267; police killings **134**, **136**; quality of life 172, 173, **177**, 178, **180**, 180, 181, 182; traffic stops 191, *196*, 197, **202**, 204, **207**, **211**, **212**; use of Twitter by CBC **117**, 118, 126; of victim 129, 130, 133, **136**, 136, 140
agency 14, 16, 32, 33, 50, 57, 81, 259; and intersectional solidarity 291, 292, 294, 295
agenda builder and setter, media as 63–65
Alexander, Michelle 2, 8, 26, 37, 188
Alexander-Floyd, Nikol 289, 295, 296n1, 305

All Lives Matter movement 50, 62, 76
Alt-Right movement 6, 9
American carceral state 1–2
American democracy 1, 3, 9, 190
American Political Development (APD): and BLM 1–3, 5–11; in age of incarceration 23–29; strange fruit of 13–20
American politics 5, 6, 7, 9, 14, 16, 110, 113; Asian 268, 269; black historical subjectivity in 43; and BLM 270, 274, 282; and police killings of African-Americans 128; populist nationalism in 23, 24; and race-based movements 268; racial violence in 19–20, 95; Women's March as force in 302
American racial and ethnic politics (REP) 269, 270, 283n6, 110, 114
American racial hierarchy 32–33, 272, 273
American society 32, 39, 40, 161
American Twittersphere 108
American values 25, 129, 130, 132, 144, 145–146
anger, as emotional response to police shooting 39, 48, 89, 91–92, **93**, 94, **95**, 96, 171
anti-black discrimination 268, 274, 275, 276, 278, 280, 281, 284n15
anti-black racism 100, 129, 252, 269, 274, 282
"anti-black" society 44
anti-dehumanization 40
antidiscrimination 227
anti-lynching activism 18
Anzaldúa, Gloria 290–291
APD *see* American Political Development (APD)
Arc-en-ciel d'Afrique 250, 252, 256, 259, 260
arrests 58n7, 167, 174, 230; and traffic stops 189, 192, 193, **193**, 197, 205n2
Asian American support for BLM 268–284, **275**, *276*, **278**
Association of American Editorial Cartoonists (AAEC) 79
audience, for racial gaslighting 47, 51, **55**, 55, 56, 57, 79

autonomy, police 61, 65, 66, 67, 70, 71
availability of resources 166, 173, **176**, 176

"bad apple" police officer hypothesis 14, 192, 203, 205, 230
Baldwin, James 3, 24, 40
Baltimore Exceptionalism 166, 167–168, 168–169, 170, 172, 182
Baltimore Mayoral Democratic Primary (2016) 100–101
Baltimore Uprising 166, 167, 182, 183, 183n1; quality of life before 166–184, **175**, **176**, **177**, **178**, *179*, **180**, *181*
Bethune, Mary McLeod 43–44
bias: confirmation 130–131; media **80**, **83**; race-of-victim 215–216, *216*, 218, 220, 221, 223n6; racial *see* racial bias; social desirability 138
biographical availability 253
biological racism 26
"birtherism" 9
black activism 15, 27, 39, 40, 43; *see also* Black Lives Matter (BLM)
Black Americans, and the "crime narrative" 155–163, *159*, *162*
"black body", in the BLM era 32–44
black civil rights activism 27
black counterpublic sphere 119
black criminality 35, 64, 101, 155, 161–162, 228; and APD 2–3, 18, 25, 26, 27
black drivers 188, 190, 194, 197, 200, **202**, 204, **207**, **211**, **212**, 238
black education 32, 34, 38, 40, 41, 42, 43–44
black feminism 296
black freedom struggle 3
black historical subjectivity, in American politics 43
"black inferiority" 37, 38, 39, 41, 78, 101
black institutions 32, 34, 36, 39, 40–44
black liberation 17, 100
black life 14, 15, 24, 34, 50, 100
Black Lives Matter (BLM) 1, 2; activism of 76, 86, 102, 104, 276; APD in era of 1–3, 5–11; Asian American support for 273–282, **275**, **276**, **278**; "black body" in era of 32–44; political cartoons in era of 75–87, **80**, *82*, **83**, **84**, **85**; primes related to 127, 129, 130, 141, *142*, 142, **143**, 143–144, 144–145, 146, **151–152**, **153**; rhetoric of 144–145; scholarship on 100–105; Twitter hashtag for 14, 24, 100–105, 116, 119, 188, 226, 270–271; and women 84–85, **85**
Black "nobodies" 101, 103
Black Panther Party 62, 64
Black Power 2, 23, 105, 270
black protest 14, 16–17
black public high schools 32, 34, 38, 40, 41, 42, 43–44
black racial stereotypes 33–34
black social movements 13–14, 283n7
"Black Twitter" 76, 109

Black victims: and police killings *138*, 138; and race-of-victim effects in US executions 214, *216*, 216, *219*, 219, *220*, 220, 221, 223n3, 224n12, 224n13
blackness, politics of 32–44
Black-on-Black crime 218, 223224n11
Black-on-White crime 218, 221
"Blacktags" 109, 115, 116, *116*, 119
Bland, Bob 306
Bland, Sandra 72, 127–128
BLM *see* Black Lives Matter (BLM)
Braden, Carl and Anne 47, 51, 53–54, 55, 56, 57
Brown, Michael 10, 24, 75, 100, 101, 108, 157, 188, 226; and news coverage of killing 61, 64, 68, 69, 72; and police killings 89, 90, 95, 127, 131, 136, 141
brutality, police 6, 13, 36, 61–62, 67, 110, 156, 166, 226, 272, 283n5; and BLM scholarship 101, 103, 105; political cartoons relating to 75, 80, 83, 84, 85, 86
"Build the wall!" 23, 29
bureaucratization 16, 38, 41, 167, 170
Bush v. Gore 2000 election 9

capital prosecution 215, *216*, 216, 218
capital punishment 24, 213–224, *216*, *217*, *219*, *220*, 223n3
capital sentencing, influence of victim race in 214–215
carceral state 1–2, 2–3, 25, 26, 28, 169, 170
cartoons, political 75–87, **80**, *82*, **83**, **84**, **85**
Castile, Philando 68, 72, 146
CBC (Congressional Black Caucus) 107–121, *115*, *116*, **117**
Charlottesville, Virginia, white supremacist rally in 23, 24, 29
chattel slavery 34–35
citizen agency 16
citizen satisfaction 170, 171, 172
citizen surveys 166, 170–172, 183
Citizens' Council 25
citizenship 33, 35, 36, 40, 42, 43, 105, 190, 204; and APD 2, 6, 8, 10, 11, 14, 16, 19, 20; and Asian American support for BLM 269, 273, 278, **278**
Civil Rights Acts 15, 16, 25, 36
civil rights activism 16, 27, 28, 39
Civil Rights movement 36, 40, 51, 62, 77, 81, 102, 109, 306; and APD 1, 3, 6, 7, 8, 20, 25, 27
civil rights policies 26, 36
Civil Rights State 5–6, 8, 9, 10, 11
civil unrest 36, 166, 167, 168, 171, 183n1
Civil War 19, 35, 36, 39
class 26, 42, 43, 49, 63, 250; and Asian American support for BLM 269, 273, 274; and grassroots intersectionality 304, 305, 312, 317; and intersectional solidarity 289, 292, 294, 295, 296n2, 296–297n3; and intersectional stereotyping in policing 226, 227, 229, 230, 231, 232, 233, 237–240, 241, 242, 244, 245; and

police killings **136**, 136, 141; and quality of life before 2015 Uprising 167, 168, 169, 170, 179–180, 182, 183
cleavages: generational 281; intersectional activism 310, 312; racial and spatial 166–184, **175**, **176**, **177**, **178**, *179*, **180**, *181*
Clinton, President Bill 49–50, 56
Clinton, Hillary 9, 10, 270, 307
coding 65, 66, 79–81, 126, 163n3
Collaborative Multiracial Post-Election Survey (2016) 268, 269, 273, **275**, *276*, **278**
collective action 86, 253, 291, 293
collective action frames 81, 302, 303, 304, 306, 307, 308, 310, 312, 315, 316, 317, 318
collective identity 249, 250, 253, 305, 306
color blindness 102–103
Combahee River Collective 227, 254, 288, 290–291, 293, 304
Commonwealth of Kentucky v. Braden (1955) 47, 51, 53–55, **55**
concrete state action 51, 52, 53, 58n6
Confederacy 2
confirmation bias 130–131
Congresses 110–111, 112; 113th 113–114, 115–116, *115*, *116*, 117, 118, 119, 120
Congressional Black Caucus (CBC), use of Twitter by 107–121, *115*, *116*, **117**
conjoint survey experiments 127–148, **134**, *135*, **136**, *138*, *139*, *142*, **143**, *144*, *147*
consent searches 189, *201*, 202, 208, *211*
conservatism 28, 118
Constitution (US) 34, 58n5, 222
content analysis 66, 113, 114, 121, 163n2
contraband 188, 193, 198, 200, **200**, *201*, **202**, 203, **207**, **210**, *210*, *211*, **212**, 233
contraband hit rates 191, 192, 202, 204, 205, 208
Cooper, Anna Julia 3, 40, 43–44
Crenshaw, Kimberlé W. 227, 254, 255, 304, 305; and intersectional solidarity 288, 289, 290, 291, 293–294, 295
"crime narrative", Black Americans and 155–163, *159*, *162*
criminal charges 89, 91, 92, 93, **93**, 94–95, **95**
criminal justice system 8, 10, 96, 100, 116, 222–223, 245; and Asian American support for BLM 271, 283n5; and traffic stops 188, 190
criminal punishment 13–14, 17, 20, **55**, 55, 56, 101, 229; for police killings of unarmed African Americans 89, 91, 92–94, **93**, 94
criminality 25, 89, 90, 91, 93, 94–95, **95**, 160; black *see* black criminality; societal 90; stereotypes of 229, 230, 238
cross-racial coalitions and interactions 96, 268, 269, 271–273, 279, 281
crowd wisdom 170, 171
Cullors, Patrisse 14, 24, 76, 116
culture 39–40, 78, 102, 103, 119, 161, 227, 270, 272, 304; an intersectional solidarity 295, 296–297n3; and LGBTQ people of color 251, 254, 255, 262–263n2; and quality of life before 2015 Uprising 173, 175, **175**; and racial gaslighting 47, 49, 50, 52

Death Penalty Information Center (DPIC) 214, 216
defendant race 215
dehumanization 40, 50, 100
democracy 3, 8, 14, 15, 32, 292; *see also* American democracy
Democracy in Black: How Race Still Enslaves the American Soul 100
Democratic Party 109, 111–112, 119
democratization 8, 28
demographics 91, 96n2, 160, 173, 174, 202, **202**, **207**, **211**, **212**
deprivation 168, 170, 171
"digital divide" 108
disappointment, as emotional response to police shooting 89, 91, 92, **93**, 93, **93**, 95
discrimination: anti-black 268, 274, 275, 276, 278, 280, 281, 284n15; racial 16, 51, 101, 191, 204, 233, 294
disenfranchisement 2, 48, 64
"disposable citizens" 101
DOJ (US Department of Justice) 14, 167, 188, 190–191, 200, 204, 217, 218
Douglass, Frederick 3, 40, 168
DPIC (Death Penalty Information Center) 214, 216
drivers: black *see* black drivers; female *see* female drivers; Hispanic **202**, 203–204, **207**, **211**, **212**; male 197, 200, 203, 204, 236, 237, 238, 239–240, 241
"driving while black" 188, 189
drug offenders 228–229
Du Bois, W.E.B. 18, 24, 38, 42, 43–44
due process 10, 13, 18, 19, 35

economic in/equality 2, 3, 10, 86, 167
education 11, 229, 259–260, 278, **278**, 291, **314**, **315**; police killings **134**, 143, **151**, **152**; politics of blackness 32, 34, 35, 38, 40, 41, 42, 43–44; quality of life before 2015 Uprising **178**, 179, **180**, 181, 182
elections 14, 104, 171, 270, 274, 306, 307; use of Twitter by CBC 107, 110, 112, 118
electoral reform 8, 9, 20
electoral politics 20, 63, 140, 302; local 100–105
emotional responses, to police killings of unarmed African Americans 89–96, **93**, **95**
empathy 64, 96, 229
episodic frames 156–157, 157–160, *159*, 163n5
equal citizenship and representation 16, 20, 190
equality 15, 18, 32, 34, 36, 75, 101, 103, 104; economic 3; norm of 158; political 3, 8, 39; racial 6, 10, 158; social 3
exceptionalism, politics of 6, 273; *see also* Baltimore Exceptionalism
exclusion 19, 36, 52, 75, 79, 86; of LGBTQ people of color 249, 254, 255, 256, 257

executions 24, 213–224, *216*, *217*, *219*, *220*, 223n3; race-of-victim effects in 213–224, *216*, *217*, *219*, *220*; *see also* capital punishment
Executive Order 9066, for forced removal of persons of Japanese ancestry 51
explicit-implicit media framing 156, 158, *159*
exposure: to crime 174, 182; to faces of black people 128; to news about crime 160, 161, 162; to racial gaslighting 51, **55**, 55–56, 57, 147; to violence 38

Fair Housing Act 15, 36
federal government 13, 16, 18, 52, 71, 114, 214
female drivers: intersectional stereotyping of 236, 237, 238, 239, 240, 241–242, *242*; and young men of color 197, 207–210, *208*, *209*, **210**, *210*, 211, **211**, **212**
feminism 48–49, 256, 283n7, 304, 305; and intersectional solidarity 288, 289, 290, 291, 293, 295–296
"Ferguson Effect" 76
Ferguson insurgency 24; news-coverage after 61–73, **67**, **68**, *69*, *70*
first Redemption Era 5, 6, 7–8, 9, 11
FLH (Front de libération homosexuel) 251, 263n4
foreign policy 16, 89–90
frames: alignment of 303–304, 310, 312–316, **314**, **315**, 317; collective action *see* collective action frames; episodic 156–157, 157–160, *159*, 163n5; "General Racism" 79–80, **83**, 83, **84**, 84; movement 81, 84; news *see* news framing; "Police" **67**, 80, 82, 85; "Solutions" 81; thematic 157, 158, 160
From #BlackLivesMatter to Black Liberation 100
From Protest to Politics: The Future of Civil Rights Movement 103
Front de libération homosexuel (FLH) 251, 263n4

GAO (Government Accounting Office) 214
Garner, Eric 108, 127, 128, 157, 188
Garza, Alicia 1, 14, 24, 76, 100, 102, 110, 116
Gaslight 47–48, 57
gaslighting, racial 47–58, **55**
gender identification 5, 43, 239, 240, 245, 245n2, 256, 257, 258, **267**
"General Racism" frame 79–80, **83**, 83, **84**, 84
generational cleavages 281
Glaude, Eddie 100, 101, 102, 103, 105
Goldwater, Barry 24, 25, 26
governance 3, 7, 15, 19, 25, 28, 29, 35, 166, 183
Government Accounting Office (GAO) 214
government legitimacy 167
grass roots intersectionality 302–318, *308*, *311*, *312*, **314**, **315**, *316*
Gray, Freddie 68, 72, 104, 105, 127, 136, 166, 167, 182, 183, 188
Greensboro Four 27
group consciousness 90, 274

hate crimes 65, 110
high schools 32, 34, 37, 38, 40, 41, 42, 43–44
Hill, Marc Lamont 100, 101, 102, 103
Hispanic drivers **202**, 203–204, **207**, **211**, **212**
Holiday, Billie 13, 15
"home style" 108, 119
homicides 213–214, 215, 217–219, *217*, *219*, 220–221, *220*, 223–224n11
homosexuality 250–251
Hooker, Juliet 3, 15, 24, 168, 283n7
hooks, bell 254, 260, 263n12, 288, 290, 304
House of Representatives 109, 110, 111, 112, 113, 115
Hughes, Langston 40
human rights 43, 77, 263n6, 288, 291, 292
Hurston, Zora Neale 40
hypothetical police shootings 129, 140

identities: collective 249, 250, 253, 305, 306; gender 5, 239, 240, 245, 245n2, 256, 257, 258, **267**; intersectional *see* intersectional identity; racial *see* racial identities; shared 291–292, 292–293; social 308, 312–313, **314**, **315**, 315
identity groups 172, 227, 230, **234**, 236, 237, 243–244, 294
identity-based profiling *see* profiling
identity-based stereotyping 226, 227
identity-related processes 249, 250, 253, 257–259, 262
ideology: liberal-conservative 39, 278; political 16, 269, 277, **278**; racial uplift 42, 43; as variable in police killings analysis 130, **134**, 143, 148n3
IE (implicit-explicit) model 156, 158, *159*
Illinois, analysis of traffic stop data in 226–245, **234**, **236**, *237*, *238*, *240*, *241*, *242*, *243*
immigration reform 10
implicit-explicit media framing 156, 158, *159*
incarceration 2, 10; APD in age of 23–29
inclusion 34, 38, 81, 96, 249, 261, 290, 303, 313
indifference, as emotional response to police shooting 91, 92, **93**, 93, **93**, **95**
inequalities 2, 10, 33; racial *see* racial inequalities
"inferiority, black" 37, 38, 39, 41, 78, 101
in-groups 40, 90, 92, 159
"innate black criminality" 25, 27
institutionalized oblivion, and racism 39–40
insurgency 64, 68, 71, 72–73
intercurrence 3, 7
interracial crimes 213–214, 218
interracial social capital 41
interracial tensions 269, 272
intersectional activism 302–306, 307, *308*, 308–318, *311*, *312*, **314**, **315**, *316*; and intersectional solidarity 291, 294, 297n6
intersectional advocacy 288, 289, 290, 294, 293, 297n6, 297n7, 307, 313
intersectional identity 227, 230, 231, 232, 233, **234**, 235, 236, 243, 244, 245, 257, 258, 259
intersectional marginalization 317, 318

intersectional methodology 255–256
intersectional models, of identity 234, 235, 236, **236**, *237*, 245
intersectional solidarity 288–297
intersectional stereotyping, in policing 226–245, **234**, **236**, *237*, *238*, *240*, *241*, *242*, *243*
intersectionality 121n2, 227, 231, 236, 245, 249, 250, 252–254, 255, 259, 262; at the grassroots 302–318, *308*, *311*, *312*, **314**, **315**, *316*; political 255, 259, 293–294; structural 255; theory of 231, 304; *see also* intersectional solidarity
intraracial politics, and black institutions 40–44
Is Anyone Responsible? 155
Iyengar, Shanto, on effects on public opinion formation of television news frames 155, 156–157, 160, 161

Japanese Americans 51, 52–53, 56
Jim Crow 127; and APD 2, 5, 6, 7, 8, 11, 16, 19, 26; and politics of blackness 32, 34, 35–36, 37, 38, 39, 40, 41, 42, 43
Johnson, James Weldon 18
Johnson, Lyndon B. 36
judicial system 214, 223
justice system *see* criminal justice system
justifiability, of police killing 127–148, **134**, *135*, **136**, *138*, *139*, *142*, *143*, *144*, *147*, 148n3, 148n4, **153**, *154*
Justified Hypothetical Victim 140, 141–142, 143, *144*, 144–145

King, Rodney 62, 90, 127
KKK (Ku Klux Klan) 27
Korematsu, Fred 51, 53, 55–56, 57, 58n5
Korematsu v. United States (1944) 47, 51–53
Ku Klux Klan (KKK) 27

Latinx communities 5, 10, 229–230, *237*, 237, 238, 239, 240, 241, 242, 244, **267**
law enforcement 65, **80**, 131, 166, 189, 192; and APD 13, 14, 20, 24, 25, 27, 28; and intersectional stereotyping in policing 228, 231, 233, 245
law reform 251
leadership 43, 84, 86, 104, 105, 168, 170; APD 3, 8, 18, 23; intersectionality 290, 293, 317; use of Twitter by CBC 110, 111, 112–113, **117**, 119
legislative activity, impact of post-Ferguson news coverage on 61–73, **67**, *68*, *69*, *70*
LexisNexis State Capital database 65
LGBTQ people of color activism in Canada, intersectional analysis of 249–263
Liang, Peter 271–272
liberal-conservative ideology 39, 278
liberalism 3, 7, 9
liberation 17, 24, 32, 39, 100
Lifestyle Resources variable, in quality of life study **175**, 176, **177**, *177*, 182, 184n11, 184n12

linked fate beliefs, race-based 268, 269, 281
lived experiences 89, 90, 181–182, 272; and intersectional solidarity 289, 290, 292, 293, 294–295, 296, 296–297n3
local electoral politics, implications of BLM scholarship on 100–105
"long civil rights movement" 7
Lorde, Audre 24, 40, 43, 290
lynching 8, 15, 17–18, 19, 40

McCleskey v. Kemp 221, 222, 223n2
Mckesson, DeRay 101, 104–105
male drivers 197, 200, 203, 204, 236, 237, 238, 239–240, 241
March for our Lives 308, 310, 311, 313, **315**
March for Trump 308, 310, 311, **314**, **315**
marginalization, of communities of color 10, 48, 63, 86, 103, 270, 272, 277; and intersectionality 289, 305, 309, 312, 317, 318; of LGBTQ people of color in Canada 249, 250, 254, 255, 256, 257, 258, 259, 260, 261–262
Martin, Trayvon 5, 24, 61, 67, 76, 81, 89, 90, 100, 101, 116, 127, 157, 188, 226
mass incarceration 2, 10, 24, 37, 188, 204; and political cartoons in BLM era **80**, 81, **84**, 86
Mechanical Turk platform 132
media, state response to **68**, *69*, *70*
media bias **80**, **83**
media coverage, of policing and protests post-Ferguson 61–73, **67**, *68*, *69*, *70*
media framing *see* news framing
Media Perspectives on Policing (MPOP) database 66
methodology 16, 216–218, 255–256
micro-blogging, use of by CBC 107–121, *115*, *116*, **117**
micromobilization 303, 312
militarization, of the police 1, 2, 20, 24, 83
mob violence 18
"model minority", Asian Americans stereotyped as 229–230, 273
Moore v. Dempsey 18–19
Moraga, Cherríe 290–291
Movement for Black Lives 1–2, 23, 24, 28–29, 62, 76, 89, 128
movement frames 81, 84
MPOP (Media Perspectives on Policing) database 66
multiple identities, intersection of 226–245, **234**, **236**, *237*, *238*, *240*, *241*, *242*, *243*
multiple political traditions perspective, on APD 7
murders 213–214, 215, 217–219, *217*, *219*, 220–221, *220*, 223–224n11

National Association for the Advancement of Colored People (NAACP) 8, 18–19, 23–24, 270
Native Americans 230, 232, 238, 240, 241, 242, 279
"negro, the" 35, 37, 38

"Negro problem" 33–34, 38
neighborhood conditions 166, 167, 168, 170, 171, 172
neoliberalism 3, 102, 103, 169, 170
neo-Redemption era 5–11
New Deal 9, 19
"the *new* Jim Crow" 2, 8, 11, 26
New Jim Crow 188
New York Times 10, 49, 63, 66, 77
news framing 90; of Black American "crime narrative" 155–163, *159*, *162*; of collective action 302, 303, 307, 310, 315, 316, 318; of police and protesters post-Ferguson 62, 63, 64–65, 66, 71, 72; racialized 67, 77–78, 90; of racism in political cartoons 79–81, **80**, 82–84, **83**, **84**, 85–86
news media coverage, of policing and protests post-Ferguson 61–73, **67**, *68*, *69*, *70*
news media cues, historical narratives of Black criminality as 161–162
"nobodies", Black 101, 103
Nobody: Casualties of America's War on the Vulnerable, From Ferguson to Flint and Beyond 100
"norm of equality" 158–159
North Carolina, traffic stops *see* young men of color, traffic stops of

Obama, President Barack 77–78, 86, 100, 101–102, 103, 109, 168, 269; and APD 5–6, 8–11, 14, 20
Obamacare 9, 10, 116
officer at fault, as variable in analysis of police killings **93**, **95**
oppression 1, 49, 57n1, 86, 102, 103, 254, 255, 272–273; grassroots intersectionality 302, 303, 304, 305, 309, 312, 318; intersectional solidarity 288, 289, 290, 291, 293, 294, 296, 297n4; politics of blackness 33, 34, 35, 38, 43
outcomes: of gaslighting people of color 47, 51, **55**, 55, 56, 57; traffic stop 226–245, **234**, **236**, *237*, *238*, *240*, *241*, *242*, *243*
out-groups 89, 90, 92, 159

party development 16
pathologization, of people of color 47, 50, 51, **55**, 55, 56, 57, 58n8
perceptions about police 179–182, *179*, **180**, *181*
Phule, Savitribai 288, 289, 297n6
Physical Resources variable, in quality of life study 173, 176, **177**, 177, 184n11, 184n12
polarization, political 9
police: confidence in *147*, 148n3, 148n4; perceptions about 179–182, *179*, **180**, *181*
police accountability 61, 62, 63, 64, 65, 66, 67, 70, 71
police authority 65, 73n1
police autonomy 61, 65, 66, 67, 70, 71
police brutality 6, 13, 36, 110, 156, 166, 226; and Asian American support for BLM 272, 283n5;

and local electoral politics 101, 103, 105; in news coverage post-Ferguson 61–62, 67; in political cartoons 75, 80, 83, 84, 85, 86
"Police" frame **67**, 80, 82, 85
police killings: emotional responses to 89–96, **93**, **95**; race and political evaluations of 127–148, **134**, *135*, **136**, *138*, *139*, **142**, *143*, **144**, *147*, 148n3, 148n4, **153**, *154*
police reform 61, 63, 76, **80**
police repression 64, 249, 251–252, 263n5
police violence 10, 13, 24, 25, 61–62, 169; in political cartoons 75, 76, 80, 86
police-stops *see* traffic stops
policing legislation 61, 62, 65, 66, 67, 69, 72
policy responsiveness 61, 63, 65, 71, 72
political activism 40, 43, 269, 297n6
political attitudes 129, 155, 156, 159, 160, 274; and grassroots intersectionality 308, 312, 313, **314**, 315–316, **315**
political beliefs 157, 158, 277
political cartoons, in BLM era 75–87, **80**, *82*, **83**, **84**, *85*
political change 16–17, 281
political culture 72, 78
political development *see* American Political Development (APD)
political elites 14, 15, 36, 313
political entrepreneurship 40
political equality 3, 8, 39
political expression 107
political ideology 16, 269, 277, **278**
political intersectionality 255, 259, 293–294
political involvement 312, 313, **314**, **315**, 316
political messages 33, 155, 158, 163n1
political opportunity structures 291, 292–293
political orders 1, 2, 6–7, 11
political polarization 9
politicization 254, 256
populism 10, 23, 24
portrayal, of people of color 47, 51, **55**, 55, 56, 57
post-racial America, lingering myths of 89
power dynamics 16, 254
power structure, white supremacist state 47, 49, 50, 52, 54
precarity, of black lives 15, 24, 29
Pride marches 249
primes, related to BLM 127, 129, 130, 141, *142*, 142, **143**, 143–144, 144–145, 146, **151–152**, 153
prisons 26, 27, 101, 131
privilege 57n1, 182, 183, 273, 282; and intersectional solidarity 289, 290, 292, 295; and LGBTQ people of color activism in Canada 256, 259, 260
probable cause 189, 198, **198**, 200, **200**, *201*, 202, 208, **210**, *210*
profiling 64, 65, 116, 189, 192, 280; intersectional stereotyping in policing 226, 227, 228, 230–231, 237, 244, 245
pro-police media framing 66, 67, 69, 70, 71
pro-protester media faming 66, 67, 70, 71

public opinion formation, impact of news frames on 155–163, *159*, *162*
"public peace" 28, 81
punishment: capital 24, 213–224, *216*, *217*, *219*, *220*, 223n3; criminal *see* criminal punishment

quality of life, before the 2015 Uprising 166–184, **175**, **176**, **177**, **178**, *179*, **180**, *181*
Quebec, LGBTQ people of color in 251, 252, 260, 261, 263n5, 263n6, 263n9

race politics 1, 3, 48, 56
race relations 17, 81, 89–90, 96, 108, 109, 115; and local electoral politics 101, 103, 105
race tweets 115, **117**, 118–119
race-based considerations, amongst Asian Americans 269, 273–277, *275*, *276*, 278, **278**, 279, 281, 282, 284n15
race-based linked fate beliefs 268, 269, 281
race-of-victim bias 215–216, *216*, 218, 220, 221, 223n6
race-of-victim effects, in US executions 213–224, *216*, *217*, *219*, *220*
racial and ethnic politics (REP) 269, 270, 283n6, 110, 114
racial animus 131–132, 160, 162, 221, 222
racial anxiety 10, 147
racial apartheid 55
racial bias 62, 116, 128, 188, 191, 200, 204, 233; and race-of-victim effects in US executions 213, 214, 215, 216, 221, 222, 223, 223n2
racial categorization 32, 49
racial cleavages, in satisfaction with quality of life before 2015 Uprising 166–184, **175**, **176**, **177**, **178**, *179*, **180**, *181*
racial conservatism 28
racial demagoguery 23, 24, 28–29
racial discrimination 16, 51, 101, 191, 204, 233, 294
racial disparities 95–96, 169, 179, 228, 230; in race-of-victim effects in US executions 214, 216, 221, 222; in traffic stops 188, 192, 197, 200, 203, 205, 207, 208–210
racial diversity 72
racial equality 6, 10, 158
Racial Formation in the United States 49
racial formation theory 56–57
racial gaslighting 47–58, **55**
racial group attitudes 274
"racial habits" 101, 102, 103
racial hierarchy 32–33, 96, 272, 273, 281
racial identities 6, 49, 91, **93**, **95**, 170, 175–176, **176**, 256, 259, **267**
racial inequalities 6, 10, 11, 15, 33, 36, 90, 96, 158, 269, 280
racial messaging 155, 156, 157–159, 160, 162
racial novelty 132
racial orders 3, 5, 6, 7, 8–11, 16, 105, 272
racial politics 33, 95–96, 111, 271, 281
racial power 273, 282

racial profiling *see* profiling
racial progress 5, 6, 109
racial reparation 9
racial representation, in CBC tweets 107–121, *115*, *116*, **117**
racial sedition 53–55, **55**
racial spectacles 47, 49–50, 51, 52–53, 54, 57, 58n2, 58n7
racial stereotypes 65, 77, 136, 158, 228, 272; and politics of blackness 33–34, 39, 41, 42
racial tensions 54, 96, 159
racial terrorism 53
racial uplift ideology 42, 43
racial violence 15–16, 17, 18; in American politics 19–20, 95–96; institutionalized 23, 29
racism: biological 26; symbolic 127, 129, 132, 139–140, *139*, 146, 147, **152**, **153**, *154*; systemic 36, 37, 39, 56–57, **80**, 80, 94, 260
radicalism 9
Rawlings-Blake, Mayor Stephanie C. 167, 168, 179
Reagan, Ronald 28, 103
reasonable accommodation crisis of 2006–2008 252, 263n9
Reconstruction Period 33, 35, 36, 40, 41, 49; and APD 5, 6, 7–8, 9, 11, 19, 20, 24
reform: election 8, 9, 20; immigration 10; law 251; police 61, 63, 76, **80**; prison 26; school 41
"relative deprivation", theory of 171
REP (racial and ethnic politics) 269, 270, 283n6, 110, 114
residents, opinions of Baltimore 167, 168, 169, 170, 172, 175, 182
resistance 5, 15, 25, 109, 250, 255, 283n7; and intersectional solidarity 291, 294, 295; and politics of blackness 34, 40, 41; to racial gaslighting 47, 50, 51–53, 56, 57, 58n8
resistance movement 25, 101
Rice, Tamir 68, 69, 127, 157
riots 26, 36, 58n6, 62, 65, 166, 183n1
rollcall voting, of African American legislators 120
Roosevelt, President Franklin 19, 51
Rustin, Bayard 103–104, 105

Sanders, Bernie 270, 307
Sanford, Governor Terry 27
satisfaction: as emotional response to police shooting **93**, **95**; with quality of life before the 2015 uprising 166–184, **175**, **176**, **177**, **178**, *179*, **180**, *181*
#SayHerName campaign 85, 226–227
scholarship, on BLM 100–105
school reform 41
search and arrest, targeting young men of color for 188–205, **193**, **194**, **195**, *196*, **198**, **198**, *199*, **200**, *201*, **202**
second Redemption era 8, 9, 11
segregation 51, 54, 55, 167–168, 171, 182; and APD 2, 14, 16, 20, 25, 26, 28; and politics of blackness 35, 36, 37–38, 42
September 11th attacks 9, 56, 280, 284n19

sexual orientation 245, 251, 256, 263n6, **267**, 296–297n3, 304
sexual violence 230, 304
shared blame **80**, 81, **84**, 86
shared identities 291–292, 292–293
shared interests 272, 291, 292
Shelby v. Holder 9
Shook, Teresa 306
"signifyin" 109, 119
SLAP (State Legislative Action on Policing) database 65, 66
slavery 19, 34–35, 35–36, 40, 41, 127
Social Darwinism 35, 37
social desirability bias 138
social equality 3
social identity 308, 312–313, **314**, **315**, 315
social justice 48, 50, 100, 102, 169; and intersectionality 288, 291, 302, 304, 305
social media 43, 107, 108, 168, 270, 274, 307, 308; and APD 11, 13; and local electoral politics 100, 102, 103, 104, 105; and news coverage post-Ferguson 61, 62, 72; political cartoons in 76, 77, **80**, 80, 84
social movements 145, 253, 254, 255, 262, 270, 283n7; and APD 3, 13–14, 15, 17–19; and intersectionality 288–297, 304, 305, 306, 313, 318
social norms 33, 155, 157–158, 160, 161
social policy 16, 157, 160, 292
social ties 249, 250, 253
social welfare state 9, 11, 14, 20
societal criminality 90
socio-economic status 218, 308, 312, 313, **314**, 316
solidarity: race-ing 268–284, **275**, *276*, *278*; intersectional 288–297
"Solutions" frame 81
spatial cleavages, in satisfaction with quality of life before 2015 Uprising 166–184, **175**, **176**, **177**, **178**, *179*, **180**, *181*
SRS (Symbolic Racism Scale) 127, 129, **153**
state development 2, 3, 17–19, 24, 283n7
state institutions 15, 26, 50
State Legislative Action on Policing (SLAP) database 65, 66
state legislature 61–73, 113
state power 24, 28–29; white supremacist 47, 49–50, 52–53, 54
state violence 101, 103, 110, 280; and APD 13, 14, 19, 20, 24, 29
stereotyping: of criminality 229, 230, 238; identity-based 226, 227; intersectional 226–245, **234**, **236**, *237*, *238*, *240*, *241*, *242*, *243*; racial *see* racial stereotypes; of suspicion 228–230; threat of 131
Sterling, Alton 68, 141, 146
Stewart, Maria 288, 289
stops *see* traffic stops
"Strange Fruit", of APD 13–20
structural intersectionality 255

structural-related processes 256, 259–261, 262
Supreme Court *see* US Supreme Court
suspicion: categorical compounding of 242–244, *243*; stereotypes of 228–230
symbolic interactionism 253, 254
symbolic racism 127, 129, 132, 139–140, *139*, 146, 147, **152**, **153**, *154*
Symbolic Racism Scale (SRS) 127, 129, **153**
systemic racism 36, 37, 39, 56–57, **80**, 80, 94, 260

Taylor, Keeanga-Yamahtta 24
Tea Party 6, 9, 10
television news 155, 156, 163n1
thematic frames 157, 158, 160
thematic-episodic news framing 155, 156, 158, 159–160, *159*, 162–163
theoretical context, of CBC 110–114
theoretical motivation, to resort to using stereotypes 130–131
Thurmond, Strom 25, 26
Tometi, Opal 14, 24, 76, 100
"tone policing" 49
"traditional" American values 25, 129, 130, 132, 144, 145–146
traffic stop warnings 205n2, 233, **234**, 240–241, 241–242, 244
traffic stops: and intersectional stereotyping in policing 226–245, **234**, **236**, *237*, *238*, *240*, *241*, *242*, *243*; in North Carolina 188–205, **193**, **194**, **195**, *196*, **198**, *199*, **200**, *201*, **202**, 227, 230
Trump, President Donald J.: and APD 10, 13, 20, 23, 24, 28; and grassroots intersectionality 302, 303, 306, 307, 317; March for 308, 310, 311, **314**, **315**; and police killings 129, **134**, 140, 141, **144**, 146
Trump primes 129, 141, *142*, 142, **143**, 143, 145, **151–152**, **153**
Truth, Sojourner 263n12, 288, 289–290
Twitter, use of by CBC 107–121, *115*, *116*, **117**
two-wave conjoint survey experiment 132, 145

unarmed African Americans, racialized differences in perceptions of and emotional responses to police killings of 89–96, **93**, **95**
United Klans of America 27
Unjustified Hypothetical Victim 140–141, 142–143, *144*, 144, 146
Uprising of 2015 *see* Baltimore Uprising
urbanicity 72
US carceral system 26, 28
US Constitution 34, 222
US Department of Justice (DOJ) 14, 167, 188, 190–191, 200, 204, 217, 218
US executions, race-of-victim effects in 213–224, *216*, *217*, *219*, *220*
US Supreme Court 7, 9, 18–19, 35, 189; and race-of-victim effects in US executions 215, 221, 222, 223n2, 223n10; and racial gaslighting 51, 53, 56, 58n4

"value gap" 102–103, 105
values, American 25, 129, 130, 132, 144, 145–146
victim race, influence of in capital sentencing 214–215, 217, *217*, 220
violence: mob 18; police *see* police violence; racial *see* racial violence; sexual 230, 304; state *see* state violence; white supremacist 27, 51, 57
voting 9, 18, 36, 111–112, 120, 157, 190, 277, 307
voting rights 10, 33, 35
Voting Rights Act (VRA) 8, 9, 15, 36, 104, 110

Wade, Andrew and Charlotte 53–54, 55
"war on black people" 28–29
"war on drugs" 26, 37, 188, 189
warnings, traffic stop 205n2, 233, **234**, 240–241, 241–242, 244
Washington, Booker T. 38, 43–44
Washington Post 66, 101, 168, 169
welfare state 9, 11, 14, 20
Wells, Ida B. 3, 15, 17–18, 24, 40
Which shooting is more justified? 135
"white body" 33, 38, 40
white guilt 9
white populist nationalism 23, 24

white supremacy 2, 6, 17, 24, 28, 100, 272; and politics of blackness 34, 35, 38, 39; and racial gaslighting 47, 49, 50–51, 54, 55, 56, 57, 57n1, 58n8; state power structure associated with 47, 49–50, 52–53, 54; violence associated with 27, 51, 57
White victims 213–214, 216, 220, 221, 223n3
White-on-Black crime 218, 221
White-on-White crime 218, 221
Whren v. United States (1996) 189
Wilson, Darren 61, 64, 100, 127, 157
Wilson, Representative Frederica 116, 117, 119, 120, 121n3
women: African American 112–113, 120, 303, 306; and Black Lives Matter 84–85, **85**
Women's March 49, 302, 303, 304, 306–308, *308*, 310–312, *311*, *312*, 313–318, **314**, **315**, *317*
Woodson, Carter G. 38

young men of color, traffic stops of 188–205, **193**, **194**, **195**, *196*, *198*, **198**, *199*, **200**, *201*, **202**

Zimmerman, George 24, 61, 67, 89, 100, 116, 127, 188, 226